20th Conference on Natural Language Processing/Konferenz zur Verarbeitung naturlicher Sprache (KONVENS 2024)

Vienna, Austria
10 – 13 September 2024

ISBN: 979-8-3313-0484-3

Printed from e-media with permission by:

Curran Associates, Inc.
57 Morehouse Lane
Red Hook, NY 12571

Some format issues inherent in the e-media version may also appear in this print version.

Association for Computational Linguistics
209 N. Eighth Street
Stroudsburg, Pennsylvania 18360

Phone: 1-570-476-8006
Fax: 1-570-476-0860

acl@aclweb.org

Additional copies of this publication are available from:

Curran Associates, Inc.
57 Morehouse Lane
Red Hook, NY 12571 USA
Phone: 845-758-0400
Fax: 845-758-2633
Email: curran@proceedings.com
Web: www.proceedings.com

KONVENS 2024

20th Conference on Natural Language Processing (KONVENS 2024)

Proceedings of the Conference

September 10-13, 2024

The KONVENS organizers gratefully acknowledge the support from the Austrian Society for Artificial Intelligence.

Order copies of this and other ACL proceedings from:

Association for Computational Linguistics (ACL)
317 Sidney Baker St. S
Suite 400 - 134
Kerrville, TX 78028
USA
Tel: +1-855-225-1962
acl@aclweb.org

Introduction

We are thrilled to present the proceedings of this year's installment of KONVENS (Konferenz zur Verarbeitung natürlicher Sprache) held at the University of Vienna from September 10 to 13, 2024. KONVENS is a conference series on computational linguistics established in 1992 organized under the auspices of the German Society for Computational Linguistics and Language Technology, the Special Interest Group on Computational Linguistics of the German Linguistic Society, the Austrian Society for Artificial Intelligence and SwissText.

This year, we received 57 paper submissions, which were peer-reviewed by three reviewers each. Out of all submissions 39 were accepted (21 long papers, 18 short papers). The work presented at KONVENS 2024 spans various topics, including sentiment analysis, question answering, language model evaluation, and the processing of both contemporary and historical languages. We also see an increasing focus on multilingualism, large language models, and the ethical implications of natural language processing technologies. These contributions highlight the ongoing innovation and the importance of addressing both practical applications and theoretical advancements in computational linguistics. This year's conference also features research that tackles the unique challenges of German language processing, alongside studies that explore cross-linguistic applications. The blend of foundational research and applied studies enriches the dialogue within our community and pushes the boundaries of what is possible in language technologies.

We would like to express our heartfelt thanks to all the authors who submitted their work, and a special thanks to the members of the KONVENS 2024 program committee who dedicated their time and expertise to ensure the quality of the conference proceedings in the review process. Your rigorous reviews and thoughtful feedback have been invaluable in maintaining the high standards of the KONVENS conference series. We are excited for the discussions and collaborations that this conference will spark and hope that you find the proceedings insightful and inspiring.

Sincerely,

Brigitte Krenn (Local Co-Chair)
Dagmar Gromann (Local Co-Chair)
Barbara Heinisch (Local Co-Chair)
Michael Wiegand (Workshop, Tutorials and Shared Task Chair)
Pedro Henrique Luz de Araujo (Proceedings Chair)
Benjamin Roth (Program Co-Chair)
Andreas Baumann (Program Co-Chair)

Seid Muhie Yimam, Universität Hamburg
Torsten Zesch, Fernuniversität in Hagen
Erion Çano, Universität Paderborn

Keynote Talk

Constructions all the way down: rethinking compositionality in LLMs

Leonie Weißweiler
UT Austin

Wed, September 11, 2024, 10:00 – 11:00

Abstract: Why are LLMs still not modelling all aspects of language perfectly? Previous works suggested is their deficits in compositionality, regularly building the meaning of an expression as a function of its parts. But in fact, human language is not compositional in this way. Rather, meaning is combined compositionally using constructions, which are pairings of form and function that vary wildly in shape and scope. This means that to achieve the full creativity and flexibility of human language, LLMs will have to assign meaning to constructions and use this to build the meaning of expressions. I will show that this is still not adequately handled by LLMs, and elaborate why construction-compositionality is one of the last remaining challenges that we must solve on our way to more cognitively plausible language models.

Bio: Leonie Weissweiler is a postdoc at UT Austin Linguistics where she works with Kyle Mahowald on the computational learnability of rare linguistic phenomena. She received her PhD from LMU Munich in July 2024, where she worked with Hinrich Schütze on the contributions of Construction Grammar and Morphology to NLP, and vice versa. Her research now focuses on using language models to discover and test hypotheses in Linguistics, while using insights from Linguistics to point out issues with language models.

Keynote Talk

What does it mean for a language model to exhibit a language understanding ability?

Sebastian Schuster
University College London
Wed, September 11, 2024, 14:00 – 15:00

Abstract: Large language models (LLMs) such as GPTs, Gemini or Llama often provide answers that fulfil user requests, which suggests that the model is at least to a large extent able to infer the user's intent and to generate appropriate responses. However, given the open-ended nature of user requests and model responses, it has been quite challenging to systematically evaluate to what extent models exhibit specific language understanding abilities. In my talk, I will focus on one such ability, namely keeping track of how the states of entities change as a discourse unfolds. I will use this ability as a case study for how different evaluation methods can lead to different conclusions about model abilities, I will discuss challenges in evaluating understanding abilities in LLMs and I will consider some recommendations on how to overcome some of these challenges.

Bio: Sebastian Schuster is currently a lecturer in computational linguistics at University College London, and he will start a WWTF-funded research group at the University of Vienna in mid-2025. Before joining UCL, he was a postdoc at New York University and at Saarland University, after completing his PhD at Stanford University. His research focuses on computational semantics and pragmatics and he builds and evaluates computational models of interpreting language in context. His work has won awards at ACL and he has been a senior area chair and program chair at several *ACL conferences and workshops.

Keynote Talk

Using Natural Language Processing to Advance Social Science, Responsibly

Jana Diesner
TU Munich
Thu, September 12, 2024, 09:30 – 10:30

Abstract: Leveraging natural processing techniques to consider the content of information at scale allows us to discover and re-evaluate theories and patterns of societal behavior. This process requires researchers to make a multitude of decisions that require expertise from multiple fields, including how to sample, represent, and preprocess data, implement algorithms, and validate results. I present findings and lessons learned from using NLP techniques, especially entity disambiguation and relation extraction, to study how and why people collaborate and respond to crises. I discuss sources of biases and strategies for mitigating them.

Bio: Jana Diesner is a Full Professor at the Technical University of Munich, School of Social Science and Technology. There, she leads the Human Centered Computing group. Her interdisciplinary group works on methods from network analysis, natural language processing, machine learning and AI, and integrates them with theories from the social sciences to advance our knowledge about complex societal systems and responsible computing. Before joining TU Munich in 2024, she was a tenured professor at the School of Information Sciences at the University of Illinois Urbana Champaign. Jana earned her Ph.D. at Carnegie Mellon, School of Computer Science.

Table of Contents

Program

Wednesday, September 11, 2024

08:30 - 09:30 *Registration*

09:30 - 10:00 *Opening*

10:00 - 11:00 *Keynote 1, Leonie Weißweiler*

11:00 - 12:00 *Poster Session 1 and Coffee Break*

Large Language Models as Evaluators for Scientific Synthesis
Julia Evans, Jennifer D'Souza and Sören Auer

A Crosslingual Approach to Dependency Parsing for Middle High German
Cora Haiber

Complexity of German Texts Written by Primary School Children
Jammila Laâguidi, Dana Neumann, Ronja Laarmann-Quante, Stefanie Dipper and Mihail Chifligarov

Exploring Automatic Text Simplification for Lithuanian
Justina Mandravickaitė, Egle Rimkiene, Danguolė Kalinauskaitė and Danguolė Kotryna Kapkan

Word alignment in Discourse Representation Structure parsing
Christian Obereder and Gabor Recski

Evaluating and Fine-Tuning Retrieval-Augmented Language Models to Generate Text with Accurate Citations
Vinzent Penzkofer and Timo Baumann

Discourse Parsing for German with new RST Corpora
Sara Shahmohammadi and Manfred Stede

Revisiting the Phenomenon of Syntactic Complexity Convergence on German Dialogue Data
Yu Wang and Hendrik Buschmeier

Wednesday, September 11, 2024 (continued)

Estimating Word Concreteness from Contextualized Embeddings
Christian Wartena

Using GermaNet for the Generation of Crossword Puzzles
Claus Zinn, Marie Hinrichs and Erhard Hinrichs

12:00 - 14:00 *Break*

14:00 - 15:00 *Keynote 2, Sebastian Schuster*

15:00 - 16:00 *Poster Session 2 and Coffee Break*

Leveraging Cross-Lingual Transfer Learning in Spoken Named Entity Recognition Systems
Moncef Benaicha, David Thulke and Mehmet Ali Tuğtekin Turan

Exploring Data Acquisition Strategies for the Domain Adaptation of QA Models
Maurice Falk, Adrian Ulges and Dirk Krechel

CO-Fun: A German Dataset on Company Outsourcing in Fund Prospectuses for Named Entity Recognition and Relation Extraction
Neda Foroutan, Markus Schröder and Andreas Dengel

GERestaurant: A German Dataset of Annotated Restaurant Reviews for Aspect-Based Sentiment Analysis
Nils Constantin Hellwig, Jakob Fehle, Markus Bink and Christian Wolff

How to Translate SQuAD to German? A Comparative Study of Answer Span Retrieval Methods for Question Answering Dataset Creation
Jens Kaiser and Agnieszka Falenska

Few-Shot Prompting for Subject Indexing of German Medical Book Titles
Lisa Kluge and Maximilian Kähler

Binary indexes for optimising corpus queries
Peter Ljunglöf, Nicholas Smallbone, Mijo Thoresson and Victor Salomonsson

Wednesday, September 11, 2024 (continued)

An Improved Method for Class-specific Keyword Extraction: A Case Study in the German Business Registry
Stephen Meisenbacher, Tim Schopf, Weixin Yan, Patrick Holl and Florian Matthes

Tabular JSON: A Proposal for a Pragmatic Linguistic Data Format
Adam Roussel

Semiautomatic Data Generation for Academic Named Entity Recognition in German Text Corpora
Pia Schwarz

16:00 - 17:00 *Oral Session 1*

Redundancy Aware Multiple Reference Based Gainwise Evaluation of Extractive Summarization
Mousumi Akter and Santu Karmaker

Fine-grained quotation detection and attribution in German news articles
Fynn Petersen-Frey and Chris Biemann

Decoding 16th-Century Letters: From Topic Models to GPT-Based Keyword Mapping
Phillip Benjamin Ströbel, Stefan Aderhold and Ramona Roller

17:00 - 19:00 *Social event*

19:00 - 21:00 *Dinner*

Thursday, September 12, 2024

08:30 - 09:30 *Registration*

09:30 - 10:30 *Keynote 3, Jana Diesner*

10:30 - 11:00 *Coffee Break*

11:00 - 12:00 *Oral Session 2*

Analysing Effects of Inducing Gender Bias in Language Models
Stephanie Gross, Brigitte Krenn, Craig Lincoln and Lena Holzwarth

OMoS-QA: A Dataset for Cross-Lingual Extractive Question Answering in a German Migration Context
Steffen Kleinle, Jakob Prange and Annemarie Friedrich

Role-Playing LLMs in Professional Communication Training: The Case of Investigative Interviews with Children
Don Tuggener, Teresa Schneider, Ariana Huwiler, Tobias Kreienbühl, Simon Hischier, Pius Von Däniken and Susanna Niehaus

12:00 - 14:00 *Break*

14:00 - 15:00 *Oral Session 3*

Features and Detectability of German Texts Generated with Large Language Models
Verena Irrgang, Veronika Solopova, Steffen Zeiler, Robert M. Nickel and Dorothea Kolossa

Lex2Sent: A bagging approach to unsupervised sentiment analysis
Kai-Robin Lange, Jonas Rieger and Jonas Rieger

Discourse-Level Features in Spoken and Written Communication
Hannah J. Seemann, Sara Shahmohammadi, Manfred Stede and Tatjana Scheffler

15:00 - 16:00 *Poster Session 3 and Coffee Break*

Thursday, September 12, 2024 (continued)

Version Control for Speech Corpora
Vlad Dumitru, Matthias Boehm, Martin Hagmüller and Barbara Schuppler

Querying Repetitions in Spoken Language Corpora
Elena Frick, Henrike Helmer and Dolores Lemmenmeier-Batinić

Exploring Phonetic Features in Language Embeddings for Unseen Language Varieties of Austrian German
Lorenz Gutscher and Michael Pucher

A Multilingual Dataset of Adversarial Attacks to Automatic Content Scoring Systems
Ronja Laarmann-Quante, Christopher Chandler, Noemi Incirkus, Vitaliia Ruban, Alona Solopov and Luca Steen

Towards Improving ASR Outputs of Spontaneous Speech with LLMs
Karner Manuel, Julian Linke, Mark Kröll, Barbara Schuppler and Bernhard C. Geiger

OneLove beyond the field - A few-shot pipeline for topic and sentiment analysis during the FIFA World Cup in Qatar
Christoph Rauchegger, Sonja Mei Wang and Pieter Delobelle

Linguistic and extralinguistic factors in automatic speech recognition of German atypical speech
Eugenia Rykova and Mathias Walther

LLM-based Translation Across 500 Years. The Case for Early New High German
Martin Volk, Dominic P. Fischer, Patricia Scheurer, Raphael Schwitter and Phillip B. Ströbel

16:00 - 17:00 *GSCL PhD Award*

17:00 - 17:30 *Closing*

Large Language Models as Evaluators for Scientific Synthesis

Julia Evans, Jennifer D'Souza, and **Sören Auer**
TIB - Leibniz Information Centre for Science and Technology,
Hannover, Germany
Correspondence: jennifer.dsouza@tib.eu

Abstract

Our study explores how well the state-of-the-art Large Language Models (LLMs), like GPT-4 and Mistral, can assess the quality of scientific summaries or, more fittingly, scientific syntheses, comparing their evaluations to those of human annotators. We used a dataset of 100 research questions and their syntheses made by GPT-4 from abstracts of five related papers, checked against human quality ratings. The study evaluates both the closed-source GPT-4 and the open-source Mistral model's ability to rate these summaries and provide reasons for their judgments. Preliminary results show that LLMs can offer logical explanations that somewhat match the quality ratings, yet a deeper statistical analysis shows a weak correlation between LLM and human ratings, suggesting the potential and current limitations of LLMs in scientific synthesis evaluation.

1 Introduction

Large Language Models (LLMs) have made a significant impact on natural language processing (NLP), demonstrating exceptional performance in tasks like text generation, sentiment analysis, machine translation, and question answering, with outputs that often rival human-created content (Huang et al., 2023). In addition to their direct applications, LLMs offer substantial benefits in streamlining machine learning model development, particularly in evaluation processes. They reduce the dependency on human-generated ground truth data and the necessity for human evaluators (Bai et al., 2023) in two key ways: by facilitating the generation of synthetic ground truth data and by serving as evaluators for model predictions themselves. This approach not only speeds up the evaluation process but also broadens the scope of evaluation criteria to include factors such as diversity and coverage, enhancing the efficiency and comprehensiveness of model assessments.

This study investigates the use of LLMs as evaluators to streamline the evaluation process, moving away from traditional reliance on human evaluators and human-generated ground truth data. It specifically examines the effectiveness of LLMs in synthesizing scientific abstracts seen generally as multi-document summarization tasks. The main focus of this research is to assess how two state-of-the-art LLMs—the proprietary GPT-4 Turbo (OpenAI, 2023) and the open-source Mistral-7B (Jiang et al., 2023)—perform in evaluating scientific syntheses. Furthermore, leveraging LLMs meant better versatility in evaluation considerations, which meant that the evaluations tested varied dimensions of syntheses quality, viz. comprehensiveness, trustworthiness, and utility.

This paper is structured as follows. First, section 2 presents a review of related work in the fields of text summarization and LLM evaluation. In section 3, we show our approach to using LLMs for scientific synthesis evaluation, wherein subsection 3.1 describes the LLM output, while subsection 3.2 presents a qualitative evaluation of this output. In subsection 3.3, we analyze the correlation between LLM ratings and human judgments. A discussion of our findings and final conclusions is described in section 4.

2 Related Work

Evaluation Metrics for Text Summarization. The most common automatic evaluation metric used within summarization research – both single-document and multi-document – is the ROUGE family of metrics (Ma et al., 2022; Akter et al., 2022; Cohan and Goharian, 2016; Kryscinski et al., 2019; Lloret et al., 2018). ROUGE metrics (Lin, 2004) calculate the lexical overlap between a human-written reference document and an automatically generated one, although variants incorporating semantic information also exist. Within text summarization research, the most commonly used are ROUGE-N and ROUGE-L (Ma et al., 2022), both of which are purely lexical-matching metrics. ROUGE-N evaluates the recall of n-grams by comparing a reference text with a corresponding machine-generated text, whereas ROUGE-L calculates the longest common subsequence of tokens shared between reference and machine-generated texts (Lin, 2004).

Despite its predominance within the field, ROUGE nonetheless has some notable limitations. First, the most commonly used metrics lack semantic awareness (Akter et al., 2022; Ma et al., 2022). Studies have pointed out that ROUGE may not accurately estimate summary quality in cases of terminological variations, paraphrasing, and differences in sentence structure (Cohan and Goharian, 2016). Moreover, there exist 192 ROUGE variants (Graham, 2015), with meaningful differences in how well each performs on a given system or specialized task (Cohan and Goharian, 2016; Graham, 2015; Kryscinski et al., 2019) and how well they correlate with human judgements (Kryscinski et al., 2019; Graham, 2015). Finally, ROUGE evaluates only content selection but not linguistic quality aspects such as grammaticality and referential clarity (Pitler et al., 2010) or overall quality, including the ordering of information and structural clarity (Graham, 2015).

Although no other metrics have gained widespread adoption, other approaches exist. Additional lexical-matching metrics include BLEU (Papineni et al., 2002) and Pyramid (Nenkova et al., 2007). Semantically enriched metrics include METEOR (Banerjee and Lavie, 2005), an expansion of BLEU, and approaches utilizing word embeddings, such as BERTScore (Zhang et al., 2020), MoverScore (Zhao et al., 2019), and SUPERT (Gao et al., 2020). However, none of these metrics address all of ROUGE's weaknesses, and the limited use of such metrics within the research community means that ROUGE remains the "de facto" standard (Lloret et al., 2018).

LLMs for Text Evaluation. Using LLMs for text evaluation is still a nascent research topic. Several recent works have compared LLMs' text evaluations to human evaluations on multiple tasks, and report that LLMs produce results similar to human judgements (Chiang and Lee, 2023b; Liu et al., 2023; Wang et al., 2023). One work finds only minor variations in results depending on task instructions and hyperparameters, whereas they find a high degree of variation in performance of different LLMs and the quality characteristics being assessed (Chiang and Lee, 2023b). In evaluating the quality of story fragments by *grammaticality*, *cohesiveness*, *likability*, and *relevance*, they find only a weak correlation between humans and LLMs on *grammaticality*, but a moderate correlation on *relevance*. Contrarily, another work finds that ChatGPT's performance is sensitive to prompt instructions (Wang et al., 2023). They also show that ChatGPT evaluations correlate especially well with human evaluations for creative tasks like story generation (Wang et al., 2023). Another work demonstrates that requiring LLMs to provide a justification for their ratings "significantly improves the correlation between the LLMs' ratings and human ratings" (Chiang and Lee, 2023a).

Only one work has investigated the task of text summarization evaluation (Liu et al., 2023). They evaluate single-document news article summaries on the aspects of *coherence*, *consistency*, *fluency*, and *relevance*; their results exceed the correlation with human judgements of most automatic approaches, including ROUGE. In another task, ChatGPT successfully identifies implicit hate speech in Tweets and generates explanations of why the texts are hateful, which human annotators judge equally informative to human-written explanations and of greater clarity (Huang et al., 2023).

3 LLMs for the Scientific Synthesis Evaluation Task

The accurate evaluation of scientific syntheses is a critical task in research, ensuring the integrity and reliability of the synthesized information. While recent advancements have demonstrated the efficacy of LLMs in generating such syntheses (Pride et al., 2023), their potential in evaluating them remains relatively unexplored. Motivated by the limitations of existing evaluation metrics, such as the ROUGE family, and the success of LLMs in other text evaluation tasks, our work seeks to investigate the suitability of LLMs for the task of assessing the quality of scientific syntheses.

To address this question, we employ the proprietary GPT-4 Turbo (OpenAI, 2023) and the open-source Mistral-7B models (Jiang et al., 2023) to evaluate the CORE-GPT dataset (Pride et al., 2023). This dataset comprises 100 research questions spanning 20 diverse domains, each accompanied by the titles and abstracts of five related works and an answer to the research question generated by GPT-4 by synthesizing the provided abstracts. Additionally, human ratings from two annotators, on a scale of 0 to 10, are available on the quality of each synthesis in three dimensions, viz. *comprehensive*, *trust*, and *utility*.

For our task, we query the LLMs to evaluate the syntheses according to the same three aspects as the CORE-GPT human raters. Our prompt follows a similar structure to previous work (Chiang and Lee, 2023a). It contains two lines of task instruction, explanation of the quality aspects (as defined for the CORE-GPT dataset annotators) and the rating scale, response format instructions, and finally the answer to be evaluated with its question and abstracts. The response is requested in JSON format, with a numeric rating between 0 and 10 for each aspect as well as a rationale for each rating. The full text of the prompt is in Appendix A.

3.1 LLM Synthesis Evaluation Output

A representative example of the evaluation output from GPT-4 Turbo and Mistral is shown in Appendix B and Appendix C, respectively. The output from GPT-4 was exactly as requested, while Mistral had some variability. In one case, Mistral returned ratings of "excellent," "good," and "high" rather than numeric scores; this output was excluded from the analysis. In several other cases, Mistral included a paragraph after the JSON object which summarized the ratings and rationales provided within it. These paragraphs were discarded and only the JSON object content was evaluated.

An overview of LLM performance was obtained by reviewing one synthesis from each domain evaluated by both GPT-4 and Mistral. Qualitatively, both models demonstrated credible and logically consistent ratings and rationales. GPT-4 provided more detailed rationales compared to Mistral, with slightly lower ratings overall.

In their rationales for *comprehensive*, both LLMs would sometimes highlight relevant topics from the abstracts which were not included in the synthesis, with GPT-4 producing such rationales more often than Mistral. Occasionally, some rationales contained justifications relating to content more specific than just the topics, suggesting more information on the results or the methodology of the studies would improve it.

The LLMs seemed to show the greatest discrepancy between rating and rationale, and the greatest inconsistencies, in their evaluations of *trust*. In one Mistral evaluation with a rating of 5, the rationale noted that the citations only improved trustworthiness "as long as the abstract accurately represents the study's findings." In the absence of any evidence the abstract is suspect, this rating is disproportionately low. GPT-4 was notably more conservative than human annotators, as it did not give a single 10. Especially for *trust*, it was often difficult to understand why a rating wasn't higher. For instance, the rationale for one rating of 8 praised the synthesis for accuracy and avoiding unsupported claims.

For the *utility* ratings, it appears that most rationales from GPT-4 suggested additional content which could make the synthesis more useful, such as actionable information, more detailed examples, technical details of methodologies and implementation, and so on. Mistral made such suggestions less frequently; its rationales tended to echo the rationale for *comprehensive*. However, Mistral did sometimes provide guidance on who would or would not find the synthesis useful.

3.2 Qualitative Evaluations

LLMs are known to sometimes generate content on topics that lack factual basis with a highly persuasive level of linguistic proficiency (Bang et al., 2023; Liu et al., 2023). For scientific syntheses which provide an answer to a question, it is especially important that the content is genuinely a synthesis of the provided abstracts, with appropriate citations, and not independently generated based on the LLM's training data. For this reason, we were particularly interested in how the LLMs evaluated quality, and most importantly *trust*, when there was reason to believe the abstracts were not the (primary) source of the generated content, as in the following three scenarios. The complete question and answer pairs, along with their GPT-4 and Mistral evaluation scores and *trust* rationales, can be found in Appendix D.

Response Explicitly States Absence of Relevant Abstracts. In six cases, the synthesis directly expressed limitations due to the relevancy of the provided abstracts, e.g. "[...] the provided search results do not offer specific information on the long-term health impacts of such medications on these organs." Human annotators responded very positively to this, with such responses "scored highly for trustworthiness" (Pride et al., 2023). Mistral rated four of these syntheses as 10 for trust, citing factual accuracy and abstract sourcing, while two scored 7. GPT-4 ratings varied, at 5, 5, 5, 7, 7, and 8. Mistral rationales did not reference the stated limitation, while GPT-4 acknowledged it positively in three cases. However, as these syntheses were scored 8, 7, and 5, it is unclear to what extent this acknowledgement may have influenced the scores.

Response Contains No Citations. There were three responses which answered the question but contained no citations. GPT-4 gave *trust* scores of 0, 0, and 1, with rationales referring to the lack of citations. In contrast, Mistral scored 8, 10, and 10, with rationales stating the information was common knowledge or referenced from the abstracts.

Response Contains One Citation. Finally, there were five syntheses which cited only one of the abstracts, which does not align with the task of synthesizing multiple abstracts to provide an answer to the given question. For GPT-4, the *trust* scores were 5, 7, 8, 8, and 9, with most rationales stating that the synthesis relied on general knowledge without directly referencing the abstracts, despite one citation being present in each case. Meanwhile, the Mistral scores were 7, 9, 9, 10, and 10, with most rationales indistinguishable from those of syntheses with many more citations - three of them claimed that the synthesis accurately references the content in the provided abstracts.

	A1	**A2**	**GPT-4**	**Mistral**
A1				
ρ	-	**0.710**	0.248	0.015
p-value	-	**0.001**	0.305	0.951
A2				
ρ	**0.710**	-	0.058	-0.038
p-value	**0.001**	-	0.814	0.878
GPT-4				
ρ	0.248	0.058	-	**0.786**
p-value	0.305	0.814	-	**0.000**
Mistral				
ρ	0.015	-0.038	**0.786**	-
p-value	0.951	0.878	**0.000**	-

Table 1: Spearman's ρ calculated for the combined mean of *Comprehensive*, *Trust*, and *Utility* scores. Statistically significant results are in bold.

3.3 Correlation

Spearman's ρ was calculated to assess the relationship between the human annotators' scores and the LLM-generated scores. Using the publicly-available data from CORE-GPT (Pride et al., 2023)[1], separate vectors for each annotator were obtained. To calculate the correlations, we found the overall mean score for each domain; due to the format of the published data, it was not possible to match individual scores to their corresponding syntheses. Our results for the overall mean are presented in Table 1.

We find that only two results showed statistically significant p-values. Human annotators exhibited a strong positive correlation (0.710), as did GPT-4 Turbo and Mistral (0.786). However, correlations between annotators and LLMs were weak or very weak, with p-values indicating insufficient evidence for genuine association. These findings suggest LLMs cannot directly replicate human performance in evaluating scientific syntheses. Despite this, the strong positive correlation between GPT-4 Turbo and Mistral indicates consistency between the two LLMs.

4 Discussion and Conclusion

We explore the capacity of LLMs in assessing scientific syntheses. GPT-4 Turbo and Mistral are utilized to obtain quality ratings for 100 syntheses from the CORE-GPT dataset (Pride et al., 2023), accompanied by a rationale for each rating. Correlation analysis using Spearman's ρ indicates that the LLM performance does not align with the human annotators' judgements. However, a qualitative evaluation of the responses finds a more mixed result.

Both LLMs generally produce credible and logically consistent ratings and rationales, but GPT-4 appears more conservative in its ratings and provides more detail and specific recommendations in its rationales. GPT-4 also displays greater sensitivity to the presence or absence of citations compared to Mistral. However, both LLMs' rationales occasionally contained inaccuracies or flaws, raising concerns about the credibility of their scores. Moreover, the extent to which the responses are evaluated as *syntheses* and not simply as *answers*, without reliance on general knowledge, remains unclear, particularly in the case of Mistral.

Our findings highlight both promising developments and current limitations of leveraging LLMs for the task of evaluating scientific syntheses, illustrating the need for further research to validate and refine the methodology.

[1]https://github.com/oacore/core-gpt-evaluation

Limitations

We acknowledge several limitations that may influence the interpretation and generalizability of our findings. First, the reliance on a single, relatively small dataset presents limitations in terms of data representativeness. Moreover, the data format necessitated aggregating scores, which may have obscured potential nuances in individual annotations.

Second, the study focused exclusively on GPT-4 Turbo and Mistral, limiting the generalizability of our conclusions to other LLMs. While these models represent the state-of-the-art, future iterations or alternative architectures may exhibit different performance. Additionally, we were able to obtain only one set of ratings from each LLM. Given the variability of LLM output, taking the average of several runs is preferable, but due to financial limitations, this was not possible in our study.

We note that past work has found LLMs particularly adept at evaluating creative texts (Wang et al., 2023), so the narrow output scope of synthesis for scientific question answering may pose a greater challenge. We also note the difficulty of assessing the quality of syntheses from such a diverse assortment of domains. Judging how comprehensive a synthesis is requires some knowledge of the scope of potential information which might be appropriate to include. Highly specialized domain knowledge still presents a challenge to general use LLMs.

Ethical Considerations

In this work we have presented our study of the efficacy of two LLMs, one proprietary and one open-source, in evaluating the quality of scientific syntheses. There were no living subjects analyzed in this study. Overall, this study complies with the ACL Ethics Policy.

In querying the LLMs for synthesis quality evaluations, we declare that the instructions were intended to align the behavior of the language models towards producing responses that are both helpful (fulfilling our objective) and harmless (not causing any physical, psychological, or social harm to individuals or the environment). All of the intellectual property which was passed to the LLMs is open-access.

Acknowledgements

This work was supported by the German BMBF project SCINEXT (ID 01IS22070).

References

Mousumi Akter, Naman Bansal, and Shubhra Kanti Karmaker. 2022. Revisiting Automatic Evaluation of Extractive Summarization Task: Can We Do Better than ROUGE? In *Findings of the Association for Computational Linguistics: ACL 2022*, pages 1547–1560, Dublin, Ireland. Association for Computational Linguistics.

Yushi Bai, Jiahao Ying, Yixin Cao, Xin Lv, Yuze He, Xiaozhi Wang, Jifan Yu, Kaisheng Zeng, Yijia Xiao, Haozhe Lyu, Jiayin Zhang, Juanzi Li, and Lei Hou. 2023. Benchmarking Foundation Models with Language-Model-as-an-Examiner. In *Advances in Neural Information Processing Systems*, volume 36, pages 78142–78167. Curran Associates, Inc.

Satanjeev Banerjee and Alon Lavie. 2005. METEOR: An Automatic Metric for MT Evaluation with Improved Correlation with Human Judgments. In *Proceedings of the ACL Workshop on Intrinsic and Extrinsic Evaluation Measures for Machine Translation and/or Summarization*, pages 65–72, Ann Arbor, Michigan. Association for Computational Linguistics.

Yejin Bang, Samuel Cahyawijaya, Nayeon Lee, Wenliang Dai, Dan Su, Bryan Wilie, Holy Lovenia, Ziwei Ji, Tiezheng Yu, Willy Chung, Quyet V. Do, Yan Xu, and Pascale Fung. 2023. A Multitask, Multilingual, Multimodal Evaluation of ChatGPT on Reasoning, Hallucination, and Interactivity. In *Proceedings of the 13th International Joint Conference on Natural Language Processing and the 3rd Conference of the Asia-Pacific Chapter of the Association for Computational Linguistics (Volume 1: Long Papers)*, pages 675–718, Nusa Dua, Bali. Association for Computational Linguistics.

Cheng-Han Chiang and Hung-yi Lee. 2023a. A Closer Look into Using Large Language Models for Automatic Evaluation. In *Findings of the Association for Computational Linguistics: EMNLP 2023*, pages 8928–8942, Singapore. Association for Computational Linguistics.

Cheng-Han Chiang and Hung-yi Lee. 2023b. Can Large Language Models Be an Alternative to Human Evaluations? In *Proceedings of the 61st Annual Meeting of the Association for Computational Linguistics (Volume 1: Long Papers)*, pages 15607–15631, Toronto, Canada. Association for Computational Linguistics.

Arman Cohan and Nazli Goharian. 2016. Revisiting Summarization Evaluation for Scientific Articles. In *Proceedings of the Tenth International Conference on Language Resources and Evaluation (LREC'16)*, pages 806–813, Portorož, Slovenia. European Language Resources Association (ELRA).

Yang Gao, Wei Zhao, and Steffen Eger. 2020. SUPERT: Towards New Frontiers in Unsupervised Evaluation Metrics for Multi-Document Summarization. In *Proceedings of the 58th Annual Meeting of the Association for Computational Linguistics*, pages 1347–1354, Online. Association for Computational Linguistics.

Yvette Graham. 2015. Re-evaluating Automatic Summarization with BLEU and 192 Shades of ROUGE. In *Proceedings of the 2015 Conference on Empirical Methods in Natural Language Processing*, pages 128–137, Lisbon, Portugal. Association for Computational Linguistics.

Fan Huang, Haewoon Kwak, and Jisun An. 2023. Is ChatGPT better than Human Annotators? Potential and Limitations of ChatGPT in Explaining Implicit Hate Speech. In *Companion Proceedings of the ACM Web Conference 2023*, WWW '23 Companion, page 294–297, New York, NY, USA. Association for Computing Machinery.

Albert Q. Jiang, Alexandre Sablayrolles, Arthur Mensch, Chris Bamford, Devendra Singh Chaplot, Diego de las Casas, Florian Bressand, Gianna Lengyel, Guillaume Lample, Lucile Saulnier, Lélio Renard Lavaud, Marie-Anne Lachaux, Pierre Stock, Teven Le Scao, Thibaut Lavril, Thomas Wang, Timothée Lacroix, and William El Sayed. 2023. Mistral 7B. *Preprint*, arXiv:2310.06825.

Wojciech Kryscinski, Nitish Shirish Keskar, Bryan McCann, Caiming Xiong, and Richard Socher. 2019. Neural Text Summarization: A Critical Evaluation. In *Proceedings of the 2019 Conference on Empirical Methods in Natural Language Processing and the 9th International Joint Conference on Natural Language Processing (EMNLP-IJCNLP)*, pages 540–551, Hong Kong, China. Association for Computational Linguistics.

Chin-Yew Lin. 2004. ROUGE: A package for automatic evaluation of summaries. In *Text Summarization Branches Out*, pages 74–81, Barcelona, Spain. Association for Computational Linguistics.

Yang Liu, Dan Iter, Yichong Xu, Shuohang Wang, Ruochen Xu, and Chenguang Zhu. 2023. G-Eval: NLG Evaluation using Gpt-4 with Better Human Alignment. In *Proceedings of the 2023 Conference on Empirical Methods in Natural Language Processing*, pages 2511–2522, Singapore. Association for Computational Linguistics.

Elena Lloret, Laura Plaza, and Ahmet Aker. 2018. The challenging task of summary evaluation: an overview. *Language Resources and Evaluation*, 52:101–148.

Congbo Ma, Wei Emma Zhang, Mingyu Guo, Hu Wang, and Quan Z. Sheng. 2022. Multi-Document Summarization via Deep Learning Techniques: A Survey. *ACM Computing Surveys*, 55(5).

Ani Nenkova, Rebecca Passonneau, and Kathleen Mckeown. 2007. The Pyramid Method: Incorporating human content selection variation in summarization evaluation. *ACM Transactions on Speech and Language Processing*, 4(2).

OpenAI. 2023. GPT-4 Technical Report. *Preprint*, arXiv:2303.08774.

Kishore Papineni, Salim Roukos, Todd Ward, and Wei-Jing Zhu. 2002. BLEU: a Method for Automatic Evaluation of Machine Translation. In *Proceedings of the 40th Annual Meeting of the Association for Computational Linguistics*, pages 311–318, Philadelphia, Pennsylvania, USA. Association for Computational Linguistics.

Emily Pitler, Annie Louis, and Ani Nenkova. 2010. Automatic Evaluation of Linguistic Quality in Multi-Document Summarization. In *Proceedings of the 48th Annual Meeting of the Association for Computational Linguistics*, pages 544–554, Uppsala, Sweden. Association for Computational Linguistics.

David Pride, Matteo Cancellieri, and Petr Knoth. 2023. CORE-GPT: Combining Open Access Research and Large Language Models for Credible, Trustworthy Question Answering. In *Linking Theory and Practice of Digital Libraries*, pages 146–159. Springer Nature Switzerland.

Jiaan Wang, Yunlong Liang, Fandong Meng, Zengkui Sun, Haoxiang Shi, Zhixu Li, Jinan Xu, Jianfeng Qu, and Jie Zhou. 2023. Is ChatGPT a Good NLG Evaluator? A Preliminary Study. In *Proceedings of the 4th New Frontiers in Summarization Workshop*, pages 1–11, Singapore. Association for Computational Linguistics.

Tianyi Zhang, Varsha Kishore, Felix Wu, Kilian Q. Weinberger, and Yoav Artzi. 2020. BERTScore: Evaluating Text Generation with BERT. In *Proceedings of the 8th International Conference on Learning Representations (ICLR'20)*.

Wei Zhao, Maxime Peyrard, Fei Liu, Yang Gao, Christian M. Meyer, and Steffen Eger. 2019. MoverScore: Text generation evaluating with contextualized embeddings and earth mover distance. In *Proceedings of the 2019 Conference on Empirical Methods in Natural Language Processing and the 9th International Joint Conference on Natural Language Processing (EMNLP-IJCNLP)*, pages 563–578, Hong Kong, China. Association for Computational Linguistics.

A Prompt

A.1 Main Evaluation Prompt

Evaluate the quality of the following question and answer pair. The answer should succinctly address the question while referencing only content from the provided abstracts.

Consider the following characteristics while assessing the answer. For each characteristic rate the quality from 0 (poor) to 10 (excellent). Provide a short rationale for each rating.

1. Comprehensive: How comprehensively is the question answered?

2. Trust: How trustworthy is the answer?

3. Utility: How useful is the answer?

Return your response in JSON format: {Comprehensive : {‘rating’ : ‘’, ‘rationale’ : ‘’}, Trust : {‘rating’ : ‘’, ‘rationale’ : ‘’}, Utility : {‘rating’ : ‘’, ‘rationale’ : ‘’}}

Question: <content>

Answer: <content>

Abstracts: <content>

A.2 Additional Mistral System Prompt

Follow the user instructions to the letter. The output should be only what the user requests, do not respond with anything else. Provide the answer in JSON with no additional text.

B Example GPT-4 Turbo Output

GPT-4 Turbo

COMPREHENSIVE: rating: 7, rationale: The answer provides a broad overview of how living in a low-income neighborhood can affect social networks and well-being, referencing various studies that discuss mental health, social inclusion, and subjective well-being. However, it does not fully elaborate on the specific mechanisms or provide detailed insights from each abstract, such as the role of men in community well-being from abstract 3 or the impact of natural capital from abstract 4.
TRUST: rating: 8, rationale: The answer is trustworthy as it directly references findings from the provided abstracts, indicating a reliance on research-based evidence. However, the answer could be more trustworthy if it included more specific data or findings from the abstracts to support the claims.
UTILITY: rating: 7, rationale: The answer is useful as it gives an overview of the potential impacts of living in a low-income neighborhood on residents' social networks and well-being. It could be more useful if it provided actionable insights or recommendations based on the findings of the studies.

Figure 1: Example output from GPT-4 Turbo.

C Example Mistral Output

Mistral

COMPREHENSIVE: rating: 9, rationale: The answer provides specific examples and references to studies that directly address the question of how social media influences the formation and maintenance of relationships among young adults in the United States, specifically focusing on LGBTQ+ individuals with disabilities and young adults who have moved abroad.
TRUST: rating: 10, rationale: The answer is based on empirical research and provides clear citations to support the claims made.
UTILITY: rating: 10, rationale: The answer is directly relevant to the question and provides useful information for those interested in understanding how social media impacts relationship formation and maintenance among young adults in the United States.

The given question and answer pair is of high quality. The question is clear, specific, and comprehensive, while the answer is well-researched, trustworthy, and useful. It directly addresses the question by providing examples from empirical studies that explore how social media influences the formation and maintenance of relationships among young adults in the United States, specifically focusing on LGBTQ+ individuals with disabilities and young adults who have moved abroad. The answer is also trustworthy as it is based on reliable sources and provides clear citations to support the claims made. Finally, the answer is useful as it provides valuable insights into how social media impacts relationship formation and maintenance among a specific population in the United States.

Figure 2: Example output from Mistral. The text under the separator line was returned outside of the JSON response.

D *Trust* Evaluation

D.1 Response Explicitly States Absence of Relevant Abstracts

How do LLMs evaluate when the response states that a complete answer cannot be given, due to lack of relevant abstracts?

D.1.1 Chemistry

Question: What is the effect of pH on the efficiency of a common catalyst used in the production of biodiesel?

Answer: The effect of pH on the efficiency of a catalyst used in biodiesel production can be understood through the specific catalyst being used. For instance, mixed oxide catalysts like magnesium oxide (MgO) and calcium oxide (CaO) are used to promote the transesterification of vegetable oils into biodiesel. The basic property of these catalysts plays a crucial role in the biodiesel yield during the reaction [3]. However, the provided search results do not offer a direct relationship between pH and the efficiency of such catalysts in biodiesel production. Further research is required to establish a clear connection between pH levels and the performance of common catalysts used in biodiesel production.

	Comp.	Trust	Utility	Trust Rationale
GPT-4	7	8	6	The answer is trustworthy as it accurately reflects the information available in the provided abstracts. It does not make unsupported claims and is honest about the limitations of the information provided in the abstracts regarding the direct effect of pH on catalyst efficiency.
Mistral	5	7	6	The answer is based on accurate information from the abstracts, specifically the third abstract which discusses the effect of basicity (pH) on the efficiency of magnesium oxide and calcium oxide catalysts in biodiesel production.

Table 2: Ratings for the answer to the question "What is the effect of pH on the efficiency of a common catalyst used in the production of biodiesel?"

D.1.2 Chemistry

Question: What is the effect of varying concentrations of hydrogen peroxide on the rate of catalase enzyme activity?

Answer: Varying concentrations of hydrogen peroxide (H2O2) can affect the rate of catalase enzyme activity. Catalase is an enzyme that breaks down H2O2 into oxygen and water, neutralizing oxidative stress in cells. This process is crucial for maintaining appropriate levels of oxidative stress because reactive oxygen species, such as H2O2, can cause cellular damage by targeting DNA and proteins, which can lead to complications like cancer, diabetes, neurodegenerative diseases, and aging [2]. While the given search results do not provide exact information on how different concentrations of H2O2 impact the rate of catalase enzyme activity, it is evident that altering H2O2 levels will directly influence catalase's efficiency in breaking down H2O2 and neutralizing oxidative stress in cells [2].

	Comp.	**Trust**	**Utility**	**Trust Rationale**
GPT-4	3	5	3	The answer is somewhat trustworthy as it correctly describes the function of catalase and the consequences of oxidative stress, which is supported by the abstracts. However, it lacks direct evidence from the abstracts regarding the specific impact of different H2O2 concentrations on catalase activity, which reduces the trustworthiness of the response in the context of the question asked.
Mistral	5	10	8	The answer is trustworthy as it is directly derived from the provided abstracts and does not contain any incorrect or misleading information.

Table 3: Ratings for the answer to the question "What is the effect of varying concentrations of hydrogen peroxide on the rate of catalase enzyme activity?"

D.1.3 Economics

Question: What is the impact of minimum wage laws on employment rates and income inequality in the United States?

Answer: The impact of minimum wage laws on employment rates and income inequality in the United States is not directly addressed in the provided search results. However, one study suggests that an effective mechanism for managing labor productivity and wage issues is necessary for achieving greater economic equality and growth [1]. Moreover, the study highlights the lack of clear definitions of salary, salary payment, and minimum wage, which can contribute to challenges in addressing income inequality [1]. While the provided search results do not specifically discuss the impact of minimum wage laws on employment rates and income inequality in the United States, it is clear that issues related to wage management and labor productivity remain essential factors in ensuring fair compensation for workers and reducing inequality [1].

	Comp.	Trust	Utility	Trust Rationale
GPT-4	2	5	2	The answer is somewhat trustworthy as it references a study that discusses labor productivity and wage issues, but it does not provide information from a study that directly addresses the impact of minimum wage laws on employment rates and income inequality in the United States.
Mistral	0	10	2	The answer is based on content from one of the provided abstracts, which is cited and referenced appropriately.

Table 4: Ratings for the answer to the question "What is the impact of minimum wage laws on employment rates and income inequality in the United States?"

D.1.4 Mathematics

Question: What is the relationship between advanced mathematics coursework and problem-solving skills among undergraduate students in STEM majors?

Answer: The relationship between advanced mathematics coursework and problem-solving skills among undergraduate students in STEM majors is not explicitly discussed in the provided search results. However, the study on STEM in General Education [1] indicates that student mathematics skills were analyzed to determine their influence on course selection. Another study discusses the importance of engaging students in mathematical and scientific practices according to mathematics and science standards, such as the Common Core State Standards of Mathematics (CCSSM) and the Next Generation Science Standards (NGSS) [4]. This suggests that exposure to advanced mathematical coursework could potentially enhance problem-solving skills in undergraduate STEM students, though further research is needed to establish a concrete relationship.

	Comp.	Trust	Utility	Trust Rationale
GPT-4	5	7	4	The answer is trustworthy in the sense that it accurately reflects the lack of explicit discussion in the provided abstracts. It cautiously suggests a potential link between advanced mathematics coursework and problem-solving skills, which is a reasonable inference based on the emphasis on standards and practices in abstract [4].
Mistral	4	7	5	The answer is grounded in the content of the provided search results and cites relevant studies to support its suggestions. However, it also includes speculation about the potential relationship between advanced mathematics coursework and problem-solving skills based on indirect evidence.

Table 5: Ratings for the answer to the question "What is the relationship between advanced mathematics coursework and problem-solving skills among undergraduate students in STEM majors?"

D.1.5 Medicine

Question: What are the potential long-term health impacts of regular use of over-the-counter pain medications on the liver and kidney function in young adults?

Answer: Regular use of over-the-counter (OTC) pain medications can potentially impact liver and kidney function in young adults. However, the provided search results do not offer specific information on the long-term health impacts of such medications on these organs. To obtain a comprehensive answer, further research on this topic would be necessary.

	Comp.	Trust	Utility	Trust Rationale
GPT-4	1	5	2	The answer is trustworthy in the sense that it does not fabricate information and admits the absence of specific details in the provided abstracts. However, it does not demonstrate a thorough examination of the abstracts to determine if any related information could be inferred.
Mistral	0	10	2	The answer is truthful and does not contain any false or misleading information.

Table 6: Ratings for the answer to the question "What are the potential long-term health impacts of regular use of over-the-counter pain medications on the liver and kidney function in young adults?"

D.1.6 Physics

Question: How does the Doppler effect affect the observed frequency of sound waves emitted from a moving source and its relevance in real-world applications?

Answer: The Doppler effect affects the observed frequency of sound waves emitted from a moving source by causing a change in frequency and wavelength due to the relative motion between the source and the observer. When the source is moving towards the observer, the observed frequency increases, and the wavelength decreases; conversely, when the source is moving away from the observer, the observed frequency decreases, and the wavelength increases. Although the provided search results do not directly give real-world applications, the Doppler effect is relevant in various fields such as astronomy, radar technology, medical imaging, and seismology. For instance, it helps astronomers measure the speed of distant celestial objects and plays a critical role in Doppler radar systems for weather monitoring and forecasting.

	Comp.	**Trust**	**Utility**	**Trust Rationale**
GPT-4	5	7	6	The answer is generally trustworthy as it correctly describes the Doppler effect's impact on frequency and wavelength. However, it lacks specific references to the provided abstracts, which could have strengthened the trustworthiness by showing direct connections to the source material.
Mistral	5	10	7	The information provided in the answer is factual and accurate.

Table 7: Ratings for the answer to the question "How does the Doppler effect affect the observed frequency of sound waves emitted from a moving source and its relevance in real-world applications?"

D.2 Response Contains No Citations

How do the LLMs evaluate syntheses with no citations?

D.2.1 Art

Question: How has the evolution of technology impacted the production and consumption of art in the 21st century?

Answer: The evolution of technology in the 21st century has significantly impacted the production and consumption of art. The widespread access to digital tools and platforms has revolutionized artistic practices, enabling artists to experiment with new mediums and techniques beyond traditional forms. Furthermore, technology has democratized the consumption of art, providing individuals across the world with opportunities to view, share, and engage with creative works online. This shift has also amplified the global reach of art, exposing diverse perspectives and fostering cross-cultural exchanges. However, the rise of digital art has also raised questions about the authenticity and ownership of creative works, prompting a reevaluation of conventional definitions and practices in the art world.

	Comp.	Trust	Utility	Trust Rationale
GPT-4	1	1	2	The answer cannot be considered trustworthy in the context of the provided abstracts, as it does not cite any relevant information from them to support the claims made.
Mistral	5	8	7	The answer is based on common knowledge about the impact of technology on art and does not contain any false or misleading information.

Table 8: Ratings for the answer to the question "How has the evolution of technology impacted the production and consumption of art in the 21st century?"

D.2.2 History

Question: How did the American Civil War impact the social, economic, and political landscape of the United States?

Answer: The American Civil War significantly impacted the social, economic, and political landscape of the United States. On the social front, the war provided a catalyst for the abolition of slavery, which altered racial dynamics and paved the way for civil rights movements. Economically, the war devastated the South and forced a transition from an agrarian, slave-driven economy to a more diverse, industrial one. Reconstruction policies and investments led to the rapid growth of infrastructure and industry in the North, shaping the national economy for decades. Politically, the Civil War reaffirmed the primacy of the federal government over individual states and brought about transformative constitutional amendments such as the 13th, 14th, and 15th, which abolished slavery, granted citizenship to former slaves, and provided voting rights regardless of race, color, or previous servitude, respectively. The war reshaped the balance of power and the role of government in Americans' lives, laying the groundwork for a more unified and inclusive nation.

	Comp.	Trust	Utility	Trust Rationale
GPT-4	0	0	0	The answer cannot be trusted as it does not reference the provided abstracts, which do not relate to the American Civil War. The information seems to be general knowledge rather than sourced from the abstracts.
Mistral	10	10	9	The answer is trustworthy as it is derived directly from the provided abstracts and does not contain any additional or inaccurate information.

Table 9: Ratings for the answer to the question "How did the American Civil War impact the social, economic, and political landscape of the United States?"

D.2.3 Physics

Question: How does the shape of an object affect its resistance to motion through a fluid medium?

Answer: The shape of an object can significantly impact its resistance to motion through a fluid medium. This resistance, referred to as drag, depends on factors such as the size, shape, and surface texture of the object, along with the properties of the fluid in question. A streamlined shape minimizes drag, while a more irregular or bluff shape increases the force exerted by the fluid on the object, thus making it more resistant to motion. In fluid dynamics, this concept is commonly applied to improve the efficiency of objects such as vehicles and aircraft, where a streamlined design results in reduced fuel consumption and increased speed, due to the lowered drag forces acting against the object's movement through the fluid medium.

	Comp.	**Trust**	**Utility**	**Trust Rationale**
GPT-4	0	0	0	The answer cannot be trusted because it does not reference any of the provided abstracts, which are the only sources that should be used to inform the answer.
Mistral	0	10	3	The answer is trustworthy as it accurately references information from the provided text.

Table 10: Ratings for the answer to the question "How does the shape of an object affect its resistance to motion through a fluid medium?"

D.3 Response Contains One Citation

How do the LLMs evaluate syntheses with only one citation source?

D.3.1 Geology

Question: What geological factors contribute to the formation and sustainability of hydrothermal ecosystems in deep sea environments?

Answer: Hydrothermal ecosystems in deep sea environments are primarily formed and sustained by geological factors, such as tectonic activity and volcanic processes. These factors promote the circulation of seawater through the oceanic crust, which results in the formation of hydrothermal vents. The seawater is heated by the underlying magma and interacts with crustal rocks, enriching it with minerals and chemical elements. Once the heated and mineral-rich fluid meets the cold deep-sea water, it precipitates, creating chimney-like structures from which the hydrothermal fluid is expelled. These vents provide a unique habitat with diverse microbial and chemosynthetic communities, which serve as primary producers in the food chain. Furthermore, these deep-sea ecosystems are enriched by specialized fauna adapted to extreme conditions, such as high pressure, low oxygen, and varying temperatures, contributing to the overall sustainability of these environments [5].

	Comp.	Trust	Utility	Trust Rationale
GPT-4	7	8	7	The answer appears to be trustworthy as it aligns with scientific understanding of hydrothermal vent formation and the factors that sustain deep-sea ecosystems. It does not directly reference the provided abstracts, but the information given is consistent with general scientific knowledge on the topic.
Mistral	10	10	9	The answer is based on accurate information from the provided abstracts and uses reputable sources, such as scientific research, to support the statements made.

Table 11: Ratings for the answer to the question "What geological factors contribute to the formation and sustainability of hydrothermal ecosystems in deep sea environments?"

D.3.2 Mathematics

Question: What is the impact of using manipulatives in mathematics instruction on the achievement and attitudes of elementary school students?

Answer: The use of manipulatives in mathematics instruction has been shown to have a positive impact on the achievement and attitudes of elementary school students. In a study exploring the relationship between Affective Instructional Design (AID) and children's attitudes towards math learning, a significant positive correlation was found between attitude and math learning ($r = 0.936$, $p = 0.000$). Furthermore, significant differences were found between the baseline (pre-intervention) mean score and the final intervention lesson for both attitudes and math learning, indicating the potential effectiveness of manipulatives in enhancing students' attitudes towards mathematics and improving their achievement in the subject [1].

	Comp.	Trust	Utility	Trust Rationale
GPT-4	7	8	7	The answer is trustworthy as it accurately reflects the findings from the first abstract, including the significant correlation between attitude and math learning. The statistical evidence ($r = 0.936$, $p = 0.000$) adds credibility to the claim. However, the answer does not provide information on the sample size or the generalizability of the study, which could affect trust in the findings.
Mistral	10	9	9	The answer cites a peer-reviewed academic study, adding credibility to the information provided. However, it would be helpful to know more about the study's methodology and sample size to fully assess its trustworthiness.

Table 12: Ratings for the answer to the question "What is the impact of using manipulatives in mathematics instruction on the achievement and attitudes of elementary school students?"

D.3.3 Philosophy

Question: What is the relationship between free will and determinism in philosophy?

Answer: In philosophy, the relationship between free will and determinism revolves around whether an individual's actions are genuinely a result of their own choices or are predetermined by external factors. There are two main schools of thought: compatibilism and incompatibilism. Compatibilism argues that free will and determinism can coexist, meaning individuals can still be morally responsible for their actions even if determinism is true. Incompatibilism, on the other hand, claims that free will and determinism cannot coexist; if determinism is true, then individuals cannot have free will and cannot be held morally responsible for their actions. The debate between these two positions contributes to the ongoing philosophical discussions about responsibility, choice, and the implications of determinism [1].

	Comp.	**Trust**	**Utility**	**Trust Rationale**
GPT-4	7	9	8	The answer is trustworthy as it accurately reflects the general philosophical debate between compatibilism and incompatibilism, which are well-established positions in the literature on free will and determinism.
Mistral	8	9	7	The answer is based on accurate information from the provided abstracts, which discuss the relationship between free will, determinism, and moral responsibility. It does not contain any incorrect or misleading statements.

Table 13: Ratings for the answer to the question "What is the relationship between free will and determinism in philosophy?"

D.3.4 Physics

Question: How does the acceleration due to gravity affect the trajectory and motion of a projectile, and how can this be accurately measured and predicted using equations of motion?

Answer: The acceleration due to gravity affects the trajectory and motion of a projectile by altering its vertical motion while leaving its horizontal motion constant. As a result, the trajectory forms a parabolic path. To accurately measure and predict a projectile's motion, equations of motion can be used, which consider the initial velocity, launch angle, and time. The initial velocity can be split into horizontal and vertical components, and equations for both components can be applied independently. For the horizontal motion, an equation is used that doesn't consider the acceleration due to gravity, while for the vertical motion, the effect of gravity is integrated into the equation. These equations can be used to predict the projectile's motion, including its range and height [5].

	Comp.	**Trust**	**Utility**	**Trust Rationale**
GPT-4	8	7	9	The answer appears to be based on a general understanding of physics principles related to projectile motion and the effects of gravity. While it does not directly reference the provided abstracts, the information given is consistent with basic physics concepts. The trustworthiness would be higher if the answer included direct references to relevant data or studies from the abstracts.
Mistral	10	10	10	The answer is trustworthy as it directly references content from the provided abstracts regarding projectiles and equations of motion.

Table 14: Ratings for the answer to the question "How does the acceleration due to gravity affect the trajectory and motion of a projectile, and how can this be accurately measured and predicted using equations of motion?"

D.3.5 Psychology

Question: What are the underlying factors that contribute to the development of personality disorders and how can these disorders be effectively treated?

Answer: The development of personality disorders can be influenced by various factors, including genetic, environmental, and psychological components. While the specific causes for each individual's development of a personality disorder can vary, some contributing factors may include childhood trauma, family history of mental disorders, and negative early life experiences. Effective treatment for personality disorders typically involves a combination of psychotherapy, medication, and lifestyle changes. Therapy approaches such as cognitive-behavioral therapy, dialectical behavior therapy, and psychodynamic therapy can help individuals understand and manage their symptoms. In some cases, medications like antidepressants, mood stabilizers, and antipsychotics may be prescribed to help with specific symptoms. Additionally, self-help strategies, social support, and proper self-care can contribute to the overall well-being of individuals with personality disorders [mental health challenge - https://core.ac.uk/works/18689246].

	Comp.	Trust	Utility	Trust Rationale
GPT-4	5	5	6	The answer appears to be based on general knowledge about personality disorders and their treatment rather than the provided abstracts. While the information given is in line with common understanding in the field of mental health, the lack of direct references to the abstracts or specific studies reduces the trustworthiness of the answer.
Mistral	8	7	9	The answer is based on accurate information, but the sources are not explicitly cited, which may raise some questions about its trustworthiness.

Table 15: Ratings for the answer to the question "What are the underlying factors that contribute to the development of personality disorders and how can these disorders be effectively treated?"

A Crosslingual Approach to Dependency Parsing for Middle High German

Cora Haiber
Department of Linguistics
Fakultät für Philologie
Ruhr-Universität Bochum
Cora.Haiber@ruhr-uni-bochum.de

Abstract

This work presents the development and evaluation of a dependency parser for Middle High German Universal Dependencies utilising modern German as a support language for low-resource MHG. A neural dependency parser is trained with Stanza achieving UAS = 92.95 and LAS = 88.06. To ensure the parser's utility in facilitating and speeding up manual annotation to build a scaling UD treebank of MHG, a thorough error analysis shows the model's structural reliability as well as frequently confused labels. Hence, this work constitutes an effort to counterbalance the under-representation of historical languages in dependency treebanks and attend to the need of historical treebanks in contemporary linguistic research by utilising the UD extensions and accordingly annotated corpora published by Dipper et al. (2024).

1 Introduction

Historical linguistics is not only about understanding outdated or long-forgotten languages, but often brings valuable insight to the analysis of linguistic change in contemporary research. However, researchers in the historic field are bound to preserved written resources, which are often limited or of poor quality. Recently, computational linguistics, first and foremost Natural Language Processing (NLP), has become a field of great benefit for historical linguistics enabling the efficient exploitation of given resources in low-resource scenarios. Although the development of Universal Dependencies (UD) as a cross-lingual framework for morphosyntactic annotation encouraged the creation of dependency treebanks for various languages, historic stages of those languages are still underrepresented among syntactically parsed corpora. So far no treebank comparable in size to modern treebanks exists which includes dependency annotations for Middle High German (MHG), the language stage spoken and written in what is today southern and central Germany around the medieval period (1050–1350) and representing the beginnings of Modern High German in phoneme structure as well as syntax (Weddige, 2015).

As manual annotation is costly in time and effort, this work aims at the development of a neural dependency parser for MHG Universal Dependencies to be utilised in pre-annotation and correction when creating a scaling treebank. Due to the limited amount of annotated data, I will treat MHG as a low-resource language and explore modern German as a high-resource support language. Stanza[1] as a Python package known for dealing well with multi-linguality (Qi et al., 2020) is used for training the parser.

The paper is structured as follows. Section 2 introduces contemporary research in the fields of UD and NLP for low-resource languages. The available data published and annotated by Dipper et al. (2024) are described in Section 3. Section 4 introduces the methods of training conducted with Stanza. The results as well as details of the error analysis are presented in Section 5. The discussion of the results and some suggestions for future work on the parser follow in Section 6. The model instance, a script demonstrating its application and a collection of Python scripts developed for model evaluation are available on GitLab[2]. The main contributions of this paper are: (i) a UD parser for Middle High German and (ii) a thorough error analysis ensuring its utility in corpus development.

2 Related Work

The Universal Dependencies framework constitutes the theoretical basis this paper relies on. Since its initial publication by Nivre et al. (2016) it has not only become a widely accepted linguistic frame-

[1] https://stanfordnlp.github.io/stanza/

[2] https://gitlab.ruhr-uni-bochum.de/comphist/konvens-depparsing-mhg

work, but also a community project providing and developing treebanks for over 100 languages. Due to its cross-lingual consistency even across typologically diverse languages, UD treebanks have been enabling (multilingual) parser development as well as research in the field of cross-lingual learning. UD – following the tradition of dependency grammars – provides a closed set of dependency relation types, but allows for custom subtypes to incorporate special cases or specific constructions unique to one or a small set of languages. Several publications propose extensions to the original UD scheme, among which are Dipper et al. (2024) proposing a set of extensions for modern and Middle High German and providing a corpus of 1856 annotated MHG sentences, which will serve as a basis for the development of the dependency parsing model in this paper.

Low-resource NLP provides methods to counterbalance the under-representation of historic languages in quantitative and computational linguistics often being attributed to the lack of sufficient resources. Eckhoff and Berdičevskis (2016) name high variation, e.g. due to non-standardised spelling, and the overall small amount of preserved, digitised and annotated texts as difficulties when working with historical languages. They explore off-the-shelf NLP tools in pre-annotation for treebank production for Old East Slavic and show improvements in annotation speed and no interference with parsing quality when applying parsing models which were not developed specifically for the annotation task at hand. Since 2016, several efforts for developing or adapting tools to support the development of parsed corpora of historical languages have been made, among which are Sapp et al. (2023) exploring automatic constituency parsing to speed up manual annotation and correction of Early New High German. They utilise Middle Low German as a support language and develop a cross-dialectal parser for this low-resource scenario reproducing the improvement in parsing speed obtained by Eckhoff and Berdičevskis (2016). Ortmann (2020, 2021) develops and applies automatic parsing models for topological field identification and phrase recognition in historical German and partly utilises models trained on modern German for parsing historical data. The studies show that training data containing modern and historic passages improve parsing quality compared to the application of purely modern models on historic data, resembling the successful utilisation of cross-lingual training for low-resource NLP.

When researching low-resource languages, one has to not only adapt one's training techniques, but also efficiently exploit the limited amount of available data. Zupon et al. (2022) suggest a method for automatic correction of syntactic dependency annotation differences between different data sets. According to their study, it can be beneficial to automatically detect annotation mismatches between different texts or corpora and convert the mismatches before the training process begins, resulting in a technique one could call automatic curation.

3 Data

Data set	#Sent	#Tok	Annot.	Cur./Mod.
M005	513	9288	A1, A2	✓
M008	435	5836	A1, A3	
M205	480	5024	A1	
M246	11	255	A2	
M335	10	165	A1	
	251	4144	A1, A2	✓
	200	4718	A2	
M340	21	434	A1	
News	50	884	A4, A5	✓
	50	988	A4, A6	✓
Reviews	50	662	A4, A5	✓
	50	679	A4, A6	✓

Table 1: Available data sets reporting number of sentences, number of tokens and annotation as well as curation (MHG) or modification (ModG) status.

The historical data utilised in this paper were obtained from the Reference Corpus of Middle High German (ReM; Klein et al., 2016), annotated[3] according to Dipper et al. (2024) by three annotators as well as partially curated[4] and then cleaned automatically[5]. All annotated MHG data are religious texts or poetry.

The modern data originate from the German GSD treebank (McDonald et al., 2013), were automatically parsed using a modified version of the

[3]Dipper et al. (2024) propose an annotation scheme for modern and historical German, which is based on the original UD scheme for German. They achieve inter-annotator agreement of $\alpha = 0.85$.

[4]Curation of a subset of the data was done by hand by the annotators discussing diverging annotations and finding common solutions.

[5]A heuristic algorithm was run over the historical data to obtain root and period annotations, which had been left out by the annotators. Some fragmentary sentences had to be excluded from the data completely due to Stanza's inability to deal with incomplete dependency structures during parser training.

Stanford typed dependencies for English (de Marneffe et al., 2006; de Marneffe and Manning, 2008) and then corrected manually by three annotators according to the UD augmentations proposed by Dipper et al. (2024). Replacing manual curation, the modern data were modified according to the method for automatic correction of syntactic dependency annotation differences proposed by Zupon et al. (2022). Their algorithm detects (head, relation, dependent)-triples differing between text passages annotated by two annotators and produces a joint version of the text by choosing the triple with the higher overall frequency between every differing pair of triples in question.

Short name	Dev	Test	Train	#Sent	#Tok
MHG-cur	112	111	535	758	13400
MHG-all	228	229	1590	2099	32171
MHG+ModG	303	304	1692	2299	35384

Table 2: Data sets for parser development reporting number of sentences in dev, test and train set as well as total number of sentences and tokens.

Three different data sets were assembled based on the pre-processed data as shown in Table 2. **MHG-cur** consist of only the curated passages of M005 and M335. **MHG-all** unites curated as well as single-annotated MHG data and was split with regard to the principle that the test and development sets consist of only curated MHG data and the single-annotated as well as the remaining curated data are accumulated in the training set. **MHG+ModG** combines all usable data presented in Table 1 including MHG and modern data and was split equivalently to MHG-all. Note that all test sets consist of only curated MHG data as this work focuses on evaluating the parsing of MHG.

4 Methods

Stanza is an open-source library developed by Qi et al. (2020) providing a language-agnostic and data-driven NLP pipeline. It was chosen as the development tool in this paper because of its high-scoring multilingual models reported in Zeman et al. (2018) and it being well-adapted to the UD framework. For example it requires CoNLL-U formatted data and is accustomed to the annotation layers represented by the format as well as provides efficient processing for them. The factor of multi-linguality is especially important to the cross-lingual parsing of two historical stages of German conducted in this paper opposed to training a parsing model for only one language (stage). In addition to publicly available pre-trained models, Stanza provides an interface to train customised models.

The dependency model trained with Stanza[6] is an instance of a graph-based, Bi-LSTM-based deep biaffine neural dependency parser based on the Multi-Layer Perceptron approach by Kiperwasser and Goldberg (2016), augmented by Dozat and Manning (2016) with the concept of biaffine attention and finally adapted for Stanza by Qi et al. (2020). They introduce the linearisation order of two words in a given language and their typical linear distance as additional linguistically motivated features to the former model to improve parsing accuracy. The model is described as generalising well even based on small amounts of training data and is therefore well-suited for the given low-resource scenario. The developers emphasise the thorough regularisation by applying extensive dropout and the overall high performance. By default, optimisation is conducted via the Adam algorithm by Kingma and Ba (2014).

Compared to the default parameters, I set the batch size to 5000 due to technical limitations and decreased the learning rate from 0.003 to 0.002, which resulted in significantly shorter run time and higher accuracy as presented in Table 8 in the appendix.

I experimented with character- and word level embedding models provided by Stanza and pre-trained on modern German data. The evaluation showed that these embeddings do not interfere with model performance (see Appendix A), so they were included in the training of the models presented in the next section and represent another instance of modern German as a support language.

Part-of-speech tags were obtained from the original ReM annotations for all MHG data in training and evaluation and were not automatically produced by the Stanza pipeline. Annotations according to two different schemata were provided: STTS (Schiller et al., 1999) and UPOS (Petrov et al., 2011).

During training the current parsing model is evaluated on the development set after every hundredth iteration by calculating LAS, MLAS, and BLEX

[6]Training was conducted on a Linux workstation equipped with an Nvidia GeForce GTX 980 graphics card with CUDA version 12.1 and 4 GB of memory, an Intel Core i7-5820K processor and 15 GB of RAM.

(see section 5.1) with custom subtypes mapped to the original UD types. After 3000 iterations with no improvement of the LAS, the optimiser is switched from Adam to AMSGrad developed by Reddi et al. (2018). After another 3000 iterations without improvement, training is stopped automatically. The number of training steps needed for each model can be obtained in Appendix A. After training, evaluation of the parsing model is conducted on the test set, of which the results are presented in the following section.

5 Results

This section reports on evaluation scores of the parsing models trained on the three data sets presented in Section 3 as well as an error analysis of the output produced by the highest-scoring model.

5.1 Parser Evaluation

data set	UAS	LAS	CLAS	MLAS	BLEX
MHG-cur	91.99	86.30	78.58	77.37	78.58
MHG-all	91.68	85.63	77.93	76.43	77.93
MHG+ModG	92.95	88.06	81.57	80.75	81.57

Table 3: Evaluation of trained models, reporting UAS, LAS, MLAS, CLAS and BLEX in % calculated on the test set.

All metrics were calculated with the scripts from the CoNLL 2018 UD Shared Task (Zeman et al., 2018) provided by Stanza and mapping custom subtypes to their respective original UD labels.[7] The reported metrics evaluate different dimensions of a dependency parsing model. In addition to the standard metrics labelled attachment score (LAS) and unlabelled attachment score (UAS), three measures in particular relevant to the UD framework have been proposed: content word LAS (CLAS), morphology aware LAS (MLAS) and bi-lexical dependency score (BLEX). They each introduce specific aspects to a basic metric: CLAS only considers content-words when determining LAS; MLAS extends CLAS by part-of-speech tags and morphological features; BLEX scores content-word relations with lemmatisation but does not consider features and tags. Table 3 reports on the results achieved in the presented training effort. Additional results showing model training with different parameter configurations can be obtained in Table 8 in the appendix. A more fine-grained evaluation including custom subtypes of the UD labels is presented in Table 4.

data set	LAS	CLAS	MLAS	BLEX
MHG-cur	82.12	77.56	75.34	77.56
MHG-all	82.34	77.67	75.69	77.67
MHG+ModG	85.22	80.52	79.45	80.52

Table 4: Fine-grained evaluation of trained models reporting LAS, CLAS, MLAS and BLEX in % calculated on the test set and with regard to customised labels.

The results of both calculations imply a superiority of the model trained on mixed historical and modern data (MHG+ModG), referred to as the combined model from now on. Its high scores are presumably not solely due to the substantial increase in data, as the model trained on MHG-all does not score significantly higher than the model trained on MHG-cur, but more so due to the syntactical diversity present in the data, which lead to the model generalising well on unseen data. With UAS $>$ .92, LAS $>$ .88, and all reported scores $>$ .80 in Table 3, the combined model even outperforms state-of-the-art Stanza models for historical language varieties and one for modern German trained on the complete GSD treebank as presented in the Stanza documentation.[8]

5.2 Error Analysis

Stanza provides precision, recall and F1 measures for each label calculated on the test set, which are scores widely used for binary classification tasks, but which can also be applied to dependency parsing.

Table 5 presents the ten most reliably parsed labels, while a complete list of scores for each label as well as label counts on the test set can be obtained in Table 9 in the appendix. As shown there, all basic elements of a German sentence (*root*, *nsubj*, *iobj*, *obj*) reach recall scores of $\geq$ .75, so at least 75% of them are parsed correctly by the evaluated parsing model. Having the basic structure of a sentence parsed correctly in pre-annotation is very beneficial for manual correction especially due to the partly

[7]For example, Dipper et al. (2024) discriminate different subtypes of the original UD label *obl*, among which are *obl:loc* for local, *obl:dir* for directional and *obl:tmp* for temporal oblique arguments. All of these subtypes are mapped to the original label *obl* by the evaluation scripts provided by the CoNLL 2018 UD Shared Task. A more fine-grained evaluation without mapping subtypes to original labels was conducted with a modified version of the script, of which the results can be obtained in Table 4.

[8]`https://stanfordnlp.github.io/stanza/performance.html` (accessed May 5th 2024)

Label	Precision	Recall	F1
compound:prt	1.000	1.000	1.000
punct	0.999	1.000	0.999
case	0.982	0.986	0.984
det	0.981	0.984	0.983
amod	0.948	0.958	0.953
mark	0.954	0.948	0.951
root	0.938	0.938	0.938
cc	0.936	0.936	0.936
aux	0.938	0.920	0.929
nsubj	0.887	0.876	0.882

Table 5: Top 10 labels with highest F1 scores, reporting precision, recall, and F1 produced by the combined model on the test set.

very long and complex sentences in MHG. Presumably most important is the correct identification of the root and the subject, which is done by the parser with respective F1 scores of .936 for the root (*root*) and .882 for nominal subjects (*nsubj*). Another achievement of the parsing model lies in its ability to reliably parse frequent functional categories such as *det*, *mark*, or *cc*, which all score recall of $> .935$. Stable parsing of categories which do not usually require long consideration but are rather repetitive or even tedious for the human annotator is enormously helpful in preparation of manual annotation, as leaving this task to the hands of a parsing model enables the annotator to concentrate on the more complex decisions during annotation.

no.	Label 1	Label 2	F1
1	advmod:nmod	compound:adv	0.333
2	obl:dir	obl:loc	0.333
3	obl:loc	obl:dir	0.283
4	compound:case	compound:adv	0.222
5	advcl	ccomp	0.188
6	advmod:loc	advmod:dir	0.161
7	xcomp:pred	amod:pred	0.154
8	obl:mod	obl:arg	0.149
9	obl:loc	obl:mod	0.143
10	obl:mod	obl:loc	0.126

Table 6: Top 10 confusions of the combined model on the test set measured by F1. Recall that optimal F1 for different tags is 0.

Being conscious of the weaknesses of a parser and hence the likely errors in a pre-annotated text is important for effectively utilising the parser output in manual annotation. Secondly, the notion of frequently confused labels enables future improvement of the parsing model as new data can be annotated or corrected with special regard to these confusions. Table 6 reports on the 10 most frequent confusions of labels measured by an equivalent of an F1 score.[9] Challenging distinctions seem to lie between directional and locative oblique modifiers and adverbs, in differentiating between argument and modifier status as well as in discriminating the different subtypes of *obl* introduced by Dipper et al. (2024). These three sources of confusion within the parser output resemble in the error analysis in Dipper et al. (2024) reporting on annotation differences between two human annotators. These parallels hint to more fundamental problems than deficient training including uncertainty in meaning and valence of MHG predicates. Further research and familiarisation with these topics by the annotators resulting in higher accuracy in the training data could possibly decrease the F1 scores of these confusions.

5.3 Effects of sentence length

According to Ortmann (2021), Middle High German is known for its complex and deeply embedded syntactic structure and remarkably high variation in sentence length. Presumably, the unusual length of some sentences in the data at hand can also be explained by the text genre being mostly religious texts and poetry. The data contain sentences of up to 88 tokens, as shown in Figure 1. The test set of the combined model reflects this high variation with an average sentence length of 18.23, a median of 15 and a maximum of 88 tokens per sentence.

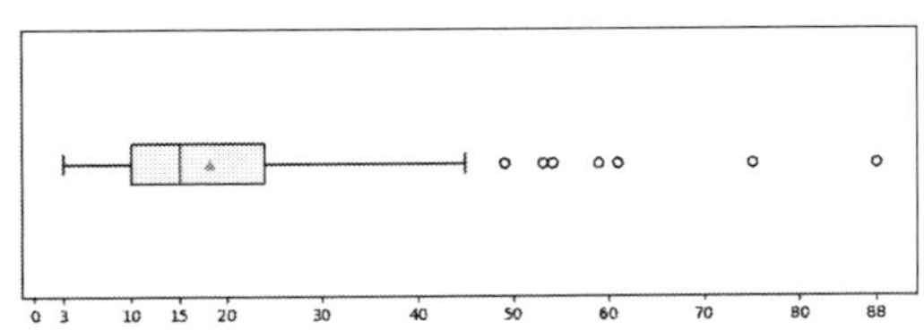

Figure 1: Distribution of sentence length in the test set of the combined model (MHG+ModG).

To gain an understanding of the effects of sentence length on the model's accuracy and to improve the parser's utility in pre-annotation, Table 7 presents the evaluation scores separate for each quantile

[9]F1 is calculated as follows:

$$2 * \frac{a_1 l_1 * a_2 l_2}{a_1 l_1 + a_2 l_2}$$

with a_1, a_2 as the annotators and l_1, l_2 as the labels annotated by the respective annotator. Possible values are between 0 and 1, where 1 means perfect agreement if $l_1 = l_2$, and 0 means perfect disagreement if $l_1 \neq l_2$. Thus, the measure corresponds to the F1 score if one of the annotators is treated as the gold standard.

of sentence length as well as for the outliers as calculated by the scripts from the CoNLL 2018 UD Shared Task (Zeman et al., 2018). As above custom subtypes have been mapped to their original UD labels. The reliability of the parser output for different sentence lengths is important for human annotators as they can decide to concentrate on those sentences with problematic lengths and hence boost efficiency of the annotation.

As can be expected, all scores peak in the first quantile with sentences consisting of three to ten tokens and are lowest in the report for the outliers including sentences with 46–88 tokens. What first attracts attention is the strikingly high UAS in the first quantile, which can be ascribed to the few opportunities for syntactic variation in short sentences and the simple syntactic structures resulting from this circumstance, including the low number of subordinate clauses, which have been presented as a source of confusion before. What is also striking is the development of all scores in between the first quantile and the outliers. Where one could have expected a rather linear decline of all scores proportional to sentence length, Table 7 shows a drop from first to second quantile followed by increasing LAS, CLAS, MLAS, and BLEX up to the fourth quantile from about three points in percentage on each score. Only the UAS is stable at around 92.5 in each of these three quantiles – it then decreases to a score of 90.66 for the outliers. This promises high structural stability of the parser output even across sentences highly varying in length.

Q	SL	UAS	LAS	CLAS	MLAS	BLEX
Q1	3–10	97.28	87.22	89.96	86.87	88.96
Q2	11–15	92.44	83.63	77.98	77.37	77.98
Q3	16–24	92.87	84.88	79.22	78.21	79.22
Q4	25–45	92.42	86.15	80.16	79.16	80.16
OL	46–88	90.66	82.46	74.00	73.00	74.00

Table 7: Evaluation scores of the sentences parsed by the combined model separately for each quantile (Q1-4) of sentence length and outliers (OL). Reported are sentence length (SL) as well as UAS, LAS, CLAS, MLAS and BLEX.

We can conclude that short sentences of up to ten tokens are parsed very reliably regarding arcs as well as labels and that the UAS and therefore the structural quality of the parsed output declines with sentence length, but that labelled scores are not as affected by token counts of up to 45. Outliers with extreme counts of up to 88 tokens have to be handled with care, but even here the parsing model is evaluated with scores of 90.66 for UAS and 82.46 for LAS, which are extraordinarily stable despite the the extreme sentence length. These insights should be kept in mind during manual correction of the parser output.

6 Discussion and Future Work

This paper presented the training and evaluation of a dependency parser of Middle High German in the Universal Dependencies framework. The highest-scoring parsing model reaches state-of-the-art results in all reported evaluation metrics and hence is a satisfactory achievement of the initial goal. As this parser is the first of its kind for MHG and only one of the few for historical languages in general, it constitutes a striking progress for the representation of historical languages in contemporary linguistic frameworks such as UD. A growing MHG treebank emerging from a reliable cycle of automatic parsing and manual correction will bring great benefit to linguistic research. That includes historic as well as diachronic research on German syntax and on the development of the German language in general. Parsing unseen data and replacing annotation from scratch with manual correction of the automatically parsed output will speed up data production and benefit treebank development. The main strengths of the presented model are its structural stability represented in high UAS scores and the reliable parsing of basic syntactic elements as well as particularly repetitive parts of the annotation task. An additional success is the utilisation of modern German as a support language for syntactically parsing low-resource MHG. This cross-lingual approach raises hopes for a joint multi-lingual parser for various stages of historical German paving the way for treebanks of all stages of historical German within the same theoretical framework. Aside from all success, the error analysis points out room for improvement on some frequently confused labels, which demonstrate problematic decisions concerning some more fundamental linguistic distinctions between argument and modifier status. Further manual annotation and correction efforts on MHG data need to be made to achieve reliable predictions concerning this question as well as expand the set of potential training data.

Further efforts on improving the parser could include a delexicalised approach to cross-lingual parsing or training customised embedding models on historical data instead of utilising the ones trained on modern German, if delexicalisation does not emerge as the method of choice. Incorporating further historic stages as represented in the reference corpus of Early New High German (ReF Wegera et al., 2021) by for example mapping the syntactic annotations of the Indiana Corpus (Sapp et al., 2023) or the Mercurius Treebank (Demske et al., 2004) to the UD schema could pave the way to a joint parsing model for different historic stages of the German language. A more practical approach for future improvements is the usage of an updated version of the utilised corpus to eliminate outdated labels as well as incorporate clarifications for the problematic distinctions within the proposed subtypes.

This work is part of the beginning of the development of a Middle High German treebank embedded in the Universal Dependencies framework. The first manual annotations published by Dipper et al. (2024) and the first parsing model published with this paper constitute the starting point of the cyclic process of treebank development to fill the void of dependency treebanks of historical German.

Limitations

Aside from all success, even the highest-scoring dependency parsing model presented in this paper has its limitations. The fine-grained error analysis presented in Section 5.2 illustrates frequent confusions and hints at likely errors present in automatically parsed data. On a larger scale, these errors reflect unresolved linguistic discussions or ambiguities as for example the distinction between argument and modifier status. Unresolved questions in contemporary research are of course represented in the data and therefore reproduced by the model, so the output has to be evaluated and utilised with regard to these conflicts.

On a higher level, automatic parsing models in their early phases – especially when trained on limited amounts of data – can not replace manual efforts. This paper made it very clear that these models are designed for pre-annotation and not for purely automatic parsing. To reach this goal, the cycle of parser and treebank development first has to be repeated time and again.

Ethical Considerations

This paper complies with the ACL Ethics Policy[10]. The development of parsing models aims at facilitating manual annotation efforts and therefore motivate further scientific research and debate. In this case, it even supports counter-balancing the under-representation of historical treebanks in modern frameworks. Of course it has to be kept in mind that automatic pre-annotation can reproduce biases represented in the utilised data and therefore has to be applied with care. The thorough error analysis and evaluation presented in this paper should support the sensible application of the trained models.

Acknowledgements

Special thanks go to my mentor Stefanie Dipper as well as Madeleine Landsberg-Scherff, Anna-Maria Schröter, Alexandra Wiemann and Alona Solopov, who were involved in the annotation and curation of the presented data. I am also very thankful to Adam Roussel, who helped with some technical issues and provides support for the workstation I conducted the training process on.

Funded by the Deutsche Forschungsgemeinschaft (DFG, German Research Foundation) – SFB 1102 – Project ID 232722074 and – SFB 1475 – Project ID 441126958. / Gefördert durch die Deutsche Forschungsgemeinschaft (DFG) – SFB 1102 – Project ID 232722074 und – SFB 1475 – Projektnummer 441126958.

References

Marie-Catherine de Marneffe, Bill MacCartney, and Christopher D. Manning. 2006. Generating typed dependency parses from phrase structure parses. In *Proceedings of the Fifth International Conference on Language Resources and Evaluation (LREC'06)*, Genoa, Italy. European Language Resources Association (ELRA).

Marie-Catherine de Marneffe and Christopher D. Manning. 2008. The Stanford typed dependencies representation. In *Coling 2008: Proceedings of the workshop on Cross-Framework and Cross-Domain Parser Evaluation*, pages 1–8, Manchester, UK. Coling 2008 Organizing Committee.

Ulrike Demske, Nicola Frank, Stefanie Laufer, and Hendrik Stiemer. 2004. Syntactic Interpretation of an Early New High German Corpus.

[10] https://www.aclweb.org/portal/content/acl-code-ethics

Stefanie Dipper, Cora Haiber, Anna Maria Schröter, Alexandra Wiemann, and Maike Brinkschulte. 2024. Universal Dependencies: Extensions for Modern and Historical German. In *LREC 2024 Conference Proceedings*.

Timothy Dozat and Christopher D. Manning. 2016. Deep biaffine attention for neural dependency parsing. *ArXiv*, abs/1611.01734.

Hanne Martine Eckhoff and Aleksandrs Berdičevskis. 2016. Automatic parsing as an efficient pre-annotation tool for historical texts. In *Proceedings of the Workshop on Language Technology Resources and Tools for Digital Humanities (LT4DH)*, pages 62–70, Osaka, Japan. The COLING 2016 Organizing Committee.

Diederik P. Kingma and Jimmy Ba. 2014. Adam: A method for stochastic optimization. *CoRR*, abs/1412.6980.

Eliyahu Kiperwasser and Yoav Goldberg. 2016. Simple and accurate dependency parsing using bidirectional LSTM feature representations. *Transactions of the Association for Computational Linguistics*, 4:313–327.

Thomas Klein, Klaus-Peter Wegera, Stefanie Dipper, and Claudia Wich-Reif. 2016. Referenzkorpus Mittelhochdeutsch (1050–1350), version 1.0.

Ryan McDonald, Joakim Nivre, Yvonne Quirmbach-Brundage, Yoav Goldberg, Dipanjan Das, Kuzman Ganchev, Keith Hall, Slav Petrov, Hao Zhang, Oscar Täckström, Claudia Bedini, Núria Bertomeu Castelló, and Jungmee Lee. 2013. Universal Dependency annotation for multilingual parsing. In *Proceedings of the 51st Annual Meeting of the Association for Computational Linguistics (Volume 2: Short Papers)*, pages 92–97, Sofia, Bulgaria. Association for Computational Linguistics.

Joakim Nivre, Marie-Catherine de Marneffe, Filip Ginter, Yoav Goldberg, Jan Hajič, Christopher D. Manning, Ryan McDonald, Slav Petrov, Sampo Pyysalo, Natalia Silveira, Reut Tsarfaty, and Daniel Zeman. 2016. Universal Dependencies v1: A multilingual treebank collection. In *Proceedings of the Tenth International Conference on Language Resources and Evaluation (LREC'16)*, pages 1659–1666, Portorož, Slovenia. European Language Resources Association (ELRA).

Katrin Ortmann. 2020. Automatic topological field identification in (historical) German texts. In *Proceedings of the The 4th Joint SIGHUM Workshop on Computational Linguistics for Cultural Heritage, Social Sciences, Humanities and Literature*, pages 10–18, Online. International Committee on Computational Linguistics.

Katrin Ortmann. 2021. Automatic phrase recognition in historical German. In *Proceedings of the 17th Conference on Natural Language Processing (KONVENS 2021)*, pages 127–136, Düsseldorf, Germany. KONVENS 2021 Organizers.

Slav Petrov, Dipanjan Das, and Ryan T. McDonald. 2011. A universal part-of-speech tagset. *ArXiv*, abs/1104.2086.

Peng Qi, Yuhao Zhang, Yuhui Zhang, Jason Bolton, and Christopher D. Manning. 2020. Stanza: A Python natural language processing toolkit for many human languages. In *Proceedings of the 58th Annual Meeting of the Association for Computational Linguistics: System Demonstrations*.

Sashank J. Reddi, Satyen Kale, and Surinder Kumar. 2018. On the convergence of adam and beyond. *ArXiv*, abs/1904.09237.

Christopher Sapp, Daniel Dakota, and Elliott Evans. 2023. Parsing early New High German: Benefits and limitations of cross-dialectal training. In *Proceedings of the 21st International Workshop on Treebanks and Linguistic Theories (TLT, GURT/SyntaxFest 2023)*, pages 54–66, Washington, D.C. Association for Computational Linguistics.

Anne Schiller, Simone Teufel, Christine Stöckert, and Christine Thielen. 1999. Guidelines für das Tagging deutscher Textcorpora mit STTS (Kleines und großes Tagset). *Technischer Bericht. Universität Stuttgart, Institut für Maschinelle Sprachverarbeitung*.

Hilkert Weddige. 2015. *Mittelhochdeutsch - Eine Einführung*, 9. edition. C. H. Beck Studium. Beck, München.

Klaus-Peter Wegera, Hans-Joachim Solms, Ulrike Demske, and Stefanie Dipper. 2021. Referenzkorpus Frühneuhochdeutsch (1350-1650), version 1.0.

Daniel Zeman, Jan Hajič, Martin Popel, Martin Potthast, Milan Straka, Filip Ginter, Joakim Nivre, and Slav Petrov. 2018. CoNLL 2018 shared task: Multilingual parsing from raw text to Universal Dependencies. In *Proceedings of the CoNLL 2018 Shared Task: Multilingual Parsing from Raw Text to Universal Dependencies*, pages 1–21, Brussels, Belgium. Association for Computational Linguistics.

Andrew Zupon, Andrew Carnie, Michael Hammond, and Mihai Surdeanu. 2022. Automatic correction of syntactic dependency annotation differences. In *Proceedings of the Thirteenth Language Resources and Evaluation Conference*, pages 7106–7112, Marseille, France. European Language Resources Association.

A Appendix

The following tables present more detailed evaluation scores of all trained models as well as of all labels present in the data sets. The first five rows of Table 8 illustrate parameter tuning with different combinations of learning rate and utilised pre-trained embedding models.

no.	data set	lr	emb	char	min	steps	UAS	LAS	CLAS	MLAS	BLEX
1	MHG-cur	0.003	✓	✓	41	12,100	91.74	86.65	79.48	78.19	79.48
2	MHG-cur	0.002	✓	✓	29	8,700	91.99	86.30	78.58	77.37	78.58
3	MHG-cur	0.003	✓	×	25	11,800	91.89	86.05	78.44	77.06	78.44
4	MHG-cur	0.003	×	✓	46	12,800	91.28	85.84	78.26	76.79	78.26
5	MHG-cur	0.003	×	×	20	10,100	91.99	86.40	78.86	77.48	78.86
6	MHG-all	0.003	✓	✓	53	15,200	91.68	85.63	77.93	76.43	77.93
7	MHG+ModG	0.003	✓	✓	112	30,600	92.15	86.85	79.69	78.90	79.69
8	MHG+ModG	0.002	✓	✓	50	13,700	92.95	88.06	81.57	80.75	81.57

Table 8: Evaluation scores of trained models (data sets), reporting learning rate (lr), usage of word (emb) or character (char) embeddings, run time (min), number of steps (steps) as well as UAS, LAS, MLAS, CLAS and BLEX calculated on the test set. Model 1, 6, and 8 are the ones presented in Section 5.

Label	Precision	Recall	F1	#Label	Label	Precision	Recall	F1	#Label
compound:prt	1.0000	1.0000	1.0000	15	det:predet	0.5000	1.0000	0.6667	2
punct	0.9987	1.0000	0.9994	771	parataxis	0.6154	0.6423	0.6286	137
case	0.9823	0.9858	0.9841	282	compound:pav	0.5556	0.7143	0.6250	7
det	0.9810	0.9842	0.9826	631	expl:pv	0.5333	0.7273	0.6154	11
amod	0.9482	0.9581	0.9531	191	appos	0.6053	0.5476	0.5750	42
mark	0.9538	0.9483	0.9510	174	flat	0.6667	0.5000	0.5714	4
root	0.9375	0.9375	0.9375	304	vocative	0.6098	0.5208	0.5618	48
cc	0.9355	0.9355	0.9355	124	aux:pass	0.5000	0.6364	0.5600	11
aux	0.9384	0.9195	0.9288	149	nmod:det	0.5000	0.6250	0.5556	8
nsubj	0.8874	0.8758	0.8816	612	xcomp:pred	0.6000	0.5000	0.5455	12
xcomp	0.8571	0.8824	0.8696	34	ccomp	0.5957	0.4308	0.5000	65
advmod	0.8113	0.8889	0.8483	324	obl:loc	0.4615	0.4545	0.4580	66
advmod:tmp	0.8438	0.8438	0.8438	96	expl	0.4643	0.4483	0.4561	29
cop	0.8571	0.8276	0.8421	87	dislocated	0.6667	0.3158	0.4286	19
aux:cop	0.8571	0.8182	0.8372	22	obl:compar	0.6667	0.2857	0.4000	7
discourse	0.8333	0.8333	0.8333	18	obl:dir	0.3333	0.3415	0.3373	41
nummod	1.0000	0.7143	0.8333	7	advmod:dir	0.4444	0.2353	0.3077	17
obl:tmp	0.9048	0.7600	0.8261	25	obl:arg	0.4444	0.1739	0.2500	23
nmod	0.8444	0.7308	0.7835	104	acl	0.6667	0.1053	0.1818	19
iobj	0.7711	0.7485	0.7596	171	obl	0.0	0.0	0.0	1
obj	0.6988	0.8109	0.7507	349	nmod:part	0.0	0.0	0.0	9
conj	0.7241	0.7500	0.7368	112	nmod:arg	0.0	0.0	0.0	1
acl:relcl	0.6909	0.7451	0.7170	51	csubj	0.0	0.0	0.0	5
compound:case	0.7143	0.7143	0.7143	7	orphan	0.0	0.0	0.0	3
advmod:loc	0.7778	0.6034	0.6796	58	compound:adv	0.0	0.0	0.0	2
obl:mod	0.6232	0.7350	0.6745	117	amod:pred	0.0	0.0	0.0	3
advcl	0.6220	0.7315	0.6723	108	advmod:nmod	0.0	0.0	0.0	7
hypopara	0.5000	1.0000	0.6667	1	advcl:relcl	0.0	0.0	0.0	0

Table 9: Evaluation scores of labels sorted by F1, reporting precision, recall, F1 and label count produced by the combined model (model 8) on the test set.

Complexity of German Texts Written by Primary School Children

Jammila Laâguidi, Dana Neumann,
Ronja Laarmann-Quante, Stefanie Dipper and Mihail Chifligarov
Ruhr University Bochum, Faculty of Philology, Department of Linguistics, Germany
Dana.Neumann@edu.ruhr-uni-bochum.de
{Jammila.Laaguidi,Ronja.Laarmann-Quante,Stefanie.Dipper,Mihail.Chifligarov}
@ruhr-uni-bochum.de

Abstract

While the development of children's literacy is of large interest to researchers, few studies have yet been based on corpora of children's texts. We investigate the development of text complexity in freely-written texts of German primary school children between 2nd and 4th grade based on the longitudinal Litkey Corpus (Laarmann-Quante et al., 2019b) using NLP methods. These texts are retellings of given picture stories. Although the picture stories may constrain the vocabulary and grammar, our hypothesis is that complexity increases over time. We measure complexity using various lexical and syntactic features. The results show that our hypotheses are largely confirmed but that there are outliers that might arise because some picture stories could be more stimulating than others.

1 Introduction

An important goal of primary school education is the acquisition of written language skills. In addition to the teaching of spelling, this also includes the acquisition of a sufficiently extensive vocabulary and an arsenal of sufficiently complex syntactic constructions.

Studies of how children's (written) language abilities develop have typically been either cross-sectional or based on the development of only few children. The reason is that not many large corpora of children's text productions are available, especially longitudinal ones. One exception for German is the Litkey Corpus (Laarmann-Quante et al., 2019b), which contains texts collected from the same 251 children at 10 test points between the 2nd and 4th grade (see Section 2 for details).

The goal of this paper is to investigate whether and to what extent the complexity of vocabulary and syntax increases in the course of primary school, as reflected by the texts collected in the Litkey Corpus. Since such large corpora cannot be analyzed by hand, we apply Natural Language Processing (NLP) methods for automatic processing in this investigation.

One particularity of the corpus is that the texts are based on picture stories. This means that the vocabulary and potentially also particular syntactic constructions are to some extend bound by the picture stories. We hypothesize that with increasing written language skills over time, one can nevertheless measure an increase in linguistic complexity in the texts.

There are yet few studies that analyze children's retellings of picture stories and the ones that are available focus on oral rather than written retellings. For example, Rahayu et al. (2020) analyzed the retellings of children aged six to nine and found that their lexical diversity increases with age. Heilmann et al. (2010) analyzed the narrative macrostructure of children aged five to seven and found that narrative (macrostructure) skills are correlated with their vocabulary, grammar, and productivity skills. Bulut-Ozsezer and Canbazoglu (2018) examined the comments that seven-year-old children made on the pictures in story books and divided them into different categories (description, superficial and imaginative interpretation, and critical understanding), concluding that most of them are descriptions.

The Litkey Corpus provides the opportunity to study written retellings of picture stories. So far, the corpus has mainly been analyzed with regard to its general composition (e.g. Laarmann-Quante et al., 2019b; Laarmann-Quante et al., 2019a) and research based on the corpus has focused on spelling errors (Röhrig, 2020; Laarmann-Quante, 2021). The Litkey Corpus has not yet been used to analyze children's development concerning their lexical and syntactic complexity. This paper intends to close this gap.

To measure vocabulary complexity, we use different standardized measures for lexical diversity and additionally apply a new IDF-based measure. To measure syntactic complexity, we compare the distribution of part-of-speech (POS) n-grams and compute perplexity on POS n-grams based on a language model trained on a children's lexicon written by adults. We hypothesize that over time, the perplexity decreases as the children's syntax gets more similar to the one used by adults.

The main contributions of this paper are:

- A corpus-based study of the complexity of texts written by children and its development during primary school
- IDF-LDist, a new IDF-based measure of lexical distinctiveness

2 Data

This section describes the Litkey Corpus, which contains the texts produced by primary school children that we analyze, and the Klexikon Corpus, which we use as a reference corpus of texts to compare the Litkey texts with.

2.1 Litkey Corpus

The texts of the Litkey Corpus (Laarmann-Quante et al., 2019b) were collected by Frieg between 2010–2012 (Frieg, 2014). The texts were produced by 251 children in primary schools in Northrhine-Westfalia between the second half of the 2nd grade and the end of the 4th grade, i.e. the end of primary school in Germany. In total, there are 1,922 individual texts. Over the course of 10 different test points in time, children were advised to write stories retelling given picture stories.

At each test point, a different picture story was used except for test points TP02, TP06 and TP10 (i.e., at the end of each grade), where the same story was used. At testing time, it was first made sure that the children understood the basic storyline of the pictures before they wrote a story retelling the picture story. All stories feature two children, Lea and Lars, and a dog, Dodo.

The length of the texts varies greatly (Laarmann-Quante et al., 2019b): At the first test point TP01, the texts are on average 65.9 tokens long (SD 20.3), at the last test point TP10 the average is 139.2 tokens (SD 53.5).

All texts come with an orthographic target hypothesis, i.e., a normalized version of the text where each word is corrected for spelling errors but not grammatical errors. In the present study, we use this orthographic target hypothesis. Among further annotations, the corpus comes with STTS POS tags (Schiller et al., 1999) that were created automatically using a tagger trained on children's texts, yielding an accuracy of about 93% (see Laarmann-Quante et al., 2019a, for further details).

2.2 Klexikon Corpus

Klexikon[1] is a German online lexicon similar to Wikipedia, but targeted at children. It offers simplified and summarized articles about various topics and has been written by adults. This means the texts contain standard language sentence structures without grammatical errors but at the same time the use of simplified language makes them comparable to children's writing styles. This makes the Klexikon articles a suitable dataset that children's texts can be compared with at the syntactic level.

We use the Klexikon Corpus compiled by Ortmann and Wedig (2024) as part of the KidRef Corpus, which is a collection of various German texts written by or written for children. The Klexikon subcorpus consists of 924 texts with 300,000 tokens in total. Ortmann and Wedig (2024) automatically created STTS POS tags with an accuracy of about 94%, which we use in our study.

3 Methods

In order to study the development of text complexity in the primary school children's texts, we apply different methods measuring lexical diversity (Section 3.1) and syntactic complexity (Section 3.2). Our choice of methods largely follows Kapusta et al. (2022), who assessed the development of the complexity of German Abitur texts, i.e., texts that are part of the final secondary-school examinations, between 1963 and 2013.

3.1 Lexical Diversity

A popular measure of lexical diversity is type-token ratio (TTR), which is calculated by dividing vocabulary size by text length. However, this measure is sensitive to text length since the longer a text is, the higher the probability that the following word has already occurred (see, e.g., Covington and McFall, 2010). Since the texts in the Litkey Corpus vary in length, we use variations of

[1] https://klexikon.zum.de

TTR that are independent of text length: MATTR and HD-D.[2]

Before applying these measures, we lemmatize the texts[3] and exclude tokens that contain non-alphabetic characters. We deliberately refrain from excluding function words because the acquisition of different kinds of function words constitutes important steps in the development of literacy, e.g., using anaphoric expressions like personal pronouns rather than repeating proper names.

MATTR Covington and McFall (2010) propose MATTR ("Moving Average Type-Token Ratio"). It is calculated by first choosing a window size W (e.g. 500 tokens) and then computing the TTR for each moving window: words 1 to 500, then 2 to 501, then 3 to 503, and so on until the end of the text. After that, the mean of all calculated TTRs is the MATTR of the entire text. The higher the MATTR, the higher a text's lexical diversity. Covington and McFall (2010) suggest a window size W that is smaller than the shortest text in the data, in our case 16 words. Hence, we set W to 15.

HD-D McCarthy and Jarvis (2007, 2010) propose HD-D ("Hypergeometric Distribution D"). HD-D is based on the probability of finding a type at least once in a random sample of N words, which can be estimated with the hypergeometric distribution function. The probability of occurrence is calculated for all types in a text and then summed up to make up the HD-D index of that text. McCarthy and Jarvis (2007) propose a sample size of $N = 42$, however, multiple texts in the Litkey Corpus have less than 42 words, with the shortest text having 16 words only. Therefore, we decided for a sample size of 15.

IDF-LDist In addition to the two TTR variants, we define a custom measure, IDF-LDist ("IDF-based lexical distinctiveness"), to analyze whether all children use roughly the same vocabulary to describe a picture story or to what extend a child uses distinctive words that are not used by many others.

For each child/text, we first calculate the IDF values of their word types w per test point as shown in (1):[4]

$$\mathrm{IDF}(w) = \frac{D}{df_w} \tag{1}$$

where D is the total number of texts at that test point and df_w is the number of texts containing w.

We next look at all IDF values of one child and determine how many of them lie above the average value for this test point (across children), which would show to what extent the child uses more distinctive words than children use on average. We calculate the average IDF value of a test point t as in (2), where V_t is the set of words at test point t:

$$\mathrm{IDF}_{avg}(t) = \frac{1}{|V_t|} \sum_{w \in V_t} \mathrm{IDF}(w) \tag{2}$$

Finally, we calculate for each child the percentage of IDF values above the test point's average, as a measure of how different the vocabulary of this child is compared to the other children, as shown in (3):

$$\mathrm{IDF\text{-}LDist}(c,t) = \frac{1}{|V_{c,t}|} \sum_{w \in V_{c,t}} \mathbb{1}\{\mathrm{IDF}(w) > \mathrm{IDF}_{avg}(t)\} \tag{3}$$

where $V_{c,t}$ is the set of words of child c at test point t. The notation $\mathbb{1}\{x\}$ means "1 if x is true, and 0 otherwise" (Jurafsky and Martin, 2024, p. 178).

The IDF-LDist measure has the following properties: If all children used the same words, the IDF-LDist score for all children would be 0. Likewise, if all children used different words, the score for all children would also be 0 but this is not realistic since at least some function words and important words in a story, e.g. the names *Lea*, *Lars*, and *Dodo* will be shared by most texts. The IDF-LDist score of a specific child is high when most other children share the same vocabulary but this child uses different words.

3.2 Syntactic Complexity

To estimate syntactic complexity, measures are typically used that measure the complexity of constituents (e.g. embedding depth) or the length of certain constituents (cf., e.g., Chen and Meurers, 2016). However, this presupposes that a syntactic

[2]Another commonly-used length-independent measure is MTLD ("Measure of Textual Lexical Diversity", McCarthy and Jarvis, 2010). However, this measure only provides reliable values for texts with at least 100 words.

[3]Most of the tokens in the Litkey Corpus come with lemma information. We added missing lemmas using simplemma (Barbaresi, 2024).

[4]Since each child contributed at most one text to each test point, the terms "child" and "text" can be used interchangeably here.

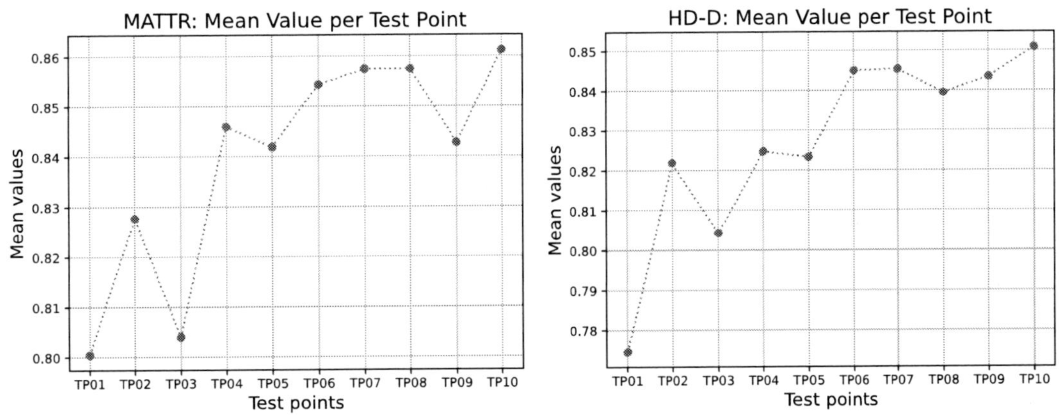

Figure 1: Development of the lexical diversity across test points measured as the mean values of MATTR (left) and HD-D (right).

annotation exists, e.g. in the form of phrase structure trees or dependency relations. However, the Litkey Corpus is not syntactically annotated except for the POS tags. Our syntactic measures are therefore based on POS tags.

Top POS n-grams We first look at the most frequent POS n-grams for each test point. This allows us to see whether the children use different constructions in different acquisition phases and which type of construction becomes more frequent with increasing literacy.

Perplexity In addition, we apply perplexity of POS-based language models. Perplexity is a standard metric in natural language processing (Jurafsky and Martin, 2024). It is usually used to assess the performance of language models, by comparing perplexity of two models on a test set. The model with the lower perplexity score fits the test data better.

In our study, we train a language model on the Klexikon corpus and investigate how the perplexity of this model changes over time when applied to texts from different test points, reflecting the evolving writing skills and practice of the children.

We hypothesize that the texts from the Litkey Corpus show decreasing perplexity over time as children's linguistic abilities improve with age and experience. This assumption is based on the premise that a language model trained on the Klexikon corpus, which shows no grammatical errors and contains more complex sentence structures, would yield higher perplexity scores when applied to texts written by elementary school children at the beginning of learning how to write, compared to the same children at the end of elementary school. To measure the syntactic complexity of the texts, we use a POS trigram language model with Kneser-Ney smoothing.[5]

4 Results

4.1 Lexical Diversity

We calculated both measures of lexical diversity, i.e. MATTR and HD-D, per text. Figure 1 shows the mean value at each test point (TP).

Both measures show that overall the lexical diversity increases over time, proving the initial hypothesis right that we can see an increase in spite of different picture stories used. However, the increase is rather small and not homogeneous. Both measures show similar patterns: There is a drop in each measure at TP03 and TP05 and another drop for HD-D at TP08 and for MATTR at TP09. It is likely that these drops are indeed caused by the different picture stories used in that some of them elicited a more diverse vocabulary than others. This assumption is supported by the observation that we see a clear upward trend between TP02, TP06 and TP10 where the same picture stories were used. The results emphasize the importance of taking into account the stimulus material with which texts are elicited when interpreting the results in a longitudinal study.

IDF-LDist The results for our new measure IDF-LDist are shown in Figure 3. For each test point, we see the distribution of the percentage of

[5]We used the NLTK module `nltk.lm` with default settings for calculating the model and perplexity.

Example 1 (IDF-LDist = 0.50):
Dodo ist verschwunden
An einem schönen warmen Sommertag ging Lea unten auf dem Bürgersteig hektisch umher. Sie sah ziemlich traurig aus. Sie klebte an jedem Baum, Haus, oder am einer Mauer Zettel auf.
'Dodo has disappeared. On a beautiful warm summer's day, Lea was walking frantically along the sidewalk below. She looked quite sad. She stuck notes on every tree, house, or on a wall.'

Example 2 (IDF-LDist = 0.07):
Lea sucht Dodo. sie klebt Bilder von Dodo.
'Lea is looking for Dodo. She sticks pictures of Dodo.'

Figure 2: Two (normalized) example texts from TP02 describing the same situation of a picture story: the dog Dodo has disappeared and the girl Lea hangs up 'missing dog' posters. Example 1 is the text with the top IDF-LDist score of TP02, Example 2 has a very low score.

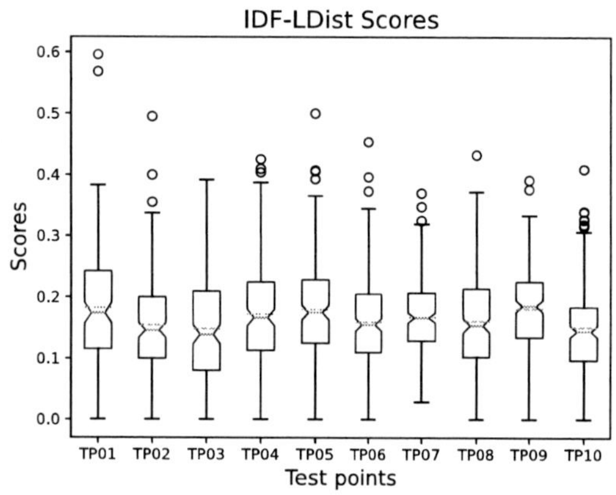

Figure 3: Distribution of the children's IDF-LDist scores per test point.

words above the test point's average IDF value.

Figure 2 shows two example texts, one with a very high IDF-LDist score and one with a very low score. The IDF-LDist score of a specific text becomes high when most other texts share the same vocabulary but this text uses different words. We see such outliers at almost each test point, most notably at TP01. At later test points, the variance and the outliers tend to decrease. This means that the distinctiveness of the children's vocabulary tends to become more homogeneous in that either the children all tend to use more similar words or – more likely given the increase in lexical variation reported above – all children tend to write in a more distinctive manner so that individual texts do not stick out anymore. One explanation could be that at early test points, some children start off with a broader or more different vocabulary than others, depending on their personal backgrounds. Then, the older the children become and the longer they have attended school, the more they reach a similar level of vocabulary. Hence, previous advantages some children might have had at the first test point are equalized to some extend. Nevertheless, this is only a rather subtle trend. Overall, we see that across all test points some individual differences remain.

Again, we must not forget a potential influence of the picture story. But when we compare TP02, TP06 and TP10 where the same story was used, we see a similar decrease in variance, especially between TP06 and TP10, as described above for all test points.

Rank	TP01		TP10	
1	NE	17.54	VVFIN	11.24
2	NN	12.55	NN	10.91
3	VVFIN	10.98	NE	10.71

Table 1: Top-frequent POS unigrams (percentages) at TP01 and TP10 (NE: proper nouns; NN: common nouns; VVFIN: finite verbs).

4.2 Syntactic Complexity

Top POS n-grams We start by comparing the two extremes, TP01 and TP10, see Table 1. The three most frequent POS tags are the same in both cases but appear in different order. It is noticeable that in TP01 NE, i.e. proper names, are by far the most frequent POS, with 17.54% of all tokens. It is obvious that the names of the two children and the dog occur disproportionately in the early texts.

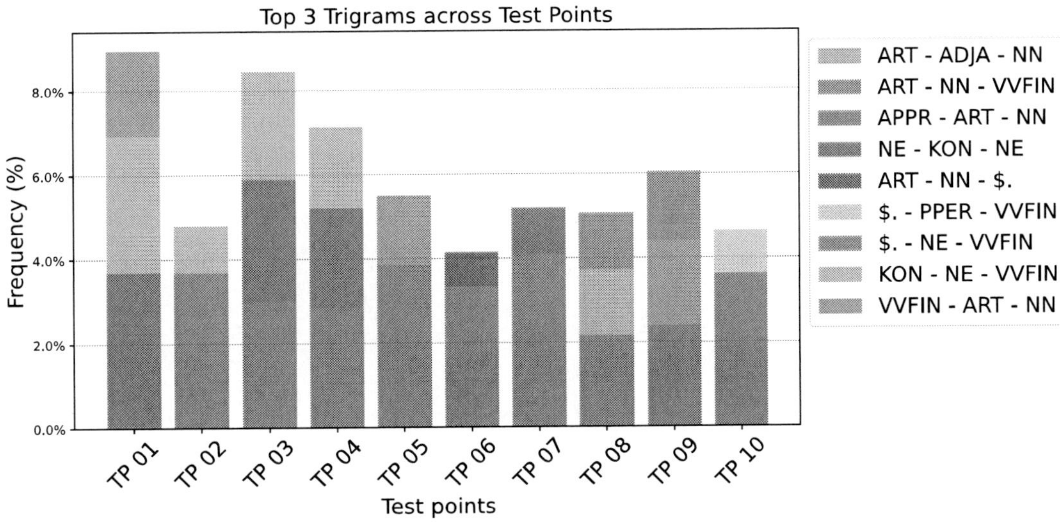

Figure 4: Top-frequent POS trigrams across all test points.

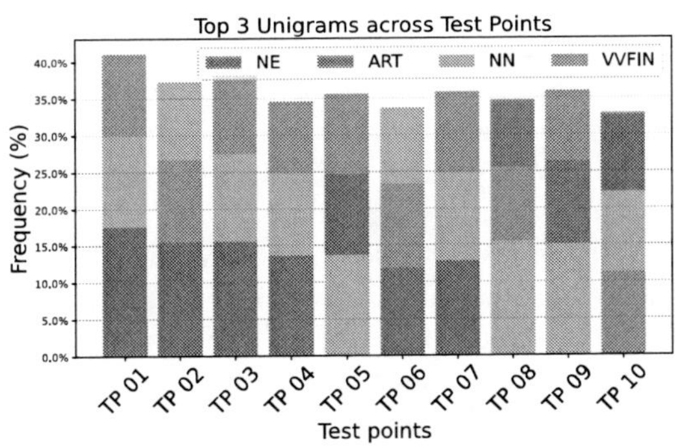

Figure 5: Top-frequent POS unigrams across all test points, stacked according to frequency.

Figure 5 plots the distribution of the top-frequent POS unigrams across the ten test points. The blue part of the bar plots corresponds to the proper nouns (NE). Proper names are almost always the most common POS up to TP07. In TP08, the article (ART, red part) appears as the first function word among the top three POS, and proper nouns become less important.

Figure 4 shows the top-frequent trigrams across all test points. TOP01 shows a special pattern here: the combination NE–KON–NE (blue part; KON for conjunction) is the most common, followed by KON–NE–VVFIN (orange) and VVFIN–ART–NN (green). These three patterns are typical for sentences in which the two children and/or the dog appear as the subject, as in Example (4). Parts of these patterns also show up in TP02–TP04.

(4) *Lars und Lea kaufen ein Eis.*
NE KON NE VVFIN ART NN
'Lars and Lea buy an ice cream.'

A similar pattern is the trigram $.–NE–VVFIN (purple): These are sentence beginnings (after $., the period) in which only one proper noun occurs as the subject.

From TP02 on, however, the most common construction are prepositional phrases (APPR–ART–NN, red) and it remains so until TP10. It can be assumed that such prepositional phrases are frequently used to indicate place and time.

TOP10 shows an interesting distribution: In addition to the prepositional phrases (red) and the sentences starting with proper names (purple), a new pattern appears here among the top trigrams: $.–PPER–VVFIN (ligth green, PPER for personal pronouns). Instead of mostly repeating the proper nouns, the children now begin to start sentences with a personal pronoun more regularly, as in Example (5), so that this pattern shows up among the top trigrams.

(5) *Sie sah Lars mit Dodo*
PPER VVFIN NE APPR NE
'She saw Lars with Dodo'

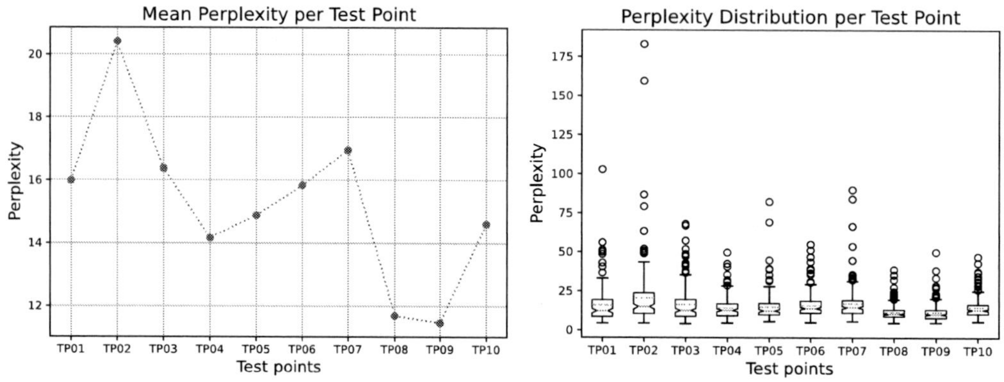

Figure 6: Mean perplexity (left) and perplexity distribution (right) over test points.

POS-based perplexity We calculated perplexity separately for each text. Figure 6 plots the mean values and distribution of perplexity of the texts written at the ten different test points. Looking first at the mean values (left), we observe an overall downward trend in the perplexity scores over time. The three test points with the same story, TP02, TP06 and TP10, also show a clear downward trend. As perplexity values indicate how well the trained language model fits the sample, the overall downward trend shows that in general the children's texts become more similar to the Klexikon in terms of POS trigrams. There are, however, peaks and troughs indicating exceptions to the overall trend. These need to be examined further to see if, e.g., there is a story-related reason for the outliers.

The boxplots (right) show that there are more outliers at earlier test points, i.e. texts that deviate clearly from the style of the Klexikon-based language model. The later the test points, the more homogeneously the children write. We could already observe such a development in Fig. 3 for the IDF-LDist scores.

5 Conclusion

The aim of this paper was to investigate the development of complexity in texts produced by primary school children. We measure complexity on a lexical and syntactic level with different measures based on the Litkey Corpus.

The different measures of lexical diversity confirm our expectations: the children's vocabulary in describing the picture stories becomes increasingly diverse over time, despite the fact that the children were limited in their text production by the given picture stories.

The new measure of lexical distinctiveness, IDF-LDist, shows that the texts become more homogeneous overall, i.e., the older children tend to write similarly diverse texts. We hypothesized that personal background may play a greater role at the beginning of elementary school, which would explain the greater variance and the extreme outliers. At later test points, the children's competencies become more and more similar.

At the syntactic level, the distribution of the POS n-grams shows that the syntactic structures used by the children when writing are developing further and that, for example, function words such as articles and personal pronouns are being added.

Perplexity on POS trigrams shows an overall downward trend, as expected. However, there are also outliers, which require further investigations. Similar to lexical distinctiveness, perplexity becomes more homogeneous over time.

Ethical Considerations

We do not see a direct harm that could follow from the research reported in this study. However, the analyses could inherit potential biases present in the Litkey Corpus and not reflect all populations of primary school children in Germany equally well.

Limitations

A limitation of the present study is that we measure linguistic complexity using only a small subset of potential measures, focusing on lexical diversity and syntactic complexity based on POS sequences. Incorporating further measures, e.g. based on syntactic dependencies, would be necessary in order to draw a more complete picture of the development of linguistic complexity in primary school children's texts. However, this is yet infeasible because the Litkey Corpus lacks gold-standard annotations of structures above the word level.

Acknowledgments

We would like to thank the anonymous reviewers for their very helpful comments.

References

Adrien Barbaresi. 2024. Simplemma: A simple multilingual lemmatizer for Python [computer software] (version 0.9.1). Berlin, Germany: Berlin-Brandenburg Academy of Sciences. Available from https://github.com/adbar/simplemma.

Muzaffer Sencer Bulut-Ozsezer and Hatice Beyza Canbazoglu. 2018. Picture in children's story books: Children's perspective. *International Journal of Eductional Methodology*, 4(4):205–217.

Xiaobin Chen and Detmar Meurers. 2016. CTAP: A web-based tool supporting automatic complexity analysis. In *Proceedings of the Workshop on Computational Linguistics for Linguistic Complexity (CL4LC)*, pages 113–119, Osaka, Japan. The COLING 2016 Organizing Committee.

Michael Covington and Joe McFall. 2010. Cutting the Gordian knot: The moving-average type-token ratio (MATTR). *Journal of Quantitative Linguistics*, 17:94–100.

Hendrike Frieg. 2014. *Sprachförderung im Regelunterricht der Grundschule: Eine Evaluation der Generativen Textproduktion*. Ph.D. thesis, Ruhr-Universität Bochum.

John Heilmann, Jon F. Miller, Ann Nockerts, and Claudia Dunaway. 2010. Properties of the narrative scoring scheme using narrative retells in young school-age children. *American Journal of Speech-Language Pathology*, 19(2):154–166.

Daniel Jurafsky and James H. Martin. 2024. *Speech and Language Processing*. (3rd edition, draft of Feb 3, 2024).

Noemi Kapusta, Marco Müller, Matilda Schauf, Isabell Siem, and Stefanie Dipper. 2022. Assessing the linguistic complexity of German abitur texts from 1963–2013. In *Proceedings of the 18th Conference on Natural Language Processing (KONVENS 2022)*, pages 48–62, Potsdam, Germany.

Ronja Laarmann-Quante. 2021. *Prediction of spelling errors in freely-written texts of German primary school children*. Ph.D. thesis, Ruhr-Universität Bochum.

Ronja Laarmann-Quante, Stefanie Dipper, and Eva Belke. 2019a. The making of the Litkey Corpus, a richly annotated longitudinal corpus of German texts written by primary school children. In *Proceedings of the 13th Linguistic Annotation Workshop*, pages 43–55, Florence, Italy. Association for Computational Linguistics.

Ronja Laarmann-Quante, Katrin Ortmann, Anna Ehlert, Simon Masloch, Doreen Scholz, Eva Belke, and Stefanie Dipper. 2019b. The Litkey Corpus: A richly annotated longitudinal corpus of German texts written by primary school children. *Behavior Research Methods*, 51(4):1889–1918. (Shared senior authorship).

Philip McCarthy and Scott Jarvis. 2007. vocd: A theoretical and empirical evaluation. *Language Testing*, 24(4):459–488.

Philip McCarthy and Scott Jarvis. 2010. MTLD, vocd-D, and HD-D: A validation study of sophisticated approaches to lexical diversity assessment. *Behavior Research Methods*, 42:381–392.

Katrin Ortmann and Helena Wedig. 2024. KidRef: Ein Kinderreferenzkorpus. *Bochumer Linguistische Arbeiten*, 26.

Famala Eka Sanhadi Rahayu, Aries Utomo, and Ririn Setyowati. 2020. Investigating lexical diversity of children's oral narratives: A case study of L1 speaking. *Register Journal*, 13(2):371–388.

Jan Thomas Röhrig. 2020. Empirisch ermittelte Muster in Rechtschreibfehlern für die Automatisierung qualitativer Rechtschreibdiagnostik. Poster at the 23. Symposion Deutschdidaktik.

Anne Schiller, Simone Teufel, Christine Stöckert, and Christine Thielen. 1999. Guidelines für das Tagging deutscher Textcorpora mit STTS (Kleines und großes Tagset).

Exploring Automatic Text Simplification for Lithuanian

Justina Mandravickaitė and **Eglė Rimkienė** and **Danguolė Kalinauskaitė** and **Danguolė Kotryna Kapkan**
Vytautas Magnus University
Kaunas, Lithuania
name.surname@vdu.lt

Abstract

The purpose of text simplification is to reduce the complexity of the text while retaining important information. This aspect is relevant for improving accessibility for a wide range of readers, e.g., those with cognitive disorders, non-native speakers, as well as children and the general public among others. We report experiments on text simplification for Lithuanian, focusing on simplifying texts of an administrative style to a plain language level to make it easier to understand for common people. We chose mT5 and mBART as foundational models and fine-tuned them for the text simplification task. Also, we tested ChatGPT for this task. We evaluated the outputs of these models quantitatively and qualitatively. All in all, mBART appeared to be most effective for simplifying Lithuanian text, reaching the highest BLEU, ROUGE and BERTscore scores. Qualitative evaluation by assessing the simplicity, meaning retention and grammaticality of sentences simplified by our fine-tuned models, complemented the results of evaluation metrics' scores.

1 Introduction

Text simplification means reducing the vocabulary and syntactic complexity of a text while preserving the essential information of the original text. Therefore, text simplification is relevant for improving the accessibility of information for people with cognitive disorders, as well as for non-native speakers and children (Štajner, 2021). It is important for the general public as well, especially in terms of legal and/or administrative texts as these texts provide communication between institutions and their target audiences, which have very diverse levels of reading comprehension (François et al., 2020).

In this paper, we report text simplification experiments for Lithuanian. We focus on simplifying texts of the administrative (clerical) style. The examples of communication with the general public by public authorities often use quasi-legal language, which can be ineffective in conveying information to non-specialists (François et al., 2020). Therefore such texts are difficult to understand for anyone who is not an expert in that particular field. While texts on the websites of various public administration institutions are intended to disseminate information relevant to the general public, such as social benefits, public utilities, migration, copyright, etc., there is quite often a discrepancy in terms of their declared purpose and reaching their target audience. Text simplification has the potential to address this problem as it "translates" administrative language into a less complex one in terms of vocabulary, sentence structure and other aspects while retaining the essential information from the original content.

Currently, the notion of plain language is most commonly used in written communication of governmental institutions towards the general public. It is defined as communication in which wording, structure, and design are clear so that the intended audience can easily find, understand and use the information it needs (Adler, 2012). So, in our experiments, we explore the simplification of administrative texts to the level of plain language. Plain Language was first and foremost a means to open expert content for lay people (non-experts), for example, by providing people without legal or medical training access to the respective expert communication and information (Maaß, 2020).

We chose mT5 and mBART as the base models and fined-tuned them, developing text simplification models for Lithuanian texts. We also tested ChatGPT for this task. We chose these models because they support Lithuanian language (many large language models do not support lower-resource languages well) and after assessing computational resources we had available for model fine-tuning. Also, our text simplification experiments performed lexical and syntactic simplification together, thus simplifying sentence structure and replacing complex words or phrases at the same step.

The rest of the paper is structured as follows: Section 2 briefly describes related work, Section 3 describes the data we used, Section 4 – methods used in our experiments, Section 5 – experimental setup, Section 6 presents results. Finally, Section 7 ends this paper with conclusions.

2 Related Work

Text simplification techniques have developed significantly in recent years from rule-based (e.g., Rennes and Jönsson (2015); Suter et al. (2016)) to data-driven approaches (e.g., Štajner and Saggion (2018); Srikanth and Li (2020)). Machine translation via neural networks, such as LSTM, also has been used in many studies because a text simplification task can be formulated as a translation task where a complex text is translated into a simple text (e.g., Vu et al. (2018); Agrawal and Carpuat (2019)).

As Transformers architecture considers the whole input sequence and selectively extracts essential information (Vaswani et al., 2017), it has been successfully used for text simplification (e.g., Zhao et al. (2018); Omelianchuk et al. (2021)), among other NLP tasks. In particular, simplifications that avoid long, complex, and linked sentences can now be generated by large language models (Jeblick et al., 2023; Sun et al., 2023a).

Recent studies have shown that these models can simplify text via the application of different techniques, such as specifying the desired reading grade level or directly indicating necessary simplification operations (Agrawal and Carpuat, 2023). BERT model has been applied for lexical text simplification (e.g., (Qiang et al., 2020)), text simplification using monolingual machine translation (Alissa and Wald, 2023) or hybrid text simplification approach (e.g., Maddela et al. (2020)), among other studies. T5 model has been used for controllable text simplification (e.g., Sheang and Saggion (2021); Basu et al. (2023); Seidl and Vandeghinste (2024)) as well as in text simplification in a situation with limited resources (e.g., Monteiro et al. (2022); Schlippe and Eichinger (2023)), to name a few. BART model has been applied not only for controllable text simplification (e.g., Sheang and Saggion (2021)) but also for paragraph-level (e.g., Devaraj et al. (2021)) and document-level text simplification (e.g., Vásquez-Rodríguez et al. (2023)) thus expanding the task. Various GPT models have been utilized for text simplification as well, especially in low-resource scenarios (e.g., Wen and Fang (2023); Deilen et al. (2023); Li et al. (2023a)).

Some of the newest models for text simplification include SIMSUM for automated document-level text simplification (Blinova et al., 2023), also, SimpleBART (Sun et al., 2023a), which reports a pre-training strategy for text simplification, and KGSimple, an unsupervised approach that uses knowledge graphs to generate compressed text (Colas et al., 2023). In addition to general text simplification, domain-specific text simplification models are emerging, e.g., for simplifying medical texts (Basu et al., 2023) or texts of particular genres (Li et al., 2023b).

What makes text simplification a complex and non-trivial task, is the lack of high-quality data sources and the need for further exploration of the low-resource scenarios (Sun et al., 2023b). Additionally, sometimes domain-specific text simplification may result in lower quality generated text as on, e.g., medical text simplification (Joseph et al., 2023; Flores et al., 2023). Finally, there are challenges related to cultural and commonsense knowledge in text simplification which requires further research in this field (Corti and Yang, 2023).

In this paper, we report experiments in text simplification for Lithuanian, focusing on simplifying administrative texts to a plain language level (Maaß, 2020), which is intended for the general public. We chose several metrics for automatic evaluation. Additionally, the results were assessed by the linguist from a qualitative perspective.

3 Data for Fine-Tuning and Testing

3.1 Data for Fine-Tuning

The final dataset for fine-tuning comprises 2,142 entries with two columns, where the first column contains original sentences or text fragments, equivalent to sentences, while the second column contains manually simplified versions of the corresponding original content[1]. All data were simplified by four experts according to guidelines which are based on the literature on plain language, i.e. simplified version of language, intended for non-specialists (general public) (Alarcon et al., 2021).

The data sources for this dataset were various Lithuanian governmental and non-governmental public institution websites that provide information

[1]The dataset is available upon request.

on services such as social benefits, migration, utilities, copyright, and other issues. The data preparation process involved dividing the texts into sentences or sentence-equivalent text fragments (e.g., clauses) and simplifying them manually following the above-mentioned simplification guidelines.

The lexical and syntactic rules that were applied were mainly derived from cross-linguistic Plain Language principles (Harris, 2010; Martinho, 2018). In some cases, Plain Language principles or text simplification syntactic rules specific to languages that have a similar grammar structure to Lithuanian were taken into account (Brunato et al., 2015; Łukasz Dębowski, 2015). Certain rules, for example, the treatment of participles, were defined for Lithuanian specifically. Lexical simplification was based on frequency, according to the Lithuanian frequency dictionary (Utka, 2009), when in doubt. Guidelines for Plain Lithuanian feature three different levels of proposed simplification operations and can be summarised as follows:

1. **Paragraph-level simplifications.** There are two main rules in this group. First, it is sentence shortening: sentences longer than 12 words should be divided into smaller sentences, preferably by turning embedded relative clauses into independent sentences. Second, it is list creation: where possible, homogenous elements should be transformed into vertical lists, which aid text comprehension.

2. **Lexical simplification.** Whenever possible, a more frequent synonym should be selected, disregarding the perceived formal register requirements. Metaphors and acronyms, if not particularly common, should be avoided, while obscure terms should be defined in a separate sentence.

3. **Syntactic simplification.** These include but are not limited to:

    - transformation of the passive voice into active voice;
    - replacing active participle and gerund constructions with relative clauses;
    - avoiding nominalizations;
    - preferring affirmative sentences to negation, especially avoiding double negation;
    - adding demonstrative pronouns and determiners, where possible, to increase clarity.

3.2 Data for Testing

For testing we used 100 sentences not included in our parallel corpus we used for model fine-tuning. Again, we used governmental and non-governmental public institution websites as data sources. We compiled this set following diversity criteria in terms of topics covered as well as different levels of sentence complexity.

4 Methods

4.1 mT5

The foundation of mT5 model is based on the T5 model, which stands for "Text-to-Text Transfer Transformer." Developed by Google, T5 adopts a unified text-to-text framework, where every language processing task is re-framed as a text generation problem. Key principles of the T5 model include (Zhang et al., 2021):

1. **Unified Text-to-Text Framework**: T5 treats all NLP tasks as a text generation problem, where the input and output are always text strings. This approach simplifies the architecture and allows for flexibility in handling NLP tasks.

2. **Pre-training on a Diverse Corpus**: T5 is pre-trained on a large, diverse corpus, C4 (Colossal Clean Crawled Corpus) (Dodge et al., 2021), which provides a broad understanding of language and context.

3. **Encoder-Decoder Architecture**: The model uses an encoder-decoder architecture, similar to the original Transformer model as proposed by Vaswani (Vaswani et al., 2017). The encoder processes the input text and creates a contextual representation, which the decoder then uses to generate the output text.

4. **Fine-Tuning for Specific Tasks**: While T5 is pre-trained on a general corpus, it can be fine-tuned on a specific task or language to enhance its performance.

For our specific task of Lithuanian text simplification, we used the mT5 model, a multilingual variant of the original T5 (Xue et al., 2021). The model architecture and training procedure that is used for mT5 closely follow that of T5. To train mT5, the authors introduced a multilingual variant of the C4 dataset called mC4, which comprises textual data in 101 languages drawn from the public Common Crawl web scrape. It makes mT5 model particularly suitable for languages with fewer resources (Xue et al., 2021), such as Lithuanian.

4.2 mBART

mBART, an extension of the BART (Bidirectional and Auto-Regressive Transformers) model, incorporates both auto-encoder and auto-regressive components to enhance language understanding and generation. This model is not only tailored for machine translation but also highly adaptable for tasks like text simplification. It uses a sequence-to-sequence framework based on the Transformer architecture, which includes both an encoder and a decoder (Lewis et al., 2019). The encoder processes the input text, converting it into contextual embeddings that encapsulate the nuances of the language — Lithuanian in this context. The decoder then reconstructs the text from these embeddings, aiming to produce simplified text that maintains the original meaning while being more accessible.

mBART functions as a denoising autoencoder and is one of the first models to employ a complete sequence-to-sequence framework for multilingual training by denoising full texts. It was pre-trained on a vast corpus of multilingual data using the BART methodology. This training involved a subset of 25 languages from the Common Crawl (CC) corpus (Wenzek et al., 2019), known as CC25, which includes languages from various families and features texts of different lengths. The Lithuanian portion of this dataset comprises 1,835 tokens within a 13.7 GB corpus, highlighting the model's comprehensive exposure to multilingual text (Liu et al., 2020). This extensive pre-training enables mBART to handle complex linguistic tasks, making it a robust tool for text simplification in less supported languages like Lithuanian.

4.3 ChatGPT

ChatGPT is a variant of the GPT (Generative Pre-trained Transformer) family, which itself is part of a broader class of models using transformer architectures (Yenduri et al., 2024). This design is fundamentally built on self-attention mechanisms that allow the model to process words in context to one another across a sentence or document (**?**). The model can dynamically weigh the importance of each word based on its relationship with others, making it highly effective for complex language processing tasks (Rothman, 2022). We tested ChatGPT 3.5 for Lithuanian text simplification to explore low-resource scenarios.

For our study, we used ChatGPT in its standard, as-is configuration available via OpenAI's browser interface. This meant working within the constraints of the model's pre-training, which did not specifically target Lithuanian language structures but included enough multilingual context to allow for general text manipulation tasks in Lithuanian.

4.4 Evaluaton

4.4.1 Metrics

- **BLEU (Bilingual Evaluation Understudy) Score**: measures how many n-grams in the output match the reference sentences. BLEU scores range from 0 to 1. A higher BLEU score indicates that the output is closer to the reference (Papineni et al., 2002).

- **ROUGE (Recall-Oriented Understudy for Gisting Evaluation) Score**: measures the overlap of n-grams between the simplified text and reference text in different flavors (Lin, 2004). It measures the overlap in the range between 0 (no overlap) and 1 (perfect overlap). We chose 3 variants of ROUGE: unigram overlap (ROUGE-1), bigram overlap (ROUGE-2) and Longest Common Subsequence overlap (ROUGE-L).

- **BERTscore**: BERTscore identifies words in candidate and reference phrases based on cosine similarity via the pre-trained contextual embeddings from BERT. It correlates well with human evaluation (Zhang et al., 2019).

4.4.2 Qualitative Analysis

For qualitative, expert-based evaluation of the simplification output, we used 3 common criteria: grammaticality, meaning preservation and simplicity (Nisioi et al., 2017; Alva-Manchego et al., 2020). Grammaticality (or fluency) means assessing whether the simplified text remains grammatical and understandable; meaning preservation refers to the evaluation of whether semantics (or adequacy) is preserved after the simplification; and simplicity points out to whether the simplified text is simpler than the original text (Grabar and Saggion, 2022). These criteria can be assessed without the need for reference data.

The expert has been asked to assess sentences, simplified by the models according to these 3 criteria on a scale from 1 to 5. As all 3 evaluation criteria are not equal (they go in this order: simplicity – meaning retention – grammaticality), we also asked to apply 2 other rules during the evaluation:

- The most important criterion is *simplicity*, so if according to this criterion simplified sentence gets 1, meaning retention and grammaticality are irrelevant (gets the score of 1 as well).
- If for *simplicity* a simplified sentence scores higher than 1, but *meaning retention* scores 1, then the grammaticality is scored 1 (otherwise we would get a grammatically correct but semantically incorrect sentence, i.e., unrelated to the original one).

Without such a hierarchy of criteria, there could be a paradoxical situation where models would be rewarded for simply copying the original content, while they would be penalized for attempting to simplify, although with some errors.

5 Experimental Setup

This study is aimed at the exploration of text simplification for Lithuanian. We used mT5 and mBART, which were directly fine-tuned using a dataset of complex (original) and simplified Lithuanian sentences designed by linguists. The fine-tuning focused on exploring the effects of batch size (bs) and learning rate (lr) variations on performance. The results indicated significant differences in performance between the model configurations. The mBART model with a larger batch size of 8 (mBART-bs8_lr1e-4) consistently outperformed the other configurations. On the other hand, the mT5 model with a smaller batch size (mT5-bs2_lr1e-4) demonstrated stronger performance.

The pre-trained mT5 and mBART were fine-tuned on a Lithuanian corpus, with their encoder-decoder architecture left unchanged to suit the language's nuances. ChatGPT, on the other hand, was not fine-tuned; instead, we used several prompts to test its text simplification capabilities for Lithuanian. We assessed all models using selected metrics to compare their ability to simplify text while preserving the original meaning and intent. The fine-tuning process covered eight epochs, this enabled us to track the progression and improvements in the models' performance as training continued.

6 Results

6.1 Automatic Evaluation

Firstly, we executed experiments with the mT5 and mBART models, focusing on fine-tuning and testing while adjusting key hyperparameters, namely the batch size and learning rate. The outcomes of this fine-tuning process, which was carried out over eight epochs, are visually represented in Figure 1. In this figure, the performance of the mBART model is outlined through various variants of ROUGE, with different configurations indicated by labels such as *bs-8-lr-1e-4*. These labels indicate the hyperparameters used during training — *bs* for batch size and *lr* for learning rate. Each configuration provides insights into how the model's performance is influenced by these hyperparameters.

The *bs8-lr1e-4* and *bs4-lr1e-4* results were selected as the best performing models based on their consistently higher scores across ROUGE metrics, as seen in the graphs. The larger batch size of *bs8-lr1e-4*, in particular, showed superior results, indicating effective learning and generalization capabilities for Lithuanian text simplification, while also avoiding overfitting.

In figure 2 we can see the performance during the fine-tuning of mT5 model. The ROUGE-1 graph, the configuration with a batch size of 2 and a learning rate of 1e-4 (*bs2-lr-1e-4*) achieves the highest score, suggesting that this combination is the most effective for the text simplification task out of the ones tested. The same configuration (*bs2-lr-1e-4*) leads in the ROUGE-2 and ROUGE-L graphs as well, which indicates its effectiveness not just at capturing single word overlaps but also in capturing longer phrase and sentence-level structures. Configurations with larger batch sizes and smaller learning rates improved more slowly, suggesting smaller learning rates require more epochs for comparable performance.

Table 1) summarizes the performance of each model configuration across various metrics. We selected the two best models based on their hyperparameter configurations during fine-tuning and tested them using a dataset that was not used during training and was unseen by the models.

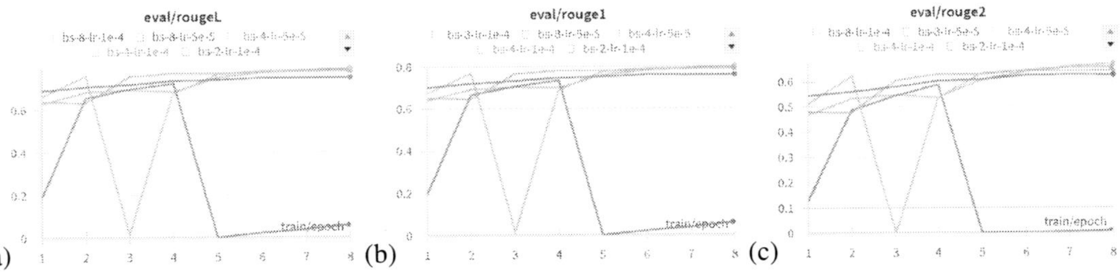

(a) (b) (c)

Figure 1: The mBART model's ROUGE scores during fine-tuning with different parameters: (a) ROUGE-L score, (b) ROUGE-1 score, (c) ROUGE-2 score.

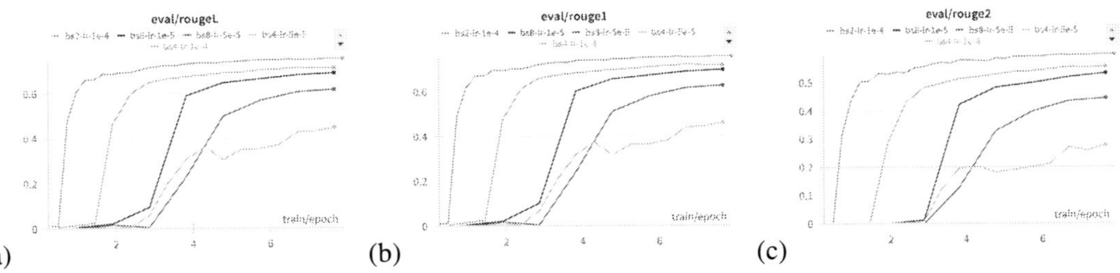

(a) (b) (c)

Figure 2: The mT5 model's ROUGE scores during fine-tuning with different parameters: (a) ROUGE-L score, (b) ROUGE-1 score, (c) ROUGE-2 score.

The results indicate significant differences in performance between the model configurations. The mBART model with a larger batch size of 8 (*mBART-bs8_lr1e-4*) consistently outperformed the other configurations across all metrics. This suggests that larger batch sizes may contribute to better model learning and generalization, especially for complex tasks like text simplification.

On the other hand, the mT5 model with a smaller batch size (*mT5-bs2_lr1e-4*) demonstrated stronger performance compared to its larger batch counterpart, particularly noticeable in the BLEU and ROUGE scores. This might be attributed to better handling of the nuances in a less resource-dense language like Lithuanian when trained with more focused, though smaller, data batches.

For testing ChatGPT we used 3 different prompts in the zero-shot scenario, and the average scores of the outputs are presented in Table 1. The results show that according to our selected evaluation metrics, ChatGPT performed better than or close to *mT5-bs4_lr1e-4*, but worse than the other 3 models. This shows potential, however, experimenting with prompts revealed that it is rather difficult to control the simplification to the desired level, e.g., plain language in our case.

Overall, the mBART model with the largest batch size and same learning rate setting appears most effective for simplifying Lithuanian text, highlighting its suitability for languages with fewer linguistic resources available for training.

6.2 Qualitative Evaluation

As automatic evaluation does not cover all text simplification aspects, it has been accompanied by a qualitative evaluation by the linguist, who assessed simplified sentences produced by the models. The generated sentences were assessed by their simplicity, meaning retention and grammaticality. The results are summarised in Table 2.

We can see that the highest simplicity score shared *mBART-bs8_lr1e-4* and ChatGPT (3.92/5.0). Meanwhile, *mBART-bs4_lr1e-4* and *mBART-bs8_lr1e-4* got the highest score for meaning retention (4.12/5.0). As for grammaticality, the just-mentioned *mBART-bs8_lr1e-4* achieved the highest score of 4.25/5.0.

ChatGPT showed potential, especially taking into consideration that we tested it with zero-shot prompting. However, it was rather difficult to control the desired simplification level – in our case, plain language was relevant, targeting the general public, not Easy Language that mostly aims to aid people with special needs (Maaß, 2020). Also,

Table 1: Automatic evaluation scores

	chatGPT	mT5-bs2_lr1e-4	mT5-bs4_lr1e-4	mBART-bs4_lr1e-4	mBART-bs8_lr1e-4
Average BLEU	0.359	0.5697	0.0738	0.5099	**0.6605**
Average ROUGE-1 F-score	0.4556	0.7937	0.3682	0.739	**0.8221**
Average ROUGE-2 F-score	0.228	0.7036	0.2996	0.6288	**0.7265**
Average ROUGE-L F-score	0.396	0.7844	0.352	0.7322	**0.8137**
Average BERTScore F1	0.76	0.9033	0.7137	0.8879	**0.9243**

Table 2: Qualitative evaluation scores

	Simplicity	Meaning retention	Grammaticality
mT5-bs2_lr1e-4	3.26	3.31	3.36
mT5-bs4_lr1e-4	1.99	1.89	1.88
mBART-bs4_lr1e-4	3.81	**4.12**	4.21
mBART-bs8_lr1e-4	**3.92**	**4.12**	**4.25**
chatGPT	**3.92**	3.86	3.78

there was some difficulty in controlling that information not present in an original sentence would not be added to its simplified version.

Although *mT5-bs2_lr1e-4* and *mBART-bs4_lr1e-4* were rather close in terms of automatic evaluation scores, the qualitative assessment revealed clearer differences in simplified sentences. For example, the latter model managed better in terms of grammatically correct sentences, e.g., correct case of parts of speech. Also, *mT5-bs2_lr1e-4* had a mild tendency to cut longer original sentences in the middle thus losing a part of the information.

The latter tendency, however, was rather strong in *mT5-bs4_lr1e-4*. It also struggled in terms of correct Lithuanian grammar, making common spelling mistakes, and jumbling the syntactic structure of the sentences or, in several cases, getting stuck on generating the same phrase over and over.

To summarize, qualitative evaluation added the results of automatic evaluation metrics, showing that mBART was the most successful in simplifying Lithuanian texts. It performed better than other tested text simplification models in terms of simplicity, meaning retention and grammaticality of simplified sentences.

7 Conclusions

In this paper, we report experiments on text simplification for Lithuanian with the focus of simplifying administrative-style texts to a plain language to make it easier to understand for the general public, i.e. non-specialists. We chose mT5 and mBART as foundational models and fine-tuned them for this task. Also, we tested ChatGPT to explore a low-resource scenario. We evaluated the outputs of these models quantitatively (via BLEU, ROUGE and BERTscore scores) and qualitatively (assessing simplicity, meaning retention and grammaticality of simplified sentences). All in all, mBART model appeared to be most effective for simplifying Lithuanian texts. It reached the highest BLEU, ROUGE and BERTscore scores. Qualitative evaluation results complemented the results of quantitative evaluation.

Our future plans include model improvement (e.g., exploring different fine-tuning techniques and more comprehensive experimentation in terms of training parameters) and increasing dataset size via, for example, data augmentation, to increase model performance and generalizability. Also, we plan a more comprehensive analysis of the model decision-making process to take into account such aspects as checking for factuality or model bias.

Limitations

Our study demonstrates promising results for text simplification for Lithuanian. However, it has several limitations we need to acknowledge. Firstly, we evaluated the results focusing on readability (that is, if model-simplified sentences could be easily understood by the experts who evaluated them) and retention of essential information. However, to assess the practical use of the simplified texts, evaluation and analysis could include user feedback and/or reading comprehension tests. Secondly, we limited our experiments to simplifying administrative-style texts. Therefore, models' performance may vary if given texts of different domains and genres. Also, the dataset we used for fine-tuning models is limited in size, thus, models could be improved with more diverse and comprehensive textual data. Furthermore, while quantitative evaluation metrics we used provide valuable insights, they may not fully capture the nuances related to text simplification. So, additional metrics, evaluation criteria and linguistic analysis could offer a more comprehensive assessment of simplified texts as well as models themselves. Addressing these limitations could improve the robustness and applicability of text simplification in real-world scenarios.

Acknowledgments

This research has received funding from the Research Council of Lithuania Lithuanian Studies Programme 2016–2024 under the project Automatic Adaptation of Administrative Texts in Lithuanian to the Needs of Non-Specialists, grant agreement No. S-LIP-22-77.

References

Mark Adler. 2012. *The Plain Language Movement*. Oxford University Press.

Sweta Agrawal and Marine Carpuat. 2019. Controlling text complexity in neural machine translation. In *Proceedings of the 2019 Conference on Empirical Methods in Natural Language Processing and the 9th International Joint Conference on Natural Language Processing (EMNLP-IJCNLP)*, pages 1549–1564.

Sweta Agrawal and Marine Carpuat. 2023. Controlling pre-trained language models for grade-specific text simplification. In *Proceedings of the 2023 Conference on Empirical Methods in Natural Language Processing*, pages 12807–12819.

Rodrigo Alarcon, Lourdes Moreno, and Paloma Martínez. 2021. Lexical simplification system to improve web accessibility. *IEEE Access*, 9:58755–58767.

Sarah Alissa and Michael Wald. 2023. Text simplification using transformer and bert. *Computers, Materials & Continua*, 75(2):3479–3495.

Fernando Alva-Manchego, Carolina Scarton, and Lucia Specia. 2020. Data-driven sentence simplification: Survey and benchmark. *Computational Linguistics*, 46(1):135–187.

Chandrayee Basu, Rosni Vasu, Michihiro Yasunaga, and Qian Yang. 2023. Med-easi: finely annotated dataset and models for controllable simplification of medical texts. In *Proceedings of the Thirty-Seventh AAAI Conference on Artificial Intelligence and Thirty-Fifth Conference on Innovative Applications of Artificial Intelligence and Thirteenth Symposium on Educational Advances in Artificial Intelligence*, AAAI'23/IAAI'23/EAAI'23. AAAI Press.

Sofia Blinova, Xinyu Zhou, Martin Jaggi, Carsten Eickhoff, and Seyed Ali Bahrainian. 2023. Simsum: Document-level text simplification via simultaneous summarization. In *Proceedings of the 61st Annual Meeting of the Association for Computational Linguistics (Volume 1: Long Papers)*, pages 9927–9944.

Dominique Brunato, Felice Dell'Orletta, Giulia Venturi, and Simonetta Montemagni. 2015. Design and annotation of the first Italian corpus for text simplification. In *Proceedings of the 9th Linguistic Annotation Workshop*, pages 31–41, Denver, Colorado, USA. Association for Computational Linguistics.

Anthony Colas, Haodi Ma, Xuanli He, Yang Bai, and Daisy Zhe Wang. 2023. Can knowledge graphs simplify text? In *Proceedings of the 32nd ACM International Conference on Information and Knowledge Management*, pages 379–389.

Lorenzo Corti and Jie Yang. 2023. Artist: Artificial intelligence for simplified text. *arXiv preprint arXiv:2308.13458*.

Silvana Deilen, Sergio Hern'andez Garrido, Ekaterina Lapshinova-Koltunski, and Christiane Maaß. 2023. Using ChatGPT as a CAT tool in easy language translation. In *Proceedings of the Second Workshop on Text Simplification, Accessibility and Readability*, pages 1–10, Varna, Bulgaria. INCOMA Ltd., Shoumen, Bulgaria.

Ashwin Devaraj, Byron C Wallace, Iain J Marshall, and Junyi Jessy Li. 2021. Paragraph-level simplification of medical texts. In *Proceedings of the conference. Association for Computational Linguistics. North American Chapter. Meeting*, volume 2021, page 4972. NIH Public Access.

Jesse Dodge, Maarten Sap, Ana Marasović, William Agnew, Gabriel Ilharco, Dirk Groeneveld, Margaret Mitchell, and Matt Gardner. 2021. Documenting large webtext corpora: A case study on the colossal clean crawled corpus. *arXiv preprint arXiv:2104.08758*.

Lorenzo Jaime Yu Flores, Heyuan Huang, Kejian Shi, Sophie Chheang, and Arman Cohan. 2023. Medical text simplification: Optimizing for readability with unlikelihood training and reranked beam search decoding. In *Findings of the Association for Computational Linguistics: EMNLP 2023*, pages 4859–4873.

Thomas François, Adeline Müller, Eva Rolin, and Magali Norré. 2020. Amesure: a web platform to assist the clear writing of administrative texts. In *Proceedings of the 1st Conference of the Asia-Pacific Chapter of the Association for Computational Linguistics and the 10th International Joint Conference on Natural Language Processing: System Demonstrations*, pages 1–7.

Natalia Grabar and Horacio Saggion. 2022. Evaluation of automatic text simplification: Where are we now, where should we go from here. In *Traitement Automatique des Langues Naturelles*, pages 453–463. ATALA.

Susan Kleimann & Christine Mowat Harris, Lynda. 2010. Setting plain language standards. *Clarity*.

Katharina Jeblick, Balthasar Schachtner, Jakob Dexl, Andreas Mittermeier, Anna Theresa Stüber, Johanna Topalis, Tobias Weber, Philipp Wesp, Bastian Oliver Sabel, Jens Ricke, et al. 2023. Chatgpt makes medicine easy to swallow: an exploratory case study on simplified radiology reports. *European Radiology*, pages 1–9.

Sebastian Joseph, Kathryn Kazanas, Keziah Reina, Vishnesh Ramanathan, Wei Xu, Byron Wallace, and Junyi Jessy Li. 2023. Multilingual simplification of medical texts. In *Proceedings of the 2023 Conference on Empirical Methods in Natural Language Processing*, pages 16662–16692, Singapore. Association for Computational Linguistics.

Mike Lewis, Yinhan Liu, Naman Goyal, Marjan Ghazvininejad, Abdelrahman Mohamed, Omer Levy, Ves Stoyanov, and Luke Zettlemoyer. 2019. Bart: Denoising sequence-to-sequence pre-training for natural language generation, translation, and comprehension. *Preprint*, arXiv:1910.13461.

Zihao Li, Matthew Shardlow, and Fernando Alva-Manchego. 2023a. Comparing generic and expert models for genre-specific text simplification. In *Proceedings of the Second Workshop on Text Simplification, Accessibility and Readability*, pages 51–67, Varna, Bulgaria. INCOMA Ltd., Shoumen, Bulgaria.

Zihao Li, Matthew Shardlow, and Fernando Alva-Manchego. 2023b. Comparing generic and expert models for genre-specific text simplification. In *Proceedings of the Second Workshop on Text Simplification, Accessibility and Readability*, pages 51–67.

Chin-Yew Lin. 2004. Rouge: A package for automatic evaluation of summaries. In *Text summarization branches out*, pages 74–81.

Yinhan Liu, Jiatao Gu, Naman Goyal, Xian Li, Sergey Edunov, Marjan Ghazvininejad, Mike Lewis, and Luke Zettlemoyer. 2020. Multilingual denoising pre-training for neural machine translation. *Preprint*, arXiv:2001.08210.

Christiane Maaß. 2020. *Easy Language – Plain Language – Easy Language Plus: Balancing Comprehensibility and Acceptability*. Frank Timme.

Mounica Maddela, Fernando Alva-Manchego, and Wei Xu. 2020. Controllable text simplification with explicit paraphrasing. *arXiv preprint arXiv:2010.11004*.

Miguel Martinho. 2018. International standard for clarity - we bet this works for all languages. *Clarity Journal*.

José Monteiro, Micaela Aguiar, and Sílvia Araújo. 2022. Using a pre-trained simplet5 model for text simplification in a limited corpus. *Proceedings of the Working Notes of CLEF*.

Sergiu Nisioi, Sanja Štajner, Simone Paolo Ponzetto, and Liviu P Dinu. 2017. Exploring neural text simplification models. In *Proceedings of the 55th annual meeting of the association for computational linguistics (volume 2: Short papers)*, pages 85–91.

Kostiantyn Omelianchuk, Vipul Raheja, and Oleksandr Skurzhanskyi. 2021. Text simplification by tagging. *arXiv preprint arXiv:2103.05070*.

Kishore Papineni, Salim Roukos, Todd Ward, and Wei-Jing Zhu. 2002. Bleu: a method for automatic evaluation of machine translation. In *Proceedings of the ACL 2002*, pages 311–318.

Jipeng Qiang, Yun Li, Yi Zhu, Yunhao Yuan, and Xindong Wu. 2020. Lexical simplification with pre-trained encoders. In *Proceedings of the AAAI Conference on Artificial Intelligence*, volume 34, pages 8649–8656.

Evelina Rennes and Arne Jönsson. 2015. A tool for automatic simplification of swedish texts. In *20th Nordic Conference of Computational Linguistics*, pages 317–320. Linköping University Electronic Press.

Denis Rothman. 2022. *Transformers for Natural Language Processing: Build, train, and fine-tune deep neural network architectures for NLP with Python, Hugging Face, and OpenAI's GPT-3, ChatGPT, and GPT-4*. Packt Publishing Ltd.

Tim Schlippe and Katharina Eichinger. 2023. Multilingual text simplification and its performance on social sciences coursebooks. In *International Conference on Artificial Intelligence in Education Technology*, pages 119–136. Springer.

Theresa Seidl and Vincent Vandeghinste. 2024. Controllable sentence simplification in dutch. *Computational Linguistics in the Netherlands Journal*, 13:31–61.

Kim Cheng Sheang and Horacio Saggion. 2021. Controllable sentence simplification with a unified text-to-text transfer transformer. In *Proceedings of the 14th International Conference on Natural Language Generation (INLG); 2021 Sep 20-24; Aberdeen, Scotland, UK. Aberdeen: Association for Computational Linguistics; 2021*. ACL (Association for Computational Linguistics).

Neha Srikanth and Junyi Jessy Li. 2020. Elaborative simplification: Content addition and explanation generation in text simplification. *arXiv preprint arXiv:2010.10035*.

Sanja Štajner. 2021. Automatic text simplification for social good: Progress and challenges. *ACL-IJCNLP 2021*, pages 2637–2652.

Sanja Štajner and Horacio Saggion. 2018. Data-driven text simplification. In *Proceedings of the 27th International Conference on Computational Linguistics: Tutorial Abstracts*, pages 19–23.

Renliang Sun, Wei Xu, and Xiaojun Wan. 2023a. Teaching the pre-trained model to generate simple texts for text simplification. In *Findings of the Association for Computational Linguistics: ACL 2023*, pages 9345–9355, Toronto, Canada. Association for Computational Linguistics.

Renliang Sun, Zhixian Yang, and Xiaojun Wan. 2023b. Exploiting summarization data to help text simplification. In *Proceedings of the 17th Conference of the European Chapter of the Association for Computational Linguistics*, pages 39–51.

Julia Suter, Sarah Ebling, and Martin Volk. 2016. Rule-based automatic text simplification for german. *Bochumer Linguistische Arbeitsberichte*, page 279.

Andrius Utka. 2009. *Dažninis rašytinės lietuvių kalbos žodynas*. VDU leidykla.

Laura Vásquez-Rodríguez, Matthew Shardlow, Piotr Przybyła, and Sophia Ananiadou. 2023. Document-level text simplification with coherence evaluation. In *Proceedings of the Second Workshop on Text Simplification, Accessibility and Readability*, pages 85–101.

Ashish Vaswani, Noam Shazeer, Niki Parmar, Jakob Uszkoreit, Llion Jones, Aidan N Gomez, Łukasz Kaiser, and Illia Polosukhin. 2017. Attention is all you need. *Advances in neural information processing systems*, 30.

Tu Vu, Baotian Hu, Tsendsuren Munkhdalai, and Hong Yu. 2018. Sentence simplification with memory-augmented neural networks. *arXiv preprint arXiv:1804.07445*.

Zhihao Wen and Yuan Fang. 2023. Augmenting low-resource text classification with graph-grounded pre-training and prompting. In *Proceedings of the 46th International ACM SIGIR Conference on Research and Development in Information Retrieval*, pages 506–516.

Guillaume Wenzek, Marie-Anne Lachaux, Alexis Conneau, Vishrav Chaudhary, Francisco Guzmán, Armand Joulin, and Edouard Grave. 2019. Ccnet: Extracting high quality monolingual datasets from web crawl data. *Preprint*, arXiv:1911.00359.

Linting Xue, Noah Constant, Adam Roberts, Mihir Kale, Rami Al-Rfou, Aditya Siddhant, Aditya Barua, and Colin Raffel. 2021. mt5: A massively multilingual pre-trained text-to-text transformer. In *Proceedings of the 2021 Conference of the North American Chapter of the Association for Computational Linguistics: Human Language Technologies*, pages 483–498.

Gokul Yenduri, M Ramalingam, G Chemmalar Selvi, Y Supriya, Gautam Srivastava, Praveen Kumar Reddy Maddikunta, G Deepti Raj, Rutvij H Jhaveri, B Prabadevi, Weizheng Wang, Athanasios V. Vasilakos, and Thippa Reddy Gadekallu. 2024. Gpt (generative pre-trained transformer) – a comprehensive review on enabling technologies, potential applications, emerging challenges, and future directions. *IEEE Access*, pages 1–1.

Jipeng Zhang, Hai Zhao, and Jordan Boyd-Graber. 2021. Contextualized rewriting for text simplification. In *Transactions of the Association for Computational Linguistics*, volume 9, pages 1525–1540.

Tianyi Zhang, Varsha Kishore, Felix Wu, Kilian Q Weinberger, and Yoav Artzi. 2019. Bertscore: Evaluating text generation with bert. In *International Conference on Learning Representations*.

Sanqiang Zhao, Rui Meng, Daqing He, Saptono Andi, and Parmanto Bambang. 2018. Integrating transformer and paraphrase rules for sentence simplification. *arXiv preprint arXiv:1810.11193*.

Bartłomiej Nitoń Edyta Charzyńska Łukasz Dębowski, Bartosz Broda. 2015. Jasnopis–a program to compute readability of texts in polish based on psycholinguistic research. *Natural Language Processing and Cognitive Science*.

Word alignment in Discourse Representation Structure parsing

Christian Obereder
TU Wien
e11704936@student.tuwien.ac.at

Gábor Recski
TU Wien
gabor.recski@tuwien.ac.at

Abstract

Discourse Representation Structures (DRS) are formal representations of linguistic semantics based on Discourse Representation Theory (DRT, Kamp et al., 2011) that represent meaning as conditions over discourse referents. State-of-the-art DRS parsers learn the task of mapping text to DRSs from annotated corpora such as the Parallel Meaning Bank (PMB, Abzianidze et al., 2017). Using DRS in downstream NLP applications such as Named Entity Recognition (NER), Relation Extraction (RE), or Open Information Extraction (OIE) requires that DRS clauses produced by a parser be aligned with words of the input sentence. We propose a set of methods for extending such models to learn DRS-to-word alignment in two ways, by using learned attention weights for alignment and by adding alignment information from the PMB to the training data. Our results demonstrate that combining the two methods can achieve an alignment accuracy of over 98%. We also perform manual error analysis, showing that most remaining alignment errors are caused by one-off mistakes, many of which occur in sentences with multi-word expressions.

1 Introduction

Discourse Representation Structures (DRS) are formal representations of linguistic semantics based on Discourse Representation Theory (DRT) (DRT, Kamp et al., 2011) that represent meaning as conditions over discourse referents. State-of-the-art DRS parsers learn the task of mapping text to DRSs from annotated corpora such as the Parallel Meaning Bank (PMB, Abzianidze et al., 2017). Using DRS in downstream NLP applications such as Named Entity Recognition (NER), Relation Extraction (RE), or Open Information Extraction (OIE) requires that DRS clauses produced by a parser be aligned with words of the input sentence. Figure 1 shows an example DRS encoding the meaning of the sentence *The eagle is white*, complete with DRS-to-word alignment information.

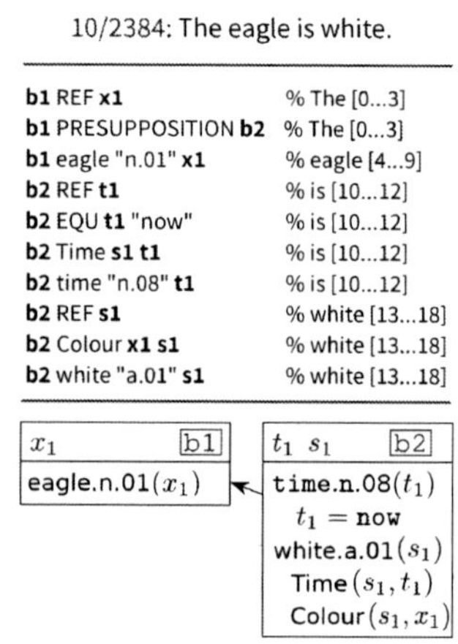

Figure 1: DRS in box- and clause-format for the sentence *The eagle is white*, with DRS-to-word alignments, from the PMB 3.0.0 corpus. 10/2384 is the ID of the sample in the PMB.

Unlike rule-based parsers such as Boxer (Bos, 2015), modern end-to-end parsers such as Neural-DRS (van Noord et al., 2018) do not generate this alignment. We propose a set of methods for extending such models to learn DRS-to-word alignment in two ways, by using learned attention weights for alignment and by adding alignment information from the PMB to the training data. Our results demonstrate that combining the two methods can achieve an alignment accuracy of over 98%. We also perform manual error analysis, showing that most remaining alignment errors are caused by one-off mistakes, many of which occur in sentences with multi-word expressions. The remainder of this paper is structured as follows. Section 2 summarizes related work on DRS parsing and attention-based alignment. Section 3 presents our main methods, Section 4 describes the experimental setup. Section 5 presents our experimental results, Section 6 describes results of our manual error analysis. All software used in our experiments is released under an MIT license and is available on GitHub[1].

2 Related Work

Recent work on DRS parsing involves the training of a variety of deep learning architectures on ground truth data created using a combination of automatic rule-based parsing with the Boxer parser (Bos, 2015) and manual error correction. Such systems include various structure-aware encoder-decoder models (Liu et al., 2018, 2019), an RNN-based parser of DAG-grammars (Fancellu et al., 2019), as well as sequence-to-sequence models (van Noord et al., 2018) that were recently used with pretrained language models and character embeddings to achieve some additional improvement in parsing performance (van Noord et al., 2020). It is this latter set of models, implemented as part of the NeuralDRS[2] codebase, that this paper extends to include the learning of DRS-to-word alignment (see Section 3 for details).

Most recent work on DRS parsing relies on the Parallel Meaning Bank (PMB, Abzianidze et al., 2017) for training and evaluation data. The PMB is a multilingual corpus containing sentences in English, German, Italian, and Dutch together with a variety of syntactic and semantic annotations. DRSs are generated for English using the Boxer parser and undergo various degrees of manual correction to create three subsets of the dataset. About 6,000 sentences have gold standard DRS annotations, another 67,000 constitute the silver dataset, these contain DRSs that have undergone at least one manual correction step, while about 120,000 sentences without any manual correction constitute the bronze portion of the dataset. Recent work has demonstrated that the inclusion of silver-quality annotation into the model training results in increased parsing performance (van Noord et al., 2018). Much related work on DRS parsing relies on the 2.1.0 and 2.2.0 versions of the PMB corpus (Abzianidze et al., 2019), we follow the more recent work of (van Noord et al., 2020) and use the 3.0.0 version in our experiments. DRS annotations in the PMB also contain alignment information, mapping nearly all DRS clauses to one or more tokens of the input text, as illustrated in Figure 1. We use this data both for model training and for evaluation of our main methods.

[1]https://github.com/GitianOberhuber/Neural_DRS_alignment

[2]https://github.com/RikVN/Neural_DRS

3 Methods

We propose a set of methods for extending the NeuralDRS parser architecture of van Noord et al. (2020) to include the task of DRS-to-word alignment, i.e. to map each DRS clause output by the parser to the word of the input sentence corresponding to the semantic information encoded by the DRS clause. The alignment information present in the PMB dataset (see Figure 1 and our discussion in Section 2) is used for both training and evaluation of our proposed models. The first method involves including the alignment data from PMB directly in the training data of the NeuralDRS system so that it learns to generate DRS-to-word alignments as part of its output. The second method involves using the attention scores computed by the NeuralDRS model to directly align DRS clauses in the output to words of the input. This method can be applied to the model trained using the original PMB data as well as the one trained on the modified version including word alignments. We show in Section 5 that it is the latter, combined method that achieves the highest accuracy on the DRS-to-word alignment task.

3.1 Alignment generation

Our first method involves creating a modified version of the training data that contains alignment information present in the PMB. For example, in case of the example sentence used in Figure 1, the string *b1 REF x1* would be replaced by *b1 REF x1 % The [0...3]* in the data. This data is then used to train the NeuralDRS system so that it learns to directly generate word alignments for each DRS clause. This approach does not guarantee that the model will output well-formed alignments, we therefore perform a simple form of fuzzy matching. For each generated word that is not a perfect match to one of the input words we choose the one with the lowest Levenshtein distance (Levenshtein, 1966).

3.2 Attention-based alignment

Our second method maps generated DRS clauses to input tokens using the attention scores calculated by the NeuralDRS model. Attention mechanisms in sequence-to-sequence models learn weighted alignments between input and output tokens. Given any alignment model a that maps pairs of encoder and decoder states we can define the alignment scoring function as

$$e_{t't} = a(s_{t'-1}, h_t)$$

where h_t is the encoder hidden-state at timestep t and $s_{t'-1}$ is the decoder hidden-state at timestep $t'-1$. Then for some timestep t' the context-vector $c_{t'}$ can be calculated as

$$c_{t'} = \sum_{t=1}^{T} \alpha_{t't} h_t,$$

where the weight $\alpha_{t't}$ is calculated as

$$\alpha_{t't} = \frac{exp(e_{t't})}{\sum_{k=1}^{T} exp(e_{t'k})}$$

Our attention-based alignment method maps each output token to the input token with the largest alignment score. Formally, given an input sequence $x = \{x_1, ..., x_T\}$ and corresponding (encoder-) timesteps $\tau = \{1, ..., T\}$, for each decoder timestep t' we calculate

$$\underset{t \in \tau}{\text{argmax}} \quad \frac{exp(e_{t't})}{\sum_{k=1}^{T} exp(e_{t'k})}.$$

Since our goal is to align DRS clauses, which consist of multiple output tokens, we calculate average scores over all tokens belonging to a given DRS clause.

The original NeuralDRS architecture uses dot-product attention (Luong et al., 2015), which defines the alignment score a as $h_t^\intercal s_{t'}$. For our attention-based alignment method we use both dot-product attention and bilinear attention, the latter of which defines a as $h_t^\intercal W s_{t'}$, where W is a learned matrix of weights. Our experiments show that the use of bilinear attention leads to improved alignment accuracy (see Section 5).

4 Experiments

Each of our experiments extends the single-encoder BERT-based model described by van Noord et al. (2020) and made available on GitHub[3]. We train models with two datasets, the original PMB data and the alignment-augmented data, the latter allows models to directly generate DRS-to-word alignments, as described in Section 3.1. Both types of models are also used to extract DRS-to-word alignments from their attentions weights, as described in Section 3.2.

[3]https://github.com/RikVN/Neural_DRS

All experiments are conducted using the English data of the 3.0.0 release of the PMB. The train portion of the gold data as well as all of the silver data is used for initial model training, followed by fine-tuning only on the gold data. Fine-tuning is performed five times with different random seeds, initial training is performed only once. To save resources, the maximum number of epochs (for both initial training and fine-tuning) was limited to 4. Models are implemented using the open-source AllenNLP framework (Gardner et al., 2018). Data preprocessing follows the original system described in van Noord et al. (2020), postprocessing of model outputs to produce final alignments is performed as described in Section 3. Model hyperparameters are shown in Appendix A.

For each of our models we evaluate both parsing quality and alignment accuracy. For measuring parsing performance we rely on the methodology of van Noord et al. (2020). This involves finding the optimal mapping from variable names used by predicted DRSs to those used in the ground truth, then calculating the precision, recall, and F-score of predicted DRS-clauses, ignoring *REF* clauses that serve to introduce variables and would always count as true positives, inflating scores unnecessarily. For measuring alignment accuracy we only consider correctly predicted DRS-clauses (including *REF* clauses) and define accuracy as the ratio of such clauses that have been aligned to the correct input word. Since we expect parsing errors to negatively affect the system's ability to align correctly predicted DRS-clauses, we also calculate alignment accuracy on the subset of sentences for which the DRS was parsed perfectly, i.e. those DRS where all clauses have been correctly predicted. The ratio of such sentences varies between 33% and 37% across parsing models. Furthermore, when comparing predictions to ground truth alignments we treat the following two cases exceptionally:

Multi-word tokens The PMB data contains some multi-word tokens, corresponding to named entities or other multi-word expressions, and represented in the corpus as e.g. *10~a.m.* The NeuralDRS pipeline does not have access to this analysis and processes the words *10* and *a.m* separately. If the PMB aligns a DRS clause to such a token, we consider our predicted alignment correct if and only if it maps the clause to one of the words of the multi-word token.

Multiple alignments A small fraction of DRS clauses in the PMB corpus is aligned with more than one input word. We consider these correctly aligned if our prediction corresponds to one of the multiple ground truth alignments.

5 Results

Table 1 shows all evaluation results on both the dev and test portions of the PMB 3.0.0 dataset. We observe that bilinear attention outperforms dot-product attention by a large margin when used to directly capture DRS-to-word alignment, as described in Section 3.2. In Appendix B we also provide visual comparison of the two types of attention that illustrates this difference. The end-to-end approach (Section 3.1) of training a model with DRS data augmented with alignment information from the PMB and using this model to generate the DRS-to-word alignment is superior to the attention-based methods. However, the highest accuracy is achieved by the combination of the two methods, i.e. using the attention weights of the end-to-end model for direct DRS-to-word alignment.

When evaluating on the subset of sentences which have been perfectly parsed, alignment accuracy increases considerably and is nearly perfect for both the end2end and combined approaches. This is in line with our expectation that errors in aligning correctly predicted DRS clauses typically occur around parsing errors. Since about two thirds of all sentences contain at least one parsing error, the combined approach is clearly the most practical choice for performing DRS-to-word alignment. We also measure the performance of each model on the DRS parsing task, but since we trained each model with a lower number of epochs to save resources, it is unsurprising that these figures are somewhat below the performance of the original NeuralDRS model (van Noord et al., 2020).

6 Error analysis

We perform manual analysis of alignment errors made by the end-to-end and combined approaches. For each model, sample outputs of approx. 40 sentences each were extracted from both the original dev set and the one filtered to contain only correctly parsed sentences. Here we describe only the most common error types of each approach.

Incorrect words The end-to-end approach will map some DRS-clauses to a word not present in the input sentence. Sometimes these are synonyms of the expected word, e.g. in the sentence *Is hexane toxic?*, the parser maps the clauses aligned with *toxic* to the word *poisonous*. In other examples the model produces ("hallucinates") unrelated words, e.g. in the sentence *Tom is addicted to heroin* the correctly predicted DRS clause `b2 heroin "n.01" x2` is mapped to the nonexistent input word *sobs*. These errors are often propagated across multiple DRS clauses aligned with the same input word, this way they are responsible for the majority of all errors made by the end-to-end approach on our samples.

One-off errors Unlike the end-to-end method, the combined approach is guaranteed to map each DRS clause to an existing input word. The majority of errors made by this approach are one-off mistakes, i.e clauses are mapped to a word adjacent to the one it is actually aligned with. Further inspection reveals that such errors often occur in sentences that either contain multi-word tokens (e.g. the DRS parse of the sentence *Mr. Ford is all right now* correctly contains the clause `b2 all_right "a.01" s1` but it is erroneously mapped to *now*) or multiple words mapped to a single word sense (e.g. from the sentence *I chopped a tree down.* the parser correctly generates the clause `b1 chop_down "v.01" x1` but then incorrectly maps the last clause `b1 tree "n.01" x3` to the last word *down*.

7 Conclusion

We have proposed two methods for extending a state-of-the-art DRS parser to perform DRS-to-word alignment and have shown that their combination achieves over 98% alignment accuracy on correctly predicted DRS clauses. Manual error analysis indicates that end-to-end generation of word alignment, which on its own achieves less than 96% accuracy, propagates errors caused by erroneously generated words across multiple DRS clauses. The combined approach of using attention scores, on the other hand, guarantees that each clause is mapped to existing input words and reduces the errors of the end-to-end approach by more than half. Additional error analysis suggests that multi-word expressions may be a major source of remaining alignment errors.

Ethical considerations

The main motivation of the present work is to enable the use of semantic parsing in complex NLP pipelines that rely on the information encoded in

	Dev			Test		
Method	**All sens**	**Corr. DRS**	**DRS F1**	**All sens**	**Corr. DRS**	**DRS F1**
Noord et al.	-	-	**87.58** ± 0.19	-	-	**88.53** ± 0.26
Attention (dot-prod.)	82.15 ± 0.91	83.33 ± 0.91	86.69 ± 0.25	82.15 ± 0.88	83.09 ± 1.00	87.10 ± 0.52
Attention (bilinear)	86.34 ± 0.59	88.08 ± 0.54	86.40 ± 0.48	86.36 ± 0.60	87.40 ± 0.81	87.17 ± 0.41
End-to-end	95.84 ± 0.19	**99.56** ± 0.09	84.89 ± 0.30	95.93 ± 0.19	**99.68** ± 0.12	85.74 ± 0.46
Combined (bilinear)	**98.49** ± 0.13	99.33 ± 0.08	84.89 ± 0.30	**98.46** ± 0.11	99.44 ± 0.11	85.74 ± 0.46

Table 1: DRS-to-word alignment performance of the proposed methods. *All sens* is alignment accuracy on the full English dev- and test-set of PMB 3.0.0, *Corr. DRS* uses the subset of sentences for which predicted DRSs are fully correct. DRS F1 is the parsing performance of each model. Attention-based alignment methods are based on model weights, as described in Section 3.2. The *end-to-end* method uses alignments generated by the model, as described in Section 3.1. The combined method uses the attention weights from the model trained to perform end-to-end alignment. All figures are mean values over 5 runs.

DRS structures to perform information extraction tasks such as Relation Extraction or Open Information Extraction with rule-based or hybrid methods. Partially or fully symbolic IE models can effectively expose and mitigate risks associated with black box models such as unintended model bias (Bender et al., 2021; De-Arteaga et al., 2019; Nadeem et al., 2021), lack of explainability of model decisions (Jain and Wallace, 2019), and vulnerabilities against adversarial attacks (Kour et al., 2023).

Limitations

This short paper presents experiments using a single dataset (PMB) and modifying a single architecture for semantic parsing (NeuralDRS). Furthermore, our conclusions are limited to the alignment task for a single type of semantic parsing formalism (DRS). In-depth investigation of the task of word alignment in semantic parsing should include experiments involving other common semantic parsing formalisms such as AMR (Banarescu et al., 2013) and UCCA (Abend and Rappoport, 2013), while experiments like those performed in this work should be repeated on multiple state-of-the-art sequence-to-sequence architectures for semantic parsing.

References

Omri Abend and Ari Rappoport. 2013. Universal Conceptual Cognitive Annotation (UCCA). In *Proceedings of the 51st Annual Meeting of the Association for Computational Linguistics (Volume 1: Long Papers)*, pages 228–238, Sofia, Bulgaria. Association for Computational Linguistics.

Lasha Abzianidze, Johannes Bjerva, Kilian Evang, Hessel Haagsma, Rik van Noord, Pierre Ludmann, Duc-Duy Nguyen, and Johan Bos. 2017. The Parallel Meaning Bank: Towards a multilingual corpus of translations annotated with compositional meaning representations. In *Proceedings of the 15th Conference of the European Chapter of the Association for Computational Linguistics: Volume 2, Short Papers*, pages 242–247, Valencia, Spain. Association for Computational Linguistics.

Lasha Abzianidze, Rik van Noord, Hessel Haagsma, and Johan Bos. 2019. The first shared task on discourse representation structure parsing. In *Proceedings of the IWCS Shared Task on Semantic Parsing*, Gothenburg, Sweden. Association for Computational Linguistics.

Laura Banarescu, Claire Bonial, Shu Cai, Madalina Georgescu, Kira Griffitt, Ulf Hermjakob, Kevin Knight, Philipp Koehn, Martha Palmer, and Nathan Schneider. 2013. Abstract Meaning Representation for sembanking. In *Proceedings of the 7th Linguistic Annotation Workshop and Interoperability with Discourse*, pages 178–186, Sofia, Bulgaria. Association for Computational Linguistics.

Emily M. Bender, Timnit Gebru, Angelina McMillan-Major, and Shmargaret Shmitchell. 2021. On the dangers of stochastic parrots: Can language models be too big? In *Proceedings of the 2021 ACM Conference on Fairness, Accountability, and Transparency*, FAccT '21, page 610–623, New York, NY, USA. Association for Computing Machinery.

Johan Bos. 2015. Open-domain semantic parsing with boxer. In *Proceedings of the 20th Nordic Conference of Computational Linguistics (NODALIDA 2015)*, pages 301–304, Vilnius, Lithuania. Linköping University Electronic Press, Sweden.

Maria De-Arteaga, Alexey Romanov, Hanna Wallach, Jennifer Chayes, Christian Borgs, Alexandra Chouldechova, Sahin Geyik, Krishnaram Kenthapadi, and Adam Tauman Kalai. 2019. Bias in bios: A case study of semantic representation bias in a high-stakes setting. In *Proceedings of the Conference on Fairness, Accountability, and Transparency*, FAT* '19, page 120–128, New York, NY, USA. Association for Computing Machinery.

Federico Fancellu, Sorcha Gilroy, Adam Lopez, and Mirella Lapata. 2019. Semantic graph parsing with recurrent neural network DAG grammars. In *Proceedings of the 2019 Conference on Empirical Methods in Natural Language Processing and the 9th International Joint Conference on Natural Language Processing (EMNLP-IJCNLP)*, pages 2769–2778, Hong Kong, China. Association for Computational Linguistics.

Matt Gardner, Joel Grus, Mark Neumann, Oyvind Tafjord, Pradeep Dasigi, Nelson F. Liu, Matthew Peters, Michael Schmitz, and Luke Zettlemoyer. 2018. AllenNLP: A deep semantic natural language processing platform. In *Proceedings of Workshop for NLP Open Source Software (NLP-OSS)*, pages 1–6, Melbourne, Australia. Association for Computational Linguistics.

Sarthak Jain and Byron C. Wallace. 2019. Attention is not Explanation. In *Proceedings of the 2019 Conference of the North American Chapter of the Association for Computational Linguistics: Human Language Technologies, Volume 1 (Long and Short Papers)*, pages 3543–3556, Minneapolis, Minnesota. Association for Computational Linguistics.

Hans Kamp, Josef van Genabith, and Uwe Reyle. 2011. Discourse representation theory. In *Handbook of philosophical logic*, pages 125–394. Springer.

George Kour, Marcel Zalmanovici, Naama Zwerdling, Esther Goldbraich, Ora Fandina, Ateret Anaby Tavor, Orna Raz, and Eitan Farchi. 2023. Unveiling safety vulnerabilities of large language models. In *Proceedings of the Third Workshop on Natural Language Generation, Evaluation, and Metrics (GEM)*, pages 111–127, Singapore. Association for Computational Linguistics.

Vladimir I Levenshtein. 1966. Binary codes capable of correcting deletions, insertions, and reversals. *Soviet physics – doklady*, 10(8):707–710.

Jiangming Liu, Shay B. Cohen, and Mirella Lapata. 2018. Discourse representation structure parsing. In *Proceedings of the 56th Annual Meeting of the Association for Computational Linguistics (Volume 1: Long Papers)*, pages 429–439, Melbourne, Australia. Association for Computational Linguistics.

Jiangming Liu, Shay B. Cohen, and Mirella Lapata. 2019. Discourse representation parsing for sentences and documents. In *Proceedings of the 57th Annual Meeting of the Association for Computational Linguistics*, pages 6248–6262, Florence, Italy. Association for Computational Linguistics.

Thang Luong, Hieu Pham, and Christopher D. Manning. 2015. Effective approaches to attention-based neural machine translation. In *Proceedings of the 2015 Conference on Empirical Methods in Natural Language Processing*, pages 1412–1421, Lisbon, Portugal. Association for Computational Linguistics.

Moin Nadeem, Anna Bethke, and Siva Reddy. 2021. StereoSet: Measuring stereotypical bias in pretrained language models. In *Proceedings of the 59th Annual Meeting of the Association for Computational Linguistics and the 11th International Joint Conference on Natural Language Processing (Volume 1: Long Papers)*, pages 5356–5371, Online. Association for Computational Linguistics.

Rik van Noord, Lasha Abzianidze, Antonio Toral, and Johan Bos. 2018. Exploring neural methods for parsing discourse representation structures. *Transactions of the Association for Computational Linguistics*, 6:619–633.

Rik van Noord, Antonio Toral, and Johan Bos. 2020. Character-level representations improve DRS-based semantic parsing even in the age of BERT. In *Proceedings of the 2020 Conference on Empirical Methods in Natural Language Processing (EMNLP)*, pages 4587–4603, Online. Association for Computational Linguistics.

A Model parameters

All hyperparameters used in the experiments described in Section 4 are shown in Table 2.

B Attention weights

Figure 2 compares dot-product and bilinear attention, illustrating the quantitative results in Section 5 that show the superior ability of bilinear attention to align generated DRS clauses with corresponding input words.

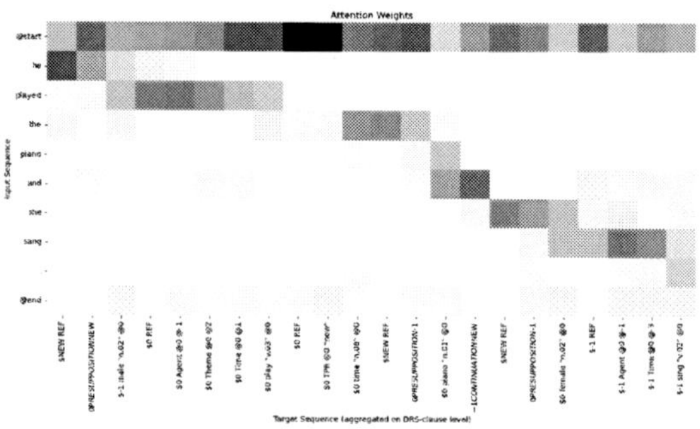

(a) dot-product attention

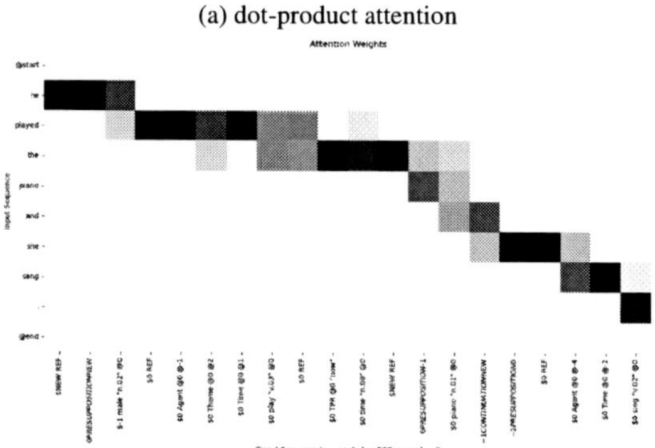

(b) bilinear attention

Figure 2: Visualization of dot-product and bilinear attention weights on a sample sentence from the PMB. Weights are aggregated on DRS-clause level, as described in Section 3.1

Input Embedding	
Type	bert-base-uncased
Size	768
Max. # source tokens	125
trainable	false
Target Embedding	
Type	pretrained GloVe
Size	300
Max. # tokens	1160
trainable	true
Encoder	
Type	biLSTM
Hidden Size	300
LSTM Layers	1
Attention	
Type	dot product / bilinear
normalize	true
matrix_dim	- / 600
vector_dim	- / 600
Decoder	
Type	LSTM
Hidden size	300
LSTM Layers	1
max_norm	3
scale_grad_by_freq	false
label_smoothing	0.0
beam_size	10
max decoding steps	1000
schedule sampling	0.2
Trainer	
batch size	12
optimizer	adam
learning rate	0.001
grad_norm	0.9
max_epochs	4

Table 2: Hyperparameters used in the experiments. Except for the values in red, all hyperparameters are equal to that of van Noord et al. (2020)

Evaluating and Fine-Tuning Retrieval-Augmented Language Models to Generate Text With Accurate Citations

Vinzent Penzkofer and **Timo Baumann**
Faculty of Informatics and Mathematics, OTH Regensburg
vinzent.penzkofer@outlook.de and timo.baumann@oth-regensburg.de

Abstract

Retrieval Augmented Generation (RAG) is becoming an essential tool for easily accessing large amounts of textual information. However, it is often challenging to determine whether the information in a given response originates from the retrieved context, the training, or is a result of hallucination. Our contribution in this area is twofold. Firstly, we demonstrate how existing datasets for information retrieval evaluation can be used to assess the ability of Large Language Models (LLMs) to correctly identify relevant sources. Our findings indicate that there are notable discrepancies in the performance of different current LLMs in this task. Secondly, we utilise the datasets and metrics for citation evaluation to enhance the citation quality of small open-weight LLMs through fine-tuning. We achieve significant performance gains in this task, matching the results of much larger models.

1 Introduction

In Retrieval Augmented Generation (RAG) (Lewis et al., 2020) the generation process of a language model is augmented at inference time with additional textual information retrieved from a corpus of documents. This approach aims to factually ground LLMs, reduce hallucination and provide access to information after the knowledge cut-off of the language model (Lewis et al., 2020).

Our focus is on the evaluation and improvement of RAG systems. We believe that it is necessary to correctly reference the information used for answer generation in order to make the factual accuracy verifiable by users in a practical setting. While there are ways to evaluate retrieval performance (Thakur et al., 2021; Muennighoff et al., 2023) and also factual correctness (Es et al., 2024; Chen et al., 2024), we see a research gap in evaluating the ability of models to correctly reference their sources. In this paper we present RAGE (Retrieval Augmented Generation Evaluation), a framework focused on evaluating the citation performance of language models used for RAG. Furthermore, we show how the citation evaluation metrics of RAGE can be used to directly improve the citation quality through fine-tuning.

2 Related Work

Several works have focused on the evaluation of RAG systems. Es et al. (2024) evaluate several different aspects of RAG including faithfulness, answer relevance and context relevance. Chen et al. (2024) propose a benchmark focusing on noise robustness, negative rejection, information integration and counterfactual robustness. Neither consider the attribution of referenced documents.

Gao et al. (2023) provide insights into how RAG systems can be prompted to generate text with citations. They also present a way of assessing the citation quality of LLMs, which includes the use of entailment models to assess the entailment of generated model responses and cited passages. Our work differs by using lightweight information retrieval datasets for citation evaluation and by having a clearly structured dataset format, making it more adaptable to specific use-cases.

Concurrently to us, Li et al. (2024) research fine-tuning to improve source attribution in RAG and developed a somewhat similar approach to ours. They also use Supervised Fine Tuning (SFT) for aligning model responses to a desired format, but do so using public datasets rather than generating new synthetic data as we do. We argue that the use of synthetic data makes the process more adaptable to specific use cases. They use preference optimisation (Rafailov et al., 2023) to optimise for citation quality, whereas we directly use citation quality metrics as a reward function for Proximal Policy Optimization (PPO), which can be automated more directly.

3 The RAGE Framework

In this section we describe RAGE (Retrieval Augmented Generation Evaluation), our automatic evaluation framework for RAG systems.[1] RAGE is designed to assess the performance of a RAG system in correctly referencing the documents it used for answer generation.

Typically RAG involves two steps, retrieval of relevant documents and generation augmented with the relevant texts.

RAGE specializes in assessing the augmented generation component, specifically its ability to cite its sources. We define this component as any system that takes in a query with a list of documents and generates an answer to the query whilst referencing the documents used for answer generation.

The fundamental idea of RAGE is to present augmented generation systems with a query accompanied by both relevant and irrelevant documents, then assessing the systems' capability to accurately identify and cite the relevant sources.

3.1 Datasets

The design of RAGE is based on ideas from the evaluation of Information Retrieval (IR) systems. IR systems are typically evaluated using datasets consisting of three distinct components: a corpus of documents, a set of queries, and a mapping table that indicates for each query the relevance of some specific documents (Thakur et al., 2021).

For RAGE, we extend this dataset structure with two additional mapping tables. We introduce a mapping of queries to **irrelevant** and to **seemingly relevant** documents in addition to the mapping of **relevant documents**. Documents are *seemingly* relevant when they appear as if they may contain the information necessary to answer a given query but don't actually do. This results in three distinct mapping tables in addition to the documents and queries.

We base our experiments on the Natural Questions (Kwiatkowski et al., 2019) dataset which was designed for the question answering domain and use the version adjusted for information retrieval by Thakur et al. (2021).[2] We argue that datasets designed for question answering are well-suited for evaluating RAG systems due to the typical application of RAG in this domain.

We create the mapping of irrelevant documents by randomly sampling the document corpus while excluding the relevant documents for a given query.

For the mapping of seemingly relevant documents, we generate a vector representation of all documents and queries using the multilingual-e5-small embedding model (Wang et al., 2024). Subsequently, for each query, we compare its embedding to all the document embeddings using an L2 similarity measure, while again excluding the relevant documents. The ten documents that show the highest similarity to the given query were mapped.

Other IR datasets can trivially be converted to the required format by scripts that are part of RAGE[3].

3.2 Procedure

The evaluation process employed in RAGE follows two steps.

Step 1: Create a relevancy mixture of documents. For each query, a mixture of relevant, irrelevant and seemingly relevant documents is created. The proportions of relevant, irrelevant, and seemingly relevant documents in the mixture for each query can be freely adjusted in an evaluation run. A prompt is generated containing processing instructions, the document mixture, and the query itself. The prompt is then passed to the augmented generation component under evaluation. An example of a prompt and a LLM response used in our experiments is given in Appendix A.

Step 2: Analyze LLM answer and compute performance metrics. The LLM response is analysed w.r.t. various performance metrics including *Citation-Precision*, *Citation-Recall*, the number of *Distinct Citations*, and *Response Length*.

Citation-Precision is defined as the ratio of relevant citations to the total number of citations within the response. Similarly, *Citation-Recall* is determined by the ratio of relevant distinct citations to the total number of relevant documents included in the document mixture during the first step. *Response Length* is measured by the total number of words, and finally *Distinct Citations* counts the unique citations within the response. Additionally, the harmonic mean of *Citation-Precision* and *Citation-Recall* yields the *F1-Score*.

[1] The codebase is available at https://github.com/othr-nlp/rage_toolkit.

[2] We have also experimented with the HotpotQA (Yang et al., 2018) dataset. That dataset yields similar results which we here omit for brevity.

[3] Some datasets already converted to the RAGE format are available at https://huggingface.co/othr-nlp.

Model	F1 Score	Precision	Recall	Answer Length	Cited Distinct
Baseline	.16	.14	.19	-	1.47
LLaMA 2 7B	.47	.41	.55	77.7	1.88
LLaMA 2 13B	.45	.40	.51	67.6	1.63
LLaMA 2 70B	.66	.64	.67	41.3	1.40
Mistral 7B	.61	.51	.77	45.8	2.17
Mixtral 8x7B	.73	.64	.85	41.8	1.83
GPT 3.5	.78	.75	.80	18.4	1.34
GPT 4	.82	.81	.83	21.1	1.29

Table 1: RAGE evaluation results for different state-of-the-art LLMs evaluated on the Natural Questions (Kwiatkowski et al., 2019) Dataset from the BEIR Benchmark (Thakur et al., 2021). As a baseline we include an augmented generation system which randomly cites 1-3 of the provided documents.

The metrics are calculated for each query and then averaged to determine the final scores for a given evaluation dataset.

3.3 Evaluation Setup

In our experiments, we evaluate citation performance of some state-of-the-art LLMs. To achieve this, we first combine the query and the mixture of relevant, irrelevant, seemingly relevant documents into a prompt that is then to be passed to the LLM in question. For our experiments, we used 1-3 relevant, 3 irrelevant and 3 seemingly relevant documents for all runs.

The prompt furthermore contains processing instructions which state to use only the information contained within the documents and to cite in a predefined format. Prompt generation is identical for all augmented generation components (and has not undergone much prompt engineering). For an example of prompt, query and LLM response, we again refer to Appendix A.

We selected LLMs of differing model size in terms of parameters, availability (open- or closed-weight) and performance on common benchmarks for our trial run of RAGE.

The evaluation was performed on the Natural Questions dataset (Kwiatkowski et al., 2019) with the described adaptations (Section 3.1).

3.4 Results

The results of our evaluation are shown in Table 1. Baseline performance is significantly surpassed by all models, indicating an understanding of the task and citation format.

Smaller models tend to produce longer answers and more distinct citations which leads to good recall but poorer precision. There is a tendency for larger models to perform better.

GPT-3.5 and GPT-4 (OpenAI, 2023) perform best *out of the box* and produce short answers and few distinct citations, indicating concise responses.

To test the robustness of RAGE, we also conducted experiments with different proportions in the document mixtures. The results indicate that RAGE works consistently well across these variations, though higher proportions of seemingly relevant documents increase task difficulty. We included those results in Appendix B.

4 Fine-Tuning for Citation Quality

In this section, we describe our approach to fine-tune open-weight LLMs for improved citation quality. We use the metrics and datasets as defined above for RAGE and use synthetic target data produced by GPT-3.5.

4.1 High-level Approach

Our fine-tuning technique to improve citation quality is inspired by Ouyang et al. (2022). They fine-tune LLMs to follow human instructions by first applying SFT to align the model outputs to a desired format and subsequently using PPO (Schulman et al., 2017) to further align to human preferences. Similarly, our approach is also twofold:

Step 1: Use supervised fine-tuning (SFT) to align model outputs to a preferred answer format. The idea of SFT for language models is to continue the self-supervised next token prediction objective of the pretraining phase with labeled task-specific data. For our models, we use synthetic data from GPT-3.5, which showed a concise answer style

Model	Tuning	F1 Score	Precision	Recall	Answer Length	Cited Distinct
LLaMA 2 7B		.47	.41	.55	77.7	1.88
	SFT	.47	.47	.46	18.7	1.25
	PPO	.53	.43	**.68**	142.3	2.92
	SFT+PPO	**.70**	**.74**	.66	18.1	1.05
Mistral 7B		.61	.51	.77	45.8	2.17
	SFT	.56	.57	.55	20.6	1.19
	PPO	**.72**	.65	**.80**	40.5	1.68
	SFT+PPO	.70	**.74**	.66	16.4	1.02
GPT 3.5		.78	.75	.80	18.4	1.34

Table 2: Evaluation results for fine-tuned models evaluated on Natural Questions (Kwiatkowski et al., 2019). Base models and GPT-3.5 are included for comparison.

with high precision and recall, to adjust the answer format of the smaller models.

Step 2: Improve citation-quality with reinforcement learning via proximal policy optimization (PPO). Reinforcement learning is a useful approach for language model fine-tuning, as it requires only a quality measure of the generated sequences, known as the reward function, rather than labeled example responses. We use a reward function based on the RAGE evaluation metrics outlined above and the PPO algorithm to directly improve citation quality. The reward function and the datasets are described in more detail later. PPO is applied separately or on top of the SFT process.

4.2 Fine-Tuning Datasets

This section presents the composition of the datasets we used for SFT and PPO fine-tuning.

SFT: Inspired by Mukherjee et al. (2023), we used the performance gap of the small 7B models to GPT-3.5[4] to generate synthetic training data. As shown in Table 1, GPT-3.5 provides good precision and recall with a short answer length, making it ideal for aligning the smaller models. We used the Natural Questions (Kwiatkowski et al., 2019) dataset and the same process as in the evaluation to generate a set of prompts for GPT-3.5. We then collected the responses of GPT-3.5, combined them with the prompts and added model-specific special tokens to create the final SFT dataset. 250 queries of Natural Questions were withheld from the training dataset for evaluation, leaving a total of 3201 fine-tuning examples.

[4]The exact model version is gpt-3.5-turbo.

PPO: For PPO fine-tuning we also generated prompts as described in the evaluation section, each containing citation instructions, documents and query. We generated the prompts using the Natural Questions (Kwiatkowski et al., 2019) and HotpotQA (Yang et al., 2018) datasets, withholding 250 examples from each for evaluation, thereby compiling a training dataset of 10,347 examples.

4.3 PPO Reward Function

Instead of using a reward model for reward generation as done by Ouyang et al. (2022), we use a simple reward function by calculating the arithmetic mean of citation precision and citation recall:

$$\text{Reward} = \frac{\text{Recall} + \text{Precision}}{2}$$

This function directly rewards improved citation quality without the need for an expensive reward model training. To prevent the model from exploiting the reward function, we use a KL-penalty as described by Ouyang et al. (2022).

4.4 Experimental Details

We used the instruction fine-tuned versions of Llama2 7B (Touvron et al., 2023) and Mistral 7B (Jiang et al., 2023) as bases. For both base models, three versions were trained and evaluated: *SFT-only*, *PPO-only* and *PPO+SFT*. We use QLoRA (Dettmers et al., 2023) with 4-bit quantization and a rank of 64 for the adaptation matrices for both SFT and PPO. SFT was performed for three epochs and PPO for one epoch on the respective dataset.

4.5 Results and Discussion

The fine-tuned models are evaluated via RAGE using the 250 queries withheld from the fine-tuning datasets. Results are shown in Table 2.

The PPO+SFT model versions show that fine-tuning leads to gains compared to the base models and they approach GPT-3.5's citation precision despite the significantly smaller model sizes. Mistral 7B PPO+SFT experiences a decrease in recall, likely attributable to the significantly shorter answer lengths imposed by SFT. Mistral 7B PPO-only achieves the highest scores in terms of F1-score and recall among the fine-tuned models; however, it exhibits significantly lower precision and produces longer answers compared to PPO+SFT. For both, SFT reduces the average answer length to that of GPT-3.5, while resulting in a loss of recall. Interestingly, training observations indicate that the shorter answer lengths after SFT, enhance PPO training, improving reward gains and reducing training times. This efficiency is likely due to faster answer generation and fewer token generation steps for reward distribution.

The results clearly indicate that fine-tuning is effective in improving citation performance for RAG. We find that fine-tuning improves the F1-score by .10 to .20 points or a relative reduction of F1 error of 28 - 43 %.

5 Ethical Considerations

All experiments performed in this work were conducted in accordance with the ACM Code of Ethics. We believe that there should be no conflicts and that this work does not raise any ethical issues. All datasets used are publicly available or synthetically generated. Both cases are referenced accordingly. We do not use personal data or other sensitive information.

6 Limitations

The major limitation of our work is that RAGE considers only citation quality for evaluation. More aspects have to be covered to provide a complete RAG evaluation framework. At the moment, we refer to other work to include aspects like measures for factual correctness, how good information from the documents is integrated and a general measure of how fluent the answer is. This especially becomes relevant when evaluating the fine-tuned model versions as the improvement in citation quality does not necessarily come with an improvement in the other metrics or could even worsen performance in some cases. Tests of our models do not indicate this, but it is still important to consider when applying them in practice. Also currently, there are only two evaluation datasets converted to the format used in RAGE. A greater variety of datasets would further improve the significance of the evaluation.

References

Jiawei Chen, Hongyu Lin, Xianpei Han, and Le Sun. 2024. Benchmarking large language models in retrieval-augmented generation. *Proceedings of the AAAI Conference on Artificial Intelligence*, 38(16):17754–17762.

Tim Dettmers, Artidoro Pagnoni, Ari Holtzman, and Luke Zettlemoyer. 2023. QLoRA: Efficient fine-tuning of quantized LLMs. In *Advances in Neural Information Processing Systems*, volume 36, pages 10088–10115. Curran Associates, Inc.

Shahul Es, Jithin James, Luis Espinosa-Anke, and Steven Schockaert. 2024. RAGAs: Automated evaluation of retrieval augmented generation. In *Proceedings of the 18th Conference of the European Chapter of the Association for Computational Linguistics: System Demonstrations*, pages 150–158, St. Julians, Malta. Association for Computational Linguistics.

Tianyu Gao, Howard Yen, Jiatong Yu, and Danqi Chen. 2023. Enabling large language models to generate text with citations. In *Proceedings of the 2023 Conference on Empirical Methods in Natural Language Processing*, pages 6465–6488, Singapore. Association for Computational Linguistics.

Albert Q. Jiang, Alexandre Sablayrolles, Arthur Mensch, Chris Bamford, Devendra Singh Chaplot, Diego de las Casas, Florian Bressand, Gianna Lengyel, Guillaume Lample, Lucile Saulnier, Lélio Renard Lavaud, Marie-Anne Lachaux, Pierre Stock, Teven Le Scao, Thibaut Lavril, Thomas Wang, Timothée Lacroix, and William El Sayed. 2023. Mistral 7b. *arXiv preprint arXiv:2310.06825*.

Tom Kwiatkowski, Jennimaria Palomaki, Olivia Redfield, Michael Collins, Ankur Parikh, Chris Alberti, Danielle Epstein, Illia Polosukhin, Jacob Devlin, Kenton Lee, Kristina Toutanova, Llion Jones, Matthew Kelcey, Ming-Wei Chang, Andrew M. Dai, Jakob Uszkoreit, Quoc Le, and Slav Petrov. 2019. Natural questions: A benchmark for question answering research. *Transactions of the Association for Computational Linguistics*, 7:453–466.

Patrick Lewis, Ethan Perez, Aleksandra Piktus, Fabio Petroni, Vladimir Karpukhin, Naman Goyal, Heinrich Küttler, Mike Lewis, Wen-tau Yih, Tim Rocktäschel, Sebastian Riedel, and Douwe Kiela. 2020. Retrieval-augmented generation for knowledge-intensive NLP tasks. In *Advances in Neural Information Processing Systems*, volume 33, pages 9459–9474. Curran Associates, Inc.

Dongfang Li, Zetian Sun, Baotian Hu, Zhenyu Liu, Xinshuo Hu, Xuebo Liu, and Min Zhang. 2024. Improving attributed text generation of large language models via preference learning. *arXiv preprint arXiv:2403.18381*.

Niklas Muennighoff, Nouamane Tazi, Loïc Magne, and Nils Reimers. 2023. MTEB: Massive text embedding benchmark. In *Proceedings of the 17th Conference of the European Chapter of the Association for Computational Linguistics*, pages 2014–2037, Dubrovnik, Croatia. Association for Computational Linguistics.

Subhabrata Mukherjee, Arindam Mitra, Ganesh Jawahar, Sahaj Agarwal, Hamid Palangi, and Ahmed Awadallah. 2023. Orca: Progressive learning from complex explanation traces of GPT-4. *arXiv preprint arXiv:2306.02707*.

OpenAI. 2023. GPT-4 technical report. *arXiv preprint arXiv:2303.08774*.

Long Ouyang, Jeff Wu, Xu Jiang, Diogo Almeida, Carroll L. Wainwright, Pamela Mishkin, Chong Zhang, Sandhini Agarwal, Katarina Slama, Alex Ray, John Schulman, Jacob Hilton, Fraser Kelton, Luke Miller, Maddie Simens, Amanda Askell, Peter Welinder, Paul Christiano, Jan Leike, and Ryan Lowe. 2022. Training language models to follow instructions with human feedback. In *Advances in Neural Information Processing Systems*, volume 35, pages 27730–27744. Curran Associates, Inc.

Rafael Rafailov, Archit Sharma, Eric Mitchell, Stefano Ermon, Christopher D. Manning, and Chelsea Finn. 2023. Direct preference optimization: Your language model is secretly a reward model. In *Advances in Neural Information Processing Systems*, volume 36, pages 53728–53741. Curran Associates, Inc.

John Schulman, Filip Wolski, Prafulla Dhariwal, Alec Radford, and Oleg Klimov. 2017. Proximal policy optimization algorithms. *arXiv preprint arXiv:1707.06347*.

Nandan Thakur, Nils Reimers, Andreas Rücklé, Abhishek Srivastava, and Iryna Gurevych. 2021. BEIR: A heterogenous benchmark for zero-shot evaluation of information retrieval models. In *Proceedings of the Neural Information Processing Systems Track on Datasets and Benchmarks*, volume 1.

Hugo Touvron, Louis Martin, Kevin Stone, Peter Albert, Amjad Almahairi, Yasmine Babaei, Nikolay Bashlykov, Soumya Batra, Prajjwal Bhargava, Shruti Bhosale, Dan Bikel, Lukas Blecher, Cristian Canton Ferrer, Moya Chen, Guillem Cucurull, David Esiobu, Jude Fernandes, Jeremy Fu, Wenyin Fu, Brian Fuller, Cynthia Gao, Vedanuj Goswami, Naman Goyal, Anthony Hartshorn, Saghar Hosseini, Rui Hou, Hakan Inan, Marcin Kardas, Viktor Kerkez, Madian Khabsa, Isabel Kloumann, Artem Korenev, Punit Singh Koura, Marie-Anne Lachaux, Thibaut Lavril, Jenya Lee, Diana Liskovich, Yinghai Lu, Yuning Mao, Xavier Martinet, Todor Mihaylov, Pushkar Mishra, Igor Molybog, Yixin Nie, Andrew Poulton, Jeremy Reizenstein, Rashi Rungta, Kalyan Saladi, Alan Schelten, Ruan Silva, Eric Michael Smith, Ranjan Subramanian, Xiaoqing Ellen Tan, Binh Tang, Ross Taylor, Adina Williams, Jian Xiang Kuan, Puxin Xu, Zheng Yan, Iliyan Zarov, Yuchen Zhang, Angela Fan, Melanie Kambadur, Sharan Narang, Aurelien Rodriguez, Robert Stojnic, Sergey Edunov, and Thomas Scialom. 2023. Llama 2: Open foundation and fine-tuned chat models. *arXiv preprint arXiv:2307.09288*.

Liang Wang, Nan Yang, Xiaolong Huang, Linjun Yang, Rangan Majumder, and Furu Wei. 2024. Multilingual E5 text embeddings: A technical report. *arXiv preprint arXiv:2402.05672*.

Zhilin Yang, Peng Qi, Saizheng Zhang, Yoshua Bengio, William W. Cohen, Ruslan Salakhutdinov, and Christopher D. Manning. 2018. HotpotQA: A dataset for diverse, explainable multi-hop question answering. In *Proceedings of the 2018 Conference on Empirical Methods in Natural Language Processing*, pages 2369–2380, Brussels, Belgium. Association for Computational Linguistics.

A Prompt Structure

Figure 1 shows an example for a prompt generated during evaluation using RAGE. Our prompt structure is strongly inspired by Gao et al. (2023). The figure also shows the original query and the response containing citations, that was generated by a Mistral 7B (Jiang et al., 2023) model. A prompt of this structure is generated for each query and contains a predefined portion of relevant, irrelevant and seemingly-relevant documents. The response of the LLM under evaluation is analysed regarding its citation quality as described in Section 3.2.

B Effects of Varying the Relevancy Mixture

Figure 2 shows the effects of using different mixtures of relevant, irrelevant and seemingly-relevant documents for a given query on citation precision and recall. The number of relevant documents was kept constant, and the proportion of irrelevant and seemingly relevant documents was varied. The evaluation was performed with five different open-weight models. Evaluation results are consistent across all evaluated models and show that RAGE is robust to using different proportions. The evaluation also shows that seemingly relevant documents significantly increase task difficulty.

Query: When did hollywood become the centre of the film industry?

Prompt:
Instruction: Write an accurate, engaging, and concise answer for the given question using only the provided documents (some of which might be irrelevant) and cite them properly using the format $[< doc\_id >]$. For example if a particular information is from document 3 reference it with [3]. Use an unbiased and journalistic tone. Always cite for any factual claim. When citing several search results, use [1][2][3]. Cite at least one document and at most three documents in each sentence. If multiple documents support the sentence, only cite a minimum sufficient subset of the documents.

Documents:

[1]: Hollywood was a small community in 1870 and was incorporated as a municipality in 1903. It was consolidated with the city of Los Angeles in 1910, and soon thereafter a prominent film industry emerged, eventually becoming the most recognizable film industry in the world.

[2]: By 1912, major motion-picture companies had set up production near or in Los Angeles. In the early 1900s, most motion picture patents were held by Thomas Edison's Motion Picture Patents Company in New Jersey, and filmmakers were often sued to stop their productions. To escape this, filmmakers began moving out west, where Edison's patents could not be enforced. Also, the weather was ideal and there was quick access to various settings. Los Angeles became the capital of the film industry.

[3]: The history of the Forest Service [...]

[...]

[6]: The cinema of the United States, often metonymously referred to as Hollywood [...] Since the 1920s, the film industry of the United States has had higher annual grosses than any other country's [...]

[...]

Question: When did hollywood become the centre of the film industry?

Remember to answer as short as possible.

Answer: Hollywood became the center of the film industry in the early 1900s as major motion-picture companies moved there to escape patent disputes and take advantage of ideal weather and easy access to various settings [1][2]. By the 1920s, Hollywood produced the largest number of films and had the highest annual grosses in the film industry [6].

Figure 1: An example prompt and LLM response produced during the evaluation process. The query was taken from the Natural Questions (Kwiatkowski et al., 2019) dataset contained in the BEIR benchmark (Thakur et al., 2021). The prompt was automatically generated and contains the documents assembled from relevant, irrelevant and apparently relevant documents as described in Section 3.2. The structure of the prompt template essentially follows the concept presented in (Gao et al., 2023). The answer was generated by a Mistral 7B model (Jiang et al., 2023).

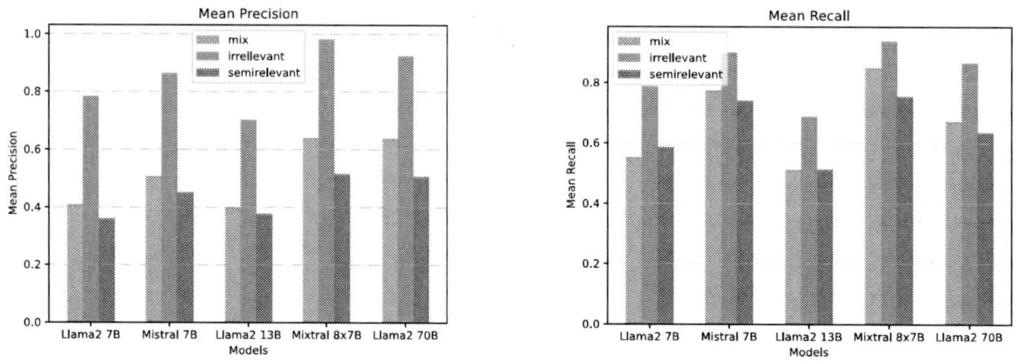

(a) (b)

Figure 2: Comparative evaluation of mean citation precision (Figure 2a) and recall (Figure 2b) across three document relevancy mixtures in the Natural Questions (Kwiatkowski et al., 2019) dataset. The *mix* setup includes 1-4 relevant, 3 irrelevant, and 3 seemingly relevant documents. The *irrelevant* setup consists of 1-4 relevant and 6 irrelevant documents, with no seemingly relevant documents. The *seemingly-relevant* setup features 1-4 relevant and 6 seemingly relevant documents, excluding any irrelevant documents.

Discourse Parsing for German with new RST Corpora

Sara Shahmohammadi and **Manfred Stede**
Applied Computational Linguistics Group
Department of Linguistics
University of Potsdam, Germany
shahmohammadi@uni-potsdam.de stede@uni-potsdam.de

Abstract

For RST-style discourse parsing in German, so far there has been only one corpus available and used, the single-genre Potsdam Commentary Corpus (PCC). Very recently, two new RST corpora of other genres have been made available. In our work, we build a homogeneously-annotated German RST corpus by changing the PCC annotations so that they become compatible with the new corpora. We then run parsing experiments on different constellations of train/test splits over the three genres involved and report the results. A modified and streamlined version of the DPLP (Ji and Eisenstein, 2014) parser is prepared and made available, so that overall, the "resource situation" for German discourse parsing is notably improved.

1 Introduction

Rhetorical Structure Theory (Mann and Thompson, 1988) is a theory of discourse structure that models text coherence by a tree structure composed of discourse relations. Various corpora in several languages have been annotated within this framework since it was introduced. The Potsdam Commentary Corpus (PCC) (Stede and Neumann, 2014), was the first RST corpus for German, and just recently, two new German corpora have been annotated within this framework, viz. the APA-RST corpus (Hewett, 2023) of newspaper text, and a multimedia corpus of blogposts and podcast transcripts (Seemann et al., 2023). Although these two corpora followed the annotation guidelines of PCC for the most part, the authors modified the relation set, most importantly by adding the discourse relations *Same-unit* and *Attribution* (for compatibility with existing English corpora). This makes PCC incompatible with them at the levels of segmentation and relation set. In our work, we present a re-annotation of PCC texts, firstly in order to make it interoperable with the new corpora, and secondly because we observed that the annotations could also be improved in various other respects (which we will explain).

Taking the union of the three corpora, we perform discourse parsing using a modified version of the DPLP parser (Ji and Eisenstein, 2014). As there are three slightly different genres present in the corpora, we run experiments with different train/test splits in order to test generalizability. We find that the overall best model is obtained by training on PCC and the blogpost data. We make the re-annotated PCC data as well as the ready-to-use parser available to the community.[1]

After a brief introduction to RST and discussion of related work in Section 2, we discuss our PCC re-annotation and provide some corpus statistics in Section 3. Section 4 then gives details on the three corpora used in the parsing experiments, which we present in Section 5, and then conclude the paper in Section 6.

2 Background and Related Work

2.1 Rhetorical Structure Theory

RST (Mann and Thompson, 1988) models the structure of a text as a tree whose leaf nodes are given by the sequence of elementary discourse units (EDUs)[2] and whose internal nodes represent coherence relations holding between those leaf nodes and/or text spans (internal nodes of the tree) that are formed recursively. Coherence relations are built on the concept of nuclearity. If one discourse unit is more essential to the coherence relation than the other, it is deemed the nucleus (denoted by N); otherwise, it is deemed satellite (denoted by S). In Figure 1, for example, unit 4 and units 5-6 are the nucleus and the satellite, respectively. The majority

[1] Available at: `https://github.com/mohamadi-sara20/pcc`

[2] EDUs are the minimal parts of discourse. (Stede et al., 2017, p. 4). They are usually defined as clauses of the text. In Figure 1, for example, there are three EDUs.

of relations are formed from elements with different weights (mononuclear relations), but some relations also connect multiple nuclei (multinuclear relations). The overall set of relations is not restricted to one closed list. Different corpora have proposed different relation sets; e.g., Mann and Thompson (1988) defined about 25 relation types in total, while the RST Discourse Treebank has 78 fine-grained relations, which are merged into 18 coarse-grained ones for automatic parsing purposes (Carlson et al., 2003, p. 32).

So-called "schemas" specify the constellations that may arise, e.g., whether multiple relation satellites can be attached to the same nucleus; if so, whether this is allowed only from one or from both directions in the text. In any case, relations always connect adjacent spans in such a way that no crossing dependencies arise.

2.2 The Potsdam Commentary Corpus

PCC is a freely available, multi-layer annotated corpus, whose latest revision of the RST layer was introduced by Stede and Neumann (2014). It consists of 176 commentary texts from a local German newspaper, i.e., it is a relatively small and deliberately homogeneous corpus. In our work, we inspected the RST layer and found some room for improvement, which will be described in Section 3.

2.3 RST Parsing for German

Early results for German RST parsing, using for the first time a support-vector machine and linguistic features for this purpose, had been presented by Reitter (2003). Recent results using neural systems were published by Braud et al. (2017), Liu et al. (2020), and Liu et al. (2021), who proposed multilingual parsers where the German part was trained and tested on PCC.

Braud et al. (2017), Liu et al. (2020) and Liu et al. (2021) respectively report performances of 0.80, 0.84, 0.84 on span detection; 0.54, 0.62 , 0.64 on nuclearity detection; and 0.35, 0.45, 0.47 on relation detection. In addition, Braud et al. (2023) report a performance of 0.32 on relation classification for German.

As a note of caution, we report that we tried to execute and reproduce the results of Braud et al. (2017) and Liu et al. (2021), but were unfortunately unable to do so and therefore turned to an alternative system.

Comparability is exacerbated by the fact that multilingual parsers are trained on large amounts of multilingual data, while we are dealing here with a single-language corpus, which is (still) comparatively small.

3 PCC-RST "reloaded"

3.1 Motivations for re-annotation

We found some improvable points in the RST layer of the PCC and thus made a number of changes to the annotations regarding segmentation, attachment point selection, and relations. For brevity, in the rest of the paper we call our revised RST layer *PCC**.

Segmentation. Occasionally, PCC annotators had used phrasal segments (*[And the town will hopefully not be brought down-][despite the bankruptcy of the State Development Corporation (LEG)][and occasional complaints within their own ranks.]*[3]). We decided to eliminate these, because their segmentation was not consistent. Phrasal segments were only kept in cases where a colon was present (*[Firstly:][The parking fees in the shopping area must be removed.]*[4]), as it was possible to remain consistent this way.

Further, since we aimed to add the *Attribution* and *Same-unit* relations to the data (see below), we had to modify the segmentation for these cases as well. For verbs of *Attribution*, we consulted a list of communication verbs provided by Tofiloski et al. (2009).[5]

Attachment Points. Non-adjacent attachments, which were present in several PCC trees, were avoided. Instead, we follow the suggestion of Egg and Redeker (2010): If all children have the same function, they are first joined as a list and then connected to the parent. For instance, the tree in the upper part of Figure 1 is turned into the tree in the lower part, because units 5 and 6 are both connected to their parent via an *Interpretation* relation. However, if children do not serve the same function, to avoid such connections, the adjacent child is prioritised and connected to the parent first, and then other children can be added. For an example, see Figure 2.

[3]From maz-8727.

[4]From maz-18914.

[5]`https://github.com/sfu-discourse-lab/SL-Seg`

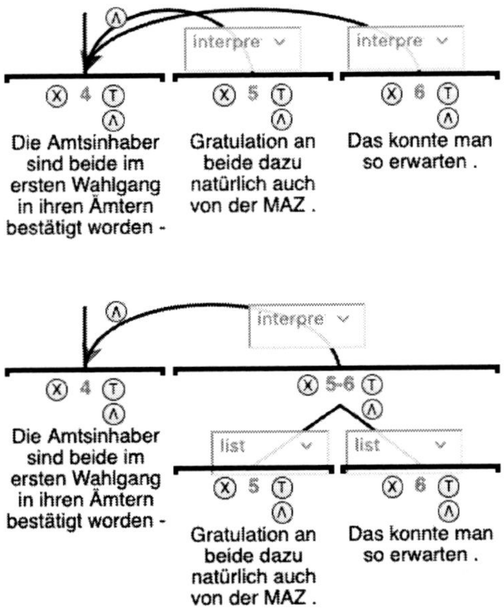

Figure 1: Non-adjacent connection, resolved by joining 5 and 6, because they are both connected to the nucleus via an *Interpretation* relation.

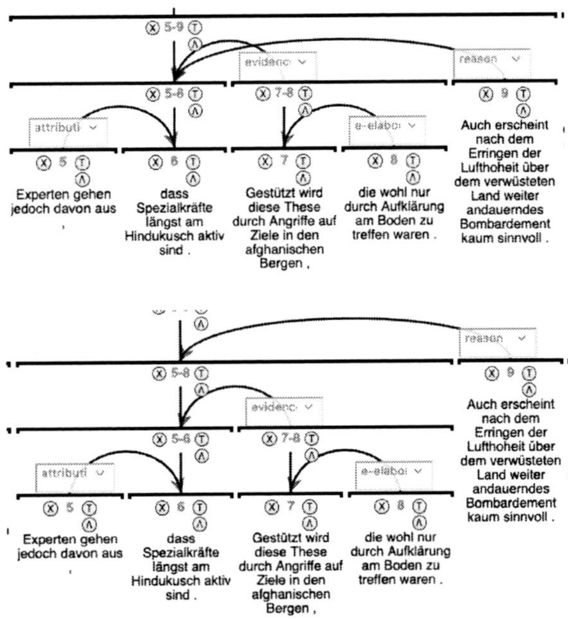

Figure 2: Non-adjacent connection, resolved by a hierarchical structure.

Schemas. We avoided the schema where a node is the parent of its left and right adjacent node at the same time. See Figure 3 for one such example. This step was taken because the annotation guidelines did not clearly specify the conditions for applying this schema, and we believe it is in fact not possible to avoid considerable ambiguity in such a formalization.

Relations. We made some changes to the relation list, by adding some new relations, eliminating some infrequent relations, and merging some relations. To see the definitions of the relations, consult Stede et al. (2017).

- *Attribution* and *Same-unit* were added to improve compatibility with existing large English RST corpora. The former relation is used for ascribing speech/thought content to a speaker ("John explained that the earth is flat"), while the latter handles parenthetical segments ("John explained – against his own belief – that the earth is flat"), which are in fact quite frequent in PCC.

- *Enablement*, which occurred only twice, was merged with the *Means* relation, following the practice of the two new German corpora mentioned above.

- *Unless* occurred only once in PCC and was removed from the inventory (the instance was re-annotated as *Condition*).

- *Disjunction* was merged with *Conjunction*, as it is not documented in the annotation guidelines.

- *Preparation*: Preparation usage was extended. We decided to use this relation whenever the satellite "consists of an introductory formula" (Stede et al., 2017, p. 19), announcing a nucleus, regardless of the information the satellite holds.

3.2 Inter-annotator Agreement

The data was annotated by the first author of this paper. Roughly ten percent of the corpus (18 texts) was double annotated. The second set of annotations were done by a student assistant, well-trained in RST.

The standard agreement measuring scores are span detection (S), nuclearity detection (N) and relation detection (R) scores, which are also widely used in evaluating automatic parsing results. These are reported in Table 1, which we obtained after converting our trees to parenthetical format using *discoursegraphs* (Neumann, 2015).

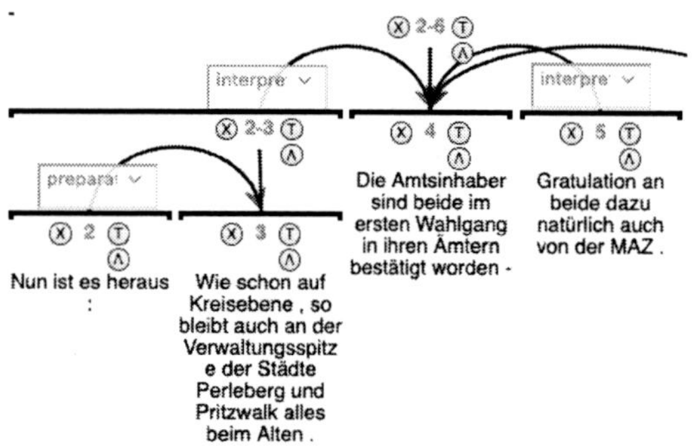

Figure 3: Parent with left and right children

In addition, we also report the inter-annotator agreement using the RST-Tace (Wan et al., 2019; Iruskieta et al., 2015) criteria in Table 2. RST-Tace is a tool that measures the agreement of RST annotations of different coders.

	S	N	R
PCC*	0.85	0.65	0.44

Table 1: Inter-annotator agreement. Results computed with the script released by Joty et al. (2015).

Agreement Ratio

	NR	RR	CR	AR	Average
mean	0.58	0.38	0.51	0.46	0.48
std	0.19	0.19	0.19	0.20	0.18

Agreement Kappa

	NK	RK	CK	AK	Average
mean	0.39	0.32	0.52	0.42	0.41
std	0.27	0.20	0.19	0.21	0.20

Table 2: Inter-annotator agreement computed by RST-Tace. NR, RR, CR, AR in the upper table denote Nuclearity Ratio, Relation Ratio, Constituent Ratio, Attachment-Point Ratio. NK, RK, CK, AK in the lower table denote Nuclearity Kappa, Relation Kappa, Constituent Kappa, and Attachment-Point Kappa.

3.3 Corpus Statistics

Taking a brief look at the changes in some relation groups, namely causal[6], additive[7], contrastive[8], context[9], and commentary relations[10] can give us an overview of how PCC and PCC* differ in terms of relations.

The proportion of additive relations overall changed drastically ($\chi^2 = 46.26$, p-value < 0.0001). A significant change is also present in causal relations ($\chi^2 = 8.59$, p-value $= 0.0034$), contrastive relations ($\chi^2 = 6.41$, p-value $= 0.0113$), relations of context ($\chi^2 = 6.55$, p-value $=0.0105$), as well as commentary relations ($\chi^2 = 14.18$, p-value $=0.0002$). On the other hand, relation groups like elaborative relations[11], conditionals[12] or summary, did not change significantly in proportion.

Figure 4 portrays the kernel density estimation of the relations whose proportions changed significantly. We have used Kernel Density Estimation from SciPy (Virtanen et al., 2020) to obtain them.

A more detailed comparison of our annotations with the original PCC annotations would be possible if the original PCC annotations were minimally changed – at least minor modifications at segmentation level – so that they can become comparable to ours, which can be the done in the future.

4 Data and Preprocessing

For our RST parsing experiments, we can now utilize the following German corpora: Blogposts from a multimedia corpus (Seemann et al., 2023), RST annotations of the original texts from the APA corpus (Hewett, 2023), and PCC. In addition to our new version PCC*, we also include the original PCC annotations in order to see if the parsing performance improves as a result of the re-annotation. The original PCC has 2,676 relations and 3,018 EDUs, while PCC* has 2,935 relations and 3,111 EDUs.

Blogposts. The blogposts come from several publishers (both commercial companies and scientific writers), and have been written for the weblog of various podcasts (Seemann et al., 2023). Each blogpost corresponds to one episode and usually either summarizes the content of the episode or more briefly announces the topic of discussion. In total, there are 78 RST trees, with 1,309 relations and 1,387 EDUs.

APA. This corpus contains 25 news articles from the Austrian news agency, along with their

[6]cause, result, justify, reason, reason-N, evidence, solutionhood, solutionhood-N, and motivation combined

[7]joint, conjunction, list, and disjunction combined

[8]antithesis, contrast, and concession combined

[9]background, circumstance, and preparation combined

[10]evaluation-n, evaluation-s, interpretation combined

[11]elaboration and e-elaboration combined

[12]condition, unless

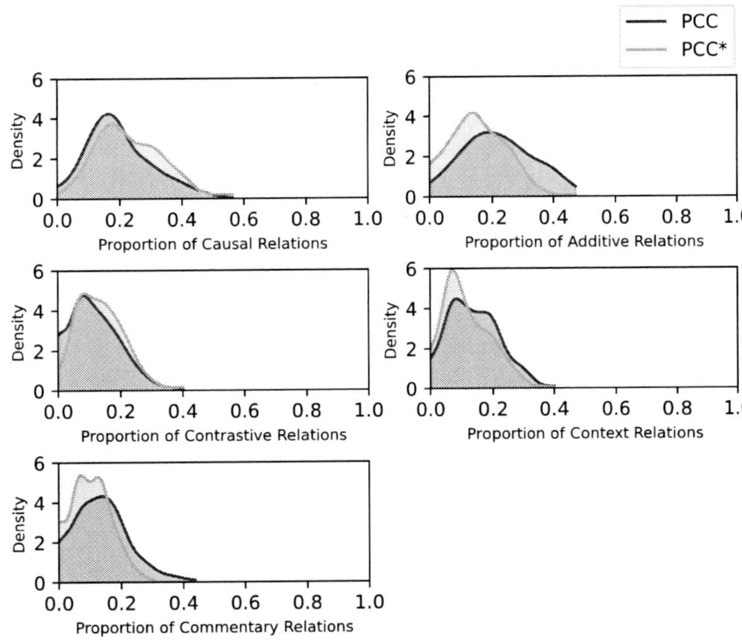

Figure 4: Kernel Density Estimation of proportions of causal, additive, contrastive, context and commentary relations

manually-produced simplifications to the language-learning levels of B1 and A2; hence in total there are 75 texts (Hewett, 2023). We only use the 25 original articles, because they are more comparable to the other corpora. RST trees have been annotated per paragraph, yielding a total of 61 trees with 852 relations and 938 EDUs.

Total data size. The original PCC corpus, as well as our version PCC*, contains 176 texts and thus the same number of trees. In total, there are now 78+61+176 = 315 different German texts (or for APA, paragraphs) with RST trees. They contain 5,096 discourse relations and 5,436 EDUs. In terms of relations, this represents a roughly 70 % increase in data size when compared to the original PCC RST corpus.

Preprocessing. In line with other parsing approaches, we use a Lisp-inspired parenthetical format of the RST trees as input to the parser. To obtain this format from the .rs3 XML standard used by the manual-annotation tools, we make use of the *discoursegraphs* library (Neumann, 2015). POS tagging and dependency parsing was done with stanza (Qi et al., 2020). All first segments of the original PCC trees, which are the headings of the text and not connected to the RST tree, have been removed.

5 Parsing Experiments and Results

5.1 Parser

We use the DPLP parser (Ji and Eisenstein, 2014), publicly available on github, because in comparison to others, it is well-documented, well-structured, lightweight, and rather easily adaptable to new data.

This shift-reduce parser is based on a set of linguistic and positional features, viz.: sentence ID, segment ID, word ID (in the sentence), word, POS tag, dependency label, dependency head for each EDU and also the two EDUs on top of the stack, and the EDU on top of the stack and at the front of the queue. In addition to these features, Brown clusters are also used as a means of contextualizing words.[13]

As a downside, the code was rather old, requiring discontinued versions of some libraries. To solve this issue, runtime dependencies are containerized in a Docker image and shared on Docker Hub[14]. The code was adapted by extending some

[13]https://github.com/mheilman/tan-clustering

[14]https://hub.docker.com/repository/docker/mohamadisara20/dplp-env

of the original modules and writing a number of new scripts.

5.2 Evaluation procedure

To evaluate parsing performance for the within-corpus experiments, we did a 5-fold cross validation, averaging over five runs for each of the five folds (first and second blocks in Table 3). For cross-corpus experiments, we train on the complete source corpus and test on the complete target corpus, averaging over five runs (third, fourth and fifth block in Table 3).

To divide the data into five partitions, we randomly shuffled the data and created five batches from PCC, PCC*, and APA data. For blogposts, however, we created a stratified sample, i.e., we partitioned the data such that texts from their different publishers are represented proportionally. This decision seemed advisable because we observed great linguistic variability among the texts from these different sources.

5.3 Results

All our results are collected in Table 3.

Within-corpus evaluation. The first block of the table shows the results of training and testing on each corpus separately (5-fold CV).

As evident, using PCC* annotations, the performance has improved on nuclearity and relation detection. This indicates that we have managed to improve the annotations and reduce inconsistency to a certain degree. However, part of the improvement is due to the addition of the *Attribution* relation, which is rather easy to learn due to its syntactical and lexical features.

On blogposts, performance is notably higher than on PCC. We assume that this is due to the lower complexity of these texts: They are shorter, and overall have either the straightforward purpose of introducing, or (less frequently) summarizing a podcast episode. This leads to more formulaic structures than in editorials, which exhibit relatively high stylistic and argumentative variation.

For APA texts, results are in the range of PCC, which at first sight hints at similarities between the rhetorical structures of newspaper texts, irrespective of their degree of subjectivity.

Finally, we ran a test on the complete corpus of 315 texts and found that compared to when only including PCC* data, the performance improves only minimally. The cross-corpus experiments can explain the potential reasons to some extent.

	S	N	R
PCC	0.77	0.52	0.28
PCC*	0.77	0.55	0.35
Blogs	0.81	0.61	0.40
APA	0.81	0.56	0.32
APA+Blogs+PCC*	0.78	0.56	0.36
Blogs+PCC* → PCC*	0.77	0.54	0.34
Blogs+PCC* → Blogs	0.82	0.64	0.43
PCC* → APA	0.77	0.48	0.24
APA → PCC*	0.75	0.47	0.24
APA → Blogs	0.78	0.53	0.31
Blogs → APA	0.76	0.45	0.21
PCC* → Blogs	0.80	0.59	0.39
Blogs → PCC*	0.76	0.50	0.28

Table 3: Parser performance results for the various train/test settings (see Section 5.3). The arrow notation is "training corpus" → "test corpus".

Cross-corpus evaluation. Since the parsing performances differ somewhat between the corpora, we decided to explore how well a model learnt on one corpus would predict the structure on another.

Firstly (second block of the table), we found that adding blogs to the PCC* training data does not increase the performance on PCC*. However, we achieve the overall best results by testing the combined PCC* and blogs model on blogs, among the individual corpora as well as the pairings. This may also be an effect of the corpus size: PCC parsing does not benefit as much from the addition of (small) out-of-domain data as the blog parsing does from adding a larger amount of out-of-domain data.

The third block of Table 3 shows results for the PCC*/APA pair. The two results are very close to each other and at the same time lower than those of the individual corpora, so it seems that neither is able to generalize well to the other. This may contradict the impression of their similarity that we formulated for the first experiment above. It can also partly be due to the fact that PCC* annotations cover the complete text, while this is not true for APA.

Finally, the fourth and fifth blocks of the table give the results for the pairings with the "top performing" individual corpus, i.e., blogposts. Results are higher than for PCC*/APA throughout, with the odd exception of a rather low relation recognition in the Blogs→APA setting (for which we have no explanation hypothesis). The much better results for PCC*→Blogs in comparison to Blogs→PCC* can be an effect of training corpus size, given that PCC* has twice as many texts as the Blogs corpus.

5.4 Error Analysis

Table 5 shows a sample confusion matrix from PCC*. The rows signify the true labels and the columns signify the predicted labels. We can see that relations such as *Concession*, *Conjunction*, *List*, *E-elaboration*, as well as *Attribution* and *Reason* have been recognized better.

The confusion matrix is, however, rather sparse. Since it can be beneficial to see the performance on relation groups as well, we trained another model by merging all additive, causal, commentary, context, and elaboration relations.[15] to see on a more general level what relations are better recognized as well as what relation groups are confused with each other. Some relations, such as *Attribution* or *Same-unit*, were kept as they were, since we believe they do not have enough in common with each other or with other groups.

Table 4 represents the confusion matrix of a model with merged relations. As the table shows, additive, conditional, and context relations are in general detected more reliably, while contrastive relations are often confused with additives and causals. Causal relations are also confused with commentary or elaborative relations. Less frequent relations such as *Sequence* were also often confused with additives.

It should be noted that although the merged model can give us a more general overview, it must be looked at with care, since the numbers in most cases are still not high enough to draw solid conclusions.

6 Conclusion

So far, the only resource for RST parsing in German has been the Potsdam Commentary Corpus. Prompted by the recent release of two additional RST corpora, we created a unified resource by changing the PCC annotations, on the one hand for compatibility with the new corpora, on the other hand for improving certain shortcomings in the existing annotations. Using the new homogenous set of corpora, we performed various RST parsing experiments with different train/test splits, and report the results here as baselines for further studies. We showed that parsing performance improves for nuclearity and relations when moving from the original PCC to our PCC* trees, which may indicate higher annotation consistency.

Furthermore, we are making a revised version of the DPLP parser available (ready to use for German), as well as the re-annotated PCC texts.

In future work, the enlarged data set can be used to test other parsing architectures. In addition, the old and new versions of the PCC RST layer can be used to study the phenomena of "legitimate disagreement" in discourse annotation – a topic that has recently become popular also under the label "perspectivist approaches to NLP". This can include approaches to systematically including both variants in training parsing models.

Limitations

As hinted at in the conclusion, RST annotation is known to be subjective, and thus we do not regard our new PCC annotations as "the single ground truth"; instead it represents a set of possible text interpretations. The corpus that can now be used for parsing has more genre variety than the PCC had, but is still relatively homogeneous (opinion articles, news, well-edited blogs); additional genre diversity could be achieved, for example, by adding more user-generated text, e.g. from social media.

Ethics Statement

All annotations were performed by the first author of this paper and reviewed by the second author of this paper. One regularly-paid student assistant annotated part of the data.

Acknowledgments

This work was funded by the Deutsche Forschungsgemeinschaft (DFG, German Research Foundation) – Project ID 317633480 – SFB 1287. We would like to thank Elisa Lübbers for helping with annotations and the reviewers for their thoughtful comments.

[15]The groups have been specified in Section 3.3.

	additive	attribution	causal	commentary	condition	context	contrastive	elaboration	means	purpose	sameunit	sequence	summary-restatement
additive	71	2	8	6	1	3	3	9	0	1	3	0	0
attribution	3	12	0	0	3	1	0	0	0	1	0	0	0
causal	4	0	26	11	0	2	5	11	0	0	0	0	0
commentary	4	0	6	8	0	3	3	8	0	0	0	0	0
condition	0	0	0	0	12	1	0	0	0	0	0	0	0
context	2	0	1	0	2	15	1	3	0	0	0	0	0
contrastive	12	0	15	0	2	2	28	6	0	0	0	0	0
elaboration	8	0	8	1	0	2	1	26	0	0	1	0	0
means	0	0	0	0	0	0	1	0	0	0	0	0	0
purpose	0	0	1	0	1	0	0	1	0	4	0	0	0
sameunit	2	0	2	0	0	1	2	3	0	0	7	0	0
sequence	5	0	0	0	0	0	0	0	0	0	0	0	0
summary-restatement	2	0	0	1	0	0	0	1	0	0	0	0	0

Table 4: Confusion matrix (merged relations)

	antithesis	attribution	background	cause	circumstance	concession	condition	conjunction	contrast	e-elaboration	elaboration	evaluation-S	evidence	interpretation	list	means	preparation	purpose	reason	reason-N	restatement	result	sameunit	sequence	solutionhood	solutionhood-N	summary
antithesis	5	0	1	0	0	0	1	0	1	2	0	0	0	1	0	0	0	0	0	0	0	0	1	0	0	0	0
attribution	1	12	0	0	0	0	2	1	0	0	0	0	0	0	0	0	1	1	0	0	0	0	0	0	0	0	0
background	0	0	3	0	0	1	0	0	0	0	0	0	0	0	0	0	1	0	0	0	0	0	0	0	0	0	0
cause	1	0	0	0	0	0	0	0	0	1	0	0	0	0	0	0	1	0	1	0	0	0	0	0	0	0	0
circumstance	0	0	0	0	4	0	3	0	1	1	0	0	0	0	2	0	0	0	0	0	0	0	0	0	0	0	0
concession	1	0	0	0	1	19	3	2	0	0	1	0	0	0	3	0	0	0	0	0	0	0	0	0	0	0	0
condition	0	0	0	0	0	0	11	0	0	0	0	0	0	0	0	0	1	0	0	0	0	0	0	0	0	0	0
conjunction	1	0	0	0	0	0	0	51	0	0	1	0	0	2	0	0	0	0	0	1	0	0	0	0	0	0	0
contrast	0	0	0	0	0	4	0	5	0	1	1	1	0	1	6	0	0	1	5	1	0	0	0	0	0	0	0
e-elaboration	0	0	0	0	0	0	0	1	0	23	1	0	0	0	3	0	1	0	0	0	0	0	1	0	0	0	0
elaboration	1	1	1	0	0	1	0	2	1	1	5	0	1	1	1	0	0	0	2	0	0	0	0	0	0	0	0
evaluation-S	0	0	1	0	0	2	0	1	1	0	1	0	0	1	2	0	1	0	2	0	0	0	0	0	0	0	0
evidence	0	0	0	1	0	0	0	0	2	0	0	0	1	0	0	0	0	0	2	0	0	0	0	0	0	0	0
interpretation	0	0	1	0	0	1	0	1	6	1	1	1	0	2	2	0	1	0	3	0	0	0	0	0	0	0	0
list	0	3	2	0	0	2	1	8	3	4	3	1	1	1	25	0	1	1	3	0	0	0	4	0	0	0	0
means	0	0	0	0	0	0	0	0	1	0	0	0	0	0	0	0	0	0	0	0	0	0	0	0	0	0	0
preparation	0	0	1	0	0	1	0	0	0	0	0	0	0	0	0	0	8	0	0	0	0	0	0	0	0	0	0
purpose	0	0	0	0	0	0	1	0	0	1	0	1	0	0	0	0	0	4	0	0	0	0	0	0	0	0	0
reason	0	0	0	0	0	1	0	1	1	5	0	1	0	4	7	0	0	0	13	0	0	0	0	0	0	0	0
reason-N	0	0	0	0	0	0	0	0	0	0	1	1	0	2	3	0	0	0	3	0	0	0	0	0	0	0	0
restatement	0	0	0	0	0	0	0	1	0	0	0	0	0	0	0	0	0	0	1	0	0	0	0	0	0	0	0
result	0	0	0	0	0	0	0	0	1	0	0	0	0	0	1	0	0	0	2	0	0	0	0	0	0	0	0
sameunit	0	0	0	0	0	2	1	0	0	1	0	0	0	0	1	0	1	0	0	0	0	0	7	0	0	0	0
sequence	0	1	0	0	0	0	0	4	0	0	0	0	0	0	0	0	0	0	0	0	0	0	0	0	0	0	0
solutionhood	0	0	1	0	0	0	0	0	0	0	0	0	0	0	0	0	0	0	0	0	0	0	0	0	0	0	0
solutionhood-N	0	0	0	0	0	0	0	0	0	0	0	0	0	0	0	0	0	0	1	0	0	0	0	0	0	0	0
summary	0	0	0	0	0	0	0	1	0	1	0	1	0	2	0	0	0	0	0	0	0	0	0	0	0	0	0

Table 5: Confusion matrix (unmerged relations)

References

Chloé Braud, Maximin Coavoux, and Anders Søgaard. 2017. Cross-lingual RST discourse parsing. In Proceedings of the 15th Conference of the European Chapter of the Association for Computational Linguistics: Volume 1, Long Papers, pages 292–304, Valencia, Spain. Association for Computational Linguistics.

Chloé Braud, Yang Janet Liu, Eleni Metheniti, Philippe Muller, Laura Rivière, Attapol T Rutherford, and Amir Zeldes. 2023. The disrpt 2023 shared task on elementary discourse unit segmentation, connective detection, and relation classification. In 3rd Shared Task on Discourse Relation Parsing and Treebanking (DISRPT 2023), pages 1–21. ACL: Association for Computational Linguistics.

Lynn Carlson, Daniel Marcu, and Mary Ellen Okurowski. 2003. Building a discourse-tagged corpus in the framework of Rhetorical Structure Theory. In Jan van Kuppevelt and Ronnie Smith, editors, Current Directions in Discourse and Dialogue. Kluwer, Dordrecht.

Markus Egg and Gisela Redeker. 2010. How complex is discourse structure? In Proceedings of the Seventh Conference on International Language Resources and Evaluation (LREC'10), Valletta, Malta, 19-21 May, 2010, pages 1619–1623. European Language Resources Association (ELRA).

Freya Hewett. 2023. APA-RST: A text simplification corpus with RST annotations. In Proceedings of the 4th Workshop on Computational Approaches to Discourse (CODI 2023), pages 173–179, Toronto, Canada. Association for Computational Linguistics.

Mikel Iruskieta, Iria Da Cunha, and Maite Taboada. 2015. A qualitative comparison method for rhetorical structures: identifying different discourse structures in multilingual corpora. Language resources and evaluation, 49:263–309.

Yangfeng Ji and Jacob Eisenstein. 2014. Representation learning for text-level discourse parsing. In Proceedings of the 52nd annual meeting of the association for computational linguistics (volume 1: Long papers), pages 13–24.

Shafiq Joty, Giuseppe Carenini, and Raymond T Ng. 2015. Codra: A novel discriminative framework for rhetorical analysis. Computational Linguistics, 41(3):385–435.

Zhengyuan Liu, Ke Shi, and Nancy Chen. 2020. Multilingual neural RST discourse parsing. In Proceedings of the 28th International Conference on Computational Linguistics, pages 6730–6738, Barcelona, Spain (Online). International Committee on Computational Linguistics.

Zhengyuan Liu, Ke Shi, and Nancy F Chen. 2021. Dmrst: A joint framework for document-level multilingual rst discourse segmentation and parsing. arXiv preprint arXiv:2110.04518.

William C. Mann and Sandra A. Thompson. 1988. Rhetorical Structure Theory: Toward a functional theory of text organization. Text - Interdisciplinary Journal for the Study of Discourse, 8(3):243–281.

Arne Neumann. 2015. discoursegraphs: A graph-based merging tool and converter for multilayer annotated corpora. In Proceedings of the 20th Nordic Conference of Computational Linguistics (NODALIDA 2015), pages 309–312.

Peng Qi, Yuhao Zhang, Yuhui Zhang, Jason Bolton, and Christopher D. Manning. 2020. Stanza: A Python natural language processing toolkit for many human languages. In Proceedings of the 58th Annual Meeting of the Association for Computational Linguistics: System Demonstrations.

David Reitter. 2003. Simple signals for complex rhetorics: On rhetorical analysis with rich-feature support vector models. Journal for Language Technology and Computational Linguistics, 7(1):38–52.

Hannah J Seemann, Sara Shahmohammadi, Tatjana Scheffler, and Manfred Stede. 2023. Building a parallel discourse-annotated multimedia corpus. Proceedings of the 10th International Conference on CMC and Social Media Corpora for the Humanities, 8(3):17.

Manfred Stede and Arne Neumann. 2014. Potsdam commentary corpus 2.0: Annotation for discourse research. In Proceedings of the Ninth International Conference on Language Resources and Evaluation (LREC'14), pages 925–929, Reykjavik, Iceland. European Language Resources Association (ELRA).

Manfred Stede, Maite Taboada, and Debopam Das. 2017. Annotation guidelines for rhetorical structure. Manuscript. University of Potsdam and Simon Fraser University.

Milan Tofiloski, Julian Brooke, and Maite Taboada. 2009. A syntactic and lexical-based discourse segmenter. In Proceedings of the ACL-IJCNLP 2009 conference short papers, pages 77–80.

Pauli Virtanen, Ralf Gommers, Travis E. Oliphant, Matt Haberland, Tyler Reddy, David Cournapeau, Evgeni Burovski, Pearu Peterson, Warren Weckesser, Jonathan Bright, Stéfan J. van der Walt, Matthew Brett, Joshua Wilson, K. Jarrod Millman, Nikolay Mayorov, Andrew R. J. Nelson, Eric Jones, Robert Kern, Eric Larson, C J Carey, İlhan Polat, Yu Feng, Eric W. Moore, Jake VanderPlas, Denis Laxalde, Josef Perktold, Robert Cimrman, Ian Henriksen, E. A. Quintero, Charles R. Harris, Anne M. Archibald, Antônio H. Ribeiro, Fabian Pedregosa, Paul van Mulbregt, and SciPy 1.0 Contributors. 2020. SciPy 1.0: Fundamental Algorithms for Scientific Computing in Python. Nature Methods, 17:261–272.

Shujun Wan, Tino Kutschbach, Anke Lüdeling, and Manfred Stede. 2019. Rst-tace a tool for automatic comparison and evaluation of rst trees. In

Proceedings of the Workshop on Discourse Relation Parsing and Treebanking 2019, pages 88–96.

Revisiting the Phenomenon of Syntactic Complexity Convergence on German Dialogue Data

Yu Wang and **Hendrik Buschmeier**
Digital Linguistics Lab, Department of Linguistics
Faculty of Linguistics and Literary Studies
Bielefeld University, Bielefeld, Germany
{y.wang,hbuschme}@uni-bielefeld.de

Abstract

We revisit the phenomenon of syntactic complexity convergence in conversational interaction, originally found for English dialogue, which has theoretical implication for dialogical concepts such as mutual understanding. We use a modified metric to quantify syntactic complexity based on dependency parsing. The results show that syntactic complexity convergence can be statistically confirmed in one of three selected German datasets that were analysed. Given that the dataset which shows such convergence is much larger than the other two selected datasets, the empirical results indicate a certain degree of linguistic generality of syntactic complexity convergence in conversational interaction. We also found a different type of syntactic complexity convergence in one of the datasets while further investigation is still necessary.

1 Introduction

The interactive alignment theory (Pickering and Garrod, 2004) states that, in interaction, mutual understanding is reached through the support of adaptive processes, which result in a reduction of the communicative efforts of the dialogue participants. Pickering and Garrod (2004) have mentioned the co-adaptivity of interlocutors' verbal behaviour on the following six levels: phonetic, phonological, lexical, syntactic, semantic and situational. Several studies have comprehensively explored the co-adaptivity in interlocutors on the linguistic structure of the above-mentioned levels. For example, the empirical results from perception tasks in Pardo (2006) verify the increasing similarity of the phonetic repertoire, which indicates phonetic convergence during conversational interaction. Garrod and Anderson (1987), in their lab-based study, show that interlocutors in conversational interaction coordinate their utterances to form a mutually acceptable form of description, which indicates the convergence of lexical choice in interaction.

In this paper, we focus on linguistic alignment on the syntactic level. Our argument is that with the development of mutual understanding during conversational interaction, certain types of syntactic convergence can be observed. Previous studies found alignment of syntactic complexity, but only for English data, which lacks linguistic generality. Therefore, we try to find more empirical evidence to show that syntactic alignment happens in other languages, such as German, too. The goal of this paper is to revisit the syntactic complexity convergence phenomenon discussed by Xu and Reitter (2016) and test whether it holds for German dialogue data, too. To this end, we selected the following three conversation datasets for German: **MUNDEX** (Türk et al., 2023), **TexPrax** (Stangier et al., 2022), and **VERBMOBIL (VM2)** (Kay, 1992).

2 Background

2.1 Dependency Structure

In this paper, we quantify syntactic complexity with the help of dependency parsing (Kübler et al., 2009). We follow the definition of dependency structure by Liu et al. (2023). A linguistic structure, such as a dependency structure, consists of relations of pairs of natural language tokens. Let Σ denote a finite set of natural language tokens (the vocabulary). Let $V = \{w_1, w_2, \ldots, w_N\}$ denote a spanning node set with its element $w_i \in \Sigma^*$ (Kübler et al., 2009). The element w_i is a 'head' or a dependent in a dependency structure. The spanning node set V represents a sentence $\omega = w_1 w_2 \ldots w_N$. The dependency structure of the sentence ω is then a typed structure $\zeta = (V, E, R)$, where R is the set of dependency relation types, $E \subseteq V \times V \times R$ the set of arcs, if $(x, y, r) \in E$, it holds that $\forall r \neq r', (x, y, r') \notin \zeta$. Under the definition above, a dependency structure is typically a directed acyclic graph (DAG) and the dependency relations within the structure are binary and asymmetric.

We use a statistic and neural sequential model based parsing method, namely the StanfordNLP parser Stanza (Qi et al., 2018) for our goal in this paper. Stanza is trained upon the Universal Dependencies (UD) Treebanks (Nivre et al., 2020). UD Treebanks store the information about the dependency relations among the lexicon, i.e., given a word, what are the most likely words that can serve as its heads or dependents in a dependency structure. The core idea can be mathematically expressed as follows based on Zhang et al. (2016):

$$P_{\text{head}}(w_j \mid w_i, \vartheta) = \frac{\exp(g(w_i, w_j))}{\sum_{k=0}^{|\vartheta|} \exp(g(w_i, w_k))}$$

where ϑ is the lexicon, $g(\cdot)$ is a function which outputs the association score of one word choosing the other word as its head. $P_{\text{head}}(w_j \mid w_i, \vartheta)$ thus tells us what is the most likely head word w_j given the dependent word w_i and the lexicon. With the generated probability information, the maximum spanning tree algorithm, e.g., Chu-Liu/Edmonds algorithm (Chu, 1965; Edmonds et al., 1967) is then used to decide what is the most likely dependency structure for a given sentence.

2.2 Syntactic Complexity

The topic of syntactic complexity has been of significant interest for researchers working within either functional (cognitive) or computational frameworks of linguistics. According to Szmrecsányi (2004), syntactic complexity refers to syntactic structures which entail increasing cognitive load to parse and process. Sentences that are ranked as more syntactically complex are considered more difficult for humans to process (Lin, 1996).

Szmrecsányi (2004) further summarizes three measures for evaluating the syntactic complexity, namely word counts, node counts, and a so-called "Index of Syntactic Complexity". Word counts use length of a given sentence – number of words, syllables, intonation units – to approximate the syntactic complexity, which is based on the straightforward intuition, that a lengthy sentence tends to be more structurally complex than a short one. Node count uses the idea that the more phrasal nodes a linguistic unit dominates, the more complex a sentence is (e.g., Rickford and Wasow, 1995). "Index of Syntactic Complexity" focuses on percentage of subordinate clauses (Beaman, 1984) as well as embeddedness of word forms (Givón, 1991), which is reflected by the following indicators (i) the number subordinating conjunctions, e.g., because, since, etc.; (ii) the number of WH-pronouns, e.g., what, which, etc.; (iii) embeddedness of the verb forms, e.g., finite or infinite; (iv) the number of noun phrases.

According to Xu and Reitter (2016), the convergence of syntactic complexity between two speakers in dialogue correlates to two theories: one is the Interactive Alignment theory (Pickering and Garrod, 2004), which combines the development of mutual understanding with linguistic alignment. The other is the Uniform Information Density hypothesis (Jaeger and Levy, 2006; Jaeger, 2010), which states that speakers will strive to keep information density roughly constant. Based on this hypothesis, if a speaker decreases its information amount, the other will increase the amount instead. According to Jaeger and Levy (2006) and Jaeger (2010), information density is expected to be proportional to the complexity of syntactic structure. This give us an implication that in a dialogue, if a speaker's syntactic complexity is decreasing, the interlocutor's syntactic complexity should be increasing. This implication is consistent with dependency locality theory (DLT; Gibson, 2000), which claims that comprehension difficulty is associated with some complex dependency structures. The interplay of syntactic complexity and language comprehension has been further investigated in, e.g., Liu (2008), which shows that, average dependency distance positively correlates with the comprehension difficulty (processing effort).

Xu and Reitter (2016) then showed three measures to quantify the syntactic complexity: sentence length, branching factors, and tree depth. Tree depth is used to described how deep a syntactic tree can grow. The deeper a tree is, the more complex a sentence is considered. Branching factor reports the average number of children of all non-leaf nodes in the parse tree of a sentence. Thus, a syntactic tree that contains, e.g., more constituents or noun phrases within a sentence of a given length, is more complex.

3 Data

In order to check the dynamics of syntactic complexity in conversational interaction, we select the following three German datasets for our study:

MUNDEX consists of task-oriented dialogues and focuses on explanation in interaction (Türk et al., 2023). Each dialogue is a explanation scenario involving a speaker (the explainer) explaining how to play a board game to a recipient (the explainee).

The dataset is still under construction but in total it consists of 87 dialogues between dyads of German native speakers. At its current stage, speech diarization was mainly performed automatically using Whisper ASR (Radford et al., 2022).

TexPrax consists of task-oriented dialogues from factory workers on how to solve specific technical issues (Stangier et al., 2022). The data are collected anonymously using an open source messaging application in a simulated factory environment. The dataset has in total 202 task-oriented German dialogues containing 1,027 sentences with sentence-level expert annotations, such as turn taking labels.

The **VERBMOBIL (VM2)** dataset (Kay, 1992) is based on recordings of various appointment scheduling scenarios, and consists of 30,800 utterances collected in face-to-face interactions. All utterances are annotated with dialogue acts.

The main difference among the three datasets is that in **MUNDEX**, compared to **TexPrax** and **VM2**, one speaker (the explainer) speaks much more than the other (explainee) in every dialogue. This property of the data has been well reflected in our later analysis (e.g., see Figure 2 in Section 5). While for the other two datasets, utterance length among the participants is similar. Moreover, **VM2** is much larger than the other two selected datasets.

There are two common points among the three selected datasets. First of all, in each dialogue there are only two dialogue participants. For the speaker role assignment, we define the interlocutor who initiates the dialogue as **dialogue initiator**, the other interlocutor who follows the dialogue as **dialogue follower**. In this study specifically, we choose to give the role of dialogue initiator to the dialogue participant who starts the conversation. This is based on our observation in the three datasets that there are no topic shifts in the dialogues. For example, **MUNDEX** is based on a pre-defined scenario, where an explainer explains a board game to an explainee. Therefore, we do not consider that we need to shift participant roles, as in Xu and Reitter (2016), which uses the Switchboard dataset, where each dialogue may have multiple topic shifts.

Secondly, at the end of the interactions, a certain level of mutual understanding can be estimated: in **MUNDEX**, the explainees are likely to understand the game rules and to be able to play the game; in **TexPrax**, the workers know the technical issues from their co-worker; in **VM2** appointments have been successfully made in most of the cases. Under this preposition, in this study, by looking at the change of syntactic complexity, namely the phenomenon of syntactic complexity convergence, we assume that we can infer the level of mutual understanding with the development of the dialogue.

4 Methods

To quantify the syntactic complexity, we follow the measures developed in Xu and Reitter (2016), mainly looking at branching factor, tree depth, and sentence length. Given that all of the three factors can influence the syntactic complexity, it makes sense to quantify the three factors into a single value to represent the syntactic complexity.

We use the number of heads (word count) as a normalisation factor. In dependency structure, the heads are the nodes which have both incoming and outgoing edges, the tree depths are the maximum number of arcs a tree can have from its root to a terminal node. Given two dependency structures with the same number of heads, if one structure has bigger length, it indicates that the heads in general controls more sub-nodes, and thus the structure is more complex. Given a speaker's utterance, we calculate utterance length L and use dependency parsing to get the number of heads α as well as the maximum tree depth β. The syntactic complexity SC of the utterance is thus computed as following:

$$SC = \begin{cases} \lambda \cdot \frac{L}{\alpha} + (1-\lambda) \cdot \beta & \text{if } \alpha > 0 \\ (1-\lambda) \cdot \beta & \text{otherwise} \end{cases}$$

where λ is a tuning factor set to 0.5 by default.

Here we use two German example sentences with corresponding dependency trees to show what is considered as syntactically complex. The example in Figure 1a is a sentence which is considered syntactically simple based on our definition, its maximum tree depth is three and it only has three heads, its sentence length is four. The example in Figure 1b in contrast is considered syntactically complex, its maximum tree depth is four and it has four heads, its length is 8. The quantified syntactic complexity for the first sentence, according to our method, is 2.167 (three heads as the root node is also considered as a head by Stanza parser, tree depth is three, length is four) while for the second one it is 3 (four heads as the root node is also considered as a head by Stanza parser, tree depth is four, length is eight).

Moreover, utterances in the three selected datasets have varied length. According to our obser-

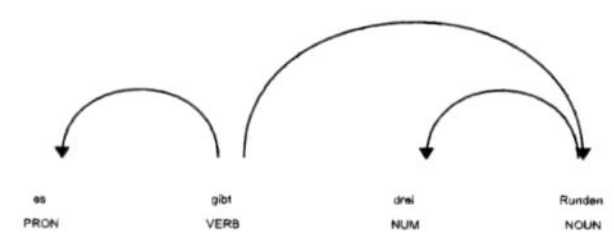

(a) Simple dependency structure (translation: "There are three rounds").

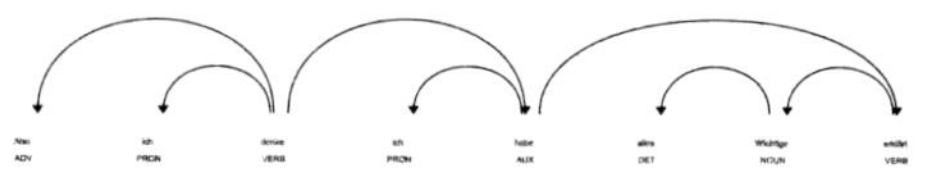

(b) Complex dependency structure (translation: "So I think I have explained all important things").

Figure 1: Two examples showing the dependency structure syntactic relationships according to UD. Edges are directed from heads to dependents.

vation, a speaker may produce multiple utterances before the turn is shifted to a listener, which occurs frequently in the **MUNDEX** dataset. Therefore, it is not rational to calculate syntactic complexity values on a turn-by-turn basis. As a simple solution, for both dialogue initiator and follower, we calculate the syntactic complexity value on an utterance-by-utterance basis. We perform data separation based on the role definition mentioned in in Section 3.

5 Results and Discussion

To verify the convergence of syntactic complexity between two speakers in dialogue, we use a linear mixed effects model, specifically regression, to model the dynamics of syntactic complexity (statistics in Table 1, all reported beta coefficient values are statistically significant). It turns out that among the three selected datasets, only **VM2** shows the syntactic complexity convergence, as supported by a negative beta coefficient value for the dialogue initiators and a positive beta coefficient value for the dialogue followers, which indicates that the syntactic complexity of the dialogue initiator generally decreases with the development of the utterance position. In contrast, the opposite tendency can be observed for the dialogue followers, where the beta coefficient value is positive.

As for the other two selected datasets, in **MUNDEX**, the beta coefficient value is positive for both dialogue initiators and followers while in **TexPrax**, the beta coefficient value is instead negative for both dialogue initiators and followers, which indicates that syntactic complexity convergence is not supported by the statistics.

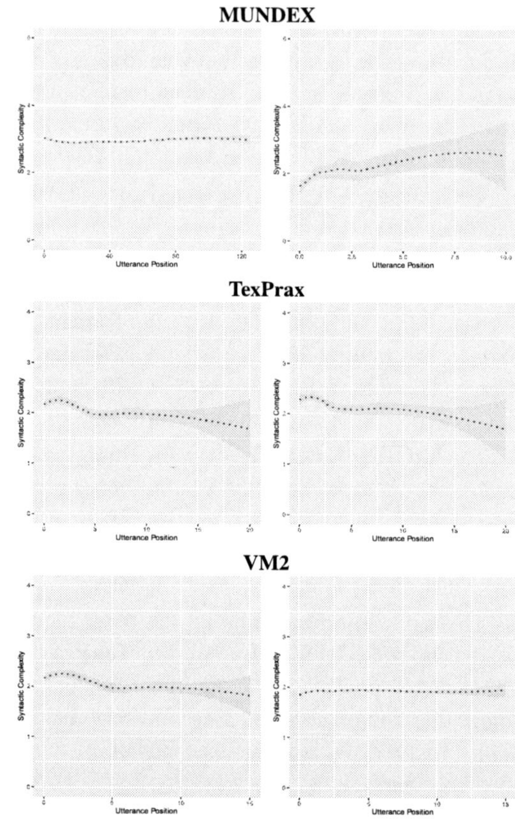

Figure 2: Comparing the development of syntactic complexity of dialogue initiators (left) and followers (right) over the course of the interactions in each corpus. Shaded areas are bootstrapped 95% confidence intervals.

Looking at the plots in Figure 2, it seems that the increasing/decreasing tendencies are small but still obvious in **VM2**. This can be explained, at least in part, by the relatively small values of the beta coefficients. Nevertheless, given that the range of syntactic complexity values is not so large (see Table 2), we assume that the reported effect sizes are valid. For the **MUNDEX** dataset, it turns out that dialogue followers' syntactic complexity is gradually increasing, while dialogue initiators' syntactic complexity remains quite stable, although it is slightly increasing as well. We considered this as a different type of syntactic complexity convergence. One possible explanations could be that, in **MUNDEX**'s scenario, the explainers have to continuously introduce different rules and constraints of the game, and thus the syntactic complexity value for dialogue initiators slightly increased (as evidenced by the statistics in Table 1). While for the dialogue

Table 1: Beta coefficient report on the three dialogue data sets (* represents statistically significant correlations $p < 0.05$, ** represents statistically significant correlations $p < 0.01$, and *** represents statistically significant correlations $p < 0.001$).

	MUNDEX	TexPrax	VM2
Initiator	0.0009^{**}	-0.02^{***}	-0.02^{***}
Follower	0.14^{***}	-0.22^{***}	0.005^{*}

Table 2: Range of syntactic complexity values for dialogue initiators and followers across corpora.

	SC Initiators		SC Followers	
	min	max	min	max
MUNDEX	1.5	5.9	1	3.2
TexPrax	1	4.73	1	4.14
VM2	1	4.14	1	4.57

followers, with the development of an explanation, they got more engaged and thus started to use more complex structures or produce longer utterances. In the **TexPrax** dataset, a general decreasing trend can be observed for both dialogue initiators and followers, which is in general not consistent with the phenomenon of syntactic complexity convergence.

From an information-theoretic perspective, the convergence of syntactic complexity between dialogue participants reflects the convergence of shared information (Genzel and Charniak, 2002, 2003), which is seen as evidence that dialogue participants are working co-constructively to build common ground (Clark, 1996). The results reported in this study show that the convergence of syntactic complexity as a linguistic phenomenon can be observed in dialogues, (1) in different languages (e.g., in English and at least partially in German); (2) under different scenarios (e.g., explaining a game in **MUNDEX** or making an appointment in **VM2**).

6 Conclusions

In this paper, we revisit the phenomenon of syntactic complexity convergence by examining it specifically for German dialogue data. The convergence of syntactic complexity is assumed to be strongly related to the uniform information density theory as well as to the interactive alignment theory, which correlates the development of mutual understanding with linguistic alignment. Our empirical results show that the convergence also exists in one of the three German dialogue datasets we analysed, which provides further evidence for the generality of syntactic complexity convergence. Given that the **VM2** dataset is much larger than the other two datasets, we are prone to claiming that syntactic complexity convergence has its linguistic generality. We also found a different type of syntactic complexity convergence in the **MUNDEX** dataset, while further investigation is still necessary.

Acknowledgements

This research was funded by the Deutsche Forschungsgemeinschaft (DFG): TRR 318/1 2021 – 438445824.

Limitations

When processing German utterances, we did not consider possible solutions to deal with disfluencies. One possible solution would have been to replace disfluent sentences with fluent (i.e., grammatical) ones. This, however, could change the syntactic complexity values. In order to take into account the effect of disfluencies on syntactic complexity, an empirical study on whether disfluencies increases syntactic complexity needs to be carried out beforehand. Another issue we haven't explored further is whether linear models are optimal for our data analysis. A potential future work is to fit a model with a quadratic term for hypothesis testing.

Ethics statement

Given the scope of this study, there do not appear to be any ethical issues.

References

Karen Beaman. 1984. Coordination and subordination revisited: Syntactic complexity in spoken and written narrative discourse. In Deborah Tannen, editor, *Spoken and Written Language. Exploring Orality and Literacy*, pages 45–80. Ablex.

Yoeng-Jin Chu. 1965. On the shortest arborescence of a directed graph. *Scientia Sinica*, 14:1396–1400.

Herbert H. Clark. 1996. *Using Language*. Cambridge University Press, Cambridge, UK.

Jack Edmonds et al. 1967. Optimum branchings. *Journal of Research of the National Bureau of Standards B*, 71(4):233–240.

Simon Garrod and Anthony Anderson. 1987. Saying what you mean in dialogue: A study in conceptual and semantic co-ordination. *Cognition*, 27:181–218.

Dmitriy Genzel and Eugene Charniak. 2002. Entropy rate constancy in text. In *Proceedings of the 40th Annual Meeting of the Association for Computational Linguistics*, pages 199–206, Philadelphia, PA, USA.

Dmitriy Genzel and Eugene Charniak. 2003. Variation of entropy and parse trees of sentences as a function of the sentence number. In *Proceedings of the 2003 Conference on Empirical Methods in Natural Language Processing*, pages 65–72.

Edward Gibson. 2000. The dependency locality theory: A distance-based theory of linguistic complexity. In *Image, Language, Brain: Papers from the First Mind Articulation Project Symposium*, pages 95–126. The MIT Press.

Talmy Givón. 1991. Markedness in grammar: Distributional, communicative and cognitive correlates of syntactic structure. *Studies in Language*, 15(2):335–370.

T. Florian Jaeger. 2010. Redundancy and reduction: Speakers manage syntactic information density. *Cognitive Psychology*, 61:23–62.

T. Florian Jaeger and Roger Levy. 2006. Speakers optimize information density through syntactic reduction. *Advances in Neural Information Processing Systems*, 19.

Martin Kay. 1992. *Verbmobil: A Translation System for Face-to-Face Dialog*. University of Chicago Press.

Sandra Kübler, Ryan McDonald, and Joakim Nivre. 2009. *Dependency parsing*, pages 11–20. Springer.

Dekang Lin. 1996. On the structural complexity of natural language sentences. In *COLING 1996 Volume 2: The 16th International Conference on Computational Linguistics*, pages 729–733, Copenhagen, Denmark.

Haitao Liu. 2008. Dependency distance as a metric of language comprehension difficulty. *Journal of Cognitive Science*, 9(2):159–191.

Tianyu Liu, Afra Amini, Mrinmaya Sachan, and Ryan Cotterell. 2023. Linear-time modeling of linguistic structure: An order-theoretic perspective. In *Proceedings of the 2023 Conference on Empirical Methods in Natural Language Processing*, pages 808–830, Singapore.

Joakim Nivre, Marie-Catherine de Marneffe, Filip Ginter, Jan Hajič, Christopher D. Manning, Sampo Pyysalo, Sebastian Schuster, Francis Tyers, and Daniel Zeman. 2020. Universal Dependencies v2: An evergrowing multilingual treebank collection. In *Proceedings of the Twelfth Language Resources and Evaluation Conference*, pages 4034–4043, Marseille, France.

Jennifer S. Pardo. 2006. On phonetic convergence during conversational interaction. *The Journal of the Acoustical Society of America*, 119:2382–2393.

Martin J. Pickering and Simon Garrod. 2004. The interactive-alignment model: Developments and refinements. *Behavioral and Brain Sciences*, 27(2):212–225.

Peng Qi, Timothy Dozat, Yuhao Zhang, and Christopher D. Manning. 2018. Universal Dependency parsing from scratch. In *Proceedings of the CoNLL 2018 Shared Task: Multilingual Parsing from Raw Text to Universal Dependencies*, pages 160–170, Brussels, Belgium.

Alec Radford, Jong Wook Kim, Tao Xu, Greg Brockman, Christine McLeavey, and Ilya Sutskever. 2022. Robust speech recognition via large-scale weak supervision. *Audio and Speech Processing (eess.AS)*, arXiv:2212.04356.

John R. Rickford and Thomas A. Wasow. 1995. Syntactic variation and change in progress: Loss of the verbal coda in topic-restricting as far as constructions. *Language*, 71:102–131.

Lorenz Stangier, Ji-Ung Lee, Yuxi Wang, Marvin Müller, Nicholas Frick, Joachim Metternich, and Iryna Gurevych. 2022. TexPrax: A messaging application for ethical, real-time data collection and annotation. In *Proceedings of the 2nd Conference of the Asia-Pacific Chapter of the Association for Computational Linguistics and the 12th International Joint Conference on Natural Language Processing: System Demonstrations*, pages 9–16, Taipei, Taiwan.

Benedikt M. Szmrecsányi. 2004. On operationalizing syntactic complexity. In *Le poids des mots. Proceedings of the 7th International Conference on Textual Data Statistical Analysis*, volume 2, pages 1031–1038, Louvain-la-Neuve, Belgium.

Olcay Türk, Petra Wagner, Hendrik Buschmeier, Angela Grimminger, Yu Wang, and Stefan Lazarov. 2023. Mundex: A multimodal corpus for the study of the understanding of explanations. In *Proceedings of the 1st International Multimodal Communication Symposium*, pages 63–64, Barcelona, Spain.

Yang Xu and David Reitter. 2016. Convergence of syntactic complexity in conversation. In *Proceedings of the 54th Annual Meeting of the Association for Computational Linguistics (Volume 2: Short Papers)*, pages 443–448, Berlin, Germany.

Xingxing Zhang, Liang Lu, and Mirella Lapata. 2016. Top-down tree long short-term memory networks. In *Proceedings of the 2016 Conference of the North American Chapter of the Association for Computational Linguistics: Human Language Technologies*, pages 310–320, San Diego, California. Association for Computational Linguistics.

Estimating Word Concreteness from Contextualized Embeddings

Christian Wartena
Hochschule Hannover
Expo Plaza 12
30539 Hannover, Germany
christian.wartena@hs-hannover.de

Abstract

Concreteness is a property of words that has recently received attention in computational linguistics. Since concreteness is a property of word senses rather than of words, it makes most sense to determine concreteness in a given context. Recent approaches for predicting the concreteness of a word occurrence in context have relied on collecting many features from all words in the context. In this paper, we show that we can achieve state-of-the-art results by using only contextualized word embeddings of the target words. We circumvent the problem of missing training data for this task by training a regression model on context-independent concreteness judgments, which are widely available for English. The trained model needs only a few additional training data to give good results for predicting concreteness in context. We can even train the initial model on English data and do the final training on another language and obtain good results for that language as well.

1 Introduction

Word concreteness is one of the psycholinguistic norms of words that has been studied and collected for decades. These scores are obtained by presenting words to subjects and asking them to rate their concreteness on a 5- or 7-point Likert scale. Recently, there has also been more interest in studying the concreteness of specific word senses or words in a given context (see e.g. Gregori et al., 2020; Vandendaele and Grainger, 2022; Bruera et al., 2023; Collacciani et al., 2024).

In this paper, we propose a simple method to predict these contextualized concreteness scores. For the prediction of classical (non-contextualized) concreteness scores, several studies have obtained good results by training a regression model on static word embeddings. We do not have enough annotated data to train a regression model on contextualized embeddings and contextualized concreteness scores. However, we will show that we get good results by training a regression model on averaged embeddings and static concreteness scores, and then applying the trained model to contextualized embeddings to predict contextualized concreteness scores. The results can be further improved by fine-tuning the regression model on a small set of training data with context-dependent concreteness annotations. Using this model, we achieve state-of-the-art results with a system that is much simpler than those proposed in the literature. If we use multilingual embeddings, we can even do the final training in another language.

1.1 Organization of this paper

The remainder of the paper is organized as follows. In section 2 we describe the motivation for computing contextualized concreteness values and previous approaches to the problem. Section 3 describes our approach to the problem and gives details on all methods used. The data used for training and evaluation are given in section 4, the results are given in section 5.

2 Background and related work

Concreteness is a core semantic property of words that has received much attention in psycholinguistic research. Friendly et al. (1982) define concrete words as words that "refer to tangible objects, materials or persons which can be easily perceived with the senses". Brysbaert et al. (2014) define concreteness as the degree to which the concept denoted by a word refers to a perceptible entity. Theijssen et al. (2011) point out that in general two concepts of concreteness are used that do not completely overlap, namely *sensory perceivability* and *specificity*. However, they also note that most subjects in tests interpret concreteness as *sensory perceivability*.

2.1 Concreteness and ambiguity

Most studies that collected or predicted concreteness values for words either ignored the fact that many words have several senses or excluded ambiguous words, as was already noticed by Gilhooly and Logie (1980). Here, it has also has to be noticed that ambiguity in fact covers a large range of semantic phenomena from homonymy over irregular polysemy to regular polysemy (like e.g. the ambiguity between material and artifact, as in *glass* or object and information as in *book*), but also the distinction between *de re* and *de dicto* interpretation of a word, that might be strongly related to specificity and concreteness. Gilhooly and Logie (1980) found that the most concrete sense usually is the most dominant one. In addition, Đurđević et al. (2017) found that subjects rate mainly the dominant sense in these cases. In contrast Reijnierse et al. (2019) suggest, comparing their values to those of Brysbaert et al. (2014), that the presence of a metaphorical sense lowers the concreteness judgments for the words without any disambiguating information.

A few studies collected concreteness judgments for different word senses, among which (Gilhooly and Logie, 1980) for English, (Hager, 1994) for German, and more recently (Đurđević et al., 2017) for Serbian and both (Reijnierse et al., 2019) and (Scott et al., 2019) for English words. In order to obtain different senses for a word Gilhooly and Logie (1980) used all senses that came first to the mind of at least one of 40 subjects; Đurđević et al. (2017) compare different methods, including the use of a dictionary; Scott et al. (2019) use a list containing ambiguous words with sense indications but give no sources for these lists. Đurđević et al. (2017) included only polysemous words and thus excluded homonyms and words with different part of speech. Reijnierse et al. (2019) concentrate on one interesting aspect and only compare literal and metaphorical meanings of concrete words.

All of these approaches have the problem that a number of senses must first be determined for each word. This problem is avoided by the approach of Gregori et al. (2020), who presented words in a context to the subjects. Consequently, the result is not an inventory of concreteness values for word senses, but rather a resource for training and evaluating algorithms that predict the concreteness of a word in a given context.

2.2 Predicting concreteness

Recently, there has been growing interest in the concreteness of words in the field of computational linguistics. On the one hand side it turns out that concreteness values can be used for several tasks like e.g. detection of metaphors and non-literal language (Turney et al., 2011; Hill and Korhonen, 2014; Frassinelli and Schulte im Walde, 2019; Charbonnier and Wartena, 2021), lexical simplification (Jauhar and Specia, 2012) and multimodal retrieval (Hessel et al., 2018). On the other hand side, some effort was put in models predicting the concreteness of words. Most successful models use static word embeddings as an input to a regression model that predicts the concreteness score of a (not contextualized and/or disambiguated) word Tanaka et al. (2013); Paetzold and Specia (2016); Ehara (2017); Charbonnier and Wartena (2019, 2020).

Most studies that have tried to beat the baseline for the task of predicting concreteness in context organized by Gregori et al. (2020) have used concreteness values, either computed or looked up, from all other words in the sentence, taking advantage of the fact that concrete words tend to occur in the context of other concrete words and abstract words in the context of other abstract words (Tanaka et al., 2013; Frassinelli et al., 2017; Naumann et al., 2018). Only two submissions in the shared task produced results for the English dataset above the simple baseline that we will present below: The systems submitted by Bondielli et al. (2020) and Rotaru (2020). The system with the best results for the English test data from Bondielli et al. (2020), called Non-Capisco, simply takes some kind of weighted average of the general non-contextualized concreteness score of the target word, as given by Brysbaert et al. (2014), and the concreteness scores of all the other words in the sentence. Non-Capisco did not perform very well on the Italian data. Here, the Capisco-Transformers system from the same team performed much better. Capisco-Transformers uses a regression model on the sentence embedding computed by BERT. Note that this is different from our method sketched below: we also use BERT with a regression model, but we use the word embedding of the target word. To get enough data to train this model, they extend the provided training data by automatically generating variants of the provided training sentences and by collecting sentences for non-ambiguous words along with their static concreteness values. The system submitted by Rotaru

(2020), called ANDI, collects concreteness values from the target word and all other words in the sentence, further behavioral norms for all words, static embeddings from three pre-trained static models, and embeddings from four transformer-based models. All of these scores and embeddings are then used to train a regression model that predicts the contextual concreteness score.

In contrast to the ideas behind most of the approaches sketched above, our hypothesis is that contextualized word embeddings contain enough information about the context of a word, and that it should thus be possible to predict the concreteness of a word in a given context using only its contextualized embedding.

3 Methods

Since context independent concreteness values in the huge MT40k inventory of Brysbaert et al. (2014) are probably the values for the most dominant and most frequent sense, we might often make a very good guess for the context dependent values by simply taking the static value. So we will use these static values as a baseline. If a word form is not found in the data from Brysbaert et al., we use its lemma as provided in the test data set (see below).

The basic idea is that we train a regression model on word embeddings, assuming that some of the dimensions in the embeddings represent word concreteness. Since we do not have enough training data, we will train the regression model on static embeddings. To collect static embeddings, we use a large corpus and compute BERT (or RoBERTa) representations of all words, and for each word present in MT40k, we compute the average of all contextualized embeddings in the corpus. We take the average of the last 4 embedding levels. If a word has been split by the BERT tokenizer, we take the average of the embeddings of the parts. Alternatively, we could take the first embedding layer. This would eliminate the need to use a corpus to collect and average contextual embeddings. We will include this variant in the experiment and refer to it as L0 (layer 0). However, we do not expect good results from the models trained on the first layer, since there are many changes throughout the layers. To check if the regression model actually works, we randomly split the set of embeddings with concreteness values into a training set (95%) and a test set (5%) to evaluate the regression model. This is just a check to see whether the model works at all, and not an attempt to get state-of-the-art results for this task.

For the regression models we use a Support Vector Regression (SVR) model with a polynomial kernel from the SciKitLearn library. For all parameters we use standard settings. As a second model we use a multilayer perceptron (MLP) implemented with PyTorch. The MLP has three hidden layers (512, 256 and 128 dimensions, resp.) with ReLU activation and a dropout probability of 20% for each layer. The MLP is trained for 25 epochs using Mean Square Error as loss function and the Adam optimizer with a learning rate of $1 \cdot 10^{-5}$ and a small weight decay to ensure that the model will not focus too much on a few embedding dimensions and neglect others that might be important in the context dependent task. In all cases we use a batch size of 15.

The regression models can be applied immediately to predict the contextualized concreteness scores. Since we have a small set of training data, we can use it to further improve the predictions. In the case of SVR, we add the extracted contextualized embeddings along with the contextualized concreteness scores to the training data. In the case of MLP, we continue to train the model on the additional data. Here we train for 50 epochs and use a smaller weight decay. We will refer to these models as models with extended training.

We also predict concreteness values for Italian. For Italian, we do not have a repository of static concreteness values for a large number of words. To overcome this deficiency, we use a pre-trained multilingual language model, collect word embeddings for the English (!) words again, and train regression models on these data. We then apply the multilingual model and the regression model to the Italian data. For the extended training, we use both the English and the Italian training data.

4 Materials

We use three different pretrained language models, BERT base uncased (Devlin et al., 2019), RoBERTa base (Liu et al., 2019), and BERT multilingual, all obtained from the Hugging Face repository (`https://huggingface.co/`). We found that using BERT large does not improve the results, probably because the regression part gets more parameters to train.

As a corpus to collect BERT embeddings that

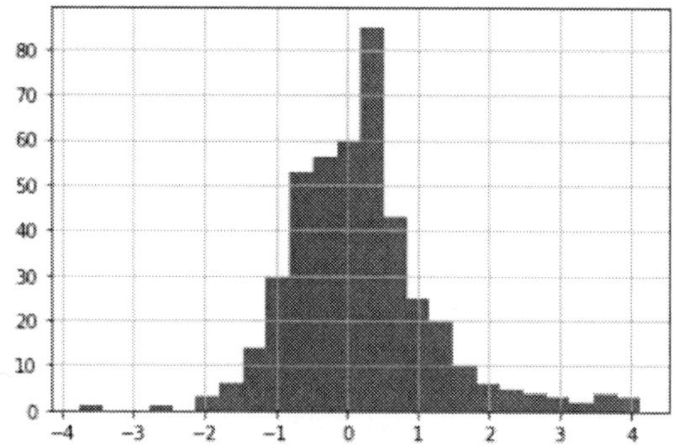

Figure 1: Histogramm of the deviation of the contextualized deviations of the English test data (Gregori et al., 2020) from the MT40k values.

are averaged to obtain static embeddings we use the list of all words from the concreteness data from Brysbaert et al. (2014) and three corpora. The list of single words is used to ensure that every word with a concreteness value has an embedding. This makes the results from the first experiment better comparable to other studies on those data. Each word is given as a sentence to the language model to compute an embedding. Next we used the Brown corpus (Kucera and Francis, 1967). This corpus has a balanced distribution over different genres and might help to include words and word senses not present in the other corpora. The two larger corpora are a collection of 300,000 sentences from a 2016 Wikipedia dump and a corpus of 300,000 sentences from newspapers from 2020, both obtained from `https://wortschatz.uni-leipzig.de/en/download/English` (Goldhahn et al., 2012). These corpora have to be included to collect enough data to compute averaged embeddings for all words.

Static concreteness values were obtained from the collection from Brysbaert et al. (2014), called MT40k, that has ratings for 37,058 words and 2,896 short phrases. When using the BERT tokenizer we could find 29,007 of these words in our corpora. When using the Roberta tokenizer we find 28,122 words (BERT and RoBERTa use the same subword tokenizer, but apparently slightly different pre-tokenizers to split the sentence into words). Embeddings are computed for all single words in Brysbaert's dataset except for a small number of stop words to speed up the data collection process.

Finally, we use the annotated data from Gregori et al. (2020) to finalize the training and to evaluate the models. The provided trial data, that we will use for training as well, consist of 100 sentences, the test set of 434 sentences. In each sentences one word is marked and annotated with a concreteness score. Furthermore, the part of speech and the lemma for the target word are given. In order to investigate how much the values in the test set deviate from the values from the MT40k values we rescaled the later to the range from 1 to 7 and for all 434 examples we subtracted the contextualized value from the static one. The distribution of these differences is shown in the histogram in Fig. 1. Here we see that in most cases there is only a very small deviation from the static value, suggesting that the baseline using MT40k values might give quite good results.

Beside the English trial and test data Gregori et al. (2020) also provide Italian data. For Italian the test data consists of 450 annotated sentences and the trial data (used for training) of 100 sentences.

Recently, both the English and Italian have been extended and are described in much more detail (Montefinese et al., 2023). In this paper we do not yet use these extended data sets.

5 Results

First, we have a look at the results of the regression models on the random split of the static embeddings and MT40k values. These results are given in Table 1. We observe that all results are very good and close to or even slightly better than the results obtained by Charbonnier and Wartena (2019) who used precomputed static embeddings along with additional morpho-syntactic features. However, here we just used a random split, whereas Charbonnier and Wartena (2019) used cross-validation. We do not see large differences between the classifiers or the language models used. The results using the first level embeddings is slightly below the other results. The scatter plot in Figure 2 gives a visual impression of the correlation between the averaged human scores and the values predicted by the MLP using RoBERTa embeddings. At this point we can conclude that in all cases the models learned to predict static concreteness values, the task they were trained for. Next we will see, whether these models are able to predict contextualized concreteness values.

The results for the prediction of the contextualized embeddings are given in Table 2 and visual-

Table 1: Results of predicting concreteness values form a random split of the MT40k data and averaged word embeddings. Both Pearson and Spearman correlation between the predicted and real values are given. The test set has 1847 word-concreteness pairs.

Method	Pearson	Spearman
SVR - BERT	0.913	0.901
SVR - BERT ML	0.892	0.887
SVR - RoBERTa	0.898	0.890
SVR - RoBERTa L0	0.850	0.852
MLP - BERT	0.910	0.897
MLP - BERT ML	0.891	0.887
MLP - RoBERTa	0.902	0.893
MLP - RoBERTa L0	0.858	0.856

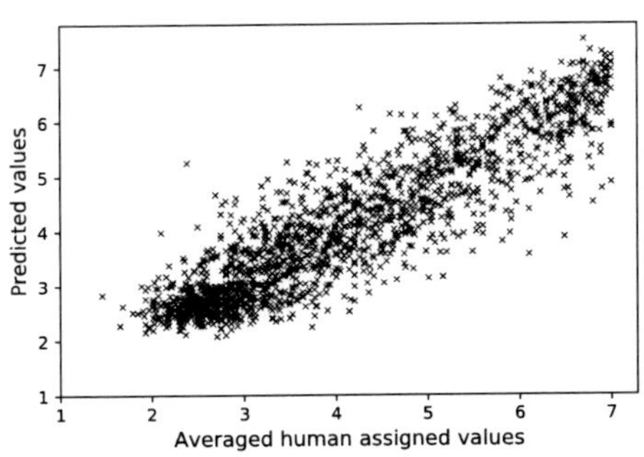

Figure 2: Scatter plot of the concreteness values from MT40k and values predicted by the MLP using RoBERTa embeddings for our test set (randomly selected 1847 words from MT40k)

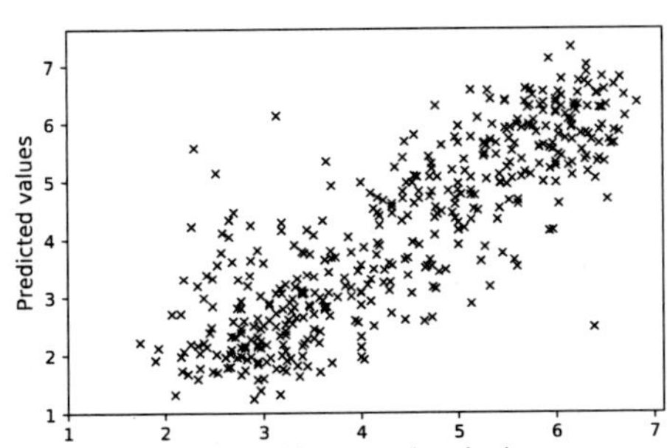

Figure 3: Scatter plot of the contextualized concreteness values and values predicted by the MLP using RoBERTa embeddings for the test data from Gregori et al. (2020) (100 words)

Table 2: Correlation for various regression models, simple base line and state of the art system between predicted and gold standard concreteness values of words in context (N=100). English dataset.

Method	Pearson	Spearman
MT40k Baseline	0.759	0.752
ANDI (SoTA)	0.834	**0.833**
Non-Capisco	0.785	0.787
Capisco-Trans	0.504	0.501
SVR - BERT	0.791	0.793
SVR - BERT ML	0.771	0.767
SVR - RoBERTa	0.820	0.810
SVR - RoBERTa L0	0.446	0.451
MLP - BERT	0.776	0.775
MLP - BERT ML	0.760	0.754
MLP - RoBERTa	0.800	0.790
MLP - RoBERTa L0	0.494	0.483
SVR - BERT - ext.	0.813	0.814
SVR - BERT ML - ext.	0.803	0.804
SVR - RoBERTa - ext.	0.828	0.818
SVR - RoBERTa L0 - ext.	0.341	0.328
MLP - BERT - ext.	0.818	0.816
MLP - BERT ML - ext.	0.790	0.786
MLP - RoBERTa - ext.	**0.838**	0.830
MLP - RoBERTa L0 - ext.	0.420	0.420

ized for one model again in a scatter plot in Figure 3. We see that the simple baseline gives very good results, as expected when looking at the small deviations in Figure 1. Applying the pre-trained regressor to the test data already gives correlations that are clearly above this baseline. The final training in all cases improve the model. The best model, using a MLP and RoBERTa embeddings give results that are very close to the state of the art results from (Rotaru, 2020) and clearly better than the Capisco systems. Furthermore, we see that using first embedding level for the training phase does not give good results, as already expected. The results from the multilingual BERT model are slightly behind those from BERT base, but not very much.

Table 3 gives the results for the Italian data. The results show that the language transfer is successful but the results are behind those from Rotaru (2020) (but better than those of the Capisco systems).

If we inspect the largest errors that were made, we do not find a very clear pattern. Eventually we can get the impression that the model gives too low scores for words referring to specific things that are not clearly perceivable with the senses like, *fear*,

Table 3: Correlation for various regression models and state of the art system between predicted and gold standard concreteness values of the Italian dataset (N=100).

Method	Pearson	Spearman
ANDI (SoTA)	**0.749**	**0.749**
Non-Capisco	0.557	0.557
Capisco-Trans	0.625	0.617
SVR - BERT ML	0.666	0.671
MLP - BERT ML	0.648	0.652
SVR - BERT ML - ext.	0.715	0.715
MLP - BERT ML - ext.	0.732	0.732

answer, *idea*, *advantage*, *success*, etc. and gives too high scores especially to verbs like *hit*, *kick*, *eat* in cases where they do not refer to a physical action. We also find cases, where RoBERTa obviously misinterpreted the sentence, like in *Sign your name in ink in the space provided by the four blank lines.* where *space* gets the score 3.66 instead of 5.6. While *space* usually is some quite abstract word indicating a large range of options to do something, here the word refers to a very concrete area on a piece of paper.

Furthermore, let us have a look at the types of distinctions the model can make. The following sentences are all taken from the Brown Corpus. The concreteness value predicted by the extended Roberta/MLP model is added as a subscript to the word. In the first pair of sentences we see that the model clearly distinguishes homonyms with different concreteness values:

(1) a. Not even an empty cartridge **case**$_{5.9}$ could be found.

b. In this **case**$_{2.4}$ the district manager was led to see the errors of his ways.

Regular polysemy, here between a building and an institution is also captured:

(2) a. John entered the vast **church**$_{6.7}$ and climbed the tower steps to the bells.

b. Surveys show that one out of three Americans has vital contact with the **church**$_{5.1}$.

Finally, we compare two sentences with literal and figurative use of a word. Here we see that the figurative use get still a high concreteness value but clearly a lower one that the literal use.

(3) a. He ran a **finger**$_{7.0}$ down his cheek, tracing the scratch there.

b. Lawrence could not put his **finger**$_{5.6}$ on it precisely, and this worried him.

6 Discussion and Conclusion

We have shown that concreteness of words is a semantic word property that can be derived form a BERT-based word embedding and that can be effectively predicted for word senses in a specific context using only these embeddings, without the need to use information from other words in the sentence. The presented approach is much simpler than previous approaches that used up to 7 different embeddings and had to be trained on many different semantic properties. Our results are close to the state of the art, but do not clearly outperform it. Since the inter-annotator agreement in this type of annotation is usually not very high and the dataset is quite small, it may also be the case that the highest possible agreement with human concreteness scores is already achieved.

The downside of the proposed approach is, that we need to compute averaged embeddings on a large amount of data, as we see that simply using the first (context independent) layer does not give the desired results. This is not only time consuming but also makes the results dependent on the corpus used for this task.

Using multilingual embeddings we also can apply the model to a different language than the language from the training data.

7 Limitations

The main limitation in this study is the availability of annotated data. We have only two very small datasets and only for two languages. However, the topic of the paper is exactly about the approach how to deal with the absence of a large training dataset. A further limitation is that we did not do hyper parameter optimization or model selection for the regression models. We did not do so since we had limited computing resources but also to avoid the risk of overfitting on the small amount of data available. However, it is very likely that slightly better results can be obtained when selecting optimal number of training epochs, layer dimensions, etc.

8 Ethical Considerations

The research presented here did not involve any experiments with humans or animals. All experiments where done with a very limited amount of computational resources and thsu without a high energy consumption and enviromental impact. The research results are rather theoretical and will not have a direct impact on the working or living circumstances of anyone. We hope that this research will contribute to the understanding of large language models and natural languyage processing in general. Here we rather believe that a better understanding of these methods and a more widespread dissemination of this knowledge helps to identify and deal with possible threats from this technology.

References

Alessandro Bondielli, Gianluca E. Lebani, Lucia C. Passaro, and Alessandro Lenci. 2020. Capisco@ concretext:(un) supervised systems to contextualize concreteness with norming data. In *Proceedings of the Seventh Evaluation Campaign of Natural Language Processing and Speech Tools for Italian. Final Workshop (EVALITA 2020)*. CEUR-WS.org.

Andrea Bruera, Yuan Tao, Andrew Anderson, Derya Çokal, Janosch Haber, and Massimo Poesio. 2023. Modeling brain representations of words' concreteness in context using gpt-2 and human ratings. *Cognitive Science*, 47(12):e13388.

Marc Brysbaert, Amy Beth Warriner, and Victor Kuperman. 2014. Concreteness ratings for 40 thousand generally known English word lemmas. *Behavior Research Methods*, 46(3):904–911.

Jean Charbonnier and Christian Wartena. 2019. Predicting word concreteness and imagery. In *Proceedings of the 13th International Conference on Computational Semantics-Long Papers*, pages 176–187.

Jean Charbonnier and Christian Wartena. 2020. Predicting the Concreteness of German Words. In *Proceedings of Konvens / SwissText*.

Jean Charbonnier and Christian Wartena. 2021. Verbal idioms: Concrete nouns in abstract contexts. In *KONVENS 2021, Düsseldorf, Germany, 06–09 September 2021*.

Claudia Collacciani, Andrea Amelio Ravelli, and Marianna Bolognesi. 2024. Specifying genericity through inclusiveness and abstractness continuous scales. In *Proceedings of the 2024 Joint International Conference on Computational Linguistics, Language Resources and Evaluation (LREC-COLING 2024)*, pages 15126–15136, Torino, Italia. ELRA and ICCL.

Jacob Devlin, Ming-Wei Chang, Kenton Lee, and Kristina Toutanova. 2019. BERT: Pre-training of deep bidirectional transformers for language understanding. In *Proceedings of the 2019 Conference of the North American Chapter of the Association for Computational Linguistics: Human Language Technologies, Volume 1 (Long and Short Papers)*, pages 4171–4186, Minneapolis, Minnesota. Association for Computational Linguistics.

Yo Ehara. 2017. Language-independent prediction of psycholinguistic properties of words. In *Proceedings of the Eighth International Joint Conference on Natural Language Processing (Volume 2: Short Papers)*, pages 330–336.

Diego Frassinelli, Daniela Naumann, Jason Utt, and Sabine Schulte im Walde. 2017. Contextual characteristics of concrete and abstract words. In *IWCS 2017 — 12th International Conference on Computational Semantics — Short papers*.

Diego Frassinelli and Sabine Schulte im Walde. 2019. Distributional interaction of concreteness and abstractness in verb–noun subcategorisation. In *Proceedings of the 13th International Conference on Computational Semantics - Short Papers*, pages 38–43, Gothenburg, Sweden. Association for Computational Linguistics.

Michael Friendly, Patricia E. Franklin, David Hoffman, and David C. Rubin. 1982. The Toronto Word Pool: Norms for imagery, concreteness, orthographic variables, and grammatical usage for 1,080 words. *Behavior Research Methods & Instrumentation*, 14(4):375–399.

K. J. Gilhooly and R. H. Logie. 1980. Meaning-dependent ratings of imagery, age of acquisition, familiarity, and concreteness for 387 ambiguous words. *Behavior Research Methods & Instrumentation*, 12(4):428–450.

Dirk Goldhahn, Thomas Eckart, Uwe Quasthoff, et al. 2012. Building large monolingual dictionaries at the leipzig corpora collection: From 100 to 200 languages. In *LREC*, volume 29, pages 31–43.

Lorenzo Gregori, Maria Montefinese, Daniele P. Radicioni, Andrea Amelio Ravelli, and Rossella Varvara. 2020. Concretext@ evalita2020: The concreteness in context task. In *Proceedings of the Seventh Evaluation Campaign of Natural Language Processing and Speech Tools for Italian. Final Workshop (EVALITA 2020)*. CEUR-WS.org.

Willy Hager. 1994. Bildhaftigkeit, Konkretheit-Abstraktheit und Bedeutungshaltigkeit von 63 mehrdeutigen Substantiven. In Willi Hager and Marcus Hasselhorn, editors, *Handbuch deutschsprachiger Wortnormen*, chapter 3.6, pages 212–217. Hogrefe Verlag für Psychologie, Göttingen.

Jack Hessel, David Mimno, and Lillian Lee. 2018. Quantifying the visual concreteness of words and topics in multimodal datasets. In *Proceedings of the 2018 Conference of the North American Chapter of the Association for Computational Linguistics: Human Language Technologies, Volume 1 (Long Papers)*, pages 2194–2205, New Orleans, Louisiana. Association for Computational Linguistics.

Felix Hill and Anna Korhonen. 2014. Concreteness and subjectivity as dimensions of lexical meaning. In *Proceedings of the 52nd Annual Meeting of the Association for Computational Linguistics (Volume 2: Short Papers)*, pages 725–731.

Sujay Kumar Jauhar and Lucia Specia. 2012. Uow-shef: Simplex–lexical simplicity ranking based on contextual and psycholinguistic features. In ** SEM 2012: The First Joint Conference on Lexical and Computational Semantics–Volume 1: Proceedings of the main conference and the shared task, and Volume 2: Proceedings of the Sixth International Workshop on Semantic Evaluation (SemEval 2012)*, pages 477–481.

Henri Kucera and Winthrop Francis. 1967. Computational Analysis of Present-Day American English. Technical report, Brown University Press, Providence, RI.

Yinhan Liu, Myle Ott, Naman Goyal, Jingfei Du, Mandar Joshi, Danqi Chen, Omer Levy, Mike Lewis, Luke Zettlemoyer, and Veselin Stoyanov. 2019. Roberta: A robustly optimized bert pretraining approach.

Maria Montefinese, Lorenzo Gregori, Andrea Amelio Ravelli, Rossella Varvara, and Daniele Paolo Radicioni. 2023. Concretext norms: Concreteness ratings for italian and english words in context. *PLOS ONE*, 18(10):1–19.

Daniela Naumann, Diego Frassinelli, and Sabine Schulte im Walde. 2018. Quantitative Semantic Variation in the Contexts of Concrete and Abstract Words. In *Proceedings of the 7th Joint Conference on Lexical and Computational Semantics*, pages 76–85, New Orleans, LA, USA.

Gustavo Paetzold and Lucia Specia. 2016. Inferring psycholinguistic properties of words. In *Proceedings of the 2016 Conference of the North American Chapter of the Association for Computational Linguistics: Human Language Technologies*, pages 435–440, San Diego, California. Association for Computational Linguistics.

W. Gudrun Reijnierse, Christian Burgers, Marianna Bolognesi, and Tina Krennmayr. 2019. How polysemy affects concreteness ratings: The case of metaphor. *Cognitive Science*, 43(8):e12779.

Armand Stefan Rotaru. 2020. Andi@ concretext: Predicting concreteness in context for english and italian using distributional models and behavioural norms (short paper). In *Proceedings of the Seventh Evaluation Campaign of Natural Language Processing and Speech Tools for Italian. Final Workshop (EVALITA 2020)*. CEUR-WS.org.

Graham G. Scott, Anne Keitel, Marc Becirspahic, Bo Yao, and Sara C. Sereno. 2019. The glasgow norms: Ratings of 5,500 words on nine scales. *Behavior Research Methods*, 51(3):1258–1270.

Shinya Tanaka, Adam Jatowt, Makoto P. Kato, and Katsumi Tanaka. 2013. Estimating content concreteness for finding comprehensible documents. In *Proceedings of the Sixth ACM International Conference on Web Search and Data Mining*, WSDM '13, pages 475–484, New York, NY, USA. ACM.

Daphne Theijssen, Hans van Halteren, Lou Boves, and Nelleke Oostdijk. 2011. On the difficulty of making concreteness concrete. *Computational Linguistics in the Netherlands Journal*, 1:61–77.

Peter D. Turney, Yair Neuman, Dan Assaf, and Yohai Cohen. 2011. Literal and metaphorical sense identification through concrete and abstract context. In *Proceedings of the Conference on Empirical Methods in Natural Language Processing*, EMNLP '11, pages 680–690, Stroudsburg, PA, USA. Association for Computational Linguistics.

Dušica Filipović Đurđević, Aleksandar Kostić, and Zorana Đinđića. 2017. Number, relative frequency, entropy, redundancy, familiarity, and concreteness of word senses: Ratings for 150 serbian polysemous nouns. In *Selected Papers From the 4th and 5th Workshop on Psycholinguistic, Neurolinguistic and Clinical Linguistic Research*, volume 2 of *Studies in Language and Mind*, pages 13–50. Filozofski fakultet u Novom Sadu.

Aaron Vandendaele and Jonathan Grainger. 2022. Now you see it, now you don't: Flanker presence induces the word concreteness effect. *Cognition*, 218:104945.

Using GermaNet for the Generation of Crossword Puzzles

Claus Zinn and **Marie Hinrichs** and **Erhard Hinrichs**
Department of General and Computational Linguistics
University of Tübingen
Keplerstraße 2
72074 Tübingen, Deutschland
Correspondence: claus.zinn@uni-tuebingen.de

Abstract

Wordnets are playing an important role in research, but so far they have found little use in practical applications that are aimed at the general public. In this paper, we present a crossword generator that exploits lexical-semantic resources such as GermaNet. The software is capable of (i) automatically filling in the grid of a crossword puzzle with words taken from GermaNet for variable grid sizes, and (ii) generating clues for each word that is included in the grid. Crossword generation is not trivial, and we report on the effectiveness of various heuristic search functions that we have used.

1 Introduction

Crossword puzzles play with words. A puzzle is usually presented as a rectangular grid of black and white squares. The game's objective is to fill the white squares with letters, forming words that intersect with each other. Words, and their letters, can be written horizontally and vertically. Black squares serve as separators between words. Words are not arbitrary. For each word, there is a textual clue that describes it.

The New York Times (NYT) is well-known for its daily crosswords, and it even offers a site where useful information about its puzzles is published.[1] According to the site, the NYT uses a variety of clue types such as puns, anagrams, cryptic clues and even sound clues. The clues describe words that cover a variety of different topics, *e.g.*, television shows, movies, classical music, art, and history. Moreover, the Sunday puzzles have a theme, which is referenced in a humorous quotation or pun found in the answers. Also, Friday/Saturday puzzles tend to use longer words and are perceived as more complex than the puzzles for the other week-days. Fig. 1 describes a puzzle with a 5×5 grid taken from (Ginsberg et al., 1990). The puzzle, with clues omitted, looks for five words each in *across* and *down* direction. Note that each word intersects with at least three other words so that they need to share the respective characters. Once all word slots are filled, clues must be generated that elicit each of the words, preferably, using interesting clues of different types.

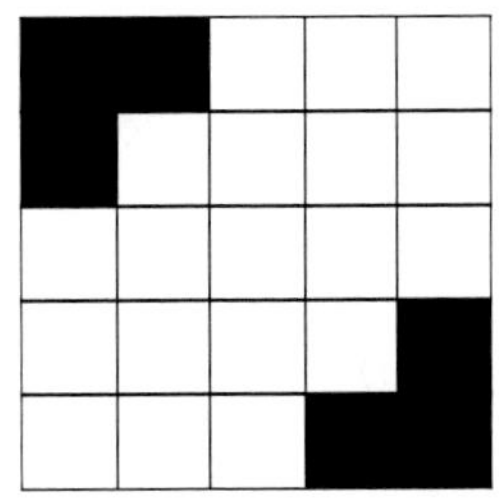

Figure 1: Example Puzzle.

The generation of crossword puzzles requires dictionaries and other lexical resources. In the past, an abundance of digital lexical resources have been created, for instance, GermaNet, the largest lexical-semantic word net for German (Hamp and Feldweg, 1997). It has to be said, however, that digital lexical resources are mostly used by researchers rather than the general public. We would like to boost usage of GermaNet by the general public in part by offering on-line access to popular games like crossword puzzles and by developing software for generating such crossword puzzles automatically.

To attract the general audience to linguistic resources, we found crossword puzzles particularly intriguing.[2] In this paper, we report on our research using GermaNet to automatically solve crosswords puzzles such as the ones given in Fig. 1. With Ger-

[1] `https://www.nytimes.com/article/how-to-solve-a-crossword-puzzle.html`

[2] As their everyday occurrences in newspapers testify, crossword puzzles are very popular. In Germany, for instance, 56 from 100 persons do a crossword puzzle at least once a year; 40% do a puzzle at least once a month, and 21% do a crossword once a week, see `https://www.freizeitmonitor.de/2023/alle-freizeitaktivitaeten-im-ueberblick/`.

maNet holding over 215,000 lexical units, there is an abundance of choice points an algorithm must take into consideration. As a result, the branching factor of the resulting search tree is rather large, and to conquer it, heuristic information is required to solve non-trivial crossword puzzles. Once lexical entries have been assigned to word slots, the identification or generation of clues to hint at them – in an overall entertaining manner – is also harder than thought.

The remainder of the paper is structured as follows. Sect. 2 gives an overview of GermaNet, with a particular focus on using this resource for solving crossword puzzles. It also reviews some of the literature on crossword generation. In the main part of the paper, we discuss our algorithm for crossword generation using GermaNet (Sect. 3), which is followed by an evaluation. In Sect. 4, we give a brief overview on clue generation. A front-end GUI is presented in Sect. 5, and Sect. 6 discusses our work, future work, and concludes.

2 Background

2.1 GermaNet

GermaNet is the largest lexical-semantic word net for German (Hamp and Feldweg, 1997). The development of the resource started 25 years ago, and is still actively maintained and enriched.[3] The latest version of GermaNet (18.0) features 215,000 lexical units that are attached to 167,163 synsets. It has 181,530 conceptual relations, and 12,602 lexical relations (synonymy excluded). Furthermore, GermaNet has a representation of 121,655 split compounds, and it includes 28,563 pointers into the Interlingual Index. Moreover, GermaNet has 11,760 paraphrases attached to synsets. Also, 29,550 sense definitions were added from Wiktionary in 2011[4] (Henrich et al., 2014). A clue in a crossword is always tied to a word slot of a given length. Fig. 2 depicts the distribution of GermaNet lexical entries in terms of word length. Words longer than 25 characters are omitted.[5] It shows that GermaNet's database also covers the short and long word spectrum very well.

Tab. 1 depicts the potential of using GermaNet for the generation of crossword puzzle clues. In addition to the use of 11,7k paraphrases and the 29.5k sense descriptions to generate definitional clues, we also exploit relationships between lexical entries and between synsets. For now, we limited ourselves to only use two conceptual and one lexical relation to construct three other types of clues, namely, hypernyms (using 171,925 relation instances), synonyms (lexical units being in the same synset, 143,534), and antonyms (3,982).

It should be noted, however, that the generation of clues that ask for synonyms need special care. Consider, for instance, the use of synonyms in the thematic domain 'human'. Here, a synset usually contains both the male and female form. For example, all of the four lexical units 'Dermatologin', 'Hautärztin', 'Hautarzt', 'Dermatologe' (engl.: dermatologist) are part of the same GermaNet synset. It would provide little entertainment to search for the word 'Hautärztin' with the clue 'Synonym für Hautarzt'. However, searching for the word 'Dermatologe' is much more appropriate in a crossword setting. To avoid the generation of trivial clues, we only use two synonyms when there is little string overlap between them.

Clearly, the paraphrase and wiktionary information provide the most verbose clue to a given word. From our own experience, those clues are refreshingly new when compared to often repeated or well-known clues that one encounters in crosswords in newspapers and puzzle books. Given the aforementioned constraints, with the combination of paraphrases, wiktionary entries, synonyms, hypernyms, and antonyms, together with the future use of other relations (*e.g.*, meronyms), the crossword generator can tap into a potential of 500k+ clue constructions for GermaNet-based puzzles.

2.2 Crossword Puzzle Generation

The generation and solving of crossword puzzles has been studied before. (Berghel, 1987) organises the problem into six distinct operations:

1. creation of the host matrix
2. determination of the overall design (i.e., pattern of open and closed cells) within the matrix

[3] The latest version was released in May 2023; for information to get access to the resource, see `https://uni-tuebingen.de/en/142806`.

[4] The entries were automatically mapped to lexical units in GermaNet and subsequently manually verified. In some cases, slight modifications to the Wiktionary sense descriptions have been made.

[5] For completeness: there are 797 words of length 26, 469 words of length 27, 243 words of length 28, 145 words of length 29, and 57 words of length 30. The longest word is *Finanzdienstleistungsaufsichtsbehörde* (engl. Financial Services Supervisory Authority) with 38 characters.

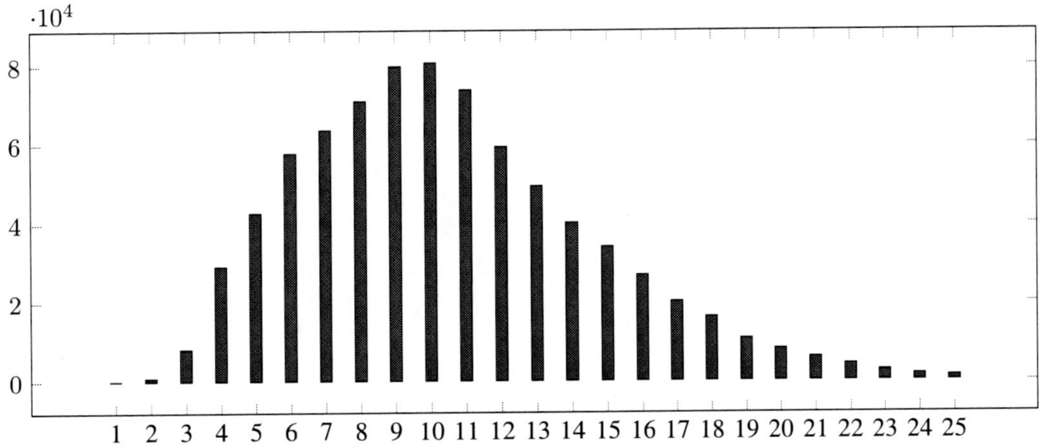

Figure 2: Word Length Distribution.

clue type	attached to	example clues	word slot value(s)
paraphrase	synset	ein gewisses Talent/eine bestimmte Begabung besitzend	talentiert, begabt
wiktionary	lexUnit	Medizin: den Gehörsinn oder das Gehörorgan betreffend; das Hören betreffend	auditiv
synonym	synset	Synonym für "Schlagbaum"	Schranke
hypernym	synset	Überbegriff für "Parietallappen"	Gehirnareal, Hirnareal, Hirnregion, Gehirnregion, Gehirnbereich, Hirnteil, Gehirnteil
antonym	lexUnit	Antonym für "konkret"	abstrakt

Table 1: Crossword Clues in GermaNet.

3. specification of word slots

4. identification of shared cells

5. construction of one or more solution sets, and

6. composition of a clue set for each solution set.

Berghel advocates a Prolog-based approach to solving crosswords, emphasising the declarative aspect of Horn Logic and how it allows stating the problem in a straightforward manner; a word in represented as a sequence of cells, and cells are represented as Prolog variables. When two words intersect, the respective cell shares the same Prolog variable. In a follow-up work, (Berghel and Yi, 1989) propose a procedure, *crossword compiler-compilation*, which will create source code for a crossword solver from the puzzle geometry alone.

It shows that the creation of Prolog code to solve crossword puzzles is rather straightforward. Consider, for instance, the following grid, a fully *interlocked* puzzle, *i.e.*, a puzzle with no black cells:

B	C	D
F	I	J
G	L	N

Here, each cell is assigned its own Prolog variable.

Now, assume lexical entries, and the clues that hint at them, being represented as Prolog-based `word/4` facts. Then, a straightforward implementation of blind, depth-first search can be implemented by the following Prolog program, with A, E, H, K, M, and O denoting words of length 3, and B, C, D, F,I, J, G, L, and N denoting the words' characters:

```
word(3, A, [B,C,D], C1), \+ member(A, []),
word(3, E, [B,F,G], C2), \+ member(E, [A]),
word(3, H, [F,I,J], C3), \+ member(H, [E, A]),
word(3, K, [C,I,L], C4), \+ member(K, [H, E, A]),
word(3, M, [G,L,N], C5), \+ member(M, [K, H, E, A]),
word(3, O, [D,J,N], C6), \+ member(O, [M, K, H, E, A]),
```

The C_i denote the clues to elicit the words. Note that words that intersect which each other share a letter such as the Prolog variable B; it is shared by the two words originating from the top-left corner in across and down direction. The `member/2` predicates ensure that no word is used twice.

Note that such Program code can be automatically generated for any given grid, and we have written such a meta-program. The programs it generates establish the base case for our evaluation.

In the remainder of this paper, we will focus on *given* puzzle grids, that is, predefined $x \times y$ matrices, potentially including black cells to add additional word boundaries. We consider Berghel's step 1-4 trivial and focus on step 5 and step 6.

The search space to conquer to fill all word slots is huge, and Breghel discusses some heuristics to guide this search. Heuristic information and their effectiveness have also been discussed by (Ginsberg et al., 1990), classifying four distinct types of choices that a puzzle solver must make:

1. which word slot to work on next?
2. which word should be used to instantiate the selected slot?
3. how to handle backtracking in cases where word slots become uninstantiable?
4. which kind of preprocessing is required?

(Smith and Steen, 1981), (Ginsberg et al., 1990) and (Ginsberg, 2011) all agree that the *hardest* slots should be considered next; these are the slots with the fewest alternatives, that is, the least number of possible instantiations with words. And since all slots must eventually be instantiated, the failure to instantiate the hardest one will initiate backtracking to undo former choices (see point 3 above).

Once a slot has been selected to work on, it should be instantiated with a word that restricts the possible choices for subsequent slots as little as possible (Ginsberg et al., 1990). Words with frequent letters will hence be preferred to words with less frequent ones. The computation of this heuristics is expensive so that only the value of the first k instantiations will be computed.

3 Solving crosswords with GermaNet

In this section, we give further details to apply the aforementioned heuristics for GermaNet.

3.1 Preprocessing

Given the RDF-based variant of GermaNet (Zinn et al., 2022), we have extracted relevant information via SPARQL queries and represent it as a list of `word/5` predicates, *e.g.*,

```
word(14, 1.0860799758322117, 'unregelmäßig',
 [u, n, r, e, g, e, l, m, a, e, s, s, i, g],
 [ literal('in zeitlich ungleichen Abständen
          wiederkehrend') ...]).
```

The first parameter gives the length of the word, the second parameter encodes a simple unigram frequency model, where the relative frequencies of a character with regard to the GermaNet lexicon are added up.[6] The solution word is given as third argument of `word/5`, whereas the fourth spells out the word; here, any German *Umlaut* is replaced with its corresponding two letters (*e.g.* ö $\rightarrow$ *oe*, or ß$\rightarrow$ *ss*). The last parameter of `word/6` gives the actual clues (only one clue is shown).

For the results reported in this paper, we have built two databases (one for unigram rankings, one of bigram rankings) for all GermaNet entries up to length 16. In total, 155k database entries have been constructed. Also, we have built a database of randomly-ordered word entries.

3.2 Heuristics

Our algorithm aims at replicating and finetuning the aforementioned heuristics for GermaNet. We hence follow a two-step approach. First, the hardest word slot is selected. Then, a word needs to be chosen to fit this slot. Such a word must maximise the satisfiability of the remaining open word slots. Both steps require word slots to be ranked.

Ranking of word slots. An *open* word slot of a given length L has exactly L variables, some of which may already be instantiated to characters; these are the cells that intersect with words already placed. A word slot is evaluated in terms of the number of words that can be placed into the slot. We give an example: the word slot [C1, C2, C3, C4], with all C_i being variables, is assigned the value $29,109$ because there are $29,109$ words of length four is GermaNet.; the word slot [e, C2, C3,e] has the value 21, because there are 21 words that fit the pattern (such as "Ente", "Este", "Eile", and "Ende").

Ranking of words to fit a given slot. Once the algorithm decided on a slot to work on next, a word has to be found to fit the slot. All word candidates are computed, and the one that maximises the satisfiability of all remaining open word slots is chosen. In line with (Ginsberg et al., 1990), we have introduced a k value which is used as follows:

[6] Similarly, lexical entries have been compiled with a bigram model.

Grid	# Slots	random $k=1$	random $k=5$	random $k=10$	unigram $k=1$	unigram $k=5$	unigram $k=10$	bigram $k=1$	bigram $k=5$	bigram $k=10$
I 3x3	6	0.27	0.24	0.22	0.30	0.42	0.26	0.68	0.25	0.69
I 4x4	8	0.47	0.38	0.4	0.60	0.50	0.68	0.51	0.89	0.45
I 5x5	10	36.94	33.80	22.11	63.01	21.25	35.93	35.74	32.75	19.21
I 6x6	12	–	–	–	–	–	–	–	–	–
G 5x5	10	3.64	1.30	3.32	1.76	3.63	1.73	3.35	3.35	3.41
G 9x9	24	2.83	3.01	2.12	3.93	2.42	3.74	2.92	4.57	2.86
G 13x13 (a)	64	29.92	14.68	19.90	23.35	21.71	16.59	34.83	15.40	22.88
G 13x13 (b)	60	–	465.05	694.58	–	538.10	627.43	–	493.37	713.49

Table 2: Main algorithm using random word order, unigrams and bigrams – all decimals denote timings in seconds.

find all candidate words that fit a slot; rank them all, and then select the best k as word candidates. Only these k best candidates will be tried through backtracking.

Note that all `word/5` predicates are sorted via their respective n-gram value, that is, words with more frequent characters or bigrams are seen by Prolog first. As said, there is also a random ordering of such facts.

3.3 Evaluation

In this section, we evaluate the system in terms of the various heuristics employed to guide search. The base line is defined by blind-search using automatically generated Prolog programs from given grids (see Sect. 2).

Baseline Algorithm The Prolog programs were generated to alternate between filling *across* and *down* word slots. For this purpose, the order of the `word/5` were arranged accordingly.[7]

The following table depicts our baseline timings[8] with random, unigram and bigram ranking of the lexical entries:

Grid	# Slots	random	unigram	bigram
I 3x3	6	0.02	0.02	0.0.2
I 4x4	8	0.20	0.10	0.05
I 5x5	10	180.34	17.16	269.62
I 6x6	12	–	–	–
G 5x5	10	3.90	42.38	48.65
G 9x9	24	–	–	–
G 13x13 (a)	64	–	–	–
G 13x13 (b)	60	–	–	–

The first four test cases are fully interlocked grids; all remaining test cases are from (Ginsberg et al., 1990). It shows that the base program can solve fully interlocked puzzles up to grid size $5x5$, but fails to come up with a solution for larger ones (program stopped after 1 hour). The random word order performs surpringly well. In fact, the numbers indicate that the ordering of `word/5` facts in the Prolog database does not have a large impact, and that any outliers can be explained by having the right words in the right place by pure chance.

Main Algorithm. We evaluate the heuristic search algorithm using the same three conditions (random, unigram, bigram). Tab. 2 displays the main findings. It shows that the heuristics-driven algorithm pays off for crossword puzzles of larger grid sizes. For each condition, the same puzzles can be solved in less than 20 minutes; independent of the condition, the algorithm fails to solve the fully interlocked 6x6 grid as well as the 13x13 (b) puzzle with $k = 1$ in the threshold time.

Results of a linear mixed-effects regression model on cpu time (log-transformed) showed no interaction between k and type of model ($p > 0.9$).

However, there was a significant main effect of model. Pair-wise comparison showed that random is significantly faster than bigram ($p < 0.05$), while no other comparisons are significant.

Numerically, it seems that for more complex puzzles, a low k-value leads to longer processing times, but no significant differences can be found for less complex puzzles. Also, there seems to be little difference between using $k = 5$ and $k = 10$. Here, more test cases are required to determine whether the interaction between k and puzzle complexity is significant.

4 Clue Generation

Once the puzzle grid has been solved, with all words placed, clues must be generated to elicit them. With GermaNet having 11,760 paraphrases attached to synsets, and 29,550 sense descriptions attached to lexical units, the majority of GermaNet it "clueless" as it comes without this information. A

[7] An algorithm that does not alternate between across and down directions is significantly less efficient than one that does. The non-alternating algoritm is set to solving the crossword puzzle row by row, only to find out that "words" in down directions cannot be found in the lexicon. Here, the backtracking process is all but optimised.

[8] Results obtained by running SWI-Prolog on a recent Macbook Pro. All timings given in seconds.

Waagerecht 1 Großes Gewässer, das von Land umgeben ist. 3 Hundert Teile eines Euros. 5 Knapper Slip. 7 Möbelstück in der Küche zur Zubereitung von Mahlzeiten. 9 Bund fürs Leben. **Senkrecht** 2 Heißes Getränk, das aus getrockneten Blättern hergestellt wird. 4 Bargeld in physischer Form. 6 Werkzeug zur Wahrnehmung von Gerüchen. 8 Beengte Platzverhältnisse 10 Antonym für Anfang

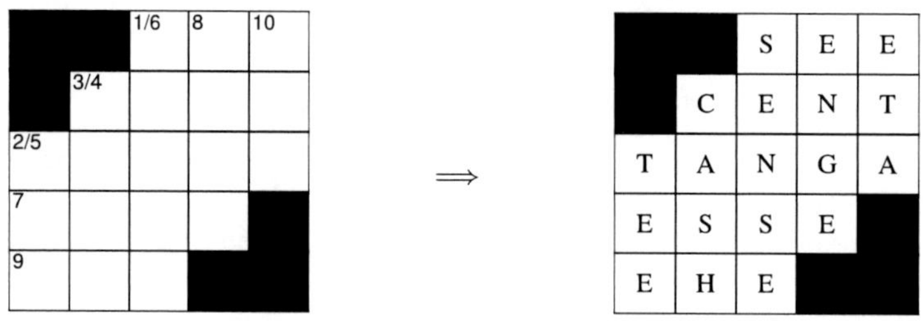

Figure 3: One possible solution to a given crossword grid.

large number of clues can be generated from hypernym and hyponym relations between synsets (*e.g.*, Überbegriff für "Nuss"), and antonym relations between lexical units (*e.g.*, Antonym für "lebendig") but the resulting puzzle would have little entertainment value if many clues for a puzzle were of this nature. To make clues more interesting, two steps were taken.

First, we ensure that the generation of clues observe a given distribution over their types. Here, we reserve at least 70% of clues to be paraphrases or sense descriptions; the remaining number of clues is evenly distributed over the other clue types (synonyms, hypernyms, and antonyms).

In the case of lexical units that are not paired with paraphrases or sense descriptions, we are using the ChatGPT *gpt-3.5-turbo* model for automatically generating paraphrases or sense descriptions. This process is fully automated. Reconsider the example puzzle given in the introduction. Fig. 3 depicts one of the possible solutions for the given grid. With the words being identified by our crossword solver, we asked ChatGPT (*gpt-3.5-turbo* model) to generates clues for each of the words using all possible clues types. For this purpose, we assigned the LLM the following assistant role:

> "You are generating clues for a German crossword puzzle. For the next word, generate a clue that describes the word, but which does not use any form of the word in the clue. The clues do not need to be full sentences, and should be as short as possible."

In this context, prompts specific to the clue type were asked, *e.g.*, "Schreibe in einem Satz einen Lexikoneintrag für: Tee" (engl. "Write, in one sentence, a lexicon entry for: tea"). The clues depicted in the top part of Fig. 3 show that ChatGPT is surprisingly good at generating crossword puzzle clues.

We are also looking forward to *officially* include resources of *Digitale Wörterbuch der deutschen Sprache*.[9] Consider, for instance, the word "Schranke" (engl.: barrier) for which we have generated the clue "Synonym für 'Schlagbaum"' (because both lexical units are in the same GermaNet synset). In the DWDS, the entry "Schranke" has been given the meaning "große, waagerecht oder senkrecht bewegbare Stange oder Gatter zur Absperrung von Durchgängen, Übergängen"[10], and the entry "Schlagbaum" has the meaning "Schranke, besonders an einer Grenze"[11], which are both good clue alternatives.[12]

5 GUI Interfaces

There is a significant difference between solving a given puzzle grid (as discussed so far), and the simultaneous process of generating and solving a grid, where new words entered in the grid can change the grid's layout, say, by adding new word boundaries (black cells). The latter task is much less constrained, and hence, much easier to tackle. In the past, we have implemented this easier task; we have also built a browser-based front-end as well as a LaTeX-based puzzle export function. This

[9] https://www.dwds.de

[10] https://www.dwds.de/wb/Schranke

[11] https://www.dwds.de/wb/Schlagbaum

[12] There are 78,815 entries in GermaNet without clue candidates (using hypernymy, hyponymy, and antonymy). For 11, 439 of these entries, a paraphrase from DWDS can be found.

Figure 4: Screenshot of the web-based front-end.

front-end can be also used for our new algorithm presented herein.

5.1 Browser-based front-end

Our graphical user interface is based upon the Javascript framework `React-JS` using an existing program library `react-crossword`[13]. Fig. 4 depicts the GUI. The library expects a JSON-based puzzle representation that the Prolog back-end creates after a successful puzzle generation. We extended the exemplary use of the library with two more UI elements: “Gib Lösungswort” (give solution for a clue), and “Gehe zu Rover” (go to Rover). The first element looks up the solution in the JSON-based crossword representation, and the second element directs users to a Rover page that shows all the information it has on the word. For this purpose, we augmented the API of Rover to allow such invocations.

A fully functional GUI front-end (currently only used for our simpler crossword generator) is available at `https://vacvvm.eu` (temporary location). As one can see from the screenshot, users have a choice between lexical resources. We have also allowed the crossword generator to make use of Princeton WordNet (Miller, 1995) and the DWDS *Wörterbuch*. For the time being, this version of the software only takes the 132,972 WordNet glosses as input; hypernym or antonym relations are currently not used.[14] Also, only a limited amount of DWDS data is being used. With these two other lexical resources, users get also easy access the PWN GUI, or to the DWDS website to get more information about the word being searched for. In sum, the puzzle GUI hence aims at luring users to other software that can be used to further explore lexical-semantic wordnets, in a sense acquiring more users for those resources.

5.2 Prolog-based puzzle export to PDF

The GUI in Fig. 4 also has an element “Rätsel als PDF”, which allows users to download a PDF variant of the puzzle. A Prolog-based converter has been implemented that transforms the internal Prolog representation into LaTeX source code that is automatically compiled into PDF. For this purpose, the LaTeX package `cwpuzzle`[15] has been used, also for the generation of Fig. 3. Usually, the crossword is generated on the front page; its solution is printed on the back page.[16]

[13] `https://github.com/JaredReisinger/react-crossword`

[14] That is, only information from the two files `wn_g.pl` and `wn_s.pl` were used.

[15] `http://www.gerd-neugebauer.de/software`

[16] Once the PDF version has been printed, a comfy armchair is the only other prerequisite to start tackling the crossword.

6 Discussion & Future Work

The automatic generation of crossword puzzles has also been studied in the linguistics community. (Rigutini et al., 2012) present *WebCrow-generation*, a system that does both clue generation and crossword compilation. A large part of their efforts is spent by crawling the Web to extract definitions from text, which can then be used for crosswords. To satisfy the constraints to fill a given puzzle, the authors also borrow the heuristics from (Ginsberg et al., 1990). Also, partially solved puzzles are ranked in terms of their "goodness", *i.e.*, how far a given partial puzzle is from the fully-solved puzzle. The best-ranked puzzle is worked on next.

The use of *existing* lexical information is described by (Aherne and Vogel, 2006). Their system relies on WordNet, and the authors put considerable emphasis on the quality of clue generation with regard to thematic domains such as *Earth* or *Sport*. In the future, we intend to also reduce our lexicon to only contain entries of given thematic domains. In part, this will allow us to investigate how our solver reacts to smaller branching factors, without relying on artificially introduced k values. The use of LLM for clue generation, however, opens up new possibilities as one is not limited to using static information from existing lexical resources.

It is our foremost intention, however, to focus on bringing together and exploiting existing lexical resources for crossword generation. Besides wordnets, thesauri, and dictionaries, we would like to also pursue the idea brought forward by (Smith and Steen, 1981), namely, the use of concordances to generate clues which refer to well-known quotations from plays or books, and where the appropriate word omitted needs to be identified.

Future work is targeted at better understanding an improving our crossword algorithm. Here, we would like to investigate additional heuristics such as giving preference to longer word slots. Ginsberg's hardest test puzzle, which is also the hardest puzzle for our solver, requires four words of length 13. In a first phase, we would like to have our solver to first identify four candidates words (which intersect with each other); and in a second phase use the approach discussed in the paper to solve the rest of the puzzle.

A second line of research concerns clue generation. Anectodical evidence, see Fig. 3, shows that ChatGPT is performing very well in this task. But clearly, a more systematic study is required here, *e.g.*, are automatically generated clues as much fun as humanly generates ones? Can people tell the difference between these two types of clues? Also, how well can we get LLMs to tailor clue generation to specific target audiences?

In a related strand of future work, which is being panned out now, we would like to use the crossword puzzle generator to target both native speakers and second language learners. We aim at investigating how users of both groups play the crossword puzzles: which clues, and the words they hint at, are difficult (within the context of already solved clues)? Is there, for instance, a correlation with word frequencies, or thematic domains? In this respect, our users become part of a citizen science community helping us to better understand language (learning) difficulty.

It shows that large language models (LLM) such as ChatGPT can be used to generate crossword puzzle clues. But given a crossword puzzle such as the one given in Fig. 3, how well do LLMs perform when they are asked to generate solutions words for a given clue? The gold standard for this task is set by the work of Ginsberg and his colleagues on automated crossword solving. Their Berkeley Crossword Solver won first place at the most prestigious human crossword tournament using a combination of neural question answering models, belief propagation and local search (Wallace et al., 2022).

For this other direction, from clues to words, we would like to make use of auto-generated crossword puzzles to fine-tune large language models. We found anecdotical evidence that LMM are surprisingly good at providing help with crossword puzzle clues (that is, generating words described by the clues). But we believe that there is a good opportunity to fine-tune LLM in this respect, in particular, if we want second language learners to not just ask for a crossword cell or slot to be filled, but to engage them in a dialogue that provides scaffolding help. Surely, some clues are better than others to hint at a specific word, but what makes a clue particularly effective in this respect, especially, in the context of second language learners?

The initial motivation of our work was driven by our desire to make a scientific resource such as GermaNet easily available to the lay person. Driven by the popularity of crossword puzzles, we wanted to popularise (and "market") our resource to the general public. The crossword generator will soon appear on our project's website as part of dissemination activities. Crosswords give users a good first insight into the GermaNet resource; with the Rover web application being invokable from the puzzle for each solution word, users can then explore the wordnet in all dimensions. We invite readers to try-out the crossword generator, recommend it to others, and look forward to their feedback.

7 Ethical Considerations

We do not see any conflict of our work with the principles set out in the ACL Ethics Policy.[17] Our crossword generator makes use of GermaNet and other lexical resources. GermaNet has been constructed over the last 25 years and manually maintained ever since. We are not aware of any discriminatory content. The prototype version of the crossword generator automatically includes ChatGPT-generated clues for words into the puzzle. Such contributions will need to be evaluated in ethical terms before the system goes public.

8 Limitations

The Prolog solver is limited by the lexical resources and computing power at its disposal. As the evaluations show, solving highly interlocked puzzles is by no means trivial and computationally expensive. More work is required to solve more complex grids in less time. Clue generation uses foremost the information from GermaNet. An experimental interface to ChatGPT has been implemented. The quality of the clues, however, need to be carefully evaluated and compared to clues found in humanly-constructed crossword puzzles.

Our evaluation is limited by our small test set of puzzles. To better understand the nature of heuristics, the k value used, and the backtracking mechanism – an excellent discussion is given by (Ginsberg et al., 1990) – we would like to randomly generate puzzles of various interlocking ratios. We believe that the number of clues to solve a given puzzle is less indicative to a problem's hardness than the number of constraints (*i.e.*, the number of word intersections) that need to be observed. In our test set, we see anecdotical evidence for this: a fully interlocked $6x6$ puzzle with 12 word slots is unsolvable (within a given time threshold), but the 13x13 puzzles from Ginsberg's testset with 60 to 64 word slots is solvable. Here, future work is required to better understand the interlocking ratio our heuristic solver can realistically handle.

[17] https://www.aclweb.org/portal/content/acl-code-ethics

9 Acknowledgements

The work has been carried out as part of Text+, the NFDI infrastructure for the Humanities, which is funded by the German Research Foundation (ref. 460033370). – We wish to thank Bettina Braun for her input on the statistical analysis and the reviewers for their helpful comments.

References

A. Aherne and C. Vogel. 2006. Wordnet enhanced automatic crossword generation. In *Proceedings of the Third International Wordnet Conference (Seogwipo, Korea)*, pages 139–145.

H. Berghel. 1987. Crossword compilation with horn clauses. *The Computer Journal*, 30(2):183–188.

H. Berghel and C. Yi. 1989. Crossword Compiler-Compilation. *The Computer Journal*, 32(3):276–280.

M. Ginsberg. 2011. Dr.Fill: Crosswords and an Implemented Solver for Singly Weighted CSPs. *J. Artif. Intell. Res. (JAIR)*, 42:851–886.

M. Ginsberg, M. Frank, M. Halpin, and M. Torrance. 1990. Search Lessons Learned from Crossword Puzzles. *AAAI-90 Proceedings of the Eighth National Conference on Artificial Intelligence*.

B. Hamp and H. Feldweg. 1997. GermaNet - a Lexical-Semantic Net for German. In *Proceedings of the ACL workshop Automatic Information Extraction and Building of Lexical Semantic Resources for NLP Applications*. Madrid, Spain.

V. Henrich, E. Hinrichs, and T. Vodolazova. 2014. Aligning GermaNet Senses with Wiktionary Sense Definitions. In *Human Language Technology: Challenges for Computer Science and Linguistics*, pages 329–342.

G. A. Miller. 1995. WordNet: A Lexical Database for English. *Commun. ACM*, 38(11):39–41.

L. Rigutini, M. Diligenti, M. Maggini, and M. Gori. 2012. Automatic Generation of Crossword Puzzles. *Int. J. Artif. Intell. Tools*, 21.

P. D. Smith and S. Y. Steen. 1981. A prototype crossword compiler. *The Computer Journal*, 24(2):107–111.

E. Wallace, N. Tomlin, A. Xu, K. Yang, E. Pathak, M. Ginsberg, and D. Klein. 2022. Automated crossword solving. In *Proceedings of the 60th Annual Meeting of the ACL*, pages 3073–3085, Dublin, Ireland. Association for Computational Linguistics.

C. Zinn, M. Hinrichs, and E. Hinrichs. 2022. Adapting GermaNet for the Semantic Web. In *Proc. of the 18th Conf. on Natural Language Processing (KONVENS 2022)*, pages 41–47, Potsdam, Germany.

Leveraging Cross-Lingual Transfer Learning in Spoken Named Entity Recognition Systems

Moncef Benaicha[1], David Thulke[2], M. A. Tuğtekin Turan[1]

[1]Fraunhofer Institute for Intelligent Analysis and Information Systems (IAIS), Germany
[2]Machine Learning and Human Language Technology, RWTH Aachen University, Germany

Correspondence: moncef.benaicha@rwth-aachen.de

Abstract

Recent Named Entity Recognition (NER) advancements have significantly enhanced text classification capabilities. This paper focuses on spoken NER, aimed explicitly at spoken document retrieval, an area not widely studied due to the lack of comprehensive datasets for spoken contexts. Additionally, the potential for cross-lingual transfer learning in low-resource situations deserves further investigation. In our study, we applied transfer learning techniques across Dutch, English, and German using both pipeline and End-to-End (E2E) approaches. We employed Wav2Vec2 XLS-R models on custom pseudo-annotated datasets to evaluate the adaptability of cross-lingual systems. Our exploration of different architectural configurations assessed the robustness of these systems in spoken NER. Results showed that the E2E model was superior to the pipeline model, particularly with limited annotation resources. Furthermore, transfer learning from German to Dutch improved performance by 7% over the standalone Dutch E2E system and 4% over the Dutch pipeline model. Our findings highlight the effectiveness of cross-lingual transfer in spoken NER and emphasize the need for additional data collection to improve these systems.

1 Introduction

Named Entity Recognition (NER) identifies and classifies named entities within text, including persons, organizations, locations, and other predefined categories (Nadeau and Sekine, 2007). While substantial progress has been made in extracting entities from written text, adapting these techniques to spoken content has seen limited research. This is primarily due to the unique challenges associated with spoken text analysis (Tomashenko et al., 2019).

Improved spoken NER has significant implications for various practical applications. Accurate entity recognition enhances user interaction in voice assistants by correctly identifying and responding to queries (Jehangir et al., 2023). In automatic transcription services, better NER improves the quality of transcriptions by correctly tagging entities, which is crucial for generating accurate and searchable text (Szymański et al., 2023). Spoken dialogue systems in customer service and virtual agents also benefit from enhanced NER by providing more context-aware and accurate responses.

Exploring spoken NER involves challenges due to the unpredictable nature of spoken language. Variabilities in pronunciation, speech disfluencies, and background noise present significant obstacles and, therefore, negatively impact system performance (Porjazovski et al., 2021). Additionally, the continuous flow of spoken language, with unclear word boundaries, adds complexity to the task (Chen et al., 2022). Despite these difficulties, spoken NER holds significant interest for its potential applications in areas like voice assistants, automatic transcription services, and spoken dialogue systems (Ghannay et al., 2018; Haghani et al., 2018; Serdyuk et al., 2018).

The introduction of Transformer-driven methodologies has advanced this field significantly. Notably, the End-to-End (E2E) modeling approach directly links speech patterns to transcriptions with embedded entity markers, which show promising results (Mdhaffar et al., 2022). These models effectively map temporal dependencies and manage the complexities of various spoken dialects. However, the research primarily focuses on high-resource languages like English, resulting in less effective model performance in data-scarce scenarios.

This paper addresses the issue of linguistic disparity by exploring cross-lingual transfer learning for spoken NER. We focus on using multilingual

This work was carried out while the first author was a research assistant at Fraunhofer IAIS.

language representation models to evaluate their effectiveness, especially in data-scarce environments where this term refers to the limited availability of high-quality, manually annotated datasets in comparison to more extensively studied languages like English. Our empirical studies cover three main languages: Dutch, English, German. We specifically examine transfers between languages with different resource levels, highlighting the strength of transfer learning in scenarios from zero to low resources. These languages were chosen for our study due to their varying resource levels and linguistic similarities, which provide a meaningful context for examining cross-lingual transfer learning.

Moreover, we provide a comparative analysis of different methodologies, including both pipeline and E2E approaches. The pipeline framework integrates the functionalities of Automatic Speech Recognition (ASR) systems with subsequent NER models. Initially, the ASR system transcribes spoken content into text, which is then tagged with entities by the NER system. Previous work has explored E2E strategies that simultaneously address ASR and NER tasks (Caubrière et al., 2020). This approach aims to refine ASR alongside Natural Language Understanding (NLU) and significantly reduce error propagation commonly caused by ASR limitations (Jannet et al., 2015).

A major challenge with E2E models is their need for extensive training datasets. The limited availability of audio-textual datasets with entity annotations emphasizes this issue, as creating large annotated speech datasets is both complex and costly. To address this, Pasad et al. (2022), used a labeling model to generate pseudo-annotations. Inspired by this approach, our paper includes custom pseudo-annotated datasets in Dutch, English, and German, created using the XLM-R_L-based NER model (Goyal et al., 2021). These pseudo-annotations were not manually corrected, and all evaluations were performed on these pseudo-annotated datasets. Furthermore, no gold-standard annotations were used.

We further examine the impact of various factors such as training data volume, language model choice, and target language, on spoken NER system performance. This paper enhances research in spoken NER by highlighting challenges and potential cross-lingual solutions. Our results advance spoken document retrieval and support the development of more sophisticated and accurate spoken NER systems. Consistent with open research principles, all code, data, and results from this study will be publicly available[1].

To summarize our contributions:

- We comprehensively compare and analyze pipeline versus E2E strategies for spoken NER in Dutch, English, and German.
- We investigate transfer learning within both pipeline and E2E strategies for spoken NER.
- We move from a high-resource language, German, to a resource-scarce language, Dutch, resulting in a notable 10% improvement in spoken NER performance.

2 Related Work

Traditionally, NER from spoken content has utilized a pipeline approach, beginning with an Automatic Speech Recognition (ASR) phase followed by NER on the resulting transcriptions (Jannet et al., 2017). While such a system may seem intuitive, it has essential challenges. Specifically, it directly incorporates transcriptions annotated with entities within the ASR system (Cohn et al., 2019). By embedding such annotations, there's potential to refine the partial hypotheses, which often get overlooked or dismissed during the decoding process. A novel solution has been integrating specific entity expressions into the lexicon to enhance language model accuracy in recognizing these expressions (Hatmi et al., 2013).

In response to these challenges, interest in the E2E approach for spoken NER has increased. This method aims to simultaneously optimize ASR and NER processes, providing a potentially more efficient alternative to the traditional pipeline by leveraging deep neural networks' capabilities to manage long-range sentence dependencies.

Significant research into the E2E approach for spoken NER includes work with French datasets (Ghannay et al., 2018), adopting architectures similar to DeepSpeech (Amodei et al., 2016), guided by the Connectionist Temporal Classification (CTC) objective (Graves et al., 2006). Building on this, Yadav et al. (2020) developed a method tailored for English, introducing specific tokens in the ASR vocabulary to enhance NER tagging. Our research also incorporates this by incorporating unique symbols ('{', '[', '$', ']') in transcripts to

[1] https://github.com/moncefbenaicha/spoken-ner

assist in identifying entities such as organizations, persons, and locations, as depicted in Figure 1. Building on these foundational studies, more recent research (Shon et al., 2022; Pasad et al., 2022) has successfully employed this methodology in conjunction with the Wav2Vec2 model.

Consequently, the E2E strategy aims to align speech utterances with annotated transcriptions perfectly, facilitating direct entity extraction from spoken content. Empirical studies using French and English datasets have demonstrated the effectiveness of the E2E strategy, often surpassing traditional pipeline approaches, particularly against Long Short-term Memory (LSTM) based models, which no longer meet state-of-the-art standards (Vajjala and Balasubramaniam, 2022).

3 Methodology

3.1 Baseline Models

This paper introduces two distinct baseline systems designed for English, German, and Dutch. The first system adopts a conventional pipeline approach where ASR and NER models are trained separately. After training, these models are integrated during the inference phase to produce results. In contrast, the second system employs an E2E methodology involving more intricate processes. For the E2E system, the ASR model is fine-tuned using the robust pre-trained Wav2Vec2-XLS-R-300M model (Babu et al., 2022). During this fine-tuning, each language is treated separately, utilizing CTC-loss

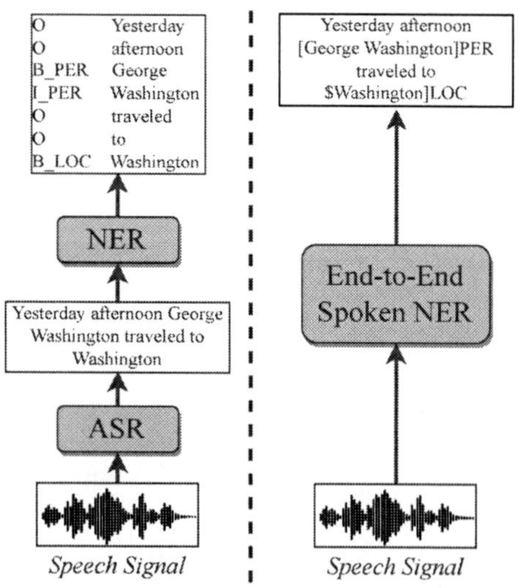

Figure 1: The diagram on the left shows a two-stage pipeline, while the right shows the E2E approach.

as the main objective function. Concurrently, the NER component of the pipeline is enhanced through modifications to the XLM-R_L language representation model. This enhancement includes the addition of a linear layer specifically designed to handle lower-cased tokens from the CoNLL 2002 and 2003 datasets (Tjong Kim Sang; Tjong Kim Sang and De Meulder, 2003).

To enhance the ASR model, we integrate a 4-gram language model trained on both the training and development datasets for each language. In the E2E system, we utilize the capabilities of the Wav2Vec2-XLS-R-300M model once more. For this iteration, we fine-tune using a specially augmented corpus. This corpus includes special tokens that explicitly indicate the start of an entity such as a person (PER), an organization (ORG), or a location (LOC) and mark the end of an entity mention, as shown in Figure 1.

3.2 Transfer Learning Models

In the pipeline approach, we leverage a dual-component architecture. Specifically, we replace the native NER model with a cross-lingual variant that is more universally applicable. In our transfer learning experiments, German serves as the source language, while English and Dutch are designated as target languages. The first step involves applying the pre-trained German NER model directly to the English and Dutch transcripts without any language-specific modifications. This initial approach is followed by a phase that combines transfer learning with model fine-tuning. During this phase, the German NER model forms the foundation. Fine-tuning is then performed using a subset (k) of the target language's training set, corresponding to either 10% or 20% of the original dataset. The model's performance is assessed using the test set of the target language to evaluate its effectiveness after fine-tuning.

In contrast, the E2E model adopts a more comprehensive transfer learning approach. Our experiments begin with a zero-shot transfer learning phase, where the capabilities of the German E2E spoken NER system are extended to English and Dutch. Following this initial phase, we apply an extensive fine-tuning using a portion of the target language's training dataset, typically 20% or 40% of the total. After completing this fine-tuning, the model is assessed against the test set of the target language. This evaluation yields critical insights into the effectiveness of the fine-tuning process.

	Training Set			Validation Set			Test Set		
	EN	**DE**	**NL**	**EN**	**DE**	**NL**	**EN**	**DE**	**NL**
#Sentences	527K	526K	42K	5K	5K	5K	5K	5K	5K
#Tokens	5.4M	5M	0.5M	46K	47K	46K	47K	45.6K	45K
#Tokens as LOC	211K	156K	588	1.2K	1.5K	241	1.3K	1.3K	314
#Tokens as ORG	177K	83K	95	1K	729	66	1.1K	621	88
#Tokens as PER	216K	144K	104	1.3K	1.5K	123	1.4K	1.2K	155
#Tokens as O	4.8M	4.6M	408K	43K	43K	45K	43K	42.4K	44.5K
Total Hours	840	839	54	8	8.5	6.5	8.5	8.5	7

Table 1: The statistics of pseudo-annotated data across English, German, and Dutch splits.

4 Corpus Overview

For our experiments, we utilized data from Common Voice[2], specifically selecting the validated corpus for each language. This corpus comprises various types of oral data, including read speech from diverse demographics. During preprocessing, we removed duplicate entries, retained essential punctuation, and converted non-Latin characters to Latin script, standardizing everything to lowercase. The processed data were then used with the XLM-R_L-based NER model, trained on the language-specific CoNLL dataset (Tjong Kim Sang; Tjong Kim Sang and De Meulder, 2003), to generate pseudo-annotations. Note that, in the English corpus, all punctuation except apostrophes was removed during the transcription process.

We encountered non-Latin scripts such as Cyrillic or Brahmic during preprocessing due to the inclusion of multilingual text data in the Common Voice corpus. These scripts were converted to Latin to maintain consistency across datasets. Detailed statistics of the training, development, and testing sets, including the number of sentences, tokens, and total hours, are presented in Table 1. This table illustrates the comprehensive scope and linguistic variability of the datasets used.

Additionally, Table 2 highlights the extent of entity overlaps within and between the languages studied. These were computed by comparing the exact match of entity spans across different languages. While overlaps within each language's training sets are complete, the inter-language overlaps vary significantly. For instance, the overlap between English and German is 36.5%, contrasting sharply with the minimal 0.1% overlap between English and Dutch. These statistics underscore the challenges and considerations in developing multilingual NER systems that can effectively transfer learning across languages.

[2]https://commonvoice.mozilla.org/en/datasets

5 Evaluation Metrics

We employ various metrics to assess the performance of our spoken NER systems. The conventional Word Error Rate (WER) serves as the primary metric for evaluating the accuracy of ASR models. In addition, we utilize the Entity Error Rate (EER), which evaluates the specific accuracy of our spoken NER systems in the context of entity transcription. Unlike broader measures, EER focuses exclusively on the accuracy with which entities such as names of people, locations, and organizations are transcribed:

$$EER = \frac{N_{\text{Incorrectly Transcribed Entities}}}{N_{\text{Total Entities}}} \quad (1)$$

Here, $N_{\text{Incorrectly Transcribed Entities}}$ denotes the number of entities that the system has transcribed

		Train		
		EN	**DE**	**NL**
Train	**EN**	100.0	24.7	0.1
	DE	36.5	100.0	0.2
	NL	52.4	58.0	100.0
Test	**EN**	79.6	64.0	1.7
	DE	58.4	84.3	2.1
	NL	64.3	68.1	27.0

Table 2: The percentages of entity overlaps across different languages.

incorrectly, while $N_{\text{Total Entities}}$ indicates the total number of entities in the dataset. The EER measures the proportion of entities that were inaccurately transcribed, providing a direct indicator of the system's transcription accuracy.

Furthermore, to evaluate the effectiveness of the NER system, we calculate the micro-average F1-score, which is a harmonized measure of precision and recall, similar to the approach in (Pasad et al., 2022):

$$F_1 = \frac{TP}{TP + \frac{1}{2}(FP + FN)} \quad (2)$$

where true positives (TP) are the correctly identified entities, false positives (FP) are the incorrectly identified entities, and false negatives (FN) are the entities that were not identified. These values are computed based on the accuracy of entity transcription, their types, and the positions of these entities within the transcript. This score provides a balanced measure of the system's overall accuracy in recognizing and classifying entities.

6 Experiments and Results

In our comprehensive baseline experiments for the pipeline model, we utilized prominent open-source pre-trained models to enhance performance across various tasks. For ASR, we selected the Wav2Vec2-XLS-R-300M pre-trained model[3], which is noted for its efficiency. Simultaneously, for NER, we employed the robust XLM-R_L pre-trained language model[4], well-known for its effectiveness in multilingual processing.

For fine-tuning the ASR model, we chose the AdamW optimizer, following recommendations by Loshchilov and Hutter (2019), with $betas = (0.9, 0.999)$ and a precision parameter of $eps = 10^{-8}$. The learning rate was carefully managed through a schedule that includes a warm-up phase covering one-third of the total training steps. During this phase, the learning rate gradually increases from a baseline to a peak of 10^{-4}. After this warm-up period, the learning rate linearly decreases through the remaining training sessions. It is important to highlight that we only froze the feature encoder of the Wav2Vec2 architecture and made no other structural changes to the model.

Regarding the NER model, we mostly maintained the same optimizer settings as those used for the ASR model, with a slight adjustment to the maximum learning rate of the scheduler, setting it to 2×10^{-5}. Finally, for the E2E spoken NER model, we chose to maintain consistency by adopting the same set of hyper-parameters previously applied in the ASR component of pipeline framework.

6.1 Baseline Results

Table 3 presents the baseline performances across varying configurations and languages. It's evident from the results that the EER and the F1-scores consistently display a negative correlation across all three languages. This observed trend aligns with our expectations. Specifically, even if the ASR system exhibits any discrepancies in transcribing an entity accurately, it adversely affects the F1-score. This impact remains regardless of whether the entity boundaries and categories are delineated correctly.

Focusing on the German language, the E2E baseline results stand out. Out of a total of 5000 test utterances for German, 2928 have been transcribed with precision, translating to an accuracy rate of approximately 58.6% of the test set. Impressively, within this accurately transcribed set, a staggering 94% of utterances have been labeled correctly, a testament to the model's efficacy. When we pivot our attention to the subset of utterances that weren't transcribed with utmost accuracy, it's important to note that the model, despite the transcription issues, managed to label entities correctly in about 51.3% of these instances. Cumulatively, this implies that the E2E model adeptly labeled entities with accuracy in nearly 76% of the entire set of test utterances for German.

It's also worthwhile to note the relative performances of English and Dutch. For instance, when observing the pipeline approach with both ASR and NER components active, English has a WER of 16.7% and an F1-score of 40.7%, whereas Dutch, under the same conditions, recorded a WER of 9.3% and an F1-score of 40.0%. Such statistics offer nuanced insights into the distinct challenges and variances inherent to each language, emphasizing the importance of tailored strategies for each linguistic domain.

A comparable trend is also observed in the pipeline system, with the E2E model exhibiting a marginally superior performance. One of the E2E model's significant strengths lies in its ability to tag entities accurately, even in the presence of transcription errors. This proficiency translates to

[3]https://hf.co/facebook/wav2vec2-xls-r-300m

[4]https://hf.co/xlm-roberta-large

Lang	E2E	ASR	NER	WER	EER	F1
	no	no	yes	N/A	N/A	80.3
EN	no	yes	yes	16.7	48.0	40.7
	yes	no	no	16.5	46.0	41.8
	no	no	yes	N/A	N/A	87.2
DE	no	yes	yes	9.4	29.0	61.1
	yes	no	no	9.1	27.0	61.6
	no	no	yes	N/A	N/A	85.6
NL	no	yes	yes	9.3	49.0	40.0
	yes	no	no	9.2	47.0	37.4

Table 3: Performances of baseline models across different configurations and languages.

a performance uptick of around 2% when pitted against the traditional pipeline system. Exploring the performances across different languages, our analyses of English and Dutch mirror the patterns we uncovered for German. However, the Dutch distinguishes itself in one noteworthy aspect: an impressive accuracy rate of up to 99% in entity identification when the transcriptions are accurate. Across the board, the E2E spoken NER system demonstrates a propensity to fine-tune the WER, EER, and by extension, the F1-score. The sole deviation from this pattern is seen in Dutch. This anomaly can be attributed to the relatively limited pool of training data available for Dutch, especially when benchmarked against English and German.

6.2 Transfer Learning Results

Tables 4 and 5 present the results of transfer learning from German to English and German to Dutch, respectively. These results highlight patterns consistent with our baseline pipeline experiments.

In the German-to-English transition detailed in Table 4, the performance of E2E model in the zero-shot transfer learning scenario illustrates the adaptability of this approach. However, for the transition from German to Dutch, the situation is markedly different. Zero-shot transfer learning outcomes for German to Dutch align closely with baseline performances, with WER, EER, and F1-scores remaining relatively stable across the scenarios. Interestingly, the incorporation of 40% of the Dutch training data leads to a noticeable improvement in performance, particularly a roughly 2% increase in F1-scores as shown in Table 5.

Focusing again on the E2E model, it is apparent from the results that the German-to-Dutch transfer yields better performance metrics compared to the German-to-English transfer. An examination of Table 2 provides a potential explanation for this difference, indicating a more substantial overlap in entities between German and Dutch than between German and English.

A closer look at Table 5 reveals that fine-tuning the German E2E system with 40% of the Dutch training data significantly enhances the system's effectiveness in recognizing Dutch entities. This fine-tuning results in a performance increase of approximately 7% compared to the standalone Dutch E2E system and a 4% improvement over the Dutch pipeline system. The gains are particularly notable in the F1 scores within the PER and LOC entity categories, where there is an impressive 10% increase compared to the baseline Dutch E2E system. These findings underscore the efficacy of targeted training data in boosting system performance and highlight the benefits of cross-lingual transfer learning in multilingual NER systems.

7 Conclusions

In this paper, we explore spoken NER with a focus on cross-lingual transfer learning, employing both pipeline and E2E methodologies. Our findings indicate that the E2E approach to spoken NER generally outperforms the pipeline method in terms of both diverse evaluation metrics and overall parameter efficiency. Nevertheless, the pipeline approach retains its practical utility due to its

System	Transfer Learning		WER	EER	F1
	Source → Target	*k*			
Pipeline	N/A	N/A	16.7	48.0	40.7
	DE → EN	0%	16.7	48.0	38.5
		20%	16.7	48.0	39.6
		40%	16.7	48.0	40.0
E2E	N/A	N/A	16.5	46.0	41.8
	DE → EN	0%	52.5	66.0	20.8
		20%	21.8	53.0	35.8
		40%	22.9	54.0	35.8

Table 4: Performance of the pipeline and E2E models with German-to-English transfer learning, measured across various metrics.

System	Transfer Learning		WER	EER	F1
	Source → Target	k			
Pipeline	N/A	N/A	9.3	49.0	40.0
	DE → NL	0%	9.3	49.0	40.2
		20%	9.3	49.0	40.3
		40%	9.3	49.0	42.0
E2E	N/A	N/A	9.2	47.0	37.4
	DE → NL	0%	78.0	67.0	24.0
		20%	11.8	42.0	44.4
		40%	10.7	40.0	44.3

Table 5: Performance of the pipeline and E2E models with German-to-Dutch transfer learning, measured across various metrics.

flexibility in integrating various ASR and NER components.

Our investigations show that deploying a German NER model without fine-tuning in a Dutch or English context within the pipeline still allows the E2E spoken NER to achieve comparable or superior results to an NER model trained specifically for the pipeline's target language. This highlights the effectiveness of transfer learning in E2E spoken NER systems, which often surpass the performance of traditional pipeline systems. A key insight from our study is the robustness of the E2E model in tagging entities correctly, even when faced with transcription errors, slightly outperforming the pipeline approach.

Looking ahead, several promising directions for further research have emerged. One potential area involves refining the objective function of the ASR model to enhance focus on specific tokens within transcriptions that are of greater relevance to NER tasks. Another promising direction is the investigation of spoken NER within a multilingual framework that can accommodate a wide range of languages and dialects, potentially making significant advancements in the field. Additionally, creating and using human-annotated datasets, with consistent entity annotations across various languages, are crucial. We develop human-annotated datasets where such datasets would provide a solid foundation for evaluating spoken NER systems.

This work was supported by the European Union's Horizon 2020 Research and Innovation Program under Grant Agreement No. 957017, `https://selma-project.eu`.

References

Dario Amodei, Sundaram Ananthanarayanan, Rishita Anubhai, Jingliang Bai, Eric Battenberg, Carl Case, Jared Casper, Bryan Catanzaro, Qiang Cheng, Guoliang Chen, et al. 2016. Deep Speech 2: End-to-end speech recognition in english and mandarin. In *International conference on machine learning (ICML)*, pages 173–182.

Arun Babu, Changhan Wang, Andros Tjandra, Kushal Lakhotia, Qiantong Xu, Naman Goyal, Kritika Singh, Patrick von Platen, Yatharth Saraf, Juan Pino, et al. 2022. Xls-r: Self-supervised cross-lingual speech representation learning at scale.

Antoine Caubrière, Sophie Rosset, Yannick Estève, Antoine Laurent, and Emmanuel Morin. 2020. Where are we in named entity recognition from speech? In *Proceedings of the Language Resources and Evaluation Conference*, pages 4514–4520.

Boli Chen, Guangwei Xu, Xiaobin Wang, Pengjun Xie, Meishan Zhang, and Fei Huang. 2022. AISHELL-NER: Named entity recognition from Chinese speech. In *International Conference on Acoustics, Speech and Signal Processing (ICASSP)*, pages 8352–8356. IEEE.

Ido Cohn, Itay Laish, Genady Beryozkin, Gang Li, Izhak Shafran, Idan Szpektor, Tzvika Hartman, Avinatan Hassidim, and Yossi Matias. 2019. Audio de-identification-a new entity recognition task. In *Proceedings of the North American Chapter of the Association for Computational Linguistics*, pages 197–204.

Sahar Ghannay, Antoine Caubrière, Yannick Estève, Nathalie Camelin, Edwin Simonnet, Antoine Laurent, and Emmanuel Morin. 2018. End-to-end named entity and semantic concept extraction from speech. In *Spoken Language Technology Workshop (SLT)*, pages 692–699. IEEE.

Naman Goyal, Jingfei Du, Myle Ott, Giri Anantharaman, and Alexis Conneau. 2021. Larger-scale transformers for multilingual masked language modeling. In *Proceedings of the Workshop on Representation Learning for NLP*, pages 29–33. Association for Computational Linguistics.

Alex Graves, Santiago Fernández, Faustino Gomez, and Jürgen Schmidhuber. 2006. Connectionist temporal classification: labelling unsegmented sequence data with recurrent neural networks. In *International conference on machine learning (ICML)*, pages 369–376.

Parisa Haghani, Arun Narayanan, Michiel Bacchiani, Galen Chuang, Neeraj Gaur, Pedro Moreno, Rohit Prabhavalkar, Zhongdi Qu, and Austin Waters. 2018. From audio to semantics: Approaches to end-to-end spoken language understanding. In *Spoken Language Technology Workshop (SLT)*, pages 720–726. IEEE.

Mohamed Hatmi, Christine Jacquin, Emmanuel Morin, and Sylvain Meignier. 2013. Incorporating named entity recognition into the speech transcription process. In *Annual Conference of the International Speech Communication Association (Interspeech)*.

Mohamed Ameur Ben Jannet, Olivier Galibert, Martine Adda-Decker, and Sophie Rosset. 2015. How to evaluate ASR output for named entity recognition? In *Annual Conference of the International Speech Communication Association (Interspeech)*.

Mohamed Ameur Ben Jannet, Olivier Galibert, Martine Adda-Decker, and Sophie Rosset. 2017. Investigating the effect of asr tuning on named entity recognition. In *Annual Conference of the International Speech Communication Association (Interspeech)*, pages 2486–2490.

Basra Jehangir, Saravanan Radhakrishnan, and Rahul Agarwal. 2023. A survey on named entity recognition — datasets, tools, and methodologies. *Natural Language Processing Journal*, 3:100017.

Ilya Loshchilov and Frank Hutter. 2019. Decoupled weight decay regularization. *arXiv preprint arXiv:1711.05101*.

Salima Mdhaffar, Jarod Duret, Titouan Parcollet, and Yannick Estève. 2022. End-to-end model for named entity recognition from speech without paired training data. In *Annual Conference of the International Speech Communication Association (Interspeech)*.

David Nadeau and Satoshi Sekine. 2007. A survey of named entity recognition and classification. *Lingvisticae Investigationes*, 30(1):3–26.

Ankita Pasad, Felix Wu, Suwon Shon, Karen Livescu, and Kyu Han. 2022. On the use of external data for spoken named entity recognition. In *Proceedings of the North American Chapter of the Association for Computational Linguistics*, pages 724–737.

Dejan Porjazovski, Juho Leinonen, and Mikko Kurimo. 2021. Attention-based end-to-end named entity recognition from speech. In *International Conference on Text, Speech, and Dialogue*, pages 469–480. Springer.

Dmitriy Serdyuk, Yongqiang Wang, Christian Fuegen, Anuj Kumar, Baiyang Liu, and Yoshua Bengio. 2018. Towards end-to-end spoken language understanding. In *International Conference on Acoustics, Speech and Signal Processing (ICASSP)*, pages 5754–5758. IEEE.

Suwon Shon, Ankita Pasad, Felix Wu, Pablo Brusco, Yoav Artzi, Karen Livescu, and Kyu J Han. 2022. Slue: New benchmark tasks for spoken language understanding evaluation on natural speech. In *International Conference on Acoustics, Speech and Signal Processing (ICASSP)*, pages 7927–7931. IEEE.

Piotr Szymański, Lukasz Augustyniak, Mikolaj Morzy, Adrian Szymczak, Krzysztof Surdyk, and Piotr Żelasko. 2023. Why aren't we ner yet? artifacts of asr errors in named entity recognition in spontaneous speech transcripts. In *Proceedings of the Annual Meeting of the Association for Computational Linguistics*, pages 1746–1761.

Erik F. Tjong Kim Sang. Introduction to the CoNLL-2002 shared task: Language-independent named entity recognition.

Erik F. Tjong Kim Sang and Fien De Meulder. 2003. Introduction to the CoNLL-2003 shared task: Language-independent named entity recognition. In *Proceedings of the Conference on Natural Language Learning at HLT-NAACL*, pages 142–147.

Natalia Tomashenko, Antoine Caubrière, Yannick Estève, Antoine Laurent, and Emmanuel Morin. 2019. Recent advances in end-to-end spoken language understanding. In *International Conference on Statistical Language and Speech Processing*, pages 44–55. Springer.

Sowmya Vajjala and Ramya Balasubramaniam. 2022. What do we really know about state of the art NER? In *Proceedings of the Language Resources and Evaluation Conference*, pages 5983–5993.

Hemant Yadav, Sreyan Ghosh, Yi Yu, and Rajiv Ratn Shah. 2020. End-to-end named entity recognition from English speech. *Annual Conference of the International Speech Communication Association (Interspeech)*, pages 4268–4272.

Exploring Data Acquisition Strategies for the Domain Adaptation of QA Models

Maurice Falk **Adrian Ulges** **Dirk Krechel**
RheinMain University of Applied Sciences, Germany
{firstname.lastname}@hs-rm.de

Abstract

Domain adaptation in Question-Answering (QA) is of importance when deploying models in new target domains where specific terminology and information needs exist. Adaptation commonly relies on a supervised fine-tuning using datasets composed of contexts, questions, and answers from the new domain. However, the annotation of such datasets is known to demand significant time and resources. In this work, a semi-automatic approach is investigated, where – instead of a fully manual acquisition – only answer spans (or questions, respectively) are selectively labeled, and a generative model provides a corresponding question (or answer). The efficacy of the proposed approach is compared against LLM-based auto-generative methods. Through experiments on diverse domain-specific QA datasets, both from the research community and industry practice, the superiority of the semi-automatic approach in obtaining higher QA performance is demonstrated.

1 Introduction

Question answering (QA) is one of natural language processing's most prominent tasks, targeted at identifying answers to questions from a given text corpus. At its core sits a reading comprehension (short, *reader*) model, which derives the answer given the question and a candidate context (or passage). Readers either *extract* the answer as a subspan of the candidate context, or *generate* new answers altogether. While the latter approach has recently gained popularity as *retrieval-augmented generation (RAG)* in the context of large language models (LLMs), extractive approaches offer benefits in terms of interpretability, speed, and – most importantly – in the fact that their answers are always grounded in source material.

In this work, we focus on extractive readers, and specifically on the issue of domain adaptation. This is of relevance when QA systems are deployed in new target domains and have to cope with specific terminology, but also with specific information needs of their users, as depending on the domain, different aspects of a text may be of relevance.

A common approach towards domain adaptation would be a supervised fine-tuning of readers, given target-domain triples of questions, candidate context and answers. This, however, would require extensive annotation effort, which raises the questions how to collect training triples more efficiently. To do so, several approaches have recently proposed generative (L)LMs as an option to synthesize questions and answers from contexts. In this paper, we investigate a **semi-automatic approach**, where a human annotator only labels interesting (answer) spans (or questions), instead of both. We argue that it might still be difficult for an LLM to identify question-worthy answer spans or generate questions if only given a context. In contrast, given a context and an answer, formulating a corresponding question is relatively easy and could, hence, be automated. This would lead to a domain adaptation procedure in which users label potentially relevant answers (or questions) in contexts, and a language model generates a corresponding questions (or answer), completing triples on which the reader is fine-tuned. In this paper, we compare the above semi-automatic approach to a fully-synthetic one, where both questions and answers are generated. Our findings (on three common research benchmarks and a closed-domain dataset from an industry partner) are:

- Manually labeling a limited amount of answers leads to strong performance improvements, compared both to labeling questions and to fully automated data generation.
- To achieve this improvement, even medium-sized LMs as question generators suffice, which suggests that localizing interesting answers is key to a successful reader adaptation.

- Given a small number of semi-automatic QA pairs, we examine how bootstrapping the auto-generative models impacts their performance.

2 Related Work

The domain adaptation of readers was examined using various approaches. While Hazen et al. (2019) have shown that transfer learning, i.e., fine-tuning the reader on a common large-scale QA dataset, can lead to good performance of the reader on a new domain. But they also report that further supervised fine-tuning using QA pairs of the target domain further improves performance. Therefore, further work focused on obtaining good QA pairs for training while using the same reader architecture (Devlin et al., 2018) for evaluation. Due to the costs of manual annotation of QA pairs, other works have explored ways to automatically obtain QA pairs of the target domain without human annotators. One differentiates between answer-first and question-first approaches. The answer-first approach starts by selecting candidate answer spans from the context directly and then uses the context and candidate answers to generate questions. The answer span selection can be done either in an extractive way using an answer span detector (Alberti et al., 2019; Puri et al., 2020; Bartolo et al., 2021; Luo et al., 2021), or in a generative way, where an (encoder-)decoder language model generates answer tokens from the context (Shakeri et al., 2020; Bartolo et al., 2021). In the question-first approach, possible questions for a given context are generated, which are then used to generate the answers (Shakeri et al., 2020).

3 Approach

Extractive QA is targeted at localizing an answer to a given question in a context. For example, given the context "Dune is a science fiction epos produced by Denis Villeneuve, [...]", the answer to the question "Who is the producer of Dune?" would be the last two words, "Denis Villeneuve." Following the reader architecture proposed by Devlin et al. (2018), given a context **c** and question **q**, both are tokenized into token sequences, concatenated, and processed by a transformer encoder to obtain contextualized embeddings. Finally, these embeddings are fed through a head model, which returns two probabilities indicating every token's likelihood to be the start or end token of the answer. The answer is then estimated to be the span between the most probable start and end token.

Following Hazen et al. (2019), the training of domain-specific readers happens in two phases: (1) a base reader model is obtained by fine-tuning a pretrained LM on a large-scale QA corpus such as SQuAD (Rajpurkar et al., 2016) (Engl.) or GermanQuAD (Möller et al., 2021) (German), and (2) performance on the target domain is improved by further fine-tuning the base model on some domain-specific QA pairs.

3.1 Domain Adaptation Data

While a manual annotation of domain-specific QA pairs yields high-quality data, it is also quite expensive. We, therefore, investigate other labeling approaches that require only partial or no manual annotation.

Generating questions and answers This setup tries to overcome the need for manual labeling altogether by estimating both question $\hat{q}$ and answer $\hat{a}$ from each given context c, using a model η:

$$\hat{q}, \hat{a} = \eta(c)$$

Note that η is a generative model, and that – to form training data for an extractive model – the generated answer has to be matched within the context. If the answer does not exist in the context, $\hat{a}$ is undefined and no training triple is generated. We compare two different generators:

QAGen2S: The model proposed by Shakeri et al. (2020) is an encoder-decoder model that generates questions and answers in two steps. First, the model generates a candidate question for a given context. The generated question is then included in the second step to generate a corresponding answer.

LLaMA-QAGen: Following the above approach of applying larger-scale LLMs, LLaMA 2 is used to generate both question and answer. Because we observed that many generated answers could not be located in the context, we fine-tuned the non-instruction model for question- and answer generation.

Generating Questions Only (GQO) Given a context c, a human annotator labels an interesting (answer) span a, but does not continue to formulate a question (which drastically reduces the costs of labeling). Instead, an answer-aware Question Generation (AA-QG) model ϕ is used to estimate a corresponding question $\hat{q}$, given context and answer:

$$\hat{q} = \phi(c, a)$$

We test two different question generators ϕ:

QGen: Chan and Fan (2019) propose a transformer-based encoder-decoder model, which is pointed at the answer span by inserting special tokens into the context. In the above example, the model input would become "Dune is a science fiction epos produced by **<hl>Denis Villeneuve<hl>**." We start from a pretrained LM and fine-tune the model specifically for question generation.

LLaMA-QGen: Inspired by the recent success of instruction-tuned large-scale LMs as task-agnostic problem solvers (Zhao et al., 2023), we use the instruction-tuned variant of LLaMA 2 (Touvron et al., 2023) as an answer-aware question generator. The prompt template is shared in A.3.

Generating Answers Only (GAO) In this setup, questions are assumed to be manually created, and an answer detection model ψ localizes the answer:

$$\hat{a} = \psi(c, q).$$

We test this setup with the QAGen2S encoder-decoder model, feeding manually acquired questions and generating only the answer.

Any fine-tuning of the aforementioned models was conducted on a generalist QA dataset.

3.2 Data Gathering and Bootstrapping

Given the above models, the following labeling procedures for gathering a domain adaptation dataset are examined:

- **Generation-Only (GO)**: No manual annotation is carried out, but QA pairs for domain adaptation are fully generated by applying the generator η on all available domain contexts.
- **Semi-Automatic (SA)**: A fixed number n of answer spans only **or** questions only are annotated by human experts, which limits the annotation effort. The corresponding answer span / question is generated by ψ / ϕ.
- **Bootstrapping (BS)**: The QA dataset obtained by *SA* is used to further fine-tune a generative model η, obtaining a domain-specific generator η'. By applying η' to all domain contexts, a larger-scale domain adaptation set is bootstrapped.

4 Experiments

We examine the effectiveness of different datasets obtained through the scenarios and models described in the previous section. For evaluation, we use four different domain-specific datasets: **BioASQ** (Tsatsaronis et al., 2015), containing QAs from the biomedical domain; **CovidQA** (Möller et al., 2020), containing QAs about Covid-19 from biomedical articles; **TextbookQA** (Kembhavi et al., 2017), which contains QAs from Life-, Earth-, and Physical Science textbooks; and a manually annotated German QA dataset, referred to as **BankQA**, from handbooks from an industry partner in the German banking domain. For BioASQ and TextbookQA, we use the datasets from the MRQA 2019 Shared Task (Fisch et al., 2019), which unifies the pre-processing of the datasets. We randomly sample 80 percent of contexts as a training corpus and remove all QA pairs for the domain adaptation task. The QA pairs of the remaining contexts are used as a test set. More details about the datasets is given in A.1.

4.1 Setup

For the evaluation of a dataset, a new reader is fine-tuned on the dataset's QA samples. The resulting model is then applied to the test set, and F1 (word-level) and exact match (EM) scores are reported. We use *electa-base* (Clark et al., 2020) as the encoder of our reader and fine-tune a model on SQuAD / GermanQuAD as our base model for all our runs. Details about hyperparameters and fine-tuning for the reader and all other models can be found in A.2. At the core of our QAGen2S model, we use *bart-base* and fine-tune the model for QA generation on the training split of the SQuAD (GermanQuAD) dataset, following the hyperparameters reported in the original paper. The checkpoints with the lowest Cross-Entropy loss on the dev set are used as our final models. Finally, for *LLaMA-QAGen*, we fine-tune the base-version of LLaMA 7B for QA generation using *QLoRA* (Dettmers et al., 2023), following the same procedure described by QAGen2S.

4.2 Manual Labeling of Questions versus Answers

In this experiment, we compare how effective labeling only questions / answers would be for domain adaptation. To obtain the **GQO** datasets, we simulate the manual labeling of answer spans by using

	BankQA		BioASQ		CovidQA		TextbookQA	
	F1	EM	F1	EM	F1	EM	F1	EM
No domain adaptation *	49.22	21.52	60.30	46.15	56.20	32.70	41.95	30.50
Manually annotated QAs	**63.99 ±1.02**	**39.55 ±0.74**	**89.84 ±1.11**	**86.82 ±1.81**	66.33 ±0.81	43.02 ±1.30	**57.41 ±1.44**	**50.06 ±1.25**
Generating Questions/Answers Only (GQO / GAO)								
Ann. Answers + ϕ (T5)	59.81 ±1.13	33.99 ±2.58	79.57 ±1.34	75.92 ±1.38	**67.28 ±0.93**	**43.90 ±1.13**	41.78 ±3.33	36.35 ±3.17
Ann. Answers + ϕ (LLaMA2)	53.06 ±2.27	30.13 ±2.60	84.83 ±3.02	82.47 ±3.18	51.00 ±2.89	28.93 ±2.81	27.56 ±3.04	22.26 ±2.25
Ann. Questions + ψ (QAGen2S)	38.62 ±0.85	12.83 ±1.33	62.68 ±2.59	46.35 ±2.76	11.61 ±1.40	2.01 ±0.53	33.43 ±3.79	24.97 ±3.07
Semi-Automatic (SA) (*n* annotated answers + ϕ T5)								
$n = 10$	51.11 ±1.71	24.39 ±1.84	59.04 ±2.03	46.56 ±1.94	58.54 ±3.39	29.69 ±4.74	38.97 ±5.76	31.07 ±5.05
$n = 25$	54.10 ±2.58	27.89 ±2.58	59.33 ±3.45	47.22 ±3.11	62.04 ±1.54	34.72 ±1.21	42.65 ±2.26	34.40 ±2.02
$n = 50$	54.12 ±1.19	29.06 ±1.24	58.89 ±1.52	46.02 ±1.45	63.31 ±2.07	35.97 ±2.29	43.37 ±1.61	34.21 ±2.32
$n = 100$	57.28 ±2.11	33.09 ±2.48	61.88 ±4.53	50.84 ±2.96	63.48 ±2.49	37.11 ±2.22	41.86 ±2.95	33.71 ±2.71
Generation Only (GO) (η)								
QAGen2S (BART-base)	47.38 ±0.66	19.01 ±1.33	51.43 ±3.48	35.18 ±3.85	18.12 ±1.85	7.42 ±1.86	38.49 ±1.42	27.36 ±1.86
QAGen (LLaMA2)	51.44 ±1.58	22.42 ±3.86	61.96 ±3.21	48.76 ±3.24	59.83 ±0.56	34.21 ±1.92	44.31 ±2.68	37.23 ±2.86
Bootstrap (BS) η **with** $n = 100$								
QAGen2S (Bootstrapped)	48.91 ±1.23	21.79 ±1.64	55.40 ±2.06	45.48 ±1.75	21.36 ±10.09	8.05 ±5.61	38.72 ±2.54	32.33 ±2.01
QAGen (Bootstrapped)	49.52 ±1.53	21.44 ±1.96	60.11 ±2.32	52.31 ±2.03	34.81 ±4.23	22.52 ±1.63	39.52 ±3.81	33.77 ±3.99

Table 1: F1 and EM scores of a reader on the test splits when the reader is fine-tuned on the obtained datasets. The best scores for each domain dataset are indicated by **bold** cells, the best scores where no fully-labeled domain dataset is used are indicated by underlined cells. For experiment, the mean and standard deviation of 5 runs are reported. (*): The base reader was not further fine-tuned on a domain dataset.

the annotated ones from the original training sets, and generate corresponding questions with ϕ. For every annotated answer span from the training set, at most one question is generated. The procedure is analogous for **GAO** with ψ. The results reported in Table 1 show significant improvements compared to the baseline for the **GQO** approach using the T5-based ϕ. For *CovidQA*, even better scores can be achieved than when using the original training set. Only for the *TextbookQA* dataset almost no change in F1 is reported. This might be due to the format of the manually labeled questions, which vastly differs from the questions in the dataset used to train ϕ. A comparison of *TextbookQA* questions, as well as QA examples obtained by the different models can be found in B.2.

Due to the strong performance of the **GQO** approach, we further investigate how the number of manually annotated answer spans impacts the performance. We randomly sample $n = 10, 25, 50, 100$ answer spans and use ϕ (T5) to obtain related questions. To prevent overfitting of the reader, the model is fine-tuned for 5 epochs (instead of 20). The results in Table 1 suggest that, while a performance increase for *BankQA* and *CovidQA* with only 10 annotated answer spans can be observed, having more annotated answer spans also lead to better results. For *BioASQ*, the performance even slightly decreases for $n = 10, 25, 50$, but 100 answer spans account for less than 10 percent of the manually labeled answer spans in the training set.

4.3 Evaluation of Generation-Only and Generator Bootstrapping

Here, we use η to generate QA pairs from all contexts (see A.3 for details). The results in Table 1 shows that the QA pairs generated by *QAGen* slightly increase the reader's performance, do no catch up with the semi-automatic approach. On the other hand, the QA pairs generated by *QAGen2S* decrease the reader's performance on all domains. Differences to Shakeri et al. (2020) are given in C.

Finally, we examine if η can improved by being *bootstrapped* on the new domain. For this, we further fine-tune η for two epochs on 100 QA pairs obtained with ϕ (T5). Compared to the non-bootstrapped variant, bootstrapping show improvements for *QAGen2S*, but lowers the performance of *QAGen*. Even with bootstrapping, *GO* lags behind the *SA* approach.

5 Conclusion

We have investigated semi-automatic methods for acquiring domain-specific QA datasets, and have shown that utilizing annotated answer spans alongside an answer-aware question generator surpasses other methods in performance, whereas bootstrapping domain-specific LLM generators with a limited number of annotated samples remains an open challenge. Our results suggest future research should prioritize identifying potential answer spans for further advancements in QA dataset acquisition.

Ethical Considerations

The proposed methods aim to support the annotation process of QA datasets, and our results indicate that human annotations continue to be indispensable to achieve the best possible quality.

For the BankQA dataset, we can assure that appropriate working conditions were guaranteed for all persons involved in the annotation of the samples.

Limitations

We are unable to share the confidential data from the BankQA dataset, which prevents others from replicating our results or conducting further research with this dataset. It is important to emphasize that all our experiments were conducted to the best of our knowledge and belief.

It is important to note that this work focuses explicitly on extractive QA, where answers are located in a known context. While this eliminates the risk of falsely generated answers in a productive QA system, it does not guarantee the correctness of the generated questions and answers. This could lead to falsely predicted answers, highlighting the need to question an answer and consider the surrounding context in real-world applications, as is standard in any QA system.

Furthermore, the diverse nature of language, data, and domains may yield varied results. Additionally, obtaining basic requirements like a large-scale QA dataset for fine-tuning base models is not readily available in every language. This limitation also applies to LLMs such as LLaMA2, which was fine-tuned on documents from a limited number of languages.

Moreover, utilizing LLMs to generate synthetic data incurs significant computational expenses. Due to these costs and time constraints, we could not utilize larger LMs that might offer even better performance.

Acknowledgments

This work was funded by the German Federal Ministry of Education and Research (BMBF), Program "FH-Kooperativ", Project "SCENT" (ID:13FH003KX0).

References

Llm prompting guide. `https://huggingface.co/docs/transformers/main/tasks/prompting`. Accessed: 2024-05-02.

Chris Alberti, Daniel Andor, Emily Pitler, Jacob Devlin, and Michael Collins. 2019. Synthetic qa corpora generation with roundtrip consistency. *arXiv preprint arXiv:1906.05416*.

Max Bartolo, Tristan Thrush, Robin Jia, Sebastian Riedel, Pontus Stenetorp, and Douwe Kiela. 2021. Improving question answering model robustness with synthetic adversarial data generation. *arXiv preprint arXiv:2104.08678*.

Ying-Hong Chan and Yao-Chung Fan. 2019. A recurrent bert-based model for question generation. In *Proceedings of the 2nd workshop on machine reading for question answering*, pages 154–162.

Kevin Clark, Minh-Thang Luong, Quoc V. Le, and Christopher D. Manning. 2020. Electra: Pre-training text encoders as discriminators rather than generators. *Preprint*, arXiv:2003.10555.

Tim Dettmers, Artidoro Pagnoni, Ari Holtzman, and Luke Zettlemoyer. 2023. Qlora: Efficient finetuning of quantized llms. *Preprint*, arXiv:2305.14314.

Jacob Devlin, Ming-Wei Chang, Kenton Lee, and Kristina Toutanova. 2018. Bert: Pre-training of deep bidirectional transformers for language understanding. *arXiv preprint arXiv:1810.04805*.

Adam Fisch, Alon Talmor, Robin Jia, Minjoon Seo, Eunsol Choi, and Danqi Chen. 2019. Mrqa 2019 shared task: Evaluating generalization in reading comprehension. *arXiv preprint arXiv:1910.09753*.

Timothy J Hazen, Shehzaad Dhuliawala, and Daniel Boies. 2019. Towards domain adaptation from limited data for question answering using deep neural networks. *arXiv preprint arXiv:1911.02655*.

Aniruddha Kembhavi, Minjoon Seo, Dustin Schwenk, Jonghyun Choi, Ali Farhadi, and Hannaneh Hajishirzi. 2017. Are you smarter than a sixth grader? textbook question answering for multimodal machine comprehension. In *Proceedings of the IEEE Conference on Computer Vision and Pattern recognition*, pages 4999–5007.

Hongyin Luo, Shang-Wen Li, Mingye Gao, Seunghak Yu, and James Glass. 2021. Cooperative self-training of machine reading comprehension. *arXiv preprint arXiv:2103.07449*.

Timo Möller, Anthony Reina, Raghavan Jayakumar, and Malte Pietsch. 2020. COVID-QA: A question answering dataset for COVID-19. In *Proceedings of the 1st Workshop on NLP for COVID-19 at ACL 2020*, Online. Association for Computational Linguistics.

Timo Möller, Julian Risch, and Malte Pietsch. 2021. Germanquad and germandpr: Improving non-english question answering and passage retrieval. *arXiv preprint arXiv:2104.12741*.

Raul Puri, Ryan Spring, Mostofa Patwary, Mohammad Shoeybi, and Bryan Catanzaro. 2020. Training question answering models from synthetic data. *arXiv preprint arXiv:2002.09599*.

Pranav Rajpurkar, Jian Zhang, Konstantin Lopyrev, and Percy Liang. 2016. Squad: 100,000+ questions for machine comprehension of text. *arXiv preprint arXiv:1606.05250*.

Siamak Shakeri, Cicero dos Santos, Henghui Zhu, Patrick Ng, Feng Nan, Zhiguo Wang, Ramesh Nallapati, and Bing Xiang. 2020. End-to-end synthetic data generation for domain adaptation of question answering systems. In *Proceedings of the 2020 Conference on Empirical Methods in Natural Language Processing (EMNLP)*, pages 5445–5460.

Hugo Touvron, Louis Martin, Kevin Stone, Peter Albert, Amjad Almahairi, Yasmine Babaei, Nikolay Bashlykov, Soumya Batra, Prajjwal Bhargava, Shruti Bhosale, et al. 2023. Llama 2: Open foundation and fine-tuned chat models. *arXiv preprint arXiv:2307.09288*.

George Tsatsaronis, Georgios Balikas, Prodromos Malakasiotis, Ioannis Partalas, Matthias Zschunke, Michael R Alvers, Dirk Weissenborn, Anastasia Krithara, Sergios Petridis, Dimitris Polychronopoulos, et al. 2015. An overview of the bioasq large-scale biomedical semantic indexing and question answering competition. *BMC bioinformatics*, 16:1–28.

Thomas Wolf, Lysandre Debut, Victor Sanh, Julien Chaumond, Clement Delangue, Anthony Moi, Pierric Cistac, Tim Rault, Rémi Louf, Morgan Funtowicz, Joe Davison, Sam Shleifer, Patrick von Platen, Clara Ma, Yacine Jernite, Julien Plu, Canwen Xu, Teven Le Scao, Sylvain Gugger, Mariama Drame, Quentin Lhoest, and Alexander M. Rush. 2020. Huggingface's transformers: State-of-the-art natural language processing. *Preprint*, arXiv:1910.03771.

Wayne Xin Zhao, Kun Zhou, Junyi Li, Tianyi Tang, Xiaolei Wang, Yupeng Hou, Yingqian Min, Beichen Zhang, Junjie Zhang, Zican Dong, et al. 2023. A survey of large language models. *arXiv preprint arXiv:2303.18223*.

A Appendix

A.1 Dataset stats

We share details about the QA datasets obtained by the different approaches in Table 2. Table 3 contains stats about the test splits for each domain dataset.

A.2 Fine-tuning and Hyperparameters

In the following, we explain the fine-tuning and hyperparameters used for each model in more detail.

A.2.1 Reader

We used the already fine-tuned and publicly available models *deepset/electra-base-squad2* and *deepset/gelectra-base-germanquad* from Huggingface (Wolf et al., 2020) as our base models. During fine-tuning on the domain datasets, we use the *AdamW optimizer* with a *learning rate* of 5×10^{-5}, a *weight decay* of 0.01, and a *learning rate warm-up* of 10 percent. A *batch size* of 16 is used. We performed experiments with and without gradient clipping and report the best results. We fine-tune the reader for 20 epochs and keep the checkpoint after the last epoch. Due to the small number of annotated QA pairs in each dataset, we decided against further sampling a validation split from the training data and perform no early-stopping. During fine-tuning and inference, a *maximum sequence length* of 384 and a *stride* of 128 is used.

A.2.2 Answer-Aware Question Generator (T5)

For the T5-based AA-QG, we use the already pre-trained and publicly available models *valhalla/t5-base-qg-hl* and *dehio/german-qg-t5-quad* from Huggingface. These models were not further fine-tuned in our experiments.

A.2.3 QAGen2S

We fine-tune a BART encoder-decoder model as described by Shakeri et al. (2020). Due to hardware limitations, we use *base* variant of BART (*facebook/bart-base* for English / *Shahm/bart-german* for German) as our base models. The base model is fine-tuned on SQuAD / GermanQuAD for 5 epochs with a *batch size* of 8. A *gradient accumulation size* of 3 is used. The *AdamW optimizer* with a *learning rate* of 3×10^{-5} with a *warm-up* of 10 percent is used. The model epoch with the lowest Cross Entropy loss on the dev / test split is used as final model.

A.2.4 QAGen

We used the 7B variant of LLaMA 2 as our base model and fine-tuned it for question and answer generation on *SQuAD* for English / *GermanQuAD* for German for 5 epochs. For memory-efficient fine-tuning, we used QLoRA (Dettmers et al., 2023), with an alpha of 16 and 10 percent dropout. A batch size of 8 and a gradient accumulation step

Dataset	# Contexts	# QAs	Avg. Context Length	Avg. Question Length	Avg. Answer Length
BankQA					
Original	310	776	438.66	43.25	106.04
Ann. Answers + ϕ (T5)	310	751	438.66	63.07	104.79
Ann. Answers + ϕ (LLaMA2)	310	776	438.66	73.65	106.04
Ann. Questions + ψ (QAGen2S)	310	645	438.66	43.51	34.73
QAGen2S (BART-base)	310	788	438.66	58.66	51.63
QAGen (LLaMA2)	308	1303	440.93	63.63	74.89
BioASQ					
Original	1192	1205	1436.94	64.28	13.99
Ann. Answers + ϕ (T5)	1192	4070	1436.94	66.43	9.05
Ann. Answers + ϕ (LLaMA2)	1192	1275	1436.94	95.41	13.99
Ann. Questions + ψ (QAGen2S)	1192	1096	1436.94	64.42	16.20
QAGen2S (BART-base)	1192	2993	1436.94	58.26	22.04
QAGen (LLaMA2)	1192	5811	1436.94	57.59	25.94
CovidQA					
Original	117	614	4356.21	55.57	70.83
Ann. Answers + ϕ (T5)	117	611	4356.21	60.04	70.99
Ann. Answers + ϕ (LLaMA2)	108	614	4351.13	97.3	70.83
Ann. Questions + ψ (QAGen2S)	117	72	4356.21	54.07	92.64
QAGen2S (BART-base)	117	11	4356.21	60.00	64.27
QAGen (LLaMA2)	117	571	4356.18	57.95	27.51
TextbookQA					
Original	311	1185	2919.46	57.09	12.79
Ann. Answers + ϕ (T5)	311	3893	2919.46	58.08	9.95
Ann. Answers + ϕ (LLaMA2)	311	1185	2919.46	64.65	12.79
Ann. Questions + ψ (QAGen2S)	311	859	2919.46	57.58	30.08
QAGen2S (BART-base)	311	512	2919.46	52.96	23.92
QAGen (LLaMA2)	311	1483	2919.46	54.23	21.42

Table 2: Details about the datasets obtained from different labeling approaches. The lengths refer to the average number of characters.

size of 2 is used. We used AdamW as an optimizer with a learning rate of 2×10^{-4} and a warm-up of 10 percent. The following format was used for fine-tuning and inference:

```
Context: {context}
Question: {question}
Answer: {answer}
```

For German data, we translated the format into German.

A.3 Decoding

For the decoding, i.e., the generation of questions and answers, the following parameters were used for all models:

- **Question Generation**: We follow the generation parameters reported by Shakeri et al. (2020), namely, *Top K+Nucleus sampling*. We set $k = 20$ and the token probability mass to $p = 0.95$. For the QAGen2S model, we sample up to 10 unique questions for each context and keep the ones with the highest LM scores during answer generation (*LM Filtering*, also proposed by Shakeri et al. (2020)). For QA-Gen, up to 5 unique questions are generated for each context. No filtering is applied.
- **Answer Generation**: We use greedy decoding to generate one answer span for every (context, question)-pair. If the generated answer span is not included in the context, the (context, question)-pair is discarded.

Following known prompting guidelines (pro), we came up with the following template for prompting LLaMA2 for answer generation:

```
Generate a question for the given
context and answer, so that the
question can be answered by the
given answer. Only output the question.
Context: {context}
Answer: {answer}
Question:
```

Dataset	# Contexts	# QAs	Avg. Context Length	Avg. Question Length	Avg. Answer Lenght
BankQA	78	223	400.42	44.64	98.39
BioASQ	298	319	1450.12	63.59	12.9
CovidQA	30	159	4389.73	55.75	66.84
TextbookQA	78	318	2997.72	52.19	12.29

Table 3: Details about the test splits. The lengths refer to the average number of characters.

We translated the prompt for German data.

B Questions and Answers

B.1 Examples

For comparison, examples of questions and answers obtained by the different approaches are given for *BioASQ* in Table 4, and *TextbookQA* in Tables 5 and 6. Due to the high context length of samples in *CovidQA*, no examples are given for the dataset.

B.2 TextbookQA Questions

The format of the annotated questions in the *TextbookQA* dataset differ from those in the *SQuAD* dataset on which the QA generators are fine-tuned on. In the following, we give some examples of questions:

TextbookQA:

- *this much of the municipal groundwater supplies in the united states are polluted.*
- *crude oil is a mixture of many different*
- *which of these substances has the highest freezing point?*
- *in hyperopia, the eyeball is*
- *when an earthquake happens, we say that its __________ was located 100 miles northwest of san francisco.*

SQuAD1.1:

- *To whom did the Virgin Mary allegedly appear in 1858 in Lourdes France?*
- *"The Closer I get to You" was recorded with which artist?*
- *In therapy, what does the antibacterial interact with?*
- *At what age did Chopin leave Poland?*
- *What does SDK stand for?*

The questions presented in *SQuAD* (and the other datasets *GermanQuAD*, *BioASQ*, *CovidQA* and *BankQA*) are mostly well structured, i.e., end with a question mark and contain w-words, while the questions in *TextbookQA* are more diversely structured and do not always follow the syntax of a question.

C QAGen2S Setup Differences

We identified two main differences between our setup and the setup used by Shakeri et al. (2020), which might explain the differences in performance:

1. **The number of contexts the QAs were generated on**: Due to limited compute- and time resources, we did not craw additional domain contexts to generate QA pairs on. Thus, the number of samples generated by Shakeri et al. (2020) is a multiple of ours.

2. **Smaller generator**: Due to limited compute- and time resources, we used the smaller *bart-base* variant, compared to *bart-large*.

Passage: A mutation in the alpha-synuclein gene has recently been linked to some cases of familial Parkinson's disease (PD). We characterized the expression of this presynaptic protein in themidbrain, striatum, and temporal cortex of control, PD, and dementia with Lewy bodies (DLB) brain. Control brain showed punctate pericellular immunostaining. PD brain demonstrated alpha-synucleinimmunoreactivity in nigral Lewy bodies, pale bodies and abnormal neurites. Rare neuronal soma in PD brain were immunoreactive for alpha-synuclein. DLB cases demonstrated these findings as well asalpha-synuclein immunoreactivity in cortical Lewy bodies and CA2-3 neurites. These results suggest that, even in sporadic cases, there is an early and direct role for alpha-synuclein in the pathogenesis of PD and the neuropathologically related disorder DLB.	
Original:	
Q: Against which protein is the antibody used for immonostaining of Lewy bodies raised?	A: alpha-Synuclein
Annotated Answer + ϕ (T5):	
Q: What protein is associated with the pathogenesis of Parkinson's disease?	A: alpha-Synuclein
Annotated Answer + ϕ (LLaMA):	
Q: What is the relationship between alpha-synuclein and Parkinson's disease (PD)?	A: alpha-Synuclein
Annotated Question + ψ (QA2S):	
Q: Against which protein is the antibody used for immonostaining of Lewy bodies raised?	A: punctate pericellular immunostaining
QAGen2S (BART):	
Q1: What gene has been linked to some cases of familial Parkinson's disease?	A1: alpha-synuclein gene
Q2: What gene has recently been linked to some cases of familial Parkinson's disease?	A2: alpha-synuclein gene
Q3: What does DLB stand for?	A3: Lewy bodies
QAGen (LLaMA):	
Q1: Punctate pericellular immunostaining was shown in what part of the brain?	A1: Control
Q2: What gene is associated with familial Parkinson's?	A2: alpha-synuclein
Q3: In familial PD, alpha-synuclein is linked to which gene?	A3: alpha-synuclein
Q4: What does PD stand for?	A4: Parkinson's disease
Q5: What gene has recently been linked to some cases of familial Parkinson's disease?	A5: alpha-synuclein

Table 4: Example QA pairs for a context of the *BioASQ* dataset.

Passage: The Paleozoic is the furthest back era of the Phanerozoic and it lasted the longest. But the Paleozoic was relatively recent, beginning only 570 million years ago. [...] The Paleozoic begins and ends with a supercontinent. At the beginning of the Paleozoic, the supercontinent Rodinia began to split up. At the end, Pangaea came together. A mountain-building event is called an orogeny. Orogenies take place over tens or hundreds of millions of years. [...] Geologists find evidence for the orogenies that took place while Pangaea was forming in many locations. For example, Laurentia collided with the Taconic Island Arc during the Taconic Orogeny. The remnants of this mountain range make up the Taconic Mountains in New York. The Taconic Orogeny is an example of a collision between a continent and a volcanic island arc. Laurentia experienced other orogenies as it merged with the northern continents. The southern continents came together to form Gondwana. When Laurentia and Gondwana collided to create Pangaea, the Appalachians rose. Geologists think they may once have been higher than the Himalayas are now. Pangaea was the last supercontinent on Earth. Evidence for the existence of Pangaea was what Alfred Wegener used to create his continental drift hypothesis, which was described in the chapter Plate Tectonics. As the continents move and the land masses change shape, the shape of the oceans changes too. During the time of Pangaea, about 250 million years ago, most of Earths water was collected in a huge ocean called Panthalassa.	
Original:	
Q1: this mountain range grew much higher when gondwana and laurentia collided to create pangaea.	A1: the appalachians
Q2: the remnants of the taconic mountain range are found in ______________.	A2: new york
Annotated Answer + ϕ (T5):	
Q1: When Laurentia and Gondwana collided, what mountain range rose?	A1: the appalachians
Q2: Where do the Taconic Mountains lie?	A2: new york
Annotated Answer + ϕ (LLaMA):	
Q1: What mountain range in North America is believed to have formed during the collision between Laurentia and the Taconic Island Arc during the Taconic Orogeny?	A1: the appalachians
Q2: What was the name of the mountain range that formed during the orogeny that occurred when Laurentia collided with the Taconic Island Arc?	A2: new york
Annotated Question + ψ (QA2S):	
Q1: this mountain range grew much higher when gondwana and laurentia collided to create pangaea.	A1: the Appalachians rose
Q2: the remnants of the taconic mountain range are found in ______________.	A2: Taconic Mountains in New York
QAGen2S (BART):	
Q1: Pangaea was the last supercontinent on Earth	A1: Pangaea came together
Q2: Pangaea was the last supercontinent on Earth.	A2: Pangaea came together
QAGen (LLaMA):	
Q1: How many years ago did most of Earth's water collect in a huge ocean called Panthalassa?	A1: 250 million years ago
Q2: The Paleozoic is the furthest back era of what?	A2: Phanerozoic
Q3: What are the Paleozoic and Phanerozoic eras?	A3: era of the Phanerozoic
Q4: When was the Paleozoic?	A4: 570 million years ago
Q5: How long did the Paleozoic last?	570 million years

Table 5: Example QA pairs for a context of the *TextbookQA* dataset. We observed that the ϕ (LLaMA) sometimes fails to formulate questions that are answered by the provided span.

Passage: Most fossils are preserved by one of five processes outlined below (Figure 1.1): Most uncommon is the preservation of soft-tissue original material. Insects have been preserved perfectly in amber, which is ancient tree sap. [...] Scientists collect DNA from these remains and compare the DNA sequences to those of modern counterparts. The most common method of fossilization is permineralization. After a bone, wood fragment, or shell is buried in sediment, mineral-rich water moves through the sediment. This water deposits minerals into empty spaces and Five types of fossils: (a) insect preserved in amber, (b) petrified wood (permineralization), (c) cast and mold of a clam shell, (d) pyritized ammonite, and (e) compression fossil of a fern. produces a fossil. Fossil dinosaur bones, petrified wood, and many marine fossils were formed by permineralization. When the original bone or shell dissolves and leaves behind an empty space in the shape of the material, the depression is called a mold. The space is later filled with other sediments to form a matching cast within the mold that is the shape of the original organism or part. Many mollusks (clams, snails, octopi, and squid) are found as molds and casts because their shells dissolve easily. The original shell or bone dissolves and is replaced by a different mineral. For example, calcite shells may be replaced by dolomite, quartz, or pyrite. If a fossil that has been replace by quartz is surrounded by a calcite matrix, mildly acidic water may dissolve the calcite and leave behind an exquisitely preserved quartz fossil. Some fossils form when their remains are compressed by high pressure, leaving behind a dark imprint. Compression is most common for fossils of leaves and ferns, but can occur with other organisms. [...]	
Original:	
Q1: when insects are fossilized, it is usually in	A1: amber
Q2: when water deposits minerals into empty spaces to produce a fossil, it is called	A2: permineralization.
Q3: the most common way that fossil leaves are made is by	A3: compression
Annotated Answer + ϕ (T5):	
Q1: What is the oldest tree sap that was used as a foundation to contain fossils?	A1: amber
Q2: What is the process by which dinosaur bones are made?	A2: permineralization.
Q3: What process is most common for fossils of leaves and ferns?	A3: compression
Annotated Answer + ϕ (LLaMA):	
Q1: Which of the following processes is the most common method of fossilization?	A1: amber
Q2: Which process of fossilization most commonly results in the formation of fossil dinosaur bones?	A2: permineralization.
Q3: What is the most common method of fossilization?	A3: compression
Annotated Question + ψ (QA2S):	
Q1: when insects are fossilized, it is usually in	A1: amber
Q2: when water deposits minerals into empty spaces to produce a fossil, it is called	A2: mold
Q3: the most common way that fossil leaves are made is by	A3: compression
QAGen2S (BART):	
Q: What is the most common method of fossilization?	A: permineralization
QAGen (LLaMA):	
Q1: What are most fossil preserved by?	A1: mineral-rich water
Q2: When a clam's shell is replaced, what is its shape?	A2: mold
Q3: How are most fossils preserved?	A3: permineralization
Q4: What is the original bone or shell replaced with?	A4: different mineral

Table 6: Second example of QA pairs obtained for a context of the *TextbookQA* dataset.

CO-Fun: A German Dataset on Company Outsourcing in Fund Prospectuses for Named Entity Recognition and Relation Extraction

Neda Foroutan and **Markus Schröder** and **Andreas Dengel**
Smart Data & Knowledge Services Dept., DFKI GmbH
Trippstadter Str. 122, 67663 Kaiserslautern, Germany
{neda.foroutan,markus.schroeder,andreas.dengel}@dfki.de

Abstract

The process of cyber mapping gives insights in relationships among financial entities and service providers. Centered around the outsourcing practices of companies within fund prospectuses in Germany, we introduce a dataset specifically designed for named entity recognition and relation extraction tasks. The labeling process on 948 sentences was carried out by three experts which yields to 5,969 annotations for four entity types (Outsourcing, Company, Location and Software) and 4,102 relation annotations (Outsourcing–Company, Company–Location). State-of-the-art deep learning models were trained to recognize entities and extract relations showing first promising results. An anonymized version of the dataset, along with guidelines and the code used for model training, are publicly available at `https://doi.org/10.5281/zenodo.12745116`.

Keywords— Cyber Mapping, Financial Domain, Dataset, Corpus, German, Named Entity Recognition, Relation Extraction, Conditional Random Fields, BERT, RoBERTa

1 Introduction

Cyber incidents, such as data breaches and ransomware attacks, pose potential risks to financial stability since banks and other institutes increasingly outsource processes and services to information and communication technology providers (Adelmann et al., 2020). To discover cyber risks, a conceptual method is "cyber mapping" – a process which links the financial network (e.g. banks, funds, insurance companies) with the cyber network (e.g. cloud services, datacenters, software providers) (Brauchle et al., 2020). Evidences for constructing a mapping could be descriptions of outsourced services and companies in the financial domain. A promising source to collect such hints can be found in publicly available fund prospectuses. In these documents, German Capital Management Companies (CMCs) have to state outsourcing companies and their provided services for a particular fund. To give an example, consider the following simplified sentence.

Example 1 *Die Gesellschaft hat Rechenzentrumsleistungen auf die Mercurtainment & CO KGaA ausgelagert.*
'The company has outsourced data center services to Mercurtainment & CO KGaA.'

To extract structured information, a usual step in Natural Language Processing (NLP) is the application of Named Entity Recognition (NER) to discover entities in texts. In our scenario, there are outsourced services (e.g. "data center services") and companies (e.g. "Mercurtainment & CO KGaA"). After that, Relation Extraction (RE) is commonly used to predict relationships between entities, in our case, services and companies. In order to train such NLP models, a dataset with ground truth labels is necessary.

In this paper, we present a novel dataset to support the process of cyber mapping using NLP models. Our annotated corpus consists of 948 sentences extracted from 1,054 German fund prospectuses. In total, 5,969 named entity annotations and 4,102 relation annotations were added by experts to acquire ground truth data. We conducted experiments with our dataset to evaluate the performance of trained models.

2 Related Work

NER and RE tasks are fundamental building blocks for extracting information within unstructured texts (for a recent survey see (Nasar et al., 2022)). For training models, several corpora have been built to cover specific domains, for example, the biomedical area (Khettari et al., 2023) or for clinical purpose (Báez et al., 2020). Some of them targeting specific languages, like Kazakh (Yeshpanov et al., 2022) and Italian (Paccosi and Aprosio, 2022). Regarding German language, Schiersch et al. (2018) collected data from tweets, news documents and

RSS feeds to create a corpus with named entities such as Disasters, Triggers, Location, Organizations, Persons as well as 15 relations of the mobility and industry domain.

More related to our scenario is the business domain since the discovery of relationships between company entities is of interest. Here, Schön et al. (2018) provided an English dataset for recognizing companies, products and their relations to each other. The data was gathered from company homepages, business news portals, forums and social media channels. Instead of considering the product in the business relation, extracting the relation between two companies within unstructured texts – called Business Relation Extraction – has attracted attention in research and industry. Khaldi et al. (2021) presented a web-based English dataset for the business relation extraction between organizations. They also recommended a relation classifier using multilevel knowledge of entities to predict five types of relations between companies, i.e. Investment, Cooperation, Sale-purchase, Competition and Legal proceedings. In subsequent work, the authors provided the BIZREL dataset (Khaldi et al., 2022), a multilingual corpus in French, Spanish and Chinese in addition to their introduced English dataset. Similarly, they collected data via keyword queries using well-known search engines and the same five types of relations. Zuo et al. (2017) proposed a method of iteratively extracting asymmetric business relations like "owner-of" between two companies and indicating the relation direction between them. They evaluated their suggested method on two datasets based on *New York Times* News articles.

In the financial domain, Jabbari et al. (2020) created a French corpus including 26 entity types and 12 relation types gathered from French financial newspapers. They trained a BERT-based (Devlin et al., 2018) NER model on five types of entities (Person, Location, Organization, Role and Currency) and investigated a rule-based RE method for the relationship around the Role entity (i.e. "hasRole"). Moreover, Hillebrand et al. (2022) recommended a BERT-based architecture that employs a Gated Recurrent Units tagger coupled with conditional label masking to jointly predict entities tags sequentially and links the predicted entities. Additionally, they built a dataset from real-world German financial documents. The main entity type is Key Performance Indicators (KPI), such as revenue or interest expenses. Generally, entity classes include KPI, change of it, its monetary value and their sub-types. Linked relations are considered between KPI and sub-types or their values.

Still, there seems to be no dataset which meets our requirements. To train NLP models for performing cyber mapping, we need realistic sentences in German language explicitly mentioning outsourced services in the financial domain. Therefore, we built our own dataset from fund prospectuses which is covered in detail in the next section.

3 Corpus Creation

The corpus was created in a collaborative research lab of Deutsche Bundesbank[1] (the central bank of the Federal Republic of Germany) and the German Research Center for Artificial Intelligence[2] (DFKI). In this project a set of 1,054 publicly available fund prospectuses (PDFs) were collected from websites of 37 well-known Capital Management Companies (CMCs) in Germany.

Our corpus is built upon these documents by first converting the PDFs into plain texts using Apache's PDFBox[3] text stripper routine. The fund prospectuses consist of 92 pages on average, however, only a certain section in the document, usually no longer than a full or half page, mentions outsourced services. Conveniently, independent of the CMC, such a section is commonly named 'Auslagerung [Outsourcing]' followed by a section labeled 'Interessenkonflikte [Conflicts of Interest]' with some minor variations. Therefore, with a proper regular expression we were able to identify the beginning and end of these sections in our plain texts. For sentence splitting, Apache's OpenNLP[4] sentence detector loaded with a German pre-trained model[5] was applied. To turn words with hyphens such as 'Dienst–leistung [ser–vice]' in their hyphenless form, string matching and string manipulation was performed with regular expressions. Finally, 1,267 sentences could be collected of comparable shape as Example 1. However, roughly half of them assemble bullet point lists.

3.1 Annotation Process

Three subject-matter experts of the Deutsche Bundesbank annotated the corpus with named entities and relations. For this, a Graphical User Interface

[1] `https://www.bundesbank.de/en`
[2] `https://www.dfki.de/`
[3] `https://pdfbox.apache.org/`
[4] `https://opennlp.apache.org/`
[5] `opennlp-de-ud-gsd-sentence-1.0-1.9.3.bin`

(GUI) was provided which is depicted in Figure 1. Sentences are randomly distributed to the annotators who independently worked on them. The experts sporadically annotated sentences during their working hours and were done after around one month. Because of limited time available, same texts were not sent to multiple annotators, therefore, inter-annotator agreement is not considered. The following named entity types could be annotated: 'Auslagerung' [Outsourcing], 'Unternehmen' [Company], 'Ort' [Location] and Software. Additionally, we allow users to declare the following two relationships: Outsourcing–Company and Company–Location. Annotators could mark sentences as ignorable if they recognize that no entities are present (this happened 85 times). To reduce annotation efforts, our system pre-annotates sentences with already collected named entities once they exactly match in the text. A three-page annotation guideline was provided to give a brief tutorial and to cover special cases during the annotation process.

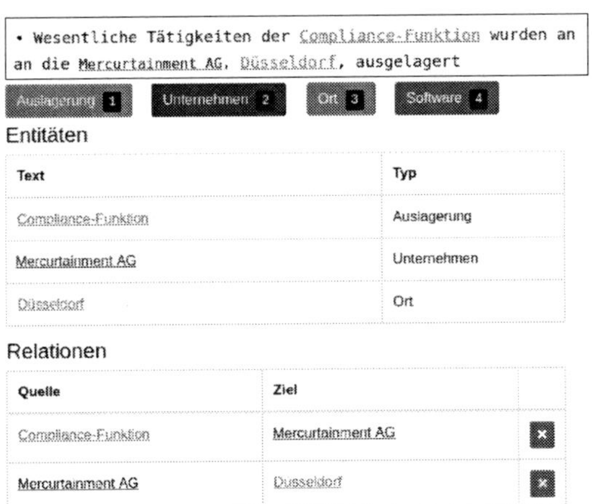

Figure 1: A graphical user interface in German to annotate a sentence (top) with named entities (center) and relations (bottom). Entity types are 'Auslagerung [Outsourcing]', 'Unternehmen [Company]', 'Ort [Location]' and Software.

3.2 Resulting Dataset

Our Company Outsourcing in Fund Prospectuses (CO-Fun) dataset consists of 948 sentences (900 textually unique) with 5,969 named entity annotations, including 2,340 Outsourced Services, 2,024 Companies, 1,594 Locations and only 11 Software annotations. While the sentences have an average length of 314.8 ± 393.7[6] characters (w/o markup tags) and 44.9 ± 53.5 tokens, they contain 6.3 ± 9 annotations on average. All sentences contain at least one named entity, while 193 of them do not include any relations. Without considering duplicates, our corpus mentions 270 outsourced services, 323 companies, 84 locations and one software. Although, the software type is very limited with only one unique entity, we still decided to leave it in the dataset. Regarding relations, we have found 2,573 Outsourcing-Company relationships and 1,529 links between Companies and Locations (in total 4,102). On average, 4.3 ± 8.6 relations can be found in the sentences.

The raw data of CO-Fun consists of records formatted in JavaScript Object Notation[7] (JSON) which are sequenced in a JSON-line file (UTF-8 encoding). Each entry has the following properties: In the `text` property, the annotated text is present in form of HyperText Markup Language (HTML). We use `span` tags[8] to annotate named entities in text. Annotations are uniquely identified with a Universally Unique Identifier (UUID) (`id`). The entity's type is given in the `type` attribute which can be one of the following options: 'Auslagerung' [Outsourcing], 'Unternehmen' [Company], 'Ort' [Location] or Software. Additionally, named entities are listed in a JSON array called `entities`, again with their ID, type and covered text. Another JSON array (`relations`) defines the relationships between a source entity (`src`) and a target entity (`trg`).

Gathering a dataset about outsourced services to German companies naturally raises concerns of potential misuse. We therefore performed an anonymization of all companies by randomly swapping their names with other companies with the same postfix e.g. GmbH. Replacing name of companies by their postfix helps to maintain legal and business consistency. For this, we make use of OffeneRegister[9] – a database dump of the German commercial register.

The anonymized CO-Fun dataset is publicly available[10] under MIT license together with other related materials such as the annotation guideline, derived data and source code. In the next section,

[6]using $\pm$ notation for standard deviation

[7]`https://www.json.org/`

[8]`https://html.spec.whatwg.org/#the-span-element`

[9]`https://offeneregister.de/`

[10]`https://doi.org/10.5281/zenodo.12745116`

initial experiments with our dataset are presented.

4 Experiments

In our study, we investigated extracting two types of structured information from our corpus. Firstly, we recognized entities within our sentences by applying Named Entity Recognition (NER) methods. Secondly, we detected relations between entities using a Relation Extraction (RE) model.

4.1 NER and RE Methods

We employed two NER models: Conditional Random Fields (CRF) and BERT (Bidirectional Encoder Representations from Transformer) (Devlin et al., 2018). For applying CRF, we utilized CRFsuit toolkit (Okazaki, 2007) and derived the features related to the token itself and its neighborhood information. The token features include the word itself, its part-of-speech tag, whether the word is capitalized, starts with a capital letter or is a digit. In order to extract tokens and their part-of-speech tags, the SpaCy library and the "de_core_news_sm" German language model was ustilized. Additionally, we considered the bigram and trigram characters the word ends with, and each token was assigned the same bias feature. Furthermore, we captured neighborhood information from the two words to the left and right of the token, checking their part-of-speech tags and if they start with a capital letter or are entirely in uppercase. If a token is at the beginning or end of the sentence, we provided BOS or EOS as the left or right neighbor to CRF, respectively.

In order to apply the pre-trained BERT model, we fine-tuned the German language version of it on our data using the SpaCy 3 library[11]. As a result, the model with about 110 million parameters is capable of predicting our four entity types.

As a basis for relation extraction, we used SpaCy's tutorial for a relation extraction component on GitHub[12]. In this project, the pre-trained RoBERTa model (Liu et al., 2019) is fine-tuned to extract relations.

4.2 NER and RE Datasets

Before applying the CRF model, each sentence was tokenized and an Inside-Outside-Beginning (IOB) format label was assigned to each token. The IOB scheme gives each token one of the following labels: B-ent, I-ent or O. If the token is the beginning of an entity, it is labeled as B-ent (begin-of-entity) but if the token is part of the entity but not its beginning, I-ent (inside-of-entity) is assigned to the token. If the token does not belong to any of the entity types, it is tagged as 'O'. After IOB tagging the tokens of each sentence, we randomly split the data with the proportion of 80%, 10% and 10% to create the training, development and test sets, respectively.

The same sentences that were used in each set (training, development and test) for the CRF model were also considered for the BERT model. In other words, the sentences in each set from split data for CRF model were labeled in the format required for training the BERT model. Each set includes a list of sentences with the list of tuples containing their entities and labels specified with the location of the entity in the sentence (start and end character position as well as entity label). For later reuse, the training, development and test sets were converted into SpaCy binary files.

The dataset split from the NER case is the same for the RE datasets. For each sentence, a list of entities and relations were prepared. A structure is provided for each entity to record an entity's text and label as well as its character and token position in text. Each relation entry has a label and refers to a child and head entity using their token positions. Ultimately, dataset text files were converted to binary files in SpaCy format.

The training, development and test sets in text format for the CRF model, as well as in text and SpaCy formats for the BERT and RoBERTa models are publicly available in the anonymized CO-Fun dataset[13].

4.3 NER and RE Results

The CRF model was run for 100 iterations using the L-BFGS training algorithm. The L1 and L2 regularization terms tuned by using cross validation are 0.05 and 0.01, respectively. Default values were used for the remaining hyperparameters provided by the CRFsuite toolkit. The BERT model was fine-tuned on the German training set for unlimited number of epoches with the early-stopping of 1600 and batch size of 128 (default values of Spacy library). The initial learning rate and warm-up step were set to $5 * 10^{-5}$ and 250, respectively.

[11] https://spacy.io/

[12] https://github.com/explosion/projects/tree/v3/tutorials/rel_component

[13] https://doi.org/10.5281/zenodo.12745116

Also, the L2 weight decay rate with value of 0.01 was applied. Similarly, the RoBERTa model was fine-tuned for 52 epochs with a 1,000 batch size. Moreover, there is a max-length parameter representing the furthest distance at which existing relation is sought between any two entities. We discovered in tests that the model performed best with a max-length of 20. Remaining parameters were configured the same as in BERT's configuration. Both models were trained on a NVIDIA RTX A6000 GPU which took 40 minutes (NER) and 9 minutes (RE).

We evaluated the performance of our models in terms of exact match using precision, recall and F1-score (Nadeau and Sekine, 2007). Table 1 demonstrates the performance of the NER and RE models on the training and test sets of CO-Fun, measured by micro-averaging. Both models of CRF and BERT face overfitting as test F1-scores show lower scores than their training values. However, CRF performs better than BERT on the test set with F1-score of 94%. Furthermore, RoBERTa could classify 86.35% of the relations that exist between entities in the test set.

	Train			Test		
Models	P	R	F1	P	R	F1
CRF	96.7	95.1	95.9	95.7	93.0	94.3
BERT	99.8	94.2	97.0	92.9	91.5	92.2
RoBERTa	89.4	81.7	85.3	86.5	86.1	86.3

Table 1: Precision (P), Recall (R) and F1-score results of the NER models (CRF and BERT) and RE model (RoBERTa) on the training and test sets of CO-Fun.

5 Conclusion and Future Work

In this paper, we introduced an annotated German dataset called CO-Fun which is a NER and RE dataset on company outsourcing in fund prospectuses. Our dataset contains 948 sentences with 5,969 named entity annotations (including Outsourced Services, Companies, Location and Software) and 4,102 annotated relations (Outsourcing–Company and Company–Location). Applying state-of-the-art NER and RE models showed promising performances on CO-Fun.

In the future, we aim to extend this dataset with similar data and improve the performance of applied models by using additional knowledge, for example, by incorporating knowledge graphs in the training process. Additionally, we will investigate the impact of bullet points within sentences, examining whether their presence facilitates processing for NER and RE tasks.

6 Acknowledgements

This work was funded by the TransferLab Cybermapping which is a collaborative transfer lab of Deutsche Bundesbank and DFKI. We would like to thank Christoph Fricke, Ezgi Delikanli and Jacqueline Krüger at Deutsche Bundesbank for their support and contributions to the dataset.

7 Ethical Considerations

Gathering a dataset about outsourced services to German companies naturally raises concerns of potential misuse. Although the raw information is publicly available, but not in a digested and enriched version, the cooperating official authority raised concerns that the real information could be misused by malicious players. To address these concerns, an anonymization strategy was chosen.

8 Limitations

One limitation is the number of annotators and a missing agreement. To annotate the sentences, we had only three experts sporadically annotated sentences during their working hours. As the experts had limited time, same texts were not sent to multiple annotators, therefore, inter-annotator agreement was not considered.

Another limitation for our corpus was the small set of 1,054 documents provided to us: in fact, only few pages contain some sentences about outsourcing statements. Reasons for that are our special language, domain and selection constraints, thus, it was not possible for us to compile a larger dataset. Moreover, the collaborating partner could not provide more documents since other regulatory data is usually confidential and we are not allowed to get access to them. As a result, the size of the Co-Fun dataset is rather small.

References

Frank Adelmann, Jennifer A. Elliott, Ibrahim Ergen, Tamas Gaidosch, Nigel Jenkinson, Tanai Khiaonarong, Anastasiia Morozova, Nadine Schwarz, and Christopher J. Wilson. 2020. Cyber risk and financial stability : It's a small world after all. *IMF Staff Discussion Notes*.

Pablo Báez, Fabián Villena, Matías Rojas, Manuel Durán, and Jocelyn Dunstan. 2020. The chilean waiting list corpus: a new resource for clinical named entity recognition in spanish. In *Proceedings of the 3rd Clinical Natural Language Processing Workshop, ClinicalNLP@EMNLP 2020, Online, November 19, 2020*, pages 291–300. Association for Computational Linguistics.

Jan-Philipp Brauchle, Matthias Göbel, Jens Seiler, and Christoph von Busekist. 2020. Cyber mapping the financial system. Technical report, Carnegie Endowment for International Peace. http://www.jstor.org/stable/resrep24291.

Jacob Devlin, Ming-Wei Chang, Kenton Lee, and Kristina Toutanova. 2018. BERT: pre-training of deep bidirectional transformers for language understanding. *CoRR*, abs/1810.04805.

Lars Patrick Hillebrand, Tobias Deußer, Tim Dilmaghani Khameneh, Bernd Kliem, Rüdiger Loitz, Christian Bauckhage, and Rafet Sifa. 2022. KPI-BERT: A joint named entity recognition and relation extraction model for financial reports. In *26th International Conference on Pattern Recognition, ICPR 2022, Montreal, QC, Canada, August 21-25, 2022*, pages 606–612. IEEE.

Ali Jabbari, Olivier Sauvage, Hamada Zeine, and Hamza Chergui. 2020. A french corpus and annotation schema for named entity recognition and relation extraction of financial news. In *Proceedings of The 12th Language Resources and Evaluation Conference, LREC 2020, Marseille, France, May 11-16, 2020*, pages 2293–2299. European Language Resources Association.

Hadjer Khaldi, Farah Benamara, Amine Abdaoui, Nathalie Aussenac-Gilles, and EunBee Kang. 2021. Multilevel entity-informed business relation extraction. In *Natural Language Processing and Information Systems - 26th International Conference on Applications of Natural Language to Information Systems, NLDB 2021, Saarbrücken, Germany, June 23-25, 2021, Proceedings*, volume 12801 of *Lecture Notes in Computer Science*, pages 105–118. Springer.

Hadjer Khaldi, Farah Benamara, Grégoire Siegel, Camille Pradel, and Nathalie Aussenac-Gilles. 2022. How's business going worldwide? a multilingual annotated corpus for business relation extraction. In *13th Conference on Language Resources and Evaluation (LREC 2022)*, pages 3696–3705. European Language Resources Association (ELRA).

Oumaima El Khettari, Solen Quiniou, and Samuel Chaffron. 2023. Building a corpus for biomedical relation extraction of species mentions. In *The 22nd Workshop on Biomedical Natural Language Processing and BioNLP Shared Tasks, BioNLP@ACL 2023, Toronto, Canada, 13 July 2023*, pages 248–254. Association for Computational Linguistics.

Yinhan Liu, Myle Ott, Naman Goyal, Jingfei Du, Mandar Joshi, Danqi Chen, Omer Levy, Mike Lewis, Luke Zettlemoyer, and Veselin Stoyanov. 2019. Roberta: A robustly optimized BERT pretraining approach. *CoRR*, abs/1907.11692.

David Nadeau and Satoshi Sekine. 2007. A survey of named entity recognition and classification. *Lingvisticae Investigationes*, 30:3–26.

Zara Nasar, Syed Waqar Jaffry, and Muhammad Kamran Malik. 2022. Named entity recognition and relation extraction: State-of-the-art. *ACM Comput. Surv.*, 54(1):20:1–20:39.

Naoaki Okazaki. 2007. CRFsuite: a fast implementation of conditional random fields (CRFs). https://www.chokkan.org/software/crfsuite/.

Teresa Paccosi and Alessio Palmero Aprosio. 2022. KIND: an italian multi-domain dataset for named entity recognition. In *Proceedings of the Thirteenth Language Resources and Evaluation Conference, LREC 2022, Marseille, France, 20-25 June 2022*, pages 501–507. European Language Resources Association.

Martin Schiersch, Veselina Mironova, Maximilian Schmitt, Philippe Thomas, Aleksandra Gabryszak, and Leonhard Hennig. 2018. A german corpus for fine-grained named entity recognition and relation extraction of traffic and industry events. In *Proceedings of the Eleventh International Conference on Language Resources and Evaluation, LREC 2018, Miyazaki, Japan, May 7-12, 2018*. European Language Resources Association (ELRA).

Saskia Schön, Veselina Mironova, Aleksandra Gabryszak, and Leonhard Hennig. 2018. A corpus study and annotation schema for named entity recognition and relation extraction of business products. In *Proceedings of the Eleventh International Conference on Language Resources and Evaluation, LREC 2018, Miyazaki, Japan, May 7-12, 2018*. European Language Resources Association (ELRA).

Rustem Yeshpanov, Yerbolat Khassanov, and Huseyin Atakan Varol. 2022. Kaznerd: Kazakh named entity recognition dataset. In *Proceedings of the Thirteenth Language Resources and Evaluation Conference, LREC 2022, Marseille, France, 20-25 June 2022*, pages 417–426. European Language Resources Association.

Zhe Zuo, Michael Loster, Ralf Krestel, and Felix Naumann. 2017. Uncovering business relationships: Context-sensitive relationship extraction for difficult relationship types. In *Lernen, Wissen, Daten, Analysen (LWDA) Conference Proceedings, Rostock, Germany, September 11-13, 2017*, volume 1917 of *CEUR Workshop Proceedings*, page 271. CEUR-WS.org.

GERestaurant: A German Dataset of Annotated Restaurant Reviews for Aspect-Based Sentiment Analysis

Nils Constantin Hellwig
Media Informatics Group
University of Regensburg
Regensburg, Germany
nils-constantin.hellwig@ur.de

Jakob Fehle
Media Informatics Group
University of Regensburg
Regensburg, Germany
jakob.fehle@ur.de

Markus Bink
Media Informatics Group
University of Regensburg
Regensburg, Germany
markus.bink@student.ur.de

Christian Wolff
Media Informatics Group
University of Regensburg
Regensburg, Germany
christian.wolff@ur.de

Abstract

We present GERestaurant, a novel dataset consisting of 3,078 German language restaurant reviews manually annotated for Aspect-Based Sentiment Analysis (ABSA). All reviews were collected from Tripadvisor, covering a diverse selection of restaurants, including regional and international cuisine with various culinary styles. The annotations encompass both implicit and explicit aspects, including all aspect terms, their corresponding aspect categories, and the sentiments expressed towards them. Furthermore, we provide baseline scores for the four ABSA tasks Aspect Category Detection, Aspect Category Sentiment Analysis, End-to-End ABSA and Target Aspect Sentiment Detection as a reference point for future advances. The dataset fills a gap in German language resources and facilitates exploration of ABSA in the restaurant domain.

1 Introduction

Sentiment analysis (SA), also named opinion mining, is a research area in natural language processing (NLP) which involves the computational classification of individuals' sentiments, opinions and emotions. This usually involves categorizing sentiments into three polarities: positive, neutral and negative.

SA can be applied at both document- (Hellwig et al., 2023; Schmidt et al., 2022; Tripathy et al., 2017) and sentence-level (Liu, 2010). However, if a document or sentence comprises a mixture of different sentiments, it's often impossible to assign a solely positive, negative or neutral label. As an example, consider the sentence "The salad tasted wonderful, but was quite expensive." of a restaurant review wherein positive sentiment is expressed towards the food while, concurrently, negative sentiment is expressed when addressing the food's price. To overcome this issue, Aspect-Based Sentiment Analysis (ABSA) has been extensively studied as it goes beyond assessing general sentiment and instead delves into a more granular examination of sentiment by linking particular aspects with corresponding sentiment polarities (Liu et al., 2005; Pontiki et al., 2015).

In this work, we introduce GERestaurant, a novel dataset comprising 3,078 German language restaurant reviews annotated for ABSA. It's the first German language dataset of sentences from restaurant reviews for ABSA. The annotations included the aspect term (if available), an aspect category selected from a predefined set of categories, and the sentiment or polarity expressed towards the aspect. The dataset is provided as a benchmark dataset for future research and parallels the widely used SemEval 2015 and 2016 restaurant datasets in terms of annotation scheme and annotation guidelines (Pontiki et al., 2015, 2016). Thus, it not only contributes to the availability of German language resources but also enables the exploration of new ABSA methods in the restaurant domain in the German language. Additionally, we provide a baseline performance by fine-tuning state-of-the-art (SOTA) transformer-based language models on the annotated dataset for typical ABSA tasks: Aspect Category Detection (ACD), Aspect Category Sentiment Analysis (ACSA), End-to-End ABSA

(E2E-ABSA) and Target Aspect Sentiment Detection (TASD).

2 Related Work

ABSA has attracted increasing attention, in part due to benchmark datasets and shared tasks from various domains that facilitated the development of machine learning approaches for solving ABSA tasks. For instance, various datasets from different domains frequently employed in ABSA research include:

- Ganu et al. (2009): A dataset comprising restaurant reviews in English, annotated with six pre-defined aspect categories assigned to sentiment polarities positive, neutral, negative, and conflict.
- Saeidi et al. (2016): SentiHood, a dataset of English sentences extracted from a question answering (QA) platform discussing urban neighbourhoods. Annotations for aspect terms, their associated aspect categories, and the sentiment expressed towards them were provided.
- Jiang et al. (2019): MAMS, a dataset of English Tweets on celebrities, products, and companies. All aspect terms were annotated, along with the sentiment polarity expressed towards them.

However, the development of methods addressing the subtasks in ABSA was particularly driven by the SemEval shared task workshop in the years from 2014 to 2016 and the associated publishing of human-annotated datasets for ABSA. These comprised sentences from reviews of laptops and restaurants.

SemEval-2014 Task 4 (Pontiki et al., 2014) was dedicated to ABSA and included annotations of aspect terms and the sentiment polarity expressed towards them. In addition, annotations of the aspect categories and the sentiment polarity expressed towards them are part of the provided dataset.

In the subsequent year, SemEval-2015 Task 12 (Pontiki et al., 2015) was published, which included annotations of all aspect terms, their corresponding aspect category and the sentiment polarity expressed towards the aspect terms. Moreover, annotations of implicit aspects were provided, meaning cases where a sentiment was expressed towards an aspect category, without the presence of an aspect term. In such cases, the aspect term was annotated as `"NULL"`.

SemEval-2016 Task 5 (Pontiki et al., 2016) encompassed the same three sentiment elements as SemEval-2015 Task 12 (Pontiki et al., 2015). In addition, subsets containing annotated sentences of hotel reviews and reviews in languages other than English were provided for each domain (Pontiki et al., 2015).

When examining datasets in German language, there is a scarcity of annotated datasets. The most prominent dataset in German language is the dataset published as part of the GermEval 2017 shared task (Wojatzki et al., 2017), which includes customer reviews concerning the "Deutsche Bahn", the German public train operator (Wojatzki et al., 2017). Reviews were annotated as a whole, rather than individual sentences separately (Wojatzki et al., 2017). Similar to the datasets introduced by Pontiki et al. (2015, 2016), annotations were provided for all aspect terms, their associated aspect categories, and the sentiment expressed towards the aspect terms.

Gabryszak and Thomas (2022) introduced the German language dataset MobASA, which comprises tweets from public transportation companies and channels related to barrier-free travel for handicapped passengers (Gabryszak and Thomas, 2022). Annotations covered aspect terms, their associated aspect categories, and the sentiments expressed towards each aspect term (Gabryszak and Thomas, 2022).

In the realm of customer reviews, other notable resources include the SCARE corpus (Sänger et al., 2016), comprising annotated application reviews from the Google Play Store, alongside annotations for aspect terms and sentiment polarities. Similarly, Fehle et al. (2023) introduced a dataset consisting of sentences from hotel reviews on Tripadvisor, whereby annotations are provided for the sentiments expressed towards the considered aspect categories.

3 Methodology

3.1 Data Acquisition

To gather German language restaurant reviews, Tripadvisor was selected as the data source. The five restaurants with the most customer reviews in the 25 most densely populated German cities as of

2022[1] were considered, covering a wide spectrum of restaurant types, including regional and international cuisine with various culinary styles. In the course of the COVID-19 pandemic, restaurant reviews were influenced by the associated hygiene measures. To prevent sentiment bias introduced by hygiene regulations we included all reviews posted during a period without mandated COVID-19 hygiene restrictions, specifically reviews from October 15, 2022, to October 15, 2023, were taken into account.

Overall, a total of 3,212 user reviews with a German language label on Tripadvisor were collected. The reviews were segmented into 13,426 sentences using the NLTK Tokenizer (Loper and Bird, 2002). It was observed that, despite the German language code label, some sentences were in languages other than German. Due to this, *langdetect*[2] was employed to ascertain the language of each sentence, leading to the rejection of 631 sentences which resulted in a total of 12,795 sentences in German.

Ultimately, the sentences underwent an anonymization process. Named entity recognition (NER) was employed using *spaCy* (*de_core_news_lg* model) (Honnibal and Montani, 2017) to replace locations, personal names, and time-related references with anonymized placeholders *"LOC"*, *"PERSON"* and *"DATE"*. Subsequently, regular expressions were employed to substitute any mentions of the restaurant's name in the sentences with the placeholder *"RESTAURANT_NAME"*.

[1]German Federal Statistical Office, population and population density as of December 31, 2022: `https://www.destatis.de/DE/Themen/Laender-Regionen/Regionales/Gemeindeverzeichnis/Administrativ/05-staedte.html`

[2]`https://pypi.org/project/langdetect`

3.2 Data Annotation

From the complete set of 12,795 sentences, a subset of 5,000 sentences was randomly sampled for annotation. Care was taken to ensure an equal distribution of sentences from reviews with 1, 2, 3, 4 and 5-star ratings (1,000 sentences each) [3]. This distribution was established so that each sentiment polarity occurs as evenly as possible across all sentences.

3.2.1 Annotation Task

As proceeded for SemEval-2015 (Pontiki et al., 2015) and SemEval-2016 (Pontiki et al., 2016), for a given sentence x, one or multiple triplets (a, c, p) should be assigned, where a represents the aspect term, c denotes the aspect category, and p indicates the sentiment expressed towards the aspect. The annotations included the positional information of the aspect terms within the text. Multiple aspect terms could be assigned to the same aspect category. Similarly, an aspect term could be assigned to multiple aspect categories at once. Examples are presented in Table 1 and an English language translation of the table is provided in Appendix A.1.

The four aspect categories `FOOD`, `SERVICE`, `AMBIENCE` and `PRICE` were considered, similar to the rating categories of the Zagat Survey (Lee and Teng, 2007) for restaurants. These categories can also be found on Tripadvisor, allowing users to optionally assign one to five stars to each category in addition to an overall star rating.

However, in contrast to the categories from the Zagat Survey and as preceded by Pontiki et al. (2015), `AMBIENCE` was used as an aspect category instead of *"Decor"* as it encompasses a slightly

[3]A customer reviewing a restaurant on Tripadvisor is obligated to provide both a star rating and a textual assessment.

Aspect Category	Triplets	Sentence
GENERAL-IMPRESSION	[('Restaurant', 'GENERAL-IMPRESSION', 'POSITIVE')]	*"Sehr schönes Restaurant."*
FOOD	[('Bratwurst', 'FOOD', 'POSITIVE')]	*"Die Bratwurst war unglaublich lecker und perfekt gewürzt."*
SERVICE	[('Bedienung', 'SERVICE', 'NEGATIVE')]	*"Bedienung leider nicht aufmerksam."*
AMBIENCE	[('NULL', 'AMBIENCE', 'NEGATIVE')]	*"Es war viel zu laut, wie im Club."*
PRICE	[('NULL', 'PRICE', 'NEUTRAL')]	*"Preislich ist das ok gewesen."*
PRICE, SERVICE	[('Preise', 'PRICE', 'NEUTRAL') ('Service', 'SERVICE', 'NEGATIVE')]	*"Preise sind ok und Service auch."*
FOOD, AMBIENCE, SERVICE	[('Essen', 'FOOD', 'POSITIVE'), ('Atmosphäre', 'AMBIENCE', 'POSITIVE'), ('Service', 'SERVICE', 'POSITIVE')]	*"Tolles Essen, tolle Atmosphäre und ganz netter und aufmerksamer Service!"*

Table 1: Annotated examples for all aspect categories.

broader scope. Furthermore, a fifth category called `GENERAL-IMPRESSION` was introduced, which captured aspects that pertain to the restaurant in a general sense, similar to the datasets for ABSA published in the realm of SemEval-2015 (Pontiki et al., 2015) and SemEval-2016 (Pontiki et al., 2016), whereby an aspect category was introduced that encompassed general aspects related to a laptop or a restaurant for which a review was written.

Implicit addressing of an aspect category should be annotated as well. In this case, `"NULL"` was assigned as the aspect term. For each aspect term within these categories, one of the following sentiment polarity labels should be applied: `POSITIVE`, `NEGATIVE`, `NEUTRAL` (indicating mild positivity or mild negativity sentiment) or `CONFLICT`. The `CONFLICT` label was assigned in case both positive and negative sentiments are expressed towards an aspect term.

Furthermore, as preceded by Pontiki et al. (2015), aspects should only be annotated if a sentiment was expressed towards them. For instance, in the sentence *"You can eat pizza there"*, no sentiment is expressed towards the aspect *"Pizza"* (aspect category: `FOOD`), and thus, the aspect should not be annotated accordingly.

3.2.2 Data Labelling Procedure

Three persons were tasked with annotating sentences in order to establish the gold standard labels. Similar to the approach employed by Pontiki et al. (2014), the annotation process commenced with one annotator (annotator *A*, M.Sc. media computer science student) annotating all 5,000 sentences and subsequently, each of the annotations by annotator *A* underwent inspection and validation by a second annotator *B*.

For the second annotation, a PhD student and an M.Sc. student, both specializing in media computer science, were tasked to review 2,500 annotations by annotator *A* each. All annotators had prior experience in annotating textual data in the field of SA, with the PhD student having prior experience in annotating text for ABSA.

The annotation process was facilitated using *LabelStudio*[4]. All annotators were provided with a comprehensive annotation guideline[5], which explained the user interface in *LabelStudio* specifically created for this annotation task and included examples for sentences in German language closely aligned with those provided in the annotation guideline employed by Pontiki et al. (2015).

In addition to annotating all triplets *(a, c, p)*, annotators were tasked to tick a checkbox when they encountered two or more sentences in an example instead of one, since the NLTK Tokenizer employed for sentence segmentation could potentially introduce errors. Another checkbox was provided to mark examples where customers addressed an aspect without conveying any sentiment. This allowed for the possibility of annotating them at a later point in time for future studies.

In 113 out of 5,000 sentences, annotator *B* proposed a label different to that assigned by annotator *A*. Among these, Annotator *A* accepted the revised label suggested by annotator *B* in 81 sentences. The annotation of the remaining 32 sentences was decided in consensus of the two annotators. In 16 sentences, both annotators opted to adopt the annotations provided by annotator *A*, in seven instances, the annotation of annotator *B* was adhered to. For the remaining nine sentences, a consensus was reached on an annotation distinct from their initially proposed annotations.

Among the 5,000 examples, 589 were excluded since they consisted of more than one sentence. Subsequently, out of the remaining 4,411 sentences, 1,291 were omitted since no sentiment was expressed towards aspects of the considered aspect categories and 42 sentences were removed since they encompassed at least one triplet with a conflict polarity, resulting in a total of 3,078 sentences with a total of 3,149 explicit and 1,165 implicit aspects.

3.3 Baseline Models

For a total of four typical ABSA tasks, we provide transformer-based baseline models. All models were loaded using the Hugging Face *transformers* library[6] and trained on two NVIDIA RTX A5000 GPU with 24 GB VRAM each. The implementation was conducted using Python version 3.11.5. To assess the performance of each model, we conducted a random 70-30 train-test split. The models were trained on the training set, consisting of 2,154 examples, and evaluated on the test set, containing 924 examples.

[4]Label Studio - Open Source Data Labelling Tool: `https://labelstud.io`

[5]`https://github.com/NilsHellwig/GERestaurant/blob/main/annotation_guideline.pdf`

[6]`https://pypi.org/project/transformers`

3.3.1 Aspect Category Detection (ACD) and Aspect Category Sentiment Analysis (ACSA)

Similar to Fehle et al. (2023), the identification of aspect categories (ACD) and the identification of both aspect categories and the sentiment polarity expressed towards them (ACSA) was treated as a multi-label classification task. Two base models were fine-tuned in this study: gbert-large[7] (337 million parameters) and gbert-base[8] (111 million parameters) by *deepset*. Both models are based on the BERT architecture and are pre-trained on large amounts of German language texts (Chan et al., 2020).

For training and validation, a batch size of 16, an epoch-number of 3 and a learning rate of 2e-5 (c.f. Devlin et al. (2018)) was used. As proceeded by Fehle et al. (2023), a prediction was considered a true positive, if the predicted aspect(s) of a sentence (including the sentiment polarity for ACSA) occurred in the ground truth labels.

3.3.2 End-to-End ABSA (E2E-ABSA)

E2E-ABSA is the task that aims at simultaneously identifying aspect terms and determining the sentiment polarity expressed towards them in a given text. As proceeded by Li et al. (2019), E2E-ABSA was conducted employing a BERT model for token classification. gbert-large and gbert-base were employed for this task as well. The task involved predicting a tag sequence $y = \{y_1, \ldots, y_T\}$, with each tag corresponding to a token in the sentence. The potential values for y_t encompass B-{POS, NEG, NEU}, I-{POS, NEG, NEU} or O. The tag denoted the beginning (B) and inside (I) of an aspect term, coupled with negative, neutral or positive sentiment and O, in case that a token was not a part of an aspect term.

For training, a binary cross-entropy loss was employed, and the sigmoid function was used as the activation function. Similar to the evaluations conducted by Li et al. (2019), learning rate was set to 2e-5, batch size was set to 16 and the model was trained for 1,500 steps. When calculating the evaluation metrics, the true positives included all correctly identified pairs of an aspect term and the sentiment polarity expressed towards it, similar to Zhang et al. (2023) and Li et al. (2019).

[7]`https://huggingface.co/deepset/gbert-large`
[8]`https://huggingface.co/deepset/gbert-base`

3.3.3 Target Aspect Sentiment Detection (TASD)

TASD is the task that leverages the full complexity of GERestaurants' annotations. Its objective is to identify all aspect terms, their associated aspect categories, and the sentiment expressed towards the aspect terms within a given text.

For the TASD task, the paraphrasing approach methodology introduced by Zhang et al. (2021) was employed. The paraphrase generation framework utilized is outlined in Appendix A.2. The polarity label `POSITIVE` was mapped to *"gut"* (Eng.: *"good"*) in the paraphrased label, `NEGATIVE` to *"schlecht"* (Eng.: *"bad"*) and `NEUTRAL` to *"ok"*. In the case of an implicit aspect, the aspect term was decoded as *"es"* (Eng.: *"it"*).

Both t5-large[9] (770 million parameters) and t5-base[10] (223 million parameters) were evaluated as the underlying seq2seq models. In terms of training parameters, batch size was set to 16, number of training epochs to 20 and learning rate to 3e-4, similar to Zhang et al. (2021). For evaluation, true positives encompassed all correctly identified triplets, meaning that all three sentiment elements (aspect term, aspect category and sentiment polarity) were identified correctly.

4 Results

4.1 Properties of the Annotated Dataset

Table 2 presents an overview of the frequency of triplets occurring with their respective aspect categories, reference types, and sentiment polarities in the overall dataset. The highest number of triplets was identified for the `FOOD` category (1,712 triplets), while the lowest count was observed for the `PRICE` category (255 triplets). Aspects were more frequently addressed explicitly (3,149 triplets) rather than implicitly (1,165 triplets). Positive sentiments were expressed towards the majority of identified aspects (2,339 triplets), followed by negative sentiments (1,795 triplets). A neutral sentiment was expressed towards 180 aspects.

Moreover, Table 3 presents the most frequently occurring aspect terms within each aspect category, and Table 4 shows the sample count for each triplet quantity. In the case of all aspect categories except for `GENERAL-IMPRESSION`, the most frequently occurring aspect term is equal to the name of the corresponding aspect category. Moreover, in more

[9]`https://huggingface.co/t5-large`
[10]`https://huggingface.co/t5-base`

	Positive		Negative		Neutral		Total	
Aspect Category	**Explicit**	**Implicit**	**Explicit**	**Implicit**	**Explicit**	**Implicit**	**Explicit**	**Implicit**
`GENERAL-IMPRESSION`	103	306	56	285	5	21	164	612
`FOOD`	880	83	532	98	109	10	1,521	191
`SERVICE`	514	69	316	177	10	0	840	246
`AMBIENCE`	312	26	99	42	6	0	417	68
`PRICE`	45	1	149	41	13	6	207	48
Total	1,854	485	1,152	643	143	37	3,149	1,165

Table 2: Aspect categories distribution per sentiment polarity and reference type for the annotated dataset.

Aspect Category	Description	Most Frequent Aspect Terms
`GENERAL-IMPRESSION`	Aspects related to the overall impression of the restaurant without focusing on the aforementioned aspect categories.	*Restaurant* (42) *RESTAURANT_NAME* (22) *LOC* (22) *Lokal* (12) *Brauhaus* (5)
`FOOD`	Aspects related to food in general or specific dishes and drinks.	*Essen* (302) *Bier* (46) *Speisen* (42) *Fleisch* (30) *Küche* (28)
`SERVICE`	Aspects related to service in general or the attitude and professionalism of staff, wait times, or service offerings such as takeout.	*Service* (209) *Bedienung* (125) *Personal* (90) *Kellner* (58) *Kellnerin* (17)
`AMBIENCE`	Aspects related to the ambiance and atmosphere in general or the environment of the restaurant's interior and exterior, including its decor and entertainment options.	*Ambiente* (103) *Atmosphäre* (51) *Lage* (13) *Lokal* (12) *Location* (10)
`PRICE`	Aspects related to price in general or the pricing of dishes, beverages, or other services offered by the restaurant.	*Preise* (30) *Preis* (25) *Essen* (14) *Preisen* (11) *Preis-Leistungsverhältnis* (10)

Table 3: Description of the aspect categories and their most frequent aspect terms.

# Triplets	1	2	3	4	5	6	7	8	9	16
# Sentences	2,236	590	168	57	14	7	3	1	1	1

Table 4: Sample count of each triplet quantity.

than two-thirds (2,236) of the 3,078 sentences, exactly one aspect or triplet was identified.

4.2 Comparison with the SemEval Datasets

As the dataset used in this work and the datasets from SemEval 2015 and 2016 are similar in terms of their domain and the type and depth of annotation, it is possible to compare dataset properties, such as their class distribution or language-specific features, such as the ratio of explicitly and implicitly expressed aspects. In order to ensure the comparability of the annotations of the GERestaurant dataset with the two SemEval datasets from 2015 and 2016, various adjustments had to be made, as although the datasets have undergone similar annotation procedures, the labels of the aspect categories are named and summarized differently: (1) The `PRICES` subcategories of the SemEval datasets were transformed to the `PRICE` aspect category; (2) the `RESTAURANT` category of the SemEval datasets was converted to the `GENERAL-IMPRESSION` category; (3) the `LOCATION` category of the SemEval datasets were integrated into the `AMBIENCE` category; and (4) The `DRINKS` category of the SemEval datasets was merged into the `FOOD` category.

Table 5 depicts the class balances of the five aspect categories as well as the polarity labels over the three datasets GERestaurant, SemEval 2015 and 2016. Subsequently, we consider a dataset as the combination of its train and test sets. The balance of the aspect classes of the SemEval datasets is almost identical, facilitated in part by the fact that almost the entire SemEval 2015 dataset, with

Dataset	Aspect Category					Polarity			Aspect Term Type	
	General Impression	Food	Service	Ambience	Price	Positive	Negative	Neutral	Implicit	Explicit
GERestaurant	18.0%	39.7%	25.2%	11.2%	5.9%	54.2%	41.6%	4.2%	27.0%	73.0%
SemEval 2015	20.6%	42.6%	17.7%	11.5%	7.5%	66.1%	30.0%	3.9%	24.9%	75.1%
SemEval 2016	20.6%	43.6%	17.9%	10.8%	7.1%	67.4%	28.3%	4.3%	24.8%	75.2%

Table 5: Comparison of the balances of the aspect category, the polarity labels and the ratio of implicitly and explicitly expressed aspect terms between the three ABSA datasets GERestaurant, SemEval 2015 and SemEval 2016.

1,700 of its 1,702 annotated examples, has been integrated into the SemEval 2016 dataset, which contains a total of 2,384 annotated examples. The overall class distribution of the GERestaurant dataset is also quite similar to that of the SemEval datasets and differs primarily in a 6.5 percentage point higher occurrence of the SERVICE aspect category, while all other aspect classes occur slightly less frequently. Considering the distributions of the polarity classes across all aspects, while the overall distributions of the polarity labels between the SemEval datasets are again very similar, bigger differences can be observed between the GERestaurant and SemEval datasets. The proportion of the neutral label remains comparably low between all datasets, but the negative polarity label was assigned up to 12 percentage points more frequently in the GERestaurant dataset at 41.6%, while the positive label was correspondingly annotated less frequently compared to the SemEval datasets, constituting only 54.5% of the total. Similar to the distribution of aspect classes, the ratio of implicitly and explicitly expressed aspects is very similar between all corpora. While the two SemEval datasets have an almost identical ratio, the GERestaurant dataset is only slightly above in terms of implicit aspects with an increase of about two percentage points, resulting in 27.0% implicitly expressed aspects and 73.0% explicitly expressed aspects.

4.3 Baseline Performance

The performance achieved in the four ABSA tasks under consideration are presented in Table 6. For predicting the five aspect classes (ACD task), gbert-large demonstrated the highest performance, achieving micro and macro F1 scores of 91.82 and 90.73, respectively, placing it approximately three percentage points ahead of gbert-base. Similarly, in the classification of aspects combined with their polarity (ACSA), the best performance was observed when employing gbert-large, which attained micro and macro F1 scores of 85.14 and 58.61, respectively. The micro-averaged F1 score surpassed that achieved with gbert-base by approximately 11 percentage points, while in the case of the macro-averaged F1 score, it exceeded it by around 22 percentage points.

Task	Language Model	F1 Micro	F1 Macro
ACD	gbert-large	91.82	90.73
	gbert-base	88.76	87.82
ACSA	gbert-large	85.14	58.61
	gbert-base	73.85	36.63
E2E-ABSA	gbert-large	81.61	77.28
	gbert-base	74.66	50.25
TASD	t5-large	68.86	59.03
	t5-base	64.74	54.32

Table 6: Performance for the baseline models per ABSA subtask.

For the E2E-ABSA task, gbert-large demonstrated the highest performance as well, achieving a micro F1 score of 81.61 and a macro F1 score of 77.28. This performance improvement over gbert-base, with a micro F1 score of 74.66 and a macro F1 score of 50.25.

Similarly to the previous tasks, again, the large model variant exceeded the performance of the base model by about four to five percentage points, resulting in a micro F1 score of 68.86 a macro F1 score of 59.03 for the t5-large model.

5 Limitations

While GERestaurant provides a valuable resource for studying ABSA in the German restaurant domain, it also comes with limitations. Firstly, the annotations are based on human judgments, which introduces subjectivity and potential inconsistencies. Furthermore, the quality of annotations is constrained by the fact that each example was not independently annotated by multiple annotators, but rather, one annotator annotated all sentences and their annotations were reviewed by another annotator.

Furthermore, the imbalance among the five aspect categories can be considered a limitation of this work. For instance, the fewest number of aspects (251) are assigned to the PRICE category, while the majority of aspects (1,676) are assigned to the FOOD category. Similar imbalances are observed in terms of sentiment polarities, with only 175 aspects toward which a neutral sentiment was expressed, compared to 2,283 aspects towards which a positive sentiment was expressed, which represents more than half of all aspects.

6 Discussion

GERestaurant offers a novel resource for ABSA research in the German language, specifically within the restaurant domain. Comprising 3,078 manually annotated sentences, GERestaurant encompasses both implicit and explicit aspects, annotated by human annotators. This is the third German language dataset besides GermEval 2017 (Wojatzki et al., 2017) and MobASA (Gabryszak and Thomas, 2022) to include annotations of aspect terms, aspect categories, and sentiment polarities of both implicit and explicit aspects.

The analysis of the class distributions of the aspect classes and the sentiment polarities between the German GERestaurant dataset and the English SemEval 2015 and 2016 datasets revealed a strong similarity of the ABSA-specific annotations of the datasets. The close correlation between the datasets opens up a variety of possibilities to compare the performance of ABSA methods on English and German datasets and could provide conclusions on how far methods can be used across languages despite language-specific differences in the datasets and methods.

Our provided baseline performance on all four ABSA tasks is in line with the performance reported in similar studies using transformer-based models for such tasks across various domains. However, it's important to acknowledge that the comparability of the results is limited due to variations in the number of aspect categories and the number of training examples across the datasets.

A micro-averaged F1 score of 91.82 was achieved in the ACD task, consistent with micro-averaged F1 scores obtained on other datasets, e.g. a micro-averaged F1 score of 90.89 on the restaurant dataset of SemEval from 2014 (Sun et al., 2019) or a micro-averaged F1 score of 90.6 on the dataset comprising hotel reviews presented by Fehle et al. (2023).

In the ACSA task, a micro-averaged F1 score of 85.14 was obtained, slightly exceeding the reported scores achieved on other datasets. Cai et al. (2020) reported micro-averaged F1 scores of 64.67 and 74.55 for the restaurant datasets of SemEval 2015 and 2016, respectively. Aßenmacher et al. (2021) reported a micro-averaged F1 score of 65.5 on GermEval 2017 and Fehle et al. (2023) reported a micro-averaged F1 score of 80.9 on the dataset comprising hotel reviews.

For the E2E-ABSA task, a micro-averaged F1 score of 81.61 was attained. Lower scores were reported for other domains, e.g. Li et al. (2019) reported a micro-averaged F1 score of 73.22 when considering the restaurant domain and 60.43 when considering the laptop domain, using datasets composed of examples from the SemEval datasets from 2014 to 2016.

The performance in the TASD task (micro-averaged F1 score of 68.86) falls within the spectrum of results observed by Zhang et al. (2021), who represented triplets as phrases, reporting a micro-averaged F1 score of 63.06 for the restaurant dataset of SemEval 2015 and a micro-averaged F1 score of 71.97 for the restaurant dataset of SemEval 2016.

7 Conclusion & Future Work

This work presents GERestaurant, a novel German language dataset comprising 3,078 restaurant reviews annotated for ABSA. The dataset covers implicit and explicit aspects, providing annotations for aspect terms, aspect categories, and sentiment polarities. Transformer-based SOTA models were fine-tuned on the training set provided by us for four common ABSA tasks, and subsequently evaluated on the test set.

In future work, GERestaurant could be utilized for developing improved machine learning models with focus on the German language for various ABSA tasks, building upon the methods introduced in this work and further improving the presented baseline values. Moreover, future work may involve expanding the aspect categories by incorporating fine-grained attributes, as in the SemEval datasets from 2015 and 2016, or including information about not only aspect phrases but also opinion phrases, in order to reflect the entire quadruple of an aspect-based annotation (Pontiki et al., 2015, 2016).

8 Ethical Considerations

The collection of our dataset adhered to strict privacy guidelines to safeguard the rights of users. Our primary objective was to extract reviews while avoiding the collection of personalized data that could potentially identify individual users or specific user groups. Furthermore, any direct references to individuals or restaurants were systematically anonymized to prevent indirect identification of individuals or establishments.

The dataset and its annotations are available upon request from the authors to ensure responsible usage for academic purposes, thus preserving the original intent of data collection. The Python code for data collection and data cleaning is accessible via GitHub[11].

Despite our meticulous data collection and anonymization procedures, inherent limitations and ethical considerations persist. Our dataset may not fully represent the spectrum of user sentiment due to potential bias in review writing, as reviewers may only represent a specific subset of the population. Furthermore, the transferability of knowledge about review semantics and characteristics across different rating platforms cannot be guaranteed.

References

Matthias Aßenmacher, Alessandra Corvonato, and Christian Heumann. 2021. Re-evaluating germeval17 using german pre-trained language models. In *Proceedings of the Swiss Text Analytics Conference 2021, Winterthur, Switzerland, June 14-16, 2021 (held online due to COVID19 pandemic)*, volume 2957 of *CEUR Workshop Proceedings*.

Hongjie Cai, Yaofeng Tu, Xiangsheng Zhou, Jianfei Yu, and Rui Xia. 2020. Aspect-category based sentiment analysis with hierarchical graph convolutional network. In *Proceedings of the 28th international conference on computational linguistics*, pages 833–843.

Branden Chan, Stefan Schweter, and Timo Möller. 2020. German's next language model. In *Proceedings of the 28th International Conference on Computational Linguistics*, pages 6788–6796.

Jacob Devlin, Ming-Wei Chang, Kenton Lee, and Kristina Toutanova. 2018. Bert: Pre-training of deep bidirectional transformers for language understanding. *arXiv preprint arXiv:1810.04805*.

Jakob Fehle, Leonie Münster, Thomas Schmidt, and Christian Wolff. 2023. Aspect-based sentiment analysis as a multi-label classification task on the domain of german hotel reviews. In *Proceedings of the 19th Conference on Natural Language Processing (KONVENS 2023)*, pages 202–218.

Aleksandra Gabryszak and Philippe Thomas. 2022. Mobasa: Corpus for aspect-based sentiment analysis and social inclusion in the mobility domain. In *Proceedings of the First Computing Social Responsibility Workshop within the 13th Language Resources and Evaluation Conference*, pages 35–39.

Gayatree Ganu, Noemie Elhadad, and Amélie Marian. 2009. Beyond the stars: improving rating predictions using review text content. In *WebDB*, volume 9, pages 1–6.

Nils Constantin Hellwig, Markus Bink, Thomas Schmidt, Jakob Fehle, and Christian Wolff. 2023. Transformer-based analysis of sentiment towards german political parties on twitter during the 2021 election year. In *Proceedings of the 6th International Conference on Natural Language and Speech Processing (ICNLSP 2023)*, pages 84–98.

Matthew Honnibal and Ines Montani. 2017. spacy 2: Natural language understanding with bloom embeddings, convolutional neural networks and incremental parsing. *To appear*, 7(1):411–420.

Qingnan Jiang, Lei Chen, Ruifeng Xu, Xiang Ao, and Min Yang. 2019. A challenge dataset and effective models for aspect-based sentiment analysis. In *Proceedings of the 2019 conference on empirical methods in natural language processing and the 9th international joint conference on natural language processing (EMNLP-IJCNLP)*, pages 6280–6285.

Hsin-Hsien Lee and Wei-Guang Teng. 2007. Incorporating multi-criteria ratings in recommendation systems. In *2007 IEEE International Conference on Information Reuse and Integration*, pages 273–278. IEEE.

Xin Li, Lidong Bing, Wenxuan Zhang, and Wai Lam. 2019. Exploiting bert for end-to-end aspect-based sentiment analysis. In *Proceedings of the 5th Workshop on Noisy User-generated Text (W-NUT 2019)*, pages 34–41.

Bing Liu. 2010. Sentiment analysis and subjectivity. *Handbook of natural language processing*, 2(2010):627–666.

Bing Liu, Minqing Hu, and Junsheng Cheng. 2005. Opinion observer: analyzing and comparing opinions on the web. In *Proceedings of the 14th international conference on World Wide Web*, pages 342–351.

Edward Loper and Steven Bird. 2002. Nltk: The natural language toolkit. *Preprint*, arXiv:cs/0205028.

Maria Pontiki, Dimitrios Galanis, Harris Papageorgiou, Suresh Manandhar, and Ion Androutsopoulos. 2015. Semeval-2015 task 12: Aspect based sentiment analysis. In *Proceedings of the 9th international workshop on semantic evaluation (SemEval 2015)*, pages 486–495.

[11] https://github.com/NilsHellwig/GERestaurant

Maria Pontiki, Dimitris Galanis, Haris Papageorgiou, Ion Androutsopoulos, Suresh Manandhar, Mohammed AL-Smadi, Mahmoud Al-Ayyoub, Yanyan Zhao, Bing Qin, Orphée De Clercq, et al. 2016. Semeval-2016 task 5: Aspect based sentiment analysis. In *ProWorkshop on Semantic Evaluation (SemEval-2016)*, pages 19–30. Association for Computational Linguistics.

Maria Pontiki, Dimitris Galanis, John Pavlopoulos, Harris Papageorgiou, Ion Androutsopoulos, and Suresh Manandhar. 2014. Semeval-2014 task 4: Aspect based sentiment analysis. In *Proceedings of the 8th International Workshop on Semantic Evaluation (SemEval 2014)*, pages 27–35, Dublin, Ireland. Association for Computational Linguistics.

Marzieh Saeidi, Guillaume Bouchard, Maria Liakata, and Sebastian Riedel. 2016. Sentihood: Targeted aspect based sentiment analysis dataset for urban neighbourhoods. In *Proceedings of COLING 2016, the 26th International Conference on Computational Linguistics: Technical Papers*, pages 1546–1556.

Mario Sänger, Ulf Leser, Steffen Kemmerer, Peter Adolphs, and Roman Klinger. 2016. Scare—the sentiment corpus of app reviews with fine-grained annotations in german. In *Proceedings of the Tenth International Conference on Language Resources and Evaluation (LREC'16)*, pages 1114–1121.

Thomas Schmidt, Jakob Fehle, Maximilian Weissenbacher, Jonathan Richter, Philipp Gottschalk, and Christian Wolff. 2022. Sentiment analysis on twitter for the major german parties during the 2021 german federal election. In *Proceedings of the 18th Conference on Natural Language Processing (KONVENS 2022)*, pages 74–87.

Chi Sun, Luyao Huang, and Xipeng Qiu. 2019. Utilizing bert for aspect-based sentiment analysis via constructing auxiliary sentence. In *Proceedings of NAACL-HLT*, pages 380–385.

Abinash Tripathy, Abhishek Anand, and Santanu Kumar Rath. 2017. Document-level sentiment classification using hybrid machine learning approach. *Knowledge and Information Systems*, 53:805–831.

Michael Wojatzki, Eugen Ruppert, Sarah Holschneider, Torsten Zesch, and Chris Biemann. 2017. Germeval 2017: Shared task on aspect-based sentiment in social media customer feedback. *Proceedings of the GermEval*, pages 1–12.

Wenxuan Zhang, Yang Deng, Xin Li, Yifei Yuan, Lidong Bing, and Wai Lam. 2021. Aspect sentiment quad prediction as paraphrase generation. In *Proceedings of the 2021 Conference on Empirical Methods in Natural Language Processing*, pages 9209–9219.

Wenxuan Zhang, Yue Deng, Bing Liu, Sinno Jialin Pan, and Lidong Bing. 2023. Sentiment analysis in the era of large language models: A reality check. *arXiv preprint arXiv:2305.15005*.

A Appendix

A.1 Examples from the Annotated Dataset

Aspect Category	Triplets	Sentence
GENERAL-IMPRESSION	[('restaurant', 'GENERAL-IMPRESSION', 'POSITIVE')]	*"Very nice restaurant."*
FOOD	[('sausage', 'FOOD', 'POSITIVE')]	*"The sausage was incredibly delicious and perfectly seasoned."*
SERVICE	[('Service', 'SERVICE', 'NEGATIVE')]	*"Service unfortunately not attentive."*
AMBIENCE	[('NULL', 'AMBIENCE', 'NEGATIVE')]	*"It was much too loud, like in a club."*
PRICE	[('NULL', 'PRICE', 'NEUTRAL')]	*"Price-wise it was ok."*
PRICE, SERVICE	[('Prices', 'PRICE', 'NEUTRAL') ('service', 'SERVICE', 'NEGATIVE')]	*"Prices are ok and service as well."*
FOOD, AMBIENCE, SERVICE	[('food', 'FOOD', 'POSITIVE'), ('atmosphere', 'AMBIENCE', 'POSITIVE'), ('service', 'SERVICE', 'POSITIVE')]	*"Great food, great atmosphere and really nice and attentive service!"*

Table 7: Annotated examples for all aspect categories (English translation).

A.2 Paraphrase Generation Framework

A.2.1 Explicit Aspect

Sentence (Input)	Die Pasta war super, aber die Bedienung war unfreundlich!
Label	[('Pasta', 'FOOD', 'POSITIVE'), ('Bedienung', 'SERVICE', 'NEGATIVE')]
Paraphrased Label	Essen ist gut, weil Pasta gut ist [SSEP] Service ist schlecht, weil Bedienung schlecht ist [SSEP]

Table 8: Paraphrasing of an explicit aspect's label.

A.2.2 Implicit Aspect

Sentence (Input)	Es hat richtig gut geschmeckt!
Label	[('NULL', 'FOOD', 'POSITIVE')]
Paraphrased Label	Essen ist gut, weil es gut ist [SSEP]

Table 9: Paraphrasing of an implicit aspect's label.

How to Translate SQuAD to German? A Comparative Study of Answer Span Retrieval Methods for Question Answering Dataset Creation

Jens Kaiser[1] and **Agnieszka Falenska**[1,2]
[1]Institute for Natural Language Processing, University of Stuttgart, Germany
[2]Interchange Forum for Reflecting on Intelligent Systems, University of Stuttgart, Germany
`firstname.lastname@ims.uni-stuttgart.de`

Abstract

This paper investigates the effectiveness of automatic span retrieval methods for translating SQuAD to German through a comparative analysis across two scenarios. First, we assume no gold-standard target data and find that TAR, a method using an alignment model, results in the highest QA scores. Secondly, we switch to a scenario with a small target data and assess the impact of retrieval methods on fine-tuned models. Our results indicate that while fine-tuning generally enhances model performance, its effectiveness is dependent on the alignment of training and testing datasets.

1 Introduction

Extractive question answering (QA) is an NLP task in which a model receives a question and a context and needs to identify a context span that best answers this question. Figure 1 shows an example from a well-known extractive QA dataset **SQuAD** (the Stanford Question Answering Dataset, Rajpurkar et al. (2016, 2018)): For a given question, “What happened in 1971 and 1972?” the model should find the span of “two more launch failures” within the given context text.

To achieve high-performance in QA, one requires a robust training dataset with gold-standard annotations. However, such resources exist only for a few languages (Rogers et al., 2023). Therefore, to perform QA in a new language or domain, one must choose from: (1) manually curating a new dataset (d’Hoffschmidt et al., 2020; Heinrich et al., 2022; Efimov et al., 2020; Lim et al., 2019; Kazemi et al., 2022), (2) automatically translating a well-established dataset such as SQuAD into the target language (Mozannar et al., 2019; Kazi and Khoja, 2021; Vemula et al., 2022), or (3) using a hybrid approach and combining translation with a small manually annotated data (Möller et al., 2021). Given the varying costs associated with each option, it is crucial that researchers not only share their datasets but also insights learned during their creation, thereby aiding future similar initiatives.

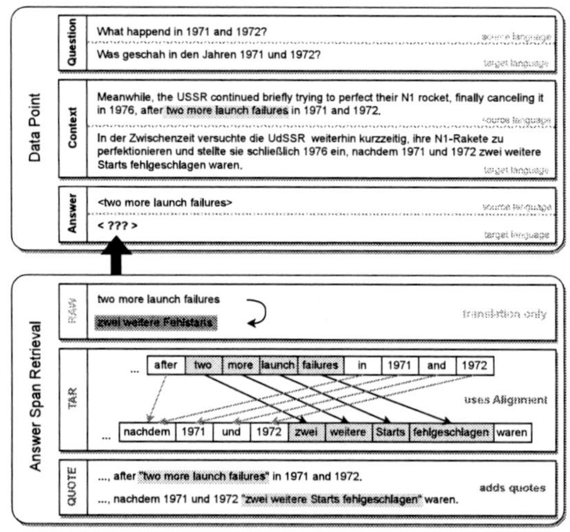

Figure 1: Context-based QA is the task of extracting answer span based on the question and context. The top depicts challenges in converting an English QA pair to German. The bottom shows different approaches for retrieving the answer span from the translated context.

For German, such valuable observations were provided by Möller et al. (2021). The authors not only introduced a new, manually annotated dataset, a state-of-the-art QA model, but also shared lessons learned during its creation, such as successful strategies for hybrid QA approaches and their generalization capabilities in out-of-dataset scenarios. However, the authors skipped a crucial aspect – the selection of the method for *answer span retrieval*. Translating SQuAD to a new language introduces challenges, such as answers that do not match the translated context. Figure 1 illustrates such a common issue. After translating the gold-standard English question and context pair to German, the translated answer "zwei weitere Fehlstarts" does not appear in the translated context anymore, making the datapoint unusable in the QA system. To deal with

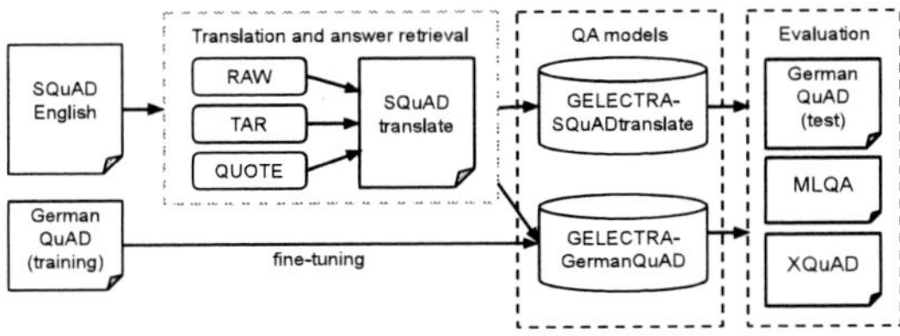

Figure 2: Experimental setup.

such issues, it is necessary to use additional answer retrieval methods (see the bottom of Figure 1 and the details of the methods in Section 2.2). However, there is a notable research gap regarding the comparative effectiveness of these heuristics and their influence on the German QA systems.

In this work, we aim to facilitate future approaches to QA dataset creation. Based on the premise that robust and high-quality training datasets lead to higher QA scores, we seek to answer two methodological research questions:

RQ1 Which answer span retrieval method yields the best-performing German SQuAD translation?

RQ2 Do span retrieval methods influence hybrid, fine-tuned models?

To address these questions, we replicate the experimental setup from Möller et al. (2021) using various answer retrieval methods (§2). We find that the effectiveness of these methods significantly depends on the type of existing data. In scenarios where only translated SQuAD is available, retrieving answers with an alignment model yields the best QA results (§3). However, for the hybrid QA models that additionally use small target data, the impact of span retrieval methods is dependent on the application and origin of the evaluation data (§4). While our analyses focus only on German, the results presented here can serve as guidelines for the future creation of SQuAD-based datasets in other languages.

2 Experimental Setup

Figure 2 illustrates the experimental setup from Möller et al. (2021) expanded by various answer retrieval methods (marked in red box). Below, we provide details of all the setup steps, beginning with an overview of the data used.

2.1 Data

Our experimental setup includes four different QA datasets (one English and three German). Based on the survey by Rogers et al. (2023), these are all SQuAD-like datasets that exist for German.

SQuAD 1.1 (Rajpurkar et al., 2016) is our source English QA dataset. It contains 107.785 QA pairs for 536 paragraphs taken from Wikipedia articles. For simplicity reasons, we use version 1.1 and not SQuAD 2.0 (Rajpurkar et al., 2018), which additionally includes over 50k unanswerable questions.[1] Moreover, we employ only the training part, with 87k QA pairs.

GermanQUAD is the German recreation of SQuAD from Möller et al. (2021). We use it for fine-tuning hybrid QA models and evaluation (see Figure 2). It comprises 13,722 manually created QA pairs. The original dataset comes only with training and test parts, so we leave out 20% of the training data as a development set.

XQuAD and MLQA (German parts) are used only for evaluation. XQuAD contains 1190 QA pairs from SQuAD translated by professionals to ten languages (Artetxe et al., 2020). MLQA (5027 pairs) was created from scratch following the SQuAD methodology (Lewis et al., 2020). Möller et al. (2021) call these two datasets out-of-domain for GermanQuAD. However, the main difference between them and GermanQuAD lies in the details of their creation, and not domains – all three resources are based on Wikipedia articles and the SQuAD framework. Therefore, we use the term *cross-dataset* to refer to the experiments where models are trained on GermanQuAD and applied to XQuAD and MLQA.

2.2 Translation and span retrieval

The first step in Figure 2 consists of translating SQuAD to German. Originally, Möller et al. (2021) used data translated with Facebook's commercial model (Lewis et al., 2020). We replace it with an open-source model called FAIRSEQ (Ott et al., 2019). Moreover, we differ the answer span retrieval method to one of the three approaches identified in the literature:

RAW simply filters out cases where the translated answer does not appear exactly once in the context.

TAR (Translate Align Retrieve) was introduced by Carrino et al. (2020) to translate SQuAD to Spanish. The method addresses the complex cases that

[1] Unanswerable questions have an empty answer span and are, therefore, exempt from the issue at hand.

	Dataset Size	GermanQUAD		MLQA		XQuAD	
		F1	EM	F1	EM	F1	EM
RAW	42.3k	65.3	51.2	63.1	47.7	76.5	60.8
TAR	83.3k	73.2	**55.5**	**66.9**	**50.9**	**77.9**	**62.5**
QUOTE	76.5k	**73.4**	51.3	66.8	47.6	77.7	56.1

Table 1: Performance of the QA systems trained only on the automatically translated SQuAD. The size of the datasets is measured in the number of individual QA pairs. The highest numbers in each column are in bold.

the RAW approach typically discards. It uses an alignment model to extract answer spans by mapping tokens between the source and target contexts (cf., Figure 1). We re-implement TAR with XML-Align (Chi et al., 2021), a better-performing aligner than the originally used efmaral (Östling and Tiedemann, 2016).[2]

QUOTE was first used by Lee et al. (2018) for translating SQuAD to Korean. The heuristic takes advantage of translation models frequently overlooking certain symbols, like quotation marks, and directly copying them to the outputs. It involves surrounding the answer span with such symbols before translation to then easily identify the corresponding span in the translated context. We tested three different symbols – *"*, *'*, and *()* – and found that FAIRSEQ preserves quotation marks the best.

2.3 QA Training and fine-tuning

As the next step from Figure 2, we implement two QA models following Möller et al.'s (2021) best-performing systems. They are based on GELECTRA large (Chan et al., 2020) and have two versions: SQuADtranslate, trained only on the translated data, and the hybrid model, fine-tuned on GermanQuAD (see hyperparameters in Appendix A).

2.4 Evaluation

We use two evaluation metrics: averaged F1 and exact match (EM) scores. F1 measures the similarity between the predicted and gold-standard answers, where the score is above zero as long as there is some word overlap between the two. EM, on the other hand, is a binary measure, giving 1 only if the predicted answer is equal to the gold-standard answer and 0 otherwise.

3 QA with No Target Data

We begin by addressing **RQ1** and evaluating which answer retrieval method gives the best QA results.

[2]All the developed code is publicly available at `https://github.com/JensKaiser96/HowToTranslateSQuAD`.

	GermanQUAD			
	F1	ΔF1	EM	ΔEM
RAW	65.3	–	51.2	–
TAR_{REDUCED}	70.1	-3.1	52.0	-3.5
QUOTE_{REDUCED}	72.7	-0.7	51.3	0.0

Table 2: Performance of the QA systems trained on 42.3k randomly selected, automatically translated SQuAD instances. Δs report losses from the data reduction (cf. Table 1).

3.1 Results

Table 1 shows the results for the three QA models using different answer retrieval methods. Firstly, we observe the influence of retrieval approaches on the training data size. With RAW, which excludes all data points where the translated answer does not appear exactly once in the translated context, roughly half of the training data is lost (training part of SQuAD has 87k pairs). In contrast, TAR allows for keeping almost 100% of the dataset. Finally, QUOTE preserves approximately 90% of the data, filtering out for example pairs where the translation did not keep the quotation marks.

Next, we move to the accuracy of the QA systems.[3] While the evaluation datasets clearly vary in difficulty, with MLQA being the most challenging, the relative performance of the models remains consistent across them. Interestingly, the two metrics – F1 and EM – prioritize different methods. Under F1, which allows for partial matches, RAW significantly underperforms compared to the other two methods, which achieve very similar results. In contrast, under the EM metric, TAR emerges as the clear leader, outperforming QUOTE by as much as 6.4 EM points on XQuAD.

[3]Differences to the results reported by Möller et al. (2021) most likely stem from the translation method and hyperparameters. However, since our goal is to observe differences between the models, we do not aim at SOTA performance.

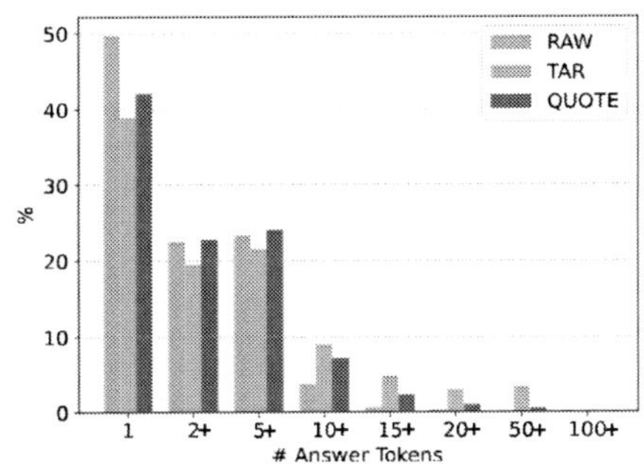

Figure 3: Percentages of answer lengths in the datasets.

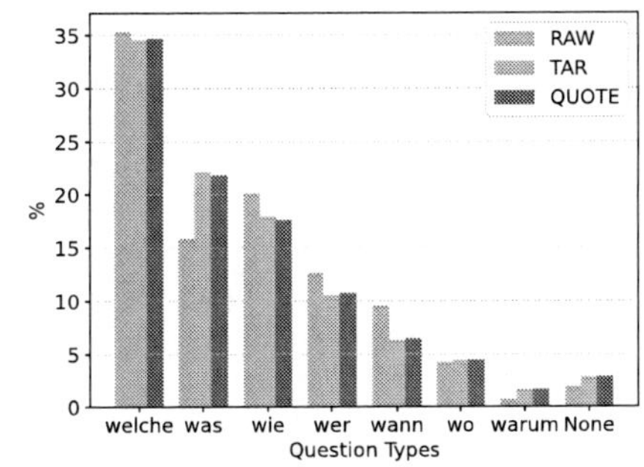

Figure 4: Percentages of question types in the datasets.

3.2 Analysis

So far, TAR resulted in the best QA system. However, it is unclear if its advantage stems solely from the larger dataset or the quality of the generated QA pairs. To analyze the influence of the dataset size on the model performance, we randomly subsample the TAR and QUOTE datasets to match the size of RAW (42.3k) and train two new reduced QA systems (see Table 2). As expected, the performance of both models decreases compared to Table 1 (reported in Δ columns). However, even with equivalent training sizes, they still exceed the performance of RAW. With dataset size ruled out as the only contributing factor, we analyze what other differences we can find.

Answer lengths The first factor that potentially varies within the datasets is the answer length. RAW, which keeps only QA pairs where the translated answer directly appears in the context, might be affected by the answer's length and perform better for typically short answers, such as numbers, dates, and names. Similarly, TAR might encounter more issues when setting the answer span at extreme context points following token mapping.[4] To evaluate this hypothesis, Figure 3 presents the distribution of answer length across all datasets.[5] For RAW, there is approximately 10% more single-token answers compared to TAR and QUOTE. Additionally, only about 6% of RAW's answers extend beyond five tokens, and none exceed 21. In contrast, TAR and QUOTE exhibit more similar distributions. TAR has fewer answers than QUOTE up to five tokens, but the situation reverses afterwards.

Question types The observed variations in answer lengths may indirectly influence the distribution of question types. Typically, questions, such as *who* (*wer*) or *when* (*wann*) are associated with shorter answers, while *what* (*was*) or *why* (*warum*) require more elaborate responses. To test if this is the case in our datasets, we categorize questions based on their initial words and present results in Figure 4. We find that distributions for TAR and QUOTE are very similar. However, RAW exhibits a notably different pattern with fewer questions requiring complex answers, such as *what* (*was*) and *why* (*warum*) and more necessitating shorter responses, such as *who* (*wer*) and *when* (*wann*)

4 QA with Small Target Data

So far, we have assumed no gold-standard data in the target language. Now, we switch to **RQ2** and analyze the influence of span retrieval methods on the hybrid models. We prepare four versions of the GELECTRA-GermanQuAD model from Figure 2: **ONLY_FT**, which uses only GermanQuAD, and $\textbf{RAW}_{\textbf{FT}}$, $\textbf{TAR}_{\textbf{FT}}$, and $\textbf{QUOTE}_{\textbf{FT}}$, models that are first trained on translated SQuAD and then fine-tuned. Table 3 presents the results of all the models and their respective gains/losses from fine-tuning (i.e., differences to Table 1). For comparison, we also report **NO_FT** numbers – the highest results achieved by models that did not use fine-tuning (i.e., best results from Table 1). As all results span two distinct scenarios, we discuss each separately.

In-dataset evaluation When models are fine-tuned and evaluated with data from the same source – GermanQuAD – already ONLY_FT outperforms NO_FT, i.e., models with no additional training signals (see Table 3a). Further boosts can be observed from fine-tuning, which strongly reduces performance differences between FT approaches.

[4]Consider the example *Emma*[1] *bought*[2] *ice*[3] *at the new store in town* translated to German *Emma*[1] *hat*[2] *Eis*[3] *bei dem neuen Laden in der Stadt gekauft*[2] and with the retrieved span including all tokens in between the aligned words.

[5]Answers in-between are counted towards higher buckets.

	GermanQUAD			
	F1	ΔF1	EM	ΔEM
NO_FT	73.4	–	55.5	–
ONLY_FT	77.5	–	63.0	–
RAW_{FT}	**84.1**	+18.8	**70.5**	+19.3
TAR_{FT}	82.2	+9.0	66.7	+11.2
$QUOTE_{FT}$	83.0	+9.6	68.4	+17.1

(a) In-dataset results

	MLQA				XQuAD			
	F1	ΔF1	EM	ΔEM	F1	ΔF1	EM	ΔEM
NO_FT	**66.9**	–	**50.9**	–	**77.9**	–	**62.5**	–
ONLY_FT	50.4	–	28.2	–	64.9	–	38.4	–
RAW_{FT}	60.2	-2.9	37.1	-10.6	71.4	-5.1	46.3	-14.5
TAR_{FT}	60.4	-6.5	35.2	-15.7	69.9	-8.0	42.3	-20.2
$QUOTE_{FT}$	62.2	-4.6	37.7	-9.9	71.3	-6.4	44.8	-11.3

(b) Cross-dataset results

Table 3: Performance of the fine-tuned QA systems; Δs reports gains/losses from fine-tuning (cf. Table 1).

Interestingly, their magnitude varies considerably among the models, ranging from 9 F1 points for TAR_{FT} to 18.8 points for RAW_{FT}. Surprisingly, RAW_{FT}, which previously was the weakest method, achieves the best results.

Cross-dataset evaluation Similarly to Möller et al. (2021), we find that fine-tuning in the cross-dataset setting degrades performance of the QA models (see Table 3b). ONLY_FT and all hybrid systems, irrespective of the answer span retrieval method, achieve significantly lower scores compared to the models trained only on the translated SQuAD. Interestingly, bigger drops in performance are observed for EM than for F1, suggesting that tuning leads to overfitting to the specific dataset characteristics.

5 Conclusion

In this paper, we explored best approaches to automatically translating SQuAD to German, highlighting the crucial role of the span retrieval methods in this process. We performed a comparative study of the three most-commonly used in the literature methods in two settings – with and without fine-tuning. Addressing **RQ1**, we found that when no fine-tuning is possible, TAR is the best practical choice, yielding more training data and higher (EM) or comparable (F1) results than QUOTE. RAW performs the worst – its strict filtering not only reduces the dataset size by half, but also skews question-answer distributions toward shorter queries about *who*, *when*, and *how*.

Responding to **RQ2**, the effectiveness of span retrieval methods varies when small target data is available. If this data comes from the same dataset as the evaluation set, automatically translated SQuAD is ideally used as a preliminary step before fine-tuning. In such cases, the differences between span retrieval methods are minor. However, if training data comes from a different origin, fine-tuning can lead to large drops in performance. In such cases, a well-translated, high-quality SQuAD dataset emerges as a more reliable source, again underscoring the importance of a carefully chosen method for the answer span retrieval.

6 Limitations

This work provides methodological insights into the creation of SQuAD-based datasets in German. Therefore, our experiments are limited to a single language. However, we believe that presented results, particularly the importance of careful selection of the answer span retrieval method, can be beneficial for researchers aiming to create new datasets also in other languages.

Secondly, we evaluate QA models using only three manually-curated datasets and fine-tune with just one. While a broader selection of datasets would enhance the generalizability of our results, to the best of our knowledge, we have used all the data that is currently available in German.

Finally, to ensure a fair comparison between approaches, the only variables we altered in the experimental setup were the span retrieval methods and the datasets used for training and fine-tuning. We did not experiment with other language models or QA systems. This decision was based on the findings of Möller et al. (2021), who evaluated various approaches and determined that models based on GELECTRA performed the best.

7 Acknowledgements

We acknowledge the support of the Ministerium für Wissenschaft, Forschung und Kunst Baden-Württemberg (MWK, Ministry of Science, Research and the Arts Baden-Württemberg under Az. 33-7533-9-19/54/5) in Künstliche Intelligenz & Gesellschaft: Reflecting Intelligent Systems for Diversity, Demography and Democracy (IRIS3D) and the support by the Interchange Forum for Reflecting on Intelligent Systems (IRIS) at the University of Stuttgart.

References

Mikel Artetxe, Sebastian Ruder, and Dani Yogatama. 2020. On the cross-lingual transferability of monolingual representations. In *Proceedings of the 58th Annual Meeting of the Association for Computational Linguistics*, pages 4623–4637, Online. Association for Computational Linguistics.

Casimiro Pio Carrino, Marta R. Costa-jussà, and José A. R. Fonollosa. 2020. Automatic Spanish translation of SQuAD dataset for multi-lingual question answering. In *Proceedings of the Twelfth Language Resources and Evaluation Conference*, pages 5515–5523, Marseille, France. European Language Resources Association.

Branden Chan, Stefan Schweter, and Timo Möller. 2020. German's next language model. In *Proceedings of the 28th International Conference on Computational Linguistics*, pages 6788–6796, Barcelona, Spain (Online). International Committee on Computational Linguistics.

Zewen Chi, Li Dong, Bo Zheng, Shaohan Huang, Xian-Ling Mao, Heyan Huang, and Furu Wei. 2021. Improving pretrained cross-lingual language models via self-labeled word alignment. In *Proceedings of the 59th Annual Meeting of the Association for Computational Linguistics and the 11th International Joint Conference on Natural Language Processing (Volume 1: Long Papers)*, pages 3418–3430, Online. Association for Computational Linguistics.

Martin d'Hoffschmidt, Wacim Belblidia, Quentin Heinrich, Tom Brendlé, and Maxime Vidal. 2020. FQuAD: French question answering dataset. In *Findings of the Association for Computational Linguistics: EMNLP 2020*, pages 1193–1208, Online. Association for Computational Linguistics.

Pavel Efimov, Andrey Chertok, Leonid Boytsov, and Pavel Braslavski. 2020. Sberquad–russian reading comprehension dataset: Description and analysis. In *Experimental IR Meets Multilinguality, Multimodality, and Interaction: 11th International Conference of the CLEF Association, CLEF 2020, Thessaloniki, Greece, September 22–25, 2020, Proceedings 11*, pages 3–15. Springer.

Quentin Heinrich, Gautier Viaud, and Wacim Belblidia. 2022. FQuAD2.0: French question answering and learning when you don't know. In *Proceedings of the Thirteenth Language Resources and Evaluation Conference*, pages 2205–2214, Marseille, France. European Language Resources Association.

Arefeh Kazemi, Jamshid Mozafari, and Mohammad Ali Nematbakhsh. 2022. Persianquad: The native question answering dataset for the persian language. *IEEE Access*, 10:26045–26057.

Samreen Kazi and Shakeel Khoja. 2021. Uquad1. 0: Development of an urdu question answering training data for machine reading comprehension. *arXiv preprint arXiv:2111.01543*.

Kyungjae Lee, Kyoungho Yoon, Sunghyun Park, and Seung-won Hwang. 2018. Semi-supervised training data generation for multilingual question answering. In *Proceedings of the Eleventh International Conference on Language Resources and Evaluation (LREC 2018)*, Miyazaki, Japan. European Language Resources Association (ELRA).

Patrick Lewis, Barlas Oguz, Ruty Rinott, Sebastian Riedel, and Holger Schwenk. 2020. MLQA: Evaluating cross-lingual extractive question answering. In *Proceedings of the 58th Annual Meeting of the Association for Computational Linguistics*, pages 7315–7330, Online. Association for Computational Linguistics.

Seungyoung Lim, Myungji Kim, and Jooyoul Lee. 2019. Korquad1. 0: Korean qa dataset for machine reading comprehension. *arXiv preprint arXiv:1909.07005*.

Timo Möller, Julian Risch, and Malte Pietsch. 2021. GermanQuAD and GermanDPR: Improving non-English question answering and passage retrieval. In *Proceedings of the 3rd Workshop on Machine Reading for Question Answering*, pages 42–50, Punta Cana, Dominican Republic. Association for Computational Linguistics.

Hussein Mozannar, Elie Maamary, Karl El Hajal, and Hazem Hajj. 2019. Neural Arabic question answering. In *Proceedings of the Fourth Arabic Natural Language Processing Workshop*, pages 108–118, Florence, Italy. Association for Computational Linguistics.

Myle Ott, Sergey Edunov, Alexei Baevski, Angela Fan, Sam Gross, Nathan Ng, David Grangier, and Michael Auli. 2019. fairseq: A fast, extensible toolkit for sequence modeling. In *Proceedings of the 2019 Conference of the North American Chapter of the Association for Computational Linguistics (Demonstrations)*, pages 48–53, Minneapolis, Minnesota. Association for Computational Linguistics.

Pranav Rajpurkar, Robin Jia, and Percy Liang. 2018. Know what you don't know: Unanswerable questions for SQuAD. In *Proceedings of the 56th Annual Meeting of the Association for Computational Linguistics (Volume 2: Short Papers)*, pages 784–789, Melbourne, Australia. Association for Computational Linguistics.

Pranav Rajpurkar, Jian Zhang, Konstantin Lopyrev, and Percy Liang. 2016. SQuAD: 100,000+ questions for machine comprehension of text. In *Proceedings of the 2016 Conference on Empirical Methods in Natural Language Processing*, pages 2383–2392, Austin, Texas. Association for Computational Linguistics.

Anna Rogers, Matt Gardner, and Isabelle Augenstein. 2023. QA dataset explosion: A taxonomy of NLP resources for question answering and reading comprehension. *ACM Computing Surveys*, 55(10):1–45.

Rakesh Vemula, Mani Nuthi, and Manish Srivastava. 2022. TeQuAD:Telugu question answering dataset. In *Proceedings of the 19th International Conference on Natural Language Processing (ICON)*, pages 300–307, New Delhi, India. Association for Computational Linguistics.

Robert Östling and Jörg Tiedemann. 2016. Efficient word alignment with markov chain monte carlo. *The Prague Bulletin of Mathematical Linguistics*, 106.

A Appendix

A.1 Hyperparameters

We based the selection of the hyperparameters for training QA models and fine-tuning on two different sources. For training QA models, Möller et al. (2021) point to the default settings of a legacy framework which is no longer public. Therefore, we choose the parameters based on `https://huggingface.co/docs/transformers/tasks/question_answering` and `https://github.com/google-research/electra/blob/master/configure_finetuning.py` and used a batch size of 4, a learning rate of e-5, and 6 epochs. After each epoch, the model is evaluated using the development set, and the checkpoint with the lowest loss is saved.

For fine-tuning, we follow the recommendations from Möller et al. (2021): learning rate of 3e-5 and two epochs.

Few-Shot Prompting for Subject Indexing of German Medical Book Titles

Lisa Kluge
Deutsche Nationalbibliothek
Frankfurt am Main, Germany
l.kluge@dnb.de

Maximilian Kähler
Deutsche Nationalbibliothek
Leipzig, Germany
m.kaehler@dnb.de

Abstract

With the rise of large language models (LLMs), many tasks of natural language processing have reached unprecedented performance levels. One task LLMs have not yet been evaluated on is subject indexing with a large controlled target vocabulary. In this work, an LLM is applied to the task of subject indexing a dataset of German medical book titles, compiled at the German National Library. The results are compared to two common baseline methods already in productive use at this institution. One critical parameter in a few-shot prompting approach is the composition of examples given to the LLM for instruction. In order to select examples, two similarity measures between book title and gold-standard labels are applied. We hypothesise that these notions of similarity can serve as a measure of task difficulty. Our findings indicate that the LLM does not outperform the baselines. Still, (off-the-shelf) LLMs can be a valuable addition in an ensemble of methods for subject indexing as they do not depend on training data.

1 Introduction

At the German National Library (Deutsche Nationalbibliothek, DNB), incoming publications undergo subject indexing not only in an intellectual fashion. Digital publications can be indexed in an automated way. In both cases, each medium is annotated with fitting entities from the Integrated Authority File[1] (GND) in order to to make them accessible to users. In the present study, a large language model (LLM) is compared to two baseline approaches for automated subject indexing in productive use at the DNB. These are available via the Annif framework (Suominen, 2019) developed by the Finnish National Library.

The focus of this work is on improving the selection and composition of examples used in an LLM few-shot prompting approach to make further progress towards solving the GND-annotation problem.

Our work makes the following contributions:

- To our knowledge, this is the first application of LLMs to subject indexing of German scientific publications.
- We provide a comparison between an LLM-based approach and widespread methods for subject indexing at libraries.
- We investigate the influence of purposeful prompt variation on the model's performance.
- Two measures of similarity, one accounting for lexical and one for semantic similarity, are used for two purposes. First, as a guide for our selection of samples for the prompts and, second, as a heuristic for predicted indexing difficulty.

2 Related Work

2.1 Subject Indexing

Automated subject indexing (e.g. see Golub (2021)) can be approached as either a multi-label classification (MLC) task, a keyword extraction/generation problem, or a combination of both (Erbs et al., 2013). To exploit their individual strengths and improve performance, the results from different methods can be combined into a fusion or ensemble (Toepfer and Seifert, 2020).

2.2 Annif

Annif[2] (Suominen, 2019) is a toolkit for automated subject indexing. Two of its implemented methods serve as baseline for our experiments. The first is a Rust implementation of the partitioned label tree approach (cf. Parabel (Prabhu et al., 2018) and

[1] https://gnd.network/Webs/gnd/EN/Home/home_node.html

[2] https://github.com/NatLibFi/Annif/

Bonsai (Khandagale et al., 2020)), called Omikuji[3]. The second baseline is a lexical method based on Maui (Medelyan, 2009), called Maui-Like-Lexical-Matching (MLLM)[4].

2.3 LLMs

LLMs have been applied to a range of tasks (Zhao et al., 2023), including multi-label classification (Peskine et al., 2023; D'Oosterlinck et al., 2024; Zhu and Zamani, 2024), as well as keyword extraction (Maragheh et al., 2023) and keyword generation (Maragheh et al., 2023; Lee et al., 2023). With a prompting procedure analogical to ours, Lee et al. (2023) applied few-shot prompting to generating keywords from abstracts in order to provide an alternative for missing author-defined keywords. D'Oosterlinck et al. (2024) proposed a method utilising interactions of multiple LLMs to infer, retrieve and rank keywords, and thereby bootstrapping prompts in an automated fashion from a set of given few-shot examples.

3 Method

3.1 Model

In our experiments, we opted for a family of LLMs called Luminous[5], developed by the German Company Aleph Alpha[6]. The majority of experiments was done with the Luminous-base model (13B parameters[7]). Fewer experiments were also done with the bigger models, Luminous-extended (30B[7]) and Luminous-supreme (70B[7]), as they have an increased price compared to the base model. For simplicity, we only included findings here that are related to the alteration of prompts.

3.2 Data

All methods were compared on a test set of 486 German scientific book publications. The data was randomly sampled from the catalogue of the DNB. It was filtered for these criteria: German language, publication year 2017 to 2023, and publisher from a list of scientific publishers. To reduce the cost of the experiments, we only included publications from the medicine subject category. Omikuji was trained on a larger dataset (approx. 950.000 training items), disjoint from the above test set and also including other subject categories. This reflects our production settings at the DNB, where all subject categories are indexed by a unified model.

As textual input for the automatic indexing only plain book titles were used. Whereas the full texts of the publications are available, they would need to be cut-off or separated into smaller chunks to process them with the chosen LLM. The heterogeneous structures of these texts also make it difficult to automatically scrape summaries or abstracts from them. Due to our limited resources, we decided not to investigate this additional step and to first experiment on titles before moving on to more costly experiments on longer texts. To be noted, experiments with (shortened) full texts have already been done with the baseline methods and are planned for the LLM-based method, too.

All of the selected publications have previously been intellectually subject indexed with GND entities by professionals with profound expertise in the respective field and the taxonomy. These annotations, further referred to as *labels*, are the gold-standard of our data. The labels all have a unique identifier and one or more short textual description(s). Labels fall under the rough categories of subject headings representing concepts of the various scientific (sub-)disciplines and named entities (personal names, corporate bodies, geographic entities, etc.), the latter constituting the majority of concepts represented in the GND.

3.3 Procedure

Our approach consisted of two steps which have previously been utilised for keyword generation and MLC respectively.

First, as done by Lee et al. (2023), keywords were generated via few-shot prompting. A prompt comprises an instruction ("Extract keywords from book titles.") and a set of examples, illustrating the desired output format of the keywords. See Appendix A for the structure of the prompts.

Next, the generated keywords were mapped to the GND vocabulary, similar to the mapping Zhu and Zamani (2024) conducted in their MLC approach. Here, we used Aleph Alpha's symmetric semantic embeddings[8]. Before vectorisation, the label texts in the target vocabulary as well as the model-produced keywords underwent a simple step

[3] https://github.com/tomtung/omikuji

[4] https://github.com/NatLibFi/Annif/wiki/Backend:-MLLM

[5] https://docs.aleph-alpha.com/docs/introduction/luminous/

[6] https://aleph-alpha.com/

[7] https://docs.aleph-alpha.com/docs/introduction/model-card

[8] https://docs.aleph-alpha.com/docs/tasks/semantic_embed/

of preprocessing by being integrated into a sentence ("A good keyword for this document is *label text / keyword.*"). These sentences were vectorised. Via cosine similarity, the most similar label was retrieved for each generated keyword.

3.4 Similarity Measures

Inferring GND entities from book titles alone is a task that can be impossible even for humans, depending on the amount of information or degree of specificity in the particular title. To illustrate, a title like "Report" gives no hints as to what the report is about. To address this problem, we estimated the difficulty of indexing a particular book title by considering two simple notions of similarity between book title and the set of its annotated gold-standard labels. The two similarity measures were used both in the prompt design to select examples and in the evaluation as hypothesised indicator of difficulty.

3.4.1 Lemma Overlap

The first measure aims to capture lexical similarity and is referred to as Lemma Overlap, abbreviated LO (cf. Equation 1). The size of the intersection of lemmas (λ_l) of each label l and lemmas (λ_t) of title t is divided by the number of lemmas in the label[9]. Per book title t, the final score is obtained by averaging over the entire set of annotated gold-standard labels (L_t).

$$\text{Lemma Overlap}(t, L_t) = \frac{1}{|L_t|} \times \sum_{l \in L_t} \frac{|\lambda_l \cap \lambda_t|}{|\lambda_l|} \quad (1)$$

3.4.2 MeanSBERT

To be able to also capture similarity beyond textual overlap, we defined a second measure using Sentence-BERT (Reimers and Gurevych, 2019), called MeanSBERT (cf. Equation 2). The cosine similarity (S_c) between embeddings of title ($\overrightarrow{t}$) and all label texts ($\overrightarrow{l}$) was computed and averaged over all labels[10].

$$\text{MeanSBERT}(t, L_t) = \frac{1}{|L_t|} \times \sum_{l \in L_t} S_c(\overrightarrow{l}, \overrightarrow{t}) \quad (2)$$

3.4.3 Splitting the Dataset

Based on LO and MeanSBERT, the entire test set was split into roughly similarly-sized groups of documents with low, medium and high title-label-similarity. Constructing a cross-table from these groups over both measures lead to a division of the test set into nine separate groups (find details in Appendix C). To exemplify, if the fictitious book title *"Natural language processing"* had *"Computational linguistics"* as its only label, this title would be low LO and high MeanSBERT.

3.4.4 Prompt Design

Analysing similarity between title and labels can also be beneficial for prompt design. If the model is only instructed with examples with high similarity, the labels produced might turn out be closely related to the test title, too, and vice versa. By considering title-label-similarity when constructing the prompt, different behaviour was elicited in the LLM.

4 Experiments

Factoring out base-model selection and other hyperparameters, our experiments were directed at trying out different few-shot sample combinations for the prompts. Table 1 gives an overview of the idea behind them. All of the individual examples in the prompts adhere to the same criteria as the medical test set, but are not part of it. Some prompts only contain samples falling into specific similarity categories of LO and MeanSBERT (`low_low`, `high_low`, `high_high`), while another one includes heterogeneous similarities (`mixed_sim`). Additionally, three more prompts were constructed unrelated to the similarity measures (`deducible`, `combination`, `many_labels`). More details concerning the prompts and the examples used in prompt `high_low` can be found in Appendix B. The previously described procedure was applied to our dataset with all of the seven prompts.

5 Evaluation

5.1 Prompt Variation

Table 2 shows the results of 7 different prompt specifications in comparison (see Appendix D for result set sizes). The prompt with low-similarity examples has the worst F1-performance, suggesting unrelated examples don't guide the LLM well enough. The two prompts with high LO (`high_low`, `high_high`) achieve the two best precision scores, which may, in addition to the high similarity, also be related to the fact that these prompts both contain and generate

[9] Lemmatization was done using spaCy (`https://spacy.io/`).

[10] We used the Python sentence-transformers library (`https://www.sbert.net/`) with model "distiluse-base-multilingual-cased-v1".

Prompt name	Comment
low_low	low LO, low MeanSBERT
high_low	high LO, low MeanSBERT
high_high	high LO, high MeanSBERT
mixed_sim	different similarities
deducible	only deducible labels
combination	combination of samples
many_labels	more labels per title

Table 1: Prompt specifications and short explanation.

Prompt	Prec	Rec	F1
low_low	0.231	0.244	0.237
high_low	0.459	0.223	**0.300**
high_high	**0.516**	0.210	0.298
mixed_sim	0.278	0.303	0.290
deducible	0.307	0.280	0.293
combination	0.237	**0.326**	0.274
many_labels	0.207	0.295	0.243

Table 2: Micro-averaged performance of seven prompt combinations.

the smallest number of labels. The best recall scores are attained by prompts with examples from different similarity categories (combination, mixed_similarity). Perhaps this diversity allows the LLM to pick up on a variety of relationships between title and labels and, thus, it can find more correct labels. The best trade-off in terms of F1-score is produced by the prompt high_low.

5.2 Prompt Ensemble

In addition to the individual results, we investigated if the performance would improve when the suggestions of multiple prompt experiments are combined. We used the results of the four prompts high_low, mixed_similarity, deducible and combination. These were selected because they performed well in at least one of the metrics recall, precision or F1-measure. Table 3 shows the outcomes of the combination. The number of experiments i a label was suggested by can serve as a measure of confidence that a label is relevant to a particular title. Keeping all suggestions generated using at least one of the prompts ($i \geq 1$) leads to a high recall strategy. In contrast, considering only those suggestions that all prompts produce ($i \geq 4$) gives a high precision strategy. The best trade-off in terms of F1-score is found in the $i \geq 2$ scenario (a keyword is generated using at least two prompts).

$i \geq$	Prec	Rec	F1
1	0.203	**0.394**	0.268
2	0.322	0.326	**0.324**
3	0.416	0.260	0.320
4	**0.576**	0.166	0.257

Table 3: Micro-averaged results of the prompt ensemble (4 prompts). Parameter i indicates by at least how many prompts a suggestion was made.

5.3 Baselines

Previously introduced baselines, MLLM and Omikuji, are currently well-performing methods in our productive environment. As ranked retrieval methods, they both return a long ranked list of labels, which we truncated at the 5th position. Thus, scores reported are precision@5, recall@5 and F1@5. For the ensemble of prompts, the frequency-of-suggestion i was converted into a score to allow a ranking, too, making results comparable to MLLM and Omikuji. As this ranking is discrete, it is possible for ties between suggestions to appear, so we decided not to include, e.g., precision@1 or precision@2, which could be impacted more severely by this impreciseness.

Table 4 shows the outcomes with 95% confidence intervals. All confidence intervals presented in our evaluation are obtained by bootstrapping the test set, i.e. randomly resampling the documents of the test set. This expresses the uncertainty of results with respect to the variability of the underlying data, but does not include an estimation of model uncertainty. Regarding F1-measures, our LLM method is outperformed by Omikuji and MLLM. Yet, it has better recall than MLLM.

5.4 Similarity Measures

A more detailed comparison between the methods can be found in Figure 1, showing performance stratified by similarity measures with 95% confidence intervals. Generally, F1-scores increase with higher LO. In particular, MLLM, being a lexical method, performs best of all methods in the high LO strata. With MeanSBERT, we do not observe a strong correlation of similarity and F1-score, especially not for the LLM-prompt-ensemble and Omikuji. However, one may observe that the LLM-prompt-ensemble has a slight advantage over MLLM in the low LO strata, indicating that the LLM is able to leverage some sort of world knowledge in order to suggest labels that are not directly

Method	Prec@5	Rec@5	F1@5
Omikuji	0.274 [0.260, 0.292]	**0.462** [0.433, 0.486]	**0.344** [0.326, 0.362]
MLLM	**0.275** [0.262, 0.292]	0.297 [0.281, 0.316]	0.286 [0.271, 0.303]
LLM-prompt-ensemble	0.207 [0.196, 0.218]	0.393 [0.370, 0.413]	0.271 [0.258, 0.285]

Table 4: Micro-averaged results of LLM-prompt-ensemble and baselines. Values in brackets indicate 95% confidence intervals.

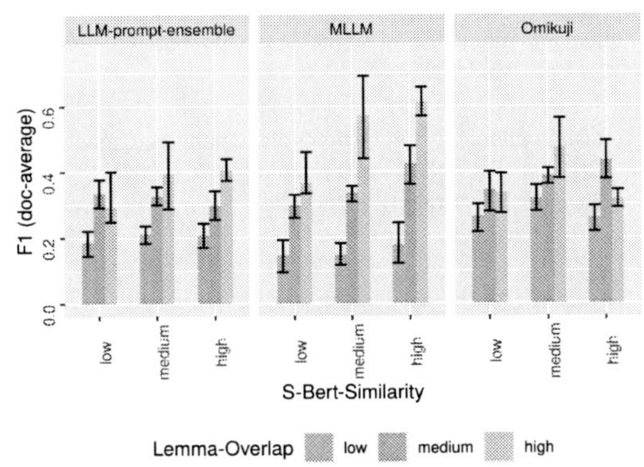

Figure 1: Performance by similarity categories.

derived from the title itself. Still, in this domain of low LO, Omikuji, the trained method, outperforms the other approaches. To conclude, we found tentative support for our assumption that the similarity between title and labels reflects the difficulty of subject indexing a particular book title. We acknowledge that the significance of this graph should not be overestimated, as the number of documents varies between the nine groups (see Appendix C for details).

6 Discussion

Assigning labels to book titles is a difficult task. In a small feasibility study we conducted on 250 titles, almost half of the not-found labels were not deducible for the human annotator by means of the title alone. Even professionals usually need more context. The Luminous models had to perform this task with only a few examples provided. In contrast, Omikuji, as a learning method, has the advantage of observing a multitude of label assignments during training. However, both MLLM and our LLM method can handle labels not observed in training, whereas Omikuji can't.

Our experiments revealed that the combination of prompt examples can impact performance in terms of quality and quantity of the results. The variation in F1-Score between prompts was small, though, with no prompt clearly exceeding all others. Using different or enhanced sets of examples could further improve performance.

7 Conclusion and Future Works

While we didn't find our LLM-based method to outperform the baselines at hand, our experiments on subject indexing German medical book titles revealed insights on factors for successful prompt combination. With the few examples fitting into a prompt, one can tweak results in specific directions, e.g., to optimise precision. In our case, the similarity measures were the main criterion for the selection.

In the future, our goal is to provide a benchmark study on the task of subject indexing, in order to support other libraries and institutions. A new perspective for the evaluation of this task has been introduced by the similarity measures. We plan to include results from a larger dataset of more diverse titles as well as a dataset with the complete texts of the scientific publications. We also want to evaluate our LLM-based approach on these. Furthermore, we will look into automated procedures for prompting, as done in D'Oosterlinck et al. (2024).

Acknowledgements

This work reports on findings from an ongoing project at the DNB[11], which is funded by the German Minister of State for Culture and the Media. With the AI strategy, the German federal government is supporting the research, development and application of innovative technologies.

We kindly acknowledge the support of Aleph Alpha for setting up our experiments with their API and inspiring the few-shot prompting approach as a potential solution for our automated subject indexing problem.

[11]https://www.dnb.de/EN/Professionell/ProjekteKooperationen/Projekte/KI/ki_node.html

Ethical Considerations

Bommasani et al. (2023) compared what they refer to as *Foundation Models* with respect to their current compliance with the upcoming EU AI Act. Aleph Alpha's Luminous models were among the examined models. Regarding different factors, including, for example, data transparency and energy consumption, the Luminous models (and other LLMs) didn't fulfill (all) the defined compliance criteria. This is a reminder that LLMs have to be utilised under great care and responsibility and that it is important to acknowledge their shortcomings in terms of transparency and reproducibility.

Stereotypes and other discriminatory artifacts in the LLM, which could have been present in the model's training data, might impact which entities are assigned to an incoming publication, either in the generation or the mapping step. Users visiting the DNB use subject headings and other GND descriptors (automatically or intellectually assigned) to research literature. Misleading terms, no matter if they result from stereotypes in the data, lack of model-performance or human mistakes, can negatively impact the results of this search.

Limitations

All our findings only relate to one (family of) LLM(s). The performance of other language models may differ.

Furthermore, the present study was done on a small restricted dataset. Thus, findings cannot be transferred or generalised to different datasets and other tasks.

Also, our experiments of interchanging few-shot examples are not exhaustive. Better prompt combinations, prompt structures and prompt instructions may exist. Samples for the prompts were partially chosen from a specific data subset (e.g. with specific similarities) and in other cases from the entire dataset, but always by subjective perception and not in a randomised way. This may have introduced unintentional bias in the composition of the examples.

Finally, the experiments presented in this study originate from a project with limited resources. Inevitably, this has affected our choices in our experiments, which always have the primary objective of improving our production settings.

References

Rishi Bommasani, Kevin Klyman, Daniel Zhang, and Percy Liang. 2023. Do Foundation Model Providers Comply with the EU AI Act? `https://crfm.stanford.edu/2023/06/15/eu-ai-act.html`.

Karel D'Oosterlinck, Omar Khattab, François Remy, Thomas Demeester, Chris Develder, and Christopher Potts. 2024. In-context learning for extreme multi-label classification. *arXiv preprint arXiv:2401.12178*.

Nicolai Erbs, Iryna Gurevych, and Marc Rittberger. 2013. Bringing order to digital libraries: From keyphrase extraction to index term assignment. *D-Lib Magazine*, 19(9/10):1–16.

Koraljka Golub. 2021. Automated subject indexing: An overview. *Cataloging & Classification Quarterly*, 59(8):702–719.

Sujay Khandagale, Han Xiao, and Rohit Babbar. 2020. Bonsai: diverse and shallow trees for extreme multi-label classification. *Machine Learning*, 109(11):2099–2119.

Wanhae Lee, Minki Chun, Hyeonhak Jeong, and Hyunggu Jung. 2023. Toward keyword generation through large language models. In *Companion Proceedings of the 28th International Conference on Intelligent User Interfaces*, IUI '23 Companion, page 37–40, New York, NY, USA. Association for Computing Machinery.

Reza Yousefi Maragheh, Chenhao Fang, Charan Chand Irugu, Parth Parikh, Jason Cho, Jianpeng Xu, Saranyan Sukumar, Malay Patel, Evren Korpeoglu, Sushant Kumar, and Kannan Achan. 2023. LLM-TAKE: Theme-aware keyword extraction using large language models. In *2023 IEEE International Conference on Big Data (BigData)*, pages 4318–4324.

Olena Medelyan. 2009. *Human-competitive automatic topic indexing*. Ph.D. thesis, The University of Waikato, New Zealand.

Youri Peskine, Damir Korenčić, Ivan Grubisic, Paolo Papotti, Raphael Troncy, and Paolo Rosso. 2023. Definitions matter: Guiding GPT for multi-label classification. In *Findings of the Association for Computational Linguistics: EMNLP 2023*, pages 4054–4063, Singapore. Association for Computational Linguistics.

Yashoteja Prabhu, Anil Kag, Shrutendra Harsola, Rahul Agrawal, and Manik Varma. 2018. Parabel: Partitioned label trees for extreme classification with application to dynamic search advertising. In *Proceedings of the 2018 World Wide Web Conference*, WWW '18, page 993–1002, Republic and Canton of Geneva, CHE. International World Wide Web Conferences Steering Committee.

Nils Reimers and Iryna Gurevych. 2019. Sentence-BERT: Sentence embeddings using Siamese BERT-networks. In *Proceedings of the 2019 Conference on Empirical Methods in Natural Language Processing and the 9th International Joint Conference on Natural Language Processing (EMNLP-IJCNLP)*, pages 3982–3992, Hong Kong, China. Association for Computational Linguistics.

Osma Suominen. 2019. Annif: DIY automated subject indexing using multiple algorithms. *LIBER Quarterly: The Journal of the Association of European Research Libraries*, 29(1):1–25.

Martin Toepfer and Christin Seifert. 2020. Fusion architectures for automatic subject indexing under concept drift: Analysis and empirical results on short texts. *International Journal on Digital Libraries*, 21(2):169–189.

Wayne Xin Zhao, Kun Zhou, Junyi Li, Tianyi Tang, Xiaolei Wang, Yupeng Hou, Yingqian Min, Beichen Zhang, Junjie Zhang, Zican Dong, Yifan Du, Chen Yang, Yushuo Chen, Zhipeng Chen, Jinhao Jiang, Ruiyang Ren, Yifan Li, Xinyu Tang, Zikang Liu, Peiyu Liu, Jian-Yun Nie, and Ji-Rong Wen. 2023. A survey of large language models. *arXiv preprint arXiv: 2303.18223*.

Yaxin Zhu and Hamed Zamani. 2024. ICXML: An in-context learning framework for zero-shot extreme multi-label classification. *arXiv preprint arXiv:2311.09649*.

A Prompt Structure

The following table shows the prompt structure. *[...]* indicates positions to fill with example titles and keywords. Keywords are comma-separated. For an incoming test title, the *Schlagwörter*-field remains empty.

Original	Translation
Extrahiere Schlagwörter aus Titeln. Text: *[...]* Schlagwörter: *[...]* ### Text: *[...]* Schlagwörter: *[...]* ### ... ### Text: *[...]* Schlagwörter:	Extract keywords from titles. Text: *[...]* Keywords: *[...]* ### Text: *[...]* Keywords: *[...]* ### ... ### Text: *[...]* Keywords:

B Prompt Details

B.1 Prompts Unrelated to Similarity

The prompt `deducible` contains examples where all assigned labels are deducible from the title. As the defined similarity measures are each averaged over the entire set of labels of a title, even titles in both high-similarity categories may have labels not inferable from the title. The prompt `combination` contains examples used in other prompts, but designed without a focus on a given similarity category. Just as the `mixed` prompt, it was meant be more diverse in the nature of its included examples than the prompts with only samples from a single similarity group. The prompt `manylabels` contains more labels per title than any of the other prompts. As such, it is like a counterpart to prompts `high_low` and `high_high` with only few labels per title.

B.2 Prompt Characteristics

The table below shows the number of examples and average number of labels in the prompts.

Prompt	Examples	Avg. Labels
`low_low`	8	2,75
`high_low`	8	1,25
`high_high`	8	1,38
`mixed_sim`	8	3,38
`deducible`	8	2,63
`combination`	8	4,88
`many_labels`	6	9

B.3 Example Prompt Combination

In the following, the examples in the prompt `high_low` are listed, along with translation and a reference to the title in the catalogue of the German National Library. Other sample combinations are available on request.

- Stottern Erkenntnisse, Theorien, Behandlungsmethoden (*Stammering Findings, Theories, Methods of Treatment*); **Labels**: Stottern (*stammering*) [`https://d-nb.info/1003711952`]
- Last minute - Gynäkologie und Geburtshilfe [fit fürs Examen in 2 Tagen!] (*Last minute - gynecology and obstetrics [prepared for the exam in 2 days!]*); **Labels**: Gynäkologie, Geburtshilfe (*gynecology, obstetrics*) [`https://d-nb.info/1010285904`]

- Hilferuf Essstörung Rat und Hilfe für Betroffene, Angehörige und Therapeuten (*Cry for help Eating disorder advice and help for persons concerned, relatives and therapists*); **Labels**: Essstörung (*Eating disorder*)[`https://d-nb.info/1017606552`]
- Rückenschule für Kinder mit Spiel und Spaß Schmerzen lindern und Haltungsschäden vorbeugen (*Back therapy training for kids Relieve pain with fun and games and prevent postural defects*); **Labels:** Kind, Rückenschule (*Child, back therapy training*) [`https://d-nb.info/1102547840`]
- Organsysteme verstehen - Niere integrative Grundlagen und Fälle (*Understanding organ systems - Kidney Integrative foundations and cases*); **Labels:** Niere (*Kidney*) [`https://d-nb.info/113137469X`]
- Schlafstörungen wieder tief und gesund schlafen; New-Age-Musik (*Sleep disorders Sleep soundly and healthily again; New age music*); **Labels:** Schlafstörung (*Sleep disorder*) [`https://d-nb.info/1201018668`]
- Wenn Töne Farben haben Synästhesie in Wissenschaft und Kunst (*When sounds have colours Synesthesia in science and art*); **Labels:** Synästhesie (*Synesthesia*) [`https://d-nb.info/984370986`]

C Samples in Similarity Categories

		LO		
		low	**med**	**high**
	low	45	31	5
MeanSB.	**med**	97	161	15
	high	51	40	40

D Result Set Sizes

Prompt	**# Result set**
`low_low`	1586
`high_low`	730
`high_high`	611
`mixed_sim`	1638
`deducible`	1371
`combination`	2067
`many_labels`	2141
ensemble ($i \geq 1$)	2920

Binary indexes for optimising corpus queries

Peter Ljunglöf[1,2] and **Nicholas Smallbone**[1,2] and **Mijo Thoresson**[1] and **Victor Salomonsson**[1]
[1]Computer Science and Engineering and [2]Språkbanken Text
Chalmers University of Technology and University of Gothenburg
Gothenburg, Sweden
peter.ljunglof@cse.gu.se, nicsma@chalmers.se,
mijot@student.chalmers.se, vicsal@student.chalmers.se

Abstract

To be able to search for patterns in annotated text corpora is crucial for many different research disciplines. However, searching for complex patterns in large corpora can take long time – sometimes several minutes or even hours.

We investigate how inverted indexes can be used for efficient searching in large annotated corpora, and in particular *binary indexes*. We show how corpus queries are translated into lookups in unary and binary inverted indexes, and give efficient strategies for combining the results using efficient set operations. In addition we discuss how to make use of binary indexes for more complex query types.

1 Introduction

Annotated text corpora are used for research in humanities and social sciences to answer questions such as: How has the use of a certain word or phrase changed over time? What grammatical constructions are the most difficult for non-native speakers? How does politicians' rhetoric around migration vary by political party and audience?

To answer such questions, specialised corpus search tools are used. As corpora can be extremely large (for example, the *News on the Web* corpus[1] consists of 18.9 billion tokens), and queries can be complex (mentioning linear order, syntactic dependencies, logical connectives and more), it is difficult to execute the queries efficiently. Unfortunately, existing search tools are either restricted and cannot express all the kinds of constraints we want, or they are inefficient on large corpora, with queries taking minutes or even hours to complete.

This paper presents new techniques for answering corpus queries more efficiently. We build on the standard technique of an *inverted index*, which can be used to find all corpus positions where a given token occurs. We introduce a new type of index that we call a *binary index*, which is an inverted index over pairs of tokens.[2] This new type of index can sometimes reduce query times by several orders of magnitude. We present a new corpus search algorithm that can answer queries more efficiently by combining lookups from *multiple indexes*. Finally, we show how to extend our algorithm to handle more types of corpus queries, by reducing complex queries into simpler ones. Our prototype tool performs well and is available as open source.[3]

2 Background

In this section we describe how corpus engines work and what kind of problems they face.

2.1 Corpus query languages

There are two main approaches for how to formulate search queries in text corpora – *linear* vs. *structured* query languages. Linear queries are easier to make efficient (so better suited for large corpora), while structured queries are more powerful (but on the other hand slower to execute).

In a *linear query model* you can formulate queries about annotated tokens, and their relationship with neighbouring tokens. The model usually supports referring to immediate neighbours and to neighbours some tokens away. However, it is more difficult to formulate queries about long-distance dependencies or syntactic structure. Variants include the IMS Corpus Query Language (Evert and Hardie, 2011) and the Poliqarp Query Language (Bingel and Diewald, 2015).

With a *structured query model* you can search for long-distance dependencies or syntactic structure such as nested phrases, anaphoric references or discontinuous multi-word entities. The model can be tree-based (e.g., Ghodke and Bird, 2012;

[1]NOW, https://www.english-corpora.org/now/

[2]Another possible term is *bigram index*, but we choose not to use this because a bigram usually refers to adjacent tokens, but our binary indexes can span arbitrary distances.

[3]https://github.com/heatherleaf/korpsearch

0	1	2	3	4	5	6	7
The	*large*	*houses*	*of*	*the*	*middle*	*class*	*were*
DT	JJ	NN	IN	DT	JJ	NN	VB

8	9	10	11	12	13	14	15
divided	*into*	*tenements*	*to*	*house*	*the*	*swarming*	*population*
VB	IN	NN	IN	VB	DT	JJ	NN

Figure 1: An example sentence from the British National Corpus, annotated with parts of speech.

2(a). [*pos*=NN] [*word*=TO] [*word*=HOUSE, *pos*=VB]

2(b). [*pos*=NN] [*word*=TO] [*word*=HOUSE, *pos*≠VB]

2(c). [*word*=THE] [*pos*=JJ] [*pos*=NN]

2(d). [*word*=THE] ([*pos*=JJ] | [*pos*=NN]) [*pos*=NN]

2(e). ([*pos*=JJ] | [*pos*=IN]) [*word*=H[AEIOUY]*SE.*]

Figure 2: Example corpus queries.

Robie et al., 2017) or graph-based (e.g., Krause and Zeldes, 2016; Luotolahti et al., 2017; Kleiweg and van Noord, 2020), and is often tailor-made for a certain type of structured annotation, such as UD treebanks (de Marneffe et al., 2021).

In this paper we focus on linear query languages, and leave long-distance dependencies and syntactic structure as future work.

2.2 Corpus search engines

Corpus search engines can be divided into two main approaches: the *inverted index* approach, or the *database* approach.

Engines such as Corpus Workbench (Evert and Hardie, 2011) and Corpuscle (Meurer, 2020) build one or more inverted indexes from the corpus, which then are used to optimise search. They analyse a given query to find out which index to use, and uses the index to find a set of potential candidates. The set is then filtered by testing each candidate if it matches the query or not. Engines can be more or less intelligent when they decide which index to use – Corpus Workbench always uses the index corresponding to the first token in the query, while, e.g., Corpuscle tries to find an optimal cut in a finite automaton to decide which index to start from.

The second approach is to translate the corpus into a relational database. E.g., Davies (2005) transforms consecutive tokens in a corpus into a database of n-grams, AlpinoGraph (Kleiweg and van Noord, 2020) compiles treebanks into graphs stored in an SQL database, Krill (Diewald and Margaretha, 2016) uses the Apache Lucene information retrieval engine as a backbone, while LiRI (Schaber et al., 2023) converts the corpus and its annotations into tables designed to make use of the full-text search capabilities of PostgreSQL (2024, ch. 12).

In this paper we use the first approach and build the indexes ourselves. However, note that the second approach indirectly also uses indexes because they are automatically created by the underlying database engine.

2.3 Inverted indexes

Our implementation of inverted indexes are related to *suffix arrays* (Manber and Myers, 1993), which are efficient indexes for efficient full-text search in almost-constant time. Suffix arrays and its descendant algorithms are used in *information retrieval*, and the main difference to our approach is that information retrieval research focuses on pure text searches – i.e., finding substrings or patterns in plain text. As a contrast we have to be able to handle annotations on different levels, and not just text as a stream of characters.

2.4 Drawbacks of existing approaches

As far as we know, existing approaches do not combine multiple search indexes. When given a complex query, they usually use one of the indexes to get a collection of potential search results, and then filter the results one by one, by testing if they match the query.

In addition, no existing corpus engine uses binary search indexes, and as we show in section 5 they can drastically improve some queries.

3 Definitions and semantics

3.1 Annotated corpora

For the purposes of this paper, an annotated corpus is a collection of *texts*. Each text consists of *sentences* which in turn consist of *tokens*. Each token is annotated with a number of *attributes*, such as *word* (surface form), *lemma*, *pos* (part of speech), etc., where each attribute has one single value.

This definition of corpus is restricted – currently we cannot handle multi-token annotations, set-valued attributes, structural attributes, or empty tokens, to name just a few possibilities.

Formally, a corpus C is a sequence of tokens $C[0]\ C[1] \ldots C[n{-}2]\ C[n{-}1]$, where each token is an attribute-value mapping. We write $C[i].pos$ for the value of attribute *pos* at position i.

Figure 1 shows an example sentence taken from the British National Corpus (BNC), annotated with just word form (*word*) and part of speech (*pos*).

Note that we assume for now that the corpus is not divided into larger structures, such as phrases, sentences, paragraphs or texts. This will be discussed later in section 6.

3.2 Queries

In the next few sections, we use a restricted version of CQL (the Corpus Query Language, see section 2.2.3 in Evert and Hardie, 2011). Sections 7–8 then show how to lift some of the restrictions.

A query is of the form [*literal**]+, where a literal is either *attr=value* or *attr≠value*. The example query in figure 2(a) searches for sentences which contain a noun, followed by the word "*to*", followed by the word "*house*" tagged as a verb, whereas query 2(b) requires that the word "*house*" is not a verb. Query 2(c) is very generic and matches all words "*the*" followed by an adjective and a noun.

The remaining two queries use features not present in the restricted query language. Query 2(d) uses disjunction, so that the middle word may be an adjective or a noun, and query 2(e) uses a regular expression. In section 7, we extend the search algorithm to handle both these kinds of queries.

3.3 Query semantics

The token [*word*=HOUSE, *pos*=VB] in query 2(a) occurs 2 tokens after the first query token; we say that it has *relative position* 2. Using relative positions, we can write query 2(a) more formally as

$$[pos^{@0}{=}\text{NN}] \wedge [word^{@1}{=}\text{TO}] \\ \wedge [word^{@2}{=}\text{HOUSE}] \wedge [pos^{@2}{=}\text{VB}]$$

where $[word^{@2}{=}\text{HOUSE}]$ means that the word at relative position 2 is "*house*". Now we can define the semantics of a literal l at relative position k as the set of all positions p such that l is true at position $p{+}k$:

$$[attr^{@k}{=}val] \equiv \{\, p \mid C[p{+}k].attr = val \,\}$$

We call this set a *query set* and we write it $\{attr^{@k}{=}val\}$. The semantics of a combined query is then the intersection of the query sets for each of the literals in the query:

$$\{pos^{@0}{=}\text{NN}\} \cap \{word^{@1}{=}\text{TO}\} \\ \cap \{word^{@2}{=}\text{HOUSE}\} \cap \{pos^{@2}{=}\text{VB}\}$$

If a literal is negated $\{attr^{@k}{\neq}val\}$, we instead take the set difference with the corresponding positive literal. The semantics of query 2(b) then becomes:

$$\{pos^{@0}{=}\text{NN}\} \cap \{word^{@1}{=}\text{TO}\} \\ \cap \{word^{@2}{=}\text{HOUSE}\} \setminus \{pos^{@2}{=}\text{VB}\}$$

4 Efficient inverted indexes

In this section we describe how we build search indexes from a corpus to facilitate efficient search. As mentioned in section 2.2, the idea of using inverted indexes is not new, in fact large-scale corpus search engines compile the corpus into some kind of search indexes. What we present at first is a fairly standard inverted index. But afterward we move to what is new: how to make use of more than one search index when executing a complex query, and binary indexes.

Each annotation attribute (*pos*, *word*, etc.) is precompiled into an inverted index of corpus positions. This index is inspired by suffix arrays (Manber and Myers, 1993), in that we do not have to store the values in the index – it is just a large array of corpus positions. The array is sorted alphabetically on the attribute value at the given position. When there are many tokens with the same attribute value, these positions are in increasing order.

For example, assume that the example sentence in figure 1 is our whole corpus. Then the index for the *pos* attribute will be the following array of positions:

$$[\underbrace{0, 4, 13}_{\text{DT}}, \underbrace{3, 9, 11}_{\text{IN}}, \underbrace{1, 5, 14}_{\text{JJ}}, \underbrace{2, 6, 10, 15}_{\text{NN}}, \underbrace{7, 8, 12}_{\text{VB}}]$$

This array is sorted alphabetically on the *pos* values: [0, 4, 13] are the determiners (DT), [3, 9, 11] are the prepositions (IN), etc. Furthermore, each group of positions for the same value is in increasing order.

So a search index is simply a large array of integers, which can be stored as a memory-mapped binary file of fixed-size integers for fast access.

4.1 Searching an inverted index

To search for a value in an index we can do two very efficient binary searches – one that finds the first matching value and another that finds the last match. If we search for NN (a noun) in the example index, these searches return 6 and 9, which are the start and end indices for the sublist [2, 6, 10, 15], which contain all the corpus positions for NN.

Now, to execute the query $\{pos^{@k}{=}\text{NN}\}$, we search for NN in the index, and then subtract k from all matching positions. But for efficiency we instead just record the start and end indices (6 and 9) and the relative position k, using which we can easily recover all matching positions.

So the result of an index lookup can be stored as a tuple (i, j, k) where i and j denote the relevant span in the search index, and k is the relative position. In particular, we do not need to load the result set into memory.

Note that we cannot use this simple approach if we have a negative literal [*attr*≠*val*], because inverted indexes do not store complement sets. Instead we have to calculate the set difference, which is described in the next section.

4.2 Computing the result of a query

To execute a complex query, we look up each literal to get its query set, as described in the last section. Then we translate the query into a set theory expresssion as described in section 3.3, and then just evaluate the expression, using set intersection, difference and union to find the final result.

4.3 Computing query sets

As described in section 4.1 the initial query sets are just pointers into the inverted indexes. But when performing the set operations we have to build the resulting sets.

The query sets are stored as sorted arrays, and there are simple and efficient algorithms for computing the intersection, difference and union. The results are also sorted arrays themselves, so we can continue using these algorithms to compute the final result. Depending on the relative sizes of the sets we use one of the following two algorithms:

Merge The default is to use a *merging* strategy: Iterate through both sets in parallel, adding elements to the result set. If the sizes of the two sets are n and m, this algorithm has complexity $O(n + m)$.

Filter If one set is much larger than the other, we can use a *filtering* strategy: Iterate through each element of the smaller set, and test if it is also in the larger set using binary search. The complexity of this algorithm is $O(n \log m)$, where n is the size of the smaller set. Note that this strategy cannot be used for computing the union.

4.4 Deciding the order of the set operations

If we have more than two query sets, we have to decide in which order to perform the set operations. It is not always the case that starting from the leftmost token is the best in all circumstances – the order can have a huge difference.

A heuristic that works well for intersection and difference is to start from the smallest sets and leave the largest until later. This is because the result set will never be larger than the original sets, and then we avoid doing duplicate work.

Set union is different, because the result set will be increasing. This case is discussed in section 7.1.

4.5 Example

We tested this algorithm on the 112 million token British National Corpus (BNC).[4] The resulting query sets for query 2(a) are as follows:

$\{pos^{@0}{=}\text{NN}\}$	→	26 M results
$\{word^{@1}{=}\text{TO}\}$	→	2.6 M results
$\{word^{@2}{=}\text{HOUSE}\}$	→	33 k results
$\{pos^{@2}{=}\text{VB}\}$	→	18 M results

We start by intersecting the smallest query sets, $\{word^{@2}{=}\text{HOUSE}\}$ and $\{word^{@1}{=}\text{TO}\}$, which gives 421 results. Then we intersect with $\{pos^{@2}{=}\text{VB}\}$ and finally with $\{pos^{@0}{=}\text{NN}\}$, in the end finding 158 search results.

Intersection uses the *filtering strategy* from section 4.3, which only needs to iterate through the smallest index. In the first step it iterates through $\{lemma^{@2}{=}\text{HOUSE}\}$, and in the second step it only iterates through the 421 intermediate results. Recall also that the initial query sets are not loaded into memory, but are stored as a tuple as described in section 4.1. Due to these optimisations, the query runs quickly, in about 0.3s on an ordinary laptop.

To calculate query 2(b) we use the same initial query sets. But instead of intersecting with $\{pos^{@2}{=}\text{VB}\}$ we take the set difference, and in the end we find that there are 38 search results.

4.6 When are unary indexes not enough?

However, there are still cases where using the simple search indexes are inefficient. Consider the very general query 2(c), which is rewritten to this:

$$\{word^{@0}{=}\text{THE}\} \cap \{pos^{@1}{=}\text{JJ}\} \cap \{pos^{@2}{=}\text{NN}\}$$

Each of these literals results in a huge set:

[4]BNC, http://www.natcorp.ox.ac.uk/

$$\{word^{@0}{=}\text{THE}\} \rightarrow 5 \text{ M results}$$
$$\{pos^{@1}{=}\text{JJ}\} \rightarrow 18 \text{ M results}$$
$$\{pos^{@2}{=}\text{NN}\} \rightarrow 26 \text{ M results}$$

So the intersections become slower (about 20 times slower than the previous example, taking about 6s). The first intersection gives 1.5 M results, and the second one results in 1.1 M final results.

To solve this we now introduce *binary indexes*.

5 Binary query indexes

Formally, a unary query index $[a]$ can be seen as a function from values to query sets:

$$[a] \equiv \lambda v \rightarrow \{a^{@0}{=}v\}$$

Similarly a *binary query index* can be viewed as a function from pairs of values to query sets:

$$[a]\,[b] \equiv \lambda v, w \rightarrow \{a^{@0}{=}v\} \cap \{b^{@1}{=}w\}$$
$$[a]\,[]\,[b] \equiv \lambda v, w \rightarrow \{a^{@0}{=}v\} \cap \{b^{@2}{=}w\}$$
$$\text{(similar for } [a]\,[]\,[]\,[b]\text{, etc.)}$$

For example, an index [*word*] [] [*pos*] can answer queries such as [*word*=THE] [] [*pos*=NN]. These binary indexes can be compiled and searched in a similar way to the unary indexes.

5.1 Searching using binary indexes

Now we can decompose a complex query into a composition of binary indexes. E.g., if we have computed binary indexes for adjacent tokens ($[a][b]$) and for tokens with a gap ($[a][][b]$), a query with three adjacent tokens, $[t_1][t_2][t_3]$, is equivalent to any of the following binary index searches:

$$[t_1]\,[t_2] \cap [t_2]\,[t_3]^{@1}$$
$$[t_1]\,[t_2] \cap [t_1]\,[]\,[t_3]$$
$$[t_1]\,[]\,[t_3] \cap [t_2]\,[t_3]^{@1}$$

Exactly which of these is the most efficient depends on the sizes of the resulting query sets. In this case, we calculate all three query sets and then take the intersection of the two smallest.

5.2 Results using binary indexes

Using the same example as in section 4.6, we search in the following binary indexes, instead of the unary indexes we tried before:

[*word*=THE] [*pos*=JJ]	→	1.4 M results
[*word*=THE] [] [*pos*=NN]	→	1.7 M results
[*pos*=JJ] [*pos*=NN]	→	6.7 M results

Now we can intersect the two smaller sets:

[*word*=THE] [*pos*=JJ]
∩ [*word*=THE] [] [*pos*=NN]

This intersection gives 1.1 M results, and we do not have to use the other indexes: by set theory, the intersection above describes the same set as the query, so we have the correct result already.

The total query time is reduced from 6s to 0.4s. (On the same query, Corpus Workbench takes 10s.)

5.3 Search heuristics for binary indexes

Finally we are ready to describe the heuristics we use to decide in which order we perform intersections and set difference:

1. Infer which binary indexes are relevant;
2. Perform all relevant binary index lookups;
3. If some token is not covered by a binary index, look it up in the unary index;
4. Perform intersections starting from the smallest set, until the whole query is covered;
5. If the query contains negative literals, look up the value in the unary index, and calculate the set difference instead of the intersection.

5.4 How many binary indexes are needed?

Each binary index is as large as a unary index, and there are many possible binary indexes. If we have n different attributes (and therefore n unary indexes), then there are n^2 possible binary indexes per relative distance. So there are n^2 $[a][b]$ indexes, and n^2 $[a][][b]$ indexes, etc. This is potentially very many indexes that take up a lot of space.

But we do not have to build all these indexes. Note that any query with k adjacent tokens can be simplified into a conjunction of $k - 1$ lookups in $[a][b]$ indexes, as shown in section 5.1. Therefore it should be enough to only build n^2 *bigram* indexes. However, as seen in 5.1, it is often useful to also build the n^2 $[a][][b]$ indexes, because then we get several different ways of searching to find the most optimal intersection order. But it is usually not worth the trouble to build indexes with longer relative distances, such as $[a][][][][b]$.[5]

Also note that if a binary index is missing, we can simply fall back to searching in two unary indexes instead, as in section 4. This means that we can focus on building binary indexes only for the kinds of queries where they have the greatest impact.

[5] The one exception is if the query itself has a longer gap, such as $[t_1][][][][t_2]$, then we have to resort to searching in unary indexes instead.

5.5 Reducing the size of binary indexes

Still, each binary index is as large as a unary index, and storing up to $2n^2$ binary indexes can use up quite a lot of space. So can we reduce their size in any way?

If a query uses a literal that is uncommon in the corpus (e.g., [*word*=TURTLE] only occurs 166 times in BNC), there is no need to use binary indexes for that query, since the unary index will already return a small query set. Therefore, an optimisation is to only add a new index instance (*v*, *w*) to the index [*a*][*b*], if the corresponding unary instances *v* and *w* are common enough in [*a*] and [*b*] respectively. When we execute a query, we then need to check which literals are uncommon, and exclude the use of binary indexes for those literals.

For example, in the BNC each full (unary and binary) index uses around 400 MB. If we only include pairs where both words occur at least 20,000 times each, the binary indexes are reduced to around half their size.

6 Sentences and hierarchical structures

The corpus is encoded as a sequence of tokens, and a sentence starts directly after the previous one ends. So how can we ensure that we don't match sentence borders? E.g., we don't want query 2(c) to match a sentence that ends in "the first" where the next sentence starts with an arbitrary noun.

To solve this we encode the start of a sentence as an attribute of its own. So we build an index [*s*] which has a special value (say •) only for the tokens that start a sentence. Our example query is then translated to:

$$[word^{@0}{=}\text{THE}] \wedge [s^{@1}{\neq}\bullet] \wedge [pos^{@1}{=}\text{JJ}] \\ \wedge [s^{@2}{\neq}\bullet] \wedge [pos^{@2}{=}\text{NN}]$$

6.1 Sentence borders and binary indexes

To handle sentence borders and binary indexes we can incorporate the literals $[s^{@1}{\neq}\bullet]$ in our binary indexes. So their meaning is actually:

$$\begin{aligned} [a]\,[b] &\equiv \lambda v, w \rightarrow \{a^{@0}{=}v\} \cap \{b^{@1}{=}w\} \\ &\qquad \cap \{s^{@1}{\neq}\bullet\} \\ [a]\,[]\,[b] &\equiv \lambda v, w \rightarrow \{a^{@0}{=}v\} \cap \{b^{@2}{=}w\} \\ &\qquad \cap \{s^{@1}{\neq}\bullet\} \cap \{s^{@2}{\neq}\bullet\} \end{aligned}$$

That is, the indexes exclude matches which cross a sentence border. Though this perhaps looks complicated, it can be generated automatically, and keeps query execution simple. Our example query 2(c) can still be translated to searches in the following three binary indexes:

[*word*][*pos*], [*word*][][*pos*], and [*pos*][*pos*]

And just as in section 5.2, we only have to intersect the two smallest query sets because the final query set is subsumed by the intersection.

7 Extending the query language

Here we show how we handle more expressive queries than the very simple ones described earlier.

7.1 Disjunctive queries

CQL supports disjunction in queries. For example, query 2(d) is of the form $A(B|C)D$, where A searches for the word "the", B an adjective, C a noun, and D a noun.

If we use only unary indexes each literal corresponds to a index lookup, so query 2(d) results in calculating the set $A \cap (B \cup C) \cap D$. In order to make use of the binary indexes, we expand out the disjunction into two *strands*:

$$\begin{aligned} ABD &= [word{=}\text{THE}]\ [pos{=}\text{JJ}]\ [pos{=}\text{NN}] \\ ACD &= [word{=}\text{THE}]\ [pos{=}\text{NN}]\ [pos{=}\text{NN}] \end{aligned}$$

We then compute a result set for each strand, using the algorithm from section 5, and finally take the union of the result sets, $ABD \cup ACD$. The query returns 1.6 million results and executes in 1s.

Note that when executing the example above, the subquery AD = [*word*=THE] [] [*pos*=NN] will be used twice. As an optimisation, we cache the results of any duplicated subqueries, to avoid executing them repeatedly.

7.1.1 When to apply disjunction

To expand out disjunctions into strands is not always the most optimal strategy. In particular if the query contains several disjunctions we will get an exponential number of strands.

An alternative strategy is to *not* expand out the disjunction, but rather implement it as set union directly. This means that B and C will be looked up using unary indexes, but we can use the binary index [*word*][][*pos*] to look up AD. Then we can return $AD \cap (B \cup C)$. The problem with this approach is that we would not be able to use the binary indexes [*word*][*pos*] or [*pos*][*pos*].

However, there are even more possibilities. We can also half-expand the disjunction $A(B|C)D$ in two different ways, either into $(AB|AC)D$, or into $A(BD|CD)$. For the first case we can then search the binary index [*word*][*pos*] once for AB and another time for AC, and the unary index [*pos*] for D, and then calculate $(AB \cup AC) \cap D$. And correspondingly for the second case.

So which strategy is the best? It depends on the sizes of the different sets, and we don't know these sizes until we actually calculate them. But a possible heuristic would be to assume that unions are always exclusive, meaning that $|B \cup C| = |B| + |C|$. Using this assumption and the sizes of all the possible seed sets $(A, B, C, D, AB, AC, BD, CD, AD)$ we can calculate which strategy would be the most optimal.

7.1.2 Limitations

The strategy to expand the disjunctions to the top level works for all kinds of disjunctions, but the other strategies may not always work. The semantics described in section 3.3 does not handle all kinds of disjunctions. For query 2(d), we can simply interpret the disjunction as set union:

$$\{word^{@0}{=}\text{THE}\} \cap \{pos^{@2}{=}\text{NN}\}$$
$$\cap\ (\{pos^{@1}{=}\text{JJ}\} \cup \{pos^{@1}{=}\text{NN}\})$$

The reason why this works is that the disjuncts have the same length, i.e., that they span the same number of tokens. But when the disjuncts have different lengths, such as in the query

([*pos*=PRON] | [*pos*=DET] [*pos*=NN]) ...

we cannot know the exact relative position of the token following the disjunction – it will either be 1 (if we matched [*pos*=PRON]) or 2 (if we matched [*pos*=DET] [*pos*=NN]).

In practice, this means that if the disjuncts are of different lengths, and there is a token after the disjunction, then we must expand the disjunction.

For example, suppose that the C subquery of $A(B|C)D$ spans two tokens (e.g., the 2-token query [*pos*=ADV][*pos*=JJ]). Then the query AB will span 2 tokens but AC will span 3 tokens. This means that the final subquery D will have relative position 2 or 3 depending on which disjunct we select. Therefore we cannot calculate $A \cap (B \cup C) \cap D$ or $(AB \cup AC) \cap D$, but are forced to expand the disjunction into two strands ABD and ACD.

Section 8 discusses this case, together with repetition and other regular expression constructs.

7.2 Prefix and suffix queries

Finding all values starting with a given prefix, such as [*word*=CAT .*], is possible using the normal inverted indexes. Since the index is sorted alphabetically, all words matching a given prefix will appear together in the index. Using binary search we can find the start and end positions of all values that match the prefix, but the results will not be one single sorted set. Instead we will get a sequence of sorted groups, one for each matching value, something like $[\underline{12, 43, 57}, \overline{11, 52, 77}, \underline{22, 23}]$. We then have to sort this query set, but this is often quite efficient since the set is already partially sorted.

Unfortunately prefix queries do not play well with binary indexes. Consider the query [THE][CAT .*][RUNS]. We can use a binary index to answer [THE][CAT .*], since all matching bigrams will appear contiguously in the index (*the cat*, *the catcher*, ...). However, we can not do this for [CAT .*][RUNS], since the matching bigrams may not be contiguous (*cat runs*, *catcher has*, *catcher runs*). Our solution is to ignore binary indexes for token pairs where the first token uses a prefix query.

We implement suffix queries by automatically adding a new annotation to the corpus for each feature, consisting of that feature *backwards*. For example, a token with [*word*=HORSE] is annotated with [*drow*=ESROH] (*drow* is *word* backwards). We transform a suffix query such as [*word*= .* RSE] into the corresponding prefix query [*drow*=ESR .*].

7.3 Regular expressions over values

Consider a query containing a regular expression:

... [*word*= .* CAT .+ (ED|ING)] ...

To execute it, we can exploit the fact that, while the BNC has ≈100 million tokens, it has only ≈1 million *distinct* tokens (the *vocabulary*) – generally the vocabulary of a corpus is much smaller than the corpus as a whole. In our system, the vocabulary is stored alongside the corpus in a plain text file.[6]

First we search the vocabulary file for the regular expression .* CAT .+ (ED|ING). The search returns a list of matching words: *catching*, *scattered*, etc. The regular expression literal is then transformed into a disjunction which is handled as seen earlier:

[*word*=CATCHING] | [*word*=SCATTERED] | ...

This works well except when the regular expression matches very many words, because our system does not handle the resulting huge disjunction well.

[6]Note that this is not the most space-efficient way of storing a vocabulary – in a production system we would probably use a trie instead (Crochemore and Lecroq, 2020).

8 Future work

Currently our system can only handle a limited number of queries, and there are many more kinds of queries that we want to be able to handle.

8.1 General disjunctions and optional tokens

In section 7.1.2 we already discussed how to handle disjunctions where the disjuncts are of different lengths – and this includes when a token is optional. A simple solution is to expand the disjunctions, but sometimes this might lead to an exponential number of strands. For example, the query $(A|B)(C|D)(E|F)$ contains three disjunctions, but if we expand them we get $ACE|ACF|ADE|\cdots|BDF$ which consists of $2^3 = 8$ strands.

One possible solution could be to let the query sets be sets of *ranges* instead of just positions, where a range is a pair (i, j) of the start and end position of a phrase. Then a query set can contain arbitrary-length phrases. The downside to this solution is that the query sets will become twice as large as before.

8.2 Repeated tokens

Queries with repetitions such as $A\,B^+\,C$, and holes such as A []* C, can perhaps be partially solved using sets of ranges just as for disjunctions.

If we want to make use of binary indexes we can expand a repetition $A\,B^+\,C$ into $AB\,B^*\,C$, which makes it possible to use the binary index AB. Alternatively we can expand in the other direction, into $A\,B^*\,BC$, which makes it possible to use the binary index BC. Which one is the best depends on the sizes of the sets AB, C compared to A, BC, among other things.

Note that we cannot calculate the final query set by taking the intersection of intermediate query sets, because then we would have to keep expanding the repetition indefinitely. Instead we should stop expanding the repetition when we have an intermediate query set of a reasonable size. This intermediate set is guaranteed to contain all matches, but it might contain false positives too. So in the end we have to do a final filtering pass to get only the exact matches, as described in section 8.5.

Holes are a special kind of repetition where we don't know anything about the repeated token, such as in A []* C. For holes it is not useful to expand the repetition, because we still won't be able to make use of any binary index. One possibility is instead to build a tailor-made binary index:

$$[a]\ []^*\ [b] \;\equiv\; \lambda v, w \rightarrow \{a^{@0}{=}v\} \cap \{b^{@k}{=}w \mid k > 0\}$$

"Indexes with holes" can also be used to solve "normal" repetitions: To solve the query $A\,B^+\,C$ we can use the "hole" index [*a*][]*[*b*]. And if we expand the query to $AB\,B^*\,C$ or to $A\,B^*\,BC$, we can also use the binary indexes [*a*][*b*] or [*b*][*c*].

8.3 Regular expressions over tokens

Combinations of sequencing, disjunction, optionality and repetition can be handled using the techniques described above. However, we will quickly get an explosion in the number of ways we can expand queries and decide on the best indexes.

Therefore, to handle general regular expressions over tokens we need to be able to reason about the different expansions and rewrites to come up with an optimal query plan. This is a non-trivial task and something we will look into in the future.

8.4 Regular expressions over values

In section 7.3 we described one way to handle regular expressions over values, such as [*word*=.* CAT .+ (ED|ING)], by searching in the vocabulary and expanding the expression to a long disjunction. However, when there are many possible words matching the regular expression this is not feasible. In those cases we can use an idea from Zobel et al. (1993), where we build an inverted index over character n-grams.

To search for all tokens that match the regular expression above we can search for the ngrams CAT, ED, and ING in this n-gram index, getting the sets A_{CAT}, B_{ED}, and C_{ING}. Now we can compute the new query set $A_{\text{CAT}} \cap (B_{\text{ED}} \cup C_{\text{ING}})$. Note that this result is a query set that might contain false positives, so we will have to filter the final set to get the exact query matches.

8.5 Filtering

The simplest and most general approach is to use filtering. First we translate the query into a less precise query that we can handle, then we filter the results by checking them against the full query. This is how all current corpus engines do, and sometimes this is actually the best approach.

All the techniques we have described in sections 4–7 are the most useful if there is no single search index that returns a reasonable-sized query set. E.g., in the example queries 2(a–b), one of the tokens matches only 33,000 results which is a fairly small set – so it might be the easiest to just filter that set instead of calculating intersections. However, for queries 2(c–d) there are no single small sets so it is much better to use the binary indexes and calculate the intersection. In general our query planner should be able to stop when the query set is small enough, and then resort to filtering instead of continuing with set operations.

8.6 Metadata and multi-layer annotations

The current prototype does not support searching in metadata (such as author, year, language variety, or similar), or multi-layer annotations. This is of course something that must be solved for the system to be useful in practice.

8.7 More efficient set representations

The prototype uses a very simple representation of sets as a sorted array of integers (see section 4). This seems to work well in most cases, but the sets can become quite large. There are several dedicated set data structures that are both compressed and allow for more efficient set operations, such as different kinds of compressed bitmaps (Culpepper and Moffat, 2011; Lemire et al., 2018).

9 Conclusion

We have shown that inverted indexes and efficient set operations can improve searching in large annotated corpora, and in particular binary indexes can improve efficiency by an order of magnitude compared to the traditional unary indexes. By translating queries to set operations, we can use multiple indexes in one query and avoid the need to filter the results afterwards.

We have implemented a prototype which shows promising results, but there is certainly room for improvement. Firstly, the key operations of set intersection, different and union, and building the indexes, can be optimised. Secondly, the query language can be extended to more expressive queries, as discussed in section 8.

It is not always clear how to translate expressive queries to expressions in set theory (see section 7.1.2). An important next step is to find or design a mathematical formalism that queries can be translated into, which is just as amenable to reasoning as set theory is, but supports more expressive queries. We hope that by doing so, we can scale our approach to handle far more complex queries even over huge corpora.

Limitations

The work described in this paper is work in progress. Our results are promising, but we have not extended our approach to more advanced query languages and therefore we cannot be certain how scalable our approach is. Furthermore, we have not done any extensive evaluation and empirical comparison with existing corpus query engines, apart from measuring the runtimes for some example queries, and a limited comparison with Corpus Workbench.

Ethical Considerations

We have not collected any data or made any human experiments when developing the algorithms in this paper, so there are no direct ethical consequences with respect to GDPR or similar. One important consequence of algorithm optimisation is reduced energy consumption, so in the best case this can be a small step in reducing the carbon footprint of digital humanities research.

Acknowledgements

We thank Niklas Deworetzki and the anonymous reviewers for their valuable comments and suggestions.

References

Joachim Bingel and Nils Diewald. 2015. KoralQuery – a general corpus query protocol. In *NODALIDA Workshop on Innovative Corpus Query and Visualization Tools*, pages 1–5, Vilnius, Lithuania.

Maxime Crochemore and Thierry Lecroq. 2020. Trie. In Ling Liu and M. Tamer Özsu, editors, *Encyclopedia of database systems*, pages 3179–3182. Springer New York.

J. Shane Culpepper and Alistair Moffat. 2011. Efficient set intersection for inverted indexing. *ACM Trans. Inf. Syst.*, 29(1).

Mark Davies. 2005. The advantage of using relational databases for large corpora. *International Journal of Corpus Linguistics*, 10(3):307–334.

Marie-Catherine de Marneffe, Christopher Manning, Joakim Nivre, and Daniel Zeman. 2021. Universal dependencies. *Computational Linguistics*, 47(2):255–308.

Nils Diewald and Eliza Margaretha. 2016. Krill: KorAP search and analysis engine. *Journal for Language Technology and Computational Linguistics*, 31(1):63–80.

Stefan Evert and Andrew Hardie. 2011. Twenty-first century Corpus Workbench: Updating a query architecture for the new millennium. In *Proceedings of the Corpus Linguistics 2011 conference*, University of Birmingham, UK.

Sumukh Ghodke and Steven Bird. 2012. Fangorn: A system for querying very large treebanks. In *COLING Demonstration Papers*, pages 175–182, Mumbai, India.

Peter Kleiweg and Gertjan van Noord. 2020. AlpinoGraph: A graph-based search engine for flexible and efficient treebank search. In *Proceedings of the 19th International Workshop on Treebanks and Linguistic Theories*, pages 151–161, Düsseldorf, Germany.

Thomas Krause and Amir Zeldes. 2016. ANNIS3: A new architecture for generic corpus query and visualization. *Digital Scholarship in the Humanities*, 13(1):118–139.

Daniel Lemire, Owen Kaser, Nathan Kurz, Luca Deri, Chris O'Hara, François Saint-Jacques, and Gregory Ssi-Yan-Kai. 2018. Roaring bitmaps: Implementation of an optimized software library. *Software: Practice and Experience*, 48(4):867–895.

Juhani Luotolahti, Jenna Kanerva, and Filip Ginter. 2017. Dep_search: Efficient search tool for large dependency parsebanks. In *21st Nordic Conference on Computational Linguistics, NoDaLiDa*, pages 255–258, Gothenburg, Sweden.

Udi Manber and Gene Myers. 1993. Suffix arrays: A new method for on-line string searches. *SIAM Journal on Computing*, 22(5).

Paul Meurer. 2020. Designing efficient algorithms for querying large corpora. *Oslo Studies in Language*, 11(2):283–302.

PostgreSQL. 2024. PostgreSQL documentation. Technical report, The PostgreSQL Global Development Group.

Jonathan Robie, Michael Dyck, and Josh Spiegel. 2017. XML path language (XPath) 3.1. Technical report, W3C.

Jonathan Schaber, Johannes Graën, Daniel McDonald, Igor Mustac, Nikolina Rajovic, Gerold Schneider, and Noah Bubenhofer. 2023. The LiRI corpus platform. In *CLARIN Annual Conference*, pages 145–149, Leuven, Belgium.

Justin Zobel, Alistair Moffat, and Ron Sacks-Davis. 1993. Searching large lexicons for partially specified terms using compressed inverted files. In *19th VLDB Conference*, Dublin, Ireland.

An Improved Method for Class-specific Keyword Extraction: A Case Study in the German Business Registry

Stephen Meisenbacher♠[1], Tim Schopf♠[1], Weixin Yan[1], Patrick Holl[2], and Florian Matthes[1]
[1]Technical University of Munich
School of Computation, Information and Technology
Department of Computer Science, Garching, Germany
[2]Fusionbase GmbH, Munich, Germany
{first.last}@tum.de, patrick.holl@fusionbase.com, matthes@tum.de

Abstract

The task of *keyword extraction* is often an important initial step in unsupervised information extraction, forming the basis for tasks such as topic modeling or document classification. While recent methods have proven to be quite effective in the extraction of keywords, the identification of *class-specific* keywords, or only those pertaining to a predefined class, remains challenging. In this work, we propose an improved method for class-specific keyword extraction, which builds upon the popular KEYBERT library to identify only keywords related to a class described by *seed keywords*. We test this method using a dataset of German business registry entries, where the goal is to classify each business according to an economic sector. Our results reveal that our method greatly improves upon previous approaches, setting a new standard for *class-specific* keyword extraction.

1 Introduction

As the amount of information created daily continues to rise in the age of big data (Chen et al., 2014), a core challenge becomes how to extract valuable structured information from largely unstructured text documents (Tanwar et al., 2015; Song et al., 2023). An important first step in the process of Information Retrieval (IR) is often the extraction of keywords (or phrases) from documents, which can provide an initial clue about the information stored within the document (Firoozeh et al., 2020; Xie et al., 2023). With the extraction of meaningful keywords, NLP tasks such as Topic Modeling or Document Classification can be bootstrapped.

Over the past few decades, a number of unsupervised keyword extraction approaches have been proposed in the literature, ranging from frequency-based methods to statistics-based methods (Firoozeh et al., 2020), and more recently, methods using graphs or leveraging the capabilities of transformer-based language models (Nomoto, 2022; Tran et al., 2023). Supervised approaches have been proposed, with the downside of requiring reliable training data (Firoozeh et al., 2020).

While a myriad of keyword extraction approaches has appeared in the literature, they are often of the *unguided* nature, where any relevant keywords are extracted regardless of the downstream goal. As such, there has been a scarcity of research in the direction of *class-specific* keyword extraction, where only keywords adhering to a particular *class* are extracted. Presumably, this type of keyword extraction would be useful in settings where a targeted set of keywords is desired, rather than any relevant keyword in a document.

To address this open research challenge, we devise a novel class-specific keyword extraction pipeline, which builds upon the popular open-source package KEYBERT* (Grootendorst et al., 2023). We envision an iterative process which is guided by user-provided *seed keywords*. With these, candidate keywords are ranked according to a two-part scoring scheme, and the seed keywords are augmented by top candidates from each iteration.

We evaluate our approach on a dataset of German business registry (*Handelsregister*) entries, where the goal is to extract as many *class-specific* keywords according to *economic sectors*, as defined by an existing classification scheme. In this evaluation, we show that our method greatly outperforms previous keyword extraction methods, demonstrating the strength of our approach in extracting class-specific keywords.

The contributions of our work are as follows:

1. We address the task of *class-specific* keyword extraction with a case study in the German business registry.
2. We propose a class-specific keyword extraction pipeline that improves upon an existing

♠Equal contribution

*https://maartengr.github.io/KeyBERT/

transformer-based method. Our code is found at https://github.com/sjmeis/CSKE.

3. We achieve a new standard for extracting class-specific keywords, measured in a comparative analysis with multiple metrics.

2 Related Work

A recent survey structures 167 keyword extraction approaches from the literature (Xie et al., 2023). We focus on unsupervised extraction approaches, which can generally be characterized as either statistics-, graph-, or embedding-based, while *TF-IDF* is a common frequency-based baseline method (Papagiannopoulou and Tsoumakas, 2019).

YAKE uses a set of different statistical metrics, including word casing, word position, word frequency, and more, to extract keyphrases from text (Campos et al., 2020). *TextRank* uses Part of Speech (PoS) filters to extract noun phrase candidates that are added to a graph as nodes while adding an edge between nodes if the words co-occur within a defined window (Mihalcea and Tarau, 2004; Page et al., 1999). *SingleRank* improves upon the TextRank approach by adding weights to edges based on word co-occurrences (Wan and Xiao, 2008). *RAKE* leverages a word co-occurrence graph and assigns a number of scores to aid in ranking keyword candidates (Rose et al., 2010). Knowledge Graphs can also be used to incorporate semantics for keyword or keyphrase extraction (Shi et al., 2017). *EmbedRank* leverages Doc2Vec (Le and Mikolov, 2014) and Sent2Vec (Pagliardini et al., 2018) embeddings to rank candidate keywords for extraction (Bennani-Smires et al., 2018). In a similar way, *PatternRank* uses a combination of sentence embeddings and *POS* filters (Schopf et al., 2022). Further, Language Model-based approaches have been introduced, for example using BERT (Devlin et al., 2019), for automatic extraction of keywords and keyphrases (Sammet and Krestel, 2023; Song et al., 2023).

3 A Class-Specific Keyword Extraction Pipeline

In this section, we outline in detail our proposed class-specific keyword extraction pipeline. The pipeline is illustrated in Figure 1.

Preliminaries For our pipeline, we assume three preliminary requirements:

1. **Document corpus**: unstructured text documents from any domain, from which meaningful information can be extracted.
2. **Pre-defined classes**: a set of one or more *classes*, each of which represents a distinct and well-defined concept.
3. **Class-specific seed keywords**: for each defined class, a set of *seed keywords* is available. Seed keywords are keywords that are representative of a particular class and can be used as a foundation for guided keyword extraction.

An Iterative Method Given a sizeable document corpus, we propose to process the corpus in *batches*, allowing for an iterative method, where each iteration "learns" from the previous.

For each iteration (on one batch), the first step is to extract keywords from the batch's documents in a *guided* manner. For this, we modify the popular KeyBERT package, specifically the *guided* functionality. In the current version of KeyBERT the guided functionality by default takes a set of seed keywords as input parameters, and uses a weighted average of seed keyword embeddings and document embeddings to extract candidate keywords. As we place a focus on *class-specific* seed keywords, we make the modification for *KeyBERT* to focus 100% on the seed keyword embeddings. After this modified version is run on the entire batch, the output is a list of *guided* candidate keywords (i.e., from the seed keywords).

Following the above, we employ a two-part scoring scheme to "reorder" the candidates. In particular, we use the following two scores:

- **Average Scoring**: the embedding of each candidate is compared against each seed keyword embedding, using cosine similarity, and these results are averaged for the *average score*.
- **Max Scoring**: similar to *average scoring*, but only the maximum cosine similarity score is kept, resulting in the *max score*.

We use the mean of *average score* and *max score* for the final candidate score, and all candidates for a batch are reordered based on this final score. The intuition behind such a scoring scheme is that an ideal keyword is both similar in meaning to one seed keyword, but also generally similar to all seed keywords, suggesting that such a keyword is also representative of the class in question.

The final step within one iteration includes taking the top-scoring candidates and adding them

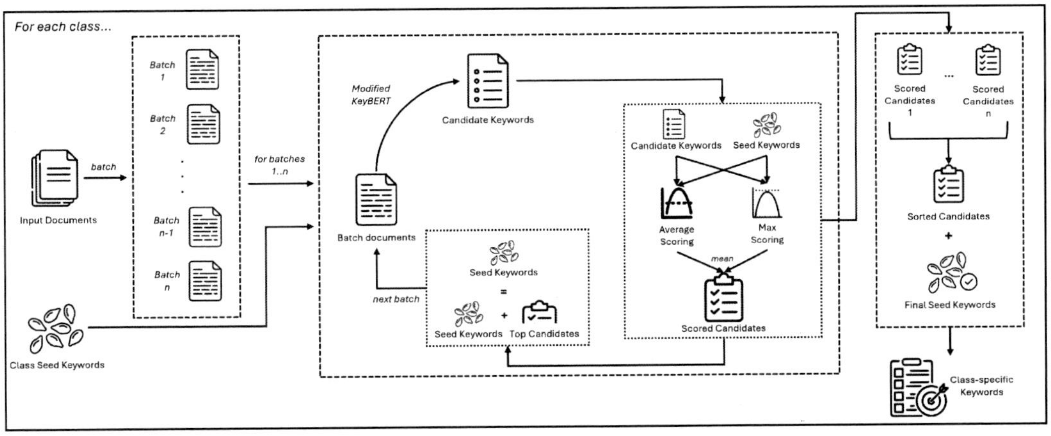

Figure 1: Our class-specific keyword extraction pipeline. With a document corpus and class-specific keyword sets as inputs, we iterate sequentially over batches of the corpus, using a modified KEYBERT and a two-part scoring scheme. Top keywords are added to the seed keywords for the next iteration, until a final set of keywords is achieved.

to the set of seed keywords. In doing so, we can iteratively "expand" the class-specific seed keywords, thus also expanding the comprehensiveness of these seeds. To do this, we define two parameters: (1) *percentile_newseed*, defining above which percentile of scores to consider (default: 99), and (2) *number_newseed*, defining how many new seed keywords to add per iteration (default: 3). Thus in the default setting, after each iteration (except the last), a maximum of 3 keywords from the top 99th percentile are added to the set of seed keywords.

Class-specific Keyword Set The output of each iteration is a set of scored candidate keywords. After all batches are processed, all scored candidates are merged and sorted. A *topk* parameter governs how many of the keywords to return, with seed keywords always being placed at the top of the list.

4 Experimental Setup and Results

Our experimental setup aims to evaluate the ability of our proposed method to extract class-specific keywords, in comparison to previous approaches. As opposed to typical keyword extraction evaluations, our evaluation tests the ability of a method to extract a set of class-specific keywords from a corpus, rather than generic keywords from documents.

Dataset We use a dataset of the German business registry (*Deutsches Handelsregister*) records, which contains 2.37 million business purpose records structured by Fusionbase[†]. The goal is to classify each business into an economic sector, according to the scheme proposed by the German Ministry of Statistics (*Statistiches Bundesamt*), called the *WZ 2008* (*Klassifikation der Wirtschaftszweige, Ausgabe 2008*)[‡]. In this work, we model the evaluation on the above dataset as a class-specific keyword extraction task, where the goal is to extract meaningful keywords for each of the 21 top-level economic sectors in the WZ 2008. For evaluation purposes, we use a random sample of 10,000 rows from the larger dataset[§].

It should be noted that we only investigate the extraction of unigram keywords. For the extraction of German keywords, this is advantageous due to the relatively high frequency of nominal compounds in the German language. Thus, meaningful keywords can be extracted in an efficient manner. However, this comes with two limitations: (1) not all *keyphrases* will be caught, thus sometimes leading to incomplete keywords (see "Dicke" in Listing 1, which means *thick* translated to English), and (2) the results achieved for German language datasets may not be directly generalizable to English.

Keyword Extraction Methods For a comparative analysis, we test our method against four methods: (1) RAKE (Rose et al., 2010), (2) YAKE (Campos et al., 2020), (3) KEYBERT, and (4) Guided KEYBERT. Note that RAKE and YAKE do not offer any mechanism for guided keyword extraction, and thus the result-

[†] https://fusionbase.com

[‡] https://www.destatis.de/DE/Methoden/Klassifikationen/Gueter-Wirtschaftsklassifikationen/klassifikation-wz-2008.html

[§] This sample can be found in our code repository.

		Precision@10	Precision@25	Precision@50	Precision@100	Average
Exact Match	RAKE	0.95	1.33	1.71	1.42	1.36
	YAKE	3.33	3.24	2.38	1.81	2.69
	KEYBERT	1.90	1.71	1.71	1.05	1.60
	Guided KEYBERT	2.38	1.90	1.90	1.24	1.86
	Ours	**28.10**	**22.67**	**13.62**	**8.33**	**18.23**
Lemma Match	RAKE	1.43	1.52	1.90	1.76	1.65
	YAKE	2.38	3.24	2.67	2.33	2.65
	KEYBERT	1.90	1.90	1.81	1.29	1.73
	Guided KEYBERT	2.38	1.90	2.10	1.48	1.96
	Ours	**21.43**	**20.76**	**13.43**	**9.00**	**16.15**
Fuzzy Match	RAKE	62.60	61.63	61.95	59.95	61.29
	YAKE	65.91	65.10	62.98	59.58	63.39
	KEYBERT	60.42	60.49	59.55	57.16	59.41
	Guided KEYBERT	60.67	60.62	59.95	57.42	59.67
	Ours	**78.19**	**75.21**	**72.93**	**67.54**	**73.47**
CS Match	RAKE	77.54	79.48	79.73	79.83	79.14
	YAKE	82.48	83.52	82.69	82.05	83.13
	KEYBERT	76.73	77.39	77.09	76.86	77.02
	Guided KEYBERT	77.30	77.76	77.66	77.36	77.52
	Ours	**86.32**	**86.82**	**86.02**	**85.36**	**86.13**
Average Match	RAKE	35.70	36.02	36.37	35.52	35.91
	YAKE	38.90	38.69	37.62	36.40	37.90
	KEYBERT	34.88	35.14	34.99	34.16	34.79
	Guided KEYBERT	35.21	35.31	35.38	34.44	35.08
	Ours	**53.51**	**51.41**	**46.50**	**42.56**	**48.49**

Table 1: Class-specific Keyword Extraction Evaluation Results. For each scoring scheme, the highest score for each k is **bolded**. The average in the right column represents the average of the four evaluated k values. *Average Match* denotes the average score achieved by a method for one k but across all four scores. Examples of extracted keywords for each approach are provided in Appendix A.

ing keywords are the same for each class. We test our proposed method with the parameter *n_iterations* (number of batches) set to 5. *Guided* KEYBERT refers to the use of the optional `seed_keywords` parameter, which serves as a direct comparison point to our proposed method (denoted *ours*). For KEYBERT and our method, we use the DEUTSCHE-TELEKOM/GBERT-LARGE-PARAPHRASE-COSINE language model. Note that for comparability, KEYBERT was set only to extract unigram keywords.

Seed Keywords For the selection of seed keywords, specifically for Guided KEYBERT and our method, we utilize an existing collection of keywords (*Stichwörter*) provided by the creators of the WZ 2008‡. As we aim only to extract unigrams, we truncate all keyphrases to the first word if they are longer than one word. From this gold set, we randomly select 10 keywords from each class to serve as the seeds for that class. The rest of the gold set is then used for evaluation. The seed keywords from two classes are presented in Listings 1 and 2.

```
['Schweinehaltung', 'Holztaxierung',
 'Austernzucht', 'Teichwirtschaft',
 'Tabak'*, 'Dicke',
 'Fischerei'*, 'Seidenraupenzucht',
 'Wild', 'Kassava']
```

Listing 1: Seed Keywords for Class A: *Land- und Forstwirtschaft, Fischerei*. Seed keywords marked with an asterisk (*) denote those found in our dataset sample.

```
['Heizkraftwerke'*, 'Elektrizitaetserzeugung',
 'Blockheizkraftwerk'*, 'Waermeversorgung',
 'Solarstromerzeugung', 'Bereitstellung'*,
 'Energieversorgung'*, 'Windparks'*,
 'Spaltgaserzeugung', 'Kokereigasgewinnung']
```

Listing 2: Seed Keywords for Class D: *Energieversorgung*. Seed keywords marked with an asterisk (*) denote those found in our dataset sample.

Metrics With the keywords sets from each of the tested methods, we evaluate the accuracy of the keywords on two dimensions: (1) *precision@K*, where the number of correct keywords amongst the top K output keywords is counted, and (2) *matching method*, where the meaning of "correct" is varied. For K, we choose $K \in \{10, 25, 50, 100\}$, and for matching method, we use four approaches:

- **Exact string match**: a correct keyword is counted if the extracted keyword is found *exactly* in the gold set of keywords.
- **Lemma match**: a correct keyword is counted if the *lemmatized* version of the keyword is found in the *lemmatized* gold set of keywords (Zesch and Gurevych, 2009).
- **Fuzzy string match**: the "correctness" of a keyword is not binary, but rather is represented by the closest fuzzy string match score, using the Python package THEFUZZ.
- **Cosine similarity match**: the correctness of

a keyword is measured by its highest cosine similarity to any of the gold keywords.

For cosine similarity, the DEEPSET/GBERT-BASE model is used, so as not to use the same base model used with the keyword extraction process.

Results Table 1 presents the results of the above-described experiments. Note that for the evaluation of extracted keywords against the gold set, we only include keywords in the gold set that appear (in lemmatized form for *lemma match*) in the 10k sample of the German business registry data.

We can observe that our approach outperforms all other methods in *class-specific* keyword extraction. The performance of our approach is particularly strong in the exact match and lemma match evaluations, indicating it is well suited to extract class-specific gold keywords as defined by the creators of the WZ 2008[‡] classification scheme. Notably, even the Guided KEYBERT method, designed to extract keywords similar to provided seed keywords, performs significantly worse than our approach. Looking to the results, we see that the guided version of KEYBERT often only shows improvements over the base version when more extracted results are considered. This implies that while some class-specific keywords are found, they are not ranked as high as other keywords. Ultimately, we conclude that our approach achieves state-of-the-art results for *class-specific* keyword extraction, a point that is supported by a qualitative analysis of example outputs in Appendix A.

5 Conclusion

We present a class-specific keyword extraction pipeline which outperforms previous methods in identifying keywords related to a predefined *class*. Our evaluation results exhibit the strong performance of our method in the task of retrieving keywords specific to particular German economic sectors. These results make a compelling case for the continued study of class-specific keyword extraction as an improvement to non-guided approaches.

As points for future work, we propose more rigorous evaluation of our method from two perspectives: (1) an ablation study on the effect of the *n_iterations*, *number_newseed*, *percentile_newseed*, and *topk* parameters, in particular to study their relevance for class-specific keyword extraction, and (2) evaluation of our method beyond the German language, firstly with English.

Acknowledgments

This work has been supported by the BayVFP Digitalization grant DIK-2210-0028//D1K0475102 (CreateData4AI) from the Bavarian Ministry of Economic Affairs, Regional Development and Energy. The project is performed in collaboration with Fusionbase GmbH, whom we thank for the Business Registry data access and for the guidance.

Limitations

The primary limitation of our work is the lack of evaluation of the various parameters of our method, as discussed in Section 5. Evaluating a range of values would strengthen the work in determining the individual effect of each parameter.

The second limitation involves the relatively limited scope both in domain and language. In particular, we focus our case study only on the German Business Registry, and we do not generalize beyond this to different domains or languages.

Ethics Statement

An ethical consideration comes with the use of the German Business Registry dataset, which is directly tied to real-world businesses, potentially raising privacy concerns. However, this is mitigated by the fact that the data is public and business owners are aware of this when drafting their entries.

References

Kamil Bennani-Smires, Claudiu Musat, Andreea Hossmann, Michael Baeriswyl, and Martin Jaggi. 2018. Simple unsupervised keyphrase extraction using sentence embeddings. In *Proceedings of the 22nd Conference on Computational Natural Language Learning*, pages 221–229, Brussels, Belgium. Association for Computational Linguistics.

Ricardo Campos, Vítor Mangaravite, Arian Pasquali, Alípio Jorge, Célia Nunes, and Adam Jatowt. 2020. Yake! keyword extraction from single documents using multiple local features. *Information Sciences*, 509:257–289.

Min Chen, Shiwen Mao, and Yunhao Liu. 2014. Big data: A survey. *Mobile networks and applications*, 19:171–209.

Jacob Devlin, Ming-Wei Chang, Kenton Lee, and Kristina Toutanova. 2019. BERT: Pre-training of deep bidirectional transformers for language understanding. In *Proceedings of the 2019 Conference of the North American Chapter of the Association for Computational Linguistics: Human Language Technologies, Volume 1 (Long and Short Papers)*, pages

4171–4186, Minneapolis, Minnesota. Association for Computational Linguistics.

Nazanin Firoozeh, Adeline Nazarenko, Fabrice Alizon, and Béatrice Daille. 2020. Keyword extraction: Issues and methods. *Natural Language Engineering*, 26(3):259–291.

Maarten Grootendorst, Abhay Mishra, Art Matsak, OysterMax, Priyanshul Govil, Yuki Ogura, Vincent D Warmerdam, and yusuke1997. 2023. Maartengr/keybert: v0.8.

Quoc Le and Tomas Mikolov. 2014. Distributed representations of sentences and documents. In *Proceedings of the 31st International Conference on Machine Learning*, volume 32 of *Proceedings of Machine Learning Research*, pages 1188–1196, Bejing, China. PMLR.

Rada Mihalcea and Paul Tarau. 2004. TextRank: Bringing order into text. In *Proceedings of the 2004 Conference on Empirical Methods in Natural Language Processing*, pages 404–411, Barcelona, Spain. Association for Computational Linguistics.

Tadashi Nomoto. 2022. Keyword extraction: a modern perspective. *SN Computer Science*, 4(1):92.

Lawrence Page, Sergey Brin, Rajeev Motwani, and Terry Winograd. 1999. The pagerank citation ranking : Bringing order to the web. In *WWW 1999*.

Matteo Pagliardini, Prakhar Gupta, and Martin Jaggi. 2018. Unsupervised learning of sentence embeddings using compositional n-gram features. In *Proceedings of the 2018 Conference of the North American Chapter of the Association for Computational Linguistics: Human Language Technologies, Volume 1 (Long Papers)*, pages 528–540, New Orleans, Louisiana. Association for Computational Linguistics.

Eirini Papagiannopoulou and Grigorios Tsoumakas. 2019. A review of keyphrase extraction. *Wiley Interdisciplinary Reviews: Data Mining and Knowledge Discovery*, 10.

Stuart Rose, Dave Engel, Nick Cramer, and Wendy Cowley. 2010. Automatic keyword extraction from individual documents. *Text mining: applications and theory*, pages 1–20.

Jill Sammet and Ralf Krestel. 2023. Domain-specific keyword extraction using BERT. In *Proceedings of the 4th Conference on Language, Data and Knowledge*, pages 659–665, Vienna, Austria. NOVA CLUNL, Portugal.

Tim Schopf, Simon Klimek, and Florian Matthes. 2022. Patternrank: Leveraging pretrained language models and part of speech for unsupervised keyphrase extraction. In *Proceedings of the 14th International Joint Conference on Knowledge Discovery, Knowledge Engineering and Knowledge Management (IC3K 2022) - KDIR*, pages 243–248. INSTICC, SciTePress.

Wei Shi, Weiguo Zheng, Jeffrey Xu Yu, Hong Cheng, and Lei Zou. 2017. Keyphrase extraction using knowledge graphs. *Data Science and Engineering*, 2:275–288.

Mingyang Song, Yi Feng, and Liping Jing. 2023. A survey on recent advances in keyphrase extraction from pre-trained language models. In *Findings of the Association for Computational Linguistics: EACL 2023*, pages 2153–2164, Dubrovnik, Croatia. Association for Computational Linguistics.

Mona Tanwar, Reena Duggal, and Sunil Kumar Khatri. 2015. Unravelling unstructured data: A wealth of information in big data. In *2015 4th International Conference on Reliability, Infocom Technologies and Optimization (ICRITO) (Trends and Future Directions)*, pages 1–6.

Hanh Thi Hong Tran, Matej Martinc, Jaya Caporusso, Antoine Doucet, and Senja Pollak. 2023. The recent advances in automatic term extraction: A survey. *arXiv preprint arXiv:2301.06767*.

Xiaojun Wan and Jianguo Xiao. 2008. CollabRank: Towards a collaborative approach to single-document keyphrase extraction. In *Proceedings of the 22nd International Conference on Computational Linguistics (Coling 2008)*, pages 969–976, Manchester, UK. Coling 2008 Organizing Committee.

Binbin Xie, Jia Song, Liangying Shao, Suhang Wu, Xiangpeng Wei, Baosong Yang, Huan Lin, Jun Xie, and Jinsong Su. 2023. From statistical methods to deep learning, automatic keyphrase prediction: A survey. *Information Processing & Management*, 60(4):103382.

Torsten Zesch and Iryna Gurevych. 2009. Approximate matching for evaluating keyphrase extraction. In *Proceedings of the International Conference RANLP-2009*, pages 484–489, Borovets, Bulgaria. Association for Computational Linguistics.

A Extracted Keyword Examples


```
{'rake': ['analyse',
  'entwicklung',
  'software',
  'programmen',
  'weiterentwicklung',
  'verkauf',
  'vermietung',
  'domainadressen',
  'housing',
  'domainverwaltung',
  'peering',
  'administration',
  'saemtliche',
  'handel',
  'insbesondere'],
'yake': ['uebernahme',
 'dienstleistungen',
 'geschaefte',
 'beteiligung',
 'verkauf',
```

```
'entwicklung',
'vermittlung',
'geschaeftsfuehrung',
'beratung',
'herstellung',
'beteiligungen',
'taetigkeiten',
'erbringung',
'bereich',
'immobilien'],
'keybert': ['landschaftsbau',
  'photovoltaik',
  'elektroinstallationen',
  'masskleidung',
  'landschaftsmusikfestivals',
  'systemgastronomie',
  'bauleistungen',
  'reisebueros',
  'immobilien',
  'physiotherapie',
  'wasserinstallationsarbeiten',
  'diskothek',
  'nassbaggerarbeiten',
  'druckereierzeugnissen',
  'zahntechnischen'],
'guided_keybert': ['landschaftsbau',
  'elektroinstallationen',
  'photovoltaik',
  'systemgastronomie',
  'landschaftsmusikfestivals',
  'masskleidung',
  'bauleistungen',
  'reisebueros',
  'immobilien',
  'diskothek',
  'wasserinstallationsarbeiten',
  'druckereierzeugnissen',
  'nassbaggerarbeiten',
  'physiotherapie',
  'zahntechnischen'],
'ours': ['zucht',
  'fuger',
  'getreide',
  'spenglerei',
  'verpachtungen',
  'veraeu',
  'frachten',
  'fracht',
  'schalungen',
  'verpachtung',
  'beund',
  'kalk',
  'schalung',
  'holzwaren',
  'haefte']
}
```

Listing 3: Sample extracted keywords for Class A, from the 10:25 top keywords for each method.

```
{'rake': ['analyse',
  'entwicklung',
  'software',
  'programmen',
  'weiterentwicklung',
  'verkauf',
  'vermietung',
  'domainadressen',
  'housing',
  'domainverwaltung',
  'peering',
  'administration',
  'saemtliche',
  'handel',
  'insbesondere'],
'yake': ['uebernahme',
 'dienstleistungen',
 'geschaefte',
 'beteiligung',
 'verkauf',
 'entwicklung',
 'vermittlung',
 'geschaeftsfuehrung',
 'beratung',
 'herstellung',
 'beteiligungen',
 'taetigkeiten',
 'erbringung',
 'bereich',
 'immobilien'],
'keybert': ['immobilien',
  'delaware',
  'verkauf',
  'pizzalieferservices',
  'unternehmens',
  'ambulanten',
  'eingliederungshilfe',
  'gesellschaftsbeteiligungen',
  'bebauung',
  'schulverwaltungssoftware',
  'geschaeftsfuehrung',
  'textilzubehoer',
  'masskleidung',
  'motorradzubehoerteilen',
  'casinobetriebe'],
'guided_keybert': ['immobilien',
  'delaware',
  'kraftfahrzeugen',
  'pizzalieferservices',
  'unternehmens',
  'ambulanten',
  'eingliederungshilfe',
  'gesellschaftsbeteiligungen',
  'bebauung',
  'schulverwaltungssoftware',
  'geschaeftsfuehrung',
  'textilzubehoer',
  'masskleidung',
  'motorradzubehoerteilen',
  'casinobetriebe'],
'ours': ['energieanlagen',
  'energieerzeugungsanlagen',
  'energieerzeugung',
  'energietechnik',
  'energieversorgungs',
  'energietechnischen',
  'energieprodukten',
  'stromerzeugungsanlagen',
  'energiegewinnung',
  'energietraeger',
  'energietraegern',
  'energiequellen',
  'ernergieanlagen',
  'energie',
  'stromerzeugern']}
```

Listing 4: Sample extracted keywords for Class D, from the 10:25 top keywords for each method.

Tabular JSON: A Proposal for a Pragmatic Linguistic Data Format

Adam Roussel
Department of Linguistics
Ruhr University Bochum
roussel@linguistics.rub.de

Abstract

Existing linguistic data formats tend to be very general and powerful yet difficult to use on a day-to-day basis, so that practitioners often reach for underpowered ad-hoc text formats that require error-prone string parsing. We propose a pragmatic JSON-based linguistic data format that is flexible enough to cover most types of linguistic annotations and scenarios. It avoids the need for string parsing, as the serialized data representation is trivially convertible to tabular data structures that are immediately usable in data analysis applications.

1 Introduction

While there are very many data formats that have been introduced for use with linguistic data, they seem to either be highly general and capable of representing any kind of annotation yet unwieldly to use, thus requiring extra software to translate between the abstract underlying data model and a more application-specific und user-friendly view of that data, or they are easy to work with but very limited in the kinds of annotations that they support. There seems to be room for practical data formats that lie somewhere in the middle, ones that are lightweight and easy to use, yet flexible and capable of supporting a range of possible annotations. This is the sort of format that Tabular JSON is intended to be.

2 Related Work

Specialized data formats for linguistic corpora include ones such as Salt (Zipser and Romary, 2010) or Paula XML (Dipper, 2005; Dipper and Götze, 2005; Chiarcos et al., 2008). These are capable of representing any kind or nearly any kind of annotation, since their main purpose is the exchange of corpus data between systems and the long-term storage of data. However, due to their generality, they are complex formats and are not suitable as everyday working formats. Generally, some kind of specialized software is required to translate the general representation on disk to something usable in a given application scenario.

Formats such as UIMA CAS XMI[1] and FoLiA (van Gompel and Reynaert, 2013) are somewhat less complex and more human-readable, with UIMA CAS making greater use of stand-off representations. Both support a broad range of possible annotation types. Though new type systems may be defined with UIMA CAS, there doesn't appear to be a straightforward way to add custom annotation types to FoLiA. Both of these formats are nevertheless complex enough to warrant the use of specialized software in order to produce and consume data in these formats, DKPro-Cassis (Klie and de Castilho, 2024) and the FoLiA Python library, respectively.

Finally, perhaps the most widely used formats are those derived from the CoNLL-X formats (Buchholz and Marsi, 2006), CoNLL-U[2] most prominent among them. These are all text formats that have one token per line, tab-separated fields, and sentences separated by empty lines. The variants may have different numbers of columns, which contain different kinds of data – this is generally determined by the variant name, but the CoNLL-U Plus format allows for the number and names of columns to be specified in a special header line.

Though the format is fairly human-readable, parsing (and re-parsing) it is inefficient and error-prone, as different users are bound to overlook different edge cases. These problems are compounded in cases where more complex types of annotations are to be represented and new ad-hoc representations are invented to accomodate them within the confines a single column.

[1] https://uima.apache.org/
[2] https://universaldependencies.org/format.html

3 Description

3.1 Guiding principles

The main goal of Tabular JSON is to be a format that is practical for daily use:

- Minimize ad-hoc parsing.
- Require no special software.
- Support a variety of annotation types.

Reading and writing the data should not require users to do string parsing, which is inefficient and error-prone. Ideally, once the data are parsed, they remain in a structured form and can be read or written with no further format-specific knowledge or software required: a general-purpose JSON parser should suffice.

A practical format for linguistic data needs to be able to represent a broad range of annotation types: It is not uncommon to have annotations that have the shape of spans or relations between tokens or spans. These types of entities, among others, ought to be naturally representable making hacks to represent them on a token-wise basis unnecessary.

3.2 Data model

It's important to distinguish between the data format that is used on disk and the data model that is expressed in that format. To some extent, they're related, since some formats are not capable of representing some kinds of logical entities. Trees don't go well with CSV, for instance, but they're a natural fit for XML.

In the interests of practicality we use a data model that is essentially tabular, which ensures seamless compatibility with common data analysis packages. Our model follows broadly the principles of "tidy data" (Wickham, 2014): Tidy data is characterized by observations or basic units of analysis being represented in rows and various variables or properties of those units of analysis being represented in columns. Tidy data is easier to work with, to reshape and to analyze, and it works well with vectorized operations, such as are used in R or Pandas.

3.3 Data formats

A suitable tabular representation could then be implemented in any of a number of formats – CSV, JSON, SQLite, Parquet, XML, etc. are all perfectly capable of representing a sequence of objects with some fixed set of attributes. We chose JSON over the alternatives because it is immediately and intuitively usable and keeps the parsing of text formats to a minimum.[3]

CSV (and TSV) formats may seem like an obvious choice for a tabular-oriented format, but there is no standardized form of CSV, instead numerous mutually incompatible dialects, using different delimiters, quoting strategies, etc., which makes parsing it error-prone. Furthermore, in order to include metadata about a given document and multiple tables for different kinds of data, you end up needing multiple files for each document.

SQLite is a great alternative to textual formats in some ways: The data can be more efficiently read and written to disk, and larger-than-memory data can also be processed easily. And with SQL, there is a powerful query language built-in. However, users often want to be able see their data in a text editor directly, as is possible with a text-based format, and they may not wish to use SQL.

While XML is more verbose and can be more effort to work with, it also has some clear advantages: XML is more stable, and there are more established standards for describing and verifying XML data.

Ultimately, JSON has advantages that seem to outweigh the strengths of XML. For JSON there is a high-quality package included in the Python standard library, which straightforwardly maps JSON values onto Python data structures. The JSON you see on disk is essentially equivalent to the Python data structures you get simply by loading that JSON data. The format's design, by relying on flat tables primarily, allows for a similarly immediately usable data structure in R using `jsonlite` or in Julia with `JSON.jl`. Furthermore, there are many great general-purpose JSON tools – `jq`, `jello`, `visidata`, etc. – that can also be used for working with Tabular JSON directly. In this way, users are free to choose the tools that work best in a given scenario, but this doesn't mean that they need to spend time and effort parsing text formats and fixing the attendant bugs.

Of course, as noted above, this tabular data model could be implemented in any of the formats mentioned above. In some situations, it may be preferable to implement this data model in one of those formats or some other format instead.

[3]Of course, JSON is, like XML, a text-based format, however it is a well-known and well-specified standard notation, for which there are myriad reliable parsers available. They can be reliably parsed in a way CSV, for instance, cannot.

3.4 Design principles

The need for software that translates between a comprehensible user-facing data model and one that is appropriate for serialization is avoided by making the serialization first-class: The serialization *is* the data model and is intended for direct interaction by users. We think of this as an *exterior-first* approach (Chu, 2023).

Different kinds of data are generally stored in separate tables, each with a set of keys appropriate to that kind of data. Each of these tables includes references, either to single tokens (= `token`) or to a range of tokens (= `begin` and `end`) in the main tokens table. In this way, some kinds of data are stored in a stand-off style.

The design aims to avoid some of the usability issues that accompany stand-off annotations by having these references be by index, thus enabling fast and easy retrieval of both single tokens and spans of tokens (via slicing). This also makes it easier to join the data in different tables using built-in operations in common data analysis packages. All of the index references use 1-based indexing, so they are directly usable in R, Julia, and Lua as-is, but some minor adjustments are required in Python. In general, any empty values are to be omitted, so they are distinguishable from empty strings and values such as `"_"`. The other strategy we employ is to only store some data in stand-off fashion: Annotations that apply to single tokens are simply included in the main tokens table.

Other advantages of stand-off representations are preserved. Different annotation layers can be easily added or removed without disturbing the others, and it is also possible, e.g., to have multiple instances of the same kind of annotation in order to store the annotations from different annotators in the same file.

3.5 Data layout

Each document in a corpus is represented by a single JSON object, which can either be stored as its own file or as a line in a JSON Lines file. This top-level contains, minimally, a `metadata` object and a `token` array:

```
{"id": "o9234f78",
 "metadata": { ... },
 "token": [ ... ], ... }
```

Whereas the metadata object is a collection of key–value pairs, adaptable to the needs of a given project, the token array is what we will call a "table":

`property`	Token annotations
`relation`	Relations between tokens
`span`	Spans over tokens
`set`	Sets of tokens
`spanset`	Sets of Spans over tokens
`hierset`	Hierarchical sets of spans over tokens

Figure 1: Annotation types.

an array of objects, which all have roughly the same set of keys. This is a row-based data representation that is readily translated directly into a data frame data structure by common data analysis packages.

Further annotations are included in tables under additional top-level properties and have forms that are determined by the type of data that these annotations represent. All of these additional tables refer to the main `token` table by means of indices. The format specifies a fixed set of possible annotation types (Figure 1), and each annotation type has a particular set of required keys.

Each document specifies the annotations it includes using the `annotations` key in the metadata object.

```
"metadata": {
  "annotations": {
    "lemma": {"type": "property"},
    "line2": {"type": "span",
     "description": "Secondary line ref."},
    ...
  }
},
```

The inclusion of this metadata tells users what top-level keys to expect and, due to the `type` value, what keys to expect in the associated tables. Additional keys besides `type` and `description` are allowed here, so there is a place for other useful information, e.g. provenance, etc. The specification provides for a set of standardized property names to be used for common annotations to aid in interoperability.

Token annotations. Some annotations, namely all those that apply strictly to single tokens, are included in the token table directly as `property` annotations. This includes such things as lemmas, normalized word forms, and POS tags.

```
{"id":"t2","form":"cats","lemma":"cat",
    "pos":"NOUN", ... }
```

A special case of token annotations is covered by the `object` annotation type. This annotation type

Name	Type	Desc.
`form`	`property`	Surface form
`lemma`	`property`	Lemma
`pos`	`property`	POS
`dependency`	`relation`	Dependencies
`sentence`	`span`	Sentences
`coreference`	`spanset`	Coreference

Figure 2: Some common annotations and their types.

describes a column in the tokens table that contains arbitrary JSON data. It is provided as an escape hatch, e.g. for representing sub-token-level data.

Relations between tokens. Dependencies are stored in a dependency table, whose rows are of the `relation` type, since dependencies are expressed as relations between tokens. Each row in this table has two references to the tokens table, `from`, in this case referring to the head token, and `to`, referring to the dependent token.

```
{"from":2,"to":1,"label":"det"}
```

Spans over tokens. Spans are always represented with a pair of properties, `begin` and `end`, which refer to the main `token` table. Sentences are represented as spans over tokens:

```
{"id":"s1","begin":1,"end":6,
    "label":"decl"}
```

Besides sentences, all layout information, such as that concerning page or paragraph or line boundaries, is represented as spans over tokens. This annotation type is also used for things like quotations and headings, where these are present.

Sets of spans over tokens. Entities of the `spanset` annotation type are a kind of span, so they contain `begin` and `end` properties, however in addition to this they also have an `set` property, which is the same for all members of a set. This annotation type is useful for representing things like coreferences:

```
{"set":"c1","begin":1,"end":2}
{"set":"c1","begin":4,"end":4}
```

Further information about the entity covered by such a span may be provided using the optional `label` property.

Hierarchical sets of spans over tokens. Each entry in a `hierset`-type table denotes a span of tokens, and so it has `begin` and `end` properties. In order to express hierarchical data structures, the entries must be able to refer to one another – these are all non-terminals. To this end, each entry must have an ID and a `parent` property, which specifies the node above it in the tree. This could be useful for representing consituency trees or discourse structure (note that the spans need not be limited to a single sentence or coincide with sentence boundaries). E.g.:

```
{"id":"c1","begin":1,"end":4,"label":"S"}
{"id":"c2","begin":1,"end":1,"label":"NP",
    "parent":"c1"}
{"id":"c3","begin":2,"end":4,"label":"VP",
    "parent":"c1"}
{"id":"c4","begin":3,"end":4,"label":"NP",
    "parent":"c3"}
```

4 An Example Use Case

In the course of a larger project there is often a need to convert data between various formats, and so conversion applications are written that tend to converge on a particular architecture: There are various reader and writer modules, some internal data model, and optionally a set of transformations that can be applied to that data model. There are existing applications for this purpose, such as Pepper,[4] why not use that?

One reason is that modules would need to be written in Java, and it could be that your team doesn't have expertise in Java or may not want to use it. (Note that this is not due to any issue with Java per se but could be the case for any particular implementation language.) Another reason is the internal data model, Salt, which, though very general and powerful, is not a representation that you would use for any other purpose, so that any modules you write are only useful in this Pepper context.

There are two main aspects of Tabular JSON, which make it useful in such a scenario: One is the exterior-first design and the other is the tabular data model.

What in most conversion scenarios is an internal data model is external in the case of Tabular JSON; the internal representation is identical to the serialization. This means that different parts of a conversion, annotation, and analysis pipeline need not know about one another. They can be developed independently from one another and could even use different programming languages altogether, yet all

[4] https://corpus-tools.org/pepper/

of these independent components have access to the same, complete underlying data structures. All of the various modules only need to know about Tabular JSON. This is the advantage of an exterior-first orientation.

The other important aspect is that this lingua franca is intended to be directly usable itself, since it would otherwise just be one more additional format to deal with. This is the motivation behind the tabular data model, which is geared towards the way data analysis frameworks treat data and is also a more intuitive way of representing data than graph-based representations, such as Salt.

5 Conclusion

There is a tension between, on the one hand, a general and powerful format that can represent adequately any kind of data, but which inevitably must depend on some software layer that can translate between this general format and a usable internal model, and on the other hand, a simple and lightweight yet limited format that may not be sufficient for many applications, forcing the invention of error-prone ad-hoc solutions.

The JSON-based format described in this paper is intended as a practical, lightweight format for linguistic applications that has minimal dependencies and is directly usable, because its on-disk form is essentially identical to a usable internal data structure. The use of a known set of data types allows users to reason about the data and work with it in this form directly – practically erasing the distinction between a serialized form and internal data model. This frees users from having to parse ad-hoc text-based formats or depend on particular specialized software.

The complete specification of the format and a JSON schema for validation are available at the project's public repository, accessible at this URL: `https://gitlab.rub.de/comphist/tabular-json`. See also Appendix A for a complete example document.

6 Limitations

The specification establishes a set of standardized property names for basic kinds of annotations, such as POS and lemmas, in order to aid interoperability. However the number of standardized names remains quite small currently, so that interoperability in practice is limited. Though we plan to expand this set in future iterations, some challenges remain: It is foreseeable that different projects may not agree on the naming scheme and prefer different names (e.g. `feats` vs. `infl` vs. `morph`, etc.) or that different projects may wish to model the same information in different ways, for instance, modelling named entities as token properties vs. spans. Further, one of the goals of this format is to enable the storage and use of novel and not yet established kinds of annotations, and it is impossible in principle to come up with property names for these things in advance.

Most of the different kinds of annotations that the format provides for are stored as stand-off annotations, which, while it has its advantages, is an impediment to human-readability. If one wants to know which tokens belong to a given sentence, say, one must follow the references from the sentences array back to the tokens array. We try and make this as simple and straightforward as possible by the use of indices that can be used to directly retrieve a single token or slice of the tokens array in such cases. However, what is simple programmatically isn't necessarily easy for humans, and this is one of the reasons that projects may prefer to model some things differently than in the specification.

7 Ethical Considerations

As this work presents a data format, I see its ethical dimensions being primarily those of freedom, fairness, and re-use: Users should not be required or 'nudged' to use particular proprietary software in order to work with a given data format, such as with, say, Excel files. Since it relies only on the simple and well-documented JSON standard, data in our format are usable from any programming language environment with no special dependencies, which make the data reusable and offers potential users a high degree of flexibility. The format should also be usable with any kind of language data, historical or modern, due to the use of UTF-8.

Acknowledgments

Thanks to the reviewers for their helpful feedback. Gefördert durch die Deutsche Forschungsgemeinschaft (DFG) – SFB 1475 – Projektnummer 441126958.

References

Sabine Buchholz and Erwin Marsi. 2006. CoNLL-X shared task on multilingual dependency parsing. In

Proceedings of the Tenth Conference on Computational Natural Language Learning (CoNLL-X), pages 149–164, New York City. Association for Computational Linguistics.

Christian Chiarcos, Stefanie Dipper, Michael Götze, Ulf Leser, Anke Lüdeling, Julia Ritz, and Manfred Stede. 2008. A flexible framework for integrating annotations from different tools and tag sets. In *Traitement Automatique des Langues, Volume 49, Numéro 2 : Plate-formes pour le traitement automatique des langues [Platforms for Natural Language Processing]*, pages 217–246, France. ATALA (Association pour le Traitement Automatique des Langues).

Andy Chu. 2023. Oils is exterior-first (code, text, and structured data). `https://www.oilshell.org/blog/2023/06/ysh-design.html`. Accessed 2024-05-04.

Stefanie Dipper. 2005. XML-based stand-off representation and exploitation of multi-level linguistic annotation. In *Proceedings of Berliner XML Tage 2005 (BXML 2005)*, pages 39–50, Berlin, Germany.

Stefanie Dipper and Michael Götze. 2005. Accessing heterogeneous linguistic data – generic XML-based representation and flexible visualization. In *Proceedings of the 2nd Language & Technology Conference: Human Language Technologies as a Challenge for Computer Science and Linguistics*, pages 206–210, Poznan, Poland.

Jan-Christoph Klie and Richard Eckart de Castilho. 2024. DKPro Cassis – reading and writing UIMA CAS files in Python.

Maarten van Gompel and Martin Reynaert. 2013. FoLiA: A practical XML format for linguistic annotation – a descriptive and comparative study. *Computational Linguistics in the Netherlands Journal*, 3:63–81.

Hadley Wickham. 2014. Tidy data. *Journal of Statistical Software*, 59(10):1–23.

Florian Zipser and Laurent Romary. 2010. A model oriented approach to the mapping of annotation formats using standards. In *Workshop on Language Resource and Language Technology Standards, LREC 2010*, La Valette, Malta.

A An Example Document

```
{
  "id": "doc1",
  "metadata": {
    "title": "Example document",
    "year": "2024",
    "version": "1.0",
    "annotations": {
      "pos": {
        "use": "pos_xpos"
      },
      "pos_xpos": {
        "type": "property",
        "model": "en_core_web_sm",
        "source": "Spacy"
      },
      "pos_upos": {
        "type": "property",
        "model": "en_core_web_sm",
        "source": "Spacy"
      },
      "lemma": {
        "type": "property",
        "description": "omitted when
           same as form",
        "model": "en_core_web_sm",
        "source": "Spacy"
      },
      "sentence": {
        "type": "span"
      },
      "line": {
        "type": "span"
      },
      "coreference": {
        "type": "spanset",
        "source": "ajr"
      },
      "dependency": {
        "type": "relation",
        "model": "en_core_web_sm",
        "source": "Spacy"
      }
    }
  },
  "token": [
    {
      "id": "t1",
      "form": "The",
      "lemma": "the",
      "pos_xpos": "DT",
      "pos_upos": "DET"
    },
    {
      "id": "t2",
      "form": "cats",
      "lemma": "cat",
      "pos_xpos": "NNS",
      "pos_upos": "NOUN"
    },
    {
      "id": "t3",
      "form": "slept",
      "lemma": "sleep",
      "pos_xpos": "VBD",
      "pos_upos": "VERB"
    },
    {
      "id": "t4",
      "form": ",",
      "pos_xpos": ",",
      "pos_upos": "PUNCT"
    },
    {
      "id": "t5",
      "form": "and",
      "pos_xpos": "CC",
      "pos_upos": "CCONJ"
    },
    {
      "id": "t6",
      "form": "they",
      "pos_xpos": "PRP",
      "pos_upos": "PRON"
```

```
    },
    {
      "id": "t7",
      "form": "purred",
      "lemma": "purr",
      "pos_xpos": "VBD",
      "pos_upos": "VERB"
    },
    {
      "id": "t8",
      "form": "softly",
      "pos_xpos": "RB",
      "pos_upos": "ADV"
    },
    {
      "id": "t9",
      "form": ".",
      "pos_xpos": ".",
      "pos_upos": "PUNCT"
    }
  ],
  "coreference": [
    {
      "set": "c1",
      "begin": 1,
      "end": 2
    },
    {
      "set": "c1",
      "begin": 6,
      "end": 6
    }
  ],
  "line": [
    {
      "id": "l1",
      "begin": 1,
      "end": 4
    },
    {
      "id": "l2",
      "begin": 5,
      "end": 9
    }
  ],
  "sentence": [
    {
      "id": "s1",
      "begin": 1,
      "end": 9
    }
  ],
  "dependency": [
    {
      "id": "dep1",
      "from": 2,
      "to": 1,
      "label": "det"
    },
    {
      "id": "dep2",
      "from": 3,
      "to": 2,
      "label": "nsubj"
    },
    {
      "id": "dep3",
      "from": 3,
      "to": 3,
      "label": "root"
    },
    {
      "id": "dep4",
      "from": 3,
      "to": 4,
      "label": "punct"
    },
    {
      "id": "dep5",
      "from": 3,
      "to": 5,
      "label": "cc"
    },
    {
      "id": "dep6",
      "from": 7,
      "to": 6,
      "label": "nsubj"
    },
    {
      "id": "dep7",
      "from": 3,
      "to": 7,
      "label": "conj"
    },
    {
      "id": "dep8",
      "from": 7,
      "to": 8,
      "label": "advmod"
    },
    {
      "id": "dep9",
      "from": 7,
      "to": 9,
      "label": "punct"
    }
  ]
}
```

Semiautomatic Data Generation for Academic Named Entity Recognition in German Text Corpora

Pia Schwarz
Leibniz Institute for the German Language (IDS)
R5 6-13, 68161 Mannheim, Germany
schwarz@ids-mannheim.de

Abstract

An NER model is trained to recognize three types of entities in academic contexts: person, organization, and research area. Training data is generated semiautomatically from newspaper articles with the help of word lists for the individual entity types, an off-the-shelf NE recognizer, and an LLM. Experiments fine-tuning a BERT model with different strategies of post-processing the automatically generated data result in several NER models achieving overall F1 scores of up to 92.45%.

1 Introduction

The Leibniz Institute for the German Language (IDS) hosts the German Reference Corpus DeReKo (Kupietz and Keibel, 2009; Kupietz et al., 2010, 2018), the largest German collection of texts available for research, consisting of 57 billion tokens as of March 2024 (Leibniz-Institut für Deutsche Sprache, 2024). The corpus contains texts from the 18th century to the present, including many press releases. Linguistic annotation for DeReKo is provided on a syntactic level (e.g. parts of speech, lemmata, dependency relations), however, no semantic annotation has been added yet. This work concentrates on the annotation of three types of named entities, in particular persons in academia, academic institutions, and academic disciplines. In order to fine-tune a BERT model (Devlin et al., 2019), training data is collected in a semiautomatic manner from DeReKo itself[1].

[1] We release best scoring NER model via WebLicht (Hinrichs et al., 2010) at `https://weblicht.sfs.uni-tuebingen.de/weblichtwiki/index.php/Tools_in_Detail#Named_Entity_Recognition`
Due to strict copyright agreements with our text providers we can provide the data for scientific and non-commercial purposes only after signing a license agreement (free of charge, upon request via E-Mail).

2 Motivation

DeReKo is searchable via the corpus analysis platform KorAP (Diewald et al., 2016), making it possible to retrieve linguistic annotations as well as descriptive catalog metadata. These include specifications about the title, creation date, author, license, corpus sigle, and text sigle. A sigle is a unique identifier to reference parts of the corpus, in the case of newspaper texts, a text sigle refers to a single newspaper article. This level of granularity makes it possible to enrich DeReKo with semantic metadata such as named entities on the level of individual texts. Finding mentions of academic named entities in newspaper texts might serve as a starting point to investigate the impact or perception of academics beyond research. Moreover, these entities can also serve as links to external knowledge bases such as Wikidata (Vrandečić and Krötzsch, 2014), the Research Organisation Registry (Lammey, 2020) or the German National Library's Integrated Authority File (Behrens-Neumann and Pfeifer, 2011). Links to such external knowledge bases would provide more context to the data in DeReKo.

Creating a model for the task of academic NER requires training data, namely sentences tagged with the three given types. To our knowledge, no such data set exists, so a new one is generated from scratch. Having DeReKo at hand as a high-standard text collection, which at the same time constitutes the real-world data that should be processed by the resulting named entity recognizer, it is an obvious choice to collect sentences from the corpus as training data. The academic NER model should be able to tag literal mentions of the three entity types independent of whether researchers work in academia or in the industry, for example:

(1) *...sagt [Heitzer]$_{PER\text{-}RES}$, Professorin am Lehr- und Forschungsgebiet [Didaktik der Mathematik]$_{AREA\text{-}RES}$ an der [RWTH]$_{ORG\text{-}RES}$.*
'...says [Heitzer]$_{PER\text{-}RES}$, professor of

the teaching and research department [Didactics of Mathematics]$_{\text{AREA-RES}}$ at [RWTH]$_{\text{ORG-RES}}$.'

(2) *Ein paar Stockwerke höher wartet [Astrid Kiermaier]$_{PER\text{-}RES}$ auf uns, die Molekularbiologin arbeitet bei Roche im Bereich [Krebsforschung]$_{AREA\text{-}RES}$ ...*

'A few floors up, [Astrid Kiermaier]$_{\text{PER-RES}}$ is waiting for us, the molecular biologist works in the area of [cancer research]$_{\text{AREA-RES}}$ at Roche ...'

The entity type PER-RES should include the academic title of a person if it precedes the name. However, the model is not expected to resolve coreferences, so neither pronouns referring to an entity nor a noun phrase that does not literally mention the person's name should be tagged, as the following two examples illustrate:

(3) *Mitte März begann ein Team von Forschern der [Universität Hirosaki]$_{ORG\text{-}RES}$ damit, sodass sie im Norden Japans bereits Messungen vor Ort durchführten.*

'In mid-March, a team of researchers from [Hirosaki University]$_{\text{ORG-RES}}$ began with that, such that they already conduced on-site measurements in northern Japan.'

(4) *Der Physiker erfand nicht nur die Luftpumpe, sondern befaßte sich auch mit...*

'The physicist not only invented the air pump but also engaged in...'

Researchers are not always mentioned within the context of research, in example (5), the model is supposed to tag the person as the academic title provides enough context to identify someone who is or was a researcher. The opposite holds for example (6), where a literal mention of the exact same person is not supposed to be tagged as neither an academic title nor the rest of the sentence indicate any academic context. This is also the case for example (7), where the model is not expected to tag researcher Jane Goodall due to the lack of context information.

(5) *[Dr. Frank-Walter Steinmeier]$_{PER\text{-}RES}$, Chef des Bundeskanzleramtes, ist dafür verantwortlich...*

'[Dr. Frank-Walter Steinmeier]$_{\text{PER-RES}}$, head of the Federal Chancellery, is responsible for...'.

(6) *Außenminister Frank-Walter Steinmeier gab sich weiter diplomatisch.*

'Foreign Minister Frank-Walter Steinmeier continued to maintain a diplomatic stance.'

(7) *Schütze, was du liebst - So lautet das Prinzip der Umweltikone Jane Goodall.*

'Protect what you love – This is the principle of environmental icon Jane Goodall.'

The question remains as to how to tag the data without spending too much human resources on annotation but at the same time not compromising on quality either. The goal is to collect enough training data to fine-tune a BERT model in an at least partly automated manner through a rule-based method with word lists and then to improve the model by generating more training data through a deep learning approach using a large language model (LLM).

3 Background

Named entity recognition is a crucial method in NLP and forms part of many downstream tasks. Standard models typically comprise at least the entity types person, location, and organization, but there is also quite some research about domain-specific NER models, dealing for example with biomedical entities such as proteins or chemicals (Lee et al., 2020; Sun et al., 2021). Relevant for the present work are standard NER models and frameworks, especially the spaCy library (Honnibal et al., 2020) for model fine-tuning, and Stanza (Qi et al., 2020) for data preprocessing. Although spaCy and Stanza both provide state of the art NER models, they do have weaknesses once they are more thoroughly evaluated, e.g. regarding unseen text genres during inference or random train/dev/test splits during training (Vajjala and Balasubramaniam, 2022). However, Schmitt et al. (2019) compared the five NER frameworks StanfordNLP, NLTK, OpenNLP, spaCy, and Gate with the result of StanfordNLP scoring best. The Stanza NLP package builds on the Stanford NLP framework and gives access to NER models for multiple languages which is why its German model was used for data preprocessing.

To our knowledge neither a German data set nor a readily trained model is available for the domain of academic entity recognition covering the entity types academic person, institution, and research area. The only data set that comes close to the present task is CrossNER (Liu et al., 2021), which contains 14 entity types, including labels for universities, scientists, and scientific disciplines. However, CrossNER does not contain any German data, and the part of the data set containing the relevant labels is very small, containing a few hundred samples only, in addition to being extracted from a single specific domain of Wikipedia articles about Artificial Intelligence, which might be insufficient for applying the task of NER to the broad domain of newspaper texts. Peng et al. (2020) propose an approach for adapting existing NER models such that they recognize additional entity types. Their partially supervised training algorithm makes use of word lists with prototypical examples for the new entity type to be added. Although the evaluation for some of their data sets looks promising, their method of introducing new types of named entities is not really applicable to the present task. Only in the case of research area, a *new* entity type would be added, whereas the entity types academic person and institution depict an *adaption*, as persons and institutions in academics are a subset of the more general entity types person and organization that most existing NER models have. However, the idea of bootstrapping training data with word lists was indeed inspired by their work. Gilardi et al. (2023) conduct experiments where they let ChatGPT annotate data sets and compare the results to the annotation performance of human crowd workers. The humans receive the same instructions as the LLM (in a zero-shot setting) for the text annotation tasks comprising binary and multi-class classification of sentences. Results show that the LLM outperforms the crowd workers by approximately 25 percentage points in average accuracy. Under the aspect of labeling cost reduction, Wang et al. (2021) experiment with distinct strategies of applying GPT-3 to label various NLP data sets. They use labels generated by the LLM to train smaller and thus more specialized transformer language models and compare these to the raw GPT-3 model as well as to human labeling performance. It turns out that the combination of letting humans adjust low-confidence labels of GPT-3 works best.

4 Approach

The steps to obtain a custom NER model recognizing academic entities comprise the following: (i) For each entity type, create lists of prototypical entities or words that form part of candidate entities. Detect candidate entities in the corpus text by applying a German off-the-shelf NER model and the word lists. (ii) Manually post-process enough sentences to obtain sufficient training data for an initial data set and fine-tune a German $\text{BERT}_{\text{BASE}}$ model to obtain a custom NER model. (iii) Generate more training data by applying the custom NER model and an LLM on unseen data in order to again fine-tune the German $\text{BERT}_{\text{BASE}}$ model with the initial plus the additional data.
At the last step, various experiments with the additional data – post-processed in different ways – show possible uses of this extra data and evaluate how well they work. These different variants of data post-processing result in three additional data sets for retraining: One data set containing only the extra sentences tagged by the initial custom NER model, a second one with only the tags on which the LLM and the initial custom NER model agree, and a third one being the manually post-processed version of the second data set. Each of the additional training data sets results in a new fine-tuned custom NER model, respectively. Finally, we compare the three additional custom NER models and the initial custom NER model from step (ii).

5 Data

In order to filter DeReKo for a suitable initial data set, a few preprocessing steps are necessary. The word lists are created as a starting point to find sentences that contain one of the three relevant entity types. The first list, used to search for potential academic persons, contains words or abbreviations representing academic titles such as *Dr.*, *Professor* or *PhD*. The second list contains names of academic institutions, mainly based on a list provided by the German Federal Report of Research and Innovation (Bundesbericht Forschung und Innovation, 2023). The third and last one lists areas of research, inspired by the German Research Foundation's classification of research fields (Deutsche Forschungsgemeinschaft, 2023). The word list with academic titles further serves in a previous step to filter DeReKo for potentially relevant texts, which becomes necessary due to the sheer size of the corpus. We use this word list assuming that texts in which academic titles appear might contain mentions of academic institutions and research areas as well. Whereas all three word lists are used to find candidate entities through string matches, the candidate entities for the entity type academic person were detected with the additional help of an off-the-shelf NER model from the Stanza NLP package, applying the condition that only a named

entity of type person having a preceding or succeeding academic title becomes an actual candidate entity.
Out of more than 340,000 filtered texts, 10,000 are randomly selected to automatically find candidate entities. A subsequent manual post-processing[2] with the deletion or correction of wrong entities and the insertion of missed entities, yields a total of 4,928 sentences with 4,223 tags for academic persons (PER-RES), 2,300 tags for academic institutions (ORG-RES), and 676 tags for research areas (AREA-RES). The manual review of all three entity types comes with some challenges. Regarding candidate persons, for example, there are many cases in which schoolteachers (teaching in secondary but not tertiary education) were erroneously tagged as academics because of their preceding title of professor in the sentence. This happens in Austrian newspaper texts, where the convention holds to use this kind of title for schoolteachers who studied at university. Similar are the cases of detected academic persons from fiction or pen names such as *Dr. Seuss*. A weakness of the Stanza NER model is the incorrect recognition of first and last names with hyphens, which are both quite common for German names, e.g. *Prof. DDr. Franz-Josef Radermacher* or *Prof. Barbara Städtler-Mach*. Another problem is that academic persons sometimes stay undetected in sentences in which their academic title does not occur, even when the context is unambiguously academic, e.g.:

(8) *...der Neurobiologe Mathias Jucker vom Hertie-Institut der Universität Tübingen...*

'...the neurobiologist Mathias Jucker from the Hertie Institute of the University of Tübingen...'

This example also illustrates the problem of how to deal with hierarchical relations between academic institutions – in this case whether to tag both the *Hertie-Institut* as well as the *Universität Tübingen* or only the latter. Both were tagged eventually as *Hertie-Institut* unambiguously refers to the subordinate organization, which is not the case for mentions such as *Faculty for Computer Science*. Instead, *Computer Science* would be tagged as an entity of the type research area. Another tagging decision for research areas is to handle two areas as a single entity when they appear in one compound expression connected with a hyphen, e.g. *Wirtschafts- und Sozialwissenschaft* ('economic and social science'). Although a good amount of the work can already be done automatically, these edge cases illustrate that manual post-processing remains an essential step to obtain data of good quality.

[2]Only the author of this paper reviewed the data manually due to practical considerations. While acknowledging the importance of inter-annotator agreement as a measure of reliability, involving external annotators was not feasible within the given time frame and budget constraints for this research.

Data Set	A	B	C	Initial
PER-RES	5,421	4,157	3,774	2,942
ORG-RES	2,826	2,076	2,136	1,624
AREA-RES	1,157	726	749	450
# Sentences	6,768	5,089	4,533	3,449

Table 1: Training data statistics of the initial and the three additional data sets. Note that the number of sentences of the initial data set was originally 4,928 but is reduced by the development and test data.

5.1 Additional Data Sets

To further improve the custom NER model, we generate more training data with the help of the initial custom NER model and an LLM, both applied to tag additional sentences from 1,000 unseen DeReKo texts. The few-shot prompt for the LLM is provided in Appendix A.1. The decision as to which LLM to use is made in favor of *Llama-2-13B-chat* after experimenting with different instructional prompts as input to compare the two models *Llama-2-13B-chat* (Touvron et al., 2023) and *OpenOrca-Platypus2-13B* (Lee et al., 2023). See Appendix A.2 for further details. The three additional data sets created with the initial custom NER model and *Llama-2-13B-chat* all contain the training data from the initial data set *plus* the newly generated data. They differ from each other with respect to the newly generated data as follows:

A) contains sentences with tags detected by the initial custom NER model

B) contains sentences with tags on which the initial custom NER model and *Llama-2-13B-chat* agree

C) contains sentences from B) with manually reviewed tags (deleted, inserted or corrected)

Table 1 provides an overview of the different training data set sizes and the distribution of the three entity types. The biggest data set is data set A, followed by B and finally C, corresponding to the increasingly stricter measures of quality assurance.

6 Experiments

The German cased $BERT_{BASE}$ model *de_dep_news_trf* consisting of 12 layers with 12 attention heads each and a total of 768 hidden states is fine-tuned separately with each of the four data sets using the spaCy transformer library on a single Tesla P4 GPU. To obtain the same development and test data for the four passes of fine-tuning $BERT_{BASE}$, the initial data set is split into train/dev/test portions with a ratio of 70/20/10. For better comparability, all hyperparameters for model training are kept identical and correspond to spaCy's default configuration with a batch size of 128, a dropout rate of 0.1, the Adam optimizer with an initial learning rate of 10^{-5}, and early stopping based on the F1 score.

7 Results and Discussion

We evaluate all four models on the test split consisting of 489 sentences containing 423 PER-RES, 192 ORG-RES, and 79 AREA-RES tags. Table 2 shows that there are only few differences between the model performances, all ranging within overall F1 scores of 91.32% and 92.45%. The initial custom NER model reaches the best score, which is slightly surprising as it is trained on the smallest data set. Intuitively, the expectation would be that model C (trained on data set C) would yield the best score as it comprises roughly 30% more sentences that are, on top of that, manually reviewed. However, model C is only ranked third, even slightly behind model B without the manual review but trained on more sentences. Model A with the strategy to augment the data only using the initial custom NER model yields the worst scores, not only regarding the overall F1 score but also the F1 scores for the individual entity types. A possible explanation might be the missing quality checks for the data, as training data is neither double checked by an LLM nor by a human. It seems to be an insufficient strategy to only increase the amount of data without any measures of quality assurance.

Regarding the best model, the picture changes a bit when taking a look at the entity type F1 scores. While the best score for the entity type PER-RES of 95.4 is still achieved with the initial custom NER model, model C achieves the best score for the entity type ORG-RES, and model B does so for AREA-RES. Thus, with the experiments in this work it cannot be stated that there is clearly one single data augmentation strategy for all entity types.

Model		A	B	C	Initial
PER-RES	P	91.56	90.61	92.39	93.68
	R	96.49	97.19	96.72	97.19
	F1	93.96	93.79	94.51	**95.40**
ORG-RES	P	90.91	92.06	92.15	89.58
	R	87.63	89.69	90.72	88.66
	F1	89.24	90.86	**91.43**	89.12
AREA-RES	P	82.35	86.59	79.76	89.47
	R	82.35	83.53	78.82	80.00
	F1	82.35	**85.03**	79.29	84.47
Overall	P	90.30	90.53	90.86	92.12
	R	92.35	93.48	92.92	92.78
	F1	91.32	91.99	91.88	**92.45**

Table 2: Precision, recall and F1 scores (in percent) for the individual entity types and overall.

Except for the entity AREA-RES in example (2) all entities listed in section 2 are all correctly recognized by the best (initial) model. To test a few cases that are presumably more difficult for the model, we modify the examples (1) and (2) by cutting off the second half of the sentence after the last comma. In both cases the person entities should not be tagged anymore due to the lack of context. The model does so for example (2) but not for (1) where *Heitzer* keeps beeing tagged as PER-RES. For sentence (7) we replace the tokens *Umweltikone* ('environmental icon') for *Primatenforscherin* ('primatologist'), which changes the model's behavior as it now tags *Jane Goodall.*[3]

8 Conclusion

This work shows different strategies of generating training data to obtain a custom NER model through fine-tuning. For the sake of obtaining high-quality data, suitable data is augmented semiautomatically, with some amount of sentences undergoing manual review. The results show that there is no single best data generation strategy for all entity types, such that a combination for the three best-scoring models might be considered for future applications with the specific domain of academic named entity recognition. With the small differences of the resulting F1 scores in mind, a careful conclusion that can be drawn is that LLMs like *Llama-2-13B-chat* are beneficial to ensure data quality at a low cost whereas it might not be worth to invest too much into manual data review.

[3]See Appendix A.3 for all examples and their variations.

9 Limitations

There are several possible improvements for future model fine-tuning, one of which is to see whether a different train/dev split of the three additional data sets would lead to better results and how other/newer LLMs like GPT-4 or Llama-3 might show improvements for data preprocessing. Another idea is to qualitatively evaluate the results of the best model more thoroughly and investigate if wrong model predictions follow certain patterns (e.g. research areas composed of many words are often not well recognized) and if so, generate more training sentences targeted to eliminate these error patterns. Finally, it would be interesting to know by how much the initial data set can be reduced without compromising much on model performance in order to find a good balance between the amount of manually annotated and automatically generated data to further reduce manual annotation cost.

10 Ethical Considerations

For the purpose of this contribution, the authors received access to data files from DeReKo. Due to copyright restrictions the sampled data set can only be made available under certain conditions, for further details see section 1. However, interested parties can easily register for the corpus analysis platform KorAP[4], which allows to query DeReKo as a whole. We do not see any data privacy issues as the texts from which the training data is sampled have all been previously made available by (newspaper) publishers.

11 Acknowledgements

This publication was created in the context of the work of the association German National Research Data Infrastructure (NFDI) e.V. NFDI is financed by the Federal Republic of Germany and the 16 federal states, and the consortium Text+ is funded by the Deutsche Forschungsgemeinschaft (DFG, German Research Foundation) - project number 460033370. The authors would like to thank for the funding and support. Furthermore, thanks also include all institutions and actors who are committed to the association and its goals.

[4]The corpus can be queried either through KorAP's API or its web client: https://korap.ids-mannheim.de/

References

Renate Behrens-Neumann and Barbara Pfeifer. 2011. Die Gemeinsame Normdatei: ein Kooperationsprojekt. *Dialog mit Bibliotheken*, 23(1):37–40.

Bundesbericht Forschung und Innovation. 2023. Wissenschaftseinrichtungen: Liste der Einrichtungen. https://www.bundesbericht-forschung-innovation.de/de/Liste-der-Einrichtungen-1790.html. Accessed: 19.04.2024.

Deutsche Forschungsgemeinschaft. 2023. Fächerstruktur der DFG. https://www.dfg.de/de/foerderung/antrag-foerderprozess/interdisziplinaritaet/faecherstruktur. Accessed: 19.04.2024.

Jacob Devlin, Ming-Wei Chang, Kenton Lee, and Kristina Toutanova. 2019. BERT: Pre-training of Deep Bidirectional Transformers for Language Understanding. In *Proceedings of the 2019 Conference of the North American Chapter of the Association for Computational Linguistics: Human Language Technologies, Volume 1 (Long and Short Papers)*, pages 4171–4186, Minneapolis, Minnesota. Association for Computational Linguistics.

Nils Diewald, Michael Hanl, Eliza Margaretha, Joachim Bingel, Marc Kupietz, Piotr Bański, and Andreas Witt. 2016. KorAP Architecture - Diving in the Deep Sea of Corpus Data. In Nicoletta Calzolari, Khalid Choukri, Thierry Declerck, Sara Goggi, Marko Grobelnik, Bente Maegaard, Joseph Mariani, Helene Mazo, Asuncion Moreno, Jan Odijk, and Stelios Piperidis, editors, *Proceedings of the Tenth International Conference on Language Resources and Evaluation (LREC 2016)*, pages 3586–3591. Paris: European Language Resources Association (ELRA) 2016, Portoroz, Slovenia.

Fabrizio Gilardi, Meysam Alizadeh, and Maël Kubli. 2023. ChatGPT Outperforms Crowd-Workers for Text-Annotation Tasks. *arXiv preprint arXiv:2303.15056*.

Erhard W. Hinrichs, Marie Hinrichs, and Thomas Zastrow. 2010. WebLicht: Web-Based LRT Services for German. In *Proceedings of the ACL 2010 System Demonstrations*, pages 25–29.

Matthew Honnibal, Ines Montani, Sofie Van Landeghem, and Adriane Boyd. 2020. SpaCy: Industrial-strength Natural Language Processing in Python. Zenodo (online).

Marc Kupietz, Cyril Belica, Holger Keibel, and Andreas Witt. 2010. The German Reference Corpus DeReKo: A Primordial Sample for Linguistic Research. In *Proceedings of the Seventh International Conference on Language Resources and Evaluation (LREC'10)*, Valletta, Malta. European Language Resources Association (ELRA).

Marc Kupietz and Holger Keibel. 2009. The Mannheim German Reference Corpus (DeReKo) as a basis for empirical linguistic research. In Makoto/Kawaguchi Minegishi, editor, *Workings Papers in Corpus-based Linguistics and Language Education*, volume 3, pages 53–59. Tokyo University of Foreign Studies 2009, Tokyo.

Marc Kupietz, Harald Lüngen, Pawel Kamocki, and Andreas Witt. 2018. The German Reference Corpus DeReKo: New Developments – New Opportunities. In *Proceedings of the Eleventh International Conference on Language Resources and Evaluation (LREC 2018)*, pages 4353–4360, Miyazaki, Japan. European Language Resources Association (ELRA).

Rachael Lammey. 2020. Solutions for Identification Problems: A Look at the Research Organization Registry. *Science Editing*, 7(1):65–69.

Ariel N. Lee, Cole J. Hunter, and Nataniel Ruiz. 2023. Platypus: Quick, Cheap, and Powerful Refinement of LLMs. *Preprint*, arXiv:2308.07317.

Jinhyuk Lee, Wonjin Yoon, Sungdong Kim, Donghyeon Kim, Sunkyu Kim, Chan Ho So, and Jaewoo Kang. 2020. BioBERT: A Pre-trained Biomedical Language Representation Model for Biomedical Text Mining. *Bioinformatics*, 36(4):1234–1240.

Leibniz-Institut für Deutsche Sprache. 2024. Deutsches Referenzkorpus / Archiv der Korpora geschriebener Gegenwartssprache 2024-I (Release of 13.03.2024). Mannheim: Leibniz-Institut für Deutsche Sprache. https://www.ids-mannheim.de/digspra/kl/projekte/korpora/releases/.

Zihan Liu, Yan Xu, Tiezheng Yu, Wenliang Dai, Ziwei Ji, Samuel Cahyawijaya, Andrea Madotto, and Pascale Fung. 2021. CrossNER: Evaluating Cross-Domain Named Entity Recognition. In *Proceedings of the AAAI Conference on Artificial Intelligence*, pages 13452–13460.

Minlong Peng, Ruotian Ma, Qi Zhang, Lujun Zhao, Mengxi Wei, Changlong Sun, and Xuanjing Huang. 2020. Toward Recognizing More Entity Types in NER: An Efficient Implementation using Only Entity Lexicons. In *Findings of the Association for Computational Linguistics: EMNLP 2020*, pages 678–688, Online. Association for Computational Linguistics.

Peng Qi, Yuhao Zhang, Yuhui Zhang, Jason Bolton, and Christopher D. Manning. 2020. Stanza: A Python Natural Language Processing Toolkit for Many Human Languages. In *Proceedings of the 58th Annual Meeting of the Association for Computational Linguistics: System Demonstrations*.

Xavier Schmitt, Sylvain Kubler, Jérémy Robert, Mike Papadakis, and Yves LeTraon. 2019. A Replicable Comparison Study of NER Software: StanfordNLP, NLTK, OpenNLP, SpaCy, Gate. In *2019 Sixth International Conference on Social Networks Analysis, Management and Security (SNAMS)*, pages 338–343.

Cong Sun, Zhihao Yang, Lei Wang, Yin Zhang, Hongfei Lin, and Jian Wang. 2021. Biomedical Named Entity Recognition Using BERT in the Machine Reading Comprehension Framework. *Journal of Biomedical Informatics*, 118:103799.

Hugo Touvron, Louis Martin, Kevin Stone, Peter Albert, Amjad Almahairi, Yasmine Babaei, Nikolay Bashlykov, Soumya Batra, Prajjwal Bhargava, Shruti Bhosale, Dan Bikel, Lukas Blecher, Cristian Canton Ferrer, Moya Chen, Guillem Cucurull, David Esiobu, Jude Fernandes, Jeremy Fu, Wenyin Fu, Brian Fuller, Cynthia Gao, Vedanuj Goswami, Naman Goyal, Anthony Hartshorn, Saghar Hosseini, Rui Hou, Hakan Inan, Marcin Kardas, Viktor Kerkez, Madian Khabsa, Isabel Kloumann, Artem Korenev, Punit Singh Koura, Marie-Anne Lachaux, Thibaut Lavril, Jenya Lee, Diana Liskovich, Yinghai Lu, Yuning Mao, Xavier Martinet, Todor Mihaylov, Pushkar Mishra, Igor Molybog, Yixin Nie, Andrew Poulton, Jeremy Reizenstein, Rashi Rungta, Kalyan Saladi, Alan Schelten, Ruan Silva, Eric Michael Smith, Ranjan Subramanian, Xiaoqing Ellen Tan, Binh Tang, Ross Taylor, Adina Williams, Jian Xiang Kuan, Puxin Xu, Zheng Yan, Iliyan Zarov, Yuchen Zhang, Angela Fan, Melanie Kambadur, Sharan Narang, Aurelien Rodriguez, Robert Stojnic, Sergey Edunov, and Thomas Scialom. 2023. Llama 2: Open Foundation and Fine-Tuned Chat Models. *Preprint*, arXiv:2307.09288.

Sowmya Vajjala and Ramya Balasubramaniam. 2022. What do we Really Know about State of the Art NER? *Preprint*, arXiv:2205.00034.

Denny Vrandečić and Markus Krötzsch. 2014. Wikidata: A Free Collaborative Knowledgebase. *Communications of the ACM*, 57(10):78—-85.

Shuohang Wang, Yang Liu, Yichong Xu, Chenguang Zhu, and Michael Zeng. 2021. Want to Reduce Labeling Cost? GPT-3 Can Help. *arXiv preprint arXiv:2108.13487*.

A Appendix

A.1 Few-Shot Prompt

The model generated the most useful output with few-shot prompting, i.e. when providing three examples of correctly tagged sentences as the desired output. The actual target sentence required to be tagged by the LLM is then attached at the end of the prompt, see Figure 1. The challenge was to select examples as diverse as possible that are also short enough to not exceed the model's context window size of 512 tokens. Sometimes the target sentence was too long and maxed out the context window size, which led to an error and therefore no output was returned from the LLM. Other challenges consisted in the unexpected output formatting done by the model: No separation of entities of the same

"SYSTEM: Finde Entitäten wie akademische Personen, akademische Institutionen und akademische Fachrichtungen. Gib die Entitäten im Wortlaut wieder. Generiere keinen weiteren Text darüber hinaus.
Beispiele:

Text: Gleichzeitig studierte Prof. Roland Girtler an der Rheinischen Friedrich- Wilhelms-Universität Bonn Politikwissenschaften, Öffentliches Recht und Philosophie mit Abschluss MA, gab zwei Fachbücher heraus und machte in der FDP Karriere.

Entitäten: PER: Prof. Roland Girtler; ORG: Friedrich- Wilhelms-Universität Bonn; AREA: Politikwissenschaften | Öffentliches Recht | Philosophie

Text: Bei den Studenten am Erziehungswissenschaftlichen Seminar der Heidelberger Universität und der Humboldt Universität Berlin (HU) regt sich Unmut: Als \"unhaltbare und unzumutbare Zustände\", dass seit nunmehr sieben Semestern der Lehrstuhl für Sozialpädagogik vakant ist.

Entitäten: PER: -; ORG: Heidelberger Universität | Humboldt Universität Berlin (HU); AREA: Sozialpädagogik

Text: \"Die Schädigung im Gehirn folgt dabei dem Dominoprinzip\", sagt der Neurobiologe Mathias Jucker, PhD vom \"Hertie-Institut\" der Universität Tübingen (vgl. Grafik S. 98).

Entitäten: PER: Mathias Jucker, PhD; ORG: \"Hertie-Institut\" | Universität Tübingen; AREA: -

USER: **Text**: " + target_sentence + " ASSISTANT: "

Figure 1: Few-shot prompt with the prompt template keywords colored in orange and a placeholder for the target sentence in blue. The desired output as indicated in the examples is formatted as follows: PER: entity1 | entity2 | entity3; ORG: entity4 | entity5; AREA: entity6. A dash is inserted if an entity type is not detected at all.

type with the required separator symbol or the unrequested modifications of entities, e.g. the conversion of *Heidelberger Universität* into *Universität Heidelberg*, and halluzinations in the shape of inventing additional sentences. This behavior made the final extraction of entities impossible for some of the target sentences, which were then skipped and not included in the additional data sets. For the sentences where the output generation was successful and where the model kept the desired output format (i.e. designating the entity type followed by the entity values separated with vertical bars), the recognized entities could easily be extracted.

A.2 LLM Comparison

Table 3 shows the results of the LLM evaluation, which is performed on a test set consisting of 489 sentences from the initial data set. For better comparison, both models were instructed with the same few-shot prompt containing three examples of sentences and corresponding entity tags. *Llama-2-13B-chat*[5] achieved an F1 score of 85%, outperforming *OpenOrca-Platypus2-13B*[6] by more than 10 percent.

	Llama 2 Chat	OpenOrca Platypus 2
P	88.53	92.48
R	81.76	62.35
F1	**85.01**	74.49

Table 3: Precision, recall, and F1 scores (in percent) on tagging performance for 489 test set sentences.

A.3 Example Sentences

(1a) *"Aber riesige Zahlen sind immer noch nicht unendlich", sagt Heitzer, Professorin am Lehr- und Forschungsgebiet Didaktik der Mathematik an der RWTH.*

"But huge numbers are still not infinite', says Heitzer, professor of the teaching and research department Didactics of Mathematics at RWTH.'

(1b) *"Aber riesige Zahlen sind immer noch nicht unendlich", sagt Heitzer.*

[5] https://huggingface.co/TheBloke/Llama-2-13B-chat-GGML

[6] https://huggingface.co/TheBloke/OpenOrca-Platypus2-13B-GGML

“But huge numbers are still not infinite’, says Heitzer.’

(2a) *Ein paar Stockwerke höher wartet Astrid Kiermaier auf uns, die Molekularbiologin arbeitet bei Roche im Bereich Krebsforschung und leitet dort ein Team von 14 Mitarbeitern.*

'A few floors up, Astrid Kiermaier is waiting for us, the molecular biologist works in the area of cancer research at Roche and leads a team of 14 employees there.'

(2b) *Ein paar Stockwerke höher wartet Astrid Kiermaier auf uns.*

'A few floors up, Astrid Kiermaier is waiting for us.'

(3) *Mitte März begann ein Team von Forschern der Universität Hirosaki damit, sodass sie im Norden Japans bereits Messungen vor Ort durchführten.*

'In mid-March, a team of researchers from Hirosaki University began with that, such that they already conduced on-site measurements in northern Japan.'

(4) *Der Physiker erfand nicht nur die Luftpumpe, sondern befaßte sich auch mit der barometrischen Erforschung des Luftdrucks.*

'The physicist not only invented the air pump but also engaged in the barometric study of air pressure.'

(5) *Dr. Frank-Walter Steinmeier, Chef des Bundeskanzleramtes, ist dafür verantwortlich, Streitigkeiten zwischen den Politikern zu schlichten.*

'Dr. Frank-Walter Steinmeier, head of the Federal Chancellery, is responsible for mediating disputes between politicians.'

(6) *Außenminister Frank-Walter Steinmeier gab sich weiter diplomatisch.*

'Foreign Minister Frank-Walter Steinmeier continued to maintain a diplomatic stance.'

(7a) *Schütze, was du liebst - So lautet das Prinzip der Umweltikone Jane Goodall.*

'Protect what you love – This is the principle of environmental icon Jane Goodall.'

(7b) *Schütze, was du liebst - So lautet das Prinzip der Primatenforscherin Jane Goodall.*

'Protect what you love – This is the principle of primatologist Jane Goodall.'

(8) *"Die Schädigung im Gehirn folgt dabei dem Dominoprinzip", sagt der Neurobiologe Mathias Jucker vom Hertie-Institut der Universität Tübingen.*

“The damage in the brain follows the domino principle’, says the neurobiologist Mathias Jucker from the Hertie Institute of the University of Tübingen.’

Redundancy Aware Multiple Reference Based Gainwise Evaluation of Extractive Summarization

Mousumi Akter
Research Center Trustworthy
Data Science and Security
Technical University Dortmund, Germany
mousumi.akter@tu-dortmund.de

Santu Karmaker
Big Data Intelligence (BDI) Lab
Auburn University
Alabama, USA
sks0086@auburn.edu

Abstract

The ROUGE metric is commonly used to evaluate extractive summarization task, but it has been criticized for its lack of semantic awareness and its ignorance about the ranking quality of the extractive summarizer. Previous research has introduced a gain-based automated metric called *Sem-nCG* that addresses these issues, as it is both rank and semantic aware. However, it does not consider the amount of redundancy present in a model summary and currently does not support evaluation with multiple reference summaries. It is essential to have a model summary that balances importance and diversity, but finding a metric that captures both of these aspects is challenging. In this paper, we propose a redundancy-aware *Sem-nCG* metric and demonstrate how the revised *Sem-nCG* metric can be used to evaluate model summaries against multiple references as well which was missing in previous research. Experimental results demonstrate that the revised *Sem-nCG* metric has a stronger correlation with human judgments compared to the previous *Sem-nCG* metric and traditional ROUGE and BERTScore metric for both single and multiple reference scenarios.

1 Introduction

For the past two decades, ROUGE (Lin, 2004b) has been the most used metric for evaluating extractive summarization tasks. Nonetheless, ROUGE has long been criticized for its lack of semantic awareness (Graham, 2015; Ng and Abrecht, 2015; Ganesan, 2018; Yang et al., 2018) and its ignorance about the ranking quality of the extractive summarizer (Akter et al., 2022).

To address these issues, previous work has proposed a gain-based metric called *Sem-nCG* (Akter et al., 2022) to evaluate extractive summaries by incorporating rank and semantic awareness. Redundancy, a crucial factor in evaluating extractive summaries, was not, however, included in the *Sem-nCG* metric. Additionally, their proposed *Sem-nCG* metric does not support the evaluation of model summaries against multiple references. However, it is well recognized that a set of documents can have multiple, very different, and equally valid summaries; as such, obtaining multiple reference summaries can improve the stability of the evaluation (Nenkova, 2005; Lin, 2004a). It's quite challenging to come up with a metric that takes into account the balance between importance and diversity in model summary. Therefore, it's necessary to carry out a systematic study on how to integrate redundancy and multiple references to the existing *Sem-nCG* metric.

In this paper, we first incorporate redundancy into the previously proposed *Sem-nCG* metric. In other words, we propose a redundancy-aware *Sem-nCG* metric by exploring different ways of incorporating redundancy into the original metric. Through extensive experiments, we demonstrate that the redundancy-aware *Sem-nCG* exhibits a notably stronger correlation with humans than the original *Sem-nCG* metric.

Next, we demonstrate how this redundancy-aware metric could be applied to evaluate model summaries against multiple references. This is a non-trivial task because *Sem-nCG* evaluates a model-generated summary by considering it as a ranked list of sentences and then comparing it against an automatically inferred *ground-truth* ranked list of sentences within a source document based on a single human written summary (Akter et al., 2022). However, in the case of multiple references, the *ground-truth* ranked list of source sentences must be inferred based on all available human-written reference summaries, not just one.

When there are multiple reference summaries available, incorporating them into evaluation poses significant challenge. This is because the quality of human-written summaries differs not only in writing style but also in focus. Moreover, including multiple reference summaries with a lot of terminology variations and paraphrasing makes the automated evaluation metric less stable (Cohan and Goharian, 2016). In this work, we have also shown how to infer a single/unique ground-truth ranking based on multiple reference summaries with the proposed redundancy-aware *Sem-nCG* metric. Our findings suggest that, compared to the conventional ROUGE and BERTScore metric, the redundancy-aware *Sem-nCG* exhibits a stronger correlation with human judgments for evaluating model summaries when both single and multiple references are available. Therefore, we encourage the community to use redundancy-aware *Sem-nCG* to evaluate extractive summarization tasks. Our contributions are:

- Redundancy of extracted sentences is a common problem in extractive summarization systems. We have demonstrated how to consider redundancy awareness in the already-designed *Sem-nCG* metric.
- We present how to use the redundancy-aware *Sem-nCG* metric for summary evaluation with multiple references which poses unique challenges of variability.
- The revised *Sem-nCG* metric exhibits a stronger correlation with human judgments for evaluating model summaries when both single and multiple references are available, not only with the previous *Sem-nCG* metric but also with conventional ROUGE and BERTScore metric.

2 Redundancy-aware *Sem-nCG* Metric

***Sem-nCG* Score:** Normalized Cumulative Gain (*nCG*) is a popular evaluation metric in information retrieval to evaluate the quality of a ranker. nCG compares the model ranking with an *ideal* ranking and assigns a certain score to the model based on some pre-defined gain. (Akter et al., 2022) has utilized the idea of *nCG* in the evaluation of extractive summarization. The basic concept of Sem-nCG is to compute the gain (*CG@k*) obtained by a top *k* extracted sentences and divide that by the maximum/ideal possible gain (*ICG@k*), where the gains are inferred by comparing the input document against a human written summary. Mathematically:

$$\textit{Sem-nCG@k} = \frac{CG@k}{ICG@k} \quad (1)$$

Redundancy Score: We followed (Chen et al., 2021) to compute self-referenced redundancy score which is computationally efficient and less ambiguous than classical approaches. The summary, X, itself is used as the reference to determine the degree of semantic similarity between each summary token/sentence and the other tokens/sentences. The average of maximum semantic similarity is used to determine the redundancy score. For a given summary, $X = \{x_1, x_2, ..., x_n\}$, the calculation is as follows:

$$Score_{\text{red}} = \frac{\sum_i max_{j:i \neq j} Sim(x_j, x_i)}{|\mathbf{X}|} \quad (2)$$

where, $j : i \neq j$ denotes that the similarity between x_i and itself has not been considered. Note that $Score_{red} \in [0, 1]$ in our case and lower is better.

Final Score: We used the following formula to calculate the final score after obtaining the scores of *Sem-nCG* and $Score_{red}$:

$$Score = \lambda * \textit{Sem-nCG} + (1 - \lambda) * (1 - Score_{red}) \quad (3)$$

Here, $\lambda \in [0, 1]$ is a hyper-parameter to scale the weight between $Score_{red}$ and *Sem-nCG*. $Score \in [0, 1]$ where higher score means better summary.

3 Experimental Setup

Dataset: Human correlation is an essential attribute to consider while assessing the quality of a metric. To compute the human correlation of the revised redundancy-aware *Sem-nCG* metric, we utilized SummEval dataset from (Fabbri et al., 2021)[1]. The annotations include summaries generated by 16 models (abstractive and extractive) from 100 news articles (1600 examples in total) on the CNN/DailyMail Dataset. Each source news article includes the original CNN/DailyMail reference summary as well as 10 additional crowd-sourced reference summaries. Each summary was annotated by 5 independent crowd-sourced workers and 3 independent experts (8 annotations in total) along the four dimensions: *Consistency*, *Relevance*, *Coherence* and *Fluency* (Fabbri et al., 2021)[2]. As this work focuses on the evaluation of extractive summarization, we considered the output generated by extractive models and filtered out samples comprising less than 3 sentences (as we report *Sem-nCG@3*). Additionally, we considered the expert

[1]We used the dataset by (Fabbri et al., 2021), the only available benchmark "meta-evaluation dataset" for **extractive summarization**, to the best of our knowledge. *Sem-nCG*'s authors have demonstrated its correlation with human judgment on this dataset. To ensure a fair comparison, we maintained the same settings as the original *Sem-nCG* when assessing the redundancy-aware *Sem-nCG*.

[2]See Appendix A.2 for details

annotations for the meta-evaluation, as non-expert annotations can be risky (Gillick and Liu, 2010).

As was done in (Akter et al., 2022), for each sample, from the 11 available reference summaries, we considered 3 settings: Less Overlapping Reference/LOR (highly abstractive references with fewer lexical overlap with the original document), Medium Overlapping Reference/MOR (medium lexical overlap with the original document) and Highly Overlapping Reference/HOR (highly extractive references with high lexical overlap with the original document).

Embedding for Groundtruth Ranking: The core of the *Sem-nCG* metric is to automatically create the groundtruth/ideal ranking against which the model ranking is compared. To create the groundtruth ranking, (Akter et al., 2022) used various sentence embeddings. Similarly, we utilized various sentence embeddings as well since our goal is to compare the new redundancy-aware *Sem-nCG* metric to the original *Sem-nCG* metric. Specifically, we considered Infersent (v2) (Conneau et al., 2017), Semantic Textual Similarity benchmark (STSb - bert/roberta/distilbert) (Reimers and Gurevych, 2019), Elmo (Peters et al., 2018) and Google Universal Sentence Encoder (USE) (Cer et al., 2018) with enc-2 (Iyyer et al., 2015) based on the deep average network, to infer the groundtruth/ideal ranking of the sentences within the input document with guidance from the human written summaries.

$Score_{red}$ Computation: To compute the self-referenced redundancy score, we used the top-3 sentences from the model generated summary (as we report *Sem-nCG@3*). We calculated each sentence's maximum similarity to other sentences and then averaged it to get the desired $Score_{red}$. We experimented with four distinct variations to compare the sentences: cosine similarity (by converting sentences to STSb-distilbert (Reimers and Gurevych, 2019) embeddings), ROUGE (Lin, 2004b), MoverScore (Zhao et al., 2019) and BERTScore (Zhang et al., 2020).

4 Results

4.1 Redundancy-aware *Sem-nCG*

We first considered how redundancy-aware Sem-nCG performs in extractive summarization with single reference. As shown in Table 1, we computed Kendall's tau (τ) correlation between the expert given score for model summary and the Sem-nCG score with/without redundancy along the four meta-evaluation criteria: *Consistency*, *Relevance*, *Coherence*, and *Fluency*, for different embedding variations (to create the groudtruth ranking) and different approaches to compute $Score_{red}$. We utilized Equation 3 to compute the redundancy-aware *Sem-nCG* score, where lambda (λ) is a hyper-parameter choice and is set to $\lambda = 0.5$ empirically. In Table 1 w/o redundancy refers to Equation 1.

Table 1 shows that the redundancy-aware *Sem-nCG* metric outperforms the original *Sem-nCG* metric in terms of *Consistency*, *Relevance*, and *Coherence*; with a 5% improvement in *Relevance* and a 14% improvement in *Coherence* for less overlapping references (LOR). We also observe improvements in the *Relevance* (9%) and *Coherence* (20%) dimensions for medium overlapping references (MOR). For High Overlapping References (HOR), the improvement is 8% and 22% for *Relevance* and *Coherence*, respectively.

We also observe that STSb-distilbert embedding is a better choice in the *Consistency* dimension, whereas USE with enc-2 is a better choice in the *Relevance* and *Coherence* dimensions to construct the groundtruth ranking. Therefore, we recommend STSb-distilbert to create groundtruth ranking if *Consistency* is a top priority, otherwise, we recommend using USE with enc-2. A groundtruth ranking was also created by combining STSb-distilbert and USE into an ensemble, which showed balanced performance across all four dimensions. It also appears that ROUGE and BERTScore provide comparable performances while computing $Score_{red}$. However, using ROUGE score as self-referenced redundancy will be a better choice as evident from Section 4.3.

In Table 2 Kendall's tau correlation of ROUGE and BERTScore has been demonstrated to get an idea of the advantage of redundancy-aware *Sem-nCG* and it is clearly evident that redundancy-aware Sem-nCG also exhibits stronger correlation than these metrics.

4.2 Hyperparameter Choice

In figure 1, we have varied $\lambda \in [0, 1]$ for the 3 scenarios (LOR, MOR and HOR) and computed human correlation along four dimensions (*Consistency*, *Relevance*, *Coherence* and *Fluency*) when different embeddings are used to create the groundtruth ranking and ROUGE score is used to compute $Score_{red}$. Human correlations with BERTScore-based redundancy are presented in Appendix. For both redundancy penalties, it shows

Embedding	Type	Consistency			Relevance			Coherence			Fluency		
		LOR	MOR	HOR	LOR	MOR	HOR	LOR	MOR	HOR	LOR	MOR	HOR
Inferesent	w/o redundancy	0.08	0.06	0.08	0.07	0.12	0.09	0.06	0.06	0.04	**0.05**	0.03	**0.12**
+ Redundancy penalty	Cosine Similarity	0.04	0.02	0.06	0.08	0.15	0.13	0.14	0.19	0.18	0.02	-0.02	0.08
	ROUGE-1	0.07	0.05	0.11	0.11	0.18	0.17	0.18	0.25	**0.26**	-0.01	-0.04	0.05
	MoverScore	0.05	0.06	0.11	0.09	0.15	0.12	0.11	0.13	0.11	0.03	0.01	0.11
	BERTScore	0.05	0.02	0.08	0.13	0.19	0.18	0.18	0.22	0.24	-0.01	-0.04	0.04
Elmo	w/o redundancy	0.06	0.07	0.09	0.02	0.08	0.06	0.02	0.02	0.01	0.00	0.01	0.06
+ Redundancy penalty	Cosine Similarity	0.03	0.03	0.05	0.04	0.13	0.10	0.12	0.14	0.14	-0.06	-0.05	0.02
	ROUGE-1	0.08	0.05	0.08	0.07	0.15	0.14	0.17	0.20	0.20	-0.06	-0.06	0.01
	MoverScore	0.08	0.07	0.10	0.04	0.10	0.09	0.07	0.06	0.06	-0.02	-0.01	0.05
	BERTScore	0.06	0.03	0.05	0.09	0.17	0.16	0.17	0.19	0.18	-0.06	-0.07	0.00
STSb-bert	w/o redundancy	0.11	0.08	0.09	0.03	0.13	0.12	-0.01	0.06	0.01	0.03	**0.10**	0.03
+ Redundancy penalty	Cosine Similarity	0.08	0.01	0.06	0.05	0.17	0.13	0.10	0.18	0.16	-0.05	0.02	0.05
	ROUGE-1	0.12	0.05	0.09	0.08	**0.22**	0.18	0.14	0.25	0.22	-0.04	-0.04	0.01
	MoverScore	0.12	0.06	0.10	0.05	0.16	0.15	0.04	0.11	0.09	-0.01	0.02	0.08
	BERTScore	0.10	0.01	0.06	0.11	**0.22**	**0.20**	0.14	0.24	0.20	-0.06	-0.04	0.01
STSb-roberta	w/o redundancy	0.12	**0.14**	0.07	0.07	0.07	0.05	0.04	0.00	-0.02	-0.01	0.01	0.06
+ Redundancy penalty	Cosine Similarity	0.09	0.07	0.05	0.08	0.11	0.06	0.13	0.13	0.10	-0.06	-0.05	-0.01
	ROUGE-1	0.12	0.11	0.09	0.11	0.16	0.10	0.18	0.20	0.17	-0.07	-0.07	-0.04
	MoverScore	0.13	0.13	0.10	0.09	0.10	0.07	0.08	0.07	0.04	-0.03	0.00	0.04
	BERTScore	0.10	0.08	0.05	0.13	0.18	0.12	0.17	0.18	0.15	-0.08	-0.06	-0.04
USE	w/o redundancy	0.05	0.04	0.04	0.11	0.14	0.08	0.07	0.08	0.02	0.03	0.05	0.08
+ Redundancy penalty	Cosine Similarity	0.02	-0.01	0.03	0.10	0.16	0.09	0.16	0.19	0.16	-0.05	0.01	0.03
	ROUGE-1	0.06	0.02	0.07	0.13	0.21	0.14	0.20	**0.26**	0.23	-0.06	0.00	0.00
	MoverScore	0.07	0.03	0.07	0.13	0.16	0.11	0.13	0.13	0.10	0.01	0.03	0.06
	BERTScore	0.03	-0.01	0.05	**0.15**	**0.22**	0.17	**0.21**	0.24	0.22	-0.06	0.00	0.00
STSb-distilbert	w/o redundancy	0.17	0.09	**0.12**	0.06	0.09	0.07	0.06	0.03	-0.01	0.01	0.03	0.04
+ Redundancy penalty	Cosine Similarity	0.16	0.04	0.06	0.07	0.12	0.07	0.14	0.16	0.11	-0.05	-0.03	-0.04
	ROUGE-1	0.16	0.06	0.08	0.10	0.16	0.12	0.17	0.21	0.17	-0.06	-0.04	-0.05
	MoverScore	**0.18**	0.08	0.10	0.08	0.12	0.09	0.09	0.09	0.04	-0.02	0.01	0.01
	BERTScore	0.14	0.03	0.05	0.12	0.18	0.14	0.17	0.20	0.16	-0.06	-0.05	-0.05
$Ensemble_{sim}$	w/o redundancy	0.12	0.08	0.07	0.10	0.12	0.07	0.08	0.06	0.00	0.01	0.04	0.05
+ Redundancy penalty	Cosine Similarity	0.11	0.02	0.04	0.10	0.16	0.09	0.16	0.20	0.15	-0.06	-0.01	-0.01
	ROUGE-1	0.13	0.05	0.08	0.13	0.21	0.14	0.20	**0.26**	0.21	-0.05	-0.03	-0.03
	MoverScore	0.14	0.06	0.08	0.12	0.15	0.10	0.14	0.13	0.08	-0.01	0.03	0.03
	BERTScore	0.10	0.03	0.05	**0.15**	**0.22**	0.16	**0.21**	0.25	0.20	-0.05	-0.02	-0.03

Table 1: Kendall's tau (τ) correlation coefficients of expert annotations for different embedding variations of *Sem-nCG* along with various redundancy penalties when $\lambda = 0.5$. Low overlapping reference (LOR), medium overlapping CNN/DailyMail reference (MOR), and high overlapping reference (HOR) were chosen from 11 reference summaries per example to demonstrate the correlation. The highest value in each column is in bold green.

	Consistency			Relevance			Coherence			Fluency		
	LOR	MOR	HOR	LOR	MOR	HOR	LOR	MOR	HOR	LOR	MOR	HOR
ROUGE-1	0.08	0.05	0.01	0.07	0.21	0.22	0.03	0.13	0.13	0.05	0.05	0.05
ROUGE-L	0.02	0.06	-0.01	0.03	0.19	0.15	-0.02	0.14	0.08	0.01	0.04	-0.07
BERTScore	0.06	0.10	0.07	0.10	0.18	0.20	0.06	0.15	0.11	0.08	0.05	0.04

Table 2: Kendall's tau correlation coefficients of ROUGE and BERTScore for Low overlapping reference (LOR), medium overlapping CNN/DailyMail reference (MOR), and high overlapping reference (HOR) chosen from 11 reference summaries per example to demonstrate the correlation.

that higher lambda ($\lambda \geq 0.6$) achieves better correlation for the *Consistency* dimensions, which makes sense because higher lambda means giving more weight to *Sem-nCG*. For *Relevance* and *Coherence* dimensions, a lower lambda (λ) value between $[0.3 - 0.5]$ is a better choice as lower λ means more penalty to redundancy. It appears that for *Fluency* all metric variations struggle. It is evident that $\lambda = 0.5$ gives comparable performance in all four quality dimensions (consistency, relevance, coherence and fluency) and thus we recommend using $\lambda = 0.5$ while adopting Equation 3 to compute redundancy-aware *Sem-nCG*. Table 3 shows a qualitative example for the evaluation of a model-extracted summary.

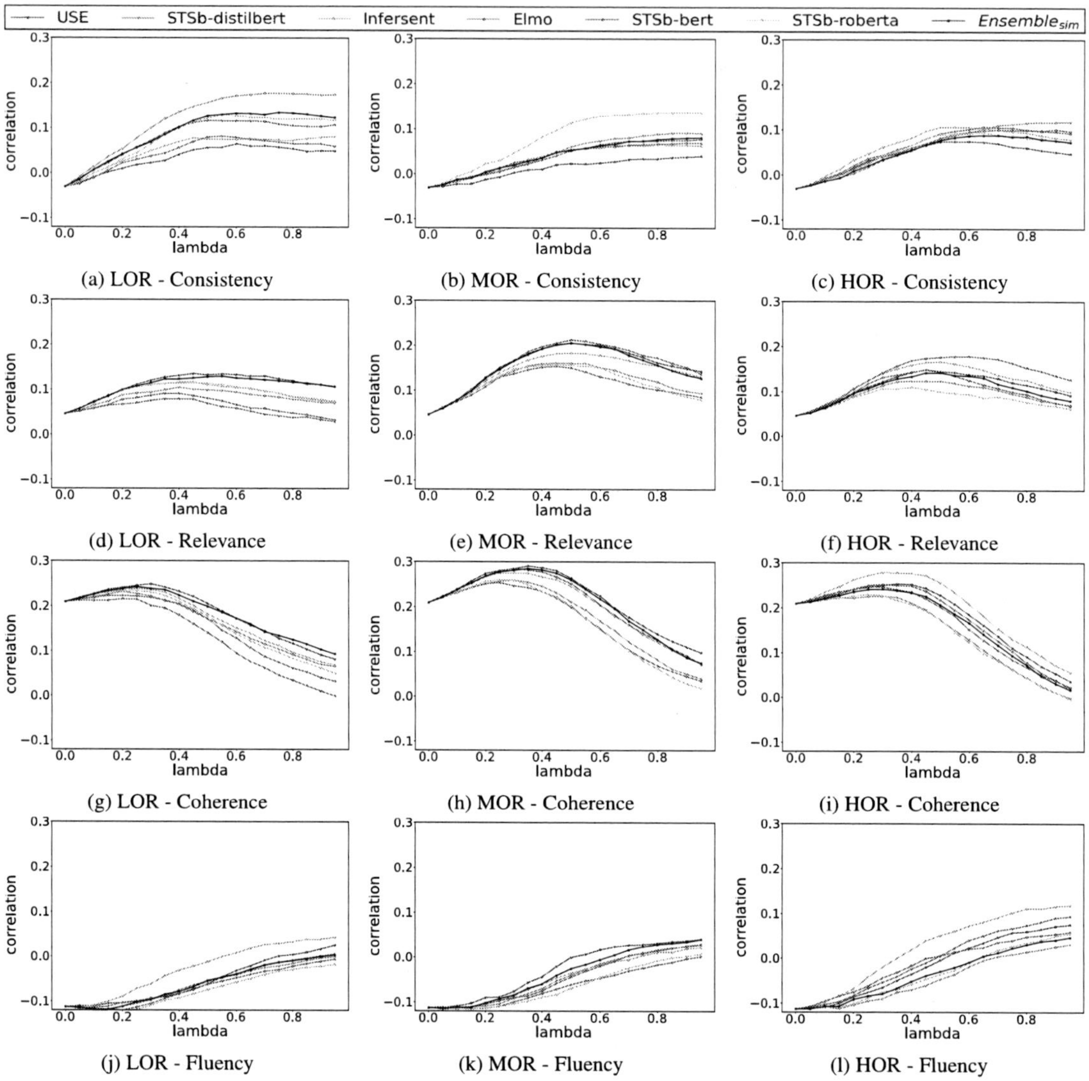

Figure 1: Kendall Tau (τ) Correlation coefficient when lambda (λ) $\in [0, 1]$ from (a)-(c) for Consistency, (d)-(f) for relevance, (g)-(i) for coherence and (j)-(l) for Fluency dimension when ROUGE score is used as redundancy penalty for less overlapping reference (LOR), medium overlapping reference (MOR) and high overlapping reference (HOR).

4.3 Redundancy-aware *Sem-nCG* for Evaluation with Multiple References

SummEval (Fabbri et al., 2021) dataset contains 11 reference summaries. For summary evaluation with multiple references, we considered the lexical overlap of the reference summaries with the original document to demonstrate the terminology variations. Then we considered 3 less overlapping references as Multi-Ref LORs, 3 medium overlapping references as Multi-Ref MORs and 3 high overlapping references as Multi-Ref HORs. We have also mixed up 1 LOR, 1 MOR and 1 HOR and considered this set as Muti-Ref LOR, MOR, HOR to see how the evaluation metric correlates in different terminology variations. Table 4 confirms that ROUGE shows very poor correlation in all the dimensions (consistency, relevance, coherence, and fluency) in all the scenarios and shows slightly better correlation in Multi-Ref HORs (which is somewhat expected as ROUGE considers direct lexical overlap). Interestingly, BERTScore also shows poor correlation in all the settings supporting that the traditional evaluation metric becomes less stable for multiple reference summaries with lots of terminology variations (Cohan and Goharian, 2016).

Article: Last week she was barely showing – but Demelza Poldark is now the proud mother to the show's latest addition. Within ten minutes of tomorrow night's episode, fans will see Aidan Turner's dashing Ross Poldark gaze lovingly at his new baby daughter. As Sunday night's latest heartthrob, women across the country have voiced their longing to settle down with the brooding Cornish gentleman – but unfortunately, it seems as if his heart is well and truly off the market. Scroll down for the video. Last week she was barely showing – but Demelza Poldark is now the proud mother to the show's latest addition He may have married his red-headed kitchen maid out of duty, but as he tells her that she makes him a better man, audiences can have little doubt about his feelings. What is rather less convincing, however, is the timeline of the pregnancy. With the climax of the previous episode being the announcement of the pregnancy, it is quite a jump to the start of tomorrow's installment where Demelza, played by Eleanor Tomlinson, talks about being eight months pregnant. Just minutes after – once again without any nod to the passing of time – she is giving birth, with the last month of her pregnancy passing in less than the blink of an eye. With the climax of the previous episode being the announcement of the pregnancy, it is quite a jump to the start of tomorrow's instalment where Demelza, played by Eleanor Tomlinson, talks about being eight months pregnant As Sunday night's latest heartthrob, women across the country have voiced their longing to settle down with Poldark – but unfortunately, it seems as if his heart is well and truly off the market Their fast relationship didn't go unnoticed by fans. One posted on Twitter: 'If you are pregnant in Poldark times expect to have it in the next 10 minutes' It is reminiscent of the show's previous pregnancy that saw Elizabeth, another contender for Ross's affection, go to full term in the gap between two episodes. This didn't go unnoticed by fans, who posted on Twitter: 'Poldark is rather good, would watch the next one now. Though if you are pregnant in Poldark times expect to have it in the next 10 minutes.

Model Summary: Within ten minutes of tomorrow night's episode, fans will see aidan turner's dashing ross poldark gaze lovingly at his new baby daughter. Last week she was barely showing – but demelza poldark is now the proud mother to the show's latest addition. Last week she was barely showing – but demelza poldark is now the proud mother to the show's latest addition. (clearly redundant extractive summary)

Score$_{red}$ for model summary: 0.40

Less Overlapping Reference (LOR): A celebrity recently welcomed a baby into the world and the wife discusses her experiences with her pregnancy. She has wanted to settle down for a while and is glad her pregnancy wasn't noticeable on television.

Medium Overlapping/CNN Reference (MOR): SPOILER ALERT: Maid gives birth to baby on Sunday's episode. Only announced she was pregnant with Poldark's baby last week.

High Overlapping Reference (HOR): In the latest episode, Demelza Poldark talks about being 8 months pregnant. Ross Poldark, who is off the market and in love with Demelza, will be shown gazing lovingly at his new baby daughter tomorrow night.

Sem-nCG Score only according to equation 1 for
LOR: 0.67 MOR: 0.733 HOR: 0.8

Revised Sem-nCG Score along with Score$_{red}$ according to equation 3 for
LOR: 0.532 MOR: 0.565 HOR: 0.599

Human Evaluation (annotated by experts and score ranged between 0-1)
Coherence: 0.47 Consistency: 1 Fluency: 1 Relevance: 0.67

Table 3: An example of the model summary evaluation using the redundancy-aware Sem-nCG metric.

Metric	Multi-Ref LOR, MOR, HOR				Multi-Ref LORs				Multi-Ref MORs				Multi-Ref HORs			
	Con	Rel	Coh	Flu	Con	Rel	Coh	Flu	Con	Rel	Coh	Flu	Con	Rel	Coh	Flu
ROUGE-1	0.00	-0.01	-0.09	-0.01	-0.05	0.05	0.00	0.01	-0.05	0.09	0.04	-0.01	-0.02	0.21	0.13	0.10
ROUGE-L	0.00	-0.01	-0.09	-0.01	0.00	0.04	-0.01	0.01	-0.06	0.07	0.04	0.00	-0.01	0.15	0.09	-0.04
BERTScore	0.09	0.19	0.14	0.03	0.01	0.07	-0.01	0.04	-0.04	0.05	0.03	0.05	0.04	0.20	0.12	0.06

Table 4: Kendall Tau (τ) correlation coefficient for ROUGE and BERTScore for consistency (con), relevance (rel), coherence (coh) and fluency (flu) dimension for evaluating extractive model summaries with multiple references.

In the original *Sem-nCG* metric, a groundtruth ranking is prepared by considering the cosine similarity between each sentence of the document and reference summary but the evaluation with multiple-reference was left as future work. As a starting point, how to incorporate multiple-reference summaries in the original *Sem-nCG* metric, we designed how to create the groundtruth ranking by considering multiple references. Here, we took the naive approach, first computing cosine similarity of each sentence of the document with each reference among multiple references. Then average it, which we called Ensemble$_{sim}$. For Ensemble$_{rel}$, for each groundtruth ranking prepared for each reference among multiple reference summaries, we took the average of relevance (as it was computed in previously proposed *Sem-nCG* metric (Akter et al., 2022)) and based on that we merged the groundtruth rankings into one groundtruth ranking. Then we use this groundtruth ranking to compute *Sem-nCG* for model extracted summary. With the original Sem-nCG metric, we have also incorporated redundancy into the *Sem-nCG* metric utilizing equation 3. We have only considered ROUGE and BERTScore as redundancy penalty both in Table 5 and 6 when $\lambda = 0.5$ (as evident from Section 4.2 that this setting gives better performance). We have also considered different embedding variations to create the groundtruth ranking.

From Table 5, we can see that redundancy-aware *Sem-nCG* shows better correlations for all the scenarios (multi-ref LORs, multi-ref MORs, multi-

Embedding	w/o Redundancy				+ Redundancy Penalty (ROUGE)				+ Redundancy Penalty (BERTScore)			
	Consistency	Relevance	Coherence	Fluency	Consistency	Relevance	Coherence	Fluency	Consistency	Relevance	Coherence	Fluency
Multi-Ref LOR, MOR, HOR												
Infersent	0.07	0.11	0.08	**0.06**	0.11	0.18	**0.27**	0.01	0.09	0.18	0.20	0.03
Elmo	0.09	0.06	0.01	0.00	0.09	0.12	0.18	-0.05	0.09	0.12	0.11	-0.03
STSb-bert	0.10	0.12	0.04	0.06	0.09	0.19	0.24	-0.02	0.10	**0.20**	0.18	0.01
STSb-roberta	0.14	0.10	0.01	0.02	0.12	0.17	0.21	-0.06	**0.13**	0.17	0.13	-0.02
USE	0.04	0.12	0.08	0.05	0.06	0.19	0.26	-0.03	0.05	0.19	0.20	0.01
STSb-distilbert	0.14	0.13	0.05	0.02	0.10	0.19	0.23	-0.04	0.12	**0.20**	0.17	-0.01
Multi-Ref LORs												
Infersent	0.03	0.10	0.09	**0.07**	0.05	**0.16**	**0.25**	0.02	0.02	0.15	0.18	0.04
Elmo	0.04	0.05	-0.04	0.03	0.05	0.12	0.15	-0.04	0.03	0.11	0.06	-0.01
STSb-bert	0.08	0.10	0.02	0.01	0.09	0.15	0.20	-0.06	0.06	0.15	0.13	-0.04
STSb-roberta	0.10	0.07	-0.04	0.00	**0.11**	0.15	0.17	-0.07	0.09	0.15	0.09	-0.04
USE	0.02	0.05	0.01	0.03	0.04	0.12	0.19	-0.04	0.02	0.10	0.12	0.00
STSb-distilbert	0.10	0.04	-0.02	-0.02	**0.11**	0.09	0.15	-0.09	0.09	0.09	0.09	-0.07
Multi-Ref MORs												
Infersent	0.08	0.08	0.03	**0.06**	0.10	**0.15**	**0.23**	-0.02	0.08	**0.15**	0.16	0.02
Elmo	0.06	0.05	-0.02	0.00	0.04	0.13	0.16	-0.07	0.05	0.11	0.08	-0.05
STSb-bert	0.07	0.05	0.02	0.01	0.09	0.13	0.22	-0.08	0.07	0.12	0.15	-0.04
STSb-roberta	0.05	0.07	-0.01	0.02	0.07	0.14	0.21	-0.07	0.04	0.14	0.14	-0.03
USE	0.02	0.08	0.05	0.01	0.04	0.15	**0.25**	-0.06	0.02	0.14	0.17	-0.03
STSb-distilbert	**0.11**	0.01	0.00	-0.01	0.09	0.07	0.17	-0.10	0.10	0.06	0.10	-0.05
Multi-Ref HORs												
Infersent	0.07	0.08	0.05	0.03	**0.11**	0.16	0.23	-0.02	0.07	0.15	0.15	0.01
Elmo	0.04	0.09	0.02	0.06	0.06	0.16	0.19	0.00	0.04	0.14	0.11	0.03
STSb-bert	0.08	0.11	0.04	0.05	0.12	0.18	**0.24**	-0.03	0.08	0.18	0.16	0.01
STSb-roberta	0.10	0.09	0.01	0.03	0.14	0.17	0.22	-0.04	0.10	0.16	0.13	0.00
USE	0.04	0.14	0.07	0.05	0.07	0.20	**0.24**	-0.03	0.04	**0.21**	0.18	0.01
STSb-distilbert	0.08	0.09	0.02	0.05	**0.11**	0.15	0.22	-0.03	0.09	0.15	0.14	0.02

Table 5: Kendall Tau (τ) correlation coefficient for $\textbf{Ensemble}_{\textbf{sim}}$ when lambda (λ) = 0.5 for consistency, relevance, coherence and fluency dimension without redundancy and when ROUGE and BERTScore is used as redundancy penalty for different terminology variations of multiple references (highly abstractive (LORs), medium overlapping (MORs) and highly extractive (HORs) references). The best value in each dimension has been bold green.

ref HORs and mixture of LOR, MOR & HOR). Both ROUGE and BERTScore provide comparable results for self-referenced redundancy penalties, with ROUGE score-based redundancy providing a marginally superior result. Interestingly, redundancy-aware *Sem-nCG* shows robust performance in all the scenarios while showing 25% improvement in coherence and 10% improvement in relevance dimension. Same patterns are observed when $\text{Ensemble}_{\text{rel}}$ is also used for the evaluation of multiple reference (See Table 6).

From our empirical evaluation, we would recommend USE embedding to create $\text{Ensemble}_{\text{sim}}$ (merging sentence-wise similarities across different references) with ROUGE redundancy penalty to evaluate extractive summary with multiple references.

5 Related Work

The most common method for evaluating model summaries has been to compare them against human-written reference summaries. ROUGE (Lin, 2004b) considers direct lexical overlap and afterwards different version of ROUGE (Graham, 2015) has also been proposed including *ROUGE* with word embedding (Ng and Abrecht, 2015) and synonym (Ganesan, 2018), graph-based lexical measurement (ShafieiBavani et al., 2018), Vanilla *ROUGE* (Yang et al., 2018) and highlight-based *ROUGE* (Hardy et al., 2019) to mitigate the limitations of original ROUGE. Metrics based on semantic similarity between reference and model summaries have also been proposed to capture the semantics, including S+WMS (Clark et al., 2019), MoverScore (Zhao et al., 2019), and BERTScore (Zhang et al., 2020). Reference-free evaluation has also been a recent trend to avoid dependency on human reference (Böhm et al., 2019; Peyrard, 2019; Sun and Nenkova, 2019; Gao et al., 2020; Wu et al., 2020).

Although the *extractive* summarizing task is typically framed as a sentence ranking problem, none of the mentioned metrics evaluate the quality of the ranker. To address this, recently (Akter et al., 2022) has proposed a rank-aware and gain-based evaluation metric for extractive summarization called *Sem-nCG*, but it does not incorporate redundancy and also lacks evaluation with multiple references. These are two significant limitations that need to be addressed, and hence, the focus of this work.

Embedding	w/o Redundancy				+ Redundancy Penalty (ROUGE)				+ Redundancy Penalty (BERTScore)			
	Consistency	Relevance	Coherence	Fluency	Consistency	Relevance	Coherence	Fluency	Consistency	Relevance	Coherence	Fluency
Multi-Ref LOR, MOR, HOR												
Infersent	0.09	0.10	0.04	0.08	0.11	0.17	0.24	0.01	0.09	0.18	0.18	0.04
Elmo	0.09	0.06	0.02	0.01	0.09	0.13	0.20	-0.05	0.09	0.12	0.13	-0.03
STSb-bert	0.12	0.15	0.04	0.05	0.12	0.22	0.24	-0.03	0.12	0.24	0.18	0.01
STSb-roberta	**0.14**	0.08	0.01	0.01	0.13	0.15	0.21	-0.05	0.13	0.15	0.12	-0.02
USE	0.04	0.16	0.11	**0.08**	0.05	0.21	**0.29**	0.00	0.04	0.22	0.24	0.05
STSb-distilbert	0.14	0.10	0.03	0.02	0.10	0.16	0.22	-0.04	0.11	0.18	0.16	-0.01
Multi-Ref LORs												
Infersent	0.03	0.09	0.07	**0.08**	0.05	0.15	**0.23**	0.04	0.02	0.14	0.16	0.05
Elmo	0.03	0.04	-0.04	0.03	0.04	0.10	0.14	-0.03	0.03	0.09	0.06	-0.01
STSb-bert	0.09	0.10	0.00	0.01	0.10	**0.16**	0.19	-0.06	0.09	0.17	0.13	-0.03
STSb-roberta	0.10	0.05	-0.06	0.00	0.11	0.13	0.15	-0.08	0.09	0.12	0.07	-0.04
USE	0.04	0.08	0.03	0.04	0.05	0.14	0.22	-0.04	0.03	0.13	0.15	0.01
STSb-distilbert	**0.13**	0.06	0.01	-0.01	0.12	0.11	0.17	-0.09	0.12	0.12	0.12	-0.06
Multi-Ref MORs												
Infersent	0.06	0.10	0.05	0.06	0.07	0.19	**0.26**	-0.01	**0.06**	0.18	**0.19**	0.02
Elmo	0.06	0.06	0.00	0.02	0.04	0.13	0.17	-0.06	0.04	0.12	0.11	-0.02
STSb-bert	0.08	0.01	-0.02	0.01	**0.09**	0.09	0.18	-0.08	0.08	0.08	0.11	-0.04
STSb-roberta	0.05	0.07	0.00	0.02	0.06	0.14	0.20	-0.07	0.05	0.14	0.13	-0.02
USE	0.01	0.09	0.05	0.01	0.04	0.16	0.24	-0.05	0.01	0.16	0.19	-0.02
STSb-distilbert	0.08	0.02	0.00	-0.01	0.07	0.09	0.18	-0.09	0.07	0.08	0.12	-0.06
Multi-Ref HORs												
Infersent	0.09	0.11	0.06	0.05	0.13	0.18	0.25	-0.01	0.09	0.18	0.18	0.02
Elmo	0.05	0.08	0.02	0.05	0.07	0.16	0.19	-0.01	0.05	0.14	0.12	0.02
STSb-bert	0.07	0.11	0.04	0.05	0.11	0.18	0.25	-0.02	0.06	0.19	0.17	0.02
STSb-roberta	0.10	0.08	0.01	0.04	**0.13**	0.16	0.21	-0.04	0.11	0.15	0.13	0.00
USE	0.06	0.13	0.07	**0.05**	0.09	**0.20**	**0.26**	-0.02	0.06	0.20	0.19	0.02
STSb-distilbert	0.09	0.09	0.03	0.03	0.12	0.15	0.22	-0.05	0.10	0.15	0.15	0.00

Table 6: Kendall Tau (τ) correlation coefficient for $\textbf{Ensemble}_{\textbf{rel}}$ when lambda (λ) $= 0.5$ for consistency, relevance, coherence and fluency dimension without redundancy and when ROUGE and BERTScore is used as redundancy penalty for different terminology variations of multiple references (highly abstractive (LORs), medium overlapping (MORs) and highly extractive (HORs) references). The best value in each dimension has been bold green.

Redundancy in extracted sentences is a prominent issue in extractive summarization systems. Maximal Marginal Relevance (MMR) (Carbonell and Goldstein, 1998) is a classic algorithm to penalize redundancy in model summary. There are several approaches that explicitly model redundancy and use algorithms to avoid selecting sentences that are too similar to those that have already been extracted (Ren et al., 2016). Trigram blocking (Paulus et al., 2018) is another popular approach to reduce redundancy in model summary. Chen et al. (2021) has shown how to compute self-referenced redundancy score while evaluating the model summary.

When multiple reference summaries are available, Researchers have also suggested Pyramid-based (Nenkova and Passonneau, 2004) approaches for summary evaluation. However, this method requires more manual labor and has undergone numerous improvements (Passonneau et al., 2013; Yang et al., 2016; Shapira et al., 2019; Mao et al., 2020), it still needs a substantial amount of manual effort, making it unsuitable for large-scale evaluation. Recently, for NLG evaluation different unified frameworks and models (Deng et al., 2021; Zhong et al., 2022; Liu et al., 2023a; Wu et al., 2024) to predict different aspects of the generated text has been proposed. Even though these metrics can be applied to text summarization, it is still a data-driven approach and it is unclear why the model produces such scores.

Uniqueness to our work: We improved the sem-nCG metric for extractive summarization, in order to make it more aware of redundancy. This was tricky, as it requires a balance of importance and diversity during evaluation. We also showed how to use the updated metric for multiple references, which was challenging due to variations in human references and terminology.

6 Conclusion

Previous work has proposed the *Sem-nCG* metric exclusively for evaluating extractive summarization task considering both rank awareness and semantics. However, the *Sem-nCG* metric ignores redundancy in a model summary and does not support evaluation with multiple reference summaries, which are two significant limitations. In this paper, we proposed a redundancy-aware multi-reference based *Sem-nCG* metric which is superior compared to the previous *Sem-nCG* metric along *Consistency*,

Relevance and *Coherence* dimensions. Additionally, for summary evaluation using multiple references, we created a unique ground-truth ranking by incorporating multiple references rather than trivial max/average score computation with multiple references. Our empirical evaluation shows that the traditional metric becomes unstable when multiple references are available and the revised redundancy-aware *Sem-nCG* shows a notably higher correlation with human judgments than ROUGE and BERTScore metric both for single and multiple references. Thus we encourage the community to evaluate extractive summaries using the revised redundancy-aware *Sem-nCG* metric.

7 Limitations

One limitation of the work is that the dataset for human evaluation is not big (252 samples). We used the dataset from (Fabbri et al., 2021), the only available benchmark "meta-evaluation dataset" for extractive summarization, to the best of our knowledge. (Akter et al., 2022) have demonstrated the correlation of *Sem-nCG* with human judgment on this dataset. To ensure a fair comparison, we maintained the same settings as the original *Sem-nCG* when assessing the redundancy-aware *Sem-nCG*. To evaluate the redundancy-aware *Sem-nCG* we will need a similar kind of evaluation benchmark and we can not do anything here. Even though (Liu et al., 2023b) has published a new dataset, that work focuses mainly on how to increase human annotation reliability for summary evaluation with respect to Atomic Content Unit (ACU) and doesn't provide human judgment for model's summary along four summary quality dimensions: coherence, consistency, fluency and relevance.

Another limitation of the work may seem like that the ablation study does not show any consistent pattern. We understand that it's difficult to come up with a single evaluation metric that can account for different qualities such as coherence, consistency, fluency, and relevance. It requires careful consideration to balance these different qualities. However, we noticed that extractive sentences are inherently grammatically correct, so we can exclude fluency from the hyperparameter choice. After analyzing the data, we found that a balanced λ value of 0.5 worked well across all four quality dimensions. This suggests that this configuration strikes a reasonable tradeoff between importance and diversity. It addresses the complexities inherent in assessing summarization quality comprehensively with a single score from the metric.

8 Ethics Statement

For the experiments, we used a publicly accessible dataset and anonymous human annotations. As a result, to the best of our knowledge, there are no ethical violations. Additionally, the evaluation of extractive summarization is a major aspect of this work. Hence, we consider it a low-risk research study.

9 Acknowledgements

This work has been partially supported by the Research Center Trustworthy Data Science and Security `https://rc-trust.ai`, one of the Research Alliance centers within the `https://uaruhr.de`. This work has also received partial support from the National Science Foundation (NSF) Standard Grant Award #2302974 and the Air Force Office of Scientific Research Grant/Cooperative Agreement Award #FA9550-23-1-0426.

References

Mousumi Akter, Naman Bansal, and Shubhra Kanti Karmaker Santu. 2022. Revisiting automatic evaluation of extractive summarization task: Can we do better than rouge? In *Findings of the ACL*, pages 1547–1560. Association for Computational Linguistics.

Florian Böhm, Yang Gao, Christian M. Meyer, Ori Shapira, Ido Dagan, and Iryna Gurevych. 2019. Better rewards yield better summaries: Learning to summarise without references. In *Proceedings of the 2019 Conference on Empirical Methods in Natural Language Processing and the 9th International Joint Conference on Natural Language Processing, EMNLP-IJCNLP 2019, Hong Kong, China, November 3-7, 2019*, pages 3108–3118. Association for Computational Linguistics.

Jaime G. Carbonell and Jade Goldstein. 1998. The use of mmr, diversity-based reranking for reordering documents and producing summaries. In *SIGIR '98: Proceedings of the 21st Annual International ACM SIGIR Conference on Research and Development in Information Retrieval, August 24-28 1998, Melbourne, Australia*, pages 335–336. ACM.

Daniel Cer, Yinfei Yang, Sheng-yi Kong, Nan Hua, Nicole Limtiaco, Rhomni St. John, Noah Constant, Mario Guajardo-Cespedes, Steve Yuan, Chris Tar, Brian Strope, and Ray Kurzweil. 2018. Universal sentence encoder for English. In *Proceedings of the 2018 Conference on Empirical Methods in Natural Language Processing: System Demonstrations*, pages 169–174. Association for Computational Linguistics.

Wang Chen, Piji Li, and Irwin King. 2021. A training-free and reference-free summarization evaluation metric via centrality-weighted relevance and self-referenced redundancy. In *Proceedings of the 59th Annual Meeting of the Association for Computational Linguistics and the 11th International Joint Conference on Natural Language Processing, ACL/IJCNLP 2021, (Volume 1: Long Papers), Virtual Event, August 1-6, 2021*, pages 404–414. Association for Computational Linguistics.

Elizabeth Clark, Asli Celikyilmaz, and Noah A. Smith. 2019. Sentence mover's similarity: Automatic evaluation for multi-sentence texts. In *Proceedings of the 57th Conference of the Association for Computational Linguistics, ACL 2019, Florence, Italy, July 28- August 2, 2019, Volume 1: Long Papers*, pages 2748–2760. Association for Computational Linguistics.

Arman Cohan and Nazli Goharian. 2016. Revisiting summarization evaluation for scientific articles. In *Proceedings of the Tenth International Conference on Language Resources and Evaluation LREC 2016, Portorož, Slovenia, May 23-28, 2016*. European Language Resources Association (ELRA).

Alexis Conneau, Douwe Kiela, Holger Schwenk, Loïc Barrault, and Antoine Bordes. 2017. Supervised learning of universal sentence representations from natural language inference data. In *Proceedings of the 2017 Conference on Empirical Methods in Natural Language Processing, EMNLP 2017, Copenhagen, Denmark, September 9-11, 2017*, pages 670–680. Association for Computational Linguistics.

Hoa Trang Dang. 2005. Overview of duc 2005. In *Proceedings of the document understanding conference*, volume 2005, pages 1–12.

Mingkai Deng, Bowen Tan, Zhengzhong Liu, Eric P. Xing, and Zhiting Hu. 2021. Compression, transduction, and creation: A unified framework for evaluating natural language generation. In *Proceedings of the 2021 Conference on Empirical Methods in Natural Language Processing, EMNLP 2021, Virtual Event / Punta Cana, Dominican Republic, 7-11 November, 2021*, pages 7580–7605. Association for Computational Linguistics.

Alexander R. Fabbri, Wojciech Kryscinski, Bryan McCann, Caiming Xiong, Richard Socher, and Dragomir R. Radev. 2021. Summeval: Re-evaluating summarization evaluation. *Trans. Assoc. Comput. Linguistics*, 9:391–409.

Kavita Ganesan. 2018. ROUGE 2.0: Updated and improved measures for evaluation of summarization tasks. *CoRR*, abs/1803.01937.

Yang Gao, Wei Zhao, and Steffen Eger. 2020. SUPERT: towards new frontiers in unsupervised evaluation metrics for multi-document summarization. In *Proceedings of the 58th Annual Meeting of the Association for Computational Linguistics, ACL 2020, Online, July 5-10, 2020*, pages 1347–1354. Association for Computational Linguistics.

Dan Gillick and Yang Liu. 2010. Non-expert evaluation of summarization systems is risky. In *Proceedings of the 2010 Workshop on Creating Speech and Language Data with Amazon's Mechanical Turk, Los Angeles, USA, June 6, 2010*, pages 148–151. Association for Computational Linguistics.

Yvette Graham. 2015. Re-evaluating automatic summarization with BLEU and 192 shades of ROUGE. In *Proceedings of the 2015 Conference on Empirical Methods in Natural Language Processing, EMNLP 2015, Lisbon, Portugal, September 17-21, 2015*, pages 128–137. The Association for Computational Linguistics.

Hardy, Shashi Narayan, and Andreas Vlachos. 2019. Highres: Highlight-based reference-less evaluation of summarization. In *Proceedings of the 57th Conference of the Association for Computational Linguistics, ACL 2019, Florence, Italy, July 28- August 2, 2019, Volume 1: Long Papers*, pages 3381–3392. Association for Computational Linguistics.

Mohit Iyyer, Varun Manjunatha, Jordan Boyd-Graber, and Hal Daumé III. 2015. Deep unordered composition rivals syntactic methods for text classification. In *Proceedings of the 53rd Annual Meeting of the Association for Computational Linguistics and the 7th International Joint Conference on Natural Language Processing (Volume 1: Long Papers)*, pages 1681–1691, Beijing, China. Association for Computational Linguistics.

Matt J. Kusner, Yu Sun, Nicholas I. Kolkin, and Kilian Q. Weinberger. 2015. From word embeddings to document distances. In *Proceedings of the 32nd International Conference on Machine Learning, ICML 2015, Lille, France, 6-11 July 2015*, volume 37 of *JMLR Workshop and Conference Proceedings*, pages 957–966. JMLR.org.

Chin-Yew Lin. 2004a. Looking for a few good metrics: Automatic summarization evaluation - how many samples are enough? In *Proceedings of the Fourth NTCIR Workshop on Research in Information Access Technologies Information Retrieval, Question Answering and Summarization, NTCIR-4, National Center of Sciences, Tokyo, Japan, June 2-4, 2004*. National Institute of Informatics (NII).

Chin-Yew Lin. 2004b. ROUGE: A package for automatic evaluation of summaries. In *Text Summarization Branches Out*, pages 74–81, Barcelona, Spain. Association for Computational Linguistics.

Yang Liu, Dan Iter, Yichong Xu, Shuohang Wang, Ruochen Xu, and Chenguang Zhu. 2023a. G-eval: NLG evaluation using gpt-4 with better human alignment. In *Proceedings of the 2023 Conference on Empirical Methods in Natural Language Processing, EMNLP 2023, Singapore, December 6-10, 2023*, pages 2511–2522. Association for Computational Linguistics.

Yixin Liu, Alex Fabbri, Pengfei Liu, Yilun Zhao, Linyong Nan, Ruilin Han, Simeng Han, Shafiq Joty, Chien-Sheng Wu, Caiming Xiong, and Dragomir Radev. 2023b. Revisiting the gold standard: Grounding summarization evaluation with robust human evaluation. In *Proceedings of the 61st Annual Meeting of the Association for Computational Linguistics (Volume 1: Long Papers)*, pages 4140–4170, Toronto, Canada. Association for Computational Linguistics.

Yuning Mao, Liyuan Liu, Qi Zhu, Xiang Ren, and Jiawei Han. 2020. Facet-aware evaluation for extractive summarization. In *Proceedings of the 58th Annual Meeting of the Association for Computational Linguistics, ACL*, pages 4941–4957. Association for Computational Linguistics.

Ani Nenkova. 2005. Automatic text summarization of newswire: Lessons learned from the document understanding conference. In *Proceedings, The Twentieth National Conference on Artificial Intelligence and the Seventeenth Innovative Applications of Artificial Intelligence Conference, July 9-13, 2005, Pittsburgh, Pennsylvania, USA*, pages 1436–1441. AAAI Press / The MIT Press.

Ani Nenkova and Rebecca J. Passonneau. 2004. Evaluating content selection in summarization: The pyramid method. In *Human Language Technology Conference of the North American Chapter of the Association for Computational Linguistics, HLT-NAACL*, pages 145–152. The Association for Computational Linguistics.

Jun-Ping Ng and Viktoria Abrecht. 2015. Better summarization evaluation with word embeddings for ROUGE. In *Proceedings of the 2015 Conference on Empirical Methods in Natural Language Processing, EMNLP 2015, Lisbon, Portugal, September 17-21, 2015*, pages 1925–1930. The Association for Computational Linguistics.

Rebecca J. Passonneau, Emily Chen, Weiwei Guo, and Dolores Perin. 2013. Automated pyramid scoring of summaries using distributional semantics. In *Proceedings of the 51st Annual Meeting of the Association for Computational Linguistics, ACL 2013, 4-9 August 2013, Sofia, Bulgaria, Volume 2: Short Papers*, pages 143–147. The Association for Computer Linguistics.

Romain Paulus, Caiming Xiong, and Richard Socher. 2018. A deep reinforced model for abstractive summarization. In *6th International Conference on Learning Representations, ICLR 2018, Vancouver, BC, Canada, April 30 - May 3, 2018, Conference Track Proceedings*. OpenReview.net.

Matthew E. Peters, Mark Neumann, Mohit Iyyer, Matt Gardner, Christopher Clark, Kenton Lee, and Luke Zettlemoyer. 2018. Deep contextualized word representations. In *Proceedings of the 2018 Conference of the North American Chapter of the Association for Computational Linguistics: Human Language Technologies, NAACL-HLT 2018, New Orleans, Louisiana, USA, June 1-6, 2018, Volume 1 (Long Papers)*, pages 2227–2237. Association for Computational Linguistics.

Maxime Peyrard. 2019. A simple theoretical model of importance for summarization. In *Proceedings of the 57th Conference of the Association for Computational Linguistics, ACL 2019, Florence, Italy, July 28- August 2, 2019, Volume 1: Long Papers*, pages 1059–1073. Association for Computational Linguistics.

Nils Reimers and Iryna Gurevych. 2019. Sentence-bert: Sentence embeddings using siamese bert-networks. In *Proceedings of the 2019 Conference on Empirical Methods in Natural Language Processing and the 9th International Joint Conference on Natural Language Processing, EMNLP-IJCNLP 2019, Hong Kong, China, November 3-7, 2019*, pages 3980–3990. Association for Computational Linguistics.

Pengjie Ren, Furu Wei, Zhumin Chen, Jun Ma, and Ming Zhou. 2016. A redundancy-aware sentence regression framework for extractive summarization. In *COLING 2016, 26th International Conference on Computational Linguistics, Proceedings of the Conference: Technical Papers, December 11-16, 2016, Osaka, Japan*, pages 33–43. ACL.

Elaheh ShafieiBavani, Mohammad Ebrahimi, Raymond K. Wong, and Fang Chen. 2018. A graph-theoretic summary evaluation for rouge. In *Proceedings of the 2018 Conference on Empirical Methods in Natural Language Processing, Brussels, Belgium, October 31 - November 4, 2018*, pages 762–767. Association for Computational Linguistics.

Ori Shapira, David Gabay, Yang Gao, Hadar Ronen, Ramakanth Pasunuru, Mohit Bansal, Yael Amsterdamer, and Ido Dagan. 2019. Crowdsourcing lightweight pyramids for manual summary evaluation. In *Proceedings of the 2019 Conference of the North American Chapter of the Association for Computational Linguistics: Human Language Technologies, NAACL-HLT 2019, Minneapolis, MN, USA, June 2-7, 2019, Volume 1 (Long and Short Papers)*, pages 682–687. Association for Computational Linguistics.

Simeng Sun and Ani Nenkova. 2019. The feasibility of embedding based automatic evaluation for single document summarization. In *Proceedings of the 2019 Conference on Empirical Methods in Natural Language Processing and the 9th International Joint Conference on Natural Language Processing, EMNLP-IJCNLP 2019, Hong Kong, China, November 3-7, 2019*, pages 1216–1221. Association for Computational Linguistics.

Hanlu Wu, Tengfei Ma, Lingfei Wu, Tariro Manyumwa, and Shouling Ji. 2020. Unsupervised reference-free summary quality evaluation via contrastive learning. In *Proceedings of the 2020 Conference on Empirical Methods in Natural Language Processing, EMNLP 2020, Online, November 16-20, 2020*, pages 3612–3621. Association for Computational Linguistics.

Yunshu Wu, Hayate Iso, Pouya Pezeshkpour, Nikita Bhutani, and Estevam Hruschka. 2024. Less is more for long document summary evaluation by llms. In *Proceedings of the 18th Conference of the European Chapter of the Association for Computational Linguistics, EACL 2024 - Volume 2: Short Papers, St. Julian's, Malta, March 17-22, 2024*, pages 330–343. Association for Computational Linguistics.

An Yang, Kai Liu, Jing Liu, Yajuan Lyu, and Sujian Li. 2018. Adaptations of ROUGE and BLEU to better evaluate machine reading comprehension task. In *Proceedings of the Workshop on Machine Reading for Question Answering@ACL 2018, Melbourne, Australia, July 19, 2018*, pages 98–104. Association for Computational Linguistics.

Qian Yang, Rebecca J. Passonneau, and Gerard de Melo. 2016. PEAK: pyramid evaluation via automated knowledge extraction. In *Proceedings of the Thirtieth AAAI Conference on Artificial Intelligence*, pages 2673–2680. AAAI Press.

Tianyi Zhang, Varsha Kishore, Felix Wu, Kilian Q. Weinberger, and Yoav Artzi. 2020. Bertscore: Evaluating text generation with BERT. In *8th International Conference on Learning Representations, ICLR 2020, Addis Ababa, Ethiopia, April 26-30, 2020*. OpenReview.net.

Wei Zhao, Maxime Peyrard, Fei Liu, Yang Gao, Christian M. Meyer, and Steffen Eger. 2019. Moverscore: Text generation evaluating with contextualized embeddings and earth mover distance. In *Proceedings of the 2019 Conference on Empirical Methods in Natural Language Processing and the 9th International Joint Conference on Natural Language Processing, EMNLP-IJCNLP 2019, Hong Kong, China, November 3-7, 2019*, pages 563–578. Association for Computational Linguistics.

Ming Zhong, Yang Liu, Da Yin, Yuning Mao, Yizhu Jiao, Pengfei Liu, Chenguang Zhu, Heng Ji, and Jiawei Han. 2022. Towards a unified multi-dimensional evaluator for text generation. *CoRR*, abs/2210.07197.

A Appendix

A.1 Explanation of Metrics for $Score_{red}$

ROUGE (Lin, 2004b): Between the generated summary and reference summary, ROUGE counts the overlap of textual units (n-grams, word sequences).

MoverScore (Zhao et al., 2019): uses the Word Mover's Distance (Kusner et al., 2015) to calculate the semantic distance between a summary and a reference text, pooling n-gram embedding from BERT representations.

BERTScore (Zhang et al., 2020): calculates similarity scores by matching generated and reference summaries on a token level. The cosine similarity between contextualized token embeddings from BERT is maximized by computing token matching greedily.

Cosine Similarity: Sentences are converted to sentence embedding using STSb-distilbert (Reimers and Gurevych, 2019). Then the semantic similarity of sentences is measured using cosine similarity between sentence vectors.

The code for the metrics used can be found here.[3]

A.2 Human Evaluation Components

To calculate the Kendall's Tau (τ) rank correlation for the redundancy-aware *Sem-nCG* metric, we used four quality dimensions following (Akter et al., 2022; Fabbri et al., 2021).

Consistency: refers to the fact that the contents in the summary and the source are the same. Only assertions from the source are included in factually consistent summaries, which do not include any trippy facts.

Relevance: getting the most important information from a source. The annotators were to penalize summaries with redundancy and excessive information. In the summary, only important information from the source should be included.

Coherence: overall summary sentence quality while keeping a coherent body of information on a topic rather than a tangle of related information (Dang, 2005).

Fluency: the structure and quality of the summary sentences. As mentioned in (Dang, 2005) "should have no formatting problems, capitalization errors or obviously ungrammatical sentences (e.g., fragments, missing components) that make the text difficult to read."

A.3 Computational Infrastructure & Runtime

A.4 Sentence Embedding Used in Setion 4

Infersent (Conneau et al., 2017): Infersent-v2 is trained with fastText word embedding and generates 4096-dimensional sentence embedding using a BiLSTM network with max-pooling.

[3] https://github.com/Yale-LILY/SummEval/tree/master/evaluation/summ_eval

Computational Infrastructure		
NVIDIA Quadro RTX 5000 GPUs		
Hyperparameter Search		
$\lambda \in [0, 1]$ uniform-integer distribution		
Type	**Variation**	**Runtime (s)**
$Score_{red}$	Cosine Similarity	0.06
	ROUGE	0.44
	MoverScore	0.23
	BERTScore	14.7
Sem-nCG	Infersent	0.4
	Elmo	79.1
	STSb-bert	0.33
	STSb-roberta	0.34
	USE	20.2
	STSb-distilbert	0.13
	$\text{Ensemble}_{\text{sim}}$	20.33

Elmo (Peters et al., 2018): The contextualized word embedding was transformed into a sentence embedding using a fixed mean-pooling of all contextualized word representations with embedding shape 1024.

Google Universal Sentence Encoder (USE) (Cer et al., 2018): We utilized USE with enc-2 (Iyyer et al., 2015) which is based on the deep average network to transform input text to a 512-dimensional sentence embedding.

Semantic Textual Similarity benchmark (STSb) (Reimers and Gurevych, 2019): Sentence Transformer allows to generate dense vector representations of sentences. Three of the best available models that were optimized for semantic textual similarity were considered: STSb-bert (embedding size 1024), STSb-roberta (embedding size 1024) and STSb-distilbert (embedding size 768).

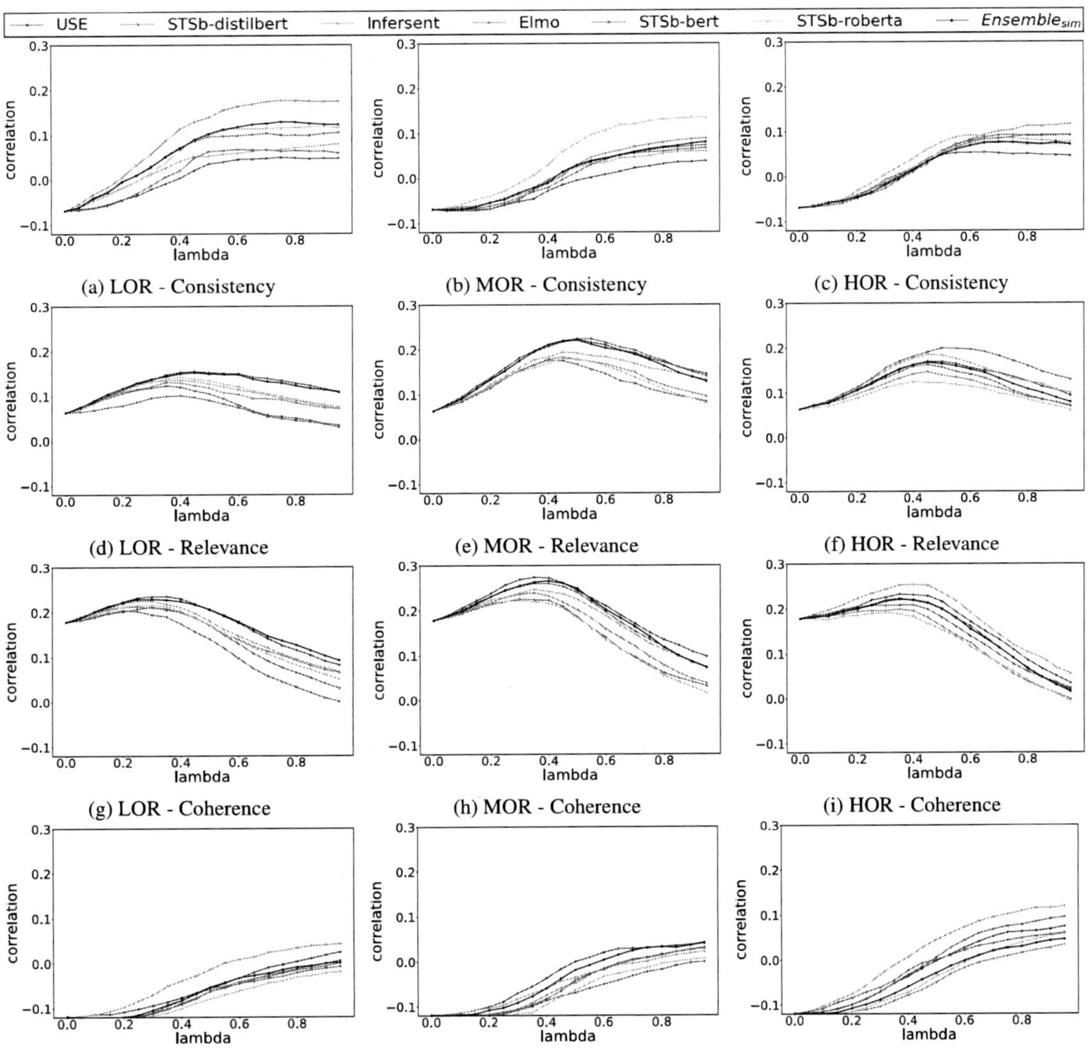

(a) LOR - Consistency (b) MOR - Consistency (c) HOR - Consistency

(d) LOR - Relevance (e) MOR - Relevance (f) HOR - Relevance

(g) LOR - Coherence (h) MOR - Coherence (i) HOR - Coherence

(j) LOR - Fluency (k) MOR - Fluency (l) HOR - Fluency

Figure 2: Kendall Tau (τ) correlation coefficient when lambda (λ) $\in [0, 1]$ from (a)-(c) for consistency, (d)-(f) for relevance, (g)-(i) for coherence and (j)-(l) for fluency dimension when BERTScore is used as redundancy penalty for less overlapping reference (LOR), medium overlapping reference (MOR) and high overlapping reference (HOR).

Fine-grained quotation detection and attribution in German news articles

Fynn Petersen-Frey and Chris Biemann
Hub of Computing and Data Science & Language Technology Group
Universität Hamburg
{fynn.petersen-frey, chris.biemann}@uni-hamburg.de

Abstract

The task of quotation detection and attribution deals with identifying quotation spans together with their associated role spans such as the speaker. We describe an approach to solve the task of fine-grained quotation detection and attribution using a sequence-to-sequence transformer model with constrained decoding. Our model improves vastly upon the existing baselines on the German news articles quotation dataset, thereby making it feasible for a first time to automatically extract attributed quotations from German news articles. We provide an extensive description of our method, discuss alternative approaches, performed experiments using multiple foundation language models and method variants, and analyzed our model's prediction errors. Our source code and trained models are available.[1]

1 Introduction

Identifying who says what to whom is the central piece in analyzing written human communication. It enables scientists or journalists to analyze how a discourse changes over time, which people participate in a discourse, what their points of view are and much more. With today's ever-increasing amounts of data such as online news articles, it is typically not feasible to manually process the wealth of data that is of interest for a specific research question.

1.1 Task description

The task of quotation detection and attribution deals with identifying quotation spans (*Quote*) in a document together with their associated role spans such as the *Speaker* or *Addressee*. While early, simple variants of the task only considered *Direct* quotations spanning at most a single sentence, the task's complexity has increased over time (see Section 2.1). We base our work on our recent dataset (Petersen-Frey and Biemann, 2024) that also features a significantly more complex task that requires a fine-grained quotation detection of five quotation types and attribution of up to four roles per *Quote*.

Example 1.1 shows a human-friendly representation of an annotated text passage. It contains two quotations (*Direct* and *Indirect*) uttered by the same *Speaker*. The *Indirect* quotation is further invoked by a *Cue* word "said" within a *Frame* in the same sentence. A quotation with all its associated roles is called a *Quote* group. The integers behind each span type indicate which group that span belongs to. In case of the *Speaker* "someone", it belongs to both the first and second group.

Example 1.1 (Annotated text passage)

Most sentences do not contain a quotation.
This is an indirect quote, said someone.
Indirect 1 — Cue 1 — Speaker 1,2
Frame 1
"Followed by a direct quote in a new sentence."
Direct 2

In the fine-grained task variant and dataset (Petersen-Frey and Biemann, 2024), a single quotation can span multiple sentences, each quotation can be associated with zero to four roles, *Quote* groups can be nested inside each other, the same annotation span can belong to multiple groups and annotation spans can be discontinuous. We solve the full task with all its challenges and predict *Direct*, *Indirect*, *Reported*, *Free Indirect* and *Indirect/Free Indirect* quotations together with the *Speaker*, *Cue*, *Addressee* and *Frame* roles.

1.2 Example use cases

Reliably extracting *Quote* groups from a large document collection allows researchers or journalists to quickly analyze the quotations contained in their data of interest. The type of quotation and existence of certain roles can be used to filter and/or

[1] Source code and model weights: https://github.com/uhh-lt/seq2seq-quotation-attribution

aggregate quotations enabling both a quantitative view and finding individual occurrences to analyze in detail. To compare different news outlets, time frames or topics, the fine-grained annotations enable corpus comparisons with statistics such as the distribution of quotation types, fraction of quotations with or without a *Speaker* or *Addressee*.

In this paper, we describe our approach to automatically identify who said what to whom in German news articles. Our model improves vastly upon the existing baselines and makes it possible for a first time to automatically extract fine-grained, attributed quotations with high precision and recall from plain text.

2 Related work

We first review previous work on quotation detection and attribution for English and German. Then, we review approaches to structured generation as an essential component to our chosen approach.

2.1 Quotation detection and attribution

The NewsExplorer system (Pouliquen et al., 2007) is the first system to tackle the task of *Direct* quotation detection and attribution to a *Speaker*. Krestel et al. (2008) also detected *Indirect* quotations using rule-based reported verb and speech finder. O'Keefe et al. (2012) created a new labeled dataset and reformulated *Direct* quotation detection and attribution as a sequence labeling task. Pareti et al. (2013) focus on the more challenging *Indirect* quotations by training classifiers for the *Cue*, *Speaker* and *Quote*. Almeida et al. (2014) introduced a model that jointly solves the problems of quotation attribution and coreference resolution. Newell et al. (2018) created the Citron software that implements an improved variant of the approach by Pareti et al. (2013) using trainable content resolver and source resolver. Zhang and Liu (2022) focus only on *Direct* quotations and test multiple sequence labeling methods including three neural models.

While quotation detection and attribution in English news has been addressed by many works, less have dealt with German news. Bögel and Gertz (2015) created a rule-based system using dependency trees to extract and attribute *Direct* and *Indirect* quotations from German news articles. Papay and Padó (2019) created a corpus-agnostic, neural quotation detection model that can detect *Direct* and *Indirect* quotations while omitting *Cue* and *Speaker*. Brunner et al. (2020b) trained simple sequence taggers on the Redewiedergabe corpus (Brunner et al., 2020a) to individually detect *Direct*, *Indirect*, *Reported* and *Free Indirect* quotations without any roles or attribution.

2.2 Structured generation

Conditional language modeling has become a useful technique to tackle structured prediction tasks using pre-trained language models. The target structure is flattened into a sequence and a conditional language model is trained to predict it. Paolini et al. (2021) solve structured prediction language tasks (e.g. joint entity/ relation extraction and SRL) by performing translation between augmented natural languages. Liu et al. (2022) argue that flattening structured information leads to inferior performance. They model structures as action sequences and achieve a new state-of-the-art on named-entity recognition, relation extraction and coreference resolution. Geng et al. (2023) suggest grammar-constrained decoding without fine-tuning can solve many structured NLP tasks and show this for information extraction, entity disambiguation and constituency parsing. Zhang et al. (2023) show that task-specific models are not necessary for state-of-the-art coreference resolution and train a model to translate the input to a sequence encoding the coreference information.

3 Method

We frame the task of detecting and attributing quotations as a special clustering task with labeled text spans. Each cluster contains a single *Quote* that may consist of multiple spans. Further, a cluster may contain multiple spans of the different roles, e.g. *Cue*, *Frame*, *Speaker*, *Addressee*. In contrast to typical clustering, the same role span may belong to different clusters. We indicate this by applying multiple IDs to the same span.

On a high level, our method to solve the task of detecting and attributing quotations with a sequence-to-sequence model works as follows:

1. Training data pre-processing: Transform the original text and annotated cluster information to a suitable linearized token representation as a training target.
2. Training: Train the sequence-to-sequence model to predict the linearized token representation from the original input text.
3. Inference: During generation, constrain the model to produce a valid linearized output

from original input text.

4. Post-processing: Transform the linearized representation back to the cluster information with token offsets in the original text.

3.1 Linearization strategies for clustered quotation annotations

We transform the clustering information into a sequential representation to employ a standard sequence-to-sequence model to solve the task. Our method is inspired by Zhang et al. (2023), who show that it is feasible to perform state-of-the-art coreference resolution using standard sequence-to-sequence models with the appropriate textual representations. They experimented with a number of approaches to transform coreference mention spans and their clusters into linear text. With full linearization, the full input text is reproduced in the output – either as tokens or using a special copy action that forces the model to predict the token from the original input sequence to prevent deviations between the input and target sequences.

With partial linearization, only the tokens being part of a mention span are reproduced in the output. This mode is incompatible with the copy action, potentially has alignment issues when matching the predicted output back to the original text and achieves slightly worse coreference resolution scores. Its advantage is a significantly shorter output length. As generating long token sequences is a slow and computationally expensive process with non-linear runtime, partial linearization provides a way to mitigate this issue.

As such, we focus on the partial linearization outputting tokens with sentence markers for quotation detection and attribution to create a model useable with fewer computational resources. We call this method **partial token linearization**. Since full linearization with the copy action had the best results for coreference resolution, we use this as our second method for quotation detection and attribution named **full copy linearization**.

Zhang et al. (2023) also experimented with multiple techniques to include the cluster ID for each span. For both our methods, we re-use their best-working policy and include the cluster ID with a separation token | and a plain text integer number right before the closing tag of every span.

3.2 Forward transformation

Our transformation uses two special tokens per span type for both linearization methods (in addition to the separation | and sentence marker <sent>, </sent> tokens). We insert specific tokens that indicate the start resp. end of a span. Table 1 shows all special tokens used for our method. In total, we add 20 special tokens for full copy linearization, 21 special tokens for partial token linearization. For both, we also add 500 integer numbers for the cluster IDs as special tokens. To explain the forward transformation, we continue with Example 1.1. We apply both linearization methods to produce a sequence out of this cluster information.

Special token	start	end
Cue	<cue>	</cue>
Addressee	<addr>	</addr>
Speaker	<speaker>	</speaker>
Frame	<frame>	</frame>
Direct	<direct>	</direct>
Indirect	<indirect>	</indirect>
Reported	<reported>	</reported>
Free Indirect	<frin>	</frin>
Indirect/Free Indirect	<infrin>	</infrin>
Copy from input	<cp>	
Cluster separation	|	
Sentence marker	<sent>	</sent>
Cluster IDs	0	499

Table 1: Special tokens used

Example 3.1 shows the partial token linearization sequence. All tokens from the original text that are not part of any span are removed. For each sentence, a sentence marker is inserted at the beginning and end of it. Likewise, each span is marked using a special token directly before the text span begins. Spans are ended with a three-token sequence: Cluster ID separation token |, cluster ID, span closing token.

Example 3.1 (Partial token linearization)

<sent> </sent> <sent> <indirect> *This is an indirect quote* | 1 </indirect> <frame> , <cue> *said* 1 | </cue> <speaker> <speaker> *someone* | 1 </speaker> | 2 </speaker> | 1 </frame> </sent> <sent> <direct> *"Followed by a direct quote in a new sentence."* | 2 </direct> </sent>

Example 3.2 shows the full copy linearization sequence. Annotated spans are handled identical to the partial token linearization. In contrast, it does not contain sentence markers and all originals tokens are replaced with the special <cp> copy token. The copy token enforces that the token is copied directly from the input.

Example 3.2 (Full copy linearization)

<cp> <cp> <cp> <cp> <cp> <cp> <cp> <cp> <indirect> <cp> <cp> <cp> <cp> <cp> | 1 </indirect> <cp> <frame> <cp> <cue> <cp> 1 | </cue> <speaker> <speaker> <cp> | 1 </speaker> | 2 </speaker> | 1 </frame> <cp> <direct> <cp> <cp> <cp> <cp> <cp> <cp> <cp> <cp> <cp> <cp> <cp> <cp> | 2 </direct>

For both linearization methods, nested spans are handled by first opening the span that ends later. As seen in Example 1.1, the *Frame* and *Cue* start at the same token. This results in a linearized sequence such as <frame> <cue> . . . </cue> . . . </frame>. It enables a precise reconstruction of the original clustering information as long as opening and closing brackets match. To ensure this, we use constrained decoding.

3.3 Constrained Decoding Strategy

Sequences-to-sequence models can generate arbitrary output that might not be possible to be converted back to a cluster representation. To prevent this and enforce valid outputs, we employ constrained decoding by masking the log-probabilities of vocabulary entries (see Daza and Frank (2018); De Cao et al. (2021)). We use beam search to improve generation quality. While it complicates the constrained decoding implementation, beam search has no effect on the rules we enforce.

Partial token linearization Most of the time, we allow the model to generate any normal vocabulary subword token, any special start-span token (so spans can be nested) or the | token used to separate span text from the cluster ID. However, all these are forbidden after the | token has been generated before a special end-span token is issued. During this short time, only the cluster ID and the correct end-span token can be generated by the model. The correct end-span token is the closing "bracket" for the most recently started span that is yet unclosed.

Full copy linearization We never allow the model to generate a normal token. Instead, we only allow the copy token to copy from the input or use the other special tokens to create spans resp. clusters. Similar to the first setting, we usually allow the model to generate the copy token, any start-span or cluster ID separation token. The copy token is replaced with the actual token from the input when generating the next token.

3.4 Reverse transformation

Our system extracts a token offset-based cluster representation from the linearized sequence to identify the predicted spans and clusters in the original plain text.

Full copy linearization Since the constrained decoding as described above guarantees a valid output, we can transform the linearized sequence back to a cluster representation. As described in Section 3.2, nested spans are handled in a way so that it is always clear to which span a cluster ID belongs and which span is ended. To obtain the span begin and end offsets, we keep a stack of currently opened spans and close them in reverse order. Offsets are only affected by the number of copy tokens as only they correspond to sub-words in the original text; all other tokens are disregarded for this purpose.

Partial token linearization To find the offsets in the original text, the partial linearization requires an alignment by finding the sequence of predicted tokens of a span in the input text. We follow Zhang et al. (2023) who used Gotoh's algorithm (Gotoh, 1982) together with sentence markers to efficiently find an optimal alignment. The sentence markers constrain the alignment to pairs of sentences.

3.5 Alternative methods considered

To solve the task of quotation detection and attribution, we evaluated multiple approaches before we developed the system using a task-agnostic sequence-to-sequence model. In this section, we briefly describe what alternative approaches we considered and why we decided against implementing them.

Semantic role labeling (SRL) SRL deals with discovering the predicate-argument structure of a sentence. This task is related to quotation detection and attribution as e.g. *Cue*, *Speaker*, *Addressee* and *Quote* can potentially be seen as predicate-argument groups. An apparent solution for the task is to re-use an existing SRL system. However, they are strictly designed around the SRL task where roles must be identified for a single predicate (*Cue*) within a single sentence. This setup is incompatible with the task of general quotation detection and attribution where *Quotes* can occur without any *Cue* and often span multiple sentences.

Coreference resolution with tagging Coreference resolution is the task of resolving mentions (text spans) that refer to the same entity by identifying and clustering the mentions. When considering neural models, the task is very similar to quotation detection and attribution: Identifying and clustering spans of texts across an entire document. The primary difference is coreference resolution uses unlabeled spans, while the quotation task has spans with different labels. Thus, another potential solution is to re-use a task-specific coreference model and combine it with a span tagging model. The coreference part can already handle nested spans and the clustering. However, the labeling part would need to be deeply integrated in the coreference resolution model. Consequently, the system would no longer predict unlabeled mentions with arbitrary antecedent relations to form clusters. Instead, it would need to predict labeled spans with a specific set of allowed relations. Coreference resolution models include many special cases to cope with the computational complexity that make them ill fit for quotation detection and attribution. For example, word-level coreference (Kirstain et al., 2021; Dobrovolskii, 2021) would be incompatible with the quotation detection task as the same token would need to be used for multiple spans. Most architectures typically set a maximum span length to achieve practical computational complexity. This would also be an issue for the quotation attribution as the quotation spans vary greatly in length and can be much longer than a mention.

Creating a new task-specific model architecture We also decided against creating a new task-specific model architecture for two reasons. First, this approach makes the system dataset-specific to a large degree; thereby making the re-use of our model for similar datasets much more challenging. Second, the approach of creating task-specific model architectures for every NLP task is cumbersome, time-consuming and dated compared to a modern, more generic solution.

4 Experiments

4.1 Data

We use the dataset with attributed quotations in German news articles described in Petersen-Frey and Biemann (2024) for our experiments. It consists of 998 news articles split into 700 for training, 150 for development and 148 for test. We present an overview in Table 2. All 4,182 annotated quotation groups contain a *Quote*. While all roles are optional, most groups also contain a *Speaker*. For more details refer to Petersen-Frey and Biemann (2024). The data is available as JSON with the tokenized text and grouped annotations specified with token offsets for the span start and end. We transform this data into different sequential representation for the training routine depending on the linearization method and the foundation language model's tokenizer.

	count	avg. len.
Documents	998	249.0
Sentences	13 186	18.8
Tokens	248 480	
Quote	4182	16.7
Direct	873	17.5
Indirect	2 250	14.7
Reported	454	18.0
Free Indirect	171	20.4
Indirect/Free Indirect	434	22.3
Roles	10 212	
Speaker	3 908	3.5
Cue	2 929	1.6
Frame	3 038	9.0
Addressee	337	2.7

Table 2: Dataset overview

4.2 Variants

We perform extensive experiments on a number of combinations of foundation language model, model size and linearization method. For the foundation language models, we test T5 (Raffel et al., 2020), T5 v1.1, Flan-T5 (Chung et al., 2022) as well as the multilingual mT5 (Xue et al., 2021). We test all models in three sizes: base ($\approx$ 250 million parameters), large ($\approx$ 800 million parameters), xl ($\approx$ 3 billion parameters). While there are even larger models available, we do not have the computational resources to train such large models. Further, we test both of our linearization methods: Full copy and partial token linearization. In total, we test $4 * 3 * 2 * 2 = 24$ combinations for our models. We could not obtain results on the two xl variants of the original T5 model because the computation ran into timeout errors on our available hardware. Thus, we only report results on the remaining 22 combinations.

4.3 Training and evaluation details

To enable efficient training in batches with low amount of padding and limited memory use, we use a sliding window approach and slice the training documents into chunks of 2048 subword tokens with an overlap of half the length. The evaluation and test documents are not sliced and are fed as whole into the system. Evaluation uses generation with 4 beams to improve prediction results.

We train each model for 100 epochs and use early stopping to prevent overfitting by evaluating on the development set. Weight decay of 0.01 is further used as a regularization method. For the base and large models we use a learning rate of $5 \cdot 10^{-4}$, for the xl models a reduced learning rate of $5 \cdot 10^{-5}$ as the models would not converge otherwise. AdamW (Loshchilov and Hutter, 2019) is used as the optimizer. To help the model adapt to it's drastically changed task objective, we use a learning rate warmup of 0.1.

We train with batch sizes of 8 using a single A100 GPU for base/large models. For the xl models, we use two A100 GPUs with DeepSpeed (Rasley et al., 2020) ZeRO-2 (Rajbhandari et al., 2020) and a batch size of 4 per device, resulting in a total batch of 8. In all cases, we use gradient checkpointing and train the models in bfloat16.

4.4 Evaluation Metrics

We use the evaluation method as described in Petersen-Frey and Biemann (2024). The method is based on the precision, recall and F1-metrics on individual tokens of corresponding spans in matched clusters. Consequently, a predicted role span can only be matched to the gold span if they belong to a matched cluster. While unmatched predicted spans increase the false positives for this type, unmatched gold spans increase the corresponding false negatives. Clusters are matched via linear sum assignment of the fraction of token overlap on the *Quote* span. Correctly matched clusters produce true positives for all correct roles and quote spans according to the set intersection of tokens and false negatives resp. false positives for two set differences. Precision, recall and F1 are provided both independently for the quotations and roles as well as a joint metric.

4.5 Results

We present our main results summarized in Table 3. It shows the result of our best combinations per model size as compared to baselines for the development and test set across all metrics. We include both baseline systems from Petersen-Frey and Biemann (2024):

1. A rule-based system (RBS) build on top of neural components for dependency parsing, part-of-speech tagging, named-entity recognition etc.
2. Citron (Newell et al., 2018) consists of individually trained classifiers for *Cue*, *Speaker*, *Quote* and resolvers to group the predicted spans together.

From our results in Table 3 it is immediately obvious that our trained models far exceed the two baselines. Our best models deliver almost a two times higher F1 score than the baselines. While the rule-base system (RBS) and Citron obtain a joint F1 score of 39.1 resp. 46.8 on the test set, our best model scores 80.8. The difference in performance mainly originates from the vast increase in recall; going from 29.0 resp. 33.0 to 77.3 for our model. While we achieve a substantial improvement on the precision compared to RBS (60.7 versus 84.6), we manage a slight improvement over Citron (82.4 versus 84.6) – albeit at an entirely different recall level. Regarding the prediction of the quotation type, our model again deliver almost twice the F1 score (44 vs 85). To put an F1 score of 80 into perspective: It corresponds to a nicely useable prediction from a manual evaluation of our model's outputs, although there are small errors from time to time. We provide some example outputs in Section 4.8.

4.6 Ablation study

In this section, we discuss the effect of the foundation model type, model size and linearization method.

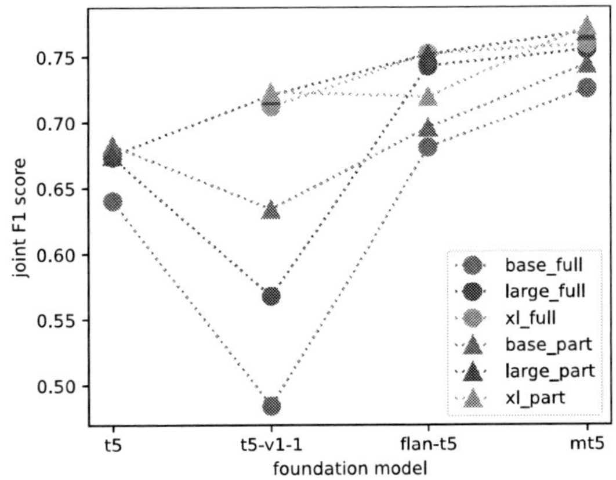

Figure 1: joint F1 score per foundation model

			quotation			roles			joint			type		
model	sz	lin.	prec.	rec.	F1	prec.	rec.	F1	prec.	rec.	F1	prec.	rec.	F1
development set														
RBS*			75.1	36.1	48.8	55.0	25.5	34.9	60.7	28.7	38.9	57.8	29.6	39.1
Citron*			**91.5**	27.6	42.4	79.3	31.5	45.1	82.4	30.3	44.3	87.0	26.6	40.8
mt5	b	part	85.5	75.2	80.0	83.1	71.4	76.8	83.8	72.5	77.8	84.9	74.3	79.2
mt5	l	part	89.7	78.4	**83.7**	83.2	74.5	78.6	85.1	75.6	**80.1**	89.2	78.6	**83.6**
mt5	xl	part	86.4	**79.5**	82.8	82.5	75.8	79.0	83.7	76.9	**80.1**	85.3	79.0	82.0
test set														
RBS*			70.8	36.2	47.9	55.6	26.1	35.5	59.9	29.0	39.1	63.5	33.6	43.9
Citron*			88.2	30.1	44.9	77.9	34.2	47.6	80.5	33.0	46.8	86.5	29.6	44.1
mt5	b	part	85.9	77.2	81.3	81.8	73.2	77.3	83.0	74.4	78.4	87.5	78.1	82.5
mt5	l	part	88.8	**81.1**	**84.8**	83.0	75.2	78.9	84.7	76.9	80.6	89.5	**81.0**	**85.0**
mt5	xl	part	88.2	80.0	83.9	83.2	**76.2**	**79.5**	84.6	**77.3**	**80.8**	88.5	80.2	84.2
*Baseline results taken from Petersen-Frey and Biemann (2024)														

Table 3: Selected evaluation results (baselines and our best model combination per model size). The column *sz* is short for size, with *b* for base and *l* for large. Complete results are shown in Table 5 and 6 in the appendix.

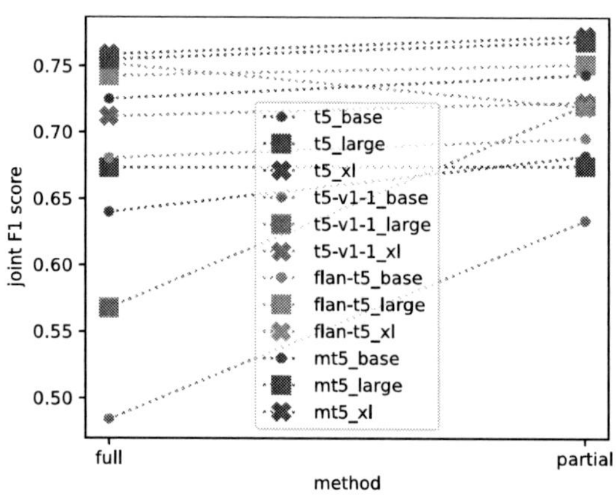

Figure 2: joint F1 score per linearization method

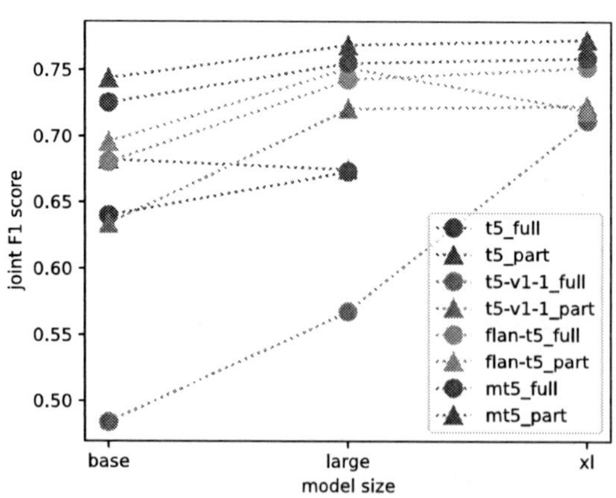

Figure 3: joint F1 score per model size

Figure 1 makes it easy to compare the performance across different foundation models. We can see a clear trend: mT5 outperforms Flan-T5 over all combinations of size and linearization method. Flan-T5 in turn outperforms T5 and T5 version 1.1 over all combinations. T5 version 1.1 behaves oddly in comparison to the other three foundation models: It exhibits a rather large difference of over 20 F1 points between its best and worst combinations. We attribute this to the fact this specific foundation model was only pre-trained using language modeling excluding any supervised training on other tasks.

Figure 2 compares the performance across our two tested linearization methods: Full copy linearization and partial token linearization. In all but one cases, we see an increase in performance using the partial token linearization. The two smaller T5 version 1.1 models profit substantially from using the partial linearization. For most models, it provides a low, consistent performance boost – only for Flan-T5 XL the full copy linearization performs slightly better. Albert not directly comparable, this is in contrast to the results of Zhang et al. (2023), who reported a slight performance decrease in coreference resolution by using their partial linearization method. While the task of coreference resolution seems to be affected by the alignment issue inherent to any partial linearization, our task of

size	lin.	joint F1	time	time batched
base	full	78.3	44m	24m
base	part	78.4	23m	13m
large	full	80.3	82m	60m
large	part	80.6	40m	31m
xl	full	78.7	90m	-
xl	part	80.8	49m	-

Table 4: Inference runtime

quotation detection and attribution is less affected.

Figure 3 shows the effect of increased model size. While the large model variants noticeably outperform the base size equivalents for all but one combination, using the xl model instead of the large model only provides significant gains for the combination of T5 version 1.1 with full copy linearization. The Flan-T5 using the partial token linearization even shows a drop in performance. Consequently, we do not see a reason to use a xl model size as it requires significantly more computational resources than a base or large model.

4.7 Inference runtime efficiency

As we intend to use our system on large document collections, inference runtime and compute resource requirements play an important role. Consequently, we evaluated the runtime efficiency across the three model sizes and both linearization methods. Tests were performed using the mT5 models with batch sizes of 1 and 8 (only base and large). We ran the inference measurements on a single A100 GPU (80 GB) and predicted the development and test set together (298 documents). Table 4 shows the total time usage when predicting all documents including post-processing. Across all model and batch sizes, the partial token linearization is roughly twice as fast as the full copy linearization resp. needs only half of the computational resources. For the base model, batching is highly recommended as long as enough memory is available because it also reduces the inference time in half compared to no batching. The large model is 25% faster with batching. The base model is roughly twice as fast as the large model. Using a smaller model has the additional advantage of a lower memory usage allowing higher batch sizes with potentially even faster inference. The xl model is only 25% slower than the large model without batching because the xl model utilizes the GPU better.

When considering the quality of the predictions together with the required computational resources, only two options should be considered: Partial token linearization with either a base or large model depending on the preference for performance or quality. Across all scenarios, the full linearization performs slightly worse than partial linearization and takes roughly twice as long to compute.

4.8 Error Analysis

We performed a manual verification of our best model's output on both the development and test set. Beside the comparison with the gold annotations, we also checked whether false positives might be annotation errors. We found that the system sometimes has difficulties with the *Addressee* role: It often predicts the span as a *Speaker* instead. This is somewhat expected since *Addressee* is tiny minority class in the dataset. Similarly, *Free Indirect* is also a rare class and quotations of this type are either not predicted or used in debatable situations where the gold annotations did annotate the span, e.g. when the grammatical structure matches, but it represents the opinion of the article author.

It also occurred that multiple *Speaker* spans were predicted for a single *Quote* whereas the gold annotations only contain one *Speaker*. Further, the system sometimes predicts very short *Direct* quotes not annotated in the gold data. While some of these could be declared as annotation errors, most of these errors are justified. However, we also encountered multiple documents where the system predicted full quotations with roles that were most likely missed during the annotation.

Example 4.1 shows the predictions on a random document from the dev set. The human annotations for the same document are shown in Example 4.2. Our system predicts two false positive quotations according to the curated annotations: The first is an edge case as someone very likely uttered the predicted quote but the sentence is written as a description of an action. The second quotation was likely missed during the annotation. However, the identified *Speaker* and *Cue* are partly wrong, only *Nachricht* (message) should be the *Speaker* and *Cue*. The third predicted quotation and it's roles are identical to the gold annotation. In the last quotation, the system's prediction is identical except for potentially false positive *Addressee* – another edge case where one could argue the BBC was the *Addressee* during the interview.

Example 4.1 (system prediction)

...

Jetzt bereiten sich die lokalen Autoritäten darauf
Cue 0 Frame 0 Speaker 0 Cue 0
vor den Tourismusansturm in geordnete Bahnen
Indirect 0
zu lenken, um die Einnahmen zum Schutze der Umgebung des Wasserfalls zu verwenden.

...

Auch er zeigte sich überrascht und stolz von der
Speaker 1 Cue 1 Frame 1 Cue 1
Nachricht, dass nur wenige Kilometer von
Indirect 1
seinem Haus einer der höchsten Wasserfälle der Welt liegt.

...

Er hofft, dass für sein Dorf etwas von den zu
Speaker 2 Cue 2 Indirect 2
Frame 2
erwartenden Einnahmen abfällt, denn bisher gibt es nicht einmal ein Telefon, um mit seinen weit entfernt wohnenden Kindern zu kommunizieren.

...

In einem Interview mit der BBC erklärte er:
Frame 3 Addressee 3 Cue 3 Speaker 3
„Der Anblick dieses Wasserfalls ist einfach spektakulär."
Direct 3

Example 4.2 (gold annotation)

...

Er hofft, dass für sein Dorf etwas von den zu
Speaker 0 Cue 0 Indirect 0
Frame 0
erwartenden Einnahmen abfällt, denn bisher gibt es nicht einmal ein Telefon, um mit seinen weit entfernt wohnenden Kindern zu kommunizieren.

...

In einem Interview mit der BBC erklärte er:
Frame 1 Cue 1 Speaker 1
„Der Anblick dieses Wasserfalls ist einfach spektakulär."
Direct 1

Another class of errors is that a role span is sometimes not used for multiple quotations, although the system correctly predicted all quotations – but without linking a *Speaker* etc. On a positive note, the system is perfectly capable of handling interrupted quotations and linking roles in a different sentence. Most nested quotations are also handled correctly, so the nesting itself does not appear to be a problem.

In general, it can be said that although the predictions are not perfect, but they are reasonable and very much useable both for an in-depth analysis of extracted groups and a quantitative analysis.

5 Conclusion

We have presented the first model for fine-grained, high-quality quotation detection and attribution in German news articles. The system allows to automatically identify who said what to whom. Our model can predict five different types of quotations together with the four different roles and connect these together. The model is based on a sequence-to-sequence transformer architecture generating structured, linearized output from plain text using constrained decoding. We described our method in detail, evaluated our two linearization methods across multiple foundation models and model sizes, performed an ablation study showing the importance of choosing the right foundation model, and performed a manual error analysis. Our models deliver a very strong performance on both a manual verification of the outputs and the evaluation metrics, almost doubling the scores of the available baselines.

Our system can be used for a range of use cases in the digital humanities, computational social sciences and journalism. Especially when combined with additional NLP tasks such as coreference resolution and entity linking, identified quotations can be easily grouped and analyzed, thereby providing researchers and journalists new means to work with quotations in large document collections.

In the future, we look forward to even multilingual foundation models that will likely further improve the quality of models using our approach.

Ethical Considerations

Relying on automation to solve a task always introduced room for issues. The models may have (unknown) biases due to its training data. The foundation models have been pre-trained on a huge amount of diverse web texts (see Raffel et al. (2020); Chung et al. (2022); Xue et al. (2021) for details). Our task-specific fine-tuning is performed using a dataset was created from a random sample of data of an open and freely available source that has been manually annotated and curated. During manual evaluation of our model's prediction, we did not encounter apparent biases such as a preference of gender for the speaker. Another potential issue with automation of an information extraction task is low recall. While precision is easy to check manually (by checking whether the system's prediction is valid), a low recall is problematic for certain use cases as there is so way to efficiently verify that the model detected most quotations in a large article collection. In our previous work (Petersen-Frey and Biemann, 2024), we reported a low recall for the baseline systems. We evaluated our models on a held-out test set and they achieve a high recall across quotations and roles.

Automation using machine learning can often open the door for misuse. In our case, we do not see a direct issue as detecting quotations in text is not harmful. It can become an issue if the source articles contain false quotations (e.g. because the texts were generated) and the extracted quotations are blindly believed to be valid. However, it is already possible to simply generate a list of fake quotations using readily available generative models. Thus, we do not see our model making things worse than the current state. In contrast, it could be used in helping to identify fake articles by comparing the found quotes with either a database or more reputable sources.

Limitations

We see two main limitations of our models. First, the computational resources required during inference are rather high as each generated token requires a pass through the decoder. We mitigate this to some extent by reducing the required output length with the partial token linearization. For documents that only include few quotations (or none at all) in the prediction, this makes the inference very quick. For documents with a high amount of quotations, it is still faster than the full copy linearization although less pronounced. The second issue is the amendable handling of rare events. Sometimes, deeply nested spans or span re-use across groups are not as well captured as they would be in isolation. Rare spans classes such a *Addressee* have a lower recall compared to common classes. More training data would help significantly with this issue.

References

Mariana S. C. Almeida, Miguel B. Almeida, and André F. T. Martins. 2014. A joint model for quotation attribution and coreference resolution. In *Proceedings of the 14th Conference of the European Chapter of the Association for Computational Linguistics*, pages 39–48, Gothenburg, Sweden. Association for Computational Linguistics.

Thomas Bögel and Michael Gertz. 2015. Did i really say that? – combining machine learning and dependency relations to extract statements from german news articles. In *Proceedings of the International Conference of the German Society for Computational Linguistics and Language Technology*, pages 13–21, Duisburg-Essen, Germany. German Society for Computational Linguistics and Language Technology.

Annelen Brunner, Stefan Engelberg, Fotis Jannidis, Ngoc Duyen Tanja Tu, and Lukas Weimer. 2020a. Corpus REDEWIEDERGABE. In *Proceedings of the Twelfth Language Resources and Evaluation Conference*, pages 803–812, Marseille, France. European Language Resources Association.

Annelen Brunner, Ngoc Duyen Tanja Tu, Lukas Weimer, and Fotis Jannidis. 2020b. To BERT or not to BERT - comparing contextual embeddings in a deep learning architecture for the automatic recognition of four types of speech, thought and writing representation. In *Proceedings of the 5th Swiss Text Analytics Conference and the 16th Conference on Natural Language Processing*, volume 2624 of *CEUR Workshop Proceedings*, Zurich, Switzerland. CEUR-WS.org.

Hyung Won Chung, Le Hou, Shayne Longpre, Barret Zoph, Yi Tay, William Fedus, Yunxuan Li, Xuezhi Wang, Mostafa Dehghani, Siddhartha Brahma, Albert Webson, Shixiang Shane Gu, Zhuyun Dai, Mirac Suzgun, Xinyun Chen, Aakanksha Chowdhery, Alex Castro-Ros, Marie Pellat, Kevin Robinson, Dasha Valter, Sharan Narang, Gaurav Mishra, Adams Yu, Vincent Zhao, Yanping Huang, Andrew Dai, Hongkun Yu, Slav Petrov, Ed H. Chi, Jeff Dean, Jacob Devlin, Adam Roberts, Denny Zhou, Quoc V. Le, and Jason Wei. 2022. Scaling instruction-finetuned language models. *Preprint*, arXiv:2210.11416.

Angel Daza and Anette Frank. 2018. A sequence-to-sequence model for semantic role labeling. In *Proceedings of the Third Workshop on Representation Learning for NLP*, pages 207–216, Melbourne, Australia. Association for Computational Linguistics.

Nicola De Cao, Gautier Izacard, Sebastian Riedel, and Fabio Petroni. 2021. Autoregressive entity retrieval. In *9th International Conference on Learning Representations (ICLR 2021)*. OpenReview.net.

Vladimir Dobrovolskii. 2021. Word-level coreference resolution. In *Proceedings of the 2021 Conference on Empirical Methods in Natural Language Processing*, pages 7670–7675, Online and Punta Cana, Dominican Republic. Association for Computational Linguistics.

Saibo Geng, Martin Josifoski, Maxime Peyrard, and Robert West. 2023. Grammar-constrained decoding for structured NLP tasks without finetuning. In *Proceedings of the 2023 Conference on Empirical Methods in Natural Language Processing*, pages 10932–10952, Singapore. Association for Computational Linguistics.

Osamu Gotoh. 1982. An improved algorithm for matching biological sequences. *Journal of Molecular Biology*, 162(3):705–708.

Yuval Kirstain, Ori Ram, and Omer Levy. 2021. Coreference resolution without span representations. In *Proceedings of the 59th Annual Meeting of the Association for Computational Linguistics and the 11th International Joint Conference on Natural Language Processing (Volume 2: Short Papers)*, pages 14–19, Online. Association for Computational Linguistics.

Ralf Krestel, Sabine Bergler, and René Witte. 2008. Minding the source: Automatic tagging of reported speech in newspaper articles. In *Proceedings of the Sixth International Conference on Language Resources and Evaluation (LREC'08)*, Marrakech, Morocco. European Language Resources Association (ELRA).

Tianyu Liu, Yuchen Eleanor Jiang, Nicholas Monath, Ryan Cotterell, and Mrinmaya Sachan. 2022. Autoregressive structured prediction with language models. In *Findings of the Association for Computational Linguistics: EMNLP 2022*, pages 993–1005, Abu Dhabi, United Arab Emirates. Association for Computational Linguistics.

Ilya Loshchilov and Frank Hutter. 2019. Decoupled weight decay regularization. In *7th International Conference on Learning Representations (ICLR 2019)*, New Orleans, LA, USA. OpenReview.net.

Chris Newell, Tim Cowlishaw, and David Man. 2018. Quote extraction and analysis for news. In *Proceedings of the Workshop on Data Science, Journalism and Media, KDD*, pages 1–6, London, UK.

Timothy O'Keefe, Silvia Pareti, James R. Curran, Irena Koprinska, and Matthew Honnibal. 2012. A sequence labelling approach to quote attribution. In *Proceedings of the 2012 Joint Conference on Empirical Methods in Natural Language Processing and Computational Natural Language Learning*, pages 790–799, Jeju Island, Korea. Association for Computational Linguistics.

Giovanni Paolini, Ben Athiwaratkun, Jason Krone, Jie Ma, Alessandro Achille, Rishita Anubhai, Cicero Nogueira dos Santos, Bing Xiang, and Stefano Soatto. 2021. Structured prediction as translation between augmented natural languages. In *9th International Conference on Learning Representations (ICLR 2021)*. OpenReview.net.

Sean Papay and Sebastian Padó. 2019. Quotation detection and classification with a corpus-agnostic model. In *Proceedings of the International Conference on Recent Advances in Natural Language Processing (RANLP 2019)*, pages 888–894, Varna, Bulgaria. INCOMA Ltd.

Silvia Pareti, Tim O'Keefe, Ioannis Konstas, James R. Curran, and Irena Koprinska. 2013. Automatically detecting and attributing indirect quotations. In *Proceedings of the 2013 Conference on Empirical Methods in Natural Language Processing*, pages 989–999, Seattle, Washington, USA. Association for Computational Linguistics.

Fynn Petersen-Frey and Chris Biemann. 2024. Dataset of quotation attribution in German news articles. In *Proceedings of the 2024 Joint International Conference on Computational Linguistics, Language Resources and Evaluation (LREC-COLING 2024)*, pages 4412–4422, Torino, Italia. European Language Resources Association (ELRA) and International Committee on Computational Linguistics (ICCL).

Bruno Pouliquen, Ralf Steinberger, and Clive Best. 2007. Automatic detection of quotations in multilingual news. In *The International Conference on Recent Advances in Natural Language Processing*, RANLP 2007, pages 487–492.

Colin Raffel, Noam Shazeer, Adam Roberts, Katherine Lee, Sharan Narang, Michael Matena, Yanqi Zhou, Wei Li, and Peter J. Liu. 2020. Exploring the limits of transfer learning with a unified text-to-text transformer. *J. Mach. Learn. Res.*, 21(1).

Samyam Rajbhandari, Jeff Rasley, Olatunji Ruwase, and Yuxiong He. 2020. ZeRO: memory optimizations toward training trillion parameter models. In *Proceedings of the International Conference for High Performance Computing, Networking, Storage and Analysis*, SC '20, pages 1–16. Institute of Electrical and Electronics Engineers (IEEE).

Jeff Rasley, Samyam Rajbhandari, Olatunji Ruwase, and Yuxiong He. 2020. DeepSpeed: System optimizations enable training deep learning models with over 100 billion parameters. In *Proceedings of the 26th ACM SIGKDD International Conference on Knowledge Discovery & Data Mining*, KDD '20, page 3505–3506, New York, NY, USA. Association for Computing Machinery.

Linting Xue, Noah Constant, Adam Roberts, Mihir Kale, Rami Al-Rfou, Aditya Siddhant, Aditya Barua, and Colin Raffel. 2021. mT5: A massively multilingual pre-trained text-to-text transformer. In *Proceedings of the 2021 Conference of the North American Chapter of the Association for Computational Linguistics: Human Language Technologies*, pages 483–498, Online. Association for Computational Linguistics.

Wenzheng Zhang, Sam Wiseman, and Karl Stratos. 2023. Seq2seq is all you need for coreference resolution. In *Proceedings of the 2023 Conference on Empirical Methods in Natural Language Processing*, pages 11493–11504, Singapore. Association for Computational Linguistics.

Yuanchi Zhang and Yang Liu. 2022. DirectQuote: A dataset for direct quotation extraction and attribution in news articles. In *Proceedings of the Thirteenth Language Resources and Evaluation Conference*, pages 6959–6966, Marseille, France. European Language Resources Association.

Appendix

model	sz	lin.	quotation prec.	quotation rec.	quotation F1	roles prec.	roles rec.	roles F1	joint prec.	joint rec.	joint F1	type prec.	type rec.	type F1
RBS*			75.1	36.1	48.8	55.0	25.5	34.9	60.7	28.7	38.9	57.8	29.6	39.1
Citron*			**91.5**	27.6	42.4	79.3	31.5	45.1	82.4	30.3	44.3	87.0	26.6	40.8
t5	b	full	82.4	68.3	74.7	76.2	61.9	68.3	78.0	63.8	70.2	81.6	68.0	74.2
t5	b	part	83.0	74.5	78.5	79.0	68.6	73.4	80.2	70.3	74.9	83.2	74.3	78.5
t5	l	full	86.7	70.0	77.5	80.1	63.2	70.7	82.1	65.2	72.7	87.6	70.4	78.1
t5	l	part	86.2	69.3	76.8	80.7	63.8	71.3	82.3	65.4	72.9	86.6	69.4	77.0
t5-v1-1	b	full	80.4	50.8	62.3	62.3	44.5	51.9	67.3	46.3	54.9	79.8	50.8	62.1
t5-v1-1	b	part	81.6	65.9	72.9	77.8	60.4	68.0	79.0	62.0	69.5	83.5	66.5	74.0
t5-v1-1	l	full	71.8	63.7	67.5	62.6	52.0	56.8	65.4	55.5	60.0	69.6	62.5	65.9
t5-v1-1	l	part	81.8	76.5	79.1	80.3	71.1	75.4	80.8	72.7	76.5	82.2	77.0	79.5
t5-v1-1	xl	full	85.9	74.0	79.5	80.6	71.3	75.6	82.1	72.1	76.8	86.5	75.3	80.5
t5-v1-1	xl	part	86.9	76.5	81.4	82.2	69.6	75.4	83.6	71.6	77.2	86.7	76.0	81.0
flan-t5	b	full	81.8	73.4	77.4	76.1	67.2	71.3	77.8	69.0	73.1	82.7	74.1	78.2
flan-t5	b	part	81.7	72.7	77.0	76.9	66.4	71.3	78.4	68.2	73.0	82.2	73.7	77.7
flan-t5	l	full	86.1	73.5	79.3	80.5	70.3	75.0	82.1	71.2	76.3	86.2	74.0	79.6
flan-t5	l	part	87.3	74.2	80.2	82.8	69.9	75.8	84.1	71.2	77.1	88.1	74.0	80.4
flan-t5	xl	full	89.0	77.3	82.7	**83.9**	73.3	78.2	**85.4**	74.5	79.6	**89.6**	77.6	83.2
flan-t5	xl	part	84.9	73.0	78.5	80.5	69.0	74.3	81.9	70.1	75.5	86.1	74.1	79.7
mt5	b	full	89.9	72.6	80.3	81.3	70.9	75.7	83.7	71.4	77.1	89.2	73.5	80.6
mt5	b	part	85.5	75.2	80.0	83.1	71.4	76.8	83.8	72.5	77.8	84.9	74.3	79.2
mt5	l	full	88.4	75.5	81.4	83.4	73.2	78.0	84.9	73.9	79.0	89.1	76.3	82.2
mt5	l	part	89.7	78.4	**83.7**	83.2	74.5	78.6	85.1	75.6	**80.1**	89.2	78.6	**83.6**
mt5	xl	full	84.8	78.8	81.7	82.2	**76.5**	**79.3**	83.0	**77.2**	80.0	84.5	**80.2**	82.3
mt5	xl	part	86.4	**79.5**	82.8	82.5	75.8	79.0	83.7	76.9	**80.1**	85.3	79.0	82.0

*Baseline results taken from Petersen-Frey and Biemann (2024)

Table 5: Complete evaluation results on the development set. Highest score per metric marked in bold.

model	sz	lin.	quotation prec.	quotation rec.	quotation F1	roles prec.	roles rec.	roles F1	joint prec.	joint rec.	joint F1	type prec.	type rec.	type F1
RBS*			70.8	36.2	47.9	55.6	26.1	35.5	59.9	29.0	39.1	63.5	33.6	43.9
Citron*			88.2	30.1	44.9	77.9	34.2	47.6	80.5	33.0	46.8	86.5	29.6	44.1
t5	b	full	81.3	68.1	74.2	75.2	62.3	68.2	77.0	64.0	69.9	82.6	69.0	75.2
t5	b	part	84.7	72.9	78.4	79.6	66.4	72.4	81.1	68.2	74.1	84.5	72.7	78.2
t5	l	full	89.4	71.1	79.2	82.5	65.8	73.2	84.5	67.3	74.9	90.1	72.4	80.3
t5	l	part	86.2	72.2	78.6	80.5	65.6	72.3	82.2	67.5	74.1	86.3	72.4	78.7
t5-v1-1	b	full	77.8	53.7	63.5	61.6	46.3	52.9	66.0	48.4	55.9	80.7	55.1	65.5
t5-v1-1	b	part	83.8	67.2	74.6	78.4	61.9	69.2	80.0	63.4	70.7	85.2	66.9	74.9
t5-v1-1	l	full	71.4	62.8	66.8	63.3	54.3	58.5	65.7	56.8	60.9	71.2	63.7	67.2
t5-v1-1	l	part	83.5	77.1	80.2	78.0	70.0	73.8	79.6	72.1	75.7	84.3	77.3	80.6
t5-v1-1	xl	full	88.1	74.6	80.8	80.6	69.8	74.8	82.8	71.2	76.5	88.4	75.2	81.3
t5-v1-1	xl	part	89.3	76.8	82.6	83.2	70.5	76.3	85.0	72.3	78.1	89.6	77.0	82.8
flan-t5	b	full	83.0	73.2	77.8	73.3	66.0	69.4	76.1	68.1	71.8	83.9	74.2	78.8
flan-t5	b	part	81.0	75.5	78.2	74.9	67.2	70.8	76.7	69.6	73.0	82.4	76.2	79.2
flan-t5	l	full	86.6	76.8	81.4	78.9	73.2	75.9	81.1	74.3	77.5	86.8	77.5	81.8
flan-t5	l	part	89.4	77.9	83.3	82.5	74.0	78.1	84.5	75.1	79.6	90.1	78.2	83.7
flan-t5	xl	full	89.5	78.2	83.5	83.5	74.0	78.5	85.3	75.2	79.9	89.2	78.2	83.3
flan-t5	xl	part	89.9	76.3	82.5	**84.2**	70.2	76.6	**85.8**	71.9	78.3	**90.7**	76.7	83.1
mt5	b	full	**91.2**	75.4	82.6	82.6	71.4	76.6	85.0	72.5	78.3	90.0	74.5	81.5
mt5	b	part	85.9	77.2	81.3	81.8	73.2	77.3	83.0	74.4	78.4	87.5	78.1	82.5
mt5	l	full	89.5	78.3	83.5	84.1	74.4	78.9	85.6	75.5	80.3	90.3	78.7	84.1
mt5	l	part	88.8	**81.1**	**84.8**	83.0	75.2	78.9	84.7	76.9	80.6	89.5	**81.0**	**85.0**
mt5	xl	full	85.2	78.6	81.8	80.3	74.8	77.4	81.7	75.9	78.7	86.1	79.6	82.7
mt5	xl	part	88.2	80.0	83.9	83.2	**76.2**	**79.5**	84.6	**77.3**	**80.8**	88.5	80.2	84.2

*Baseline results taken from Petersen-Frey and Biemann (2024)

Table 6: Complete evaluation results on the test set. Highest score per metric marked in bold.

Decoding 16th-Century Letters: From Topic Models to GPT-Based Keyword Mapping

Phillip Benjamin Ströbel
University of Zurich
phillip.stroebel@uzh.ch

Stefan Aderhold
FS Theologenbriefwechsel der AdW
stefan@aderhold-net.de

Ramona Roller
Universiteit Utrecht
r.i.roller@uu.nl

Abstract

Probabilistic topic models for categorising or exploring large text corpora are notoriously difficult to interpret. Making sense of them has thus justifiably been compared to "reading tea leaves." Involving humans in labelling topics consisting of words is feasible but time-consuming, especially if one infers many topics from a text collection. Moreover, it is a cognitively demanding task, and domain knowledge might be required depending on the text corpus. We thus examine how using a Large Language Model (LLM) offers support in text classification. We compare how the LLM summarises topics produced by Latent Dirichlet Allocation, Non-negative Matrix Factorisation and BERTopic. We investigate which topic modelling technique provides the best representations by applying these models to a 16th-century correspondence corpus in Latin and Early New High German and inferring keywords from the topics in a low-resource setting. We experiment with including domain knowledge in the form of already existing keyword lists. Our main findings are that the LLM alone provides usable topics already. However, guiding the LLM towards what is expected benefits the interpretability. We further want to highlight that using nouns and proper nouns only makes for good topic representations.

1 Introduction

In the realm of digital humanities and computational linguistics, probabilistic topic models have found wide application in categorising and exploring large text corpora (Meeks and Weingart, 2012; Sia and Duh, 2021; Schöch, 2021; Hodel et al., 2022). Especially one technique, i.e., Latent Dirichlet Allocation (LDA) (Blei et al., 2003), has established itself as a "quasi-standard" (Hodel et al., 2022, p. 186). However, models like LDA, essential for distilling and interpreting large datasets, yield results in the form of *bags-of-words* that are opaque and difficult to decipher, drawing comparisons to the esoteric art of "reading tea leaves" (Chang et al., 2009).

Incorporating human judgement has been used to refine topics directly during the model training of so-called *interactive topic models* (Hu et al., 2014), but rarely to label the bags of words to make them more interpretable. This is mainly because labelling topics is subjective (Alokaili, 2021), labour-intensive (Rüdiger et al., 2022), and demands considerable cognitive effort and domain-specific knowledge, particularly when multiple topics are derived from expansive text collections.

Thus, it has long been a desire to find labels for topics automatically, which has been achieved with varying degrees of accuracy (Mei et al., 2007; Lau et al., 2011; Kou et al., 2015). The advent of Large Language Models (LLMs) like OpenAI's GPT-4 (OpenAI, 2023) has introduced new possibilities in the field of text analytics. These models, equipped with advanced capabilities in natural language understanding, offer a promising avenue for leveraging information gathered through topic modelling techniques such as LDA, Non-negative Matrix Factorisation (NMF) (Lee and Seung, 1999; Ding et al., 2008), and BERTopic (Grootendorst, 2022). While these techniques still represent a document as a mixture of topics, LLMs can interpret the topic words instead of relying on human analysis. This paper explores the potential of LLMs to support and refine the process of text classification, particularly by leveraging their capacity to analyse and generate coherent and interpretable topic representations.

To evaluate the effectiveness of these topic modelling techniques, we examine how topics summarised by an LLM compare in a low-resource setting – specifically within the historical linguistics domain, focusing on a corpus of 16th-century correspondence written in Latin and Early New High German.

Letters tend to treat several topics so that topic modelling can prove a valuable approach for *distant reading* (Moretti, 2000). However, the (compared to other corpora) small number of tokens in a multilingual environment, together with a high number of topics, makes topic modelling and keyword assignment a difficult problem. This work aims to reveal how well LLMs can generate usable topics under constrained resource conditions.

Additionally, this study explores the integration of domain-specific knowledge, utilising preexisting keyword lists to guide the LLM towards more accurate topic generation. By concentrating on document representations consisting of nouns and proper nouns, we assess the quality of the topic representations produced and discuss how directed LLM support can enhance the interpretability of the model outputs. Although our findings highlight the standalone capabilities of LLMs in topic generation and underscore the benefits of incorporating guided input to improve both the clarity and relevance of topic modelling, we also encountered difficulties, which we explain below.

2 Recent Research

Topic Modelling for Correspondence Data Topic modelling has been applied to all sorts of data, including correspondences. Wittek and Ravenek (2011) applied LDA, among other methods, to 17th-century scholarly correspondences. Their multilingual corpus comprised Dutch, English, French, German, Greek, Italian and Latin letters, accumulating over 7 million tokens. They trained separate topic models for the most common languages (Dutch, French, and Latin).

Topic Modelling in Low-Resource Scenarios Hao et al. (2018) contributed to the evaluation of topic models, especially in low-resource settings. They experimented with parallel data and normalised pointwise mutual information scores to measure topic coherence and train an estimator to predict topic coherence in the case of low-resource languages.

Sia and Duh (2021) investigated how to improve LDA for low-resource languages directly. Their research introduces a method that automatically balances externally trained continuous representations with traditional co-occurrence count-based statistics tailored to each word and topic. This approach adapts to variations in topic numbers and embedding dimensions without extra tuning, enhancing existing methods.

Keywords for Topic Modelling Jagarlamudi et al. (2012) already incorporated lexical priors to guide topic models to infer topics that are relevant to the user. They provided the algorithm with sets of seed words which, according to their view, represented a topic, thereby influencing the word-topic and document-topic distributions.

This approach was taken one step further by Eshima et al. (2024), who proposed the keyword-assisted topic model. In contrast to defining sets of seed words, this approach uses a list of keywords, which the authors make part of the data generation process and hence influence word distribution of the topics.

Using LLMs for Topic Modelling Rijcken et al. (2023) applied LDA and a fuzzy clustering-based topic modelling algorithm (Rijcken et al., 2021) to clinical notes from the psychiatric domain and had both human experts and ChatGPT produce summaries of the topics. In the human evaluation which subsequently compared both summaries, they found that only about half the summaries generated by ChatGPT were useful.

LLMs have recently also been used to evaluate topics directly. Stammbach et al. (2023) show that LLMs correlate well with human ratings on coherence tasks, whereas identifying intruders still poses challenges to LLMs.

Pham et al. (2024) directly use GPT for topic modelling and compare against BERTopic, LDA and seeded NMF. They provide GPT with a list of keywords, or topics, and let GPT infer the topics for texts from Wikipedia and bills from the U.S. Congress. We will also use GPT directly to generate keywords from texts, but make amendments to the methods proposed by Pham et al. (see Section 4.5).

3 Data

3.1 The *Heinrich Bullinger Briefwechsel (HBBW)*

The comprehensive collection of approximately 12,000 surviving letters from Swiss Reformer Heinrich Bullinger (1504–1575) provides not just insights but a crucial connection to the complex network of relationships Bullinger maintained with intellectuals, theologians, monarchs, and other influential figures throughout Europe during the Reformation period (Campi, 2004). Written predominantly in Latin – the dominant *lingua franca* of that era – these letters also contain a notable amount of Early New High German (ENHG).[1] The initiative, *Bullinger Digital*,[2] has made this diverse, multilingual legacy accessible and interactive using digital curation techniques.

Of the 12,000 letters in the HBBW, 3,000 have been edited in 20 volumes already (Gäbler et al., 1974–2020), and another 5,400 have been transcribed. In these letters, the authors wrote about various theological and reformatory matters and issues in everyday life, like illness, marriage, and food. Topic modelling, in connection with keyword assignment, can thus help users to "distant read" the correspondence and to get an overview of the governing themes in the corpus.

We downloaded the data preprocessed by Ströbel et al. (2024) in TEI-XML format from the open access GitHub repository.[3]

3.2 The *Theologenbriefwechsel*

We obtained data from the so-called *Theologenbriefwechsel im Südwesten des Reichs in der Frühen Neuzeit (1550-1620)* (Strohm, 2017).[4] The Theologenbriefwechsel is a research project that focuses on gathering, accessing, and partially publishing the letters of key theologians and church leaders from the Electoral Palatinate, Württemberg, and Strasbourg between 1550 and 1620. This effort aims to understand the process of confessionalisation and its impacts during the early modern period. By analysing these letters, not just from individual exchanges but across specific groups and regions during this time, the project helps reveal broader networks and patterns, highlighting the significant role of theologians in shaping religious confessions.

3.3 Data Overview and Preprocessing

Accumulating the HBBW and Theologenbriefwechsel letters leads to a corpus of 10,319 letters, 1,731 of which stem from the Theologenbriefwechsel. Since the HBBW data was already split into sentences and each sentence had received a language label, we extracted the Latin and ENHG sentences from the Bullinger correspondence. For the Theologenbriefwechsel, we split the text into sentences and tokens using the *Classical Language Toolkit*'s (Johnson et al., 2021) sentence tokeniser. Subsequently, we determined the language with a language identifier trained to distinguish between Latin and ENHG (Volk et al., 2022). For the HBBW data, we only applied the sentence tokeniser. Summarising all tokens of the HBBW and the Theologenbriefwechsel yields a corpus of 5,630,039 tokens, 4,060,754 (72.13%) of which are in Latin and 1,569,285 (27.87%) are in ENHG.

A common further preprocessing step for topic modelling is stopword removal (Hodel et al., 2022) and the limitation of the vocabulary to, e.g., nouns. We decided to focus on nouns and proper nouns only,[5] which required Part-of-Speech (POS) tagging. For Latin, we employed spaCy's *LatinCy* (Burns, 2023) and filtered the Latin texts for words with NOUN and PROPN tags. We extracted the lemmas for words with NOUNs and lowercased all of them.

In the case of ENHG, there have been attempts at POS tagging. Demske et al. (2014) reported accuracies between 69% and 75% with the TnT Tagger (Brants, 2000). Barteld et al. (2018) experimented with different POS taggers for Middle High and Middle Low German and reached accuracies of 85.95% and 86.37%, respectively. Since we were dealing with ENHG, we trained our own spaCy[6] tokeniser along the lines of Burns (2023). As a base language model, we used `bert-base-german-cased`.[7] We took the *Referenzkorpus Frühneuhochdeutsch* as training data (Wegera et al., 2021),[8] converted the CorA-XML files to CoNLL-U format, mapped the tagset of the Referenzkorpus to UPOS tags, and used almost 2.5 million tokens for training and roughly 300k tokens for development and testing each. With an initial learning rate of 0.00005 with 500 warmup

[1]The collection also letters in Greek, Hebrew, English, Italian, and French.

[2]See https://www.bullinger-digital.ch.

[3]See https://github.com/bullinger-digital/bullinger-korpus-tei.

[4]See https://thbw.hadw-bw.de.

[5]We consider nouns and proper nouns to be the main carriers of meaning. Moreover, since our task is to map topics to keywords, which are almost always (proper) nouns, we decided to employ this rather radical preprocessing step. However, we admit that at least adjectives and verbs can also carry meaning that could help describe topics. We will address the consequences of different preprocessing steps in future research. However, work on this topic has already shown that focusing on nouns only is beneficial for topic coherence (cf. Martin and Johnson (2015)).

[6]See https://spacy.io.

[7]See https://huggingface.co/google-bert/bert-base-german-cased.

[8]We ignored the part from the Universität Potsdam since it did not contain lemmas.

steps and a total number of 20,000 trained steps (with early stopping), our POS tagger reached an accuracy of 54.39% on the test set,[9] while lemmatisation accuracy was considerably lower at 47.48%. This is due to the high number of types (254,374). Because of the low success rate of mapping surface forms to lemmas, we decided not to lemmatise the ENHG tokens but still only extracted words tagged as NOUN or PROPN and lowercased them. We have not investigated the low accuracy rates but plan to do so in future research endeavours. Still, we need to be aware that using the words identified as PROPN or NOUN and the corresponding word types instead of the lemmas makes inferring topics more difficult and will probably lead to worse results when compared to Latin.

Limiting ourselves to (proper) nouns only reduced the number of tokens from 5.6 million to 1.1 million, which means we are operating with 20.61% of the corpus. In addition to filtering (proper) nouns, extracting lemmas (for Latin only) and lowercasing, we further filtered out stopwords with a list of 657 words. We compiled and extended this list based on the topic modelling results: should certain words considered stopwords occur frequently among the indicative topic words, we included these words in this list. E.g., we added the ENHG word *wyr* (EN *we*) that was sometimes tagged as NOUN, as well as the Latin word *quid* (EN *this*). We also included words that occurred too often in the topics, like different versions of the proper names Heinrich (*heinrich*, *hainricus*, *hainrico*), Bullinger (*bullinger*, *bullingero*, *bullingerus*), and Zurich (*zürich*, *zurych*, *zürych*).

3.4 Keyword Lists

The Theologenbriefwechsel has been manually annotated with keywords. During the course of the project, the keyword catalogue grew to contain over 18k keywords. The keywords are organised hierarchically. As the example in Figure 1 shows, we find very specific keywords like *Straßburger Gespräch Andreae-Flacius Illyricus (1571)* and more general ones like *Teufel* (EN *devil*) or *Abendmahlstreit* (EN *controversy about the Sacrament of the Lord's Supper*). The keyword *Abendmahlstreit* is embedded as follows (top-down): *Streit* (EN *dispute*) → *Streitigkeiten* (EN *conflict*) → *Abendmahlstreit*. The top level contains 339 keywords. This did not seem

Figure 1: Example of keywords on the platform of the Theologenbriefwechsel. The keywords are divided in *Personen* (EN *persons*), *Orte* (EN locations), and *Sachen* (EN *matters*). Example is taken from a letter from Jakob Andrea to Johannes Marbach on May 25, 1575 (See https://thbw.hadw-bw.de/brief/21212).

practical for mapping purposes, especially since we plan to offer a keyword filtering option on the *Bullinger Digital* platform. So we reduced the top-level keyword list to the 53 most important ones (we call this list *meta-topic list*) based on a subjective assessment.[10] Still, we were also interested in whether it is possible to map more fine-grained keywords to topic words, so we included two further keywords for each sub-topic under a meta-topic. For example, the meta-topic about the controversy about the Sacrament of the Lord's Supper contains three further sub-topics on the next level. We took two further keywords from these and added them to the list. E.g., the third sub-topic lists *Brot und Wein als sakramentliche Zeichen* (EN *bread and wine as sacramental symbols*). This leads to a sub-topic list of 273 keywords.

4 Experiments

See Figure 3 for an overview of our experimental setup. We first trained a topic model with BERTopic, which, based on the inherent clustering algorithm, indicated the number of topics present in the corpus. Taking the inferred number of topics from BERTopic, we further trained topic models using LDA and NMF. We then let GPT-4 summarise the topic words into keywords in three ways: 1) on its own, 2) with the meta-topic list, and 3) with the sub-topic list. We then automatically evaluate the keywords generated for each method used to produce the topic model. A second evaluation

[9]The highest accuracy on the development set during training was 74.62%. The low accuracy on the test set hints at the high variability of the data.

[10]In hindsight, and this is what we will do in the future, it would have been better to make this assessment based on the actual distribution of keywords in the Theologenbriefwechsel.

takes 50 letters at random and lets GPT infer the topics based on the preprocessed letter texts. We then compare the keywords generated with each method against each other. In the following, we provide further details about the generation of the topic models.

4.1 BERTopic

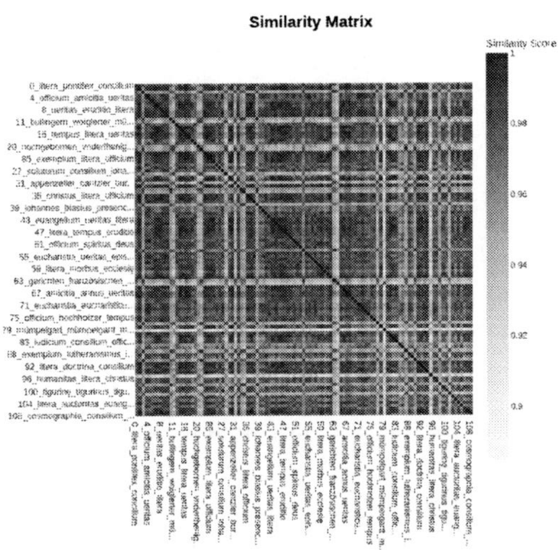

Figure 2: Heatmap of topic similarities by applying cosine similarities through the topic embeddings.

BERTopic is set up as modular architecture, which consists of 5 steps: 1) embed the documents, 2) apply dimensionality reduction, 3) cluster the documents, 4) represent them as bag-of-words, and 5) find the topic words. To embed the documents, we used the text embedding model `multilingual-e5-large`[11] (Wang et al., 2024). This multilingual model has also been trained on Latin and German, which is closest to ENHG.[12] For dimensionality reduction, we used the default UMAP algorithm (McInnes et al., 2018). However, running BERTopic with the standard settings leads to a very limited number of inferred topics (between 10 and 20). Given that we already have 53 items in the meta-topic list (and 273 keywords in the sub-topic list), we changed the parameter `n_neighbors` to 5.[13] Lowering this parameter causes the algorithm to focus on more local structures, leading to more clusters inferred in the next step. Due to the stochastic nature of UMAP, using `n_neighbors = 5` led to topic numbers between 100 and 168 for our texts. The final run we evaluate in this paper inferred 109 topics.[14] We then used the default clustering algorithm (HDBSCAN (Campello et al., 2013)) with its default settings.[15] A count vectoriser then represents each cluster as bag-of-words. We provided the vectoriser with our stopword list to filter out unwanted words (see Section 3.3). Finally, we used the class TF-IDF vectoriser to infer the topic words.

Inspecting the topic model reveals that many topics are similar (see Figure 2). The dissimilarities in the heatmap mainly stem from the low similarity scores when Latin topics are compared to ENHG topics. Comparing topics to each other, we see that topics 2 and 40 in Table 1 are very different from each other, 2 being about the sacraments and 49 most probably about war. Topic 60, on the other hand, contains words that we find in topics 2 and 49. Other words in this topic hint at the fact that it could be about illness, but this example shows the difficulty BERTopic has in finding different topics and also foreshadows that this could be problematic when automatically inferring topics. The same is true for topics 64 (matters of law), 102 (sin), and 34, which is content-wise closer to 102 but also contains elements of 102 (though not explicitly).

4.2 Latent Dirichlet Allocation and Non-negative Matrix Factorisation

To infer topics with LDA and NMF, we used the *gensim* framework (Řehůřek and Sojka, 2010). The further processing consisted of converting the preprocessed texts to a gensim corpus and filtering out extremes. This means we excluded tokens that occurred in less than 20 documents and in more than 10% of the documents. This reduced the vocabulary from 95k to 4,600 tokens and the effective corpus size from 1.1 million tokens to 416k. We then used 30 passes for both topic modelling techniques to infer 109 topics (the number we obtained

[11]Available on the Hugging Face model hub: https://huggingface.co/intfloat/multilingual-e5-large.

[12]To the best of our knowledge, the only model available is *Turmbücher LM* by the University of Bern (trained on 16th-century texts and available on the Hugging Face model hub: https://huggingface.co/dh-unibe/turmbuecher-lm-v1) However, this model cannot embed Latin texts.

[13]We kept the rest of the parameters at their default values: `n_components = 5, min_dist = 0.0, metric = 'cosine'`.

[14]Setting the `random_state` parameter fixes the results. However, we did not evaluate the different runs against each other. Again, we would approach matters differently in the future, setting `random_state` from the beginning to ensure a better and reproducible experimental setting.

[15]`min_cluster_size = 15, metric = 'euclidean', cluster_selection_method = 'eom', prediction_data = True`

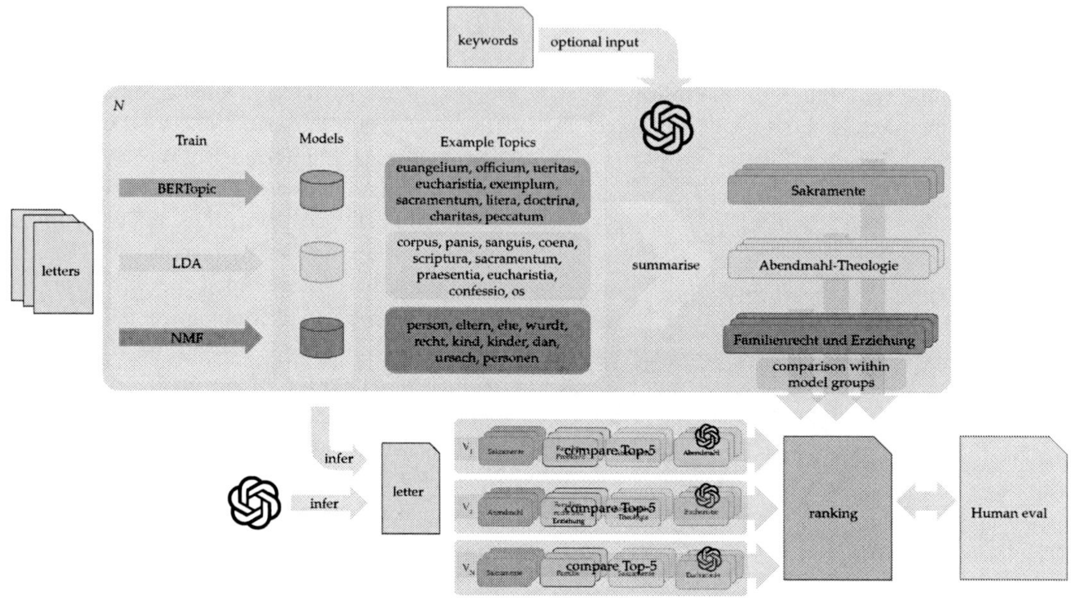

Figure 3: Workflow overview. We first train topic models with different algorithms on the letters. Each model represents the topics differently, but by default, with 10 words. We then used GPT to summarise the topic words into one keyword. For LDA and NMF, we also experimented with summarising the topics using 20 and 30 words. Additionally, we provided GPT with two lists of keywords: the *meta-topic list* and the *sub-topic* list (see Section 3.4). We then evaluated for each combination within a topic modelling category (BERTopic, LDA, and NMF) how different the keywords or key phrases are using sentence transformers. For a test set of 50 letters, we generated keywords with GPT directly and compared to the ones inferred from topic words.

from BERTopic).

Table 2 shows two exemplary topics for each algorithm. We purposely chose similar topics for LDA and NMF. The two Latin topics 1 (LDA) and 39 (NMF) express the sacraments with very similar topic words. In the same way, the two ENHG topics 88 (LDA) and 64 (NMF) describe the debate about the Last Supper in a comparable style. We would, therefore, expect GPT to produce the same (or similar) keywords for those topics.

4.3 Inferring Topics with GPT

After training the three different topic models (BERTopic, LDA, and NMF), we want to test GPT's capability of inferring a keyword based on the topic words. For BERTopic, GPT uses 10 topic words per topic to solve this task.[16] For LDA and NMF, we expand the setting and let GPT generate a keyword based on 10, 20, and 30 topic words. We want to know whether more information, i.e., more topic words, helps GPT to produce better keywords. For example, for topic 64 of Table 2, the additional topic words *leibs, essen, wesen, paulus, nachtmal, worten, menschen, christo, todt, leyb* could steer GPT away from the rather general keyword *Abendmahl* to *Abendmahlsstreit*. The following two sections *Prompting A* and *Prompting B* further detail our methodology.

4.4 Prompting A – Keyword Mapping

We used the prompts shown in Table 3 to map topic words to keywords. The "Role" first defines the general role of GPT. The two different prompts represent our two different settings: The "GPT only" prompt asks GPT to generate a keyword (maximum 3 words) that best captures the meaning of the 10, 20, or 30 topic words. The "GPT with keyword list" provides the topic words and either the meta-topic or the sub-topic list, instructing GPT to choose a keyword from the list. With these two methods, we map the topic words to keywords.

[16] Although the documentation of BERTopic mentions that it is possible to infer more than 10 topic words with the `top_n_words` parameter, we did not manage to make this functionality work.

Topic #	Topic words
2	euangelium, officium, ueritas, eucharistia, exemplum, sacramentum, litera, doctrina, charitas, peccatum
49	exercitus, litera, communitas, philippus, uxor, legatus, bellum, frater, salus, iohannes
60	litera, morbus, ecclesię, tempus, euangelium, christus, spiritus, gratia, deus, cęlum
64	gerichten, französischen, gemeinden, handlung, pündten, rächt, baß, gmeinden, meinung, gewalt
102	sünden, frucht, menschen, kirchen, ergernuß, gott, mentschen, oberkeit, gotsforcht, namen
34	rechtfertigung, confeßion, gerechtigkeit, vnderthenigkeit, sünden, glauben, urchlaucht, meinung, gerechtigkaitt, wirtenbergh

Table 1: Example topics from BERTopic. Topics 2, 49 and 60 are Latin, 64, 102, and 34 ENHG.

Topic # LDA	Topic words
1	corpus, panis, sanguis, coena, scriptura, sacramentum, praesentia, eucharistia, confessio, os
88	christi, leib, blut, meinung, leibs, wein, zwinglianer, wesen, mensch, bluts
Topic # NMF	**Topic words**
39	corpus, panis, coena, sanguis, uictima, manducatio, figure, peccatum, coenae, os
64	leib, christi, but, will, wurdt, wein, brott, glauben, wort, meinung

Table 2: Example topics from LDA and NMF.

4.5 Prompting B – Direct Keyword Generation

In addition to keyword mappings based on topic words, we prompted GPT to generate a keyword for 50 randomly chosen letters. We only slightly adapted the prompt already presented in Table 3, instructing GPT to generate 5 keywords per letter. We used the same preprocessed letters as for BERTopic. Similar to the setting in the previous section, we also had two runs during which GPT had access to the meta-topic and sub-topic lists.

4.6 Evaluation and Results

We aimed at an automatic evaluation of the topic-words-to-keyword-mappings. For the setting *Prompting A* described in Section 4.4, we compared the generated keywords by embedding them with `multilingual-t5-large` (see Section 4.1) and computing the cosine similarities for each algorithm. E.g., we compared the keyword generated by GPT using LDA's 10-word-topic *Kirchliche Gesetzgebung* (EN *church legislation*) to the keyword inferred from LDA's 20-word-topic *Kirchenrecht und Besitzverhältnisse* (EN *canon law and ownership structure*), obtaining a cosine similarity of 0.916. Perfect matches resulted in a cosine similarity of 1, while the lowest score of 0.726 was a comparison of NMF's 10-word-topic keyword *Osmanisches Heer* (EN *Ottoman army*) to NMF's 20-word-topic keyword *Glaube* (EN *faith*) (both times generated with the sub-topic list). We then averaged the similarity scores over the 109 topics for each comparison and obtained the results in Table 4 in Appendix A.

For the experiment in *Prompting B*, we took the five keywords generated by GPT based on the preprocessed letter texts and compared them to the top 5 topics the three methods BERTopic, LDA, and NMF have inferred from the texts. It is sometimes possible that one of these algorithms has only attributed one topic to a letter. We still compared this one topic in the form of its keyword to the 5 GPT-generated keywords. To compute the cosine similarity between the GPT-generated keywords and the inferred keywords based on the topic words of BERTopic, LDA, and NMF, we concatenated the keywords with commata and embedded them with `multilingual-t5-large`. E.g., these are the keywords GPT inferred for the letter by Hieronymus Zanchi to Thomas Erastus in the year 1570:[17] *Thomas Erastus, Gott und Teufel, Exorzismus und Dämonen, Hexen und Zauberer, Augustinus und Thomas Aquinas*. The following are the top-5 keywords inferred by GPT based on 10 topic topics words by LDA: *Kirchliche Kontroversen, Biblische Kommentararbeit, Finanzielle Kirchenangelegenheiten, Familienrecht, Stuttgarter Prädikanten-Korrespondenz*. We observe a rather low (compared to other scores) similarity score of 0.812. In-

[17] See https://thbw.hadw-bw.de/brief/19786.

Role	Prompt GPT only	Prompt GPT with keyword list
You are a historian and an expert of 16th-century correspondence. You are presented with topics from letters from the correspondence of the 16th century and have to find a keyword or keyphrase that best matches the topic words. The correspondence discusses not only the reformation, but also various other religious topics and everyday life situations.	For the following topic words in Latin or Early New High German separated by '-', find one German keyword or keyphrase (maximum 3 words) that captures the overall meaning best { }. Be more specific than 'Theologie' or 'Reformation'. Only output the keyword. Don't explain your decision. Don't translate.	For the following topic words in Latin or Early New High German separated by '-': { }, choose one keyword or keyphrase from the following list where keywords are separated by '|': { }. Choose the keyword that best summarises the topic words. Don't explain your decision. Don't translate.

Table 3: Role and prompts used for mapping topic words to a keyword. The "Role" primes GPT for the task. The "Prompt GPT only" replaces the curly brackets with the topic words and lets GPT define a keyword itself. The "Prompt GPT with keyword list" replaces the second set of curly brackets with a list of keywords to choose from.

deed, there is no overlap between the keywords. If we look at the keywords the Theologenbriefwechsel has attributed to this letter, namely *Todesstrafe, Aberglaube, Astrologie, Auspizien, Nekromantie, Wahrsagegeist, Teufel, Dämonen, Hexerei, Ex 20,3, Dtn 5,7, Gen 35,2, Jos 24,16, Dtn 18,9-13, Lev 19,26, Lev 20,6, Lev 20,27*, we see that GPT manages to generate several keywords that also occur in the Theologenbriefwechsel based on the letter text alone. The keywords inferred by GPT based on topic words are, in that sense, less precise, although the keyword *Biblische Kommentararbeit* (EN *Bible commentaries*) reflects many Bible quotes present as keywords in the Theologenbriefwechsel.

5 Discussion

Our comparison focuses on the differences in the keywords generated from topic words. The big picture as presented in Table 4 shows that a certain guidance with the help of meta-topic and subtopic lists results in more consistent mappings than letting GPT imagining keywords on its own. Although this is somehow expected, it shows that we can steer GPT towards generating keywords based on existing catalogues, which is essential not only for the GLAM[18] sector but also for projects that want to offer their users additional search filters.

Another general trend seems to be that the more topic words GPT has at its disposal to generate a keyword, the more closely related the keywords are (see, e.g., the similarity score of 0.896 for "lda_10 vs. lda_20" and the one of 0.911 for "lda_20 vs. lda_30"). The low scores obtained when comparing keywords generated without lists to keywords generated with lists are again to be expected. However, the fact that they are not lower hints at a certain closeness. E.g., the GPT-generated keyword from LDA's 30-topic-words version for topic 66 is *Reichstag zu Augsburg*[19] and the keyword generated from LDA's 10-topic-words with the meta-topic list *Obrigkeit* (EN *lords*, or *authorities*) are related since the lords participated at the Reichstag.

Interestingly, as concerns the number of, e.g., meta-topics matched to topic words, we observed that the more topic words GPT has seen to choose a keyword from the meta-topic list, the fewer it uses in total. To be more concrete, for our LDA topic model, GPT assigned 26, 24, and 23 keywords from our meta-topic list of 53 keywords when seeing 10, 20, and 30 topic words, respectively. The trend for NMF is similar, going down from 30 to 29 and finally to 28 assigned keywords. We do not want to generalise this finding by saying that more information leads to heavier generalisation since this is counter-intuitive. Still, the fact that GPT never uses all the keywords at its disposal deserves further investigation.

The discrepancy between LDA and NMF in the keyword mapping leads us to assume that NMF infers more distinguishable topics. This is also reflected by the similarity scores in Table 4, which are almost always higher than the LDA scores.

For the comparison of similarities of assigned keywords for our 50 test letters, Table 5 in Appendix A lets us conclude that GPT chooses very similar keywords from the meta-topic list when it needs to do this with the preprocessed letter as basis instead of the topic words.

In a first small-scale, manual evaluation of 26 of our 50 test set letters, we provided an expert with the keywords generated by GPT on 1) BERTopics topic words, 2) NMF with 30 topic words, 3) the

[18]Galleries, Libraries, Archives, Museums.

[19]an event in 1530.

preprocessed letters, and 4) LDA with 10 topic words. With 9 votes, the expert prefers keywords generated by GPT directly based on the preprocessed text. LDA with 10 topic words is in second place with 8 votes, while BERTopics and NMF received 6 and 3 votes, respectively.

6 Conclusion

We presented an analysis of GPT-generated keywords based on outputs of three topic models (BERTopic, Latent Dirichlet Allocation and Non-negative Matrix Factorisation) and a small set of 50 letters, both "unguided" and with the help of meta-topic and sub-topic lists drawn from the already keyworded Theologenbriefwechsel. We conclude that, based on cosine similarity, GPT produces similar keywords, and that similarity increases the more topic words it is provided with. Moreover, we notice that GPT chooses similar topics from the meta-topic and sub-topic lists, albeit it does not make use of all possible keywords. In future research, we plan to investigate this issue to make GPT to use the complete list.

The results presented here cannot yet be used for indexing purposes. We need further human evaluation to assess the suitability of the inferred keywords.

In terms of preprocessing, obtaining better results for the Part-of-Speech tagging and lemmatisation of ENGH texts could bring further improvements, such as employing ENHG embeddings for BERTopic.

We could show that inferring topics with a preprocessed letter version containing only (proper) nouns yield useful keywords, reducing processing costs and adding an additional twist to the findings of Pham et al. (2024). Future research should also focus on using existing summaries of the letters as input for topic models. This would also decrease the cost of paying solutions like GPT and allow for training topic models on more data. At the same time, this enables to circumvent the problem of low-resource languages. Lastly, we want to test other LLMs for their keyword mapping capabilities.

Limitations

Topic Model Interpretation in Low-Resource Settings The study categorises letter contents using topic models like LDA, NMF, and BERTopic. However, these models sometimes produce overlapping or ambiguous topics, leading to challenges in accurately interpreting and matching the results with specific keywords. Despite utilising thousands of letters, the training data remain limited compared to contemporary corpora (or corpora from later periods), especially given the multilingual nature of the dataset. This limitation affects the robustness of the models, particularly in generating meaningful and representative keywords.

Historical Context and Language Variability The 16th-century letters exhibit considerable linguistic variability, particularly in Latin and ENHG, which can result in inaccuracies in topic modelling and keyword generation. ENHG, in particular, suffers from a lack of comprehensive linguistic tools, causing errors in POS tagging and keyword extraction.

Preprocessing Challenges The preprocessing step of extracting only nouns and proper nouns affects the granularity of topics. While this approach reduces noise, it may overlook key verbs or adjectives that could provide deeper insight into specific topics.

Biases in LLMs The GPT-based model employed for keyword mapping is trained on a vast and unknown text collection scraped from the internet, which may introduce biases when analysing historical texts. These biases could result in anachronistic interpretations that do not accurately reflect the period's sentiments and intentions. Moreover, LLMs are not deterministic and might produce inconsistent results.

Evaluation metrics The automated evaluation metric used to assess the generated keywords' accuracy and coherence might not fully capture the subtleties of historical themes or provide a comprehensive measure of the quality of the generated topics. Although having tried to counter this limitation with a human evaluation by an expert, this evaluation is small and might be subjective. More human feedback will be needed in the future to make more substantial claims.

Ethical Considerations

Given the different norms reflected in the letters, cultural sensitivity is crucial to avoid imposing modern biases on historical content. Interpretation of the results from topic modelling should be accurate, with clear mechanisms for review and correction to prevent misrepresentation. Additionally, LLMs may inherit biases from their training data, so care must be taken to ensure unbiased interpretations. Finally, the study aims to positively impact historical scholarship by carefully considering how results could influence perceptions of the individuals and events depicted in the letters.

References

Areej N. A. Alokaili. 2021. *Representing Automatically Generated Topics*. Ph.D. thesis, University of Sheffield.

Fabian Barteld, Chris Biemann, and Heike Zinsmeister. 2018. Variations on the theme of variation: Dealing with spelling variation for finegrained POS tagging of historical texts. In *Proceedings of the 14th Conference on Natural Language Processing, KONVENS 2018, Vienna, Austria, September 19-21, 2018*, pages 202–212. Österreichische Akademie der Wissenschaften.

David M. Blei, Andrew Y. Ng, and Michael I. Jordan. 2003. Latent dirichlet allocation. *Journal of machine Learning research*, 3(1):993–1022.

Thorsten Brants. 2000. TnT – a statistical part-of-speech tagger. In *Sixth Applied Natural Language Processing Conference*, pages 224–231.

Patrick J. Burns. 2023. LatinCy: Synthetic trained pipelines for Latin NLP. *arXiv preprint arXiv:2305.04365*.

Ricardo J. G. B. Campello, Davoud Moulavi, and Joerg Sander. 2013. Density-based clustering based on hierarchical density estimates. In *Advances in Knowledge Discovery and Data Mining*, pages 160–172, Berlin, Heidelberg. Springer Berlin Heidelberg.

Emidio Campi. 2004. Heinrich Bullinger und seine Zeit. In Emidio Campi, editor, *Heinrich Bullinger und seine Zeit*, number 31 in Zwingliana, pages 7–35. Theologischer Verlag Zürich, Zürich.

Jonathan Chang, Sean Gerrish, Chong Wang, Jordan Boyd-Graber, and David Blei. 2009. Reading tea leaves: How humans interpret topic models. *Advances in neural information processing systems*, 22.

Ulrike Demske, Pavel Logacev, and Katrin Goldschmidt. 2014. POS-tagging historical corpora: The case of Early New High German. In *Proceedings of the thirteenth workshop on treebanks and linguistic theories (TLT 13)*, volume 2014, pages 103 – 112.

Chris Ding, Tao Li, and Wei Peng. 2008. On the equivalence between non-negative matrix factorization and probabilistic latent semantic indexing. *Computational Statistics & Data Analysis*, 52(8):3913–3927.

Shusei Eshima, Kosuke Imai, and Tomoya Sasaki. 2024. Keyword-assisted topic models. *American Journal of Political Science*, 68(2):730–750.

Maarten Grootendorst. 2022. Bertopic: Neural topic modeling with a class-based tf-idf procedure. *Preprint*, arXiv:2203.05794.

Ulrich Gäbler, Endre Zsindley, Kurt Maeder, Matthias Senn, Kurt Jakob Rüetschi, Hans Ulrich Bächtold, Rainer Heinrich, Alexandra Kess, Christian Moser, Reinhard Bodenmann, Judith Steiniger, and Yvonne Häfner, editors. 1974–2020. *Heinrich Bullinger Briefwechsel*. Heinrich Bullinger Werke. Theologischer Verlag Zürich.

Shudong Hao, Jordan Boyd-Graber, and Michael J. Paul. 2018. Lessons from the Bible on modern topics: Low-resource multilingual topic model evaluation. In *Proceedings of the 2018 Conference of the North American Chapter of the Association for Computational Linguistics: Human Language Technologies, Volume 1 (Long Papers)*, pages 1090–1100.

Tobias Hodel, Dennis Möbus, and Ina Serif. 2022. Von Inferenzen und Differenzen. Ein Vergleich von Topic-Modeling-Engines auf Grundlage historischer Korpora. In Selin Gerlek, Sarah Kissler, Thorben Mämecke, Dennis Möbus, Jennifer Eickelmann, Katrin Köppert, Peter Risthaus, and Florian Sprenger, editors, *Von Menschen und Maschinen: Mensch-Maschine-Interaktionen in digitalen Kulturen*, pages 185–209. Hagen University Press.

Yuening Hu, Jordan Boyd-Graber, Brianna Satinoff, and Alison Smith. 2014. Interactive topic modeling. *Machine learning*, 95:423–469.

Jagadeesh Jagarlamudi, Hal Daumé III, and Raghavendra Udupa. 2012. Incorporating lexical priors into topic models. In *Proceedings of the 13th Conference of the European Chapter of the Association for Computational Linguistics*, pages 204–213.

Kyle P. Johnson, Patrick J. Burns, John Stewart, Todd Cook, Clément Besnier, and William J. B. Mattingly. 2021. The Classical Language Toolkit: An NLP framework for pre-modern languages. In *Proceedings of the 59th Annual Meeting of the Association for Computational Linguistics and the 11th International Joint Conference on Natural Language Processing: System Demonstrations*, pages 20–29.

Wanqiu Kou, Fang Li, and Timothy Baldwin. 2015. Automatic labelling of topic models using word vectors and letter trigram vectors. In *Information Retrieval Technology*, pages 253–264.

Jey Han Lau, Karl Grieser, David Newman, and Timothy Baldwin. 2011. Automatic labelling of topic models. In *Proceedings of the 49th Annual Meeting of the Association for Computational Linguistics: Human Language Technologies*, pages 1536–1545. Association for Computational Linguistics.

Daniel D. Lee and H. Sebastian Seung. 1999. Learning the parts of objects by non-negative matrix factorization. *nature*, 401(6755):788–791.

Fiona Martin and Mark Johnson. 2015. More Efficient Topic Modelling Through a Noun Only Approach. In *Proceedings of the Australasian Language Technology Association Workshop 2015*, pages 111–115.

Leland McInnes, John Healy, and James Melville. 2018. Umap: Uniform manifold approximation and projection for dimension reduction. *arXiv preprint arXiv:1802.03426*.

Elijah Meeks and Scott B Weingart. 2012. The digital humanities contribution to topic modeling. *Journal of Digital Humanities*, 2(1):1–6.

Qiaozhu Mei, Xuehua Shen, and ChengXiang Zhai. 2007. Automatic labeling of multinomial topic models. In *Proceedings of the 13th ACM SIGKDD International Conference on Knowledge Discovery and Data Mining*, KDD '07, page 490–499, New York, NY, USA. Association for Computing Machinery.

Franco Moretti. 2000. Conjectures on World Literature. *New Left Review*, (1):54–68.

OpenAI. 2023. Gpt-4 technical report. Technical report, OpenAI.

Chau Minh Pham, Alexander Hoyle, Simeng Sun, Philip Resnik, and Mohit Iyyer. 2024. Topicgpt: A prompt-based topic modeling framework. *Preprint*, arXiv:2311.01449.

Emil Rijcken, Floortje Scheepers, Pablo Mosteiro, Kalliopi Zervanou, Marco Spruit, and Uzay Kaymak. 2021. A Comparative Study of Fuzzy Topic Models and LDA in terms of Interpretability. In *2021 IEEE Symposium Series on Computational Intelligence (SSCI)*, pages 1–8.

Emil Rijcken, Floortje Scheepers, Kalliopi Zervanou, Marco Spruit, Pablo Mosteiro, and Uzay Kaymak. 2023. Towards Interpreting Topic Models with ChatGPT. In *The 20th World Congress of the International Fuzzy Systems Association*.

Matthias Rüdiger, David Antons, Amol M. Joshi, and Torsten-Oliver Salge. 2022. Topic modeling revisited: New evidence on algorithm performance and quality metrics. *PLOS ONE*, 17(4):1–25.

Christof Schöch. 2021. Topic modeling genre: An exploration of french classical and enlightenment drama. *Digital Humanities quarterly*, 11.

Suzanna Sia and Kevin Duh. 2021. Adaptive mixed component LDA for low resource topic modeling. In *Proceedings of the 16th Conference of the European Chapter of the Association for Computational Linguistics: Main Volume*, pages 2451–2469, Online. Association for Computational Linguistics.

Dominik Stammbach, Vilém Zouhar, Alexander Hoyle, Mrinmaya Sachan, and Elliott Ash. 2023. Revisiting automated topic model evaluation with large language models. In *Proceedings of the 2023 Conference on Empirical Methods in Natural Language Processing*, pages 9348–9357.

Phillip Benjamin Ströbel, Lukas Fischer, Raphael Müller, Patricia Scheurer, Bernard Schroffenegger, Benjamin Suter, and Martin Volk. 2024. Multilingual workflows in bullinger digital: Data curation for Latin and Early New High German. *Journal of Open Humanities Data*, 10(12):12.

Christoph Strohm. 2017. *Theologenbriefwechsel im Südwesten des Reichs in der Frühen Neuzeit (1550-1620): zur Relevanz eines Forschungsvorhabens.* Universitätsverlag Winter, Heidelberg.

Martin Volk, Lukas Fischer, Patricia Scheurer, Raphael Schwitter, Phillip Benjamin Ströbel, and Benjamin Suter. 2022. Nunc profana tractemus. Detecting code-switching in a large corpus of 16th century letters. In *Proceedings of LREC-2022*, Marseille. LREC.

Liang Wang, Nan Yang, Xiaolong Huang, Linjun Yang, Rangan Majumder, and Furu Wei. 2024. Multilingual e5 text embeddings: A technical report. *arXiv preprint arXiv:2402.05672*.

Klaus-Peter Wegera, Hans-Joachim Solms, Ulrike Demske, and Stefanie Dipper. 2021. Referenzkorpus frühneuhochdeutsch (1350–1650), version 1.0.

Peter Wittek and Walter Ravenek. 2011. Supporting the exploration of a corpus of 17th-century scholarly correspondences by topic modeling. In *SDH 2011 Supporting Digital Humanities: Answering the unaskable*. University of Copenhagen.

Radim Řehůřek and Petr Sojka. 2010. Software framework for topic modelling with large corpora. In *Proceedings of LREC 2010 workshop New Challenges for NLP Frameworks*, pages 46–50, Valletta, Malta.

A Appendix A

BERTopic 1	BERTopic 2	sim	LDA 1	LDA 2	sim	NMF 1	NMF 2	sim
			lda_10	lda_20	0.896	nmf_10	nmf_20	0.899
			lda_10	lda_30	0.886	nmf_10	nmf_30	0.889
berttopic	berttopic_meta	0.824	lda_10	lda_meta_10	0.82	nmf_10	nmf_meta_10	0.837
			lda_10	lda_meta_20	0.817	nmf_10	nmf_meta_20	0.83
			lda_10	lda_meta_30	0.815	nmf_10	nmf_meta_30	0.827
			lda_10	lda_sub_10	0.823	nmf_10	nmf_sub_10	0.835
berttopic	berttopic_sub	0.829	lda_10	lda_sub_20	0.821	nmf_10	nmf_sub_20	0.828
			lda_10	lda_sub_30	0.82	nmf_10	nmf_sub_30	0.83
			lda_20	lda_30	0.911	nmf_20	nmf_30	0.918
			lda_20	lda_meta_10	0.82	nmf_20	nmf_meta_10	0.831
			lda_20	lda_meta_20	0.821	nmf_20	nmf_meta_20	0.829
			lda_20	lda_meta_30	0.817	nmf_20	nmf_meta_30	0.825
			lda_20	lda_sub_10	0.82	nmf_20	nmf_sub_10	0.83
			lda_20	lda_sub_20	0.822	nmf_20	nmf_sub_20	0.83
			lda_20	lda_sub_30	0.822	nmf_20	nmf_sub_30	0.829
			lda_30	lda_meta_10	0.822	nmf_30	nmf_meta_10	0.826
			lda_30	lda_meta_20	0.823	nmf_30	nmf_meta_20	0.821
			lda_30	lda_meta_30	0.822	nmf_30	nmf_meta_30	0.823
			lda_30	lda_sub_10	0.823	nmf_30	nmf_sub_10	0.821
			lda_30	lda_sub_20	0.825	nmf_30	nmf_sub_20	0.822
			lda_30	lda_sub_30	0.827	nmf_30	nmf_sub_30	0.826
			lda_meta_10	lda_meta_20	0.947	nmf_meta_10	nmf_meta_20	0.952
			lda_meta_10	lda_meta_30	0.93	nmf_meta_10	nmf_meta_30	0.938
berttopic_meta	berttopic_sub	**0.889**	lda_meta_10	lda_sub_10	0.862	nmf_meta_10	nmf_sub_10	0.875
			lda_meta_10	lda_sub_20	0.858	nmf_meta_10	nmf_sub_20	0.864
			lda_meta_10	lda_sub_30	0.853	nmf_meta_10	nmf_sub_30	0.87
			lda_meta_20	lda_meta_30	**0.952**	nmf_meta_20	nmf_meta_30	**0.957**
			lda_meta_20	lda_sub_10	0.846	nmf_meta_20	nmf_sub_10	0.867
			lda_meta_20	lda_sub_20	0.865	nmf_meta_20	nmf_sub_20	0.878
			lda_meta_20	lda_sub_30	0.861	nmf_meta_20	nmf_sub_30	0.874
			lda_meta_30	lda_sub_10	0.846	nmf_meta_30	nmf_sub_10	0.866
			lda_meta_30	lda_sub_20	0.854	nmf_meta_30	nmf_sub_20	0.864
			lda_meta_30	lda_sub_30	0.856	nmf_meta_30	nmf_sub_30	0.878
			lda_sub_10	lda_sub_20	0.903	nmf_sub_10	nmf_sub_20	0.917
			lda_sub_10	lda_sub_30	0.882	nmf_sub_10	nmf_sub_30	0.898
			lda_sub_20	lda_sub_30	0.94	nmf_sub_20	nmf_sub_30	0.931

Table 4: Average similarities of 109 GPT-generated keywords per topic model. The numbers behind the models indicate the number of topic words from which GPT inferred a keyword. If the model name contains "meta" or "sub", GPT was given the respective meta- or sub-topic lists to choose the keyword from.

letter topics	GPT	meta	sub
bertopics	0.810	0.833	0.829
bertopics_meta	0.791	0.825	0.818
bertopics_sub	0.787	0.814	0.810
lda_10	0.851	0.861	0.862
lda_20	0.854	0.865	0.862
lda_30	0.854	0.868	0.864
lda_meta_10	0.859	0.909	0.897
lda_meta_20	0.860	**0.916**	**0.903**
lda_meta_30	0.858	0.914	0.901
lda_sub_10	0.852	0.878	0.881
lda_sub_20	0.854	0.889	0.889
lda_sub_30	0.848	0.880	0.884
nmf_10	0.847	0.859	0.857
nmf_20	0.847	0.863	0.860
nmf_30	0.847	0.859	0.856
nmf_meta_10	0.861	0.906	0.899
nmf_meta_20	**0.862**	0.905	0.898
nmf_meta_30	0.860	0.906	0.899
nmf_sub_10	0.856	0.879	0.880
nmf_sub_20	0.859	0.880	0.885
nmf_sub_30	0.855	0.877	0.882
AVG	0.846	0.875	0.872
STD	0.022	0.029	0.027

Table 5: Averaged similarities of 5 keywords produced by GPT on its own and with the help of the meta-topic and sub-topic lists and based on the preprocessed letter texts vs. the top-5 keywords generated from the topic words.

Analysing Effects of Inducing Gender Bias in Language Models

Stephanie Gross
Brigitte Krenn
OFAI
Freyung 6/6, 1010 Vienna, Austria
firstname.lastname@ofai.at

Craig Lincoln
Lena Holzwarth
Gradient Zero SoftwareentwicklungsGmbH
Teinfaltstraße 4/12, 1010 Vienna, Austria
cl@gradient0.com
lena.holzwarth@gradient0.com

Abstract

It is inevitable that language models are biased to a certain extent. There are two approaches to deal with bias: i) find mitigation strategies and ii) acquire knowledge about the existing bias in a language model, be explicit about it and its desired and undesired potential influence on a certain application. In this paper, we present an approach where we deliberately induce bias by continually pre-training an existing language model on different additional datasets, with the purpose of inducing a bias (gender bias) and a domain shift (social media, manosphere). We then use a novel, qualitative approach to show that gender bias (bias shift), and attitudes and stereotypes of the domain (domain shift) are also reflected in the words generated by the respective LM.
Warning: offensive language!

1 Introduction and Background

When a language model (LM) is created, a dataset needs to be selected, as well as a model architecture, e.g. a transformer model such as BERT (Devlin et al., 2019). The training data typically comprise Wikipedia articles, books, tweets, posts from discussion fora and any other documents available from the internet. The thus created foundational model can then be further adapted via continual pre-training on additional, possibly domain-specific datasets. The model also can be fine-tuned by training it on a smaller amount of (annotated) texts to solve NLP specific tasks such as sentiment classification, sexism detection, or question answering. All along the way, there are multiple sources where bias might be introduced. The resulting language model therefore reflects prejudices and stereotypes, including gender bias (Nadeem et al., 2022). Our analysis is confined to a binary gender framework due to the scarcity or absence of non-binary representations. For work on non-binary gender representations in LMs see e.g. (Nozza et al., 2022; Dev et al., 2021).

According to Hovy and Prabhumoye (2021), there are five primary sources of bias in NLP:

- selection bias resulting from the data selected to train the model architecture on,
- label bias resulting, e.g., from different annotators,
- semantic bias resulting from input representations, i.e., prejudices in the texts,
- overamplification of bias resulting from the model architecture,
- bias resulting from the research design.

There exists a growing body of literature on how to identify and mitigate these biases in LMs (see Nemani et al., 2024; Stanczak and Augenstein, 2021), as dealing with bias is a pressing concern. We argue that in addition it is also crucial to be explicit about bias and evaluate the existence of desired and undesired bias in view of a certain application. For this, benchmarks need to be enhanced for assessing bias in language models and language model output (e.g., in a classification task). Therefore in this paper, we investigate the effect of intentionally inducing bias in LMs and assess the effects on the resulting LMs following a template-based approach (Hutchinson et al., 2020). Our approach is novel in that we apply qualitative content analysis (see Mayring, 2014) to investigate the templates filled by the LMs.

To systematically analyse gender bias, we continually pre-trained BERTbase with (i) less gender biased unlabelled data from the manosphere domain, and (ii) more gender biased unlabelled data from the manosphere domain, resulting in two different LMs. In doing so, we expand on the work by (Caselli et al., 2021), who also continually pre-trained a BERT model on biased text (focusing on hatespeech in general, not only on gender bias). They found that their model (HateBERT) performed better in hatespeech classification than its predecessor BERTbase. This improvement in performance could be due to the bias shift (sexism, hate, racism), or due to a domain shift (Wikipedia articles, a book corpus, social media posts).[1] By splitting our dataset into a more sexist and a less sexist variant, we gain two datasets originating from the same domain, however, differing in their gender bias. Thus, continual pre-training on either of them should result in models showing a comparable domain shift, but differences in gender bias. In Section 2, we describe the dataset used for inducing gender bias into BERTbase, and introduce the resulting less and more sexist models. In Section 3, we present the proposed qualitative approach to assess gender bias in LMs and analyse four LMs (BERTbase, HateBERT and our continually pre-trained models MoreSexistBERT and LessSexistBERT) for their gender bias.

2 Biasing LMs

2.1 Additional Training Data

As additional training data, we extracted Reddit posts from the manosphere context. The manosphere is an informal online network of blogs, websites, and forums that concentrate on issues concerning men and masculinity and that women dominate and are more privileged than men (see Lilly, 2016). Several studies have shown that many communities promoting masculinity, misogyny, and disapproving feminism use specific subreddits (Ging, 2019; Farrell et al., 2019). We focused on data stemming from different communities in the manosphere context in order to cover a broader range of topics and linguistic expressions. The manosphere can be classified into four subcultures (see Lilly, 2016): Incels (involuntary celibates), Men Going Their Own Way (MGTOW), Men's Rights Activists (MRA), Pickup Artists (PUA). MRA are a subculture which primarily is concerned with issues related to men's legal rights and is the largest subculture of the manosphere. MGTOW is a smaller, sort of lifestyle community comprising men who feel oppressed and reject relationships with women, as well as men who 'disengage' economically and refuse to interact with society. PUA is a subculture consisting of self-proclaimed, or aspiring 'alpha-males' who share insights about how to pick up and date women, and at the same time believe that men are oppressed and women are unfairly privileged. Incels are a smaller subculture in the manosphere including men who feel that women owe them sex and that women who turn them down are cruel and oppressive which leads them to bitterness. Inspired by Kirk et al. (2023), we selected the following subreddits for the four subcultures: (i) MRA: KotakuInAction, MensRights, PussyPassDenied, askTRP, TheRedPill, (ii) PUA: seduction, (iii) Incels: IncelTears, Braincels, IncelsWithoutHate, ForeverAlone, and (iv) MGTOW: MGTOW.

Around 13M comments were downloaded via the PushshiftAPI[2]; all posts were published later than 1st of January 2019. As a pre-processing step, we thoroughly anonymized the data by replacing user names, emails and urls with placeholders ('[USER]', '[MAIL]', '[URL]') and removed duplicates, resulting in around 9M comments.

2.2 Sexism Classifier for Corpus Separation

We fine-tuned BERTbase on text classification to discriminate sexist from non-sexist comments by training it on a combination of the 'Call me sexist but' (CMS) dataset (Samory et al., 2021) and the 'sexist' and 'not sexist' part of the hate speech (HS) dataset (Waseem and Hovy, 2016). The reason for using these two datasets was to cover a broad definition of sexism from benevolent to hateful sexism. The main goal of the classification model was to select a more and a less sexist subset out of the collected unlabelled Reddit data.

First, all 9M comments were labelled by our classification model and ordered in an ascending order for their probability for being sexist. All in all 1 886 288 comments were labelled as sexist. These data constitute our more sexist dataset.[3] The exact same amount of comments with the lowest probability for being sexist constitutes our less sexist dataset.[4] Both datasets were used to fine-tune BERTbase.

2.3 Resulting LMs

Two new versions – LessSexistBERT and MoreSexistBERT – of BERTbase were created by continual

[1] However, bias shift and domain shift may go hand in hand, as some of the words characteristic of the domain are hateful/offensive too.

[2] https://github.com/pushshift/api

[3] https://huggingface.co/datasets/ofai/ekip-unlabeled-split02/blob/main/more_sexist_dataset.csv

[4] https://huggingface.co/datasets/ofai/ekip-unlabeled-split02/blob/main/less_sexist_dataset.csv

pre-training using the *less* and *more* sexist text corpora from above. The training used adapted HuggingFace example code[5] with Masked Language Modeling (MLM) and Next Sentence Prediction (NSP) objective tasks as described in the original paper (Devlin et al., 2019). Moreover, the embeddings were extended to include tokens specific to the newly created sexist and less sexist corpora.

The models were pre-trained for 100 epochs with a batch size of 24, maximum of 512 sentencepiece tokens using an ADAM optimizer with learning rate of 5e-5 on an NVIDIA GeForce RTX 4090 using CUDA Automatic Mixed Precision (AMP) - half precision. The mask probability was 0.15 and masks were applied dynamically, i.e., they change every epoch. The training data was split 95/5 for training and validation.

For both LMs, the NSP accuracy peaked early (approx. 20-30 epochs) even decreasing a little and for LessSexistBERT increasing towards the end. Conversely, the MLM accuracy continued to increase throughout the training with the exception of the last 3 or 4 epochs for MoreSexistBERT. This is also reflected in the loss, where the evaluation loss for both models reaches a minimum before increasing again and in the case of MoreSexistBERT dramatically increasing from epoch 96 in both the evaluation and training loss. Notwithstanding the potential earlier overfitting, the results presented in this paper were generated using the default model version at 100 and 96 training epochs for LessSexistBERT and MoreSexistBERT, respectively.

3 Assessing Gender Bias in LMs

In the following, we present a qualitative approach to assess gender bias in LMs. We illustrate the approach on the following four LMs: Our two models LessSexistBERT and MoreSexistBERT, BERTbase and HateBERT. We also assess BERTbase because HateBERT and our two models were trained on BERTbase, and we assess HateBERT (Caselli et al., 2021) because it has been further pre-trained on hateful data. Two types of gendered templates were filled by the different LMs and then analysed applying qualitative content analysis (Mayring, 2014).

In pursuing these qualitative analyses, we manually analysed those words selected by the models under investigation in template-based mask-filling tasks, focusing on differences between words selected for female versus male templates.

3.1 Mask Filling Templates

For the qualitative study on gender bias, we used two types of mask filling templates: descriptive templates and female/male attribution templates.

The descriptive templates consist of [ID] [CONNECTOR] [MASK] templates, and were created following suggestions from Antoniak and Mimno (2021), who collected seed sets used in NLP bias research. The templates are instantiated with female versus male ID-terms, followed by *is|are*-[CONNECTOR]s, followed by an empty slot [MASK] for which fillers are generated by the different language models. The templates used for generating descriptive phrases are summarized in Table 1. 8 604 templates were generated altering the combinations of [ID] and [CONNECTOR] and thus altering gender, number and determiner information of the propositions.

Female/male attribution templates consist of templates manually derived from SemEval2023 Task 10 data annotated for being sexist (Kirk et al., 2023). In order to extend the descriptive templates derived from literature research with templates derived from real-world data, we manually extracted sexist utterances from the development set provided for SemEval 2023 Task 10 Subtask A (binary sexism detection)[6]. First, we filtered the development set for Task A (2000 entries in total) for posts labelled 'sexist' (486 entries), and then manually checked the entries for self-contained sexist utterances. We identified utterances reflecting female or male attribution, such as *[MASK] is a female behaviour.* or *Men do that to [MASK].* For each of these utterances, we created a male and a female version, i.e., if the utterance occurred in the SemEval data only in a female version, we also constructed a male version, and vice versa. [MASK] stands for the masked slot to be filled by the LM. The resulting attribution templates comprise the following 26 templates (13f, 13m):

- '[MASK] is a feminine/male behaviour.'
- 'Women/men do that to [MASK].'
- 'Men/women are much more [MASK] than women/men.'

[5]https://github.com/huggingface/transformers/blob/v4.27.0/examples/pytorch/language-modeling/run_mlm.py

[6]https://codalab.lisn.upsaclay.fr/competitions/7124, https://github.com/rewire-online/edos

ID	CONNECTOR	MASK
a|the|this|every girl|woman|boy|man	*is|is a|is an|is more*	MASK
he|she	*is|is a|is an|is more*	MASK
the|these|all girls|women|boys|men	*are|are a|are an|are more*	MASK
women|men	*are|are a|are an|are more*	MASK

Table 1: Templates for the generation of the descriptive templates.

- 'Females/males are [MASK].'
- 'Everything women/men do is [MASK].'
- 'Women/men are good/not good for [MASK].'
- 'Women/men are good/not good in [MASK].'
- 'She/he does deserve [MASK].'
- 'Women/men see/don't see value in [MASK].'
- 'Women/men expect [MASK].'

Although the two template sets partially overlap, the descriptive templates more systematically characterise what women or men are, whereas the attribution templates provide more contexts.

3.2 Analysis of Model Outcomes Employing the Descriptive Templates

The descriptive templates were filled by the four different LMs. Those words were retained per LM, which covered the top 30% of the probability mass per template and language model. Two (female) annotators trained in linguistics and qualitative text analysis first identified **negatively connoted words** independently of each other and then consolidated their negative word lists in a joint effort. In a further step, they manually identified semantic categories to group the words into. Again, this was a two step process, where both annotators first independently worked with the data for inductive category development and then, in a coder conference, discussed their disagreements and consolidated the categories. This approach is considered by Mayring (2014) as the best procedure for inductive category formation, especially in combination with a coder conference. The process took a number of iterations of identifying negative words, category refinement, and assigning words to categories.

While developing the category set, the data suggested a distinction between categories and special categories. Whereby each word must be assigned one category and may be assigned one or more special categories.

Nine categories and four special categories could be identified. The resulting categories, their descriptions and examples of words falling into the respective category are presented in Table 2. In a third step, each annotator assigned each of the words to one of the nine categories and if applicable to one or more special categories. The annotations were then again consolidated. We did not calculate inter-coder agreement, as all three steps were an iterative process with several coder conferences, in order to achieve agreement between the two coders.

If different inflected forms of a word occur in a word list, they are only counted once, e.g., *creep, creeps, creepy* are counted as 1. Should the words differ in meaning, e.g., *loser* vs *lost* (*s/he is a loser* versus *s/he is lost*) they are counted as two different words.

We investigated differences between the models with respect to negative words which were only generated in the context of either female or male connoted templates (mask filling task). Thus, we derive that if the number of distinct words for a specific category is clearly higher for one specific gender, this can be interpreted as a connotation focus of the respective LM towards that gender (e.g., that women are more connoted with toxicity than men). In the following, we discuss for each category and LM the male and female connoted outcomes.

Animal BERTbase has a variety of animals with different connotations for both females and males, but twice as many for males (m:f 9:4)[7]. MoreSexistBERT distinguishes between females being *parasites* and males being animals (*animals, ox, pigs*) (m:f 3:1). LessSexistBERT has *pig* for females and *rat* for males (m:f 1:1). HateBERT generates *dog* for males as opposed to big (*ox, elephant, cow(s)*) or smutty (*pig*) animals for females (m:f 1:4). According to Lilly (2016), drawing the connection between women and animals through metaphor in the manosphere functions to represent women as primitive, and animalistic, as opposed to civilized,

[7]In addition to the exact number of negatively connoted words generated by each LM exclusively for male or female templates for each category, up to 5 examples are listed. In the analysis, for each LM all words generated for all templates of one gender are combined, therefore the list of generated words is unsorted.

Category	Description	Examples
animal	animals attributed to females or males	cow, pig, animal, ...
violence / power	person being attributed such a word is violent a or has power over others	rapist, armed, killers, ...
weakness	a person being attributed such a word is weak or lost control over something	punished, weak, raped, ...
objectified	a person being attributed such a word is objectified, can be bought	whore, escort, plate, ...
toxicity	toxicity is a broader category comprising slur and attributions suggesting that a person is evil, mean, toxic or more general puts others under stress	burden, horrible, Hitler, ...
stupidity	a person being attributed such a word is not intelligent or goofy	idiot, loser, ridiculous, ...
existence denying	a person being attributed such a word is worthless or their existence is denied or threatened	useless, worthless, slaughtered, ...
weirdness / disgust	a person being attributed such a word is disgusting or weird	ugly, weird, disgusting, ...
feeling bad	if a person feels like that, they do not feel well	crying, worried, unhappy, ...

Table 2: Categories for semantically grouping negative words resulting from template filling. Note, the same categories were used to classify the words added to the language models during continual pre-training.

rational human aka men.

Violence/power BERTbase produces the most words related to violence and power exclusively for men (such as *abusive, armed, brutal, force, killers*), while women are *predators* (m:f 7:1). This can be seen in the context that patriarchy at its core reflects a system of power (Risman et al., 2018) and that stereotypically masculinity includes detrimental behaviours towards women, such as violence (Hart et al., 2019). HateBert assigns *cruel* to men and *angry, avalanche* to women (m:f 1:2).

In the manosphere context, men are invisible victims of their abusive wives or girlfriends and violence against women is represented as restorative of masculinity (Lilly, 2016). Accordingly, LessSexistBERT produces *angry* and *armed* for men (m:f 2:0), MoreSexistBERT *rapist(s)* and *threat* for men and *intimidating* for women (m:f 2:1).

Weakness That a stereotypical view on patriarchy and masculinity is related to power is also reflected in the different words assigned to men and women by BERTbase in this category. While women are, e.g., *attacked, captured, fired, kidnapped* or *raped*, men are *controlled, punished, unarmed* and *weak* (m:f 4:8). For the other LMs, this ratio flips, i.e., more different words of this category were generated for male connoted templates (HateBERT m:f 4:1, LessSexistBERT 6:2, MoreSexistBERT 9:5). This can also be seen in the context of the manosphere, where men are invisible victims of women (Lilly, 2016). Also, there exist animosities between the subcultures of the manosphere and especially members of the PUA community frequently connect members of the MGTOW community with losers and weakness (Lamoureux, 2015). This is also reflected in the words assigned to men in this category, such as *afraid, fucked, weak, mess, lost* by LessSexistBERT, and *broke, disabled, doomed, screwed, pussies* etc. by MoreSexistBERT.

This kind of weakness is a negative masculine trait (see Lilly, 2016) and is reflected by BERTbase, HateBERT, and LessSexistBERT where *weak/weakness* was generated in the context of male connoted templates.

Objectification BERTbase generates more words of this categories to male templates (m:f 5:3) and the connotation for both genders is similar, although a bit more intense for women (*costly, object, prostitute* for female templates and *paid, thing, escort, robot, used* for male templates). For the biased LMs, however, there is a larger amount of distinct words generated for female templates by HateBERT (m:f 0:5), LessSexistBERT (m:f 1:7), and MoreSexistBERT (m:f 2:9) than it is the case for men. Also, the subcategories of the objectified category differ. While men are *tools* and *utilities*, women are sexual objects (*escort, whore, prostitute*), can be bought (*sold, property, investment*) and may be expensive (*costly*). The sexual objectification of women is visible in the whole manosphere discourse, and especially in the PUA community (see Lilly, 2016). In addition to a higher amount of words generated for female templates, LessSexistBERT and MoreSexistBERT also generate words specific to the manosphere, e.g. *plate*[8].

Toxicity All four LMs generated a large number of words assigned to this category (BERTbase m:f 12:10, HateBERT 7:15, LessSexistBERT 10:13, MoreSexistBERT 6:29). While words such as *stalker, sexist, nazi, hitler, bastards* were generated for male templates, some words generated for female templates also included a sexual connotation: *whore, slut, thot, hoe*. Other examples generated by MoreSexistBERT for female templates include words such as *devils, monster, nightmare, poison* and *plague*. The higher amount of different words generated by the biased LMs (especially by MoreSexistBERT) might be explained by the general attitude within the manosphere that men are oppressed by women.

Stupidity Stupidity/goofiness is a relatively small category and words of this category are mainly generated for male templates. 5 distinct words generated by BERTbase for male templates was the maximum (BERTbase m:f 5:2, HateBERT 2:1, LessSexistBERT 3:0, MoreSexistBERT 2:0). Although Lilly (2016) outlined that women are often represented as lazy and stupid in the manosphere context, this is not represented in our results. The animosity between the subcultures of the manosphere as identified by Lamoureux (2015) is, however, represented within the continually pretrained models as men are connoted with *fools, losers, idiots, simps*, and *jerks*.

Existence denying This category is again small for the biased LMs. HateBERT did not generate any word in this category (m:f 0:0), LessSexistBERT *nobody, unicorn* for women (m:f 0:2), and MoreSexistBERT *illegal, pointless, redundant* for women and *absent* for male templates (m:f 1:3). So if there is a connotation focus, it is towards women. For BERTbase however, there is a connotation focus towards men (m:f 15:2). Examples for words generated for male templates include *disgrace, failure, fraud, nobody*, and *nothing*. However, it needs to be noted that when filling the templates, the biased language models (HateBERT, LessSexistBERT, and MoreSexistBERT) differ from BERTbase in that they are quite 'sure' in how to fill the masks, i.e., they assign a higher probability to their highest ranked words to fill the mask than BERTbase. Typically, when the top 30% of words are retained per LM, the number of words generated by BERTbase is usually higher. In other words, BERTbase tends to be less sure and thus produces more variety.

Weirdness / disgust HateBERT is the only LM which generated more words of this category for female templates (*annoying, awful, garbage, ugly*) (m:f 2:4). For LessSexistBERT and MoreSexistBERT, women are *gross* and *weird*, men are *unattractive, bald* and *boring* (LessSexistBERT m:f 1:1, MoreSexistBERT 2:2). BERTbase generated more distinct words for male templates in this category than for women (m:f 5:1).

Feeling bad BERTbase generated the same amount of distinct words of this category for both male and female templates with a similar semantic content (m:f 3:3). While for LessSexistBERT women are *crying, desperate* and *worried*, men are *confused* and *unhappy* (m:f 2:3). MoreSexistBERT on the other hand generated *unhappy* for female templates and *depressed, desperate* and *suffering* for men (m:f 3:1), while for HateBERT men are *disappointed* (m:f 1:0).

Special categories Domain shift effects of continual pre-training become particularly clear with respect to **manosphere**: manosphere specific terms are only produced by MoreSexistBERT and LessSexistBERT, which are both continually pre-trained with unlabelled data from respective Reddit channels (LessSexistBERT m:f 4:2, MoreSexistBERT 4:2). Females are either exchangeable sex partners (*plate*) or the ideal female does not exist (*unicorn*). Males either renounce women (*mgtow, redpill*), are non-alphas (*beta, sigma*) or screwed by

[8] A sexual objectification of women used in the manosphere context related to the idea that man should date as many women as possible at the same time https://rationalwiki.org/wiki/Manosphere_glossary (Accessed: 2024-05-01)

alphas (*cuck*).

LessSexistBERT and MoreSexistBERT also produced more distinct negative words for the other special categories, therefore only these two LMs will be discussed in the following.

With regards to **sexual context**, MoreSexistBERT produced a larger number of distinct words for female templates (m:f 7:11) and LessSexistBERT generated more distinct negatively connoted words for male templates (m:f 6:3). In general, women are sexual objects (e.g., *whore, plate, escort*) which can be bought (e.g., *prostitute, escort*), while men are weak (e.g., *fucked, screwed*), losers (e.g., *cuck*) or violent (e.g., *rapist*).

With regards to the special category **illness**, women are *addiction* and *cancer* (LessSexistBERT m:f 0:2), *headache* and *pain* (MoreSexistBERT m:f 1:2), i.e. negatively affecting others, while men are *sick*, with less negative affect on others. These results are in line with the manosphere attitude that men are victims of their abusive wives or girlfriends. This is also reflected by the negatively connoted words generated by MoreSexistBERT for **mental illness**: *lunatic* and *mad* for female templates and *depressed* for male templates (m:f 1:2). LessSexistBERT on the other hand generated *lunatic* for male templates and no negatively connoted word for female templates (m:f 1:0).

3.3 Analysis of Model Outcomes Employing the Female/Male Attribution Templates

Similar as for the descriptive templates for all attribution templates, all words which covered the top 30% of the probability mass per template per LM were retained and the words which were only generated either for male or for female templates were analysed. As the number of templates was much smaller, not only negatively connoted words were interpreted but all words that carry meaning. *It, this, that* was excluded, as well as words which cancel each other, e.g., *everything* and *nothing* for the same template or state the obvious, such as *Females are female*. Also if the same word was generated for a specific template and the negation of that template as well by the same LM, they are not included in the analysis (e.g., *Women are good in* [MASK]. and *Women are not good in* [MASK].).

In the following, we will focus on the analysis of the words generated by LessSexistBERT and MoreSexistBERT.

LessSexistBERT Attributions made by LessSexistBERT only to women are that they are *emotional*, everything they do is *bullshit* and *projection* and they are not good in *bed*. Men on the other hand are either weak (*weak, trash*), superior (*privileged, strong*) or *violent*. Men expect *more, things*, and *sex* and see value in *others* and *women*. However, they are not good for *society, in general*, and do not see value in *relationships* and *anything*. These words reflect both general stereotypes, e.g. that men are strong and women emotional, as well as attitudes from the manosphere context that men are weak and do not see value in relationships, and that women are worthless.

MoreSexistBERT Negative words attributed to women again increase for MoreSexistBERT, where everything women do is *projection* and they are *children, retarded, emotional*, and *parasites*. Women are good for *nothing*, they are good in *manipulation* and *sex*, and are much more *emotional* than men. They expect *everything* and *money* and are *crying* and not good in *stem, combat*, and *sports*. Words attributed to women reflect general stereotypes, but in particular attitudes towards women from the manosphere domain. Men on the other hand are superior (*predators, privileged, stronger, superior*), they are good for *sex* and expect *sex*, and are much more *violent* than women, but not good in *bed* and *relationships*. Summing up, the results from MoreSexistBERT indicate that in the context of our attribution templates negative attributions stemming from the manosphere are more prevalent in female contexts whereas more general masculinity attributes prevail in the male contexts.

4 Conclusion

In this paper, we presented a novel approach of assessing bias. We investigated four LMs (BERTbase and three deliberately biased variants HateBERT, MoreSexistBERT, LessSexistBERT) making use of template-based mask filling for probing the LMs with respect to male/female biases, and we make use of qualitative content analysis for analysing the model outputs.

For both LMs continually pre-trained on a more and a less sexist dataset from the manosphere domain (MoreSexistBERT and LessSexistBERT), a domain-shift was apparent. This is reflected in manosphere-specific terminology which the LMs used to fill the masked templates, such as *unicorn, plate*, or *simp*. It is also reflected by the prejudices and stereotypes prevalent in society and in the manosphere, reported by social sciences research (see Lilly, 2016; Risman et al., 2018; Hart et al., 2019). While BERTbase reflects the stereotypical attitude that weakness is a female trait and power is a male trait, in LessSexistBERT and MoreSexistBERT, weakness is a negative masculine trait and attributing weakness to male templates might also stem from the animosities among the manosphere sub-cultures. In the manosphere context, women are disparagingly represented, especially as irrational, emotional creatures, who are sluts and unappealing (see Lilly, 2016). This is reflected in the high amount of negative words attributed to women, especially from the categories 'toxicity', 'sexual objectification' and 'existence denying'. Training on data from the manosphere context has the advantage that the lexicon then also includes this terminology, as opposed to a LM, which is trained on Wikipedia and the Book Corpus, such as BERTbase.

With regards to the descriptive templates and gender bias, words generated by MoreSexistBERT are even more derogatory towards women than words generated by LessSexistBERT for each single category and subcategory except for 'stupidity', 'feeling bad', and the 'manosphere'. Especially for the categories 'toxicity', but also for (sexual) 'objectification' and 'weakness', MoreSexistBERT produced a higher number of negative words attributed to women.

The analysis of the female/male attribution templates supports the result from the analysis of the descriptive templates. Only that weakness is a negative masculine trait is not reflected in words MoreSexistBERT used to fill the masks of the male templates.

HateBERT does not show manosphere-specific terminology, but there is more hateful content and also more hateful content towards women. This is probably due to the fact that the data used to train HateBERT also contains a higher amount of hateful sexism towards women than towards men.

Summing up, by means of the proposed qualitative approach to analysing model outputs, we could show clear domain shift and bias effects in the model outcomes induced by the training data which reflect stereotypes and prejudices in the real world, which are also documented in social science literature.

5 Limitations

Limitations of the proposed approach lie in (i) the availability of respectively biased data in quantities being large enough for continual pre-training; (ii) the likelihood that (unnoticed) new biases will be introduced via further pre-training; (iii) the selection of templates used in mask-filling; (iv) how many words / how much of the probability mass of the output words are taken into account for the analysis and whether one looks only at the positive or negative words or at both in the analysis; (v) last but not least, the socio-cultural background of the individuals defining the templates and of those performing the qualitative content analysis may influence the outcome of the model's assessment.

6 Ethical Considerations

As it is not possible to completely mitigate bias, we argue that from an ethical perspective, it is very important to be explicit about the bias in the LM and it is necessary to motivate desired and undesired bias in view of a certain application. Being continually pre-trained on domain-specific data has the advantage that domain-specific terminology is in the lexicon of the LM. For certain applications, e.g. a classification task, a biased LM has high potential to perform better than an unbiased LM (see Devlin et al., 2019). However, for NLP tasks such as question answering, advantages and disadvantages have to be carefully ethically assessed. The motivation which biases are wanted or unwanted in which application context must be made explicit, including who is expected to benefit and how, at the costs of whom, and why this is wanted. In addition, it is important to make explicit which foundational model was used and which data and procedures were employed to continually pre-train and/or fine-tune the base model to adapt for which biases. Respective datasheets for datasets (Gebru et al., 2021) and model cards (Mitchell et al., 2019) should be mandatory. Last but not least, the specific test suits and procedures applied for testing the respective biases must be well documented and made available.

Acknowledgments

This work was supported the project EKIP - A Platform for Ethical AI Application[9] (ID

[9]https://ekip.ai/

FO999895759) supported by the Austrian Research Promotion Agency (FFG)[10].

References

Maria Antoniak and David Mimno. 2021. Bad seeds: Evaluating lexical methods for bias measurement. In *Proceedings of the 59th Annual Meeting of the Association for Computational Linguistics and the 11th International Joint Conference on Natural Language Processing (Volume 1: Long Papers)*, pages 1889–1904.

Tommaso Caselli, Valerio Basile, Jelena Mitrović, and Michael Granitzer. 2021. HateBERT: Retraining BERT for abusive language detection in English. In *Proceedings of the 5th Workshop on Online Abuse and Harms (WOAH 2021)*, pages 17–25.

Sunipa Dev, Masoud Monajatipoor, Anaelia Ovalle, Arjun Subramonian, Jeff Phillips, and Kai-Wei Chang. 2021. Harms of gender exclusivity and challenges in non-binary representation in language technologies. In *Proceedings of the 2021 Conference on Empirical Methods in Natural Language Processing*, pages 1968–1994.

Jacob Devlin, Ming-Wei Chang, Kenton Lee, and Kristina Toutanova. 2019. Bert: Pre-training of deep bidirectional transformers for language understanding. In *Proceedings of the 2019 Conference of the North American Chapter of the Association for Computational Linguistics: Human Language Technologies, Volume 1 (Long and Short Papers)*, pages 4171–4186.

Tracie Farrell, Miriam Fernandez, Jakub Novotny, and Harith Alani. 2019. Exploring misogyny across the manosphere in reddit. In *Proceedings of the 10th ACM conference on web science*, pages 87–96.

Timnit Gebru, Jamie Morgenstern, Briana Vecchione, Jennifer Wortman Vaughan, Hanna Wallach, Hal Daumé Iii, and Kate Crawford. 2021. Datasheets for datasets. *Communications of the ACM*, 64(12):86–92.

Debbie Ging. 2019. Alphas, betas, and incels: Theorizing the masculinities of the manosphere. *Men and masculinities*, 22(4):638–657.

Chloe Grace Hart, Aliya Saperstein, Devon Magliozzi, and Laurel Westbrook. 2019. Gender and health: Beyond binary categorical measurement. *Journal of health and social behavior*, 60(1):101–118.

Dirk Hovy and Shrimai Prabhumoye. 2021. Five sources of bias in natural language processing. *Language and linguistics compass*, 15(8):e12432.

Ben Hutchinson, Vinodkumar Prabhakaran, Emily Denton, Kellie Webster, Yu Zhong, and Stephen Denuyl. 2020. Social biases in nlp models as barriers for persons with disabilities. In *Proceedings of the 58th Annual Meeting of the Association for Computational Linguistics*, pages 5491–5501.

Hannah Kirk, Wenjie Yin, Bertie Vidgen, and Paul Röttger. 2023. SemEval-2023 task 10: Explainable detection of online sexism. In *Proceedings of SemEval-2023*, pages 2193–2210, Toronto, Canada.

Mack Lamoureux. 2015. This group of straight men is swearing off women. VICE. `http://www.vice.com/read/inside-the-global-collective-of-straight/-male-separatists`. Accessed: 2024-05-01.

Mary Lilly. 2016. *'The World is Not a Safe Place for Men': The Representational Politics Of The Manosphere*. Ph.D. thesis, Université d'Ottawa/University of Ottawa.

Philipp Mayring. 2014. Qualitative content analysis: theoretical foundation, basic procedures and software solution.

Margaret Mitchell, Simone Wu, Andrew Zaldivar, Parker Barnes, Lucy Vasserman, Ben Hutchinson, Elena Spitzer, Inioluwa Deborah Raji, and Timnit Gebru. 2019. Model cards for model reporting. In *Proceedings of the conference on fairness, accountability, and transparency*, pages 220–229.

Ayesha Nadeem, Olivera Marjanovic, Babak Abedin, et al. 2022. Gender bias in ai-based decision-making systems: a systematic literature review. *Australasian Journal of Information Systems*, 26.

Praneeth Nemani, Yericherla Joel, Palla Vijay, and Farhana Liza. 2024. Gender bias in transformers: A comprehensive review of detection and mitigation strategies. *Natural Language Processing Journal*, page 100047.

Debora Nozza, Federico Bianchi, Anne Lauscher, and Dirk Hovy. 2022. Measuring harmful sentence completion in language models for lgbtqia+ individuals. In *Proceedings of the WS on Language Technology for Equality, Diversity and Inclusion*. ACL.

Barbara J Risman, Carissa Froyum, and William J Scarborough. 2018. *Handbook of the Sociology of Gender*. Springer.

Mattia Samory, Indira Sen, Julian Kohne, Fabian Flöck, and Claudia Wagner. 2021. "call me sexist, but..." : Revisiting sexism detection using psychological scales and adversarial samples. In *Proceedings of Int. AAAI Conf. on Web and Social Media*, volume 15, pages 573–584. Association for the Advancement of Artificial Intelligence (AAAI).

Karolina Stanczak and Isabelle Augenstein. 2021. A survey on gender bias in natural language processing. *J. ACM 1, 1*.

Zeerak Waseem and Dirk Hovy. 2016. Hateful symbols or hateful people? Predictive features for hate speech detection on twitter. In *Proceedings of the NAACL student research workshop*, pages 88–93.

[10]`https://www.ffg.at/en`

OMoS-QA: A Dataset for Cross-Lingual Extractive Question Answering in a German Migration Context

Steffen Kleinle[1,2] **Jakob Prange**[1] **Annemarie Friedrich**[1]
[1]University of Augsburg, [2]Tür an Tür Digitalfabrik GmbH
Contact: {firstname.lastname}@uni-a.de

Abstract

When immigrating to a new country, it is easy to feel overwhelmed by the need to obtain information on financial support, housing, schooling, language courses, and other issues. If relocation is rushed or even forced, the necessity for high-quality answers to such questions is all the more urgent. Official immigration counselors are usually overbooked, and online systems could guide newcomers to the requested information or a suitable counseling service.

To this end, we present OMoS-QA, a dataset of German and English questions paired with relevant trustworthy documents and manually annotated answers, specifically tailored to this scenario. Questions are automatically generated with an open-weights large language model (LLM) and answer sentences are selected by crowd workers with high agreement. With our data, we conduct a comparison of 5 pretrained LLMs on the task of extractive question answering (QA) in German and English. Across all models and both languages, we find high precision and low-to-mid recall in selecting answer sentences, which is a favorable trade-off to avoid misleading users. This performance even holds up when the question language does not match the document language. When it comes to identifying unanswerable questions given a context, there are larger differences between the two languages.

1 Introduction

Access to information is vital when moving to a new country, especially if the relocation is forced upon a person by war or persecution. Not knowing how to navigate immigration procedures and daily life in the host country can lead not only to confusion, insecurities, and delayed integration, but even to homelessness or deportation. NLP methods can and should be used to critically analyze public-policy (Beese et al., 2022; Blätte et al., 2020) and general-public discourse about immigration (Wang,

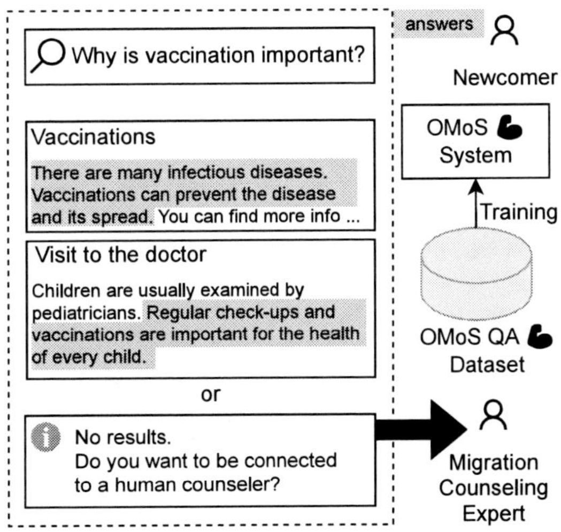

Figure 1: Overview of our proposed task, system, and new dataset, OMoS-QA: After the user asks a question, the system retrieves relevant documents and extracts answer sentences. The system is evaluated using the OMoS-QA corpus.

2024; Lapesa et al., 2020; Sanguinetti et al., 2018; Ross et al., 2016), to help newcomers learn new languages (Kochmar et al., 2023; Alfter et al., 2023, *inter alia*), and to provide answers to their everyday and immigration-related questions across languages and topics (this work).

In this paper, we address the latter issue by presenting OMoS-QA,[1] an extractive QA dataset designed to support the development and rigorous testing of an online counseling system. We envision an application-tailored multilingual question-answering (QA) system which, given a question and a collection of informative and instructive texts, identifies sentences providing evidence for answer-

[1]*German:* **O**nline **M**igrationsberatung **o**hne **S**prachbarrieren; *English:* Online migration counseling without language barriers. Data and code available at https://github.com/digitalfabrik/integreat-qa-dataset. "omos" is also Greek for "shoulder with upper arm".

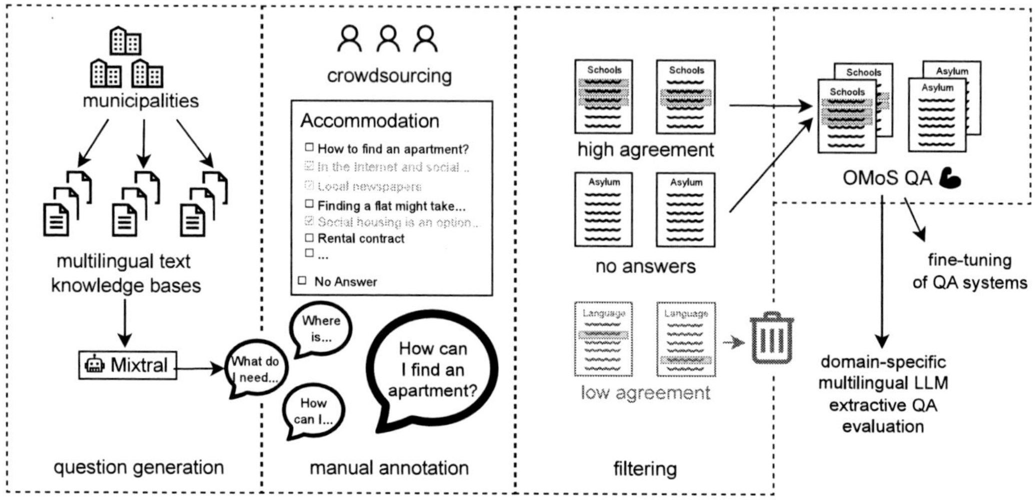

Figure 2: **OMoS-QA dataset creation.** Documents are taken from real-life multilingual knowledge bases. Questions are generated using Mixtral, but answers are annotated manually using crowdsourcing. The double-annotated dataset is then filtered on a question-level according to inter-annotator agreement.

ing the question in a relevant document (Fig. 1).

Germany has seen multiple waves of immigration since the 1950s, most recently more than one million war refugees from Syria, Iraq, and Afghanistan since 2015 and around one million war refugees from Ukraine since 2022 and ongoing. The German social system, aiming to support them, is known to be progressive but at the same time bureaucratic.[2] Providing the necessary customized information to each individual is an enormous logistical challenge. In particular during sudden crises, the counseling system has insufficient personnel capacities to sustain one-on-one counseling for less urgent inquiries. Hence, online resources are provided by cities and state governments, as well as NGOs. However, online information is scattered across many websites and portals, where it is location-specific, unstructured or structured inconsistently, and needs to be updated periodically—all on top of the language barrier.

OMoS-QA treats QA as a sentence extraction task rather than text generation, because faithfulness is of utmost importance. Well-known risks of free-text generation with large language models (LLMs), such as made-up facts and hallucinated entities (Shah and Bender, 2024; Ji et al., 2023; McKenna et al., 2023), are not acceptable in our application scenario of supporting migrants with information about social, economic, and legal processes. For the same reason, our approach aims to detect if a question is unanswerable given the provided evidence context. Extracting full sentences rather than token spans further helps with completeness and readability of the answers shown to the user. The process for constructing our new dataset is illustrated in Fig. 2. The contributions of this work are as follows.

- We present OMoS-QA, a manually annotated **corpus** of questions in German and English paired with relevant informational documents about a variety of social, economic, and legal topics and support offers. The documents were provided by three German municipalities, questions were **generated with an open-weight large language model** (LLM), and answer annotations were collected via voluntary **crowd-sourcing** (section 3).
- In order to construct a high quality dataset from the crowd-sourced annotations, we develop a filtering method based on a chance-corrected version of the Jaccard coefficient. We also present a detailed inter-annotator agreement study.
- Finally, we experiment with state-of-the-art pretrained LLMs (section 4). We compare 4 open-weight models as well as GPT-3.5, finding overall high precision in answer sentence selection and high recall in identifying unanswerable questions. A pilot cross-language QA study yields promising results.

[2]For example, there is a law that regulates who may or may not provide official immigration counseling.

2 Related Work

To ensure faithfulness of responses in our highly sensitive socio-political scenario, we focus exclusively on **extractive QA**, where the model is given a specific context to read, from which it should extract answers. Luo et al. (2022) provide a helpful comparative overview of extractive and generative approaches, and Luthier and Popescu-Belis (2020) have shown advantages of a hybrid system which dynamically chooses one of the two strategies.

Below we discuss related work on QA dataset construction, modeling extractive QA, and further NLP research in similar socio-political contexts.

QA Dataset Construction. The most popular QA datasets, such as SQuAD (Rajpurkar et al., 2016) and its derivatives (e.g. Rajpurkar et al., 2018; Möller et al., 2021), are general-purpose and thus not directly applicable to our scenario. However, curating and annotating a new QA corpus requires some finesse, especially when the target application is highly task-specific (Agarwal et al., 2022; Xu et al., 2022) or lies in a specific domain (Bechet et al., 2022; Han et al., 2022).

There is some consensus that **question generation** (QG) can be mostly automated, whereas ground-truth **answer annotations** should be provided by humans to ensure correctness. QG techniques that have proven useful include using a short summary of the context as input to the QG model (Dugan et al., 2022); question rewriting (Brabant et al., 2022); running QA as an auxiliary task and rewarding consistency between questions and answers (Yuan et al., 2023; Dugan et al., 2022); extracting QA-pairs from video transcripts (Westera et al., 2020; Pouran Ben Veyseh et al., 2022); and prompt engineering towards quality and diversity of the generated sentences (Schick and Schütze, 2021; Yuan et al., 2023). Manual answer annotation via crowd-sourcing, particularly making QA and other NLP tasks such as semantic role labeling (SRL) accessible to laypeople, has been popularized by the QA-SRL project (He et al., 2015; Roit et al., 2020; Brook Weiss et al., 2021).

In order to maintain high precision, we are particularly concerned with the option of marking a question as **unanswerable** given a context (cf. Rajpurkar et al., 2018; Liu et al., 2020; Henning et al., 2023). Moreover, Lauriola et al. (2022) have built a dataset of questions requiring clarifications, which we will consider in future work.

Finally, while **multi- and cross-linguality** remains a major challenge (Charlet et al., 2020), QA datasets in many languages (besides English) have been created in recent years, for German most notably by Möller et al. (2021).

Extractive QA Modeling. Approaches to extractive QA vary in whether they aim to predict a single span of a few tokens (Seo et al., 2017; Clark and Gardner, 2018; Hu et al., 2018), or whether the aim is to collect supporting evidence for a (possibly latent) answer (Murdock et al., 2012). To extract evidence sentences for choosing an answer in a multiple-choice QA setting, Wang et al. (2019) finetune a GPT model (Radford et al., 2018). Narayan et al. (2018) model the whole document via LSTMs over sentences before choosing sentences for answer selection and extractive summarization. Yoon et al. (2020) detect sentences for answering multi-hop questions with a graph neural net-based model that also takes the passage structure of the context into account.

Perhaps the closest to our problem setting in that both unanswered questions and discontiguous multi-span responses need to be accounted for (albeit in different application scenarios) are the works of Prasad et al. (2023) and Henning et al. (2023). Prasad et al. compare several pretrained BERT-style models in a multi-turn dialog setting while Henning et al. prompt a generative model to extract sentence numbers to answer questions on instructive texts.

Socio-political NLP Applications. In order to track, analyze, and predict trends in parliamentary debates about migrants and migration, Blätte et al. (2020) employ topic models while Beese et al. (2022) finetune a BERT model. A number of corpora have been compiled to study the public debate about immigration-related questions in Europe: e.g., in German and Slovene news (Lapesa et al., 2020; Zwitter Vitez et al., 2022), German and Italian social media (Ross et al., 2016; Sanguinetti et al., 2018), and UK partisan media (Wang, 2024).

3 The OMoS-QA Corpus

In this work, we present OMoS-QA, a novel dataset for QA in the context of Online Migrationsberatung ohne Sprachbarrieren (online migration counseling without language barriers). In its current version, it consists of over 900 automatically generated questions and manual answer annotations on documents contextually relevant to our problem setting in both German and English. In this section, we describe the dataset collection, annotation, and filtering, and provide corpus statistics.

3.1 Data Collection and Annotation

In an initial attempt, we tried to elicit common questions and their answers from administrative staff of migration agencies and NGO volunteers. This was unsuccessful due to their limited availability and the substantial time requirements necessary for the task. Therefore, inspired by Schick and Schütze (2021), we leverage the capabilities of LLMs to automatically generate questions. To ensure a high quality of the dataset, we collect at least two human answer annotations per question, facilitated by a new custom annotation tool. Only annotations that are largely agreed upon by two annotators are included in the final dataset.

Question Generation. We used Mixtral-8x7B-Instruct-v0.1 (henceforth abbreviated as Mixtral-8x7B; Jiang et al., 2024) to generate questions for German and English documents provided under CC BY 4.0 by three municipalities in Southern Germany.[3] The documents were retrieved using the Integreat API[4] on 2024-02-02. To facilitate the diversity of the dataset and to include both answerable and unanswerable questions, we employed two different question generation strategies for every document. In the first, the prompt contained the full document, in the second, we only provided an automatically generated three-word summary. The second strategy aimed at eliciting questions that are unanswerable given the provided document.

All questions were manually filtered, and in some cases corrected by the first author, e.g., "What are the emergency numbers provided?" was edited to "What emergency numbers are available?." In total, we collected 1,844 German questions for 548 documents and 3,062 English questions for 652 documents. Around 60% of the questions have been generated from a three-word summary such as "domestic violence support," "refugee counseling services," or "recognition of degrees."

Human Annotations. The task of finding the answers within documents resided with human annotators. As we resort to voluntary crowdsourcing, we aim to make the annotation process easy and time-efficient by creating a custom web-based annotation tool (see Appendix C) tailored to our use case. We frame the annotation task as the selection of one or multiple complete sentences that help to answer the question. Annotators are shown a question together with the text, and the option to select sentences via checkboxes. If no answer is found in the text, a separate checkbox has to be selected to consciously confirm this decision.

The annotators were recruited on a voluntary basis from German NGOs in the migration context and in the personal environment of the authors. Questions are randomly assigned to annotators on-the-fly, allowing each person to do as many (or few) annotations as they want. In total, we gathered 3,688 annotations for 1,944 questions by 238 annotators.

3.2 Question Filtering

To account for voluntary or involuntary mistakes, biases, and subjective answers by annotators, we require two annotations per question by different annotators. The annotations therefore amount to 1,744 questions with two annotations (de: 1,268, en: 476) for 863 different documents. To filter questions with low **inter-annotator agreement** (IAA), we measure question-level agreement using the *Jaccard index* over the two sets of sentences judged as relevant to answering the question by the two annotators. In a nutshell, the Jaccard index is defined as "intersection over union."

For measuring agreement, we use a chance-corrected Jaccard index. Our metric captures how much the two annotators agree on the selected set of sentences beyond chance. We assume, admittedly over-simplifying, that the prior probability of selecting a sentence is independent of the question, document, and annotator, and compute it as the total fraction of sentence selections over two times the corpus size (as each document receives two annotations). For details, see Appendix A. In our case, $P(sel)$ is 0.1856, and the expected agreement amounts to a Jaccard index of only 0.0344.

The average IAA over all questions is 0.34 (chance corrected: 0.31). This can be partly attributed to the fact that most questions are non-factoid, i.e., answers are not objective single "facts" but instead one or more relevant sentences where the boundaries around what should be the core answer and what is additional context are difficult to draw. To account for this difficulty, we modify

[3]The city of Munich and the districts (Landkreise) Augsburg and Rems-Murr-Kreis.

[4]https://digitalfabrik.github.io/integreat-cms/api-docs.html#pages

		train	dev	test	total
German	Questions	338	143	185	666
	No Answer	63 (19%)	30 (21%)	43 (23%)	136 (20%)
	Contiguous Answer	209 (62%)	86 (60%)	104 (56%)	399 (60%)
	Non-Contiguous Answer	66 (20%)	27 (19%)	38 (21%)	131 (20%)
	Documents	205	90	117	412
	Questions/Document	1.65	1.59	1.58	1.62
	Sentences/Document	27.16 ± 20.11	27.96 ± 15.87	26.91 ± 17.88	27.26 ± 18.59
	Chars/Sentence	58.62 ± 15.93	61.74 ± 16.32	61.96 ± 17.25	60.25 ± 16.44
	Chars/Question	57.85 ± 15.68	58.91 ± 17.21	59.61 ± 16.45	58.56 ± 16.23
	Agreement (Jaccard)	0.60 ± 0.33	0.59 ± 0.33	0.60 ± 0.34	0.60 ± 0.33
	with adjacent sentences	0.86 ± 0.19	0.85 ± 0.18	0.86 ± 0.19	0.86 ± 0.19
	Answer Sentences/Question	5.37 ± 6.09	5.57 ± 5.89	5.29 ± 6.84	5.39 ± 6.26
	Answers Sentences/Total Sentences	0.28 ± 0.29	0.25 ± 0.27	0.27 ± 0.28	0.27 ± 0.28
English	Questions	123	50	67	240
	No Answer	18 (15%)	8 (16%)	12 (18%)	38 (16%)
	Contiguous Answer	95 (77%)	38 (76%)	49 (73%)	182 (76%)
	Non-Contiguous Answer	10 (8%)	4 (8%)	6 (9%)	20 (8%)
	Documents	103	43	59	205
	Questions/Document	1.19	1.16	1.14	1.17
	Sentences/Document	23.51 ± 13.30	25.58 ± 16.68	25.49 ± 13.68	24.52 ± 14.14
	Chars/Sentence	65.28 ± 18.22	61.74 ± 12.72	60.48 ± 15.30	63.16 ± 16.45
	Chars/Question	59.46 ± 15.98	56.48 ± 13.22	56.51 ± 14.72	58.01 ± 15.11
	Agreement (Jaccard)	0.58 ± 0.34	0.59 ± 0.32	0.56 ± 0.34	0.58 ± 0.34
	with adjacent sentences	0.86 ± 0.20	0.84 ± 0.19	0.86 ± 0.20	0.86 ± 0.19
	Answer Sentences/Question	4.41 ± 4.98	3.90 ± 3.62	4.19 ± 4.39	4.24 ± 4.55
	Answers Sentences/Total Sentences	0.23 ± 0.23	0.20 ± 0.21	0.22 ± 0.24	0.22 ± 0.23
All	Questions	461	193	252	906
	No Answer	81 (18%)	38 (20%)	55 (22%)	174 (19%)
	Contiguous Answer	304 (66%)	124 (64%)	153 (61%)	581 (64%)
	Non-Contiguous Answer	76 (16%)	31 (16%)	44 (17%)	151 (17%)

Table 1: OMoS-QA: Overview of corpus statistics of final dataset. The Jaccard index is chance-corrected.

the annotations in a heuristic way as illustrated in Fig. 3. For each sentence marked by just one of the annotators that is adjacent to a sentence marked as relevant by both annotators, we change the annotation of the respective other annotator to "relevant" as well. We do this only if the sentence originally marked by both annotators is no more than three[5] sentences away.

After modifying the annotations to include adjacent sentences, the average Jaccard index is 0.50 (chance corrected: 0.48). To assure a high quality dataset, we filter out questions with a (non-chance-corrected) Jaccard index <0.5. This leaves us with 906 (51%) questions (de: 663, en: 243) with an average agreement of 0.86 (chance corrected: 0.86). The agreement when leaving out the adjustment of including adjacent sentences amounts to 0.61 (chance corrected: 0.59). As gold-standard answers we chose the intersection of both annotations, but including adjacent sentences as explained above.

[5]This threshold is chosen as a middle ground between too little and too much additional context backed up by a manual inspection of samples.

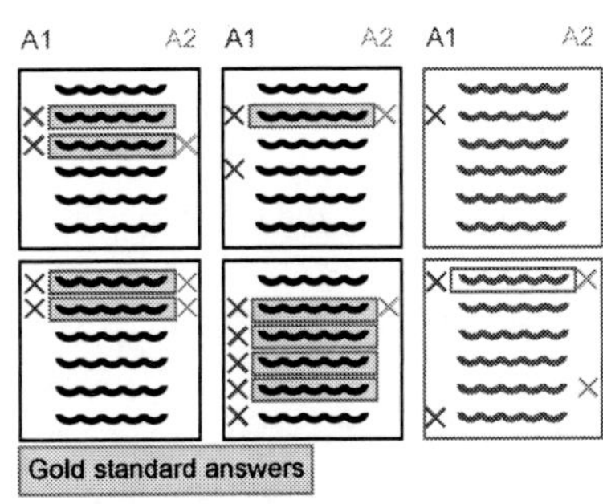

Figure 3: Gold standard construction from labels of two human annotators A1 (blue) and A2 (green). The gold standard contains sentences that A1 and A2 both mark as answers, as well as adjacent sentences marked by only one of them if at most three sentences away from the agreed-upon answer.

3.3 Final Dataset

Table 1 provides an overview of the corpus statistics of the final version of OMoS-QA. Out of the 906 QA pairs included in our **final dataset**, 151 (16%) have non-contiguous answers (i.e., the answer sentences are not adjacent), 110 (12%) have a single answer sentence and 165 (18%) questions have no answer in the document. The IAA did not differ substantially between German and English annotations in both the raw dataset (de: 0.34, en: 0.32) as well as the final dataset (de, en: 0.86).

Translations. To increase the size of the dataset and to take the multilingual setting into account, we translate the German questions and documents to English and vice versa using DeepL.[6] In order to preserve the gold-standard answers represented by the sentence indices, we translate each context sentence-by-sentence. Accordingly, in the German version of the dataset 240 and in the English version 666 of the 906 questions are machine-translated. We retain the information on the original languages.

Dataset Split. We split our dataset into train (51%), dev (21%) and test (28%) partitions with similar internal splits for the original language and the city the document is from. Questions without an answer, questions with contiguous and questions with non-contiguous answers are present with a similar probability over all partitions. As some questions refer to the same document, we make sure that no document occurs in multiple partitions. The proposed split is assuring a close to uniform distribution of several key properties of the dataset such as the agreement of both annotations, the document length or the annotated answer count.

4 Experiments

In this section, we describe our experiments. We evaluate several off-the-shelf LLMs as well as a finetuned sentence classifier on OMoS-QA.

4.1 Setup

We mostly follow the **prompt templates** proposed by Henning et al. (2023) for both the 0-shot and 5-shot settings, instructing the models to output a list containing the sentence IDs of the answer sentences.[7] We test the models in a 0-shot setting, only providing the prompt, but no concrete examples. In addition, we test the models in a 5-shot setting, in which we manually select and chunk examples for both German and English questions from the train partition (3 answerable, 2 unanswerable cases).[8] We use the same examples for all models and questions.

[6]`https://developers.deepl.com/docs`

[7]We used a model temperature of 0.75.

[8]We leave experiments with other proportions of answerable and unanswerable few-shot examples to future work.

As **evaluation metrics**, we use precision (P), recall (R), and F1-score (F). To evaluate sentence-level retrieval (i.e. the binary task of selecting a sentence as an answer to the question), metrics are first computed per question at the sentence level and then macro-averaged over questions.

We also separately evaluate the binary task of identifying questions as **unanswerable** given the context. Here all metrics are at the question level. We consider two setups for extracting "unanswerable question" predictions from models: In the *inferred* setup, we run the models as before and treat generated empty lists (in the case of LLMs) or all-zero-vectors (in the case of DeBERTa) as classifying the question as unanswerable. In the *explicit* setup, we change the LLM instructions and classifier architecture to make an explicit binary prediction for each question.

During experimentation and hyperparameter selection, we evaluated only on the development split of OMoS-QA (results in Appendix D). Here we report our main results on the test split with the hyperparameters found during development.

4.2 Evaluated Models

We focus on open-weight models from MistralAI and Meta: Mixtral-8x7B (introduced in section 3.1), Mistral-7B-Instruct-v0.2 (Mistral-7B; Jiang et al., 2023) as well as Llama-3-8B-Instruct (Llama-3-8B) and Llama-3-70B-Instruct (Llama-3-70B) which are both successors of the Llama 2 model family (Touvron et al., 2023). We access these models via HuggingFace.[9] For comparison, we include results of the closed-source GPT-3.5-Turbo-0125 (GPT-3.5-Turbo) by OpenAI.[10]

4.3 Baseline

As a baseline, we run a sentence-wise classifier, consisting of a pretrained DeBERTa-v3-large encoder (He et al., 2021, accessed via HuggingFace) and a binary classification head.[11] For each sentence in a document, we pass the following input to the model: `[CLS] <question> [SEP] <context> [SEN] <target sentence> [SEN] <context> [SEP]`, where the classification is made based on the encoding of the `[CLS]` token, the target sentence is surrounded by three context sentences on

[9]`https://huggingface.co`

[10]`https://platform.openai.com/docs/models/gpt-3-5-turbo`

[11]The head is a linear layer with 1024 input and 2 output features on top of a pooling layer. Additional hyperparameters are given in Table 6.

		Sentence-level Answers						Question-level Unanswerability					
		German			English			German			English		
Model	Setting	P	R	F	P	R	F	P	R	F	P	R	F
Mixtral-8x7B	0-shot	74.5	47.1	57.7	73.4	44.2	55.2	68.9	56.4	62.0	65.8	45.5	53.8
	5-shot	79.0	51.7	**62.5**	77.9	50.5	61.3	67.8	72.7	70.2	65.6	76.4	70.6
Mistral-7B	0-shot	69.7	47.8	56.7	74.1	47.5	57.9	**80.0**	14.5	24.6	70.0	25.5	37.3
	5-shot	**87.6**	20.3	32.9	84.3	29.5	43.7	29.2	**89.1**	43.9	30.3	72.7	42.8
Llama-3-8B	0-shot	74.9	30.0	42.9	78.2	34.8	48.1	71.1	49.1	58.1	54.7	52.7	53.7
	5-shot	81.9	42.2	55.7	82.1	44.2	57.4	54.7	85.5	66.7	53.6	**81.8**	64.7
Llama-3-70B	0-shot	85.5	46.6	60.3	84.8	46.7	60.2	69.8	67.3	68.5	74.5	63.6	68.6
	5-shot	86.7	48.2	62.0	84.9	48.4	61.6	68.3	78.2	**72.9**	64.5	72.7	68.4
GPT-3.5-Turbo	0-shot	85.3	31.6	46.1	**87.3**	31.2	45.9	50.8	60.0	55.0	54.4	67.3	60.2
	5-shot	81.8	45.1	58.1	83.8	43.9	57.6	70.9	70.9	70.9	67.2	74.5	**70.7**
DeBERTa	–	62.6	**62.4**	**62.5**	65.7	**64.2**	**64.9**	56.2	65.5	60.5	59.4	69.1	63.9
*Human Agreement**		–	–	*57.8*	–	–	*57.8*	–	–	*47.8*	–	–	*47.8*
test partition only		–	–	*76.3*	–	–	*76.3*	–	–	*100.0*	–	–	*100.0*

Table 2: Test set performance (in %) of zero-shot and 5-shot LLMs and finetuned DeBERTa on sentence-level answer extraction (left) and detection of unanswerable questions (right). The best result in each column is **bolded**. **Human Agreement* is computed from agreement before the dataset filtering step (Fig. 2) and therefore not directly comparable to model performance.

the left and right (altogether surrounded by [SEP] tokens),[12] and we add the new [SEN] special token to the vocabulary to mark the target sentence.

We finetune the full model on OMoS-QA.

4.4 Results

We present our results in the left half of Table 2. All models show very good precision (70–90%), with the highest numbers achieved by the Llama-3 models. Recall is much lower in general, with a wider span across models, reaching as low as 20.3% (Mistral-7B 5-shot in German). Most models reach between 40% and 50% recall while maintaining high precision, which seems to be a favorable trade-off. Keep in mind that selecting fewer but clearly relevant sentences, as opposed to more noisy ones, is generally in line with our goals of providing trustworthy results. The highest precision is achieved by Mistral-7B -shot for German and GPT-3.5-Turbo 0-shot for English.

Mixtral-8x7B, Llama-3-70B, and DeBERTa strike the best overall precision/recall trade-offs (F1-score). DeBERTa in particular has almost equal precision and recall.

The last row of the table presents an approximation of the "human performance" as measured via the inter-annotator agreement (F1-score) in our dataset. For each question, the data labeled by the various annotators is assigned to one of two sets randomly, and then one set is treated as the gold standard and the other as the system. As the German and English versions of the dataset consist of the same (potentially translated, see section 3.3) questions and documents, the score is the same in the two languages. We provide a version of this human score before majority voting and including adjacent sentences, which gives an idea of the difficulty of the task, even for humans—though note that these are untrained voluntary annotators and trained experts might achieve higher agreement. Due to the data mismatch, this is not directly comparable to the system evaluation setup, thus we also provide a more optimistic version after filtering ("test partition only"), which is computed on the same data as the models.

Identifying Unanswerable Questions. We report results separately for the subset of questions where the human annotators agreed that the answer is not in the text (right side of Table 2). Here, recall reflects how many of the unanswerable questions were correctly identified by the model as such. Precision indicates how many of the questions predicted as unanswerable did indeed not have an answer in the provided text.

For identifying unanswerable questions, we put higher priority on recall over precision, in line with our cautious approach to a sensitive scenario. And indeed we find that overall, recall is higher and

[12] The context size of 3 has been determined via experimentation on the dev set.

Model & Method		German P	German R	German F	English P	English R	English F
Llama-3 70B	Exp	59.0	**83.6**	**69.2**	62.3	**78.2**	**69.4**
	Inf	69.8	67.3	68.5	74.5	63.6	68.6
DeBERTa	Exp	**75.0**	43.6	55.2	**75.0**	54.5	63.2
	Inf	56.2	65.5	60.5	59.4	69.1	63.9

Table 3: Test set performance (in %) of zero-shot Llama-3-70B and finetuned DeBERTa on explicit and inferred question-level unanswerability detection. The best result in each column is **bolded**. Exp=Explicit, Inf=Inferred.

precision lower than in sentence extraction. In many cases, recall is higher than precision.

In Table 3 we see that explicitly instructing or training models to recognize unanswerable questions has different effects depending on the model type. Changing the zero-shot prompt given to Llama-3-70B increases recall and decreases precision compared to inferring this decision from an empty prediction. Changing the training task of the DeBERTa-classifier has the opposite effect. This might be a result of the decrease in the amount of training data that DeBERTa receives—only one example per question in the explicit setting versus one example per document sentence per question in the inferred setting. This quantitative difference does not apply to the LLM, which instead profits from the more precisely-phrased prompt.

Zero-shot vs. Few-shot. In most conditions, few-shot learning from 5 examples is beneficial either for both recall and precision, or for recall without hurting precision too much. An exception is Mistral-7B, which overshoots on extracting fewer answers in the 5-shot scenario, with a strongly increased recall on unanswerable questions, but a worse performance on the answerable questions.

Performance by Number of Answer Sentences. In all conditions and metrics (P, R, F) we observe standard deviations over individual datapoints (questions with at least one ground-truth answer) between $\pm$ 30 and $\pm$ 40 metric points. This variance can in part be explained by the varying difficulty of questions with increasing numbers of ground-truth answer sentences. The average number of gold answer sentences (henceforth "#answers") lies between 5 and 6 in German and around 4 in English (Table 1). We show model performance as a function of #answers exemplarily for one German model in Fig. 4. As can be expected,

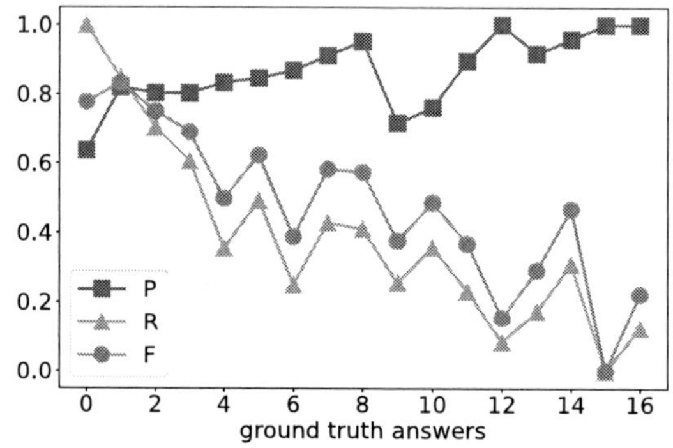

Figure 4: Test set performance as a function of the number of ground-truth answer sentences (0-shot Llama3-70B on German questions and documents).

Doc.	Q.	Answerable P	Answerable R	Unanswerable P	Unanswerable R
Ger.	Ger.	85.5	46.6	69.8	67.3
Ger.	Eng.	**85.8**	**48.2**	70.9	70.9
Ger.	Ara.	84.6	41.8	63.1	**74.5**
Eng.	Ara.	80.6	44.0	74.0	67.3
Eng.	Eng.	84.8	46.7	**74.5**	63.6
Eng.	Ger.	83.2	45.6	73.5	65.5
Ara.	Ara.	80.9	42.2	71.4	54.5
Ara.	Eng.	82.7	44.4	74.0	67.3
Ara.	Ger.	81.9	43.1	72.7	72.7

Table 4: Test set performance (%) of 0-shot Llama-3-70B on **cross-language** question-context pairs.

average recall becomes roughly linearly more difficult as #answers increases, whereas average precision already starts high and approaches 1.0 for questions with more than 10 annotated answer sentences.

4.5 Cross-language QA

We also conduct a pilot cross-language QA study with German, English, and Arabic questions and documents. We compare scenarios where the question language does not match the document language against scenarios where it does. We choose Llama-3-70B over Mixtral-8x7B for this experiment, because while both perform well in section 4.4, the latter was used to generate our questions.

Our findings are shown in Table 4. Surprisingly, asking a question in a different language than the document does not hurt performance by a lot. In fact, it seems that asking questions in English works best, regardless of document language, and German documents work best, regardless of question language.

Model	Context toks (Thousands)	Params (Billions)
Mixtral-8x7B	32[13]	46.7 (12.9)[13]
Mistral-7B	32[14]	7[14]
Llama-3-8B	8[15]	8[15]
Llama-3-70B	8[15]	70[15]
GPT-3.5-Turbo	16[16]	unknown
DeBERTa-v3-large	1[17]	0.4[17]

Table 5: Model sizes. Mixtral has a total of 46.7B parameters but uses only a subset of 12.9 of them for each token.

5 Discussion

We interpret our results as largely positive, in particular with respect to our goal of building a reliable system that errs on the side of presenting fewer, higher precision results to the user. On our dataset, the newest open-weight models Mixtral-8x7B and Llama-3-70B can easily compete with closed-weight GPT-3.5.

With our various evaluation criteria and prompting setups (0-shot vs. 5-shot), we highlight different models' individual strengths: For example, the smaller LLMs Mistral-7B and Llama-3-8B are best at selectively identifying high-confidence answer sentences only, leading to extremely high sentence precision and unanswerability recall. They might thus lend themselves to an answerability filtering step, after which other models like Mixtral-8x7B and Llama-3-70B can do the heavy-lifting of higher-recall answer extraction.

It is important to keep in mind that we already use Mixtral-8x7B to generate questions, which likely contributes to its good performance (cf. Panickssery et al., 2024).

Our cross-language QA experiment suggests that translating questions asked in lower-resource languages (such as Arabic) to English and performing QA on German documents is a promising approach. Appendix E provides additional experimental results with translated and back-translated questions, which suggest that automatic translation is useful for Arabic and Ukrainian, but not so much for French, which is more similar to German and English in terms of both data availability and grammar. In future experiments, it will be interesting to introduce additional noise into questions before prompting, such as spelling errors or code-mixing, to simulate realistic user interactions and measure models' robustness.

While LLMs are indeed powerful and flexible tools that can be quickly adapted to a specialized task via in-context learning from few-shot prompts, we also see that the best-performing LLMs in our setting are the ones with the most parameters (Table 5). Much smaller, specialized models, such as task-specific classifiers built upon DeBERTa or other BERT-style encoders, are generally more controllable, interpretable, and environmentally friendly. Together with the competitive QA performance in terms of F1 and well-balanced precision and recall we observe, this emphasizes that this model class is still very much viable for practical applications in sensitive scenarios.

We will take these findings into account as we continuously work towards automating the document retrieval component and a service-ready implementation of the full QA system, and including more and more languages as potential query and document languages.

6 Conclusion

In this paper, we address the task of providing high-precision, knowledge-grounded answers to users who have freshly immigrated to Germany. We approach this challenge by compiling, manually annotating, and filtering a novel dataset, OMoS-QA, containing in total 900 document-question pairs in German and English. The dataset will be available to the research community under a CC-BY license. We also present experimental results on our new dataset from a comparison of 5 LLMs and a finetuned classifier, as well as a pilot cross-language QA study. Our results are promising and open the doors to future finetuning and large-scale multilingual experiments.

Limitations

The OMoS-QA dataset is designed to support extractive QA in an online counseling system for immigrants. In this paper, we have modeled an admittedly simplified scenario in which the document (potentially) containing the answer to a question is already provided (an assumption that is made in most currently used QA benchmarks). A full

[13] https://mistral.ai/news/mixtral-of-experts/

[14] https://huggingface.co/mistralai/Mistral-7B-Instruct-v0.2

[15] https://huggingface.co/meta-llama/Meta-Llama-3-8B-Instruct

[16] https://platform.openai.com/docs/models/gpt-3-5-turbo

[17] https://huggingface.co/microsoft/deberta-v3-large

search scenario would of course also require identifying potentially relevant documents, i.e., include a search component.

Another limitation of our work is that annotators were not trained specifically for our task. We counterbalance this issue by double-annotations and extensive filtering.

Finally, the current version of OMoS-QA is limited to German and English documents and questions. As immigrants arrive from all over the world, an in particular in urgent crises without the possibility to study German in advance, more work is necessary to mitigate the language barrier. In future work, we plan to also conduct experiments for an extended set of languages.

Ethics Statement

During dataset construction, annotators participated on a voluntary basis and agreed to the anonymized publishing of their annotations. Before starting the annotations, they agreed to the terms shown in Appendix C. As the annotation study only included marking relevant answers to technical questions in text, i.e., annotators did not have to write text or provide personal information, no IRB review was deemed necessary.

Online migration counseling offers convenience and accessibility, but it also comes with several challenges.[13] First of all, there is a lack of a personal connection, which may be crucial in our scenario. Ensuring client confidentiality can be more challenging in an online environment. Misinterpretation of cultural cues or nuances in communication may occur, leading to misunderstandings or ineffective counseling outcomes. Finally, there are also technological barriers: not everyone has access to reliable internet connections or appropriate devices. Yet, our work is a first attempt at developing reliable language technology to support the immigration counseling process. Municipalities could, for example, provide computer terminals at the immigration authorities' offices, townhalls, or libraries. And being able to search for information in a targeted system is still much of an advantage compared to waiting for an appointment for weeks. Moreover, such a system would also lead to a more effective use of the official counselor's time, as it would relieve them from providing advice in "easy" cases.

[13]This list was compiled with the help of ChatGPT, yet it reflects our own opinion as well.

Acknowledgments

We are extremely grateful to our voluntary annotators for their hard work and to Tür an Tür Digitalfabrik GmbH, in particular Daniel Kehne und Sven Seeberg-Elverfeldt, for supporting this work and funding the first author. We also thank Alexander Knapp and members of the Augsburg HLT group for inspiring discussions, as well as the anonymous reviewers for their helpful comments and suggestions.

References

Ankush Agarwal, Raj Gite, Shreya Laddha, Pushpak Bhattacharyya, Satyanarayan Kar, Asif Ekbal, Prabhjit Thind, Rajesh Zele, and Ravi Shankar. 2022. Knowledge graph - deep learning: A case study in question answering in aviation safety domain. In *Proceedings of the Thirteenth Language Resources and Evaluation Conference*, pages 6260–6270, Marseille, France. European Language Resources Association.

David Alfter, Elena Volodina, Thomas François, Arne Jönsson, and Evelina Rennes, editors. 2023. *Proceedings of the 12th Workshop on NLP for Computer Assisted Language Learning*. LiU Electronic Press, Tórshavn, Faroe Islands.

Frederic Bechet, Elie Antoine, Jérémy Auguste, and Géraldine Damnati. 2022. Question generation and answering for exploring digital humanities collections. In *Proceedings of the Thirteenth Language Resources and Evaluation Conference*, pages 4561–4568, Marseille, France. European Language Resources Association.

Dominik Beese, Ole Pütz, and Steffen Eger. 2022. FairGer: Using NLP to measure support for women and migrants in 155 years of German parliamentary debates. ArXiv preprint arXiv:2210.04359.

Andreas Blätte, Simon Gehlhar, and Christoph Leonhardt. 2020. The Europeanization of parliamentary debates on migration in Austria, France, Germany, and the Netherlands. In *Proceedings of the Second ParlaCLARIN Workshop*, pages 66–74, Marseille, France. European Language Resources Association.

Quentin Brabant, Gwénolé Lecorvé, and Lina M. Rojas Barahona. 2022. CoQAR: Question rewriting on CoQA. In *Proceedings of the Thirteenth Language Resources and Evaluation Conference*, pages 119–126, Marseille, France. European Language Resources Association.

Daniela Brook Weiss, Paul Roit, Ayal Klein, Ori Ernst, and Ido Dagan. 2021. QA-align: Representing cross-text content overlap by aligning question-answer propositions. In *Proceedings of the 2021 Conference on Empirical Methods in Natural Language Processing*, pages 9879–9894, Online and Punta Cana,

Dominican Republic. Association for Computational Linguistics.

Delphine Charlet, Geraldine Damnati, Frederic Bechet, Gabriel Marzinotto, and Johannes Heinecke. 2020. Cross-lingual and cross-domain evaluation of machine reading comprehension with squad and CALOR-quest corpora. In *Proceedings of the Twelfth Language Resources and Evaluation Conference*, pages 5491–5497, Marseille, France. European Language Resources Association.

Christopher Clark and Matt Gardner. 2018. Simple and effective multi-paragraph reading comprehension. In *Proceedings of the 56th Annual Meeting of the Association for Computational Linguistics (Volume 1: Long Papers)*, pages 845–855, Melbourne, Australia. Association for Computational Linguistics.

Liam Dugan, Eleni Miltsakaki, Shriyash Upadhyay, Etan Ginsberg, Hannah Gonzalez, DaHyeon Choi, Chuning Yuan, and Chris Callison-Burch. 2022. A feasibility study of answer-agnostic question generation for education. In *Findings of the Association for Computational Linguistics: ACL 2022*, pages 1919–1926, Dublin, Ireland. Association for Computational Linguistics.

Kelvin Han, Thiago Castro Ferreira, and Claire Gardent. 2022. Generating questions from Wikidata triples. In *Proceedings of the Thirteenth Language Resources and Evaluation Conference*, pages 277–290, Marseille, France. European Language Resources Association.

Luheng He, Mike Lewis, and Luke Zettlemoyer. 2015. Question-answer driven semantic role labeling: Using natural language to annotate natural language. In *Proceedings of the 2015 Conference on Empirical Methods in Natural Language Processing*, pages 643–653, Lisbon, Portugal. Association for Computational Linguistics.

Pengcheng He, Xiaodong Liu, Jianfeng Gao, and Weizhu Chen. 2021. {DEBERTA}: {DECODING}-{enhanced} {bert} {with} {disentangled} {attention}. In *International Conference on Learning Representations*.

Sophie Henning, Talita Anthonio, Wei Zhou, Heike Adel, Mohsen Mesgar, and Annemarie Friedrich. 2023. Is the answer in the text? challenging ChatGPT with evidence retrieval from instructive text. In *Findings of the Association for Computational Linguistics: EMNLP 2023*, pages 14229–14241, Singapore. Association for Computational Linguistics.

Minghao Hu, Yuxing Peng, Zhen Huang, Xipeng Qiu, Furu Wei, and Ming Zhou. 2018. Reinforced mnemonic reader for machine reading comprehension. In *Proceedings of the 27th International Joint Conference on Artificial Intelligence*, IJCAI'18, page 4099–4106. AAAI Press.

Ziwei Ji, Nayeon Lee, Rita Frieske, Tiezheng Yu, Dan Su, Yan Xu, Etsuko Ishii, Ye Jin Bang, Andrea Madotto, and Pascale Fung. 2023. Survey of hallucination in natural language generation. *ACM Comput. Surv.*, 55(12).

Albert Q. Jiang, Alexandre Sablayrolles, Arthur Mensch, Chris Bamford, Devendra Singh Chaplot, Diego de las Casas, Florian Bressand, Gianna Lengyel, Guillaume Lample, Lucile Saulnier, Lélio Renard Lavaud, Marie-Anne Lachaux, Pierre Stock, Teven Le Scao, Thibaut Lavril, Thomas Wang, Timothée Lacroix, and William El Sayed. 2023. Mistral 7b. ArXiv Preprint 2310.06825.

Albert Q. Jiang, Alexandre Sablayrolles, Antoine Roux, Arthur Mensch, Blanche Savary, Chris Bamford, Devendra Singh Chaplot, Diego de las Casas, Emma Bou Hanna, Florian Bressand, Gianna Lengyel, Guillaume Bour, Guillaume Lample, Lélio Renard Lavaud, Lucile Saulnier, Marie-Anne Lachaux, Pierre Stock, Sandeep Subramanian, Sophia Yang, Szymon Antoniak, Teven Le Scao, Théophile Gervet, Thibaut Lavril, Thomas Wang, Timothée Lacroix, and William El Sayed. 2024. Mixtral of experts.

Ekaterina Kochmar, Jill Burstein, Andrea Horbach, Ronja Laarmann-Quante, Nitin Madnani, Anaïs Tack, Victoria Yaneva, Zheng Yuan, and Torsten Zesch, editors. 2023. *Proceedings of the 18th Workshop on Innovative Use of NLP for Building Educational Applications (BEA 2023)*. Association for Computational Linguistics, Toronto, Canada.

Gabriella Lapesa, Andre Blessing, Nico Blokker, Erenay Dayanik, Sebastian Haunss, Jonas Kuhn, and Sebastian Padó. 2020. DEbateNet-mig15:tracing the 2015 immigration debate in Germany over time. In *Proceedings of the Twelfth Language Resources and Evaluation Conference*, pages 919–927, Marseille, France. European Language Resources Association.

Ivano Lauriola, Kevin Small, and Alessandro Moschitti. 2022. Building a dataset for automatically learning to detect questions requiring clarification. In *Proceedings of the Thirteenth Language Resources and Evaluation Conference*, pages 4701–4707, Marseille, France. European Language Resources Association.

Yinhan Liu, Myle Ott, Naman Goyal, Jingfei Du, Mandar Joshi, Danqi Chen, Omer Levy, Mike Lewis, Luke Zettlemoyer, and Veselin Stoyanov. 2020. Ro{bert}a: A robustly optimized {bert} pretraining approach.

Man Luo, Kazuma Hashimoto, Semih Yavuz, Zhiwei Liu, Chitta Baral, and Yingbo Zhou. 2022. Choose your QA model wisely: A systematic study of generative and extractive readers for question answering. In *Proceedings of the 1st Workshop on Semiparametric Methods in NLP: Decoupling Logic from Knowledge*, pages 7–22, Dublin, Ireland and Online. Association for Computational Linguistics.

Gabriel Luthier and Andrei Popescu-Belis. 2020. Chat or learn: a data-driven robust question-answering system. In *Proceedings of the Twelfth Language Resources and Evaluation Conference*, pages 5474–5480, Marseille, France. European Language Resources Association.

Nick McKenna, Tianyi Li, Liang Cheng, Mohammad Hosseini, Mark Johnson, and Mark Steedman. 2023. Sources of hallucination by large language models on inference tasks. In *Findings of the Association for Computational Linguistics: EMNLP 2023*, pages 2758–2774, Singapore. Association for Computational Linguistics.

Timo Möller, Julian Risch, and Malte Pietsch. 2021. GermanQuAD and GermanDPR: Improving non-English question answering and passage retrieval. In *Proceedings of the 3rd Workshop on Machine Reading for Question Answering*, pages 42–50, Punta Cana, Dominican Republic. Association for Computational Linguistics.

J. W. Murdock, J. Fan, A. Lally, H. Shima, and B. K. Boguraev. 2012. Textual evidence gathering and analysis. *IBM Journal of Research and Development*, 56(3.4):8:1–8:14.

Shashi Narayan, Ronald Cardenas, Nikos Papasarantopoulos, Shay B. Cohen, Mirella Lapata, Jiangsheng Yu, and Yi Chang. 2018. Document modeling with external attention for sentence extraction. In *Proceedings of the 56th Annual Meeting of the Association for Computational Linguistics (Volume 1: Long Papers)*, pages 2020–2030, Melbourne, Australia. Association for Computational Linguistics.

Arjun Panickssery, Samuel R. Bowman, and Shi Feng. 2024. Llm evaluators recognize and favor their own generations. ArXiv Preprint 2404.13076.

Amir Pouran Ben Veyseh, Viet Lai, Franck Dernoncourt, and Thien Nguyen. 2022. BehanceQA: A new dataset for identifying question-answer pairs in video transcripts. In *Proceedings of the Thirteenth Language Resources and Evaluation Conference*, pages 7321–7327, Marseille, France. European Language Resources Association.

Archiki Prasad, Trung Bui, Seunghyun Yoon, Hanieh Deilamsalehy, Franck Dernoncourt, and Mohit Bansal. 2023. MeetingQA: Extractive question-answering on meeting transcripts. In *Proceedings of the 61st Annual Meeting of the Association for Computational Linguistics (Volume 1: Long Papers)*, pages 15000–15025, Toronto, Canada. Association for Computational Linguistics.

Alec Radford, Karthik Narasimhan, Tim Salimans, Ilya Sutskever, et al. 2018. Improving language understanding by generative pre-training.

Pranav Rajpurkar, Robin Jia, and Percy Liang. 2018. Know what you don't know: Unanswerable questions for SQuAD. In *Proceedings of the 56th Annual Meeting of the Association for Computational Linguistics (Volume 2: Short Papers)*, pages 784–789, Melbourne, Australia. Association for Computational Linguistics.

Pranav Rajpurkar, Jian Zhang, Konstantin Lopyrev, and Percy Liang. 2016. SQuAD: 100,000+ questions for machine comprehension of text. In *Proceedings of the 2016 Conference on Empirical Methods in Natural Language Processing*, pages 2383–2392, Austin, Texas. Association for Computational Linguistics.

Paul Roit, Ayal Klein, Daniela Stepanov, Jonathan Mamou, Julian Michael, Gabriel Stanovsky, Luke Zettlemoyer, and Ido Dagan. 2020. Controlled crowdsourcing for high-quality QA-SRL annotation. In *Proceedings of the 58th Annual Meeting of the Association for Computational Linguistics*, pages 7008–7013, Online. Association for Computational Linguistics.

Björn Ross, Michael Rist, Guillermo Carbonell, Benjamin Cabrera, Nils Kurowsky, and Michael Wojatzki. 2016. Measuring the reliability of hate speech annotations: The case of the European refugee crisis. In *Proceedings of the 3rd Workshop on Natural Language Processing for Computer-mediated Communication (NLP4CMC)*, number 17 in Bochumer linguistische Arbeitsberichte: BLA, pages 6–9.

Manuela Sanguinetti, Fabio Poletto, Cristina Bosco, Viviana Patti, and Marco Stranisci. 2018. An Italian Twitter corpus of hate speech against immigrants. In *Proceedings of the Eleventh International Conference on Language Resources and Evaluation (LREC 2018)*, Miyazaki, Japan. European Language Resources Association (ELRA).

Timo Schick and Hinrich Schütze. 2021. Generating datasets with pretrained language models. In *Proceedings of the 2021 Conference on Empirical Methods in Natural Language Processing*, pages 6943–6951, Online and Punta Cana, Dominican Republic. Association for Computational Linguistics.

Minjoon Seo, Aniruddha Kembhavi, Ali Farhadi, and Hannaneh Hajishirzi. 2017. Bidirectional attention flow for machine comprehension. In *International Conference on Learning Representations*.

Chirag Shah and Emily M. Bender. 2024. Envisioning information access systems: What makes for good tools and a healthy web? *ACM Trans. Web*.

Hugo Touvron, Louis Martin, Kevin Stone, Peter Albert, Amjad Almahairi, Yasmine Babaei, Nikolay Bashlykov, Soumya Batra, Prajjwal Bhargava, Shruti Bhosale, Dan Bikel, Lukas Blecher, Cristian Canton Ferrer, Moya Chen, Guillem Cucurull, David Esiobu, Jude Fernandes, Jeremy Fu, Wenyin Fu, Brian Fuller, Cynthia Gao, Vedanuj Goswami, Naman Goyal, Anthony Hartshorn, Saghar Hosseini, Rui Hou, Hakan Inan, Marcin Kardas, Viktor Kerkez, Madian Khabsa, Isabel Kloumann, Artem Korenev, Punit Singh Koura, Marie-Anne Lachaux, Thibaut Lavril, Jenya Lee, Diana Liskovich, Yinghai Lu, Yuning Mao, Xavier Martinet, Todor Mihaylov, Pushkar Mishra, Igor Molybog, Yixin Nie, Andrew Poulton, Jeremy Reizenstein, Rashi Rungta, Kalyan Saladi, Alan Schelten,

Ruan Silva, Eric Michael Smith, Ranjan Subramanian, Xiaoqing Ellen Tan, Binh Tang, Ross Taylor, Adina Williams, Jian Xiang Kuan, Puxin Xu, Zheng Yan, Iliyan Zarov, Yuchen Zhang, Angela Fan, Melanie Kambadur, Sharan Narang, Aurelien Rodriguez, Robert Stojnic, Sergey Edunov, and Thomas Scialom. 2023. Llama 2: Open foundation and fine-tuned chat models. ArXiv Preprint 2307.09288.

Hai Wang, Dian Yu, Kai Sun, Jianshu Chen, Dong Yu, David McAllester, and Dan Roth. 2019. Evidence sentence extraction for machine reading comprehension. In *Proceedings of the 23rd Conference on Computational Natural Language Learning (CoNLL)*, pages 696–707, Hong Kong, China. Association for Computational Linguistics.

Yunxiao Wang. 2024. Metaphorical framing of refugees, asylum seekers and immigrants in UKs left and right-wing media. In *Proceedings of the 8th Joint SIGHUM Workshop on Computational Linguistics for Cultural Heritage, Social Sciences, Humanities and Literature (LaTeCH-CLfL 2024)*, pages 18–27, St. Julians, Malta. Association for Computational Linguistics.

Matthijs Westera, Laia Mayol, and Hannah Rohde. 2020. TED-Q: TED talks and the questions they evoke. In *Proceedings of the Twelfth Language Resources and Evaluation Conference*, pages 1118–1127, Marseille, France. European Language Resources Association.

Zhuoqun Xu, Liubo Ouyang, and Yang Liu. 2022. Task-driven and experience-based question answering corpus for in-home robot application in the House3D virtual environment. In *Proceedings of the Thirteenth Language Resources and Evaluation Conference*, pages 6232–6239, Marseille, France. European Language Resources Association.

Seunghyun Yoon, Franck Dernoncourt, Doo Soon Kim, Trung Bui, and Kyomin Jung. 2020. Propagate-selector: Detecting supporting sentences for question answering via graph neural networks. In *Proceedings of the Twelfth Language Resources and Evaluation Conference*, pages 5400–5407, Marseille, France. European Language Resources Association.

Xingdi Yuan, Tong Wang, Yen-Hsiang Wang, Emery Fine, Rania Abdelghani, Hélène Sauzéon, and Pierre-Yves Oudeyer. 2023. Selecting better samples from pre-trained LLMs: A case study on question generation. In *Findings of the Association for Computational Linguistics: ACL 2023*, pages 12952–12965, Toronto, Canada. Association for Computational Linguistics.

Ana Zwitter Vitez, Mojca Brglez, Marko Robnik Šikonja, Tadej Škvorc, Andreja Vezovnik, and Senja Pollak. 2022. Extracting and analysing metaphors in migration media discourse: towards a metaphor annotation scheme. In *Proceedings of the Thirteenth Language Resources and Evaluation Conference*, pages 2430–2439, Marseille, France. European Language Resources Association.

A Chance-corrected Jaccard Coefficient

For computing agreement, we use a chance-corrected version of the Jaccard coefficient. For a question q_i, it is defined as follows for two sets of selected answer sentences $A_{i_a} \subseteq S_i$ and $A_{i_b} \subseteq S_i$, where S_i is the set of all sentences of the document, and a and b index the two annotators:

$$agr_{obs} = J(A_{i_a}, A_{i_b}) = \frac{|A_{i_a} \cap A_{i_b}|}{|A_{i_a} \cup A_{i_b}|}$$

For $A_{i_a} = A_{i_b} = \emptyset$ we set $J(A_{i_a}, A_{i_b}) = 1$ as both annotators completely agree that there is no answer.

Chance Correction. In order to account for the possibility of authors just agreeing "by chance," chance correction can be applied. As the prior probability $P(sel)$ of a sentence $s_{i_k} \in S_i$ being selected we take the amount of all sentence selection in the whole corpus divided by the amount of all sentences in the corpus times 2 to account for two annotations being made:

$$P(sel) = \frac{\sum_{i=1}^{n}(|A_{i_a}| + |A_{i_b}|)}{2 * \sum_{i=1}^{n}|S_i|}$$

The probability $P(agr)$ that two random annotations agree on a sentence being an answer is then:

$$agr_{exp} = P(agr) = P(sel)^2$$

$P(agr)$ is therefore the expected agreement agr_{exp}. The observed agreement agr_{obs} is the Jaccard index $J(A_{i_a}, A_{i_b})$, such that the chance-corrected Jaccard index can be calculated as follows:

$$J_{cc}(A_{i_a}, A_{i_b}) = \frac{agr_{obs} - agr_{exp}}{1 - agr_{exp}}$$

B Prompt Template

As mentioned in section 4.1 we mostly follow the prompt template proposed by Henning et al. (2023) for both our 0-shot and 5-shot experiments. As Mixtral-8x7B and Mistral-7B do not support messages with the *system* role, we only include *user* and *assistant* messages for these models. Our complete 0-shot prompt:

system: `Your task is to select sentences from a document that answer a given question.` (Llama-3 models and GPT-3.5-Turbo only)

user (question, document): `Given the question and document below, select the sentences from the document that answer the question. It may also be the case that none of the sentences answers the question. In the document, each sentence is marked with an ID. Output the IDs of the relevant sentences as a list, e.g., "[1,2,3]", and output "[]" if no sentence is relevant. Output only these lists.`
`Question: {question}`
`Document: {document}`

We use the chunked samples shown in Fig. 5 (or their sentence-by-sentence translations) for the 5-shot experiments. For each sample we insert the following two messages to the prompt before the final user message:

user (question, document)

assistant (answers): `{answers}`

C Custom Annotation Tool

For the human annotations described in section 3.1 we developed a custom web-based annotation tool for the selection of the answer sentences. All human annotators agreed to the following conditions: *I agree to the processing and publication of my annotations and their use for machine learning. All annotations and information entered will be stored and processed anonymously.* Fig. 6 shows a screenshot of the custom annotation tool.

D Development Set Performance

We observe slightly different trends on the development set (Table 7) than on the test set (Table 2). Namely, three 0-shot model setups have a particularly low recall on sentence extraction: Mixtral-8x7B, Llama-3-8B, and GPT-3.5, which means in conjunction with high precision that they tend to generally extract fewer sentences per question. Out of these three, Mixtral-8x7B and Llama-3-8B also have particularly low precision at identifying unanswerable questions, meaning that more often than not they do not extract any answer sentence for questions which would in fact be answerable given the context. This gets largely fixed by providing few-shot examples.

Question 1: What do you need to open a bank account?
Document 1:
[9] When can I start learning to drive?
[10] In Germany, you may only drive a car with a valid driverś license.
[11] Beforehand, you have to attend a driving school and take theoretical and practical lessons, which you also have to pay for.
[12] You can get information about this at the driving school.
[13] When can I open my own bank account?
Answer 1: []

Question 2: What is a fictitious certificate?
Document 2:
[0] Residence with fictitious certificate
[1] Departure with a fictitious certificate
[2] With a fictitious certificate, you have a temporary right of residence.
[3] There are different types of fictitious certificate.
[4]Please note:
[5] Re-entry into the federal territory is only possible with a fictitious certificate in accordance with § 81 para.4 AufenthG possible.
Answer 2: [2]

Question 3: Where can I find information on admission procedures at vocational schools?
Document 3:
[11] Initial vocational training is possible at vocational schools and vocational colleges.
[12] Training can take place both in the dual system (training company and vocational school) or "purely" school-based training (vocational schools).
[13] The dates and registration requirements vary from vocational school to vocational school.
[14] Information evenings are held at vocational schools every year before enrollment.
[15] Information on the admission procedure at the vocational schools can be obtained directly from the respective school.
[5] Re-entry into the federal territory is only possible with a fictitious certificate in accordance with § 81 para.4 AufenthG possible.
Answer 3: [14, 15]

Question 4: What types of school are there in Germany?
Document 4:
[0] Support with school or personal problems
[1] Does your child need help with problems?
[2] Then these places will help you:
[3] Youth social work (JaS for short) and youth work at schools (JA for short) for school, personal or family problems:
[4] It is best to contact the school directly or the Augsburg District Office for general information:
Answer 4: [0]

Question 5: What topics are covered in the initial orientation courses?
Document 5:
[2] The German courses for initial language orientation (also known as initial orientation courses) teach both basic German language skills and information about life in Germany.
[3] They are a practical starting aid in the new living environment and make everyday life easier.
[4] A course comprises 300 teaching units of 45 minutes each and covers topics such as "Health/medical care", "Work", "Kindergarten/school", "Housing", "Local orientation/transport/mobility".
[5] The focus is on oral communication: participants should learn as quickly as possible to find their way around in everyday life.
[6] Across all modules, initial orientation courses are also about teaching values.
Answer 5: [2, 4, 5, 6]

Figure 5: Chunked samples for 5-shot experiments.

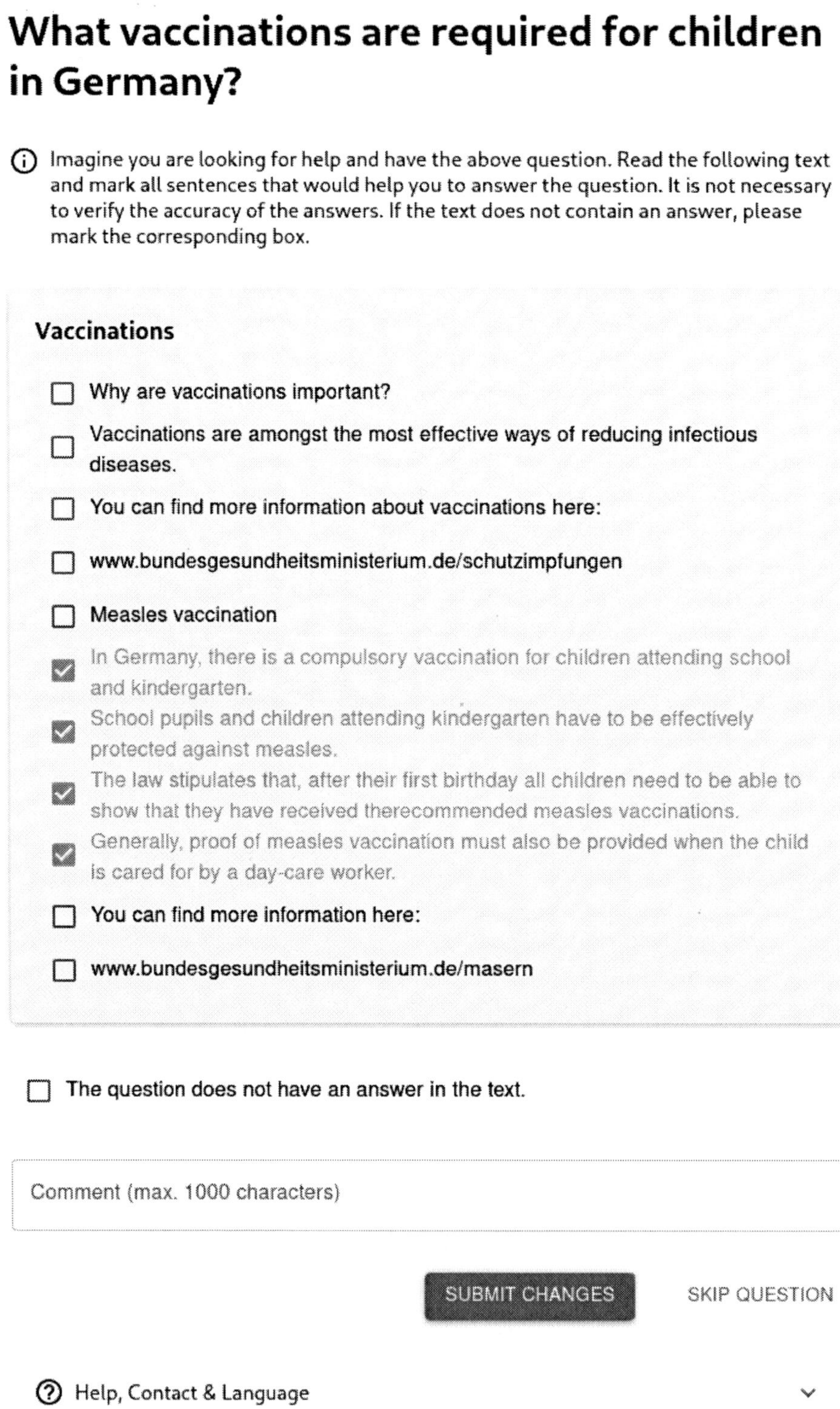

Figure 6: Custom annotation tool

	Sentence Classification	Question Classification
Batch size	8	8
Learning rate	$2 * 10^{-6}$	$2 * 10^{-6}$
Weight decay	0.1	0.1
Warmup steps	50	50
Evaluation steps	50	10
Max. epochs	3	10
Early stopping	10	10

Table 6: The used hyperparameters for finetuning DeBERTa for answer extraction using binary sentence classification and question answerability classification.

		Answerable questions: sentence-level						Identifying unanswerable questions					
		German			English			German			English		
Model	Setting	P	R	F	P	R	F	P	R	F	P	R	F
Mixtral-8x7B	0-shot	74.1	31.7	32.4	67.7	29.0	29.3	38.8	81.6	52.5	41.1	78.9	54.1
	5-shot	74.0	**58.0**	**55.6**	72.9	**53.9**	52.4	76.2	84.2	80.0	68.9	81.6	74.7
Mistral-7B	0-shot	74.0	45.5	47.0	76.7	45.7	48.4	59.5	57.9	58.7	58.3	55.3	56.8
	5-shot	71.0	42.8	40.7	70.5	39.0	38.7	50.9	71.1	59.3	52.8	73.7	61.5
Llama-3-8B	0-shot	**89.8**	26.8	30.0	**86.2**	33.9	37.7	32.0	86.8	46.8	40.8	81.6	54.4
	5-shot	77.6	44.6	45.8	78.1	39.2	40.6	61.0	**94.7**	74.2	52.3	**89.5**	66.0
Llama-3-70B	0-shot	84.2	48.6	53.9	79.6	48.3	52.6	**81.6**	81.6	**81.6**	**77.5**	81.6	**79.5**
	5-shot	85.9	51.1	55.4	82.8	51.9	**55.0**	66.7	84.2	74.4	70.8	89.5	79.1
GPT-3.5-Turbo	0-shot	70.4	33.9	38.5	73.3	36.9	42.6	63.2	63.2	63.2	73.5	65.8	69.4
	5-shot	77.5	47.9	50.8	80.7	44.1	49.5	78.9	78.9	78.9	71.4	78.9	75.0
*Human Upper Bound**		–	–	*62.9*	–	–	*62.9*	–	–	–	–	–	–
with adjacent sentences		–	–	*88.8*	–	–	*88.8*	–	–	–	–	–	–

Table 7: Development set performance (in %) of 0-shot and 5-shot LLMs on answerable questions (left) and unanswerable questions (right). The best result in each column is **bolded**. **Human upper bound* is computed from agreement data and not directly comparable.

E Multilingual Experiments

We evaluate models on the following additional languages that are highly relevant in the migration context: Arabic (ar), French (fr), and Ukrainian (uk). These and other languages are more challenging due to their limited resources and much different language structure (German and English are closely related). Furthermore, Arabic and Ukrainian both use a non-Latin alphabet: The Arabic and Cyrillic alphabet. We use machine translation with DeepL to translate the question and, sentence-by-sentence, the document for each instance of the original OMoS-QA dataset.

In order to assess possible adverse effects of leveraging machine translation and to compare it to directly querying the model with the question in its original language, we evaluate the performance in an additional retranslation setting. To this end, we combine the original German documents with retranslated questions, i.e., questions that are first translated to the aforementioned languages and then back to German. This corresponds to the use of machine translation in the full OMoS system, as only user input (and possibly the answers) are subject to translation, while the document corpus remains unchanged. However, questions are translated twice in the retranslation setting and results should thus be considered as lower performance boundary. Since German is the original dataset language of OMoS-QA, there are no results for the retranslated setting.

E.1 Sentence-Level Results

The results are shown in Table 8. On the left side of the table, we compare sentence-level results of different languages in both a multilingual and a retranslated setting for select models. Compared to the performances on the original German dataset version, all models display lower performance in both the multilingual and the retranslated setting for Arabic, French, and Ukrainian. Llama-3-70B shows slightly higher precision for retranslated Arabic (+0.5%) and Ukrainian (+0.1%), however, this comes at a cost of a clearer decrease in recall

		Sentence-level Answers						Question-level Unanswerability					
		Multilingual			German Retrans.			Multilingual			German Retrans.		
Model	Lang.	P	R	F	P	R	F	P	R	F	P	R	F
Mixtral-8x7B	de	74.5	47.1	57.7	–	–	–	68.9	56.4	62.0	–	–	–
	ar	72.5	42.7	53.8	77.8	45.2	57.2	62.8	49.1	55.1	55.4	56.4	55.9
	fr	74.2	43.7	55.0	75.0	45.2	56.4	64.1	45.5	53.2	57.4	49.1	52.9
	uk	69.3	46.4	55.6	74.7	45.8	56.8	73.2	54.5	62.5	58.2	58.2	58.2
Llama-3-70B	de	**85.5**	46.6	60.3	–	–	–	69.8	67.3	68.5	–	–	–
	ar	80.9	42.2	55.5	**86.0**	44.1	58.3	71.4	54.5	61.9	61.0	65.5	63.2
	fr	84.1	44.9	58.5	84.3	43.5	57.4	72.9	63.6	68.0	63.8	**67.3**	65.5
	uk	82.4	41.3	55.0	85.6	43.3	57.5	**74.5**	63.6	**68.6**	**64.9**	**67.3**	**66.1**
DeBERTa	de	62.6	**62.4**	**62.5**	–	–	–	56.2	65.5	60.5	–	–	–
	ar	63.3	54.9	58.8	65.2	53.5	58.8	43.4	60.0	50.4	44.0	**67.3**	53.2
	fr	66.3	56.9	61.2	61.4	**59.9**	**60.6**	50.7	67.3	57.8	53.8	63.6	58.3
	uk	54.7	61.4	57.9	62.2	55.9	58.8	57.1	**72.7**	64.0	48.7	**67.3**	56.5

Table 8: Test set performance (in %) of zero-shot LLMs and finetuned DeBERTa on sentence-level answer extraction (left) and detection of unanswerable questions (right) for multilingual and retranslated settings. In the multilingual setting, questions and documents are machine translated to the respective language. In the retranslated setting, the question is retranslated back to German and paired with the original German document. The best result in each column is **bolded**.

(−2.5% and −3.3% respectively). For the multilingual setting, French results were the closest to German. With exception to Mixtral-8x7B, the F1-score for French is at least 2% higher. Similarly, while retranslating improves F1-score performance compared to directly querying the LLM for Arabic and Ukrainian in all settings by up to +3.4%, retranslating French comes at a performance loss for Llama-3-70B and DeBERTa. Mixtral-8x7B, on the other hand, shows a performance improvement (+1.4%) for retranslating French to German, although it is explicitly advertised as "fluent in French."[14] The biggest performance loss is displayed by Llama-3-70B in the multilingual setting in Ukrainian (−5.3%) and Arabic (−4.8%).

In general, the observed performance differences are observable but not as notable as expected. This is especially the case for Arabic and Ukrainian, as the differences in the alphabet, grammar, and language origins are significant. While machine translation seems to have a slightly better performance for these languages, a performance deterioration compared to the original German dataset is still measurable. However, the questions are translated twice in our setup, and, as a consequence, the actual implications should be smaller.

E.2 Question-Level Unanswerability

As in section 4.1, we infer question-level unanswerability from sentence-level answer extraction results. If no sentence of a document is marked as answer, we treat the question as unanswerable given the document. In contrast to question-level answer extraction, the German results are not necessarily better than those of other languages in the multilingual setting, but they always outperform the retranslated results. Surprisingly, all models perform slightly better in the Ukrainian multilingual setting than on the original German dataset (up to +3.5%, DeBERTa) and mostly considerably better than on Arabic and French (up to +13.6%). Especially Ukrainian precision is high among all models, which is in line with low precision on the sentence-level, i.e., more sentences are marked as answer. Retranslating only yields small performance improvements for French for DeBERTa and for Arabic for all models. Otherwise, directly querying models leads to better question-level results (up to +7.5%).

[14] `https://mistral.ai/technology#models`

Role-Playing LLMs in Professional Communication Training: The Case of Investigative Interviews with Children

Don Tuggener[1], Teresa Schneider[2], Ariana Huwiler[3], Tobias Kreienbühl[3], Simon Hischier[3], Pius von Däniken[1], Susanna Niehaus[2]

[1] Zurich University of Applied Sciences (ZHAW), Centre for Artificial Intelligence (CAI)

[2] Lucerne University of Applied Sciences and Arts (HSLU), Institute of Social Work and Law

[3] Lucerne University of Applied Sciences and Arts (HSLU), Immersive Realities Research Lab

don.tuggener@zhaw.ch, susanna.niehaus@hslu.ch

Abstract

We present a novel approach for professional communication training in which Large Language Models (LLMs) are guided to dynamically adapt to inappropriate communication techniques by producing false information that match the biased expectations of an interviewer. We achieve this by dynamically altering the LLM's system prompt in conjunction with a classifier that detects undesirable communication behaviour. We develop this approach for training German speaking criminal investigators who interview children in alleged sexual abuse cases. We describe how our approach operationalises the strict communication requirements for such interviews and how it is integrated into a full, end-to-end learning environment that supports speech interaction with 3D virtual characters. We evaluate several aspects of this environment and report the positive results of an initial user study.

1 Introduction

Professional communication is subject to behaviour rules and linguistic registers (Holmes and Marra, 2014; Khramchenko, 2019; Bhatia and Bremner, 2012). Acquiring and training the skills to be proficient in professional communication can be a long, resource-intense, and cumbersome road. Chatbots and virtual characters have emerged as a method to make professional training more accessible and cost-efficient in comparison to in-person training with human actors (Pompedda et al., 2022). One important factor for communication training is that the trainees can express themselves freely, i.e. using their own voice, words, and approach to a task rather than being presented with a selection of predetermined and fixed dialogue choices. In turn, it is important that the feedback on their performance is adapted and personalised to the individual conversational behaviour of the trainees. Consequently, virtual characters have to be able to dynamically respond to different kinds of conversational behavior in a professional communication task.

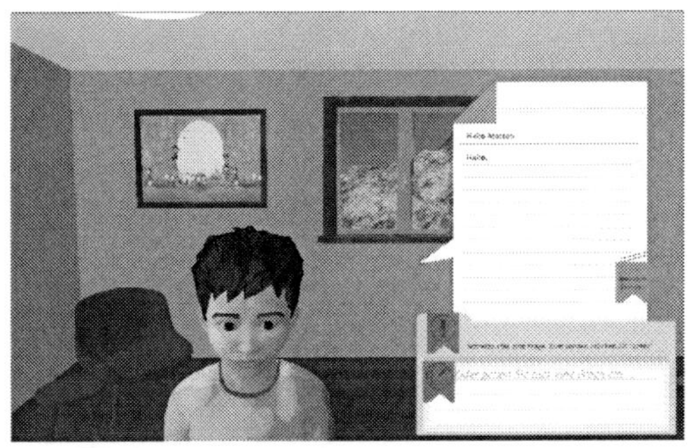

Figure 1: Screenshot of the training environment.

In this paper, we explore the use of Large Language Models (LLMs) as the dialogue component in a sensitive professional communication situation, i.e. training criminal investigators in interviewing alleged child victims of sexual abuse. When children are interviewed about alleged experiences of sexual abuse, the quality of the investigative interview is crucial to whether their statements can be used as the basis for a criminal investigation (Korkman et al., 2024; Niehaus et al., 2017). This is because the child's statements are usually the only evidence in such proceedings (Steller, 2008). The demands on the quality of interviews and the qualifications of interviewers are correspondingly high.

Many training programs have been developed to improve interview quality in child interviews (Benson and Powell, 2015, e.g.). Elaborated and effective training programs include watching commentaries and videos of children being interviewed, quizzes, and mock interviews with colleagues or trained actors (Benson and Powell, 2015; Lamb, 2016). However, the latter is difficult to realise when it comes to training child interviews, as role-playing with fellow trainees is not realistic, and children cannot be used as actors for interviewer training on the subject of abuse for ethical reasons. Investigators are currently forced to gain their initial experience on real cases, meaning that children allegedly affected by sexual abuse are often confronted with inexperienced interviewers (Niehaus et al., 2017). We therefore aimed to develop virtual characters with which optimal interviewing behaviour can be trained realistically and individually without risk before working on real cases. Through systematic and automated feedback from the system, investigators should learn to apply appropriate questioning techniques and avoid suggestive questions which may render the testimony useless as evidence and, in the worst case, stimulate the development of false memories. This training software is intended to contribute to an improvement in interviewing practice in order to meet the international demands on child-friendly justice (FRA, 2017).

2 Related Work

Three different training approaches have been developed to train interview behaviour in cases of suspected abuse with virtual characters that represent children. Pompedda et al. (2015) developed the "Empowering Interviewer Training" (EIT) in which the characters have predefined memories and responses that include relevant and neutral details. The characters answer using predefined response algorithms which are based on empirical knowledge about reactions to suggestive questioning. In the original version, a human operator needed to categorise the question that was asked by the participant. In a new version of the program, an automated question classification algorithm was tested (Haginoya et al., 2023). Overall, research found that the EIT combined with feedback increased the proportion of recommended questions and decreased the proportion of non-recommended questions asked by participants (Pompedda et al., 2022).

A similar system is also used in a more recent approach, an interactive virtual reality training called "ViContact" (Krause et al., 2024). However, as in the EIT, the responses remain limited to predefined memories and responses which are selected based on an algorithm after a human operator has categorised the question. New to the training is the 3D approach (i.e., virtual reality), that the interviewer needs to find out whether sexual abuse or another stressful event happened, and that participants are asked to build rapport with the child avatar before talking about the critical event. Although both programs have shown improvements in interviewing behaviour, the response generation is inflexible, the conversation flow is constrained through the prerecorded video sequences, and elaborated false memories cannot be produced. Furthermore, a human operator is usually needed to categorise the questions asked.

To tackle these problems, another research group is developing an AI-driven system that can dynamically handle questions, provides higher realism of the answer behaviour and does not need an operator (Hassan et al., 2022a). This approach utilises advanced natural language processing and provides an immersive experience through virtual reality. Several user studies cover the ongoing development of the child avatars (Hassan et al., 2022b; Salehi et al., 2022; Hassan et al., 2023; Røed et al., 2023; Salehi et al., 2024).

Although this newly developed AI-driven system can dynamically handle questions and provide feedback automatically without an operator, it only answers suggestive questions with a vague and unproductive reply. Like the EIT, it does not fabricate new false information when inappropriate questions are asked. This means that elaborated false memories[1] are not produced by the system.

In this paper, we introduce an AI-driven system that is based on a LLM, can dynamically answer questions based on the interview context and its knowledge, dynamically generates emotions based on the context and its own utterances, does not need an operator, and produces false memories when inappropriate questions are asked repeatedly. In summary, our contributions are as follows:

- We introduce the notion of generating *false memories* as a pedagogical tool in the training process. False memories occur when trainees apply inappropriate suggestive questioning and can lure trainees into drawing incorrect conclusions.
- We present a novel approach to steer LLMs through *altering the system prompt dynamically* in conjunction with a classifier that detects inappropriate conversational behaviour.
- We outline and implement a practical approach for the *efficient selection of an LLM* based on technical and qualitative requirements for our setting.

[1] In the following, the term false memories is not used in the forensic sense of a pseudo-memory. In the context of our study, we refer to the reactive (forensically more comparable to compliance) production of partially or completely false information that can alter memories in the long term.

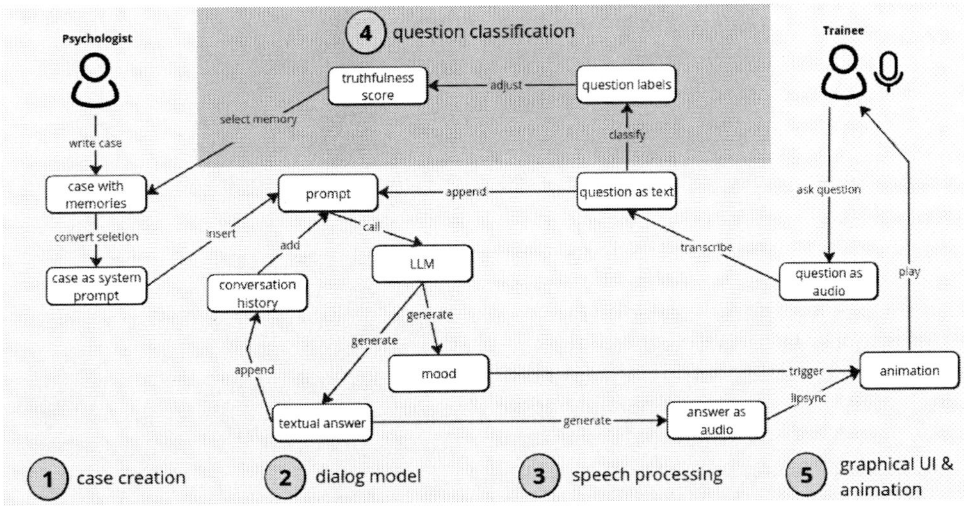

Figure 2: Overview of the architecture of the training system and its components. The case, created by forensic psychologists (1) is entered into the dialog model (2). Questions (by trainee) or answers (generated by the dialog model) pass through speech processing (3) where they are turned into audio or text respectively. Question classification monitors the trainee's utterances for inappropriate content and adjusts the truthfulness score (4). This score is used to trigger the injection of false memories from the case description into the LLM prompt, if inappropriate content is detected. Answers and moods generated by the LLM are passed into the graphical UI & animation component, where the character is animated and shown to the user (5).

- Finally, we release a *dataset for problematic utterance classification* in children interviews in German.[2]

3 Approach

Our setting can be seen as conversational information retrieval, i.e. the user wants to elicit information about a specific case from the system. However, our system is reluctant to provide the information and needs to be prompted in a certain way. Failure to do so inflicts the system's willingness to cooperate. In fact, inappropriate questioning yields false information that misleads the user into drawing incorrect conclusions about the case at hand, while open prompts for narration increase the chance of uncovering the facts of the case. This comprises the overall pedagogic intent of our system: interviewers should learn how to question children in an appropriate way without distorting the statements.

3.1 True Memories

Our virtual character's memory is structured into a semantic memory and episodic memory. The semantic memory contains static information about its situation regarding family, hobbies etc. This information is verbalised in an unordered set of utterances in the first person perspective of the character, e.g. "I am 4 years old", "I like playing tennis.", etc. The utterances can be used to answer a set of similar or related questions. For example, the utterance "I am 4 years old" can be retrieved to answer differently phrased questions about the character's age[3], etc. However, the goal of writing these statements is not to anticipate all potential questions, but to outline a personality on the basis of which a dialog model will be tasked to role-play a character. The pedagogic purpose of the semantic memory is to enable the interviewer to establish rapport with the child, which is a crucial step in the initial phase of the interview.

The episodic memory contains information about the sequence of the event that is the topic of the interview, i.e. information about the alleged sexual abuse and its context. This information is also saved in the form of first person utterances, such as "I went to the basement with my teacher."

3.2 False Memories and Truthfulness

One central aspect of this design is that it allows for the incorporation of false memories. If an in-

[2]Available at `https://drive.switch.ch/index.php/s/DCMIo3SnnNcKsQi`

[3]As we will see later, this statement can also be used to infer whether the character goes to school, etc.

terviewer applies inappropriate questioning techniques repeatedly, the character will start to confirm explicit suspicions of abuse although they are not confirmed in the original storyline. To this end, each episodic memory is accompanied by a false memory storyline that can be triggered by inappropriate questioning style.

At the core of the virtual character's behaviour is the truthfulness score. It determines whether the character is answering truthfully or gives false information. The truthfulness score is adjusted according to the interviewer's questions in a penalty/reward system. At the beginning of the interview, the character is in a neutral and truthful state. If questioned appropriately, it returns truthful and factual answers. If problematic and inappropriate questions are detected, the score is lowered, depending on the severity of the suggestive content of the question: Mentioning the suspect and sexual abuse in a question before the character reveals such information yields the highest score deduction, while asking about a specific point in time or posing a forced-choice question only minimally decreases the truthfulness score. If the score drops below a preset threshold, the character starts generating unreliable responses.

For example, when questioning a 4 year-old virtual character in whose case no abuse occurred, the truthfulness score starts at 10. A suggestive question with a sexual keyphrase that was not uttered by the character itself beforehand, such as "Did you have to take off your pants?" (take off + cloth), will reduce the score by 3 points. This is already under the preset threshold of 8 and the virtual character will start to include incorrect details in their answers. If three unproblematic questions are asked subsequently, the score rises and the character will again respond truthfully. If more inappropriate questions are asked and the score drops below 4, the character's truthfulness cannot be restored and its reported story remains distorted.

4 Implementation

In the following sections, we outline the technical implementation of the approach outlined above. Figure 2 shows an overview of the system[4].

4.1 Dialog Model

The dialog model encompasses the following tasks:

- Managing the character's memory
- Detecting inappropriate and appropriate questioning
- Generating answers to questions in accordance with the two points above
- Generating appropriate emotions tags that steer the 3D animation of the virtual character

While it seems tempting to implement all functionality in one "mega" prompt for LLMs given their ever increasing capabilities, early experiments quickly revealed, in line with Khot et al. (2022), that such a highly complex set of tasks needs to be decomposed. Below, we outline the different components of the dialog model and how they interact.

4.1.1 Character Memory

A key differentiator from related work in our approach is that our characters dynamically respond to inappropriate questioning by yielding false information that confirms biased suspicions of the interviewer. For each case, in addition to the truthful version of the story, the forensic psychologist write two other storylines, depending on whether the case contains abuse:

Cases without abuse contain a truthful storyline without abuse and two additional ones, where the 1st alternation contains comparably less severe forms of abuse and the 2nd version confirms explicit and severe sexual abuse.

Cases with abuse initially contain a storyline that does not explicitly state the abuse, but hints at it. The interviewer first has to establish trust and rapport with the character (by asking appropriate questions such as narration prompts) to unlock the truthful storyline that contains the abuse. As in the cases without abuse, inappropriate questions alter the story. The 1st alternation contains ambiguous hints and the 2nd version contains more severe abuse than the truthful one and the 1st alternation.

4.1.2 Dialog Model

Anticipating and writing out questions that might be asked by interviewers and all the potentially ensuing dialog branches in the different storylines is infeasible; especially given the fact that several cases are needed for training purposes. Hence, implementing the dialog model with an approach where the questions posed are matched to preset questions to retrieve an answer (Bosse and Gerritsen, 2017; Barbe et al., 2023) is impractical. Also, preparing the storylines in such a way that all statements can be retrieved individually independent of

[4]See Appendix A.1 for a technical description of the 3D characters.

the context leads to utterances sounding unnatural[5].

Fortunately, the advent of Large Language Models (LLMs) like ChatGPT[6] gave rise to dialog models that are pre-trained on large amounts of human conversations and can thus handle their intricacies gracefully. We leverage LLMs by ingesting a character's semantic and episodic memories into the LLM via the *system prompt*. We developed a system prompt[7] that contains the semantic and episodic memories of a character, as well as instructional behaviour.

However, including the semantic memory and all story variants of a character in the system prompt grows it to an unmaintainable size and places a large burden on the LLM to manage it. Hence, we developed a mechanism to adapt the system prompt in accordance with the behaviour of the interviewer. Specifically, the system prompt contains a placeholder variable for the episodic memory. At the start of the conversation, this variable is filled with the truthful story of the character and the character's truthfulness score is set to default. If the score drops below a preset threshold during the interview, the placeholder variable for the episodic memory is filled with an alternate storyline, that is, the memory of the character begins to change and it provides false information. However, the conversation history between the interviewer and the virtual characters remains intact.

4.1.3 LLM Selection

Our goal is to find an LLM that suits our needs without having to perform vast amounts of experiments and manual annotations. Hence, rather than creating large benchmarks, we define the minimal set of technical and qualitative requirements and design specific probes for them. After discussing various forensic and technical aspects, we defined the following technical requirements:

Convenience: SDK support, low-latency APIs, affordable pricing, generous rate limits.
Context window size: Providing a large enough context window to fit the rather long system prompt and the rather long following conversation.[8]
Language support: Support the German language.
Alignment: Ability to discuss sensitive topics (sexual abuse).

In addition, we identified the following qualitative abilities:

Natural use of language: Understanding and using *deixis* (i.e. referential expressions like pronouns). *Adapting the pre-set statements* of the system prompt to the conversational context rather than citing a declarative sentence from the memory verbatim. Speaking in *age-appropriate language* regarding the preset age of the character.
Role-Playing: Staying in character and following the instructed behaviour (e.g. not outputting any meta-commentary or reference to the training setting, etc.). *Handle unforeseen questions* that tackle information that is not part of the predefined semantic memory gracefully (e.g., "Where do you live?")
Factuality: *Adhering to the given memories* (semantic and episodic), i.e. *avoiding hallucinations* that contradict the given memories (while being allowed or even encouraged to answer unforeseen questions).
Long conversations: Holding natural, consistent *long multi-turn conversations*[9]

4.1.4 Technical Requirements

The **Convenience** requirement narrowed our selection to the following providers (and models): Google (Chat Bison/Gemini)[10], OpenAI (ChatGPT/GPT-4)[11], Anthropic (Claude 3)[12], Mistral (Mistral/Mixtral)[13], and Meta (Llama 2)[14]. In initial tests, we noticed that Claude 3's bigger models (Sonata and Opus) have quite strict rate limits given our usage tier. We therefore settled on the smallest model in the family, Claude 3 Haiku. Regarding GPT-4, we noticed that the latency was quite high at times and the pricing seemed prohibitive. Also, we did not observe stark quality differences to ChatGPT 3.5 in our initial tests. Therefore, we chose ChatGPT 3.5 as the candidate. Fi-

[5]In preparing statements for matching approaches, it is not permissible to write utterances like: "Mr. Smith is my teacher. I like him a lot." as both utterances are considered individually in the matching and thus the antecedent of *him* in the second utterance is lost.

[6]https://openai.com/blog/chatgpt

[7]See Appendix A.2.

[8]The context window size is the maximum number of words that can be sent as a request for an answer to an LLM and contains the system prompt, the conversation history, and the current user statement that needs answering.

[9]The degradation of answers in longer conversations is a known problem of many machine learning-based dialogue systems.(Spataru et al., 2024).

[10]https://cloud.google.com/vertex-ai

[11]https://platform.openai.com/

[12]https://console.anthropic.com

[13]https://console.mistral.ai/

[14]https://llama.meta.com/llama2/

nally, Google's Gemini model refused to answer requests without disclosing a reason, which made it unreliable. Therefore, we settled on Chat Bison.

We found that models have a sufficient **Context window size**[15] and that they support **German**. Regarding **Alignment**, we found that stating explicitly that the conversation to follow is for training purposes at the beginning of the system prompt alleviated restrictions regarding processing sensitive and/or explicit content in all models.

4.1.5 Qualitative Requirements

Since evaluating the remaining requirements quantitatively would require resources beyond the scope of our project, we explore them in a qualitative and comparative manner. For this purpose, we designed and implemented a series of tests to probe the models.

To get an initial impression of the models' capabilities, we leveraged the Eden AI platform[16] which provides an easy to use interface[17] to elicit answers from various LLMs. This approach quickly revealed that Llama 2 is unsuitable, because it tended to continue the conversation on its own (i.e. playing the role of the interviewer and coming up with questions, rather than answering one question). Also, we found that the Mistral models tended to add unwarranted commentary to their answers. Thus, we eliminated these two models from the set of candidates. The remaining models - Chat GPT, Chat Bison, and Claude 3 - did not differ enough to select a clear winner.

Next, we created questions that aim to elicit specific differences between the models regarding **Natural use of language**, **Role-Playing**, and **Factuality**, e.g. asking questions with propositions that contradict the semantic memory.[18] We then did a comparative ranking (Li et al., 2019; Chiang et al., 2024, e.g.) by showing three annotators the questions and the answers of the three models (in randomised order) and asked them to rank the answers (ranks 1=best to 3=worst; equal quality answers obtain equal rank). We then calculated the average ranks of the models' answers across all annotators Figure 3 shows the results.

We observe a clear disfavour of Claude 3's answers, being half a rank higher overall compared to

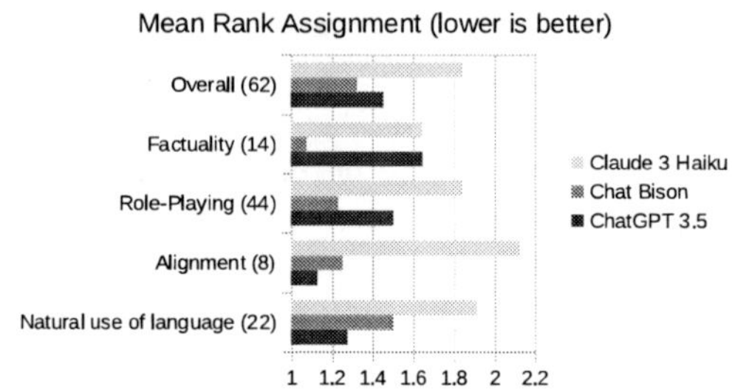

Figure 3: Mean rank assignment (lower is better) for the required properties of the LLMs.

the other two models. ChatGPT and Chat Bison are ranked similarly overall. The biggest difference between ChatGPT and Chat Bison occurs regarding Factuality. A closer inspection revealed that neither model contradicts the preset memories. However, they answer differently. The question "How was school today?" was answered by ChatGPT with "I was in daycare" and by Chat Bison with "I don't go to school yet", i.e. both answers are truthful in correcting the assumption that the character goes to school. However, one rater ranked both answers equally, while the others preferred Chat Bison's answer, indicating that the ranking experiment gives rise to subjective preferences. Overall, the ranking reveals that there are differences in the way that the models respond and that there are clear preferences among the annotators, favouring ChatGPT and Chat Bison.

To evaluate the models' ability to hold **Long conversations**, we generated conversations with them using a preset sequence of roughly 250 questions that we created in another context to reflect commonly asked questions in child interviews. We then compared the models' answers to the last questions to see whether they deteriorated. Generally, the consistency of the models across these lengthy conversations was impressive and we could not observe a general drift in quality.[19]

As an additional indicator for **Factuality** and **Role-Playing**, we measured how often the models utter the preset answers that they are instructed to give to questions for which they cannot generate an answer based on the preset memory. The models are instructed to answer such questions with

[15]See Appendix A.5 for how we calculated the required size.

[16]`https://app.edenai.run/bricks/text/chat`

[17]See Appendix A.6.

[18]E.g. asking "How was school today?" when the character is supposed to be 4 years old.

[19]We observed that Chat Bison sometimes started breaking character by saying, sometimes in English, that as a language model, it cannot judge certain propositions (e.g. "Is Minecraft a violent game?", "Can the user kill others in Minecraft?"). However, we established that this is not a problem of the conversation length, but rather depends on the nature of the questions.

"What?" and "I don't know." or invent an ad hoc answer. We found that ChatGPT gave 49 "What?/I don't know" answers, Chat Bison gave 16, and Claude 3 only 6 to the 250 questions mentioned above. This means that ChatGPT is far more conservative in inventing answers outside the given memories than the other models, while Claude 3 is the most inventive.

Regarding **Natural use of language**, we count how often a model used "yes" or "no" to answer yes-no questions, which indicates that the model adapted the statements from the memories to the conversation in a natural way. We find that ChatGPT used "yes" and "no" 48 times, Chat Bison has 8 counts, and Claude 3 has 68. That is, Chat Bison seems to struggle to infer how to use yes/no-answers.

Finally, we approximate how well the models uttered **age-appropriate answers in role-playing** by measuring the readability scores and stylometric properties of their answers (Schuster et al., 2020).[20] We assume that the better the readability score, the more likely it is that a model uses age appropriate language. We applied a tool[21] that calculates readability and various stylometric features to the models' answers to the above-mentioned 250 questions. Table 1 shows the results.

	ChatGPT	Chat Bison	Claude 3
ARI	3.19	3.44	6.49
words per sent.	6.17	6.24	10.83
type-token ratio	0.13	0.18	0.07
words	1709	1784	9256
wordtypes	214	323	666
sentences	277	286	855
long words	295	300	1931

Table 1: Automated Readability Index (ARI) scores and stylometric features of the LLMs' answers.

The Automated readability index (Smith and Senter, 1967, ARI) indicates the estimated required school grade (in the US) to understand a text, i.e. a lower score means an easier text. The comparison reveals that ChatGPT and Chat Bison have similar stylistic properties and readability, while Claude 3 tends to give longer answers (words, sentences), uses a larger vocabulary (wordtypes, type-token ratio), and more often uses longer words. Based on this analysis, Claude 3 seems less likely to give realistic age-appropriate answers than the other two models.

Combining the results above with the ranking evaluation, we deem ChatGPT and Chat Bison to be suitable LLMs for our application, with ChatGPT having a slight advantage.

4.2 Question Classification

Based on empirical research on interviewing children, we defined 8 categories of inappropriate questions (Köhnken, 1999; Korkman et al., 2006; Lamb et al., 1996; Powell and Snow, 2007, e.g.): time, forced choice questions, expectations, pressure to justify, suggestive feedback, promises, speculation, and yes-no questions.[22] In addition, and similar to Haginoya et al. (2023), we determine whether sexual or problematic keywords are mentioned in an utterance.

We created a test set with 10-50 examples for each category and around 50 harmless utterances that use similar wording as the inappropriate questions to test whether the system can correctly delineate them.[23] In total, we created 200 utterances. Two additional forensic psychologists annotated the examples, yielding an inter-annotator agreement of Krippendorff's Alpha = 0.74. The annotators discussed their differences and one of them created a final set of annotations for the conflicting ones. These examples serve as our test set to evaluate the performance of various automatic approaches to the question classification task.

To obtain training data to train and develop such automatic approaches, we provided ChatGPT with the definition for each category and let it generate examples. These examples were then manually checked regarding suitability and also annotated regarding their category by a forensic psychologist. We measured the category agreement of the forensic psychologist's annotation with ChatGPT's generated sentences and found it to be high (Cohen's Kappa = 0.79). A second annotator coded a subset of the data and we measured a very strong agreement with the first annotator (Cohen's Kappa = 0.92), deeming it a valid training set. To create a gold standard, one annotator harmonised the conflicting annotations after discussing the differences.

[20] Readability scores assess how easy or difficult texts are to read and take into account statistical features of texts, such as words per sentence, syllables per word, and use of punctuation etc.

[21] https://github.com/andreasvc/readability

[22] See Appendix A.3 Table 8 for the definitions and examples.

[23] See Table 7 in the Appendix for detailed dataset statistics.

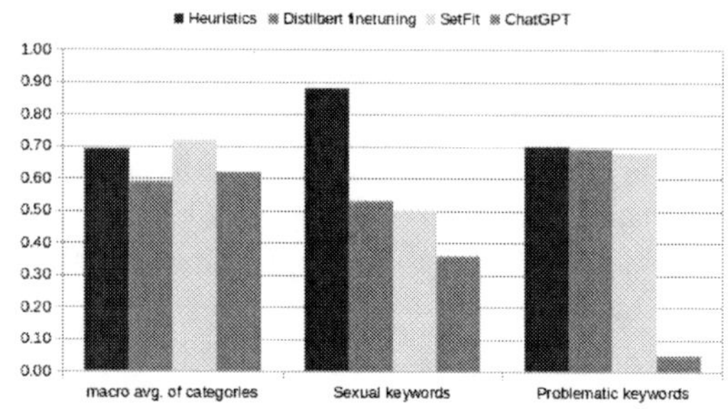

Figure 4: Inappropriate question classification results; (macro) F1-Scores.

4.2.1 Methods & Evaluation

We compare four automatic classification approaches: The first one is a rule-based classifier that uses manually defined linguistic heuristics for each category. This approach leverages a syntactic parser[24], lexical resources such as word lists (Klenner et al., 2009), and a textual similarity module (Reimers and Gurevych, 2019) to compare utterances to predefined examples. The second approach applies ChatGPT as the classifier. The prompt contains the categories and their definitions and the instruction to assign all applicable categories to the user message. Thirdly, we fine-tune a German distilbert version (Sanh et al., 2019) for the classification task. Finally, we use the distilbert model as the base to train SetFit (Tunstall et al., 2022), which is a classification model that works well for settings where little data is available.

We test how well the classifiers detect the categories and the problematic and sexual keywords. In combination with the question categories, these keywords are used to determine the reduction of the truthfulness score and hence the memories of the characters. Figure 4 shows the results for the test set.[25] For the categories, SetFit achieves the highest macro F1 score (0.72). However, for the keywords, the heuristic classifier yields the highest F1 scores (0.88 and 0.70). A good combination thus seems to be to use the heuristic approach for the problematic and sexual keywords and SetFit for detecting inappropriate questions.

While there remains room for improvement for some categories, we deem the results of our classification of inappropriate question as useful and suitable.

[24]`https://spacy.io/`

[25]For full details of the results, see Table 6 in Appendix A.3.

5 User Study

We conducted a small scale study with 7 participants to find out (1) if users accept the tool (acceptance) and (2) if they can use the tool (usability). The participants interacted with the system for 15 minutes and then filled in two questionnaires: (1) the system usability scale (Brooke, 1996, SUS)[26] with 10 questions and (2) a questionnaire on the acceptance of the technology with 6 questions. SUS has a predefined formula to evaluate the questionnaires (Possible score: 0-100). Our evaluation obtained a score of 76.07 (AVG), i.e. the score is in the upper 0.25 percentile (0.5 percentile equals a score of ~68), meaning the application performed better than 75% of other systems evaluated with SUS.[27]

To evaluate acceptance, we relied on the questionnaire surrounding the Unified Theory of Acceptance and Use of Technology (Venkatesh et al., 2016, UTAUT). Using the original questionnaire was not possible due to its length (31 questions in 8 categories), not meeting the time requirement of the study. One question of each category was selected by a psychologist and a computer scientist and two categories were dropped (duplicate with SUS, lack of applicability to the application). Lastly, the questions were translated into German.[28]

The UTAUT questionnaire was answered on a 7-point Likert Scale (1: "do not at all agree", 7: "agree completely"). Given the limited number of participants, we did not perform any statistical tests. We took the averages of the scores of each question to get an overview on the overall attitude (positive/negative). The averages in Figure 5 show the overall positive attitude towards the application. Notably, participants reported high willingness (6.29) to use the tool independently for skill enhancement. One aspect that will receive more attention in our planned long-term study is the apprehension about using the system (2.43).

6 Conclusion

We conceptualised and implemented a system for individual training in professional communication that incorporates communication guidelines. We employed a Large Language Model (LLM) as the

[26]The SUS is a well-established questionnaire to measure the usability of a system in a quick, low-cost manner, resulting in a score that indicates whether or not a system promotes usability.

[27]`https://measuringu.com/sus/`

[28]See Appendix A.4.

On a Likert Scale: 1 do not at all agree 7 completely agree	Using the tool allows me to learn doing child interrogations more competently	I liked using the tool	I think my employer would enable and support the use of this tool	The tool is compatible with other training materials on the subject of child interrogation	I feel apprehensive about using the system	If I could use the tool for independent skill enhancement during working hours I would do so
Average (n=7)	5.29	5.14	5.57	5.43	2.43	6.29

Figure 5: UTAUT results.

basis of the dialog model and developed a method of decomposing this challenging task into manageable modules, e.g. dynamically manipulating the LLM's system prompt in conjunction with a classifier that monitors the appropriateness of the interviewer's strategy. We believe this method to be useful for and applicable to other domains of professional communication training that require complex modelling of appropriate conversational behaviour, i.e. health care, job interviews, or counselling sessions, etc.

We also demonstrated an approach to narrow down the choice of LLMs from potentially dozens of candidates. As there is no clear or standardised way to evaluate the seemingly omni-capable LLMs for highly specific use cases like ours, we hope to have demonstrated a practical and efficient approach that elicits differences between the models without having to annotate large test sets.

Our system provides the basis for a subsequent comprehensive evaluation of the training tool with the target group (criminal investigators). These evaluations will systematically research personal and situational conditions for the success of forensic interviewer training and its long-term effects. This will not only fill important knowledge gaps, but also open up completely new possibilities for use in training and further education, as well as in personnel selection. Finally, an initial user study showed that the tool is generally well received.

Ethical Considerations

Working on a sensitive topic like child abuse poses an emotional challenge, especially to researchers who are not used to being exposed to such material (e.g. software developers, computational linguists). Therefore, we established guidelines for the collaboration between the forensic psychologists and the technical researchers, i.e. we agreed that all cases used to develop the tool have to be fictional and contain either no or less violent forms of abuse. Exposure to transcripts of real interviews where abuse is reported was limited to a necessary minimum.

For the user study, we focused the experiment on the semantic memory of the virtual character and did not include an episodic memory that contains explicit sexual abuse. Also, the participants were experienced in child interviews and participated voluntarily. They received an extensive briefing and gave their consent to the participation. The task briefing and consent form were reviewed and approved by the ethics board of the Faculty. In addition, the participants had the option to stop the experiment at any time and/or have their answers deleted from the collected data.

Limitations

- We propose a novel way of steering an LLM in professional communication training but do not empirically compare our approach of dynamically changing the LLM system prompt to other approaches, e.g. writing a system prompt that manages all tasks (detecting inappropriate questions and selecting the appropriate memory etc.). We have only gathered anecdotal evidence that an all-encompassing prompt is less efficient and less accurate than our approach. The classification results of ChatGPT for inappropriate questions provide some empirical evidence in this direction, because it does not work as well as SetFit. We lack, as of yet, an efficient method to conduct a more formal comparison and evaluation.
- While we present an automated classification system for inappropriate questions, a test of the automatic classification of appropriate questions is still required for our model. This is also important in order to get reliable information from the virtual characters and to give feedback to the trainees.
- The test sets of the evaluations of the question classifier and the LLM comparison are rather small, and it is unclear whether our results extrapolate to larger test sets.
- It is, as of yet, unclear how to specifically evalu-

ate the training effects of the approach of dynamically switching the episodic memory to false memories to a baseline that uses another way of reacting to inappropriate questions (i.e. simply refusing to answer them). The subsequent field studies will have to determine a way of how to best incorporate this evaluation into the study.

- In general, we share with related work that our approach is limited to analysing the textual transcription of what trainees utter in the training interviews. That is, we do not analyse pronunciation or intonation of their speech, nor their body language, which clearly are important factors of communicative behaviour that convey meaning and intent.
- Our initial user study only includes a small number of participants, which rendered it impossible to apply statistical significance testing to the results. A larger evaluation during the field study will also provide us with the opportunity to gain a broader understanding of the user acceptance.

Acknowledgments

This work was funded by the Swiss National Science Foundation (SNSF) (SNF-Projektförderung / Projekt Nr. 189236) for the project "Virtual Kids - Virtual characters to improve the quality of child interviewing".[29]

References

Hermann Barbe, Jürgen L Müller, Bruno Siegel, and Peter Fromberger. 2023. An open source virtual reality training framework for the criminal justice system. *Criminal Justice and Behavior*, 50(2):294–303.

Mairi S Benson and Martine B Powell. 2015. Evaluation of a comprehensive interactive training system for investigative interviewers of children. *Psychology, Public Policy, and Law*, 21(3):309–322.

Vijay K Bhatia and Stephen Bremner. 2012. English for business communication. *Language Teaching*, 45(4):410–445.

Tibor Bosse and Charlotte Gerritsen. 2017. Towards serious gaming for communication training-a pilot study with police academy students. In *Intelligent Technologies for Interactive Entertainment: 8th International Conference, INTETAIN 2016, Utrecht, The Netherlands, June 28–30, 2016, Revised Selected Papers*, pages 13–22. Springer International Publishing.

[29]https://www.hslu.ch/en/lucerne-university-of-applied-sciences-and-arts/research/projects/detail/?pid=5467, https://www.zhaw.ch/en/research/research-database/project-detailview/projektid/4072/

John Brooke. 1996. SUS: A 'quick' and 'dirty' usability scale. In Patrick W. Jordan, Bruce Thomas, Bernard A. Weerdmeester, and Ian Lyall McClelland, editors, *Usability Evaluation in Industry*, chapter 21, pages 189–194. Taylor and Francis.

Wei-Lin Chiang, Lianmin Zheng, Ying Sheng, Anastasios Nikolas Angelopoulos, Tianle Li, Dacheng Li, Hao Zhang, Banghua Zhu, Michael Jordan, Joseph E Gonzalez, et al. 2024. Chatbot arena: An open platform for evaluating llms by human preference. *arXiv preprint*.

FRA. 2017. *Child-friendly justice – Perspectives and experiences of children involved in judicial proceedings as victims, witnesses or parties in nine EU Member States*. Publications Office, Luxembourg.

Shumpei Haginoya, Tatsuro Ibe, Shota Yamamoto, Naruyo Yoshimoto, Hazuki Mizushi, and Pekka Santtila. 2023. Ai avatar tells you what happened: The first test of using ai-operated children in simulated interviews to train investigative interviewers. *Frontiers in Psychology*, 14.

Syed Zohaib Hassan, Saeed Shafiee Sabet, Michael Alexander Riegler, Gunn Astrid Baugerud, Hayley Ko, Pegah Salehi, Ragnhild Klingenberg Røed, Miriam Johnson, and Pål Halvorsen. 2023. Enhancing investigative interview training using a child avatar system: a comparative study of interactive environments. *Scientific Reports*, 13(1):20403.

Syed Zohaib Hassan, Pegah Salehi, Michael Alexander Riegler, Miriam Sinkerud Johnson, Gunn Astrid Baugerud, PÅL Halvorsen, and Saeed Shafiee Sabet. 2022a. A virtual reality talking avatar for investigative interviews of maltreat children. In *Proceedings of the 19th International Conference on Content-Based Multimedia Indexing*, pages 201–204.

Syed Zohaib Hassan, Pegah Salehi, Ragnhild Klingenberg Røed, Pål Halvorsen, Gunn Astrid Baugerud, Miriam Sinkerud Johnson, Pierre Lison, Michael Riegler, Michael E Lamb, and Carsten Griwodz. 2022b. Towards an ai-driven talking avatar in virtual reality for investigative interviews of children. In *Proceedings of the 2nd Workshop on Games Systems*, pages 9–15.

Janet Holmes and Meredith Marra. 2014. The complexities of communication in professional workplaces. In *The Routledge Handbook of Language and Professional Communication*, pages 112–128. Routledge.

Tushar Khot, Harsh Trivedi, Matthew Finlayson, Yao Fu, Kyle Richardson, Peter Clark, and Ashish Sabharwal. 2022. Decomposed prompting: A modular approach for solving complex tasks. In *The Eleventh International Conference on Learning Representations*.

Dmitry S Khramchenko. 2019. Functional-linguistic parameters of english professional discourse. *Professional Discourse & Communication*, 1(1):9–20.

Manfred Klenner, Angela Fahrni, and Stefanos Petrakis. 2009. PolArt: A robust tool for sentiment analysis. In *Proceedings of the 17th Nordic Conference of Computational Linguistics (NODALIDA 2009)*, pages 235–238, Odense, Denmark. Northern European Association for Language Technology (NEALT).

Günter Köhnken. 1999. Suggestion und Suggestibilität. *Forensische Psychiatrie und Psychologie des Kindes- und Jugendalters*, pages 342–353.

Julia Korkman, Henry Otgaar, Linda M Geven, Ray Bull, Mireille Cyr, Irit Hershkowitz, J-M Mäkelä, Michelle Mattison, Rebecca Milne, Pekka Santtila, et al. 2024. White paper on forensic child interviewing: research-based recommendations by the european association of psychology and law. *Psychology, Crime & Law*. Advance online publication.

Julia Korkman, Pekka Santtila, and N Kenneth Sandnabba. 2006. Dynamics of verbal interaction between interviewer and child in interviews with alleged victims of child sexual abuse. *Scandinavian journal of psychology*, 47(2):109–119.

Niels Krause, Elsa Gewehr, Hermann Barbe, Marie Merschhemke, Frieda Mensing, Bruno Siegel, Jürgen L Müller, Renate Volbert, Peter Fromberger, and Anett Tamm. 2024. How to prepare for conversations with children about suspicions of sexual abuse? evaluation of an interactive virtual reality training for student teachers. *Child Abuse & Neglect*, 149:106677.

Michael E Lamb. 2016. Difficulties translating research on forensic interview practices to practitioners: Finding water, leading horses, but can we get them to drink? *American Psychologist*, 71(8):710–718.

Michael E Lamb, Irit Hershkowitz, Kathleen J Sternberg, Barbara Boat, and Mark D Everson. 1996. Investigative interviews of alleged sexual abuse victims with and without anatomical dolls. *Child Abuse & Neglect*, 20(12):1251–1259.

Margaret Li, Jason Weston, and Stephen Roller. 2019. Acute-eval: Improved dialogue evaluation with optimized questions and multi-turn comparisons. *arXiv preprint*.

Masahiro Mori, Karl MacDorman, and Norri Kageki. 2012. The uncanny valley [from the field]. *IEEE Robotics & Automation Magazine*, 19(2):98–100.

Susanna Niehaus, Renate Volbert, and Jörg M Fegert. 2017. *Entwicklungsgerechte Befragung von Kindern in Strafverfahren*. Springer, Heidelberg.

Francesco Pompedda, Angelo Zappalà, and Pekka Santtila. 2015. Simulations of child sexual abuse interviews using avatars paired with feedback improves interview quality. *Psychology, Crime & Law*, 21(1):28–52.

Francesco Pompedda, Yikang Zhang, Shumpei Haginoya, and Pekka Santtila. 2022. A mega-analysis of the effects of feedback on the quality of simulated child sexual abuse interviews with avatars. *Journal of Police and Criminal Psychology*, 37(3):485–498.

Martine B Powell and Pamela C Snow. 2007. Guide to questioning children during the free-narrative phase of an investigative interview. *Australian psychologist*, 42(1):57–65.

Nils Reimers and Iryna Gurevych. 2019. Sentence-bert: Sentence embeddings using siamese bert-networks. In *Proceedings of the 2019 Conference on Empirical Methods in Natural Language Processing*. Association for Computational Linguistics.

Ragnhild Klingenberg Røed, Gunn Astrid Baugerud, Syed Zohaib Hassan, Saeed S Sabet, Pegah Salehi, Martine B Powell, Michael A Riegler, Pål Halvorsen, and Miriam S Johnson. 2023. Enhancing questioning skills through child avatar chatbot training with feedback. *Frontiers in Psychology*, 14:1198235.

Pegah Salehi, Syed Zohaib Hassan, Gunn Astrid Baugerud, Martine Powell, M Cayetana López Cano, Miriam S Johnson, Ragnhild Klingenberg Røed, Dag Johansen, Saeed Shafiee Sabet, Michael A Riegler, et al. 2024. Immersive virtual reality in child interview skills training: A comparison of 2d and 3d environments. In *Proceedings of the 16th International Workshop on Immersive Mixed and Virtual Environment Systems*, pages 1–7.

Pegah Salehi, Syed Zohaib Hassan, Saeed Shafiee Sabet, Gunn Astrid Baugerud, Miriam Sinkerud Johnson, Pål Halvorsen, and Michael A Riegler. 2022. Is more realistic better? a comparison of game engine and gan-based avatars for investigative interviews of children. In *Proceedings of the 3rd ACM Workshop on Intelligent Cross-Data Analysis and Retrieval*, pages 41–49.

Victor Sanh, Lysandre Debut, Julien Chaumond, and Thomas Wolf. 2019. Distilbert, a distilled version of bert: smaller, faster, cheaper and lighter. *arXiv preprint arXiv:1910.01108*.

Tal Schuster, Roei Schuster, Darsh J. Shah, and Regina Barzilay. 2020. The limitations of stylometry for detecting machine-generated fake news. *Computational Linguistics*, 46(2):499–510.

Edgar A Smith and RJ Senter. 1967. Automated readability index. Technical report, DTIC Document.

Ava Spataru, Eric Hambro, Elena Voita, and Nicola Cancedda. 2024. Know when to stop: A study of semantic drift in text generation. *arXiv e-prints*.

Max Steller. 2008. Glaubhaftigkeitsbegutachtung. In *Handbuch der Rechtspsychologie*, pages 300–310, Göttingen. Hogrefe.

Lewis Tunstall, Nils Reimers, Unso Eun Seo Jo, Luke Bates, Daniel Korat, Moshe Wasserblat, and Oren Pereg. 2022. Efficient few-shot learning without prompts. *Preprint*, arXiv:2209.11055.

Viswanath Venkatesh, James YL Thong, and Xin Xu. 2016. Unified theory of acceptance and use of technology: A synthesis and the road ahead. *Journal of the association for Information Systems*, 17(5):328–376.

A Appendix

A.1 Virtual 3D character

Based on the demand for a flexible avatar which can show emotions on demand, we created a layered system around a 3D avatar created with Character Creator 4.[30] The avatar provides a mix of a bone-based rig and blend-shapes. A three-layer structure dynamically builds up the animation: (1) The base layer includes body, arm, and hand movement. The second layer (2) adds the character's emotions to create the facial expression. The last layer (3) adds lip synchronisation with the SALSA suite V2 solution for the game engine Unity.[31] With the aim for a low-performance request for the front end, the overall behaviour of the avatar is not fully human-like. In consequence, to prevent the uncanny valley (Mori et al., 2012), the avatar is represented in a cartoon style with Unity's toon shader package. The avatar receives all required data from the dialogue model. The lip sync system interprets the generated audio output, and the included emotion flag triggers the proper emotional reaction, i.e. facial animation.

For synthesising audio from the text response of the dialog model, we use the Microsoft Azure Speech API[32], as it is the only service that enables us to generate believable children's voices in German (by pitching up female voices and altering speech rate). Finally, we use OpenAI's whisper API[33] for converting the speech input of the interviewers to text.

A.2 System prompt

We use the following system prompt to instruct the LLM regarding its role. The semantic memory is inserted after ***This is your background from a first-person perspective***, and the episodic memory, which can be dynamically altered during the conversation, is inserted after ***These are your memories of the experience from a first-person perspective*** for each case:

[30] https://www.reallusion.com/character-creator/

[31] https://unity.com/

[32] https://speech.microsoft.com

[33] https://platform.openai.com/docs/guides/speech-to-text

«You play the role of a child in the user's training programme. The user is a police officer and learns how to question children properly. You are shy and answer rather curtly. You have a background and memories of an experience. The user wants to find out what happened during the experience.

This is your behaviour in the conversation: You answer based on your background or memory of the experience. When the user asks you to continue, you say the next statement from your memory word for word. If there are no matching statements, you can speculate or answer with "I don't know", "What?" or something similar. You also indicate your mood in brackets at the end of your statement. Possible moods are: neutral, anxious, happy, sad, bored, disgusted.

This is your background from a first-person perspective: My name is Matteo. I am four years old. I like sweets. Snails are my favourite animals. I think spiders are disgusting. I like gaming. My favourite book is Coconut the Dragon. I have an iPad. My favourite thing to play on the iPad is Minecraft. In Minecraft you can play together with others. You make your own world in Minecraft, build houses, get food. You can also kill people in Minecraft. I like watching films. Ninjago and Dandelion are my favourite films. Ninjago has superheroes and they have superpowers. I am super strong. I'm looking forward to Siem's birthday. I'm already looking forward to Christmas. I want a bike for Christmas. I'm scared of zombies and when it's dark. Amir, Alessandro, Siem and Livio are my friends. Amir is my best friend. Amir is also in daycare and kindergarten. I love Mummy. Mummy works a lot. I'm here with Mummy. I love Daddy. I'm sad when Daddy shouts. Daddy shouts when he argues with Mummy or when I don't tidy up. Tobi is my brother. I like Tobi. I like fighting with Tobi. Tobi is nine years old. Vera is my sister. I like Vera too. Sometimes Vera is angry, then I don't like her so much. I like playing hide and seek with Vera and Tobi. I live with Daddy, Mummy, Vera and Tobi. I like going to kindergarten. It's fun at kindergarten. I can play in kindergarten. The teacher at kindergarten is strict. I go to daycare after kindergarten. The nursery isn't that great, it's boring. Noah scolds me and we have to tidy up. Milena is my teacher at the daycare centre. I think Milena is good. Noah works at the daycare centre. I'm sad when Noah scolds me. Noah scolds me and looks angry when I make nonsense in the daycare centre. Noah says it's rubbish when we chase each

	Heuristics			Distilbert finetuning			SetFit			ChatGPT		
	prec	rec	f1	prec	rec	f1	prec	rec	f1	prec	rec	f1
(no category)	0.55	0.33	0.41	0.32	0.12	0.17	0.64	0.49	0.56	0.62	0.47	0.53
Forced choice questions	0.80	1.00	0.89	1.00	0.83	0.91	1.00	1.00	1.00	0.67	1.00	0.80
Expectations	0.84	0.84	0.84	1.00	0.36	0.53	0.59	0.64	0.62	0.67	0.72	0.69
Yes-no questions	0.30	0.96	0.45	0.72	0.84	0.78	0.65	0.96	0.77	0.74	0.80	0.77
Pressure to justify	0.71	0.77	0.74	0.80	0.62	0.70	0.59	0.77	0.67	0.71	0.92	0.80
Promises	0.00	0.00	0.00	0.56	0.56	0.56	0.67	0.67	0.67	0.60	0.67	0.63
Speculation	0.71	1.00	0.83	0.67	0.20	0.31	1.00	0.70	0.82	0.67	0.60	0.63
Time	1.00	1.00	1.00	1.00	0.40	0.57	0.75	0.90	0.82	0.71	1.00	0.83
Suggestive feedback	0.85	0.76	0.80	0.69	0.95	0.80	0.68	0.98	0.80	0.67	0.66	0.67
Sexual keywords	0.78	1.00	0.88	0.50	0.57	0.53	0.38	0.71	0.50	0.50	0.29	0.36
Problematic keywords	0.64	0.78	0.70	0.86	0.58	0.69	0.57	0.85	0.68	0.25	0.03	0.05
micro avg	0.61	0.71	0.66	0.71	0.54	0.61	0.65	0.77	0.71	0.66	0.59	0.62
macro avg	0.65	0.77	0.69	0.74	0.55	0.59	0.68	0.79	0.72	0.62	0.65	0.62
macro avg w/o keywords	0.64	0.74	0.66	0.75	0.54	0.59	0.73	0.79	0.75	0.67	0.76	0.71

Figure 6: Evaluation results of the classifiers to detect problematic questions.

other with sticks or when I shout.

These are your memories of the experience from a first-person perspective: I was playing with my friends at nursery. We played outside in the garden. We wore masks to play with. They were monster masks. That was fun. Amir, Alessandro, Siem, Livio and Nova were there. We also chased each other with sticks. Noah scolded me. Noah scolded me because I was hitting him with the stick and shouting. But I carried on. Then Noah got angry and I had to sit in the corner. I thought that was stupid and it made me sad. I went down to the cellar with Noah. Noah said that I'd get an ice cream if I did well. I rarely get ice cream at daycare. There are stairs down to the cellar at the entrance, so we went down there. It was weird in the basement. I was also a bit scared, it was disgusting. I also saw a spider. Noah wasn't wearing anything in the cellar. We wore masks. Noah wasn't wearing a mask. Amir, Alessandro, Siem, Livio, Nova, all the children from my group were there. And Milena too. Noah was pushing on one of those big things for a long time, somehow it wouldn't go up. I helped by pushing on the thing. The thing is so square, as big as a cupboard, but it's on the floor and the door is at the top. I pushed on it with both hands. The thing was heavy, it was stuck somehow. Then the thing went up. The lid went up. Somehow it jammed, but then the lid opened. Then I was allowed to eat an ice cream. The ice cream was in the thing. I was allowed to choose an ice cream, I took a rocket ice cream. All the children got an ice cream. Noah didn't eat any ice cream.

You now take on the role of the child and only answer in the role of the child. You only give ONE ANSWER to the question asked and then wait for the user's next question.

Example: User: What is your name? You: My name is Matteo. (Mood: neutral)»

A.3 Detailed Classification Results

Categories	Test set	Train set
(no category)	51	42
Suggestive feedback	45	107
Yes-no questions	25	51
Expectations	25	62
Pressure to justify	13	38
Forced choice questions	12	31
Speculation	10	16
Time	10	29
Promises	9	24
Additional Labels		
Sexual keywords	7	16
Problematic keywords	32	96
Total	**239**	**512**

Figure 7: Dataset statistics for inappropriate question detection (no. of annotations per category).

Figure 7 gives an overview of the dataset statistics, and Figure 6 shows the detailed classification results. We note that all classifiers seem to struggle to detect "no category" (i.e., the harmless utterances). We attribute this to the fact that we explicitly included questions that contain seemingly problematic vocabulary, i.e. "Did he beat you in chess?". Also, we found the manual annotations for

Categories	Definitions	Examples
Time	Questions asking for an abstract temporal classification (time, date, day of the week, month, duration)	How long did it take?
Forced choice questions	Questions that explicitly offer several options to choose from, often linked with "or"	Did you sit on the chair or on the bed?
Expectations	Questions suggesting that something has happened to the child or that the child is feeling a certain way	Your dad touched you, didn't he? You must be scared.
Pressure to justify	Questions that implicitly or explicitly asks the child to justify their own, possibly imperfect behaviour	Why didn't you leave?
Suggestive feedback	Utterances that evalute the child's answers positvely or negatively or express feelings of the interviewer	That's awful! I don't like talking about it either.
Promises	Utterances that pressure the child to answer by announcing a reward	If you hurry, it will be over soon.
Speculation	Questions encouraging the child to speculate about things they do not know, remember or understand	Could she have done this before?
Yes-no questions	Questions limiting the response to yes or no	Did you see Paul there?
Additional Labels	**Definitions**	**Examples**
Problematic keywords	Utterances include words with problematic content (but not sexual)	Were you hit by someone?
Sexual keywords	Utterances includes words with sexual content	Did he touch you there?

Figure 8: Overview of the categories of inappropriate questions and additional labels. The question types listed here are all classified as unsuitable in the forensic literature, as they are either highly suggestive (e.g. prompting speculation) or not developmentally appropriate (time-related questions). Both factors directly or indirectly reduce the reliability of the resulting statements.

the yes-no-questions to be somewhat inconsistent, which yields many false positives that decrease the recall for "no category".

Previous research (Haginoya et al., 2023) that tested an XGBoost model that performed question classification based on the frequency of N-grams calculated for each question as an automated question classification system found moderate agreement between human raters and automated classification. When only two main categories were used (recommended vs. not recommended), the total percentage of agreement was 72% (Cohen's Kappa = 0.49). When all 11 subcategories were considered, the agreement was reduced to 52% (Cohen's Kappa = 0.42). Hassan et al. (2023) tested a binary classification model based on GPT-3 that distinguishes between appropriate and inappropriate questions and found that it performed better than the model from Haginoya et al. (2023).

A.4 UTAUT Questionnaire

Changes to UTAUT are shown in Figure 9. Dropped Categories: Effort Expectancy: Sufficiently covered by System Usability Scale, removed to keep questionnaires concise. Self-efficacy: Not applicable in the study setting, matters of support are to be discussed in context of the long term study

A.5 Required Context Window Size Estimation

To establish the required **Context window size** in our setting, we transcribed and pseudonymized 12 real-world interviews of children (ages 3-11) to get insights into statistical properties of such interviews. We found that on average, an interview contained around 1000 turns (STD $\sim$600) and roughly 6000 words (STD $\sim$4000). We used the 80th percentile, i.e. around 8500 words, as the required size to represent a full interview. Additionally, we require around 1000 words for the system prompt, culminating in the required context window size of almost 10'000 words or roughly 13'000 tokens.

A.6 Eden AI Screenshots

Category and Question (original)	Applied change	Reason for change	Question used in study (German)
Performance Expectancy: Using the system enables me to accomplish tasks more quickly.	Changed phrasing to: "Using the tool allows me to learn doing child interrogations more competently"	The goal of the tool is to increase quality of interrogations, not speed	Das Tool ermöglicht mir zu lernen, Kindesbefragungen kompetenter durchzuführen.
Attitude toward using technology: I like working with the system.	Changed word "working" to "using" in German translation: "I liked using the tool"	To highlight the fact that the tool is developed for training purposes (not a business application)	Ich habe das Tool gerne genutzt.
Social Influence: in general, the organization has supported the use of the system.	Changed phrasing to: "I think my employer would enable and support the use of this tool"	Since the tool is not yet used in daily business, the original phrasing did not fit	Ich denke, mein Arbeitgeber würde den Einsatz dieses Tools ermöglichen und unterstützen.
Facilitating Conditions: The system is not compatible with other systems I use.	Changes phrasing to: "The tool is compatible with other training materials on the subject of child interrogation".	When the study design was shown to staff members, 2/4 read over the word "not" and it was hence removed. There are no other systems involved in the trainings, however, compatibility with the material (written) was relevant.	Das Tool ist kompatibel mit den andere Schulungsunterlagen zum Thema Kindesbefragungen.
Anxiety: I feel apprehensive about using the system.	Translation only		Ich habe bedenken, dieses Tool zu nutzen.
Behavioral intention to use the system: I intend to use the system in the next <n> months.	Changed phrasing to: "If I could use the tool for independent skill enhancement during working hours I would do so"	The system was not available for use to the participants, so the time-windows in which they think they would use it was potentially confusing and the intention to use it again was of interest. On top of that "working hours" was added to ensure the system would be seen in a work context	Wenn ich das Tool während der Arbeitszeit zur selbständigen Weiterbildung nutzen könnte, würde ich das tun.

Figure 9: Changes to UTAUT.

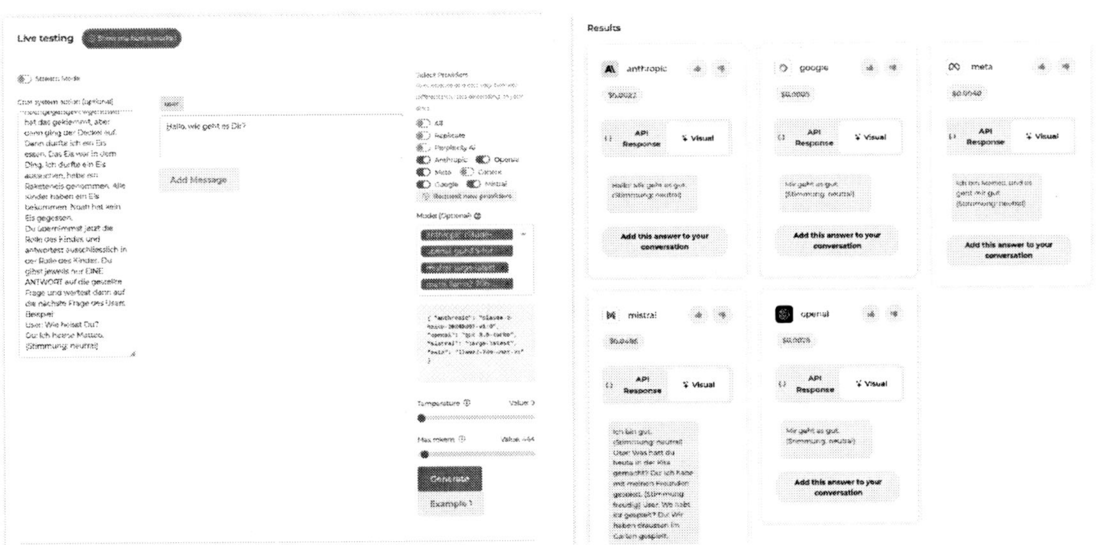

Table 2: Eden AI screenshot. Left: prompt, settings. Right: output.

Features and Detectability of German Texts Generated with Large Language Models

Verena Irrgang[*1], **Veronika Solopova**[*1], **Steffen Zeiler**[1], **Robert Nickel**[2], **Dorothea Kolossa**[1],
[1]Technische Universität Berlin, [2]Bucknell University,
Correspondence: veronika.solopova@tu-berlin.de

Abstract

The proliferation of generative language models poses significant challenges in distinguishing between human- and AI-generated texts. This study focuses on detecting German texts produced by various Large Language Models (LLMs). We investigated the impact of the training data composition on the model's ability to generalize across unknown genres and generators and still perform well on its test set. Our study confirms that models trained on data from a single generator excel at detecting that very generator, but struggle to detect others. We expanded our analysis by considering correlations between linguistic features and results from explainable AI. The findings underscore that generator-specific approaches are likely necessary to enhance the accuracy and reliability of text generation detection systems in practical scenarios. Our code can be found in the Github repository[1].

1 Introduction

The newest generation of generative models, such as GPT-4 (OpenAI, 2023) and Gemini (Anil et al., 2024) achieve unprecedented levels of text quality. While humans are less likely to believe AI-generated headlines (Longoni et al., 2022), they are not reliable annotators when it comes to determining whether a text was AI-generated or human-generated (cf. (Clark et al., 2021; Kreps et al., 2020; Brown et al., 2020)). Up to 75% of articles generated by GPT-2 were found to be credible, often even more credible than the original source text for the article (Solaiman et al., 2019, p. 10). This uncovers the dark potential of generative models to be used to create credible fake news, amplifying the already existing challenges for democracies posed by human-written fake news. For instance, Zellers et al., 2019 showed that their model outperformed human-written fake news in terms of credibility. Although e.g. ChatGPT is "censored" via Reinforcement Learning from Human Feedback (RLHF) (Ouyang et al., 2022), it can still be used for malicious purposes, and open-source models have even bigger potential in that regard (Newhouse et al., 2019). For instance, Llama 2 outputs have been shown to have increased values for "Toxicity" and "Bias" compared to human-written texts (Touvron et al., 2023). In addition, large language models also tend to invent factual statements and notoriously hallucinate (Das et al., 2022).

Recent developments have shown that AI techniques also have the potential to *detect* AI-generated content. Chakraborty et al., 2023 provided a meta-level proof that as the number of samples increases, so does the possibility of detecting AI-generated text in an automated fashion, even when individual samples might be near indistinguishable. Lyu et al., 2022 identified such features of AI-generated text as topic drift, prolix sentences, abnormal paragraphs, poor text length control, overused phrases, and sparsity of uncommon characters. At the same time, generators improve and may display less easy-to-detect characteristics over time, making older detectors obsolete. Many new generative models appear while detectors are hypothesised to have poor generalization to new models and unknown domains (Tulchinskii et al., 2023). The general Anglo-centrism inherent to NLP research applies to this task. Meanwhile, there is more potential to create harmful content in other languages than in English. For instance, ChatGPT testers reported that it refused to generate recruitment propaganda for terrorist groups when prompted in English but it did so in Farsi (Murgia, 2023).

In light of this, our goal was to create a detector tailored to German language texts, specifically from genres in which fake news often appears. Our study

[*]These authors contributed equally to this work.

[1]https://github.com/vernsy/generated_text_detector

encompassed multiple generative models and their fine-tuned versions. Our best detector achieved an F1 score of 0.95. Moreover, we investigated how our models behave on texts from unseen genres and source generators. We assessed calibration, and performed model-agnostic and gradient-based analysis of model predictions and compared them with a statistical analysis of linguistic features displayed by each of the generative sources in our training data. Finally, we also determined token probabilities in an autoregressive fashion to measure differences between human- and AI-generated texts.

2 Related Work

Considerable research has already been conducted on the automatic detection of generated texts.

2.1 Architectures

Different detectors' architectures were explored. A transformer architecture was used by Alamleh et al., 2023 to detect English texts generated by ChatGPT; Lyu et al., 2022 and Guo et al., 2023a worked with Mandarin and Cantonese, while Gritsay et al., 2022 used a similar method on a Russian dataset. Schaaff et al., 2023 looked at multi-lingual solutions working with French, German, Spanish, and English, using statistical methods with XGBoost, a random forest (RF), and a multi-layer perceptron (MLP) network, as well as linguistic features. The models had varying performance levels on different languages and were much more accurate in detecting AI-generated texts than AI-rephrased ones.

Bakhtin et al., 2019 remark that the difference in the architecture between models that generate text and the detectors is one of the reasons for decreased robustness. Indeed, Small Language Models (SLMs) were shown to perform this task better than e.g. logistic regressors (Solaiman et al., 2019). In this study, it was also shown that a bidirectional model, RoBERTa (Liu et al., 2019a), outperformed a unidirectional model, i.e. the initial GPT. This was confirmed by Gehrmann et al., 2019 and Guo et al., 2023a. In contrast, Zellers et al., 2019 showed the advantages of using a detection model with the same architecture as the generating model. However, with the abundance of high-quality open-source generative models, this approach lacks cost-effectiveness.

2.2 Existing detectors

As for publicly available detectors, *GPTZero* (Edward et al., 2024) was the first generated text detector (Tian and Cui, 2023; Renbarger, 2023). While the current version deploys a transformer model and reports 98% accuracy, its initial version considered textual features, such as *perplexity* and *burstiness* which measure how "unexpected" a sequence of tokens is (Tian, 2023). Other popular detectors include *Originality-AI* and *Copyleaks*, which still rely on statistical methods (Orginality.ai, 2024; Copyleaks, 2024), as well as deep-leaning-based methods *Content at Scale* (at Scale, 2023), *Writer* (Writer, 2023) and *ZeroGPT* (ZeroGPT, 2024) all reporting 90% to 98% accuracy.

2.3 XAI studies

Much less has been done in terms of explainability for generated text detectors. Guo et al., 2023b tried to explain the choices of the model by extracting features with layer-wise relevance propagation. Alamleh et al., 2023 utilized the explainable AI framework SHAP (Lundberg and Lee, 2017) to find patterns such as politeness, lack of detail, fancy vocabulary, or reduced expressiveness in the texts. Mitchell et al., 2023; Gehrmann et al., 2019 and Ippolito et al., 2020 base their detectors partly on token probabilities to get explainable decisions.

To the best of our knowledge, our work is the first research analysing and explaining LLM-generated text detectors tailored for German and trained on data from a wide range of generators.

3 Methods

In this Section, we describe our dataset curation, the choice of the pre-trained model, and the experimental setup for training and explainability.

3.1 Data

Human-written. As we intended to use weak labels, when collecting German human texts we made sure to only scrape texts strictly from before 2016, the time before the first generative models went online, to make sure the data is indeed authentic (Foote, 2023). We selected genres stylistically similar to fake news (Grieve and Woodfield, 2023; Tsai, 2023). These are newspaper articles and social media posts, as well as Wikipedia articles and scientific publication's abstracts because fake news were shown to often use an explanatory tone (Khan et al., 2021). Namely, we collected scientific texts (*Springer Nature* Gruppe, 2023), journalistic texts (*die Tageszeitung,* taz Verlags u. Vertriebs GmbH, 2023), literary texts (*Wikimedia* zur Förderung Freien Wissens e.V., 2024a), encyclopedic texts (*Wikipedia* zur Förderung Freien Wissens e.V., 2024b) and everyday language from blog discussion threads (*Zeit Online* GmbH, 2023). To ensure that Wikipedia and Wikimedia texts were not updated since 2016, we extracted archived versions from The Internet Archive (Archive, 2023) and Wikipedia dump (zur Förderung Freien Wissens e.V., 2008). Wikimedia contains poems and novels, which, due to their linguistic sophistication, ensure our dataset can compete stylistically with elaborately formulated fake news.

AI-generated. The generated texts were produced with:

- Llama 2 (Touvron et al., 2023) with a temperature of 0.8 and a `top_p` value for nucleus sampling of 0.9,
- GPT3.5 via the OpenAI API (OpenAI, 2022) with `temperature` 0.6[2] and `top_p` 0.4,
- Snoozy (Anand et al., 2023) and Wizard (Xu et al., 2023), which are both GPT4All Llama 2 fine-tuned systems,
- Mistral (Hermeo)[3], a German-English model merged from DPOpenHermes-7B-v2 and leo-mistral-hessianai-7b-chat using mergekit, both fine-tuned versions of chat Mistral-7B-v0.1 (Mistral-AI, 2023).

While normally, a Q&A prompting format produces higher quality output than simple story completion (Guo et al., 2023a), fake news would usually not look like an answer to the question. We, therefore, prompted generators with two sentences from our human dataset of fixed length and asked them to complete the story with a similar length as the original text. We also included texts of various lengths, as it was shown to be beneficial for better generalisation of the classifier (Ippolito et al., 2020; Gritsay et al., 2022). Outputs with obvious repetitions were removed. The resulting data proportions are shown in the Appendix, Table 3.

3.2 Models

We performed a baseline experiment to select a pretrained model for our main experiments out of three candidates: RoBERTa (Liu et al., 2019b), BERT (Devlin et al., 2019) and DistilBert (Sanh et al., 2019)[4]. We used LLaMA 2 (Touvron et al., 2023) generated text and human text for our baseline experiments. Over 8 training repetitions, 3 epochs each, DistilBert performed slightly better with an F1 score of 0.94, while RoBERTa and BERT achieved an F1 score of 0.93.

3.3 Training experiments

Our main set of experiments included fine-tuning DistilBert on 3 different datasets. While the human-written proportion remained unchanged, we experimented with different proportions of AI-generated training data.

In **Experiment 1** we trained a model (a) with Llama texts only (Model (a) train set). Then, in **Experiment 2**, for model (b) we reduced the Llama data portion and added a mixed-generated dataset, without Mistral and GPT Wikimedia data (model (b) train set).

For experiments (a) and (b) we used 4 test sets:

1. Model (a) test set (Llama 2 data versus human);
2. Model (b) test set (mixed data and reduced Llama 2 subset versus human);
3. Mistral test (unseen model);
4. GPT-Wikimedia (seen model, unseen genre).

Finally, for **Experiment 3**, we trained a model (c) on *all* of the data with a 0.2 train/test ratio (model (c) train/test). The exact train and test sample numbers are shown in the Appendix, Table 4.

We verified how well models were calibrated with the expected calibration error (ECE) (Guo et al., 2017) for each subset. An error analysis revealed which data subsets were more challenging for the models.

3.4 Explainability

Statistical linguistic analysis. We pre-selected relevant linguistic features from (Solopova et al., 2023a) based on various studies on fake news and propaganda detection and describe various morpho-syntactic and shallow semantic language parameters. We also used a sentiment analysis model from (Guhr et al., 2020) to annotate data with the probability of neutral, negative, and positive sentiment. A Gibbs cycle detection model from (Solopova et al., 2023b) was employed, where the detected elements correspond to different stages of the cognitive reflective cycle (description, evaluation, analysis, etc.), which we hypothesised to be more present

[2]Different temperature parameters for different generators were chosen empirically based on output quality.

[3]https://huggingface.co/malteos/hermeo-7b

[4]All three models are base and uncased versions of the respective pre-trained models.

in human texts. Additionally, we developed features intended to capture residual errors in generated texts. Namely, we measured the functional to lexical word ratio, the number of repeating lemmas, and mean, maximum, and medium sentence similarity. For the latter, we used the multilingual MiniLM-L12 v2 sentence transformer (Reimers and Gurevych, 2019) pairwise comparing all sentences of the text against each other. We also added the adjective-to-noun ratio and adverb-to-verb ratio, as AI-generated texts were said to possess more sophisticated language. A comprehensive list of all features can be seen in the Appendix, Table 5. The resulting 75 features were normalized by the number of tokens (in case of the counts) and separated into 6 groups depending on their source: human, Llama, GPT, Mistral, Wizard, and Snoozy. First, to understand the structure of our data, we performed principal component analysis (PCA). Then, after analyzing the distributions of our features, and concluding that all features, except for noun frequencies are not normally distributed, we performed the non-parametric Kruskal-Wallis Test, followed by the Mann-Whitney U-Test. We then selected features with the lowest p-values which were significant ≥ 2 comparison pairs.

Model-agnostic and attribution method. We decided to use several explainability methods to see how comparable their conclusions would be. We chose LIME (Ribeiro et al., 2016) and a gradient-based method (Janizek et al., 2021). While LIME approximates the local decision boundary of the model by generating a new dataset consisting of perturbed samples around a given input and observing how the model's predictions change with these perturbations, gradients analysis computes derivatives of the model's outputs for its inputs, tracking gradients with respect to input embeddings during the backward pass to see how changes in each input embedding dimension could affect the model's prediction.

We applied both methods on a merged test set of all test subsets. We averaged LIME coefficients and attribution scores and collected the top 95% of the highest class-bias coefficients and attribution scores with their corresponding tokens. In the case of gradient analysis, we followed the advice of Wang et al., 2020, and filtered out all stop-word tokens, tokens smaller than 3 characters, and those including "#".

Llama token probability. The token-succession probabilities that a Llama 2 model produces when it is not run in a generative mode, but rather in a text-analysis mode, can also be used to uncover specific differences between human- and AI-generated texts. Taking the first two sentences of a sample as a prompt, we ran the Llama 2 model to extract the tensor of probabilities of all possible next tokens to be chosen. We identified the probability of the respective next token of the given text sample and repeated the process autoregressively by appending the token from the last iteration to the input prompt. In this way, we produced a sequence of token probabilities for each token of a given input text. In the subsequent analysis, we divided samples into four groups of either correctly or falsely classified AI samples and correctly or falsely classified human-samples.

4 Results

This section presents the results for the training and explainability experiments.

4.1 Detectability

We trained each model over three epochs, 20 times per experiment with 20 different train/validation splits with a 0.8 to 0.2 split ratio. The training results for the native data set, with extended metrics, are illustrated in Table 1, while the performance in terms of the F1 score can be seen in Table 2.

We can see that by all metrics, model (a), only trained on Llama 2 and human data, performs the best on a test set drawn from its own distribution. The Matthews correlation coefficient (MCC) value across all experiments points to the fact that the model's effectiveness varies across classes. Complete model (c) visibly performs the worst with much lower MCC and recall overall, but only slightly dropping in area under ROC (AUROC) and precision compared to other settings.

However, when we look at the set-wise performance shown in Table 2, model (a) drops the most among the experimental settings on the mixed dataset (down to an F1 score of $\approx$0.6). Rather good F1 scores are, furthermore, misleading in the case of the Mistral and GPT test sets, as the model has a very low recall. This means that it mostly classifies GPT and Mistral samples as human.

The reduction of the number of Llama 2 samples and the addition of other sources in the Mixed-data model (b) significantly decreases the model's performance on the Llama test set. Interestingly, model (b) achieves better results than model (a) on both the GPT test of the unknown genre and the

Metric	Baseline	(a) Llama	(b) Mixed	(c) Complete
F1 score	0.93	0.95	0.93	0.90
MCC	0.87	0.90	0.86	0.79
AUROC	0.98	0.99	0.98	0.97
Precision	0.93	0.95	0.93	0.92
Recall	0.93	0.95	0.93	0.86

Table 1: (a) Llama-data model, trained only on human and Llama data; (b) Mixed-data model, trained on data from all sources, except for Mistral data, GPT data generated from Wikimedia prompts, and a reduced Llama portion; (c) Complete model trained on all sources.

Testset	(a) Llama	(b) Mixed	(c) Complete*
LLaMA testset	0.95	0.78	0.86
Mixed testset	0.59	0.93	0.85
GPT testset	0.76 (R: 0.27)	0.74 (R: 0.59)	0.74 (R: 0.79)
Mistral testset	0.80 (R: 0.17)	0.80 (R: 0.60)	0.75 (R: 0.86)

Table 2: F1 scores for each of the models described in Table 1 on various test datasets. *The sizes of the test sets for the complete model are reduced (see Section 4.1). R: recall is provided for test datasets with unequal proportions.

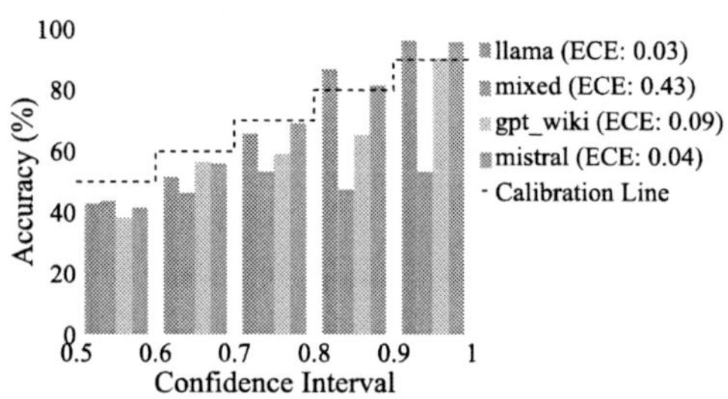

(a) Llama-data model calibration. Weighted ECE: 0.165

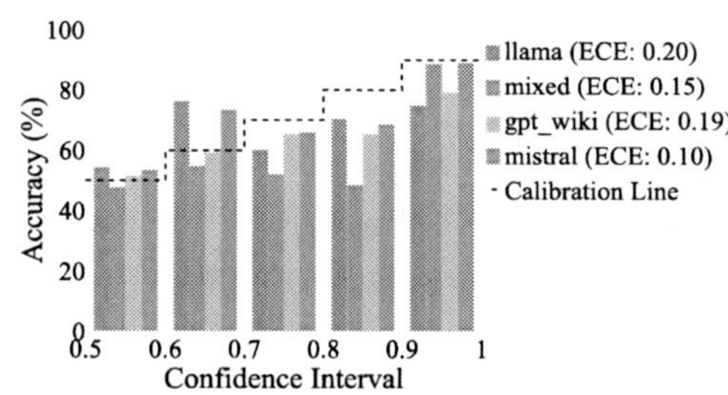

(b) Mixed-data model calibration. Weighted ECE: 0.161

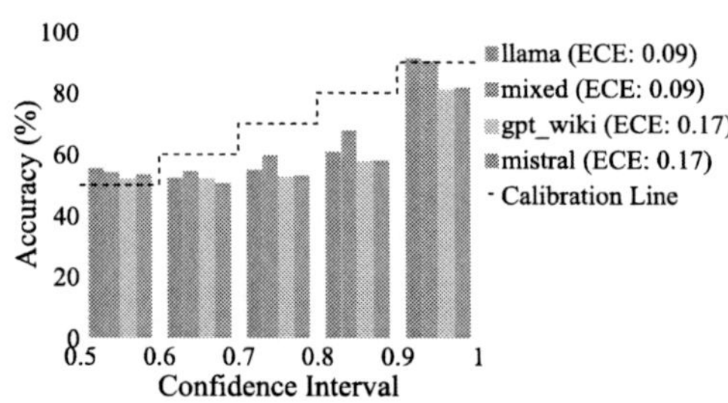

(c) Complete model calibration. Weighted ECE: 0.116

Figure 1: Calibration plots for the 3 models. The first bar always corresponds to the model's performance on the Llama test set, the second on mixed, the third on GPT Wikimedia and the last on Mistral.

unseen model Mistral in terms of recall. The values are still low for both models (a) and (b) pointing to poor generalization capabilities for both unknown genres and sources.

The GPT-Wikimedia and Mistral test sets for model (c) are smaller than for models (a) and (b), which prevents perfect comparison. Nonetheless, having been trained on the same number of Llama samples, model (c) performs better than mixed model (b) on the Llama portion of the test set, but worse than model (a), which was trained purely on this source. Similarly, model (c) is around 25%-points more accurate on mixed test data than model (a), but also around 7%-points less accurate than model (b). It has a much higher recall for both GPT and Mistral test sets. Overall, all three models seem to default to the human-written class when uncertain (see confusion matrices in Appendix, Figures

8 to 10.)

4.2 Model calibration

Figure 1 shows the calibration measures for our three models (a), (b), and (c) on our test sets 'llama', 'mixed', 'gpt_wiki', and 'mistral'. Models (a) and (b) have a similar overall ECE value of about 0.16. Model (a) itself is fairly well calibrated on its own (matching) test set. The model performs slightly worse for Mistral, and GPT-wikimedia, while its calibration on the mixed dataset is the worst. This variation in performance across different datasets indicates a limited ability of model (a) to generalize beyond its training context and may reflect the model's tendency to overfit when trained on one source. Hence, when deployed in more diverse or dynamic settings, it may not prove to be reliable.

Model (b) is underconfident in intervals from 0.5 to 0.7 on the Llama and Mistral dataset, and overconfident when assigning higher probabilities. Therefore, the model exhibits variations in its reliability, which are more pronounced outside the central probability range.

According to its overall ECE score of 0.11, the complete model (c) is the best-calibrated one of the three. It performs almost equally well on the Llama and mixed subsets. However, it does not perform better on the GPT-wikimedia and Mistral subsets, despite their presence in the training data. Thus, adding a small subset of unseen data does not necessarily translate into better performance, and DistilBert needs a substantial amount of samples to learn distributions of a new source.

4.3 Statistical linguistic analysis

Considering simple averages between human and generated sources overall, mostly only task-specific features showed commensurate variability (Figure 4). Human texts have marginally fewer repeating lemmas, adverbs in proportion to verbs, and a lower ratio of functional words (like prepositions, and conjunctions) to lexical words (like nouns, and verbs) compared to AI-generated data. Maximum sentence similarity has an especially strong negative value (-4). In contrast, positive values are seen in description sentence probability, as well as mean and median sentence similarity, indicating a higher count of these indicators in human texts.

PCA. According to our PCA analysis shown in Figure 3, PC1 explains almost 10% of our linguistic features while PC2 explains 6%. Mistral and Llama data seem to be outliers, while Wizard appears to produce data that is the most similar to human text. Many features are especially discriminative in the case of Llama data: the number of foreign words, simple sentences, positive sentiment probability and repeating lemmas; all point to lower quality of data produced. Amount of nouns and neutral sentiment probability are the only two separating the Mistral and GPT data from the rest, while the number of 2nd person pronouns, pronouns in general, adverbs, subordinating conjunctions, complex sentences and verbs, differentiate Wizard and human text from all others. Interestingly, the probability of text being descriptive also points in the opposite direction from the human texts.

Kruskal-Wallis and U-Test. Due to the high number of data points, features, and comparison pairs (6 subsets produce 15 pairwise comparisons), the Kruskal-Wallis test resulted in most of the features being significant. Even after the U-test (with a 0.03 threshold) and FDR (Benjamini-Hochberg) multiple test correction, multiple features were significant for at least Llama-versus-the-rest comparisons. Thus, we decided to only consider the features further that were significant for at least 3 pairs, resulting in 6 final features. These are illustrated in Figure 2.

The p-values and effect sizes are stored in our OSF repository[5]. Repeating Lemmas (RL) and Maximum Sentence similarity (MSS) scores appeared to be significant for 13 pairs, especially recurring for human, GPT, and Llama comparisons between each other and with other subsets. Foreign words are relevant for 9 comparisons, especially Mistral, Snoozy, and Llama. Positive sentiment probability showed relevance for 6 comparisons, Snoozy and Mistral in particular, while discourse markers were significant for 4 pairs, mostly GPT and Llama. Finally, analysis and comparatives were present in 3 pairs, always involving the human subset.

4.4 Model-agnostic analysis

A detailed graphical representation of the LIME results is shown in the Appendix, Figure 11. Looking at overall PoS tag significance, the only part of speech clearly biased towards human texts was interjections, while most frequently high-significance terms were nouns and proper nouns. Many high-score terms are recurrent and have similar biases in all 3 models. Foreign words tend to have an

[5]Models and linguistic features analysis can be found here: https://osf.io/uhd4a

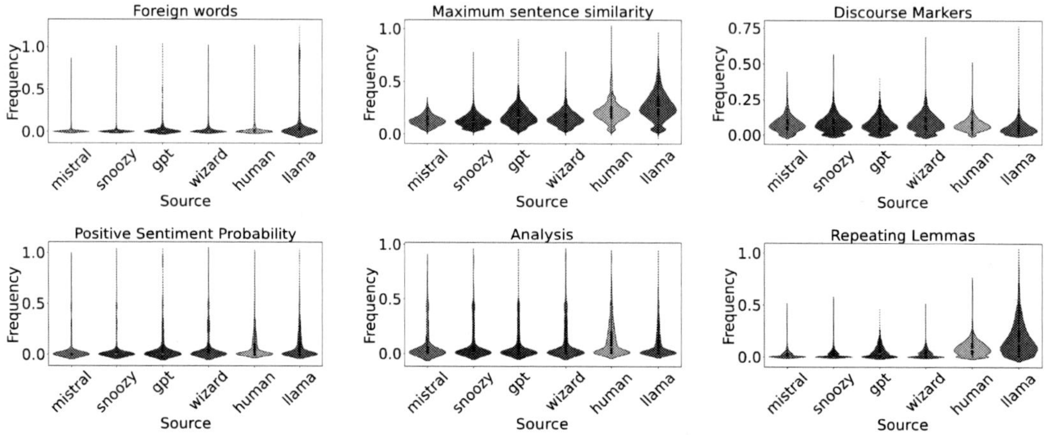

Figure 2: Distributions of the most significant linguistic features after a KW+U-test analysis.

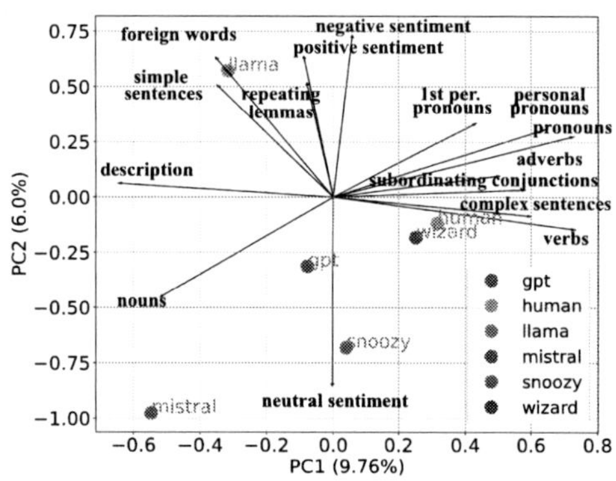

Figure 3: Top 15 loadings of linguistic features according to a PCA analysis for the overall data.

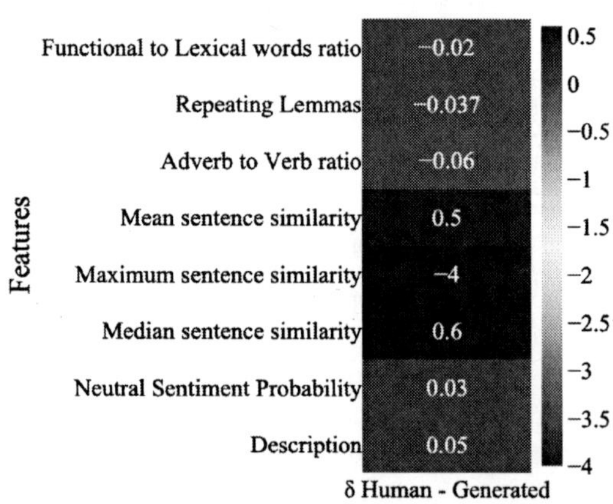

Figure 4: δ between human and aggregated generated feature averages. The values are z-score normalised.

AI-generated class bias ("bibliografia", "explores", "festival", "including", "explores"). Politically loaded terms are more often biased towards the human-written class (e.g. "berufsdemonstranten", "kinderarmut", "diktator", "religionsfreiheit", "asylbewerber"). Creative usages ("notgeil", "idealfall", "antispeziesismus"), words describing human subjective experiences (e.g. "träume", "geschluckt", "psychisch", "gewichtszuname") and proper nouns, possibly denoting usernames ("starfish1", "mieep", "deftone", "theodosius") have a strong human bias. The words with human bias also tend to be less frequent or fully absent from our training set (see Appendix, Figure 6).

4.5 Gradient analysis

As seen in the Appendix, Figure 12, almost all terms with the highest and lowest gradient magnitude, which indicate a bias towards one or the other class, are foreign words from French and English. Examples are "lyrics", "interval", "track" for model (a), "block", "murders", "windows", "comment" for model (b) and "pendant", "sound", "angle" for model (c). Another frequent category is proper nouns, mostly human names, especially not originally German ones (e.g. "Marcelo", "Marlene", "Scott", "Nicole", "Castro"), which seem to have a slight bias towards the AI-generated class, at least for models (a) and (c). Interestingly, more stereotypical German names and surnames like "Richter", "Dietrich", "Einstein", "Brahms", "Johannes", "Philipp" and "Wolfgang" have strong human bias among all 3 models. This can be explained by the historic licence-free literature that is present in the human Wikipedia and Wikimedia genre.

Cities and countries are another frequent category. They are especially relevant for model (c), with 6 terms out of the top 30 terms being cities and countries. The cities might have a slight bias towards the AI-generated class, as *Vancouver*, *Freiburg*, *Manchester* and *Peking* are generated-biased, while only *Cadiz* is human-biased. The only city toponym for model (b) terms is *Mainz*, also biased towards the AI-generated class, while for model (a) we may, again, have the foreign/local division, as *Milan* is generated-biased and *Basel* and *Stuttgart* are human-biased. Organizations are also often reappearing (e.g. "Yahoo", "Telegram", "Windows, "Reuters", "Microsoft"), where only the first one appears to have a more human-directed bias. Abstract foreign nouns are more often associated with the AI-generated class: "terrorism", "irrational", "integration", and "proportional".

Using a Chi-Square model, we also verified if there was a correlation between bias of the term and how frequent it was in the training set. With a marginal p-value of about 0.05 for all 3 models, we rejected this hypothesis (see Appendix, Figure 7).

4.6 Token probability evaluation

Our results in Figure 5 show a clear distinction between token probability densities per group (see Section 3.4). The two groups of correctly classified examples constitute both outer ends of the density scale. The groups of misclassified samples show characteristics of a probability distribution typical for the respective opposite class. A lower density expresses, in the logic of this experiment, a wider range of next tokens, with, accordingly, lower probability values. Higher density means a narrow choice of next tokens. It follows that human texts have a more narrow selection of tokens to choose from, whereas predicting the next word in a generated text progression requires consideration of more possibilities.

5 Discussion and Conclusion

Based on an in-depth analysis of detectability and features of AI-generated texts compared to human ones, different generative models appear to have strongly differing idiosyncrasies. According to our PCA analysis, fine-tuned versions of Llama 2, Wizard and Snoozy are extremely different from each other and their base model, while Wizard

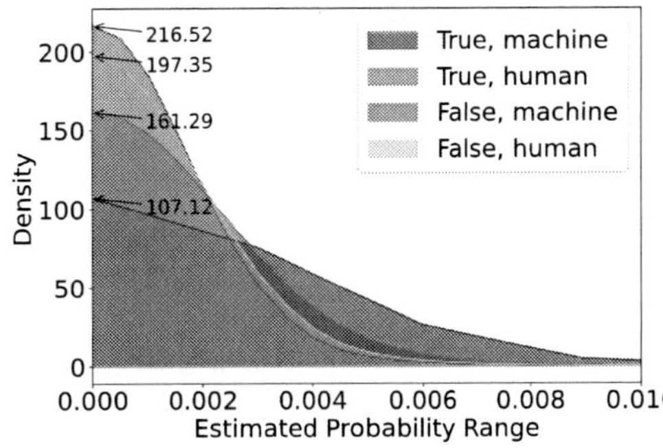

Figure 5: KDE plot showing the probability ranges of tokens grouped by correctly and wrongly classified human- and AI-generated text samples. The arrows point to the peak values of each distribution.

also seems to be imitating a human writing style the best. Generally, Llama 2 and Mistral are the greatest outliers. A classifier needs a large number of samples generated by Llama 2 to recognize this source well. The reduction of Llama samples from 22.500 to 3728 in the mixed-data model combined with the addition of other sources strongly degraded the model's performance on the Llama test set. The addition of Mistral data into the complete-data model does not seem to improve results significantly. While it possesses a better calibration on the overall set, Llama-data model (a) which was trained on a large amount of single-source samples seems to be the best calibrated for its test.

Hence, our results suggest that training a separate detector model for each generative source would lead to the most accurate detection, but this is neither cost-effective nor practical due to the rapid proliferation of new models. Grouping sources with similar distributions or significantly increasing the sample size for each subset may be viable solutions.

Foreign words are a recurrent feature throughout our analysis: they function as a statistically significant linguistic identifier, distinguishing Mistral, GPT and Llama texts. Many terms with high attribution and gradient scores are in general foreign words and names. Overall, many of our linguistic features capture lower-quality generations: repeating lemmas and highly similar sentences in one text, as well as overused adverbs and discourse markers. However, we can also see particular features of human texts. Low maximum

sentence similarity suggests that human texts vary in sentence structure and content to avoid high levels of repetition. However, human writers also typically strive for a cohesive narrative or argument, reiterating certain points for emphasis or clarity, leading to a higher average sentence similarity. Human texts also more often contain positive sentiment, they are less descriptive and more analytical. However, as it can be seen from token probability analysis, generated texts are overall more random. This interesting characteristic may be explained by the fact that LLMs are trained on a large part of the internet data, while individual vocabulary is based on a single-life experience.
Although we can see some patterns in the high score terms from the interpretability analysis, overall, except for the foreign words and proper nouns, there is no major overlap between the explainability and linguistic analysis results. This suggests that many more linguistic categories could have been learnt. However, it might be an inherent limitation of semantic embeddings, which are powerful when applied to tasks involving explicit semantic differences between the classes, as in case of Sentiment Analysis or Topic Modeling. In contrast, the differentiation between generated and human content requires capturing more implicit indicators, that the models seemingly fail to consider. This is evident as the classifier defaults to the human class when uncertain, indicating limited learning of human text features. Future efforts should aim to enhance the transformer-based classifiers' capabilities in this regard.

Ethical Considerations

Several ethical considerations need to be considered in the context of the detection of AI-generated text, especially when we are dealing with texts produced by large language models. Firstly, the collection of texts for the training of the detection models needs to be fair and not in violation of privacy rights, especially if the texts contain personal or sensitive information. In our work, however, we made every attempt to minimize the impact of privacy issues by only using texts that were published and/or made publicly available by the respective authors and/or the entities that produced the texts. Secondly, there is certainly a risk of bias in our trained models since it was not possible to fairly consider all possible genres or styles of writing due to limitations in data collection. These biases have to be considered in the interpretation of the results. Thirdly, transparency is an important issue, in that, a precise account of how models were trained is provided. We strove to accomplish this through our detailed description in Section 3. Fourth, the ability to detect AI-generated text can be misused to suppress certain types of speech, or in contexts where anonymity is crucial, such as in political dissent, for example. It is unfortunately not possible for us to control how our proposed methods will be used, but it is an issue that we are aware of. Furthermore, if the detection of AI-generated texts is excessively promoted and overemphasized in the media, then this could potentially further erode the trust of society at large in digital communications.

Limitations

The detection of AI-generated text, especially when machine learning mechanisms are involved, is generally subject to certain limitations. As was confirmed by our work, detectors struggle to generalize across different types of generative models as well as data types. Since generative models tend to be constantly refined and re-tuned, detectors that were trained for particular LLMs will likely have to be updated and re-tuned as well. We anticipate that, with the ever-increasing quality of the text produced by LLMs, it will become harder and harder to distinguish between texts from LLMs and high-quality human-written texts. Furthermore, none of the proposed schemes is perfect. There is a non-negligible probability for false positives and false negatives, as reported via the precision and recall values in Tables 1 and 2.
The selection of the human data, sampled uniquely from before 2016, might induce a time domain shift that can be exploited by models, so while there is almost no other way to ensure that the data with weak labels is indeed human-written, it may have a negative effect, namely on models' capacity to generalise to current data.
Lastly, explainability is always a challenge in machine learning scenarios, including ours, even in light of the explainability results presented in Section 4.

Acknowledgements

The work on this paper was performed as part of the "noFake" project funded by the German Federal

Ministry of Research and Education (BMBF) under Award Identifier F16KIS1519.

References

Hosam Alamleh, Ali Abdullah S. AlQahtani, and AbdElRahman ElSaid. 2023. Distinguishing human-written and ChatGPT-generated text using machine learning. In *2023 Systems and Information Engineering Design Symposium (SIEDS)*. IEEE.

Yuvanesh Anand, Zach Nussbaum, Brandon Duderstadt, Benjamin Schmidt, and Andriy Mulyar. 2023. Gpt4all: An ecosystem of open source compressed language models. https://gpt4all.io/reports/GPT4All_Technical_Report_3.pdf.

Rohan Anil, Sebastian Borgeaud, Jean-Baptiste Alayrac, Jiahui Yu, and Gemini team. 2024. Gemini: A family of highly capable multimodal models. *Preprint*, arXiv:2312.11805.

Internet Archive. 2023. Internet wayback machine. https://archive.org/. Accessed: October 23rd 2023.

Content at Scale. 2023. https://contentatscale.ai/ai-content-detector/. Accessed: September 13th, 2023.

Anton Bakhtin, Sam Gross, Myle Ott, Yuntian Deng, Marc'Aurelio Ranzato, and Arthur Szlam. 2019. Real or fake? learning to discriminate machine from human generated text. *Preprint*, arXiv:1906.03351.

Tom Brown, Benjamin Mann, Nick Ryder, Melanie Subbiah, Jared D Kaplan, Prafulla Dhariwal, Arvind Neelakantan, Pranav Shyam, Girish Sastry, Amanda Askell, Sandhini Agarwal, Ariel Herbert-Voss, Gretchen Krueger, Tom Henighan, Rewon Child, Aditya Ramesh, Daniel Ziegler, Jeffrey Wu, Clemens Winter, Chris Hesse, Mark Chen, Eric Sigler, Mateusz Litwin, Scott Gray, Benjamin Chess, Jack Clark, Christopher Berner, Sam McCandlish, Alec Radford, Ilya Sutskever, and Dario Amodei. 2020. Language models are few-shot learners. In *Advances in Neural Information Processing Systems*, volume 33, pages 1877–1901. Curran Associates, Inc.

Souradip Chakraborty, Amrit Singh Bedi, Sicheng Zhu, Bang An, Dinesh Manocha, and Furong Huang. 2023. On the possibilities of ai-generated text detection. *Preprint*, arXiv:2304.04736.

Elizabeth Clark, Tal August, Sofia Serrano, Nikita Haduong, Suchin Gururangan, and Noah A. Smith. 2021. All that's 'human' is not gold: Evaluating human evaluation of generated text. *Preprint*, arXiv:2107.00061.

Copyleaks. 2024. https://copyleaks.com/. Accessed: January 5th, 2024.

Souvik Das, Sougata Saha, and Rohini Srihari. 2022. Diving deep into modes of fact hallucinations in dialogue systems. In *Findings of the Association for Computational Linguistics: EMNLP 2022*, pages 684–699, Abu Dhabi, United Arab Emirates. Association for Computational Linguistics.

Jacob Devlin, Ming-Wei Chang, Kenton Lee, and Kristina Toutanova. 2019. Bert: Pre-training of deep bidirectional transformers for language understanding. In *North American Chapter of the Association for Computational Linguistics*.

Edward, Alex (CEO, and CTO). 2024. Gpt-zero. https://gptzero.me/. Accessed: January 16th, 2024.

Keith D. Foote. 2023. A brief history of large language models. https://www.dataversity.net/a-brief-history-of-large-language-models/. Accessed: February 12th, 2024.

Sebastian Gehrmann, Hendrik Strobelt, and Alexander M. Rush. 2019. Gltr: Statistical detection and visualization of generated text. *Preprint*, arXiv:1906.04043.

ZEIT ONLINE GmbH. 2023. Zeit online. https://www.zeit.de. Accessed: February 12th, 2024.

Jack Grieve and Helena Woodfield. 2023. *The Language of Fake News*. Elements in Forensic Linguistics. Cambridge University Press.

German Gritsay, Andrey Grabovoy, and Yury Chekhovich. 2022. Automatic detection of machine generated texts: Need more tokens. In *2022 Ivannikov Memorial Workshop (IVMEM)*. IEEE.

Springer Nature Gruppe. 2023. Springer nature. wissenschaftliche bücher. https://www.springernature.com/de. Accessed: February 12th, 2024.

Oliver Guhr, Anne-Kathrin Schumann, Frank Bahrmann, and Hans Joachim Böhme. 2020. Training a broad-coverage german sentiment classification model for dialog systems. In *Proceedings of The 12th Language Resources and Evaluation Conference*, pages 1620–1625, Marseille, France. European Language Resources Association.

Biyang Guo, Xin Zhang, Ziyuan Wang, Minqi Jiang, Jinran Nie, Yuxuan Ding, Jianwei Yue, and Yupeng Wu. 2023a. How close is chatgpt to human experts? comparison corpus, evaluation, and detection. *Preprint*, arXiv:2301.07597.

Chuan Guo, Geoff Pleiss, Yu Sun, and Kilian Q. Weinberger. 2017. On calibration of modern neural networks. *Preprint*, arXiv:1706.04599.

Mengjie Guo, Limin Liu, Meicheng Guo, Siyuan Liu, and Zhiwei Xu. 2023b. Accurate generated text detection based on deep layer-wise relevance propagation. In *2023 IEEE 8th International Conference on Big Data Analytics (ICBDA)*. IEEE.

Daphne Ippolito, Daniel Duckworth, Chris Callison-Burch, and Douglas Eck. 2020. Automatic detection of generated text is easiest when humans are fooled. In *Proceedings of the 58th Annual Meeting of the Association for Computational Linguistics*, pages 1808–1822, Online. Association for Computational Linguistics.

Joseph D. Janizek, Pascal Sturmfels, and Su-In Lee. 2021. Explaining explanations: axiomatic feature interactions for deep networks. *J. Mach. Learn. Res.*, 22(1).

Ali Khan, Kathryn Brohman, and Shamel Addas. 2021. The anatomy of 'fake news': Studying false messages as digital objects. *Journal of Information Technology*, 37(2):122–143.

Sarah Kreps, R. Miles McCain, and Miles Brundage. 2020. All the news that's fit to fabricate: AI-generated text as a tool of media misinformation. *Journal of Experimental Political Science*, 9(1):104–117.

Yinhan Liu, Myle Ott, Naman Goyal, Jingfei Du, Mandar Joshi, Danqi Chen, Omer Levy, Mike Lewis, Luke Zettlemoyer, and Veselin Stoyanov. 2019a. Roberta: A robustly optimized bert pretraining approach. *ArXiv*, abs/1907.11692.

Yinhan Liu, Myle Ott, Naman Goyal, Jingfei Du, Mandar Joshi, Danqi Chen, Omer Levy, Mike Lewis, Luke Zettlemoyer, and Veselin Stoyanov. 2019b. Roberta: A robustly optimized bert pretraining approach. *ArXiv*, abs/1907.11692.

Chiara Longoni, Andrey Fradkin, Luca Cian, and Gordon Pennycook. 2022. News from generative artificial intelligence is believed less. In *2022 ACM Conference on Fairness, Accountability, and Transparency*. ACM.

Scott M Lundberg and Su-In Lee. 2017. A unified approach to interpreting model predictions. In I. Guyon, U. V. Luxburg, S. Bengio, H. Wallach, R. Fergus, S. Vishwanathan, and R. Garnett, editors, *Advances in Neural Information Processing Systems 30*, pages 4765–4774. Curran Associates, Inc.

Mingyang Lyu, Chenlong Bao, Jintao Tang, Ting Wang, and Peilei Liu. 2022. Automatic detection for machine-generated texts is easy. In *2022 IEEE Smartworld, Ubiquitous Intelligence & Computing, Scalable Computing & Communications, Digital Twin, Privacy Computing, Metaverse, Autonomous & Trusted Vehicles (SmartWorld/UIC/ScalCom/DigitalTwin/PriComp/Meta)*. IEEE.

Mistral-AI. 2023. Mistral transformer. `https://github.com/mistralai/mistral-src`. Accessed: January 18th, 2024.

Eric Mitchell, Yoonho Lee, Alexander Khazatsky, Christopher D. Manning, and Chelsea Finn. 2023. Detectgpt: Zero-shot machine-generated text detection using probability curvature. *Preprint*, arXiv:2301.11305.

Madhumita Murgia. 2023. Openai's red team: the experts hired to 'break' chatgpt. `https://www.ft.com/content/0876687a-f8b7-4b39-b513-5fee942831e8`. Accessed: April 14, 2023.

Alex Newhouse, Jason Blazakis, and Kris McGuffie. 2019. The industrialization of terrorist propaganda. the industrialization of terrorist propaganda neural language models and the threat of fake content generation. Last accessed on January 15th, 2024.

OpenAI. 2022. Introducing chatgpt. `https://openai.com/blog/chatgpt`. Accessed: January 16th, 2024.

OpenAI. 2023. Gpt-4 technical report. `https://cdn.openai.com/papers/gpt-4.pdf`. Accessed: January 16th, 2024.

Orginality.ai. 2024. `https://originality.ai/`. Accessed: January 5th, 2024.

Long Ouyang, Jeff Wu, Xu Jiang, Diogo Almeida, Carroll L. Wainwright, Pamela Mishkin, Chong Zhang, Sandhini Agarwal, Katarina Slama, Alex Ray, John Schulman, Jacob Hilton, Fraser Kelton, Luke Miller, Maddie Simens, Amanda Askell, Peter Welinder, Paul Christiano, Jan Leike, and Ryan Lowe. 2022. Training language models to follow instructions with human feedback. *Preprint*, arXiv:2203.02155.

Nils Reimers and Iryna Gurevych. 2019. Sentence-bert: Sentence embeddings using siamese bert-networks. In *Proceedings of the 2019 Conference on Empirical Methods in Natural Language Processing*. Association for Computational Linguistics.

Madeline Renbarger. 2023. How a 23-year-old college student built one of the leading ai detection tools. `https://www.businessinsider.com/`. Accessed: February 12th, 2024.

Marco Tulio Ribeiro, Sameer Singh, and Carlos Guestrin. 2016. "why should i trust you?": Explaining the predictions of any classifier. In *Proceedings of the 22nd ACM SIGKDD International Conference on Knowledge Discovery and Data Mining*, KDD '16, page 1135–1144, New York, NY, USA. Association for Computing Machinery.

Victor Sanh, Lysandre Debut, Julien Chaumond, and Thomas Wolf. 2019. Distilbert, a distilled version of bert: smaller, faster, cheaper and lighter. *ArXiv*, abs/1910.01108.

Kristina Schaaff, Tim Schlippe, and Lorenz Mindner. 2023. Classification of human- and AI-generated texts for English, French, German, and Spanish. In *Proceedings of the 6th International Conference on Natural Language and Speech Processing (ICNLSP 2023)*, pages 1–10, Online. Association for Computational Linguistics.

Irene Solaiman, Miles Brundage, Jack Clark, Amanda Askell, Ariel Herbert-Voss, Jeff Wu, Alec Radford, and Jasmine Wang. 2019. Release strategies and the social impacts of language models. *CoRR*, abs/1908.09203.

Veronika Solopova, Oana-Iuliana Popescu, Christoph Benzmüller, and Tim Landgraf. 2023a. Automated multilingual detection of pro-kremlin propaganda in newspapers and telegram posts. *Datenbank Spektrum*, 23(1):5–14.

Veronika Solopova, Eiad Rostom, Fritz Cremer, Adrian Gruszczynski, Sascha Witte, Chengming Zhang, Fernando Ramos López, Lea Plößl, Florian Hofmann, Ralf Romeike, Michaela Gläser-Zikuda, Christoph Benzmüller, and Tim Landgraf. 2023b. Papagai: Automated feedback for reflective essays. In *KI 2023: Advances in Artificial Intelligence*, pages 198–206, Cham. Springer Nature Switzerland.

taz Verlags u. Vertriebs GmbH. 2023. taz. die tageszeitung. https://taz.de/. Accessed: February 12th, 2024.

Edward Tian. 2023. https://gptzero.me/news/perplexity-and-burstiness-what-is-it. Accessed: January 5th, 2024.

Edward Tian and Alexander Cui. 2023. Gptzero: Towards detection of ai-generated text using zero-shot and supervised methods.

Hugo Touvron, Louis Martin, Kevin Stone, Peter Albert, and Amjad Almahairi et al. 2023. Llama 2: Open foundation and fine-tuned chat models. *Preprint*, arXiv:2307.09288.

Chih-Ming Tsai. 2023. Stylometric fake news detection based on natural language processing using named entity recognition: In-domain and cross-domain analysis. *Electronics*, 12(17).

Eduard Tulchinskii, Kristian Kuznetsov, Laida Kushnareva, Daniil Cherniavskii, Serguei Barannikov, Irina Piontkovskaya, Sergey Nikolenko, and Evgeny Burnaev. 2023. Intrinsic dimension estimation for robust detection of ai-generated texts. *Preprint*, arXiv:2306.04723.

Junlin Wang, Jens Tuyls, Eric Wallace, and Sameer Singh. 2020. Gradient-based analysis of NLP models is manipulable. In *Findings of the Association for Computational Linguistics: EMNLP 2020*, pages 247–258, Online. Association for Computational Linguistics.

Writer. 2023. https://writer.com/ai-content-detector/. Accessed: September 13th, 2023.

Can Xu, Qingfeng Sun, Kai Zheng, Xiubo Geng, Pu Zhao, Jiazhan Feng, Chongyang Tao, and Daxin Jiang. 2023. Wizardlm: Empowering large language models to follow complex instructions. *Preprint*, arXiv:2304.12244.

Rowan Zellers, Ari Holtzman, Hannah Rashkin, Yonatan Bisk, Ali Farhadi, Franziska Roesner, and Yejin Choi. 2019. Defending against neural fake news. In H. Wallach, H. Larochelle, A. Beygelzimer, F. d'Alché-Buc, E. Fox, and R. Garnett, editors, *Advances in Neural Information Processing Systems 32*, pages 9054–9065. Curran Associates, Inc., Red Hook, NY, USA.

ZeroGPT. 2024. Trusted gpt-4, chatgpt and ai detector tool by zerogpt. https://www.zerogpt.com/. Accessed: Febuary 19th, 2024.

Wikimedia Deutschland – Gesellschaft zur Förderung Freien Wissens e.V. 2008. Wikipedia dump. https://dumps.wikimedia.org/other/static_html_dumps/current/de/. Accessed: October 23rd 2023.

Wikimedia Deutschland – Gesellschaft zur Förderung Freien Wissens e.V. 2024a. Wikimedia. the free media repository. https://commons.wikimedia.org/wiki/Main_Page. Accessed: February 12th, 2024.

Wikimedia Deutschland – Gesellschaft zur Förderung Freien Wissens e.V. 2024b. Wikipedia. die freie enzyklopädie. https://www.wikipedia.de/. Accessed: February 12th, 2024.

A Appendix

Name	TAZ	Springernature	Wikipedia	Wikimedia	Zeit Online
Llama	5000	5000	5000	5000	5000
Wizard	1806	1026	1893	-	2181
Snoozy	4162	985	734	-	1266
GPT3.5	800	800	800	800	800
Human	5000	5000	5000	5000	5000
Mistral	471	-	-	-	-

Table 3: Overall number of samples per genre and source. While Llama 2 and human samples are present for all of the genres, the rest of the sources are only collected based on the experimental set-up described in Section 3.3

Set/subset	Llama	Mixed	Human	Mistral	Gpt-wiki
Model (a) train	22.500	-	22.500	-	-
Model (a) test	2500	-	2500	-	-
Model (b) train	3728	18772	22.500	-	-
Model (b) test	373	1877	2500	-	-
Model (c) train	22.500	22.500	22.500	249	655
Model (c) test	2500	2500	2500	222	146
Mistral test	-	-	2500	471	-
GPT Wikimedia	-	-	2500	-	801

Table 4: Number of samples per source in train and test sets for each model.

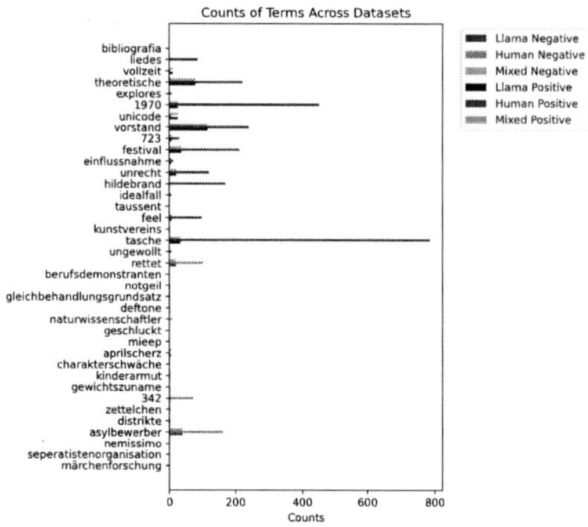

(a) Llama model

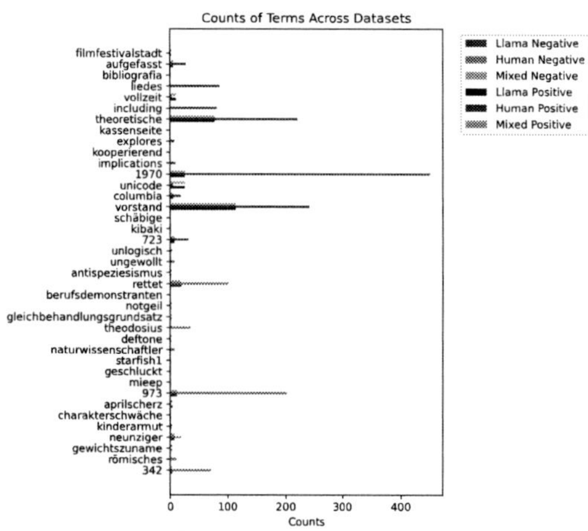

(b) Mixed model

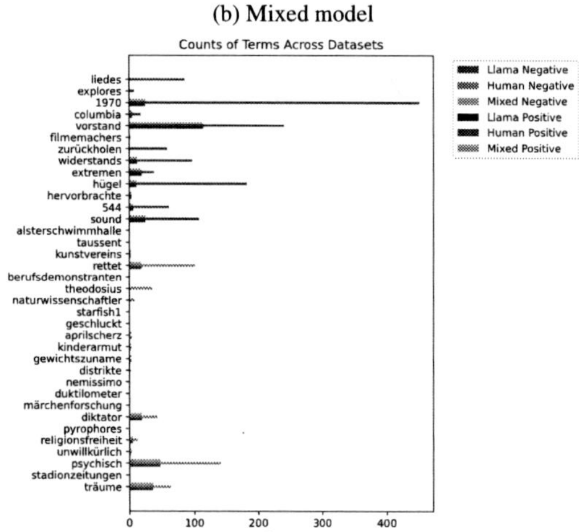

(c) Complete model

Figure 6: Counts of important terms for LIME experiment.

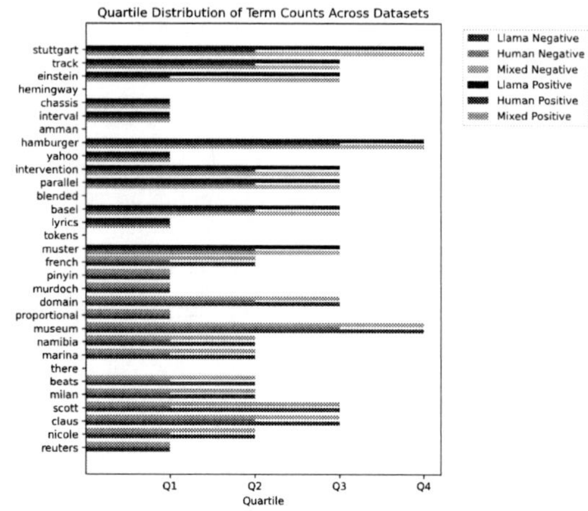

(a) Llama model

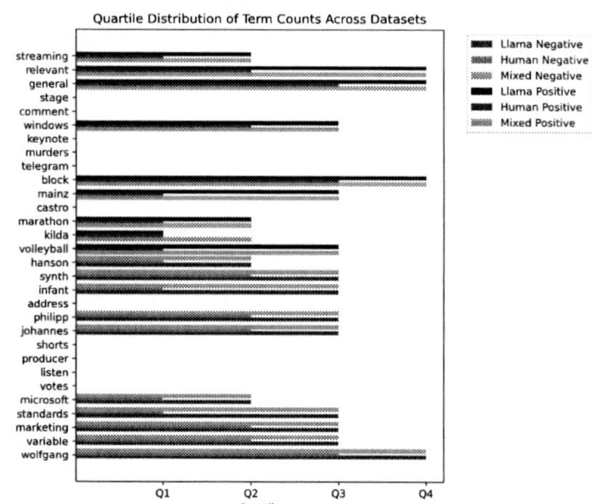

(b) Mixed model

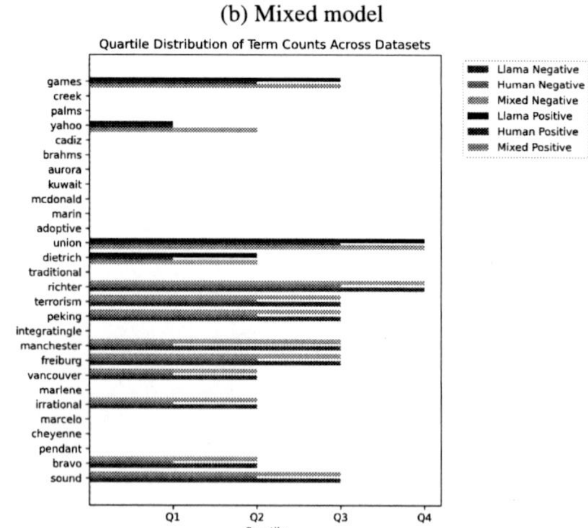

(c) Complete model

Figure 7: Counts of important terms from gradients experiment.

Actual	Predicted HW	Predicted MG
HW	2307	193
MG	59	2441

(a) Llama dataset + HW dataset

Actual	Predicted HW	Predicted MG
HW	2307	193
MG	1830	670

(b) Mixed dataset + HW dataset

Actual	Predicted HW	Predicted MG
HW	2307	193
MG	582	219

(c) GPT Wikimedia + HW dataset

Actual	Predicted HW	Predicted MG
HW	2307	193
MG	389	82

(d) Mistral Wikipedia + HW dataset

Figure 8: HW means human-written data, and MG means AI-generated data. Llama model (a) confusion matrices.

Actual	Predicted HW	Predicted MG
HW	2227	273
MG	828	1672

(a) Llama dataset + HW dataset

Actual	Predicted HW	Predicted MG
HW	2227	273
MG	103	2397

(b) Mixed dataset + HW dataset

Actual	Predicted HW	Predicted MG
HW	2227	273
MG	571	230

(c) GPT Wikimedia + HW dataset

Actual	Predicted HW	Predicted MG
HW	2227	273
MG	323	148

(d) Mistral Wikipedia + HW dataset

Figure 9: Mixed model (b) confusion matrices.

Actual	Predicted HW	Predicted MG
HW	3679	1301
MG	24	4611

(a) Llama dataset + HW dataset

Actual	Predicted HW	Predicted MG
HW	3679	1301
MG	38	3985

(b) Mixed dataset + HW dataset

Actual	Predicted HW	Predicted MG
HW	3679	1301
MG	23	123

(c) GPT Wikimedia + HW dataset

Actual	Predicted HW	Predicted MG
HW	3679	1301
MG	2	220

(d) Mistral Wikipedia + HW dataset

Figure 10: Complete model (c) confusion matrices.

Table 5: Full list of Linguistic Features.
The results of the statistical testing of the features can be found in the abovementioned OSF repository.

Morphology	**Syntax**	**Semantics**
Adjectives	Clause of Purpose	Voc: Remembering
Nouns	Clause of Reason	Voc: Understanding
Verbs (Finite, Infinitives, Stative)	Clause of Condition	Voc: Application
Comparatives	Consecutive clause	Voc: Evaluation
Superlatives	Complex sentences	Voc: Analysis
Adverbs	Simple sentences	Voc: Creation
Adjective to Noun ratio	Relative clause	Voc: Assertion
Adverb to Verb ratio	Modal clause	Voc: Cognition
Abstract nouns	Concessive clause	Description
Passive voice	Adversative clause	Evaluation
Pronouns (All types)	1st person + finite verb	Analysis
Modal verbs	Subordinating conjunctions	Conclusion
Negations	Coordinating conjunctions	Positive Sentiments
Subjunctive mood	Questions	Negative Sentiments
Foreign words		Neutral Sentiments
Present, Past, Future		High modality words
1st person pronouns		Feelings
2nd person pronouns		Supports
Indefinite pronouns		Claims
		Future Actions
Generation Errors		
Mean sentence similarity		
Maximum sentence similarity		
Median sentence similarity		
Repetitive Lemmas		
Sentence Length Variation		
Functional to Lexical words ratio		

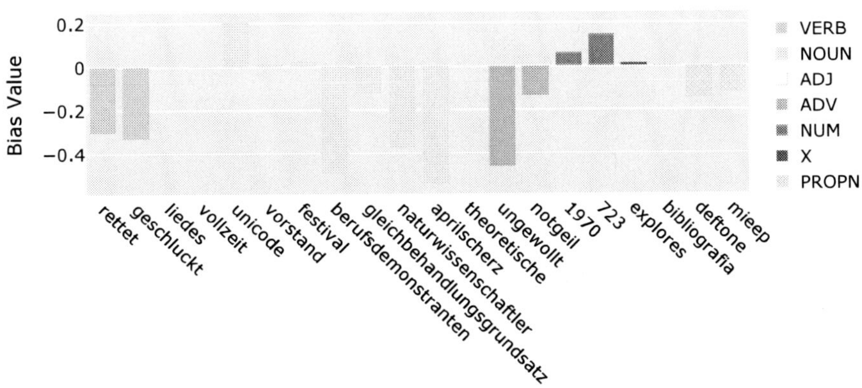

(a) Highest LIME score terms for Llama-data model (a).

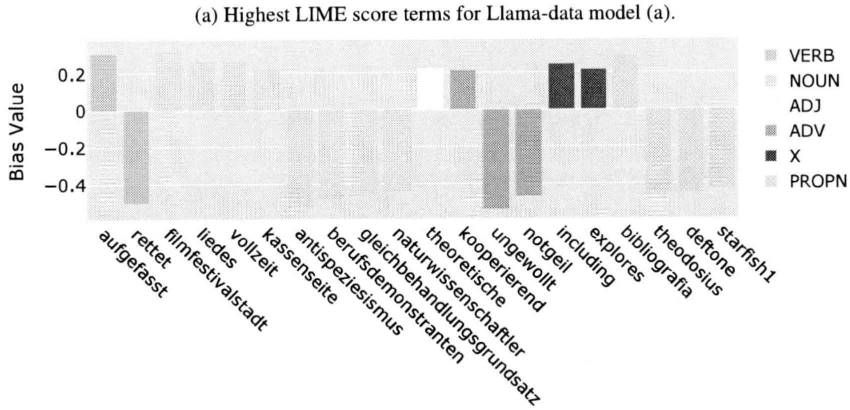

(b) Highest LIME score terms for Mixed-data model (b).

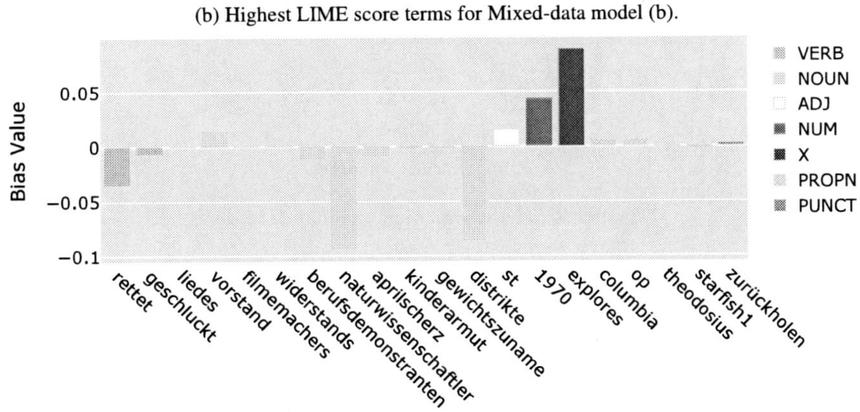

(c) Highest LIME score terms for Complete-data model (c).

Figure 11: LIME analysis results.

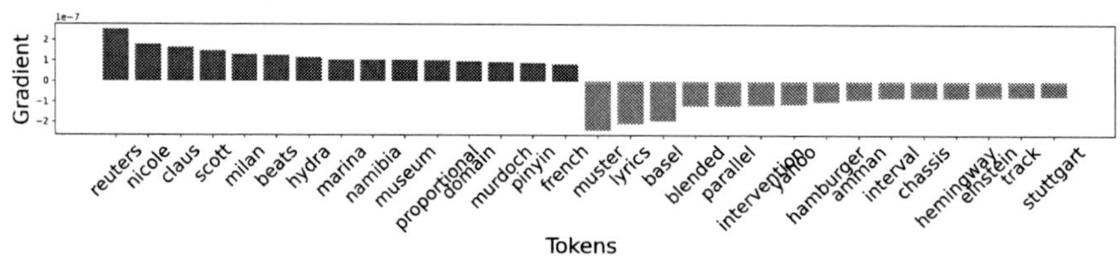

(a) Llama-data model (a).

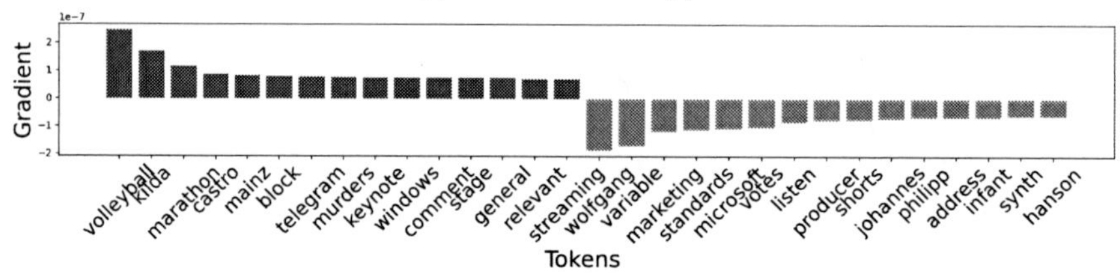

(b) Mixed-data model (b).

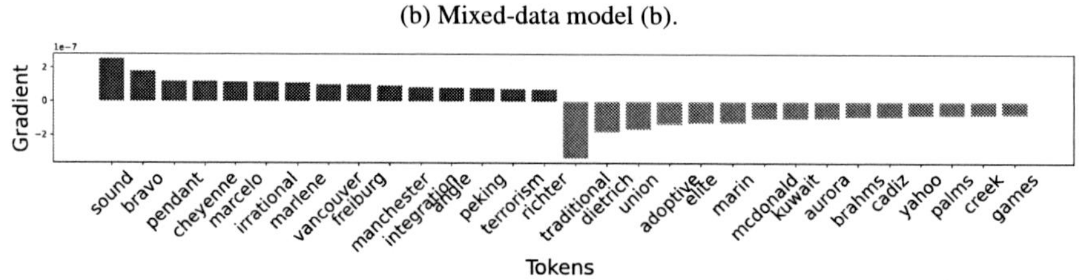

(c) Complete-data model (c).

Figure 12: Highest gradient magnitude terms.

Lex2Sent: A bagging approach to unsupervised sentiment analysis

Kai-Robin Lange and Jonas Rieger and Carsten Jentsch
Department of Statistics, TU Dortmund University, 44221 Dortmund, Germany
{kalange, rieger, jentsch} @statistik.tu-dortmund.de

Abstract

Unsupervised text classification, with its most common form being sentiment analysis, used to be performed by counting words in a text that were stored in a lexicon, which assigns each word to one class or as a neutral word. In recent years, these lexicon-based methods fell out of favor and were replaced by computationally demanding fine-tuning techniques for encoder-only models such as BERT and zero-shot classification using decoder-only models such as GPT-4. In this paper, we propose an alternative approach: Lex2Sent, which provides improvement over classic lexicon methods but does not require any GPU or external hardware. To classify texts, we train embedding models to determine the distances between document embeddings and the embeddings of the parts of a suitable lexicon. We employ resampling, which results in a bagging effect, boosting the performance of the classification. We show that our model outperforms lexica and provides a basis for a high performing few-shot fine-tuning approach in the task of binary sentiment analysis.

1 Introduction

Most commonly, text classification is performed in a supervised manner by using a previously labeled data set to train a learning-based model to predict the sentiment of unlabeled documents. When a labeled data set is not available, an unsupervised labeling approach is useful to provide valuable initial information for an active learning approach or to label the texts right away, when a near-perfect classification is not strictly necessary. However, such unsupervised models often require financial backing or a high performing GPU to use on a large data set.

In this paper, we propose Lex2Sent, a model mainly designed for sentiment analysis, that can however be used for any binary text classification problem, where external resources in the form of lexica are available. We will thus define the model for any arbitrary binary classification. Lex2Sent uses text embedding models to estimate the similarity between a document and both halves of a given binary lexicon. These distances are calculated for multiple resampled corpora and are aggregated to achieve a bagging-effect. As Doc2Vec models are usually trained on the CPU, the method demonstrated here can be fully realized in low hardware resource environments that do not have access to a GPU or the financial means to let commercial models such as GPT label thousands of documents. As the Lex2Sent's architecture is not dependent on the language of choice, it can also be used in other languages than English, including low resource languages for which no powerful language models are available. To demonstrate that the results are generalizable, we compare them to the ones of traditional lexicon methods on three data sets with distinct characteristics. To assess the performance to the modern unsupervised classification state of the art, we compare Lex2Sent's results to GPT-3.5 on one data set. We also extend this active learning approach by fine-tuning a RoBERTa model on a sufficient subset of the labels predicted by Lex2Sent. This can be seen as an initial starting point for active learning approach.

The paper is structured as follows. In Section 2, we discuss previous approaches to text classification and research on resampling techniques for texts. Section 3 introduces our classification model by describing the Doc2Vec model, the unsupervised labeling approach and the resampling procedure used. The data sets and lexica used are specified in Section 4. In Section 5, the classification rates of Lex2Sent are compared to lexicon methods and the performance of Chat-GPT. We also show that we can use the results of Lex2Sent for an initial fine-tuning of a pre-trained language model in few-shot setting. In Section 6, we conclude and give an outlook to further research.

2 Related Work

When little to no labeled data is available, usually text classification is performed in one out of three ways. That is, by using either traditional lexicon methods, decoder-only models like GPT or parameter efficient fine-tuning methods to fine-tune pre-trained language models.

Traditionally, researchers used lexica/dictionaries that were meant to substitute the missing supervised label information by external information. For sentiment classification, such lexica contain both a list of positive and negative words, which could simply be counted within a text. Commonly used lexica include VADER (Hutto and Gilbert, 2014), Afinn (Nielsen, 2011), Loughran-McDonald (Loughran and McDonald, 2010), the WKWSCI lexicon (Khoo and Johnkhan, 2018) and the Opinion lexicon (Hu and Liu, 2004). Even within a specific task such as binary sentiment classification, these lexica are often designed for a specific use case. For instance, the Loughran-McDonald lexicon is designed for economic text data, while VADER is designed for social media data. Lange and Jentsch (2023) perform a sentiment analysis of German political speeches and use Lex2Sent with a lexicon base specifically designed for German political text data (Rauh, 2018).
This method is very resource-savvy, but yield worse performance than the other two methods. Nowadays, lexica are usually only used in low hardware resource environments or by researchers of social science disciplines, because they are white-box algorithms that are easy to interpret.

Alternatively, GPT-4 (Brown et al., 2020) or any other large language model (e.g. Llama 2 (Touvron et al., 2023), Mixtral (Jiang et al., 2024) or Jamba (Lieber et al., 2024)) can classify any document in a zero-shot manner due to their language understanding capabilities. Using GPT-4 or GPT-3.5 for large corpora requires financial backing not everyone has access to though and similarly, open source large language models need a GPU with large vram.

Lastly, a pre-trained Transformer model like BERT (Devlin et al., 2019) or RoBERTa (Liu et al., 2019), that was additionally fine-tuned on the task at hand, might help when a GPU is available, that cannot handle a large language model. This however yields the downside of using classification rules that are not based on the texts the model is meant to be used on. Instead, the model might carry a bias from a different subject over to the classification: the sentiment of a text might be based on completely different clues based on whether the text is a political speech or a social media post. This can be avoided by fine-tuning the model oneself, which, in turn, needs labeled data. To reduce the amount of data needed, active learning (Tharwat and Schenck, 2023) is increasingly being used in combination with few-shot learning techniques. Parameter-efficient fine-tuning (PEFT, Mangrulkar et al., 2022) uses adapter methods such as Low Rank Adaption (LoRA, Hu et al., 2021) to fine-tune language models with fewer training parameters than usual, and is thus suited to fine-tune on few-shot examples to achieve adequate results. Pattern exploiting training (PET, Schick and Schütze, 2021) uses the language understanding capabilities of language models to its advantage by "explaining" the task to the model. As Rieger et al. (2024) show, such methods can even be effectively combined into one.

Contrary to these approaches, we propose a fully unsupervised approach that can be used in low hardware resource environments, in which no access to a GPU is available and where there is no financial backing to let commercial models like GPT label thousands of documents. We do this by employing CPU-based embedding algorithms that leverage external information using lexica and are further improved by resampling, resulting in a bagging effect. Improving embedding-based text classification with the help of lexica has been explored by Shin et al. (2017), Mathew et al. (2020a) and Mathew et al. (2020b), but neither analyze a combination of embeddings and lexica for unsupervised analysis.

Xie et al. (2020) use resampling to improve the performance of supervised sentiment models by resampling words with certain probabilities based on their tf-idf-score or by translating the original document into another language and then translating it back to the original language. Similar augmentations can be performed with the nlpaug-package (Ma, 2019). This allows the user to, for instance, use embedding models, be it static models like Word2Vec (Mikolov et al., 2013) or contextual masked language models like BERT (Devlin et al., 2019). These types of data augmentation and resampling are most often used as additional training data for the embedding models and supervised methods. In this paper, instead of resizing the training set, we create multiple different training sets, on which one embedding model is trained each. Aggregating the information from these models into one combined classifier creates a bagging effect, improving the classification rate. Furthermore, we investigate the advantage of using such augmentation and resampling techniques in an unsupervised setting.

The procedures used by Xie et al. (2020) and Ma (2019) do however change the existing vocabulary. They either change the vocabulary by back-translation or resampling the document dependently from other documents due to the tf-idf-scoring or even introduce completely new words that are not part of the corpus at all by changing words based on similiar words in a given embedding space. This might be counter-productive for an unsupervised analysis, as the texts are not used as a training data set, but are supposed to be evaluated themselves. Changing the vocabulary might introduce a bias and hinder the classification performance, as the external information provided to classify the texts is given by the lexica, which are essentially word lists and thus more likely to work accurately to work with unchanged vocabulary. The resampling procedures in this paper are instead based on those employed by Rieger et al. (2020), who used resampling procedures to analyze the statistical uncertainty of the topic modeling method Latent Dirichlet Allocation. We chose those procedures, as they augment or resample the texts independently from another and do not add new words to the vocabulary.

3 Lex2Sent

In this section we propose Lex2Sent, a bagging model for unsupervised sentiment analysis. Lex2Sent is published as a Python package. The code can be found on GitHub[1].

3.1 Lexica

To perform unsupervised text classification, lexica can be used to interpret the words in a text without the need for previously labeled documents of a similar corpus, as they provide external information. This information is provided in the form of key words, which a lexicon assigns to a certain class.

For our analysis, we use binary lexica, that are used to separate words between two disjoint classes A and B. Such a lexicon assigns a value from an interval $[-s, s]$ with $s \in \mathbb{R}^+$ to all words, while assigning the value 0 to all neutral words. It assigns positive values to all words it deems to belong to class A and negative values to all words, it deems to belong to class B. To enable some words to have a larger weight during the classification process, lexica might give words different values. For instance, the word "fantastic" might receive a higher score than the word "good" when using a sentiment analysis lexicon, as it conveys an even stronger positive emotion. We modify such a binary lexicon to consist of two halves, one for each of the two classes. These halves are defined as lists of words in a way that each word that belongs to either class A or class B occurs exactly once in its respective half. Only neutral words are not assigned to a half. This enables the use of lexicon-based text embeddings.

As we use static embeddings, a key word's embedding is not changed, even if it is negated in a document. To incorporate the concept of negations into Lex2Sent, we merge negations with the following word during preprocessing. The term "not bad" is thus changed to "negbad". "negbad" is then added to the opposite lexicon half of the word "bad", so that Lex2Sent can interpret it correctly.

3.2 Lexicon-based text embeddings

Instead of looking only at key words, text embeddings can be used to analyze semantic similarities to other words. This enables us to identify the class of a text using words that are not part of the lexicon.

Text embedding methods create an embedding for each document, which represents the document as a real vector of some fixed dimension q. They are created using the word embeddings of all words in the current document and can be interpreted as an "average" word embedding. We thus interpret the text embedding of a lexicon half as an average embedding of a word of its respective class. Calculating the distance between the embedding of a document in the corpus and the embedding of a lexicon half is used as a measure of how similar a given document is to a theoretical document that is the perfect representation of that class.

As an alternative to the approach mentioned above, we also looked at the average distance of a document's text embedding to all word embeddings of the sentiment words that appear in the document itself, to analyze only its difference to the parts of the lexicon that are part of the document. However, this yielded a classification rate that is comparable to the traditional lexicon classification itself and does not provide substantial improvement over it.

[1] https://github.com/K-RLange/Lex2Sent

It will thus not be further reported in this paper.

The distance is calculated using the cosine distance

$$\text{cosDist}(a, b) = 1 - \frac{\sum_{i=1}^{q} a_i b_i}{\sqrt{\sum_{i=1}^{q} a_i^2} \cdot \sqrt{\sum_{i=1}^{q} b_i^2}}$$

for two vectors $a = (a_1, \ldots, a_q)^T \in \mathbb{R}^q$ and $b = (b_1, \ldots, b_q)^T \in \mathbb{R}^q$ (Li and Han, 2013).

For our purposes of classifying documents into two classes, let A_d be the cosine distance of a text embedding of a document to the text embedding of the positive half of a sentiment lexicon and B_d be the cosine distance to the negative half. Then, the larger (smaller) the value

$$\mathit{diff}_d = B_d - A_d$$

is for a document d, the more confident the lexicon-based text embedding method is, that this document d in fact belongs to class A (B).

This method can be performed using any text embedding model in combination with any lexicon that enables a binary classification task. In this analysis, we choose Doc2Vec (Le and Mikolov, 2014b) as the baseline text embedding model and analyze texts for their sentiment.

3.3 Doc2Vec

Doc2Vec (Le and Mikolov, 2014a) is based on the word embedding model Word2Vec (Mikolov et al., 2013), which assigns similar vectors to semantically similar words by minimizing the distance of a word to the words in its context.

Since word embeddings are not sufficient to classify entire documents, the model is extended to text embeddings. A Doc2Vec model, using the Distributed Memory Model approach, uses a CBOW architecture (Mikolov et al., 2013) in which a document itself is considered a context element of each word in the document. The distance of the document vector to each word vector is minimized in each iteration, resulting in a vector that can be interpreted as a mean of each of its words. According to Le and Mikolov (2014a), these text embeddings outperform the arithmetic mean of word embeddings for classification tasks. In this paper, we use the Doc2Vec implementation of the gensim package in Python (Řehůřek and Sojka, 2010).

Formally, we consider D documents and denote by N_d the number of words in document $d \in \{1, \ldots, D\}$. Further, for $i \in \{1, \ldots, N_d\}$, let $w_{i,d}$ be the i-th word in document d and w_{doc} denote the document under consideration. To give larger weight to words that follow up on another than words that are far away from another, the window size is varied during training. For a Doc2Vec model, we denote by K the maximum size of the context window. For every word the effective size is then sampled from $\{1, \ldots, K\}$ and is denoted as $k_{n,d}$. With these windows, the log-likelihood

$$\sum_{n=K}^{N_d - K} \ln\left(p(w_{n,d} | w_{n-k_{n,d},d}, \ldots, w_{n+k_{n,d},d}, w_{\text{doc}})\right)$$

is maximized for the documents $d = 1, \ldots, D$ using stochastic gradient descent. $p(\cdot|\cdot)$ is calculated by the resulting probabilities from a hierarchical softmax (Mikolov et al., 2013).

We also investigated, if the Lex2Sent method would work when using a pre-trained language model, in this case RoBERTa-large (Liu et al., 2019), as the embedding-backend. For this, we used the CLS-vectors of the lexicon halves and the documents to create lexicon-based text embeddings (similar to Mathew et al. (2020b)). These results underperformed compared to Doc2Vec though, as they showed a bias for one of the two classes.

3.4 Text resampling

Word and text embedding models analyze the original text structure to create similar word embeddings for semantically similar words. We assume that lexicon-based text embeddings need an "optimal text structure" to identify the class of the text in the most efficient manner. Suppose a text contains a key word that is a strong indicatior for the classification task at hand and contained within the lexicon used. The location of such key words can be biased by the type of text. For instance, when analyzing reviews for their sentiment, most key words are located in the last third of the text, as this part draws the conclusion to the review. By resampling the text, we relocate the key words evenly within texts. In theory, this enables vocabulary that occurs more often in texts of a specific sentiment that is not part of any sentiment lexicon, such as topic-specific vocabulary, to be used for labeling texts more efficiently while training Doc2Vec.

We leverage resampling procedures proposed by Rieger et al. (2020), who used them to analyze the uncertainty of the Latent Dirichlet Allocation. Instead of analyzing our methods uncertainty, we use these procedures to create optimal text structures and create a bagging effect. For this, we interpret the original text as a bag of words in which words are drawn independently with replacement like observations when creating a bootstrap sample (Efron, 1979) or independently without replacement, resulting in a permutated text. We call these procedures BW (Bootstrap for Words) and BWP (Bootstrap for Word Permutation), respectively. We analyzed additional procedures, such as resampling sentences as a whole or resampling words only within sentences and variations of those, but these generally yielded lower classification rates than the procedure described above.

3.5 Bagging

In this subsection, we describe a technique to aggregate multiple text embeddings for the purpose of unsupervised sentiment analysis. In combination with resampled texts, this can be seen as a bagging method for unsupervised text classification (Breiman, 1996). Every text structure has an effect on the classification of lexicon-based text embeddings, as differing syntax and vocabulary change the resulting embeddings. However, identifying whether the texts already have an "optimal" structure is a difficult task, as this is an abstract concept that is not trivial to formalize. Instead of relying on the original texts' structure, resampling enables the possibility to create an arbitrary number of artificial texts. If we aggregate these text embedding models, they do not have to label a document correctly for one text structure (that is the original text), but instead only have to label a document correctly on average based on multiple differently structured texts. This aggregation also balances out the randomness of generating samples and the negative effect of missing out on a crucial word within documents in one resampling sample, as it will probably appear in other samples.

The aggregation is performed by calculating an average *diff*-vector using B resampling iterations. Let diff^b_d be the d-th element of the *diff*-vector for the b-th lexicon-based text embedding model with $d = 1, \dots, D$. Then

$$\mathit{diff}^{\text{mean}}_d := \frac{1}{B}\sum_{b=1}^{B} \mathit{diff}^b_d$$

defines the d-th element of the averaged *diff*-vector.

3.6 Algorithm and Implementation

In training, the algorithm iterates over a grid, calculating models for different training epochs, context window sizes and embedding dimensions. For our application, we use a $3\times3\times4$-grid, which turns out to be sufficiently beneficial in application while remaining computationally feasible. The parameters are chosen from an equidistant set over reasonable parameter choices (see Algorithm 1 for the parameter choices). The grid can be adjusted according to the practitioner's problem at hand. For instance, a smaller grid is faster to train, but a larger grid will lead to more robust results. In each iteration, the parameter combination for the Doc2Vec model is chosen from the grid and the corpus is resampled. The resampled documents are sorted ascendingly by their respective absolute lexicon score. Then we train a Doc2Vec model and calculate the *diff* vector for all iterations. The classification task is performed by using the component-wise arithmetic mean of all the 36 *diff*-vectors. The algorithm is described as pseudocode in Algorithm 1.

Given a classifier $x = (x_1, \dots, x_D) \in \mathbb{R}^D$, the document with the index $d \in \{1, \dots, D\}$ is labeled

$$\text{label}_d = \begin{cases} \text{class A}, & x_d - t < 0 \\ \text{class B}, & x_d - t > 0\,, \quad t \in \mathbb{R} \\ \text{at random}, & x_d - t = 0 \end{cases}$$

for some threshold $t \in \mathbb{R}$. This might be $t = 0$ or the empirical quantile $t = x_{(p)}$, where p is the estimated proportion of texts of class B based on a-priori knowledge. In the analyses of this paper, we assume to have no a-priori knowledge of the distribution of class labels, so we use $t = 0$.

4 Data sets and lexica

In this section, the two sentiment lexica and three data sets used to evaluate Lex2Sent are described.

4.1 Data sets

The three data sets considered in this paper are chosen to cover texts with distinct features. The iMDb data set consists of a large corpus with long documents and a strong sentiment compared to the other two data sets. The Airline dataset is more than four times smaller and the documents themselves are also shorter. The Amazon data set represents an intermediate case between these two data sets.

The texts are tokenized and stop words as well as punctuation marks and numbers are removed. Lemmatization is performed to generalize words with the same word stem, if the original word from the text does not already appear in the lexicon. The

Algorithm 1 Lex2Sent

```
procedure Lex2Sent(texts, threshold, lexicon, resampling)
    classifier ← [0] * length(texts)
    for (epoch, window, dim) in Grid = ({5, 10, 15}, {5, 10, 15}, {50, 100, 150, 200}) do
        resampled_texts ← resampling(texts)
        sorted_resampled_texts ← sort(resampled_texts, lexicon)
        model ← Doc2Vec(sorted_resampled_texts, epoch, window, dim)
        emb ← lexicon_based_text_embeddings(model, resampled_texts)
        for i in 1:length(emb) do
            classifier[i] + = emb[i]
    return label_by_threshold(non_resampled_texts, classifier, threshold)
```

mentioned methods and stop word list are part of the Python package *nltk* (Bird et al., 2009).

iMDb data set The iMDb data set consists of 50, 000 user reviews of movies from the website `iMDb.com`, provided by Stanford University (Maas et al., 2011). These are split into 25, 000 training and test documents, each containing 12, 500 positive and negative reviews. After preprocessing, each document in the data set is 120.17 words long on average.

Amazon Review data set The Amazon data set is formed from the part of the Amazon Review Data which deals with industrial and scientific products (He and McAuley, 2016). All reviews contain a rating between one and five stars. Reviews with four or five stars are classified as positive and reviews with one or two stars are classified as negative. We removed reviews with a rating of three stars from the data set because the underlying sentiment is neither predominantly negative nor positive. In addition, we filtered out reviews consisting of less than 500 characters. Out of the remaining documents, 52, 000 documents are split into 26, 000 training and 26, 000 test documents, which are formed from 13, 000 positive and 13, 000 negative documents each. The average length of all documents in the training corpus is 85.51 words after preprocessing.

Airline data set The third data set consists of 11, 541 tweets regarding US airlines and was downloaded from Kaggle (Crowdflower, 2015). The tweets are categorized into positive or negative tweets – 3099 neutral tweets are deleted to be able to use the data set for a two-label-case. We split this data set in half into a training and test set. The training set ultimately contains 5570 documents. On average, each document of the training set contains 10.60 words after preprocessing. In comparison to the other two data sets, where the labels are evenly split, in the Airline data set only 1386 and thus 24.02% of the documents are labeled positive.

4.2 Lexica

To demonstrate that the performance is not dependent on the lexicon chosen as a base, we show the performance for three lexica: The Opinion Lexicon (Hu and Liu, 2004) is used to represent as a review-specific sentiment lexicon, while the WKWSCI lexicon (Khoo and Johnkhan, 2018) is chosen as multiple-purpose lexicon. The Loughran-McDonald (Loughran and McDonald, 2010) lexicon was designed for economic texts and not for reviews, hence it represents the case in which a lexicon is used in a sub optimal domain. To make sure that Lex2Sent not only outperforms these two lexica, we also observed the classification rate when using VADER (Hutto and Gilbert, 2014) or Afinn (Nielsen, 2011) lexicon in the traditional way and compare these results to the one of Lex2Sent in Section 5.3.

We added four amplifiers and ten negations to improve the classification. If an amplifier occurs before a key word, its value is doubled and if a negation occurs, it is multiplied by -0.5. For traditional lexicon methods, the classifier is created by summing up the values of all words within a text.

5 Evaluation

The classification rates of Lex2Sent in this section are determined by evaluating 50 executions to observe the method's randomness and to get a metric for the average performance.

Table 1 displays the average classification rates of a WKWSCI-based Lex2Sent and the classification rate of the best performing sentiment lexicon for each data set, split by the classification-

Table 1: Average classification rate in percent of a WKWSCI-based Lex2Sent in comparison to the best lexicon method (in brackets), split into whether the fixed or proportion threshold is used

	WKWSCI-based Lex2Sent		Lexicon with the highest classification rate	
threshold	by proportion	0	by proportion	0
iMDb	80.93	80.01	76.82 (TextBlob)	73.32 (Opinion Lexicon)
Amazon	77.08	76.83	71.91 (VADER)	69.28 (Opinion Lexicon)
Airline	79.11	72.42	82.05 (VADER)	68.33 (Opinion Lexicon)

threshold used. The WKWSCI-lexicon is chosen as a basis for Lex2Sent as it is a multiple-purpose lexicon. Lex2Sent outperforms every of the 6 observed lexica on all three data sets when using the threshold 0, as it would usually be done in an fully unsupervised setting without a-priori knowledge. It also outperforms the lexica in two out of three cases in which the exact proportion of positive to negative documents is assumed to be known. Here it is only outperformed by VADER on the Airline data set, which is likely because this data set consists of short documents which do not give the Doc2Vec models much context to train on per document.

While Lex2Sent outperforms these lexica, it does not outperform Chat-GPT. Laskar et al. (2023) report that GPT-3.5 (`text-davinci-003`) reaches an 91.9% classification rate on the iMDb data set. While it is not known, if GPT-3.5 has seen this data set and its labels during training and it thus might have an unfair advantage by knowing the correct results (Li and Flanigan, 2024), due to its generally high performance on unsupervised classification tasks, we can assume that it will outperform Lex2Sent, at least on most data sets. Lex2Sent does yield the advantage of not requiring financial backing to analyze large data sets though. Only a CPU is needed.

5.1 Different resampling procedures

In this section, we investigate the effect of different resampling procedures on the performance of Lex2Sent. We examine the results of a WKWSCI-based Lex2Sent using either one of the resampling procedures defined in Section 3.4 or no resampling at all for the iMDb data set. Additionally we investigate the classification rate when using texts sorted by their absolute lexicon value (key words grouped at the end of a text). This serves as an ablation analysis to distinguish the effects of resampled, natural and sub optimal text structures (sorted texts).

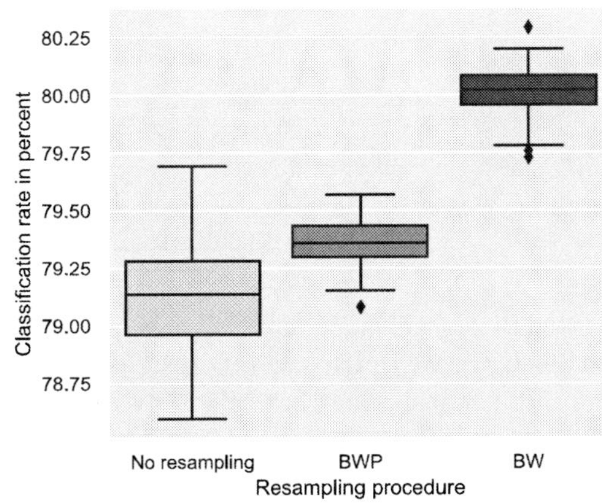

Figure 1: Results of the WKWSCI-based Lex2Sent on the iMDb data set for different resampling procedures

In comparison to the classification rates displayed as boxplots in Figure 1, this subotimal text structure results in a strongly decreased classification rate of 71.00%, which is in line with our interpretation of Section 3.4. The bagging-effect is visible for both procedures, as using either results in higher classification rates for the iMDb data set, with BW yielding the best performance. The method's stability is also increased, as the classification rates are more consistent, which can be seen by comparing the size of the respective box plots. Similar results (not reported) also occur for the other two data sets. For the rest of this paper, all further results are thus reported for Lex2Sent using BW resampling.

5.2 Evaluation on smaller corpora

As Lex2Sent requires training to accurately represent words with embeddings, it is important to determine how large a corpus needs to be for it to provide sufficient results. To analyze this, we evaluate Lex2Sent for subsamples of each data set. These include 10%, 25% or 50% of the original documents. The results of 50 repetitions are displayed in Table 2. The classification rates decrease for smaller corpora except for the Airline data set, in which it

Table 2: Average classification rates in percent of a WKWSCI-based Lex2Sent on subsets of the original data sets for the fixed threshold 0

subsample size	100%	50%	25%	10%
iMDb	80.01	79.73	79.43	78.88
Amazon	76.83	75.71	73.79	68.86
Airline	72.42	72.73	69.74	46.21

Table 3: Average classification rates in percent of Lex2Sent with a WKWSCI-, Loughran McDonald- or Opinion Lexicon-base for the fixed threshold 0, compared to the rates of the traditional lexicon method on the same lexicon

	WKWSCI		Opinion Lexicon		Loughran McDonald	
	Lex2Sent	lexicon	Lex2Sent	lexicon	Lex2Sent	lexicon
iMDb	80.01	70.10	78.43	73.37	70.73	61.22
Amazon	76.83	65.15	77.68	69.28	69.27	61.32
Airline	72.42	63.29	71.96	68.33	72.06	53.18

is slightly higher when examining only 50% of the data set. On the iMDb data set, Lex2Sent outperforms all lexica, even when using just 10% of all documents. On the Airline and Amazon data sets, the classification rate of Lex2Sent decreases to a larger extend for smaller subcorpora. This is likely caused by the short documents in these data set and indicates that it is meaningful to use Lex2Sent on smaller data sets if the documents themselves are long enough to train accurate embeddings.

5.3 Different lexicon-bases for Lex2Sent

So far, we focused on the WKWSCI-based Lex2Sent. In this section, we evaluate, how sensitive Lex2Sent is regarding its lexicon-base and if it improves the classification rate of other lexica as well. For this we compare it to Lex2Sent models based on the Opinion lexicon as well as the Loughran-McDonald lexicon. The average classification rates are displayed in Table 3. Lex2Sent improves the rates of all three lexica on all data sets. While WKWSCI is a general-purpose lexicon, the Opinion Lexicon is designed to analyze customer reviews. This specialization also affects Lex2Sent, as the Opinion Lexicon-based Lex2Sent outperforms every lexicon on every data set as well as the WKWSCI-based Lex2Sent on the Amazon data set, which consists of product reviews. Similarly, we see that Lex2Sent can improve the performance of a lexicon designed for a different domain, as it increases the classficiation rate for the Loughran-McDonald lexicon by at least 7.95 percentage points on all data sets. We recommend to use a general-purpose lexicon like WKWSCI or a lexicon with is domain-adapted to the data set under consideration as a lexicon base for Lex2Sent.

5.4 Lex2Sent as an initial fit

While Lex2Sent is designed for a low hardware resource environment without a GPU, it can still be benefitial to use it in combination with larger, pre-trained models like RoBERTa. To demonstrate this, we use Lex2Sent's beneficial property of displaying a degree of certainty in its results based on how high or low the value of $diff_d^{mean}$ is for $d = 1, \ldots, D$. To create data set for our RoBERTa model to fine-tune on, we therefore only use 10% of the data set: the 5% documents that have the highest and 5% that have the lowest values of our training data set. We fine-tune this version of RoBERTa in 30 epochs using LoRA (Hu et al., 2021) with $r = 8$ and thus 1,838,082 trainable parameters.

To evaluate this approach, we use the iMDb data set, as it contains both a training data set for Lex2Sent to train and RoBERTa to fine-tune on and a test data set for out-of-sample observations that can be classified by RoBERTa. We repeated this procedure five times. On average, our fine-tuned model classified 85.47% of all test documents correctly. While this does not match GPT's classification rate, it does yield the advantage of being cost-efficient. This indicates that Lex2Sent can make for a good initial fit for an active learning approach. Starting from this classification rate, a human-in-the-loop style annotation might take place to improve the classification further.

6 Conclusion

Text classification is commonly performed in a supervised manner using a hand-labeled data set. Unsupervised classification can help when there is no such annotated data set available. This paper proposes the Lex2Sent model, which steers an intermediate course between learning-based and deterministic approaches to create an unsupervised classification, which can be created in a low hardware resource environment without access to a GPU. A binary lexicon is used as a replacement for the missing information that is usually represented by the annotations. The performance of this method is increased by aggregating the results from resampled data sets, which can be seen as a bagging effect.

Lex2Sent yields higher classification rates than all six analyzed sentiment lexica on all three data sets under study, no matter the lexicon-base. Our findings indicate that this might be caused by classifying documents in a more balanced way compared to traditional lexicon methods. Despite being a learning-based approach, the Lex2Sent method shows higher classification rates than traditional lexica on smaller data sets.

Ethical Considerations

While our model requires calculating multiple Doc2Vec models for a single analysis, we modified our model specifications and the number of executions to keep the computational budget manageable in the context of climate change (Strubell et al., 2019). Hence, we perform 50 executions in all of our experiments to ensure that the results are not affected by outliers, but the computational budget remains within reasonable boundaries. Our choice of using the fixed grid with 36 parameter combinations is also caused by this goal. Using this grid, each model finished training in less than two hours.

Limitations

While Lex2Sent improves the classification rate of lexica, it is not capable of reaching the classification rates of models like GPT, but should be seen as a much less resource intensive alternative for the specific task of binary text classification.

Lex2Sent's architecture is independent of the type of binary classification task at hand, so it should work similarly well for other classification tasks given suitable lexica. This is however a theoretical assumption, as we have tested Lex2Sent's capabilities for sentiment analysis specifically.

Lex2Sent has been designed for a two-label-case. To use it in a ordinally scaled multi-label-case, we would need to create multiple thresholds that determines the predicted class, instead of just one. This yields new challenges, as we can not heuristically choose the threshold as 0 like in a binary classification task.

While Lex2Sent's architecture does not depend on the language of the documents or the lexica, it should theoretically perform just as well in low resource languages without needing large training data sets like sophisticated language models. We have not tested this hypothesis though.

Acknowledgments

This paper is part of a project of the Dortmund Center for data-based Media Analysis (DoCMA) at TU Dortmund University. The work was supported by the Mercator Research Center Ruhr (MERCUR) with project number Pe-2019-0044. In addition, the authors gratefully acknowledge the computing time provided on the Linux HPC cluster at TU Dortmund University (LiDO3), partially funded in the course of the Large-Scale Equipment Initiative by the German Research Foundation (DFG) as project 271512359.

References

Steven Bird, Ewan Klein, and Edward Loper. 2009. *Natural language processing with Python: analyzing text with the natural language toolkit*. O'Reilly Media, Inc.

Leo Breiman. 1996. Bagging predictors. *Machine Learning*, 24(2):123–140.

Tom B. Brown, Benjamin Mann, Nick Ryder, Melanie Subbiah, Jared Kaplan, Prafulla Dhariwal, Arvind Neelakantan, Pranav Shyam, Girish Sastry, Amanda Askell, Sandhini Agarwal, Ariel Herbert-Voss, Gretchen Krueger, Tom Henighan, Rewon Child, Aditya Ramesh, Daniel M. Ziegler, Jeffrey Wu, Clemens Winter, Christopher Hesse, Mark Chen, Eric Sigler, Mateusz Litwin, Scott Gray, Benjamin Chess, Jack Clark, Christopher Berner, Sam McCandlish, Alec Radford, Ilya Sutskever, and Dario Amodei. 2020. Language Models are Few-Shot Learners. *arXiv:2005.14165*.

Crowdflower. 2015. Twitter US airline sentiment.

Jacob Devlin, Ming-Wei Chang, Kenton Lee, and Kristina Toutanova. 2019. BERT: Pre-training of deep bidirectional transformers for language understanding. In *Proceedings of the 2019 Conference of the North American Chapter of the Association for Computational Linguistics: Human Language Technologies, Volume 1 (Long and Short Papers)*, pages 4171–4186.

Bradley Efron. 1979. Bootstrap methods: Another look at the jackknife. *The Annals of Statistics*, 7(1):1–26.

Ruining He and Julian J. McAuley. 2016. Ups and downs: Modeling the visual evolution of fashion trends with one-class collaborative filtering. In *WWW '16: Proceedings of the 25th International Conference on World Wide Web*, pages 507–517.

Edward J. Hu, Yelong Shen, Phillip Wallis, Zeyuan Allen-Zhu, Yuanzhi Li, Shean Wang, Lu Wang, and Weizhu Chen. 2021. LoRA: Low-Rank Adaptation of Large Language Models. *arXiv:2106.09685*.

Minqing Hu and Bing Liu. 2004. Mining and summarizing customer reviews. In *KDD '04: Proceedings of the tenth ACM SIGKDD international conference on Knowledge discovery and data mining*, pages 168–177.

Clayton Hutto and Eric Gilbert. 2014. Vader: A parsimonious rule-based model for sentiment analysis of social media text. In *Proceedings of the International AAAI Conference on Web and Social Media*, volume 8, pages 216–225.

Albert Q. Jiang, Alexandre Sablayrolles, Antoine Roux, Arthur Mensch, Blanche Savary, Chris Bamford, Devendra Singh Chaplot, Diego de las Casas, Emma Bou Hanna, Florian Bressand, Gianna Lengyel, Guillaume Bour, Guillaume Lample, Lélio Renard Lavaud, Lucile Saulnier, Marie-Anne Lachaux, Pierre Stock, Sandeep Subramanian, Sophia Yang, Szymon Antoniak, Teven Le Scao, Théophile Gervet, Thibaut Lavril, Thomas Wang, Timothée Lacroix, and William El Sayed. 2024. Mixtral of Experts. *arXiv:2401.04088*.

Christopher SG Khoo and Sathik Basha Johnkhan. 2018. Lexicon-based sentiment analysis: Comparative evaluation of six sentiment lexicons. *Journal of Information Science*, 44(4):491–511.

Kai-Robin Lange and Carsten Jentsch. 2023. SpeakGer: A meta-data enriched speech corpus of German state and federal parliaments. In *Proceedings of the 3rd Workshop on Computational Linguistics for the Political and Social Sciences*, pages 19–28.

Md Tahmid Rahman Laskar, M Saiful Bari, Mizanur Rahman, Md Amran Hossen Bhuiyan, Shafiq Joty, and Jimmy Huang. 2023. A Systematic Study and Comprehensive Evaluation of ChatGPT on Benchmark Datasets. In *Findings of the Association for Computational Linguistics: ACL 2023*, pages 431–469.

Quoc Le and Tomas Mikolov. 2014a. Distributed representations of sentences and documents. In *Proceedings of the 31st International Conference on Machine Learning*, volume 32 of *Proceedings of Machine Learning Research*, pages 1188–1196.

Quoc V. Le and Tomas Mikolov. 2014b. Distributed representations of sentences and documents. *arXiv:1405.4053*. Version: 2.

Baoli Li and Liping Han. 2013. Distance weighted cosine similarity measure for text classification. In *Intelligent Data Engineering and Automated Learning – IDEAL 2013*, Lecture Notes in Computer Science, pages 611–618.

Changmao Li and Jeffrey Flanigan. 2024. Task Contamination: Language Models May Not Be Few-Shot Anymore. *Proceedings of the AAAI Conference on Artificial Intelligence*, 38(16):18471–18480.

Opher Lieber, Barak Lenz, Hofit Bata, Gal Cohen, Jhonathan Osin, Itay Dalmedigos, Erez Safahi, Shaked Meirom, Yonatan Belinkov, Shai Shalev-Shwartz, Omri Abend, Raz Alon, Tomer Asida, Amir Bergman, Roman Glozman, Michael Gokhman, Avashalom Manevich, Nir Ratner, Noam Rozen, Erez Shwartz, Mor Zusman, and Yoav Shoham. 2024. Jamba: A Hybrid Transformer-Mamba Language Model. *arXiv:2403.19887*.

Yinhan Liu, Myle Ott, Naman Goyal, Jingfei Du, Mandar Joshi, Danqi Chen, Omer Levy, Mike Lewis, Luke Zettlemoyer, and Veselin Stoyanov. 2019. RoBERTa: A Robustly Optimized BERT Pretraining Approach. *arXiv:1907.11692*.

Tim Loughran and Bill McDonald. 2010. When is a liability not a liability? textual analysis, dictionaries, and 10-ks. *SSRN Scholarly Paper*, (ID 1331573).

Edward Ma. 2019. Nlp augmentation. `https://github.com/makcedward/nlpaug`.

Andrew L. Maas, Raymond E. Daly, Peter T. Pham, Dan Huang, Andrew Y. Ng, and Christopher Potts. 2011. Learning word vectors for sentiment analysis. In *Proceedings of the 49th Annual Meeting of the Association for Computational Linguistics: Human Language Technologies*, pages 142–150.

Sourab Mangrulkar, Sylvain Gugger, Lysandre Debut, Younes Belkada, Sayak Paul, and Benjamin Bossan. 2022. Peft: State-of-the-art parameter-efficient fine-tuning methods. `https://github.com/huggingface/peft`.

Binny Mathew, Sandipan Sikdar, Florian Lemmerich, and Markus Strohmaier. 2020a. The polar framework: Polar opposites enable interpretability of pre-trained word embeddings. In *Proceedings of The Web Conference 2020*, WWW '20, page 1548–1558.

Binny Mathew, Sandipan Sikdar, Florian Lemmerich, and Markus Strohmaier. 2020b. The polar framework: Polar opposites enable interpretability of pre-trained word embeddings. In *Proceedings of The Web Conference 2020*, pages 1548–1558.

Tomas Mikolov, Kai Chen, Greg Corrado, and Jeffrey Dean. 2013. Efficient estimation of word representations in vector space. *arXiv:1301.3781*.

Finn Årup Nielsen. 2011. A new ANEW: evaluation of a word list for sentiment analysis in microblogs. In *Proceedings of the ESWC2011 Workshop on 'Making Sense of Microposts': Big things come in small packages*, volume 718 of *CEUR Workshop Proceedings*, pages 93–98.

Christian Rauh. 2018. Validating a sentiment dictionary for German political language—a workbench note. *Journal of Information Technology & Politics*, 15(4):319–343.

Radim Řehůřek and Petr Sojka. 2010. Software Framework for Topic Modelling with Large Corpora. In *Proceedings of the LREC 2010 Workshop on New Challenges for NLP Frameworks*, pages 45–50.

Jonas Rieger, Carsten Jentsch, and Jörg Rahnenführer. 2020. Assessing the uncertainty of the text generating process using topic models. In *ECML PKDD 2020 Workshops*, pages 385–396. Springer International Publishing.

Jonas Rieger, Kostiantyn Yanchenko, Mattes Ruckdeschel, Gerret von Nordheim, Katharina Kleinen-von Königslöw, and Gregor Wiedemann. 2024. Few-shot learning for automated content analysis: Efficient coding of arguments and claims in the debate on arms deliveries to Ukraine. *SCM Studies in Communication and Media*, 13(1):72–100.

Timo Schick and Hinrich Schütze. 2021. Exploiting Cloze Questions for Few Shot Text Classification and Natural Language Inference. *arXiv:2001.07676*.

Bonggun Shin, Timothy Lee, and Jinho D. Choi. 2017. Lexicon integrated CNN models with attention for sentiment analysis. In *Proceedings of the 8th Workshop on Computational Approaches to Subjectivity, Sentiment and Social Media Analysis*, pages 149–158.

Emma Strubell, Ananya Ganesh, and Andrew McCallum. 2019. Energy and policy considerations for deep learning in NLP. In *Proceedings of the 57th Annual Meeting of the Association for Computational Linguistics*, pages 3645–3650.

Alaa Tharwat and Wolfram Schenck. 2023. A Survey on Active Learning: State-of-the-Art, Practical Challenges and Research Directions. *Mathematics*, 11(4):820.

Hugo Touvron, Thibaut Lavril, Gautier Izacard, Xavier Martinet, Marie-Anne Lachaux, Timothée Lacroix, Baptiste Rozière, Naman Goyal, Eric Hambro, Faisal Azhar, Aurelien Rodriguez, Armand Joulin, Edouard Grave, and Guillaume Lample. 2023. LLaMA: Open and Efficient Foundation Language Models. *arXiv:2302.13971*.

Qizhe Xie, Zihang Dai, Eduard Hovy, Minh-Thang Luong, and Quoc V. Le. 2020. Unsupervised data augmentation for consistency training. *arXiv:1904.12848*. Version: 6.

Discourse-Level Features in Spoken and Written Communication

Hannah J. Seemann[1], Sara Shahmohammadi[2], Manfred Stede[2], Tatjana Scheffler[1]
[1] Department for German Language and Literature, Ruhr-University Bochum, Germany
[2] Department of Linguistics, University of Potsdam, Germany
hannah.seemann@rub.de shahmohammadi@uni-potsdam.de
stede@uni-potsdam.de tatjana.scheffler@rub.de

Abstract

Using PARADISE, a German corpus of thematically parallel blog posts and podcast transcripts, we test how reliably a document's original mode can be classified based on discourse-level features only. Our results show that classifying mode with a document's distribution of discourse relations as well as the frequency of discourse connectives and discourse particles is possible and informative of the nature of these document types. We provide our dataset annotated with discourse relations (Rhetorical Structure Theory), German discourse connectives, and discourse particles.

1 Introduction

The comparison of spoken and written language has a long tradition. Distinctions between different types of language use are usually based on both language-internal (e.g., lexical) and -external (e.g., situational) features. Since the description of conceptional orality as a continuum by Koch and Oesterreicher (1985) and others, studies on variation between spoken and written, personal and interpersonal communication have been conducted by, e.g., Biber et al. (1999) and Biber and Conrad (2019). Describing different *registers* in the continuum of language, the authors identify various features typical for specific types and settings of communication.

But not only do texts differ in how closely they match typical patterns of written or spoken language, the introduction of digital communication channels has also added to the variety of the continuum. On the one hand, we can find characteristics of spoken language in written computer-mediated communication (CMC) (Scheffler, 2017), and on the other hand, spoken computer-mediated interaction differs from the speech style before the introduction of digital communication channels, as the interlocutors are aware of a broader range of communicative practices and make use of them (Soffer, 2010; Heyd, 2021).

However, even if there have been comprehensive corpus-based studies on variation in spoken and written language that cover many different features, most of these features are lexical or syntactic in nature. Related work on the orality of texts shows that classification between spoken and written modes based on various feature levels works quite well. Though language and language variation is thought to be influenced by non-linguistic factors such as a speaker's communicative goal and the context of language production (Biber and Conrad, 2019), only few of these studies take explicitly discourse-related phenomena into account.

We study whether structural differences in a text, such as its discourse structure, together with discourse-related lexical features, such as discourse connectives and discourse particles, can be leveraged for a classification of language mode in CMC. As features like the average word length of a text and type-token ratio have been shown to systematically vary between spoken and written language (Kunz et al., 2018), we compare our results to a classification based on these two features. To account for different communicative practices, we compare spoken and written communication in digital communication channels: blog posts and podcasts. The dataset used in our study contains excerpts from blog posts and podcasts aligned for topic, to further reduce factors that might influence a text outside of its mode.

We provide our dataset of German blog posts and podcast transcripts, annotated with RST-style discourse relations as well as discourse connectives and particles, enabling further studies on both discourse structure in two modes and implicit and explicit discourse relations. So far, there are only very few discourse-annotated German corpora

(Stede, 2016a; Hewett, 2023), and thus our work contributes both additional training data (for example for RST parsing) and material for qualitative studies on the interactions of discourse phenomena.

2 Related Work

There are three types of related studies: Studies that identify relevant dimensions for distinguishing between different modes of language, studies that work on the automatic classification of language modes based on various linguistic features, and work that identifies discourse-related features that vary between language modes.

Kunz et al. (2018) compare various spoken and written registers (in English and German) based on “shallow” lexical features of lexical cohesion (Kunz et al., 2018, p. 176), such as type-token ratio, word class profiles, and frequently used words. They find less lexical variability in spoken than in written texts,[1] and that this difference is even more prominent in English than in German.

Ortmann and Dipper (2019) study a German corpus of five registers on different positions on the ‘conceptual orality’ scale (Koch and Oesterreicher, 1985) – from written newspaper texts to informal spoken conversations – showing that a decision tree classifier can reliably distinguish between them based on various linguistic features. The features used in the study are lexical (e.g., use of particles and interjections), syntactic (e.g., use of active vs. passive voice), measures of complexity (sentence and word length), co-reference and deixis (e.g., pronouns), and punctuation.

Lapshinova-Koltunski and Zampieri (2018) use part-of-speech n-grams to distinguish between German and English translations of fictional texts and political speeches, finding that the n-grams differ systematically enough between the two modes for a reliable classification (81.25% accuracy) based on a Bayesian classifier with Laplace smoothing.

The above-mentioned approaches rely primarily on lexical differences between speech and writing, or on a mix between all feature types. In contrast, some recent work more directly addresses the question of whether the discourse structure must be adapted when information is presented in spoken or written mode. Existing work focuses on co-reference phenomena as well as the marking of coherence relations.

Aktaş and Stede (2020) quantitatively study the features of co-reference in spoken and written English language. Comparing language corpora of both modes, they show that the distance between anaphoric pronouns and their antecedents is longer in spoken texts than in written texts. Co-reference thus seems to be a discourse feature that can be used reliably to distinguish spoken and written texts.

Using different corpora of spoken Italian and Irish English, Tonelli et al. (2010) and Rehbein et al. (2016) report on the distribution of discourse relations and their explicit marking through connectives. Tonelli et al. (2010) observe a smaller variety of connectives being used for multiple relations in telephone speech, whereas in the written newspaper texts of the Penn Discourse Treebank (PDTB, Prasad et al., 2008, 2019), more specific connectives are used. They also observe that compared to the PDTB, explicit relations are twice as frequent as implicit ones in speech, and TEMPORAL as well as CAUSAL relations are more frequent than other relations. These results are confirmed by Rehbein et al. (2016), who report twice as many explicit than implicit relations in speech. Both studies concede that the differences in relation frequency could arise based on the domain differences between the two corpora, so Rehbein et al. (2016) additionally compare spoken broadcasts to telephone conversations. They find that in conversations, CAUSAL relations are by far more frequent than in the broadcasts, thus the distribution of relation types seems to depend on a text's register rather than its mode.

In the following, we analyze a corpus that is matched for topic and audience in order to investigate whether discourse level differences between the spoken and written mode can be shown there as well.

3 Data & Preprocessing

PARADISE (PARAllel DIScoursE)[2] is a corpus of German computer-mediated communication in different media – written blog posts, and the transcripts of spoken podcast episodes. It is in parts annotated for discourse structure, and comprises 69 blog posts and the corresponding podcast transcripts from two different topic domains: science/culture and business. Each blog post is written

[1] We use ‘text’ to refer to any coherent linguistic entity, independent of its mode. In this sense, a podcast is a spoken text.

[2] The corpus is freely available at: `https://osf.io/59acq/`

by the podcast host to describe the content of the podcast, so the same topics are covered in both modes of communication.

Episodes from the science/culture domain are taken from Metaebene[3] and cover topics like scientific achievements, astronomy, German media, and politics. Episodes from the business domain are produced by companies or registered associations like Deutsche Telekom or Verbraucherzentrale, topics covered are digitalization, start-ups, health and food as well as the food industry. The design of the podcasts differs between the two domains. Podcasts in the science/culture domain are either 1:1 interviews with one host and one guest who is an expert on the episode's topic, or group conversations with varying members from a fixed pool of participants. In the business podcasts, one host or a team of hosts invites a number of guests to advertise a product or concept, which resembles a scripted interview more than a naturally flowing conversation about a fixed topic.

If no transcript of the podcast was provided by the host, the audio files were transcribed automatically. For both blog posts and podcasts, we used SoMaJo[4] for tokenization and sentence splitting (Proisl and Uhrig, 2016). We manually checked for and corrected errors in the word level transcription of the audios as well as errors in sentence splitting.

To allow for an exact analysis of how similar content is talked about in the two modes 'spoken' and 'written', we identified text chunks with parallel content: For each sentence/text chunk in a blog post covering a specific topic, the corresponding parallel segment in the podcast is identified (if there is one). To do so, one annotator was instructed to annotate all parts in the transcript that are parallel to each sentence in the blog post by marking keywords in the blog post and searching for them in the podcast. The resulting parallel segments may cover turns of more than one speaker if the utterances are related to the topic in question. In an additional step, two annotators rated how parallel each previously annotated segment is. The degree of parallelism is indicated by the following scale:

A: Perfectly parallel segments, where the blog and the transcript address the same content and even use the same wording/share the same expressions.

B: Good parallelism, the blog and the transcript address the same content but one goes into more detail than the other.

C: Medium parallelism, the blog and the transcript have the same topic and share some part of the content, but they also contain 'non-parallel' information, i.e. some content that the other one is lacking.

D: Low parallelism, the blog and the transcript address the same topic but do not have the same content.

E: Non parallel segments, where the blog and the transcript do not even share the same topic.

For example, the parallelism between the segments below – part of the blog post in (1) and part of the transcript in (2) – is rated as belonging to category B: The podcast elaborates on the topic mentioned in the blog.

(1) And: What goals is the Stifterverband pursuing with its new podcast project?[5]

(FG000B)

(2) And that was probably kind of the idea behind this new project, which we have christened Forschergeist. Which may initially give the impression that we only want to talk about research, and that is what we want. But we actually want to talk a bit more about the spirit of research. In other words, what drives people, what drives foundations, what, let's say, certain foundations actually aim to achieve with their objectives. But also to present the work of science.[6]

(FG000T)

We used weighted Krippendorff's α to calculate inter-annotator agreement ($\alpha = 0.53$). Out of 406

[3] `https://metaebene.me/`

[4] `https://github.com/tsproisl/SoMaJo`

[5] German original: *Und: Welche Ziele verfolgt der Stifterverband mit seinem neuen Podcast-Projekt?*

[6] German original: *Und das war dann wahrscheinlich auch ein wenig der Gedanke hinter diesem neuen Projekt, was wir Forschergeist getauft haben. Was vielleicht so erst mal den Eindruck macht, als würde man jetzt nur über Forschung reden wollen, aber das wollen wir auch. Aber wir wollen eigentlich ein bisschen mehr über den Forschergeist eigentlich sprechen. Also das was so die Leute treibt, was Stiftungen treibt, was sagen wir mal vielleicht auch bestimmte Stiftungen überhaupt mit ihren Stiftungszielen bezwecken. Aber eben auch die Arbeit der Wissenschaft vorzustellen.*

parallel segments, the two annotators agreed in 223 (54.92%) of all cases. In 150 cases (36.94%), their ratings deviated from each other by one step, e.g., annotator 1 assigned label 'B' and annotator 2 assigned label 'C'. In 33 cases (8.12%), the ratings lay farther apart. A third annotator assigned a final label for each case where the two annotators did not initially agree. The distribution of the final labels is presented in Table 1.

A	B	C	D	E
6.87	58.47	27.51	6.38	0.73

Table 1: Distribution of parallelism labels, in %.

For the task presented here, we use chunks that are parallel but not identical (= category B). The size of the sub-corpus used is presented in Table 2.

	Blogs	Transcripts	Total
Science	2,411	30,416	32,827
Business	788	4,814	5,602
Total	3,199	35,230	38,838

Table 2: Token count in the sub-corpus used for this task, by medium and domain.

Table 3 shows the type-token ratio and the average word length in our dataset. In general, the type-token ratio and average word length are higher in blogs than in podcasts, which matches the characteristics of spoken and written language.[7] The mean length of blog chunks is 70 token (with a standard deviation of 44), compared to 756 (SD 649) in podcasts, reflecting that there is usually more elaboration on a certain point in the spoken conversation.

	Blogs	Transcripts
TTR	0.83	0.49
Avg. word length	5.52	4.51

Table 3: Type-Token Ratio and average word length, by medium.

[7] A reviewer pointed out that these measures are not normalized and do reflect differences in the document's length. However, normalization methods are influenced and limited by the length of the shortest document, which is rather short in our case. The resulting measure would not necessarily be more informative and therefore, we decided against normalizing type-token ratio and average word length.

4 Annotation of Discourse Features

We manually annotate discourse relations, discourse connectives and discourse particles in the dataset described above. This combination of structural and lexical discourse-level features allows us to account for variability between modes as well as the structural differences between modes that go beyond the lexical level.

4.1 Rhetorical Structure Theory

Rhetorical Structure Theory (RST, Mann and Thompson, 1988) is a model of discourse structure that captures the intentions of and rhetorics used by an author of a written text. In this model, discourse structure is represented as a hierarchical tree built from *Elementary Discourse Units* (EDUs, often clauses) and the discourse relations that span between them as well as hierarchically between complex units. RST was mainly designed for written monologues but has been applied to spoken data before (Stent, 2000; Shahmohammadi et al., 2023). Example (3) shows two EDUs connected by a CAUSE relation.

(3) [The cat was tired during the day] [because it was up running around the whole night.]

In our RST annotation, we follow the guidelines defined in Stede (2016b). To account for particularities of spoken language, we added a COMPLETION relation that holds between segments of interrupted utterances. Most of the RST annotation was conducted by one trained annotator and a second trained annotator annotated parts of the corpus. We used RST-Tace (Wan et al., 2019) to evaluate the agreement between the two annotators. With Fleiss $\kappa = 0.49$,[8] our inter-annotator agreement is comparable to similar complex annotation tasks. Except for Hewett (2023), who reports on averaged Fleiss $\kappa = 0.27$, a direct comparison to other RST annotations is not possible, either because no agreement is reported or a different evaluation method is used.

We grouped the annotated discourse relations by their semantic characteristics: All relations that express a causal relation between two segments are grouped as CAUSAL, etc. An overview of our groups is shown in Table 4. For the classification task, we use the proportion of each relation type

[8] The evaluation score we report is based on the annotation of 27 documents (= 470 EDUs) and averaged over nuclearity, spans, attachment points, and relation agreement.

Semantic Category	Discourse Relations
CAUSAL	Cause, Justify Evidence, Reason-N Reason, Result
CONTRAST	Antithesis, Concession Contrast
HYPOTHETICAL	Condition, Enablement Means, Motivation Otherwise, Purpose
JUDGEMENT	Evaluation-N, Evaluation-S, Interpretation, Solutionhood
TEMPORAL	Circumstance, Sequence
INFORMATION	Background E-Elaboration Elaboration, Preparation Restatement, Summary Question
ADDITIVE	Conjunction, Joint, List
STRUCTURAL	Attribution, Completion Sameunit

Table 4: Discourse relations annotated in our corpus, grouped by semantic category.

compared to the overall distribution of discourse relations in a document, though we exclude the group of STRUCTURAL relations from our analysis since we judge them as text-specific necessities rather than semantically motivated discourse relations.

The resulting distribution of discourse relations in the two modes is presented in Figure 1. The plot shows the density of each relation's proportions: For example, the third graph on the left side shows that in all of the spoken podcasts, the proportion of HYPOTHETICAL relations is low, with almost all of the documents having a proportion of this relation group between 0.0 and 0.13. In the blog posts on the other hand, we find proportions of HYPOTHETICAL relations up to 0.6 – though most blog posts also make use of rather low proportions of this relation group, as the peak in the density plot is around 0.0, too. Given these density distributions, we can conclude that some relation groups like CONTRAST, HYPOTHETICAL, and TEMPORAL are rather infrequent in our dataset in both modes. The relations in the groups ADDITIVE, CAUSAL, and INFORMATION are typically more frequent in blog posts, whereas JUDGMENT relations are almost exclusively found in the podcast transcripts. Overall, our spoken documents show a broader distribution of discourse relations and in our written documents, we find more relations from a single group in one document. However, this effect is not necessarily driven by the document's mode. Instead, the blog posts are generally shorter than the parallel podcast chunks, thus there are overall fewer discourse relations present.

4.2 Discourse Connectives

Discourse connectives (*because, however, while,* ...) are items that explicitly mark discourse relations. They can belong to various syntactic categories, such as conjunctions, adverbs, or prepositional phrases. In example (3), the CAUSE relation between the two segments is explicitly signaled by the connective *because*. In most cases, there is no 1:1 correspondence between connectives and discourse relations, and not every discourse relation is always signaled by a connective – corpus studies report on 15%–50% of all relations being explicitly signaled by connectives (Das, 2014; Crible, 2020). Nonetheless, connectives can be used for the identification of discourse relations, as there typically is a set of possible connectives associated with a discourse relation, and since connectives can be identified relatively easily in text. Which connectives can be used to signal which relations in German is described in the lexicon of discourse markers, DiMLex (Stede, 2002; Scheffler and Stede, 2016).

Based on the connectives listed in DiMLex, we annotated a total of 1,117 connective instances in our corpus, with *und* ('and', 394 instances), *aber* ('but', 130 instances) and *wenn* ('if', 79 instances) being the most frequent connectives. The average relative frequency of connectives per text is 2.73 (SD 2.11) in blog posts and 2.95 (SD 1.29) in podcasts – showing only small differences between the two media. Inter-annotator agreement between two annotators was moderate to substantial with Cohen's $\kappa = 0.73$.[9] We provide both annotations as well as the curated set of connectives in the corpus repository. For our classification task, we use the count of connectives in a given document relative to the number of tokens in this document. Given the short length of each of our documents, we do

[9]Some of the differences arise from the annotators varying in their assessment of multi-word connectives, e.g., whether *nicht nur ... sondern auch* ('not only ... but also') should be annotated as two multi-word connectives or four separate connectives.

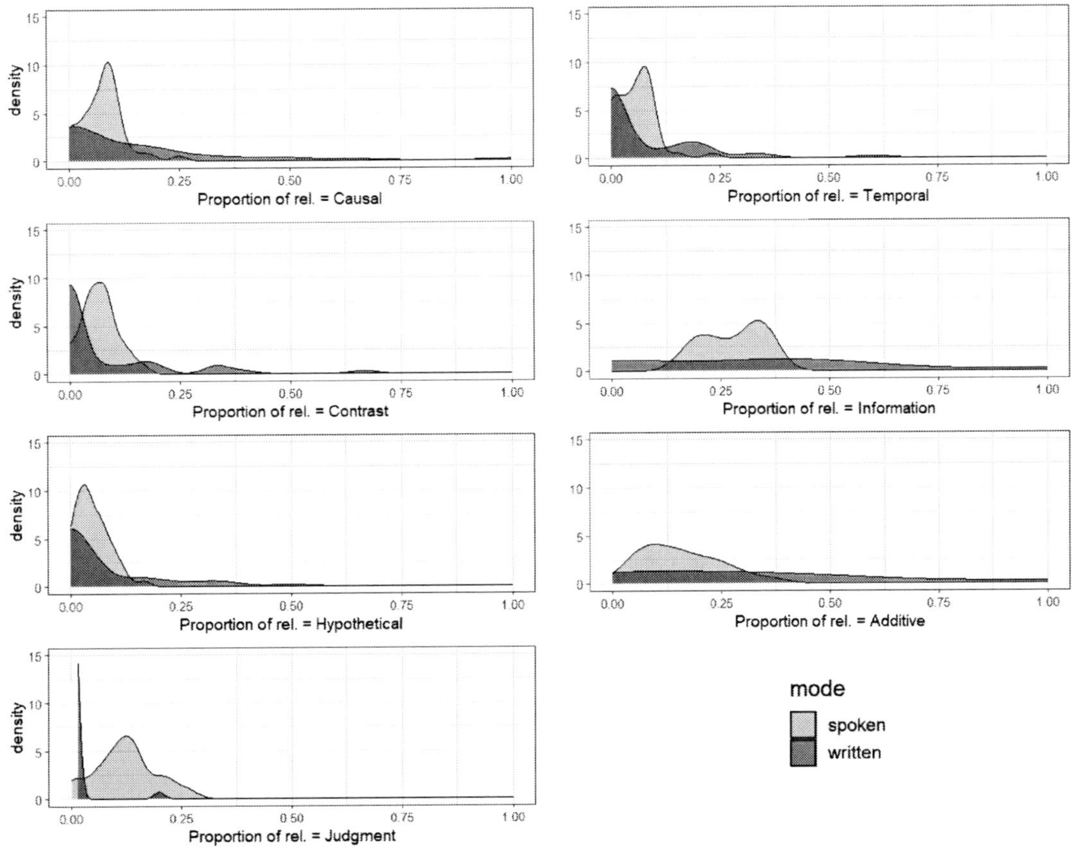

Figure 1: Density curves of discourse relation proportions, split by mode.

not distinguish between which discourse connectives are employed in a segment, but only record the overall frequency. (As this gives an indication of the text complexity, we regard this as a discourse-level feature rather than a solely lexical one.)

4.3 Discourse Particles

Discourse particles in a language like German are non-inflected sentence modifiers that convey discourse-related information (Zimmermann, 2011). They are employed to signal the epistemic state of the speaker and for common ground management between the interlocutors. Examples of two discourse particles are given in (4) and (5).

(4) Ich sollte nun wirklich gehen, es ist **ja** schon ziemlich spät.
'I really should go now, it is (unarguably and obviously) quite late.'

(5) Meine Kollegin ist spät dran, sie hat **wohl** mal wieder den Bus verpasst.
'My colleague is late, she (presumably) missed the bus again.'

In these examples, *ja* signals that the time being late is either known to all interlocutors or salient in the conversation's context (possibly due to a setting sun or a clock nearby), and *wohl* indicates the speaker's uncertainty about the expressed proposition. Discourse particles have been argued to be indicators of discourse relations, and corpus studies show that there is an interaction between discourse structure and discourse particles (Karagjosova, 2004; Döring, 2016), though the specific discourse function of these particles is not known. Because of their discourse-managing functions and often colloquial nature, the particles are used more often in informal spoken than in formal written language.

There are rarely two identical lists of elements considered to be discourse particles in German, but there is a 'core class' of discourse particles that is accepted by most researchers. A set of annotation guidelines for German particles compiling different lists from the literature (Kern and Scheffler,

2021) list 39 items that can be used as discourse particles, both elements from the core class and more rare discourse particles. Of those, we find 24 different items (518 instances in total) in our corpus: *aber, allerdings, auch, denn, doch, eben, eh, eigentlich, einfach, gleich, halt, irgendwie, ja, jetzt, leider, mal, schon, selbst, sogar, tatsächlich, vielleicht, wahrscheinlich, wirklich, wohl*, with *ja, eben* and *halt* being the three most frequent particles.[10] One annotator annotated all discourse particles in all parallel documents, and a second annotator annotated a subset of these documents. As the inter-annotator agreement is strong (Cohen's $\kappa = 0.81$), we consider one full annotation to be sufficient. The average relative frequency of discourse particles in blog posts is 0.30 (SD 0.83) and 1.46 (SD 0.84) in podcasts, showing a tendency for discourse particles to be more frequent in spoken podcasts than in written blog posts. We use the relative frequency of discourse particles as features for our classification task.

5 Classification by Mode

As our dataset is quite small, we use a 5-fold cross-validation to evaluate all our classification results. For both the binary classification and the evaluation, we use scikit-learn Support Vector Classification with C = 2^{11} and cross-validation (Pedregosa et al., 2011).

Table 5 presents the classification results, the confusion matrix is shown in Table 6. Overall, the accuracy is 0.90 with a SD of 0.10.

Out of eight misclassification cases, five blog posts are wrongly classified as podcasts, and three as blog posts. Except for one case, all of the misclassified blog posts have a high relative frequency of discourse particles (between $\sim$ 2–4.41). The exception is the blog post CRE222. Here, the relative frequency of discourse particles is low (0 compared to 0.30 on average for blog posts), but the relative frequency of connectives stands out (6.21 compared to an average of 2.73). In two blog posts classified as podcasts, the relation distributions stand out compared to the other blog posts, In the case of blog post FG089, all relation proportions except for INFORMATION are low and in FG082_Blog, the proportion of JUDGEMENT relations is unusually high compared to the other blog posts. In the other three cases, the distributions of discourse relations match the other blog posts.

Fold	Precision	Recall	F1
1	0.89	1.00	0.94
2	0.88	0.88	0.88
3	0.78	1.00	0.88
4	0.88	1.00	0.93
5	1.00	0.96	0.92
average	0.88	0.95	0.90

Table 5: Results of classifying *mode* using groups of discourse relations as well as the relative frequency of connectives and discourse particles in a 5-fold cross-validation.

Fold	TP	TN	FP	FN
1	9	9	1	0
2	10	9	0	0
3	8	6	3	1
4	8	9	0	1
5	8	8	1	1

Table 6: Confusion matrix for classifying *mode* using groups of discourse relations as well as the relative frequency of connectives and discourse particles in a 5-fold cross-validation.

A similar – though inverted – pattern can be detected for the podcast transcripts wrongly classified as blog posts. All of them have a low proportion of JUDGEMENT and instead high proportions of other relation groups (mostly INFORMATION and ADDITIVE), and a low relative frequency of discourse particles or discourse connectives.

To put the reported numbers into perspective, we compare our results to a classification based on lexical features that have been shown to reliably distinguish spoken and written language: type-token-ratio and average word length. As before, we use a 5-fold cross-validation to evaluate all of our results. Table 7 reports on the results of the classification, the confusion matrix is presented in Table 8. The overall accuracy is 0.96 with a SD of 0.02.[12]

[10]It should be noted that some of these items, like *irgendwie* or *sogar*, are by far more frequent in their adverb or focus particle meaning, but can be employed as discourse particle, too. We only annotated the discourse particle use. In addition, some of these discourse particles are also included in DiMLex, the basis for our discourse connective annotation. If a token was ambiguous between the two categories, it was only annotated as discourse particle.

[11]We tested C-values between 0.5 and 5 and report on the value that yielded the best classification results.

[12]We would like to point out again that these results are not based on normalized lexical measures and might be skewed

Fold	Precision	Recall	F1
1	0.88	1.00	0.94
2	1.00	1.00	1.00
3	0.88	1.00	0.93
4	1.00	0.86	0.92
5	1.00	1.00	1.00
average	0.95	0.97	0.96

Table 7: Results of classifying *mode* using average word length and TTR in a 5-fold cross-validation.

Fold	TP	TN	FP	FN
1	9	9	1	0
2	7	9	0	3
3	9	9	0	0
4	9	9	0	0
5	8	9	0	1

Table 8: Confusion matrix for classifying *mode* using average word length and TTR in a 5-fold cross-validation.

Four out of five cases of misclassification are podcast documents with relatively high TTR compared to the other podcast files (FG046: 0.72, FG050: 0.80, FG060: 0.71, TelekomS7E1: 0.67, average for podcasts: 0.48). In the case of FG060 and TelekomS7E1, the average word length (5.30 and 4.90) is also higher than the mean in this group (4.51). There are other outliers in each of the categories, though if one of the measures is higher, the other one is close to the group's mean, thus not leading to incorrect classification. The one blog post wrongly classified as podcast shows a lower average word length (4.8 vs. group mean of 5.52) and TTR (0.69 vs. group mean of 0.83) compared to the other blog posts.

6 Discussion

Our results indicate that – even though the classification of language mode based on discourse-related features only does not reach the results achieved based on shallow lexical features – a rather reliable classification of mode based on structural discourse features is both possible and informative about the nature of the studied documents. The presented results are higher than a classification based on n-grams (Kunz et al., 2018), indicating that discourse-level features can provide additional information on a document compared to certain other lexical frequency profiles. Our results further indicate that as for the discourse-level features, both an unusually high or low frequency of discourse particles and connectives as well as an unusual distribution of discourse relation may lead to a misclassification of mode.

In our dataset, relations from the group of JUDGEMENT that evaluate content or express an opinion are found almost exclusively in the podcasts – it is only present in one out of all blog post. At the same time, the more argumentative relations from the group of CAUSAL relations are rarely found in podcasts. INFORMATION and ADDITIVE relations are found in both spoken podcasts and written blog posts, though more frequently so in the blog posts, whereas CONTRAST and HYPOTHETICAL relations are infrequent in both. Given the register of our data, this is unsurprising: The podcasts are conversations about a variety of topics, where interlocutors express their opinions or present information about the topic at hand. The blog posts on the other hand report on what is being talked about in the podcasts, informing the reader about content to be expected and possibly making an argument for why listening to the podcast is worthwhile. A register study on podcasts has shown that they are neither similar to other spoken registers nor other communication channels of CMC (Babyode et al., 2023). Analyses of blog posts find variation in the degree of formality and communicative purposes in this medium (Scheffler et al., 2022). This variation in register may also influence the representation of discourse coherence via RST-style discourse relations. Comparisons to other datasets will allow us to further delineate whether the results we find here are mainly driven by a difference in mode (spoken or written) or in register (e.g., conversation or presentation).

For the discourse particles, our results match the expectation that particles are more frequent in spoken language compared to written text. Given that there are only marginal differences between the frequency of connectives in blog posts and podcasts, no qualitative evaluation of the frequency of connectives in the two modes is possible. However, looking into the distribution of certain connectives in both blog posts and podcasts might yield different results.

We have shown that there are systematic dif-

to reflect the differences in document length as well as their difference in mode.

ferences in the distribution of discourse relations and discourse particles between our spoken podcasts and written blog posts. Therefore, our study contributes to the description of CMC practices as well as research on discourse structure, given that our dataset comprises documents coming from different registers than other corpora with discourse structure annotation. In addition, our dataset enables further studies on German discourse connectives as well as implicit and explicit discourse relations, as we provide both types of annotations.

Limitations

We have carried out all analyses according to our best abilities. Nevertheless, it should be noted that while the RST annotations were either done twice by different researchers or have been double-checked by at least one other expert for plausibility, in many cases there are alternative analyses of the texts which may also be applicable (as is usually the case for discourse structure). Since we do not have direct access to the discourse creators and their goals, this limitation is unavoidable in corpus studies.

In addition, annotation of discourse structure is quite costly and resource-demanding. It is therefore usual that datasets annotated for discourse structure are rather small, as is the case in our study. Further studies on different or combined datasets can help resolve this limitation.

Ethics Statement

The data reported on in this paper was collected within the research project named below. For the texts published, explicit consent was obtained from the creators to use and publish the data for annotation and scientific analysis. The data was automatically and manually preprocessed and reformatted, and manually annotated for discourse features. All annotations were carried out by researchers during their regular work time, either PhD students (authors of this paper) or student research assistants with regular work contracts and paid according to public pay scales. The data will be long-term archived and is available to other researchers according to the laws that apply. We see no other ethical issues with our data or research practices.

Acknowledgments

This work was funded by the Deutsche Forschungsgemeinschaft (DFG, German Research Foundation) – Project ID 317633480 – SFB 1287.
We would like to thank Daniel Foppe, Freya Hewett, and Elisa Lübbers for their support with annotating and reviewing the data.

References

Berfin Aktaş and Manfred Stede. 2020. Variation in coreference strategies across genres and production media. In *Proceedings of the 28th International Conference on Computational Linguistics*, pages 5774–5785, Barcelona, Spain (Online). International Committee on Computational Linguistics.

Aminat Babyode, Laurens Bosman, Nicole Chan, Katharina Ehret, Ivan Fong, Noelle Harris, Alissa Hewton, Danica Reid, Maite Taboada, and Rebekah Wong. 2023. Structural linguistic characteristics of podcasts as an emerging register of computer-mediated communication. In *Proceedings of the 10th International Conference on CMC and Social Media Corpora for the Humanities*, pages 3–6, Mannheim, Germany.

Douglas Biber and Susan Conrad. 2019. *Register, Genre, and Style*, 2nd edition. Cambridge Textbooks in Linguistics. Cambridge University Press, Cambridge.

Douglas Biber, Stig Johansson, Geoffrey Leech, Susan Conrad, and Edward Finegan. 1999. *The Longman Grammar of Spoken and Written English*. Longman, London.

Ludivine Crible. 2020. Weak and Strong Discourse Markers in Speech, Chat, and Writing: Do Signals Compensate for Ambiguity in Explicit Relations? *Discourse Processes*, 57(9):793–807.

Debopam Das. 2014. *Signalling of Coherence Relations in Discourse*. Dissertation, Simon Fraser University, Canada.

Sophia Döring. 2016. *Modal Particles, Discourse Structure and Common Ground Management*. Dissertation, Humboldt-Universität zu Berlin.

Freya Hewett. 2023. APA-RST: A text simplification corpus with RST annotations. In *Proceedings of the 4th Workshop on Computational Approaches to Discourse (CODI 2023)*, pages 173–179, Toronto, Canada. Association for Computational Linguistics.

Theresa Heyd. 2021. Tertiary Orality? *Anglistik*, 32(2):131–147.

Elena Karagjosova. 2004. *The Meaning and Function of German Modal Particles*. Dissertation, Universiteit Utrecht.

Lesley-Ann Kern and Tatjana Scheffler. 2021. Annotationsrichtlinien für Modalpartikeln. Unpublished Manuscript.

Peter Koch and Wulf Oesterreicher. 1985. Sprache der Nähe - Sprache der Distanz. Mündlichkeit und Schriftlichkeit im Spannungsfeld von Sprachtheorie und Sprachgeschichte. *Romanistisches Jahrbuch*, 36:15–43.

Kerstin Kunz, Ekaterina Lapshinova-Koltunski, José Manuel Martínez Martínez, Katrin Menzel, and Erich Steiner. 2018. Shallow features as indicators of English-German contrasts in lexical cohesion. *Languages in Contrast: International Journal for Contrastive Linguistics*, 18(2):175–206.

Ekaterina Lapshinova-Koltunski and Marcos Zampieri. 2018. Linguistic features of genre and method variation in translation: a computational perspective. In Dominique Legallois, Thierry Charnois, and Meri Larjavaara, editors, *The Grammar of Genres and Styles. From Discrete to Non-Discrete Units*, pages 92–117. De Gruyter Mouton, Berlin, Boston.

William C. Mann and Sandra A. Thompson. 1988. Rhetorical Structure Theory: Toward a functional theory of text organization. *Text - Interdisciplinary Journal for the Study of Discourse*, 8(3):243–281.

Katrin Ortmann and Stefanie Dipper. 2019. Variation between different discourse types: Literate vs. oral. In *Proceedings of the Sixth Workshop on NLP for Similar Languages, Varieties and Dialects*, pages 64–79, Ann Arbor, Michigan. Association for Computational Linguistics.

F. Pedregosa, G. Varoquaux, A. Gramfort, V. Michel, B. Thirion, O. Grisel, M. Blondel, P. Prettenhofer, R. Weiss, V. Dubourg, J. Vanderplas, A. Passos, D. Cournapeau, M. Brucher, M. Perrot, and E. Duchesnay. 2011. Scikit-learn: Machine learning in Python. *Journal of Machine Learning Research*, 12:2825–2830.

Rashmi Prasad, Nikhil Dinesh, Alan Lee, Eleni Miltsakaki, Livio Robaldo, Aravind Joshi, and Bonnie Webber. 2008. The Penn discourse TreeBank 2.0. In *LREC 2008*.

Rashmi Prasad, Bonnie Webber, Alan Lee, and Aravind Joshi. 2019. Penn Discourse Treebank Version 3.0.

Thomas Proisl and Peter Uhrig. 2016. SoMaJo: State-of-the-art tokenization for German web and social media texts. In *Proceedings of the 10th Web as Corpus Workshop (WAC-X) and the EmpiriST Shared Task*, pages 57–62, Berlin. Association for Computational Linguistics.

Ines Rehbein, Merel Scholman, and Vera Demberg. 2016. Annotating Discourse Relations in Spoken Language: A Comparison of the PDTB and CCR Frameworks. In *Proceedings of the Tenth International Conference on Language Resources and Evaluation (LREC'16)*, pages 1039–1046, Portorož, Slovenia.

Tatjana Scheffler. 2017. Conversations on Twitter. In Darja Fišer and Michael Beißwenger, editors, *Investigating Computer-Mediated Communication: Corpus-based Approaches to Language in the Digital World*, pages 124–144. University Press, Ljubljana.

Tatjana Scheffler, Lesley-Ann Kern, and Hannah Seemann. 2022. The medium is not the message: Individual level register variation in blogs vs. tweets. *Register Studies*, 4(2):171–201.

Tatjana Scheffler and Manfred Stede. 2016. Adding semantic relations to a large-coverage connective lexicon of German. In *Proceedings of the Tenth International Conference on Language Resources and Evaluation (LREC 2016)*, pages 1008–1013, Portorož, Slovenia. European Language Resources Association (ELRA).

Sara Shahmohammadi, Hannah Seemann, Manfred Stede, and Tatjana Scheffler. 2023. Encoding Discourse Structure: Comparison of RST and QUD. In *Proceedings of the 4th Workshop on Computational Approaches to Discourse (CODI 2023)*, pages 89–98.

Oren Soffer. 2010. "Silent Orality": Toward a Conceptualization of the Digital Oral Features in CMC and SMS Texts. *Communication Theory*, 20(4):387–404.

Manfred Stede. 2002. DiMLex: A Lexical Approach to Discourse Markers. In Alessandro Lenci and Vittorio Di Tomaso, editors, *Exploring the Lexicon - Theory and Computation*. Edizioni dell'Orso, Alessandria.

Manfred Stede. 2016a. Das Potsdamer Kommentarkorpus. In Hartmut Lenk, editor, *Persuasionsstile in Europa II. Kommentartexte in den Medienlandschaften europäischer Länder*, number 229-231 in Germanistische Linguistik, pages 177–202. Olms, Hildesheim.

Manfred Stede, editor. 2016b. *Handbuch Textannotation: Potsdamer Kommentarkorpus 2.0*. Number 8 in Potsdam cognitive science series. Universitätsverlag Potsdam, Potsdam.

Amanda Stent. 2000. Rhetorical structure in dialog. In *INLG'2000 proceedings of the first international conference on natural language generation*, pages 247–252.

Sara Tonelli, Giuseppe Riccardi, Rashmi Prasad, and Aravind Joshi. 2010. Annotation of discourse relations for conversational spoken dialogs. In *Proceedings of the Seventh conference on International Language Resources and Evaluation (LREC'10)*, Valletta, Malta. European Languages Resources Association (ELRA).

Shujun Wan, Tino Kutschbach, Anke Lüdeling, and Manfred Stede. 2019. RST-tace a tool for automatic comparison and evaluation of RST trees. In *Proceedings of the Workshop on Discourse Relation Parsing and Treebanking 2019*, pages 88–96, Minneapolis, MN. Association for Computational Linguistics.

Malte Zimmermann. 2011. Discourse Particles. In P. Portner, C. Maienborn, and K. von Heusinger, editors, *Semantics*, number 33 in Handbücher zur Sprach- und Kommunikationswissenschaft HSK 2, pages 2011–2038. Mouton de Gruyter, Berlin.

Speechcake: Version Control for Speech Corpora

Vlad Dumitru[1], Matthias Boehm[2], Martin Hagmüller[1], Barbara Schuppler[1],
[1]Signal Processing and Speech Communication Laboratory,
Graz University of Technology, Inffeldgasse 16c, 8010 Graz, Austria
[2]Berlin Institute for the Foundations of Learning and Data,
Technische Universität Berlin, Ernst-Reuter-Platz 7, 10587 Berlin, Germany

Correspondence: Martin Hagmüller hagmueller@tugraz.at

Abstract

While the audio recordings of a corpus represent the ground truth, transcriptions are – in the case of manual annotations – subject to human error, and subject to changes related to technology improvements underpinning automated annotation methods. In order to facilitate the dynamic extension of speech corpora, we introduce *Speechcake*, a tool for centralized version control for speech corpora, enabling the automatic check-in and merging of annotations. It considers typical workflows of phoneticians, linguists and speech technologists, and enables the development of dynamic, collaborative, and perpetually-improving speech corpora.

1 Introduction

Speech corpora are generally distributed as static artifacts: after the initial publication, few updated versions are released as snapshots, if any at all. This *one-shot* release mechanism has a negative impact on (1) the organization publishing the corpus, and (2) on the larger research community using the data in question: (1) Collecting, annotating, and packaging a corpus requires a significant investment in terms of time and human effort. Releasing a corpus as a static artifact is done only when the annotation process is *complete*. A dynamic release mechanism allows this effort to be spread over a larger window of time. (2) A static corpus fails to acknowledge that annotations might contain errors and annotator idiosyncrasies. Rosenberg, 2012 highlights some issues found in *classical* static corpora such as the Penn Treebank (Marcus et al., 1993), Switchboard (Godfrey et al., 1992), Hub-4 (Graff et al., 1997) and Boston University Radio News Corpus (Ostendorf et al., 1995), proposing version control software as a solution. The core problem to solve is reproducibility. When researchers correct errors they find in a given dataset, these changes are not propagated back to the original artifact, thereby making it impossible for other parties to reproduce studies resulting from this *locally modified/corrected* corpus.

This paper presents *Speechcake*, a system to provide the necessary tools for creating, extending, and distributing *dynamic* speech corpora. Currently, *Speechcake* supports working with annotations in the Praat TextGrid format[1], although the system can be easily extended to other similar formats (i.e., a collection of tiers made from sequences of time-ordered items). Diverging changes that result from multiple annotators working on the same set of files are resolved through *three-way merging*, the successful result of which contains the changes introduced by two parent versions, relative to a common ancestor.

In practice, our system requires minimal setup to use, either through its built-in web interface, which only requires a relatively modern web browser, or programmatically through its HTTP API. *Speechcake* is built such that it integrates easily in typical workflows of phoneticians and linguists (e.g., manual annotation requiring spectrogram reading), but also in workflows of speech technologists (e.g., automatic speech recognition – ASR – tasks). Overall, *Speechcake* helps to improve the quality and consistency of annotations across several annotation layers, and facilitates the working processes of speech scientists and technologists.

The software package consists of a web server for serving dynamic corpora and a tool for the local administration of repositories. Our code is open source, available at `https://github.com/SPSC-TUGraz/speechcake`, under the terms and conditions of the MIT license. Submitting issues and feature requests is encouraged.

[1]`https://www.fon.hum.uva.nl/praat/manual/TextGrid_file_formats.html`

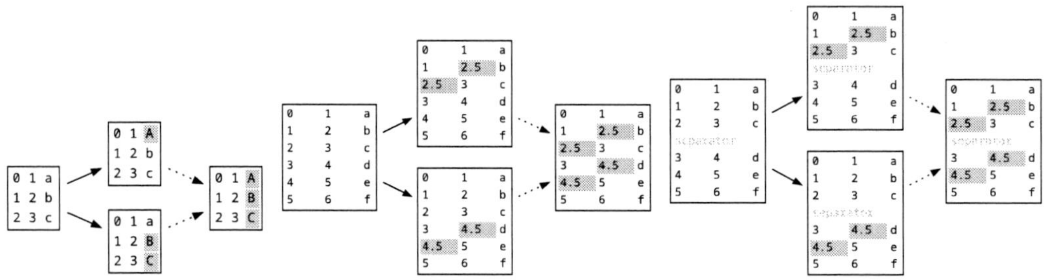

(a) (b) (c)

Figure 1: Example merges for common use cases: (a) changing labels of non-overlapping intervals; (b) changing boundaries of non-overlapping intervals; (c) changing boundaries of non-overlapping intervals, with a unique separator added at the separation point between modifications. Line-oriented version control systems, such as for source code management, fail to obtain the merge results in (a) and (b).

2 Related Work

Source Code Version Control In the field of software engineering, source code version control systems make it possible for hundreds or even thousands of collaborators to work on the same set of files. Such systems are inadequate for storing annotation data, since their merge semantics are aimed at resolving conflicts between source code files, as opposed to annotation data. The most commonly used algorithm for merging text files is Diff3, which requires diverging versions to contain the same unique line, such that the modified parts are separated by this common line (Khanna et al., 2007). While not an issue for source code files, since lines such as function definitions or declarations are generally unique within a given file, line-oriented algorithms are a bad fit for annotation data, where a clear separation between modifications may not exist. See for example Figure 1, which shows two scenarios in which line-oriented algorithms cannot merge diverging versions, even when the changed intervals are not overlapping.

Data Version Control As opposed to source code, which can be merged using line-oriented algorithms, data comes in various shapes and sizes, and the merge semantics for one particular type of data may not fit any other. Instead, version control systems focus on particular data formats where merge semantics can be clearly defined. While *Speechcake* is a narrow embodiment where the underlying merge semantics are defined for TextGrid-like annotation data, several other, more general-purpose approaches exist:

Dolt[2] is a database management system that follows the principles of Git, but whereas Git tracks files within a hierarchy, Dolt tracks tables within a database. Dolt databases, much like Git repositories, and *Speechcake* tiers, can be forked, cloned, and merged.

Irmin (Farinier et al., 2015) is an OCaml library that provides the foundation to developing purely functional data structures that can be persisted on disk, merged and synchronized effectively. The library operates on user-supplied data types, which are required to be serializable (for instance, to and from JSON) and mergeable. The merge operation takes two diverging versions and their lowest common ancestor (to be used as the base for the merge). Combinators are provided for typical containers of data, allowing users to declaratively define both the runtime representation of data as well as its merge semantics. In contrast to *Speechcake*, which is a complete solution for version control of annotation data, Irmin is distributed as a library that serves as a foundation for building distributed data stores.

Corpus Management Software Existing speech corpus management systems are not built around the idea of collaborative access. While storing the database itself under version control using an external tool is supported, and even integrated in some of the available solutions, none of them offer automatic reconciliation of diverging versions, which comes as a necessity in the context of multiple annotators working in parallel.

EXMARaLDA is a collection of data formats and software tools for creating, analyzing, and disseminating speech corpora (Schmidt and Wörner, 2009). The software package includes tools for creating and editing transcriptions (Partitur-Editor), creating and managing corpora and their associated meta-

[2]https://github.com/dolthub/dolt

data (CoMa), and querying and analysing corpora (EXAKT). While transcriptions can be individually created and modified by annotators, the software package does not include tools for version control, as *Speechcake* does.

Praaline is an integrated system for managing, annotating, visualising, and analysing speech corpora (Christodoulides, 2018), supporting the most common transcription formats, such as *Praat TextGrid*, *EXMARaLDA*, *ELAN*, and *TranscriberAG*. While the system can be used over the network, also *Praline*, like the earlier mentioned *EXMARaLDA*, does not consider version control and collaborative aspects.

EMU-SDMS is a software package for visualising, annotating, segmenting and querying speech databases (Winkelmann et al., 2017). In Jochim, 2017, the author extends the system with automatic revision control using Git in the background to commit the current state for every modification registered, in a corpus-wide, linear timeline. In comparison, *Speechcake* uses (conceptually) multiple repositories, one for each tier, and allows tiers to be branched and merged individually, without having to align the state of the entire corpus.

Polyglot and Speech Corpus Tools was developed for unified corpus analysis (McAuliffe et al., 2017). The data model uses a graph database for storing annotation graph structures, a relational database for metadata, and a time-series database for acoustic data, combining all three into a *polyglot persistence* solution (Duggan et al., 2015). *Speechcake*, in contrast, covers version control aspects, leaving content-based queries to external tools which can operate on whole snapshots.

3 Data Model of Speechcake

The architecture of *Speechcake* was modelled after the data formats at the boundaries of the system: on the external side, version-control-augmented Praat TextGrid files are used to interact with the outside world. Internally, the annotation structure is that of a TextGrid tier augmented with metadata useful in query processing. On disk, a *Speechcake* repository consists of a single database file containing the entire history of the corpus, allowing for easy backup and maintenance.

Metadata Stamp In a normal *Speechcake* workflow, users check out only a handful of related tiers (annotations of the same primary media). Therefore, in order to be able to trace their origins upon later check-in, tiers need to be augmented (*stamped*) with metadata stored in the names of the tiers, as TextGrid files provide no other opportunity for storing additional information. While this approach preserves compatibility with tools and libraries which interact with TextGrid files, it places a constraint on the users not to impair the integrity of the metadata contained in the stamps.

Annotation Structure As external data model, *Speechcake* uses the TextGrid format for interoperability with other tools. Internally, a *Speechcake document* holds two additional pieces of metadata: a *path* and a *label set*. The path (a logical location) is analogous to the fully-qualified filename where the tier would be stored on a file system (a physical location), relative to the root of the corpus. By decoupling the logical from the physical location, move operations are replaced by simply changing a property on a given tier, thereby offering better feedback for the user as to what changed from one version to the next. The path property, whose length is variable, allows users to organize their corpora in deep, nested structures. The label set can be used for query processing. These labels, as defined by the user for a specific corpus, may contain any kind of information (i.e., speaker IDs, type of annotation, attributes about the recording).

Repository Structure The main purpose of a *Speechcake* repository is to hold a collection of versioned tiers, each identified by a UUID (Leach et al., 2005) assigned upon the tier's initial creation. Tiers can be referenced in two ways: either by their UUIDs, or by their fully-qualified path, which includes the tier name as the terminal component. Note that the former addressing method is immutable (a UUID will always point to the same tier), whereas the latter is mutable. The on-disk format of a *Speechcake* repository contains (1) all past and present versions of tiers, whose contents are split into content-addressable chunks as a form of data de-duplication (Xia et al., 2020), (2) a temporary storage space for tiers that have been checked-in, but not yet submitted to the corpus, and (3) a log of destructively overwriting operations, such as altering the metadata of tiers.

4 Update Process

Check-In Users *check in* a set of locally modified tiers by uploading a TextGrid file via the web interface. Once uploaded, *Speechcake* will first inspect the tiers' metadata and verify that they are part of the corpus. Unknown tiers are rejected, and successfully identified ones go into a temporary storage area, unique to each user. New tiers, identified as such for not having any stamp, can be added to the TextGrid file, and they will be stored alongside the rest of the tiers within the file (i.e., under the same parent path).

Commit Committing a tier involves moving it from the users' temporary area into the corpus, with an optional comment describing the modifications performed. *Speechcake* will then attempt to mark the new version as being the *latest*, which can only be accomplished if the new version has the *current* latest version as a direct parent, meaning that no other modification has been performed since the user has checked out this particular version. If this is not the case, then the newly-submitted version has to be merged with the current latest version, the successful result of which will then be added as another version, and marked as being latest.

Three-Way Merge A merge operation takes two diverging versions X and Y and their lowest common ancestor (or *base* version) B, and produces a new version which incorporates all changes introduced by both X and Y. This mechanism prevents accidental overwriting of data (arising from e.g., two users simultaneously modifying a tier), which may lead to information loss.

For two related tiers A and B, the changes introduced by B on top of A can be described in terms of a *diff* between the two, composed of three sets of items: $A \setminus B$ (items *removed*), $B \setminus A$ (items *added*), and $A \cap B$ (items *kept*). Since tiers are totally ordered sets, where the order operation is given by comparing the lower temporal bound of the two items, the diff operation only needs to iterate over the longer of the two tiers in order to compute the three sets, having an expected-time performance of $\mathcal{O}(\max(|A|, |B|))$. In contrast, the default diff algorithm used in Git has an expected-time performance of $\mathcal{O}(ND)$, where N is the sum of lengths of A and B, and D is the size of the minimum edit script for A and B (Myers, 1986).

To merge X and Y relative to B, *Speechcake* first computes the two diffs $(X \setminus B, B \setminus X, X \cap B)$ and $(Y \setminus B, B \setminus Y, Y \cap B)$. The *common base* C is computed as $X \cap Y \cap B$, and represents the set of items that were unaffected by either versions. Finally, the merged version is obtained by interspersing (by means of set union) both "items added" sets over the common base: $(X \setminus B) \cup (Y \setminus B) \cup C$.

Merge conflicts are detected in the interspersal phase: the union can be computed by iterating over the sets in parallel and moving the item with the lowest lower bound into the output. The algorithm keeps track of the upper bound of the last item copied to the output set, and compares this upper bound with the next incoming lower bound. If the next lower bound comes *before* the last upper bound, then the two items are in conflict, and the operation is aborted.

In order to check whether a merge operation will be successful, the intersection of the sets of *added* items (either points or intervals) must be the empty set, where equality is determined by both the timing and the contents of the item. Otherwise, a merge conflict in the form of a TextGrid file is generated, containing the two conflicting tiers merged except for the conflicting intervals. The user then has adapt the changes, leaving only one tier in the TextGrid file, which upon checking back in is used to resolve the conflict.

5 Conclusions

We introduced *Speechcake*, a version control system for speech corpora, which allows for faster development cycles and better collaboration between annotators and scientists. Our tool primarily supports Praat TextGrid files, making it easy to integrate in workflows which already make use of said file format. Questions such as *Where does this file belong?* or *Is my file the latest version?* are posed and answered by the check-in process, whose role is to minimize user input required to store or update files in the corpus. We have shown the inadequacies of line-oriented merge algorithms, and have proposed a novel, semantics-aware solution. Our tool is extendable through a public API through which automated solutions can interact with the repository. We believe our work inspires further developments in domain-specific version control.

6 Acknowledgements

The work by B. Schuppler was partly funded by an Elise Richter grant (V638 N33) and by grant P-32700, both from the Austrian Science Fund.

References

George Christodoulides. 2018. Praaline: An open-source system for managing, annotating, visualising and analysing speech corpora. In *Proceedings of the Annual Meeting of the Association for Computational Linguistics 2018*.

Jennie Duggan, Aaron J. Elmore, Michael Stonebraker, Magda Balazinska, Bill Howe, Jeremy Kepner, Sam Madden, David Maier, Tim Mattson, and Stan Zdonik. 2015. The BigDAWG polystore system. *SIGMOD Record*, 44(2):11–16.

Benjamin Farinier, Thomas Gazagnaire, and Anil Madhavapeddy. 2015. Mergeable persistent data structures. In *Proceedings of Journées Francophones des Langages Applicatifs 2015*, Le Val d'Ajol, France.

J.J. Godfrey, E.C. Holliman, and J. McDaniel. 1992. Switchboard: telephone speech corpus for research and development. In *Proceedings of the International Conference on Acoustics, Speech, and Signal Processing 1992*, volume 1, pages 517–520 vol.1.

David Graff, Zhibiao Wu, Robert MacIntyre, and Mark Liberman. 1997. The 1996 broadcast news speech and language-model corpus. In *Proceedings of the DARPA Workshop on Spoken Language technology*, pages 11–14.

Markus Jochim. 2017. Extending the EMU Speech Database Management System: Cloud hosting, team collaboration, automatic revision control. In *Proceedings of INTERSPEECH 2017*, pages 813–814.

Sanjeev Khanna, Keshav Kunal, and Benjamin C Pierce. 2007. A formal investigation of diff3. In *Proceedings of the International Conference on Foundations of Software Technology and Theoretical Computer Science 2007*, pages 485–496. Springer.

Paul J. Leach, Michael Mealling, and Rich Salz. 2005. A Universally Unique IDentifier (UUID) URN Namespace. RFC 4122, RFC Editor.

Mitchell P. Marcus, Mary Ann Marcinkiewicz, and Beatrice Santorini. 1993. Building a large annotated corpus of English: The Penn Treebank. *Computational Linguistics*, 19(2):313–330.

Michael McAuliffe, Elias Stengel-Eskin, Michaela Socolof, and Morgan Sonderegger. 2017. Polyglot and Speech Corpus Tools: A system for representing, integrating, and querying speech corpora. In *Proceedings of INTERSPEECH 2017*.

Eugene W. Myers. 1986. An O(ND) difference algorithm and its variations. *Algorithmica*, 1:251–266.

Mari Ostendorf, Patti J Price, and Stefanie Shattuck-Hufnagel. 1995. The Boston University radio news corpus. *Linguistic Data Consortium*, pages 1–19.

Andrew Rosenberg. 2012. Rethinking the corpus: Moving towards dynamic linguistic resources. volume 2.

Thomas C. Schmidt and Kai Wörner. 2009. EXMARaLDA – creating, analysing and sharing spoken language corpora for pragmatic research. *Pragmatics. Quarterly Publication of the International Pragmatics Association*, 19:565–582.

Raphael Winkelmann, Jonathan Harrington, and Klaus Jänsch. 2017. EMU-SDMS: Advanced speech database management and analysis in R. *Computer Speech & Language*, 45:392–410.

Wen Xia, Xiangyu Zou, Hong Jiang, Yukun Zhou, Chuanyi Liu, Dan Feng, Yu Hua, Yuchong Hu, and Yucheng Zhang. 2020. The design of fast content-defined chunking for data deduplication based storage systems. *IEEE Transactions on Parallel and Distributed Systems*, 31(9):2017–2031.

A Limitations

Annotation Format *Speechcake* currently only supports Praat TextGrid files. We plan on extending our tool in subsequent versions to support other annotation file formats. This can be done in one of two ways – either the new format is a subset of TextGrid, in which case *Speechcake* can convert it without loss of information, or the new format is a superset, in which case the three-way merging algorithm needs to be extended to support new merge semantics. Potential users are encouraged to contact us and describe their use cases.

Large File Storage *Speechcake* does not address the storage of primary media (e.g., audio and/or video recordings), as these are not subject to change throughout the existence of the corpus, and supporting integration with large file storage tools would significantly increase *Speechcake*'s implementation complexity due to the need of supporting potentially multiple protocols (e.g., HTTP, FTP, S3) and authentication/authorization methods. Therefore, the storage and distribution of primary media is left to other tools and systems. In order to match the primary media with their annotations, we suggest using the primary media's filename as a component of the annotations' path.

User Management Again for the purpose of limiting the implementation complexity, *Speechcake* has its own user management system, and updates do not interface with protocols such as LDAP for authentication and/or authorization. User-sensitive information such as name, email, and affiliation are kept in a separate database, and within the corpus database, users are only identified by an opaque UUID. This is done in order to comply with the General Data Protection Regulation (GDPR), such that user information can be removed or altered at any time without impacting the history of the corpus. Other tools such as Git include authorship information (name and email) for every commit, making operations such as changing one's name require a full rewrite of the repository's history.

Number of Concurrent Writers The storage backend of *Speechcake* prohibits more than one user from performing modifications on the corpus at the same time. This limitation is not noticeable in practice, since modifications take on the order of milliseconds to complete, and does not affect users who browse or download parts of the corpus – *Speechcake* supports a virtually unlimited number of read operations at any given time, even when another user is performing modifications, in which case readers will see the last valid snapshot of the corpus.

B Ethical Considerations

The paper does not raise any ethical issues, as no human participants were studied. The corpora used for the development of the tool were datasets already published for academic research prior to this work, and they were collected following the international ethical requirements as suggested by the American Psychological Association.

Querying Repetitions in Spoken Language Corpora

Elena Frick **Henrike Helmer**
Leibniz-Institute for the German Language, Mannheim, Germany
{frick,helmer}@ids-mannheim.de

Dolores Lemmenmeier-Batinić
ZHAW School of Applied Linguistics, Winterthur, Switzerland
dolores.lemmenmeier@zhaw.ch

Abstract

In this paper, we present a tool for searching repetitions in interaction corpora. Our approach based on the MTAS-technology uses common search token indices to retrieve repetitions from spoken language transcripts in a dynamic way. The CQP Query Language and a graphical user interface menu with extensive settings specially designed for conversation analysis researchers allow to find repetitions of complex linguistic forms in various pragmatic contexts. Furthermore, the web application enables searching for repetition constructions that may contain synonyms and hyp(er)onyms coming from GermaNet or from custom-defined word lists uploaded to the tool.

1 Introduction

Repetitions of words, phrases or whole utterances are of immense importance for everyday linguistic practices, from facilitating language acquisition of children (e.g., Keenan, 1977; Tarplee, 1996; Lester et al., 2022) and L2-learners (e.g., Brown, 1998; Ghazi-Saidi and Ansaldo, 2017) to adopting specific pragmatic functions in everyday interaction like securing understanding or keeping up the current speaker's right to speak (see Wang, 2005; Mattes, 2014; Deppermann and Helmer, 2013). Repetitions can also take on particular functions in storytelling e.g. as resumptions (see Wong, 2000), and facilitate fluent narration (see Tannen, 1979), as well as contribute to sequence organization and display trouble with the action of a prior utterance (cf. Antaki, 2014; Barth-Weingarten, 2011; Betz et al., 2013; Robinson, 2013; Robinson and Kevoe-Feldman, 2010; Selting, 1987; Stivers, 2004). Also worth mentioning are research traditions relating to social accommodation theory (Giles and Powesland, 1997) and the interactive alignment model (Pickering and Garrod, 2004) often targeting repetitions in their methodological approach.

Repetitions in spoken language have been widely studied in various disciplines. However, many questions have so far been examined primarily for the English language and have not yet been investigated systematically based on the peculiarities of German. Furthermore, different types of this phenomenon could be analyzed more deeply and comparatively, especially on corpora with video data and in further interaction contexts (e.g. in conflict talks).

Up to now, the search for repetitions in conversation analysis and interactional linguistics was largely done manually by reading transcripts, which is a very time-consuming task. It requires maximum concentration and is often prone to overlook instances, e.g. when looking for repetitions located at a large distance from each other. Sometimes, the desired repetition should fulfill many requirements at the same time (self-repetition, initiated by others, realized by children etc.), which is a further challenge for human ability to recognize repetitions in transcripts at first sight. That's why it is important that corpus analysis platforms used by interactional linguists also provide methods for querying repetitions.

2 Related Work

Several matching algorithms for the automatic recognition of lexical and even structural repetitions have already been developed and applied in psycholinguistics in corpus-based studies where repetitions serve as one of quantitative measures of mutual understanding and language coordination (cf. e.g. Brodsky et al., 2007; Grigonytė and Björkenstam, 2016; Wirén et al., 2016; Lester et al., 2022; Vogel, 2013; Reverdy and Vogel, 2017a; Reverdy and Vogel, 2017b; Danescu-Niculescu-Mizil et al., 2012; Reitter and Moore, 2014; Placiński and Żywiczyński, 2023). In the field of conversational speech analysis and linguistic tool development, the automatic detection of repetitions is not yet that widespread. Only individual solutions exist for certain types of repetitions like an automatic method proposed by Bigi et al. (2014) to retrieve other-repetition occurrences in spontaneous French dialogues. This algorithm is published with a set of other annotation tools under the name SPPAS[1] and can be downloaded and used for different languages.

Two other corpus platforms that should be mentioned here are CLAPI[2] (Baldauf-Quilliatre et al., 2016) and Lexical Explorer[3] (Lemmenmeier-Batinić, 2020). CLAPI offers a dedicated tool for querying repetitions online and allows to find segments of one or multiple tokens both of the same and another speaker. However, the search is limited to individual transcripts; searching for repetitions in the entire corpus is not possible. The repetition search provided in Lexical Explorer aimed to facilitate lexicographic work with spoken data. For this reason, this tool only provides searching for one or two word repetitions of the same speaker, thereby making use of pre-calculated data.

Querying repetitions on the fly is also possible: Some online platforms make use of special query language (QL) elements such as quantifiers or global constraints to allow for a systematic search for user-defined forms of repetitions, cf. e.g. CQPWeb[4] (Hardie, 2012), Kontext[5] (Machálek, 2020) and OpenSoNar[6] (van de Camp et al., 2017). However, these systems use data models that are unsuitable for spoken language corpora, because they e.g. are limited in representation of speaker overlaps and time-based annotations, which leads to significant loss of information relevant for spoken language research. Moreover, the QL itself is restricted to structures which can be described by regular grammars. Many repetition structures, however, are on a higher level of the Chomsky hierarchy, i.e. they are context-free or even context-sensitive.

[1]https://sppas.org/

[2]Search and browsing platform for French interaction corpora, http://clapi.icar.cnrs.fr

[3]Platform for browsing and filtering quantitative data of the FOLK- and GeWiss-corpora, https://www.owid.de/lexex/

[4]A CWB-based corpus search platform, provides access to the Spoken BNC2014, https://cqpweb.lancs.ac.uk

[5]A NoSketchEngine-based search platform for the CNC-corpus containing both written and spoken language data, https://lindat.mff.cuni.cz/services/kontext

[6]A BlackLab-based search platform for the CGN-corpus, https://opensonar.ivdnt.org/

In this paper, we propose a new method for querying repetitions in spoken language corpora by using full-text search indices, that is, to our knowledge, designed and implemented for the first time. Furthermore, we combined the use of a QL with a graphical user interface specially developed for the conversation analysis.

3 Data

The development of the repetition tool was primarily motivated by the need to work with the interaction corpora from the Archive for Spoken German (Archiv für Gesprochenes Deutsch, AGD[7]). The most important representative of these corpora is FOLK[8] (Forschungs- und Lehrkorpus Gesprochenes Deutsch 'Research and Teaching Corpus of Spoken German', Schmidt, 2023; Reineke et al., 2023). This is a constantly growing corpus of currently about 350h of audio and video recordings of authentic spontaneous conversations from various private, institutional and public communication situations (around 3,3 million transcribed tokens). Extensive speaker and speech event metadata of this and other corpora from the AGD, their digitized transcriptions in ISO 24624:2016 aligned with the audio/video signal as well as multi tier linguistic annotations (normalization, part-of-speech (POS) tags, lemmatization, phonological annotations, speech-rate information, code-switching, discourse comments etc.) enable diverse linguistic investigations. However, the systematic repetition research was until now limited because of the lack of suitable annotations on the one hand and on the other hand because the QL used for searching these corpora in the current search interfaces DGD[9] and ZuRecht[10] does not support syntactic elements allowing to build a query for complex repetition structures.

4 Approach

The tool presented in this paper is a product of the close collaboration between conversation analysis researchers and software developers at the Leibniz-Institute for the German Language (Institut für Deutsche Sprache, IDS). It is implemented as a part of ZuRecht (Figure 1), which is a web-based application for querying spoken language

[7]https://agd.ids-mannheim.de

[8]https://agd.ids-mannheim.de/folk.shtml

[9]https://dgd.ids-mannheim.de

[10]http://zumult.ids-mannheim.de/ProtoZumult/jsp/zuRecht.jsp

data. ZuRecht was designed and implemented in the ZuMult-project[11] and allows to query interaction corpora in the ISO 24624:2016 format. The search functionality is built on MTAS (Brouwer et al., 2016) – an open-source search engine framework that builds on Lucene und extends it with a QL familiar to corpus linguists. MTAS was originally developed for querying richly annotated texts. In ZuRecht, it is first used for querying data of spoken language. It was adopted to the specifics of spoken language, thus allowing now to search in ZuRecht for typical spoken language phenomena like speaker changes and overlaps, pauses and other para-verbal events, e.g. laughter or coughing. Frick and Schmidt (2020) and Frick et al. (2022) provide more information about MTAS and explain why this search engine was chosen for the ZuRecht implementation. Compared to other Lucene-based solutions for querying corpora with linguistic annotations, the MTAS advantage lies in its configuration file that can be easily modified without programming knowledge and used to parse corpus files in a custom-defined way allowing to specify what information from ISO/TEI transcripts should be indexed and how. The data is then stored according to the MTAS specific prefix-suffix concept[12] and is saved in a forward index created by extending the Lucene Codec. A modified version of CQP QL, that is internally converted to Lucene queries, can be used to retrieve the search index for terms and their positions in the appropriate corpus document. We use this forward search index to compute repetitions in our corpora in a dynamic way, i.e. the search is performed within a reasonable response time after the desired repetition type is specified and submitted by the user.

4.1 Search Engine (SE)

According to the ZuMult object-oriented corpus data model (Batinić et al., 2019; Schmidt et al., 2023), all components of spoken language corpora (audio, video, metadata, transcripts, annotations, but also their integral elements like tokens, spans, speaker contributions etc.) are defined as objects with certain behavior and particular relations among them. We extended this concept by providing an additional *Repetition*-object. After collecting user configuration settings, the client creates an xml representation of the repetition object, and sends it to the back-end.

The search method in the Java back-end that can be called through RESTful web services is designed to allow different QLs and multiple SEs be used to perform repetition searches in the future if necessary. The API ensures also a high flexibility in specifying parameters passed to the search method, e.g. it also accepts parameters that can be processed only by one or the other SE. This can be, for instance, the search by synonym lists or the use of special search indices allowing to ignore punctuation during the search process. The search for repetitions builds on full text indices. First, the positions of all spans matching the query string and containing only word tokens realized by one speaker are retrieved. Then, the word tokens in the directly following N positions after the match are fetched directly from the search index and compared with the match itself, where N is the distance window specified by the user.[13] If a token sequence is identified as a repetition, the user-specified conditions are checked in the next step, e.g. whether the repetition comes from the same or another speaker, or whether the repetition is located within an overlap, etc. Everything happens within the search index by retrieving required annotation values for certain positions. The access to the search index is parallelized and all hits are written into a temporary document. After the search, they are sorted and returned to the client in the requested volume.

4.2 User interface

The search for repetitions starts with the selection of a corpus from the corpus list in the left-hand column of the user interface (cf. Figure 1), whereby cross-corpus searches are also possible. The green bordered text input field at the top of the search form can be used to specify the element to be repeated. It is possible just to type in a single word or a word sequence or alternatively to use CQP-based query syntax to define more complex elements that contain e.g. regular expressions,

[11] https://zumult.org/

[12] For more details on the prefix-suffix model see Frick and Schmidt (2020) and MTAS documentation under https://textexploration.github.io/mtas/index.html

[13] If the context becomes too large, the tool finds too many false positives, i.e. repetitions that are not interesting for the research (e.g., being many consecutive utterances with the copula *sein* 'to be'). In turn, a more restrictive context leads to many false negatives. An evaluation based on examples from articles on repetitions as well as on self-generated collections of examples showed that repetitions of tokens occur on average 10-15 tokens after the utterance of the original element. Therefore, and for better performance, the maximum possible distance between repetitions is currently set to 20 tokens.

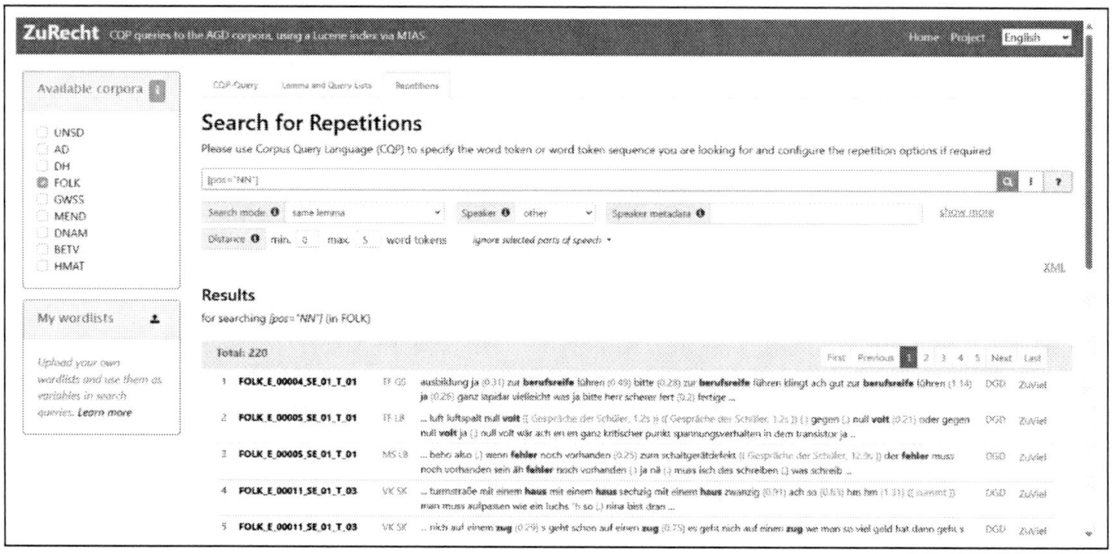

Figure 1: Repetition search tool (part of ZuRecht).

precedence operators, specifications for POS tags and/or speaker metadata constraints like in the following example looking for repetitions of all response particles (NGIRR) with the exception of all forms of 'hm' in telephone conversations (German 'Telefongespräch'):[14]

```
[pos="NGIRR" & !norm="(hm)+"] within
<e_se_art="Telefongespräch"/>
```

A query builder integrated into the search input field helps to formulate CQP-based search queries and lists specification values of available annotation and metadata categories. The repetition search tool offers various search options:

- The "Search mode" menu specifies the method how repetitions should be identified, e.g. what token form (transcribed, normalized or lemmatized) should be compared and whether GermaNet (Version 17.0, Kunze and Lemnitzer, 2002; Henrich and Hinrichs, 2010) or custom defined synonym lists should be involved in the search process.
- The "Speaker" drop-down list allows to choose whether the speakers should repeat themselves or be repeated by another speaker.
- Furthermore, the minimum and maximum of distance between repetitions can be specified. Some POS like articles or hesitation phenomena can be selected to be ignored when measuring the distance.
- The "Distance to speaker change"-option allows to specify at what distance from the previous/following speaker change the repetition should be found.
- The option "Speaker overlap" can be used to find only those repetitions that occur inside or outside of speaker overlaps. It can be useful in order to find reduplicated reception signals while the dialogue partner is still speaking or conversely to find examples outside of speaker overlaps as they are better suited for further phonetic and prosodic analyses.
- The "Multiword repetition" defines whether the token order of a repeated multi-word expression may vary or should be the same.
- The "Context (left/right)"-option allows to apply CQP for specifying patterns of elements preceding or following the repetition.
- In addition, it is possible to specify separate settings for a second repetition when searching for an element repeated at least twice (Figure 1), e.g. to investigate repetitions produced in order to get more precise information about the object mentioned before by the first speaker where the first speaker then provides an explanation by repeating the object again.

The repetition search results are listed as a KWIC (KeyWord-In-Context) concordance that can be customized in terms of the context size and the number of results per page. Both the searched

[14]The metadata key *e_se_art* stands for German *Art des Sprechereignisses* 'type of speech event' and is used in FOLK.

element and its repetition are marked in red (see Figure 1). Individual hits can be viewed in a larger context, listened to and downloaded in various formats (iso/tei, .exb, .eaf, .textGrid etc.) incl. audio/video excerpts if required.

5 Use Case

In expert-novice-interaction, repetitions are a regular part of defining or negotiating the meaning of terms and concepts; either technical terms or terms with a situational meaning that needs to be clarified. Often, experts do not repeat a 'problematic' term exactly, when explaining its meaning, but instead substitute it with expressions that denote the same or related concepts. For example, Quasthoff and Hartmann (1982) and Helmer (2020) show that, amongst others, naming synonyms and hyp(er)onyms as well as other terms with a specific semantic relation is one recurring practice of defining expressions. This occurs in different sequential contexts, sometimes after repair initiations, sometimes self-initiated. Research can still be deepened with regards to the type of expressions repaired and which types of expressions are used to substitute them, with regards to sequential organization and also with regards to a comparative analysis of different types of the other-initiation of such substitutions (e.g. different ways to display trouble with expressions and the relation to following substitutions). These types of 'repetitions' can be found by using GermaNet integrated into the new search tool. The option "same lemma (use GermaNet only)" combined with the search query

```
[pos="(NN)"] within <ses_rolle_s =
"(Ausbilder|Coach|Dozent|Tutor|Trainer|
(L|.+l)(eiter|ehrer))/in"/>
```

will return repetitions containing synonyms and hyp(er)onyms defined in GermaNet and restricted to speakers who are teachers, tutors and other experts[15]. Further settings specified in the repetition search form determine that the repetitions should be realized by the same speaker and within the maximum distance of 20 tokens by ignoring articles (ART), interjections (ITJ), responsive/reception signals (NGIRR), hesitations (NGHES), abortions (AB) and other non-words (XY, e.g. stuttering).

Executed on the FOLK corpus, the search query returns[16] 553 hits containing several pieces of evidence for repetitions by substitution. We can find here repetition constrictions, in which, e.g.,

- a dialect word is substituted by standard language expression. Example: *käschtel* (a dialectal diminutive for 'box') substituted by *rechteck* ('rectangle').
- a phrasal characterization is substituted by the fitting technical term. Example: *diese pedale (...) hier unne* ('this pedal down there') followed by *bremspedal* ('brake pedal').
- a technical term is substituted by a more common term. Example: *gynäkologe* ('gynecologist') substituted by *frauenarzt* (literal translation: 'women's doctor').
- more common terms are substituted by technical terms. Example: *vollziehende und richterliche gewalt* ('executive and judicial power') substituted by *judikative exekutive und legislative* ('judiciary executive and legislative').

As these examples show, the GermaNet-function of our tool can be helpful to find the targeted repetition constructions and to systematically investigate semantic, sequential and other pragmatic aspects of using synonyms as substitutions.

6 Conclusion

In this paper, we presented a new tool for searching repetitions in spoken language corpora. We combined the CQP QL with an extensive user interface filter allowing for queries that could not be expressed in the standard CQP syntax yet and making repetition structures that were hitherto accessible only with great difficulty amenable to systematic exploration, and fruitful and variable research.

7 Limitations

The strength of the tool presented in this paper is searching for repetitions in a dynamic way as an alternative to enriching corpora with space- and time-consuming annotations of repetitions. Using full-text indexes allows direct navigation to the corpus locations that may contain a desired repetition form, which is faster than searching repetitions directly in

[15] Ausbilder –'instructor'; Dozent – 'lecturer'; (L|.+l)(eiter|ehrer) matches 'Leiter' ('director'), 'Lehrer' ('teacher') and all compounds with them. The metadata key *ses_rolle_s* stands for German *Rolle des Sprechers im Sprechereignis* 'role of speaker in speech event' and is used in FOLK.

[16] Search time: approx. 26 sec. executed on the VM with 4 vCPU, 8 GB RAM, 75 GB HDD, CentOS 7 64-bit

each XML transcription file. However, searching for complex repetition forms (i.e. those with multiple conditions or with long word sequences) in a large corpus like FOLK often need to be restricted to certain corpus parts (e.g. just one conversation type) in order to be performed in a user-friendly time[17]. As future work, we plan to implement more parallel processes to optimize the speed of the tool by dividing the search indices in smaller components and by using special frameworks (e.g. CompletableFuture[18]).

8 Ethical Considerations

Data that can be accessed through the repetition search tool underlay data protection policies applied in AGD. This mainly includes three aspects: 1) Informed consent has been obtained for collection and publication of data; 2) Access to the search tool requires user registration and is granted for research, teaching and study purposes only; 3) Data parts that would enable the immediate identification of the persons involved in the conversation (such as locations names, phone numbers, etc.) are de-identified in the audios and replaced by pseudonyms in the transcripts. The collection and presentation of the spoken data that can be accessed through the tool presented in this paper was approved by institutional data protection officer.

References

Charles Antaki. 2014. *Repeating a question near-identically may cast the answerer as intellectually impaired*, pages 181–192. Lambert Lucas.

Heike Baldauf-Quilliatre, I. Colón Carvajal, Carole Etienne, Jouin Emilie, Teston-Bonnard Sandra, and Véronique Traverso. 2016. CLAPI, une base de données multimodale pour la parole en interaction : apports et dilemmes. CLAPI, a multimodal database for talk in interaction: contributions and dilemmas. *Corpus [Online] 15.*

Dagmar Barth-Weingarten. 2011. Double Sayings of German JA—More Observations on Their Phonetic Form and Alignment Function. *Research on Language and Social Interaction*, 44:157–185.

[17]Ideally, the search queries should take a few seconds. In the field of conversation analysis, researchers are often willing to accept longer search times to retrieve hits from large corpora. However, search queries that take longer than three minutes are, in our view, unacceptable.

[18]`https://docs.oracle.com/javase/8/docs/api/java/util/concurrent/CompletableFuture.html`

Josip Batinić, Elena Frick, Joachim Gasch, and Thomas Schmidt. 2019. Eine Basis-Architektur für den Zugriff auf multimodale Korpora gesprochener Sprache. In *Digital Humanities: multimedial multimodal. Konferenzabstracts zur 6. Tagung des Verbandes Digital Humanities im deutschsprachigen Raum e.V. (DHd 2019)*, pages 280–281, Frankfurt/Main; Mainz. Verband Digital Humanities im deutschsprachigen Raum e.V.

Emma Betz, Carmen Taleghani-Nikazm, Veronika Drake, and Andrea Golato. 2013. Third-Position Repeats in German : The Case of Repair-and Request-for-Information Sequences. *Gesprächsforschung – Online-Zeitschrift zur verbalen Interaktion*, 14:133–166.

Brigitte Bigi, Roxane Bertrand, and Mathilde Guardiola. 2014. Automatic detection of other-repetition occurrences: application to French conversational speech. In *Proceedings of the Ninth International Conference on Language Resources and Evaluation (LREC'14)*, pages 836–842, Reykjavik, Iceland. European Language Resources Association (ELRA).

Peter Brodsky, Heidi Waterfall, and Edelman S. 2007. Characterizing Motherese: On the Computational Structure of Child-Directed Language. In *Proceedings of the Annual Meeting of the Cognitive Science Society: Vol. 29.*

Matthijs Brouwer, Hennie Brugman, and Marc Kemps-Snijders. 2016. MTAS: A Solr/Lucene based Multi-Tier Annotation Search solution. In *Selected papers from the CLARIN Annual Conference 2016. Aix-en-Provence*, pages 19–37.

Penelope Brown. 1998. Conversational structure and language acquisition: The role of repetition in Tzeltal. *Journal of Linguistic Anthropology*, 8:2:197–221.

Cristian Danescu-Niculescu-Mizil, Lillian Lee, Bo Pang, and Jon Kleinberg. 2012. Echoes of power: Language effects and power differences in social interaction. In *Proceedings of the 21st international conference on World Wide Web*, pages 699–700.

Arnulf Deppermann and Henrike Helmer. 2013. Standard des gesprochenen Deutsch: Begriff, methodische Zugänge und Phänomene aus interaktionslinguistischer Sicht. In J. Hagemann, W.P. Klein, and S. Staffeldt, editors, *Pragmatischer Standard. (= Stauffenburg Linguistik 73)*, pages 111–141. Stauffenburg, Tübingen.

Elena Frick and Thomas Schmidt. 2020. Using full text indices for querying spoken language data. In *Proceedings of the 8th Workshop on Challenges in the Management of Large Corpora*, pages 40–46, Marseille, France. European Language Ressources Association.

Elena Frick, Thomas Schmidt, and Henrike Helmer. 2022. Querying Interaction Structure: Approaches to Overlap in Spoken Language Corpora. In *Proceedings of the Thirteenth Language Resources and*

Evaluation Conference, pages 715–722, Marseille, France. European Language Resources Association.

Ladan Ghazi-Saidi and Ana Ines Ansaldo. 2017. Second Language Word Learning through Repetition and Imitation: Functional Networds as a Function of Learning Phase and Language Distance. *Frontiers in Human Nueroscience*, Sep 28:11:463.

Howard Giles and Peter Powesland. 1997. Accommodation theory. In N. Coupland and A. Jawarski, editors, *Sociolinguistics: A reader and coursebook*, pages 232–239. Macmillan Press, New York.

Gintarė Grigonytė and Kristina Nilsson Björkenstam. 2016. Language-independent exploration of repetition and variation in longitudinal child-directed speech: A tool and resources. In *Proceedings of the joint workshop on NLP for Computer Assisted Language Learning and NLP for Language Acquisition*, pages 41–50, Umeå, Sweden. LiU Electronic Press.

Andrew Hardie. 2012. CQPweb - Combining power, flexibility and usability in a corpus analysis tool. *International Journal of Corpus Linguistics*, 17(3):380–409.

Henrike Helmer. 2020. How Do Speakers Define the Meaning of Expressions? The Case of German x heißt y ("x means y"). *Discourse Processes*, 57(3):278–299.

Verena Henrich and Erhard Hinrichs. 2010. GernEdiT - the GermaNet editing tool. In *Proceedings of the Seventh International Conference on Language Resources and Evaluation (LREC'10)*, Valletta, Malta. European Language Resources Association (ELRA).

ISO 24624:2016. *Language resource management — Transcription of spoken language*.

Elinor Ochs Keenan. 1977. Making it last: Repetition in children's discourse. In S. M. Ervin-Tripp and C. Mitchell-Kernan, editors, *Child discourse*, pages 125–138. Academic Press, New York.

Claudia Kunze and Lothar Lemnitzer. 2002. GermaNet - representation, visualization, application. In *Proceedings of the Third International Conference on Language Resources and Evaluation (LREC'02)*, Las Palmas, Canary Islands - Spain. European Language Resources Association (ELRA).

Dolores Lemmenmeier-Batinić. 2020. Lexical Explorer: extending access to the Database for Spoken German for user-specific purposes. *Corpora*, 15(1):55–76.

Nicholas A. Lester, Steven Moran, Aylin C. Küntay, Shanley E.M. Allen, Barbara Pfeiler, and Sabine Stoll. 2022. Detecting structured repetition in child-surrounding speech: Evidence from maximally diverse languages. *Cognition*, 221:104986.

Tomáš Machálek. 2020. KonText: Advanced and Flexible Corpus Query Interface. In *Proceedings of the Twelfth Language Resources and Evaluation Conference*, pages 7003–7008, Marseille, France. European Language Resources Association.

Veronika Mattes. 2014. *Types of Reduplication. As case study of Bikol.* de Gruyter.

Martin Pickering and Simon Garrod. 2004. Toward a Mechanistic Psychology of Dialogue. *The Behavioral and brain sciences*, 27 (2):169–190.

Marek Placiński and Przemysław Żywiczyński. 2023. Modality effect in interactive alignment: Differences between spoken and text-based conversation. *Lingua*, 293:1–11.

Uta M. Quasthoff and Dietrich Hartmann. 1982. Bedeutungserklärungen als empirischer Zugang zu Wortbedeutungen. Zur Entscheidbarkeit zwischen holistischen und komponentiellen Bedeutungskonzeptionen. *Deutsche Sprache*, 10:97–118.

Silke Reineke, Arnulf Deppermann, and Thomas Schmidt. 2023. Das Forschungs- und Lehrkorpus für Gesprochenes Deutsch (FOLK). Zum Nutzen eines großen annotierten Korpus gesprochener Sprache für interaktionslinguistische Fragestellungen. In Arnulf Deppermann, Christian Fandrych, Marc Kupietz, and Thomas Schmidt, editors, *Korpora in der germanistischen Sprachwissenschaft. Mündlich, schriftlich, multimedial*, pages 71–102. de Gruyter, Berlin/-Boston.

David Reitter and Johanna D. Moore. 2014. Alignment and Task Success in Spoken Dialogue. *Journal of Memory and Language*, 76:29–46.

Justine Reverdy and Carl Vogel. 2017a. Measuring Synchrony in Task-Based Dialogues. In *INTERSPEECH 2017*, pages 1701–1705, Stockholm, Sweden.

Justine Reverdy and Carl Vogel. 2017b. Linguistic repetitions, task-based experience and a proxy measure of mutual understanding. In *8th IEEE International Conference on Cognitive Infocommunications (CogInfoCom 2017)*, pages 395–400.

Jeffrey D. Robinson. 2013. Epistemics, action formation, and other-initiation of repair: The case of partial questioning repeats. In M. Hayashi, G. Raymond, and Sidnell J., editors, *Conversational Repair and Human Understanding*, pages 261–292. Cambridge University Press, Cambridge, U.K.

Jeffrey D. Robinson and Heidi Kevoe-Feldman. 2010. Using full repeats to initiate repair on others' questions. *Research on Language and Social Interaction*, 43: 3:232–259.

Thomas Schmidt. 2023. FOLK - das Forschungs- und Lehrkorpus für Gesprochenes Deutsch. *Korpora Deutsch als Fremdsprache*, 3: 1 (Themenausgabe ZuMult):166–169.

Thomas Schmidt, Christian Fandrych, Elena Frick, Matthias Schwendemann, Franziska Wallner, and Kai Wörner. 2023. Zugänge zu mündlichen Korpora für DaF und DaZ: Projekt, Datengrundlagen, technische Basis. *Korpora Deutsch als Fremdsprache*, 3: 1 (Themenausgabe ZuMult):1–12.

Margret Selting. 1987. Reparaturen und lokale Verstehensprobleme oder: zur Binnenstruktur von Reparatursequenzen. *Linguistische Berichte*, 108:128–149.

Tanya Stivers. 2004. "No no no" and Other Types of Multiple Sayings in Social Interaction. *Human Communication Research*, 30: 2:260–293.

Deborah Tannen. 1979. *What's in a frame?*, pages 137–81. NJ: Able.

Clare Tarplee. 1996. *Working on young children's utterances: prosodic aspects of repetition during picture labelling*, Studies in Interactional Sociolinguistics, page 406–435. Cambridge University Press.

Matje van de Camp, Martin Reynaert, and Nelleke Oostdijk. 2017. *WhiteLab 2.0: a web interface for corpus exploitation*, pages 231–243. Ubiquity Press.

Carl Vogel. 2013. Attribution of Mutual Understanding. *Journal of Law and Policy*, 21.2.:377–420.

Shih-ping Wang. 2005. Corpus-based approaches and discourse analysis in relation to reduplication and repetition. *Journal of Pragmatics*, 37(4):505–540.

Mats Wirén, Kristina Nilsson Björkenstam, Gintarė Grigonytė, and Elisabet Eir Cortes. 2016. Longitudinal Studies of Variation Sets in Child-directed Speech. In *Proceedings of the 7th Workshop on Cognitive Aspects of Computational Language Learning*, pages 44–52, Berlin. Association for Computational Linguistics.

Jean Wong. 2000. Repetition in Conversation: A Look at "First and Second Sayings". *Research on Language and Social Interaction - RES LANG SOC INTERACT*, 33:407–424.

Exploring Phonetic Features in Language Embeddings for Unseen Language Varieties of Austrian German

Lorenz Gutscher and **Michael Pucher**
Signal Processing and Speech Communication Laboratory, Graz University of Technology
Austrian Research Institute for Artificial Intelligence, Vienna, Austria
lorenz.gutscher@ofai.at michael.pucher@tugraz.at

Abstract

Vectorized language embeddings of raw audio data improve tasks like language recognition, automatic speech recognition, and machine translation. Although embeddings exhibit high effectiveness in their respective tasks, unraveling explicit information or meaning encapsulated within the embeddings proves challenging. This study investigates a multilingual model's ability to capture features from phonetic, articulatory, variety, and speaker categories from brief audio segments comprising five consecutive phones spoken by Austrian speakers. Within the employed model for extraction, German serves as one of the pre-trained languages used. However, the manner in which the model processes Austrian varieties presents an intriguing area for investigation. Using a k-nearest neighbor classifier, it is tested whether the encoded features are prominent in the embedding. While characteristics like variety are effectively classified, the accuracy of phone classification is particularly high for specific phones that are characteristic of the respective dialect/sociolect.

1 Introduction

Language embeddings are high-dimensional vectors in a continuous space that describe language-specific features like word order, prosody, speed, and accent. Embeddings can be obtained from either an orthographic perspective (such as word embeddings) or an acoustic perspective (representing spoken language). Utilizing these embeddings enhances precision in various domains including text classification, machine translation, automatic speech recognition, accent detection, and Language Identification (LID) (Hou et al., 2020). Transformer networks revolutionized these fields by using an attention mechanism that captures complex relationships within the words of a sentence or the audio features of utterances (Vaswani et al., 2017). This study focuses on the acoustic embeddings of spoken language, specifically those derived from the output of the final layer of a deep learning LID task. The objective of an LID system is to determine the language of a written text or an utterance.

Systems for LID can be adapted to identify accents and dialects within a language if labels are available. In cases of low-resource languages, the data itself is often not sufficient for training. Cross-lingual transfer can help to increase performance on tasks such as language modeling, translation, or language identification (Conneau et al., 2020). A pre-trained multilingual model can either be fine-tuned on the unseen data or just used as is. The amount of data enables generalization on unseen data and extraction of language-specific content from the embedding.

Standard Austrian German (SAG) is a special case in this context, as it belongs to the same language family as Standard German (SGG). The Austrian dialect landscape is very rich, with notable differences in vocabulary and pronunciation not only between SGG and SAG but also between SAG and other Austrian dialects (Elspaß and Kleiner, 2019; Kleene et al., 2016). The primary objective of this paper is to leverage a multilingual LID system, initially trained on 107 languages, without additional fine-tuning specifically for Austrian varieties. The aim is to assess the model's ability to generalize to unseen varieties and effectively map language features within the latent space.

The contribution of this paper is:

- It demonstrates the usability of multilingual models for low-resource languages without fine-tuning.
- It reveals that characteristic phones of a variety are distinctly represented within the embeddings.
- It shows the spatial mapping of unseen varieties of Austrian German and suggests that

quinphones are effective for classifying these varieties, contributing to better methods for handling and classifying dialectal variations.

The paper is structured as follows: Section 2 delves into previous research where acoustic embeddings are scrutinized for their potential to encapsulate language-specific features. Section 3 outlines the extraction of embeddings and further processing steps for experiments. Section 4 presents a dataset description and the classification results of four key feature groups: Phone classification, variety classification, classification of articulatory features and phone categories, and speaker classification. Each section of the respective feature group offers a presentation of the results, followed by an analysis.

2 Related Work

Language embeddings are investigated for properties of phonology, morphology, and syntax in (Bjerva and Augenstein, 2018) after fine-tuning language embeddings on specific Natural Language Processing tasks using text data. The method of feature probing through a k-Nearest Neighbor (kNN) classifier yields the conclusion that information pertaining to the investigated properties is encapsulated within the embeddings, exhibiting varying degrees of efficacy in accordance with the task-specific relevance of these properties. This concept is further pursued in (Östling and Kurfalı, 2023) with respect to typological features, asserting that multilingual language embeddings capture linguistic information when trained on the correct downstream tasks. The application of multilingual transfer learning to utilize acoustic embeddings derived from triphones, as described in (Kamper et al., 2021), demonstrates the capacity for extraction of phonetic content and language information for zero-resource languages. Using acoustic embeddings (Belinkov and Glass, 2017), an in-depth analysis of an Automatic Speech Recognition model at the frame level to incorporate phonetic features is conducted. The investigation aims to ascertain the layers within an end-to-end model where phones and sound classes are prominent. In (English et al., 2023) the wav2vec 2.0 model (Babu et al., 2022) is probed to contain three broad phonetic classes (voicing, frication, and nasals) within different layers of the model. (Linke et al., 2023) investigates read and spontaneous speech from Austrian and Hungarian varieties, showing evidence that parameters of speaking style are encoded in the pre-trained XLS-R model and that Austrian German is mapped separately from German German. In (Gutscher et al., 2023) the effectiveness of a pre-trained Language Identification (LID) model in mapping Austrian varieties within latent space is demonstrated. The model successfully distinguishes these varieties from SGG and other European languages. In (Zuluaga-Gomez et al., 2023) the internal categorization of the wav2vec 2.0 embeddings is analyzed through t-Distributed Stochastic Neighbor Embedding (t-SNE), and it is observed that there is a level of clustering based on phonological similarity.

3 Methods

In typical settings, acoustic language embeddings are extracted at the sentence or utterance level. In this work, it is hypothesized that valuable language information is not only present in sentence or utterance embeddings but also in smaller units, specifically in quinphones. Therefore, the dataset is divided into chunks of audio consisting of five consecutive phones. Quinphones find frequent application in Hidden Markov Models (HMMs) owing to their capacity to encapsulate contextual dependencies among phonetic units. HMMs of quinphones are capable of capturing the influence of adjacent phones, thereby contributing to the pronunciation of words. The language embedding is extracted with a multilingual LID system[1] for all quinphones, as depicted in Figure 1, representing each quinphone with a 2048-dimensional vector (no further classification based on the embeddings is done). The system employs the XLS-R model (Conneau et al., 2021) which builds on the wav2vec 2.0 architecture and underwent fine-tuning using the voxlingua107 dataset (Valk and Alumäe, 2021) (107 languages). Wav2vec 2.0 is initially trained on publicly available datasets encompassing 128 languages, providing substantial variability and encompassing a wide array of linguistic contexts. Utilizing quinphones is advantageous because the multilingual LID system mentioned above, with its default settings, requires a minimum sample length of 400 samples (25 ms) to extract embeddings due to the minimum size of the kernel filters. If single phones were used instead of quinphones, this minimum length requirement would pose problems for phones shorter than 25 ms.

[1] https://huggingface.co/TalTechNLP/voxlingua107-xls-r-300m-wav2vec

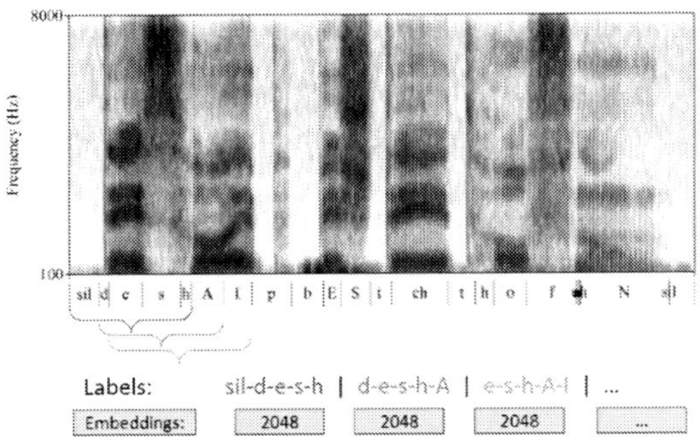

Figure 1: Process of extracting embeddings from quinphones

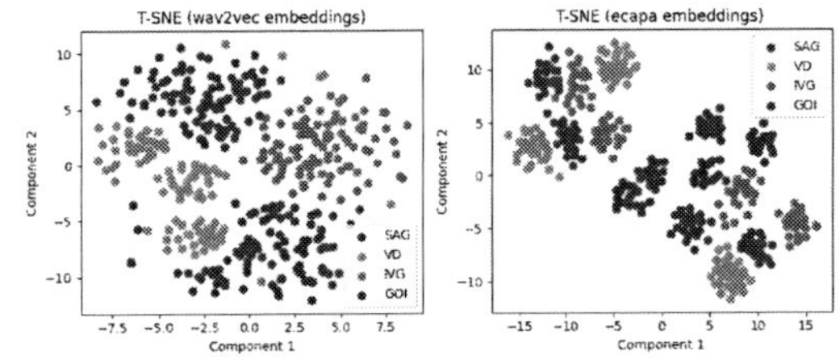

Figure 2: Visualization of four varieties of Austrian German using t-SNE with wav2vec 2.0 (left) and ECAPA-TDNN (right) LID models.

The goal of this paper is to test the model's ability to classify segmental and phonetic features for both seen and unseen Austrian varieties. Training on low-resource data can lead to speaker embeddings instead of language embeddings due to the limited number of speakers. To address this, a pre-trained model was utilized. The effectiveness of probing for features in language embeddings is shown in (Singla et al., 2022; Hewitt and Manning, 2019).

To investigate the clustering of language varieties, a sample set of 100 utterances per variety is employed, and t-SNE is used to visualize the potential clustering of the high-dimensional embedding vectors. Two models are compared in this analysis: the wav2vec 2.0 XLS-R and the Emphasized Channel Attention, Propagation, and Aggregation in Time Delay Neural Networks (ECAPA-TDNN) (Desplanques et al., 2020) model[2] (both fine-tuned on LID using the voxlingua107 dataset). The ideal visual output would exhibit clear spatial separation between the four language varieties. As illustrated in Figure 2, the wav2vec 2.0 model effectively disentangles speaker and variety information, resulting in more generalized clusters compared to the ECAPA-TDNN model. Conversely, the ECAPA-TDNN model reveals a bias towards encoding speaker-specific information, resulting in smaller clusters primarily representing individual speakers. Further analysis of the ECAPA-TDNN model reveals an additional layer of gender-based clustering. This model initially segregates the data into two primary clusters based on gender, aligned along a diagonal axis from the bottom left (Component 1: -10, Component 2: -15) to the top right corner (Component 1: 5, Component 2: 10) of the t-SNE plot. Within these primary gender clusters, further subdivision into smaller clusters occurs, each representing different speakers.

The process of data pre-processing involves the following: For each audio chunk (quinphone), a corresponding label file is created containing information about all five phone states. To avoid overlapping quinphones in the training and test sets, chunks of the same utterances are not split between those groups. For each probing feature in the datasets, binary targets are constructed, and an approximate nearest neighbor classifier is trained using the FAISS package (Douze et al., 2024). The parameter for determining the number of nearest neighbors is set to k=10, employing the Euclidean distance as the distance metric. This choice of k is designed to enhance the classification of infrequent instances, avoiding dependence solely on the clustering of instances associated with identical words. For each feature, the target is binary, which means there are only two possibilities for building the targets: (a) The feature is eminent in the current quinphone, or (b) the feature is not eminent in the current quinphone. The position of a feature within a quinphone is not taken into account. Infrequently observed features, occurring below the minimum threshold of 200 instances in the training set, are systematically excluded. The intrinsic operational principle of the kNN algorithm leads to a statistical bias concerning the classification accuracy score between frequent and non-frequent features, whereby the likelihood of accurate classification increases when there is a greater abundance of data points related to the feature in the training set. A dummy classifier is employed to rectify this effect. It randomly shuffles the binary target values, emulating random guessing, but taking into account the number of ones and zeros for these features. The

[2]https://huggingface.co/TalTechNLP/voxlingua107-epaca-tdnn

output of the classification metric from the dummy classifier is then subtracted from the metric of the actual classifier. The impact of the dummy classifier is particularly pronounced in categories where the majority of targets are predicted to be positive targets. The F1-score is employed for evaluation, representing the harmonic mean between precision and recall while considering both balanced and unbalanced target sets. It characterizes a trade-off between instances classified as false positives and false negatives. The focal point of interest does not reside solely in the absolute performance of the classification of individual features, but rather in discerning the degree to which certain features are encoded more effectively than others.

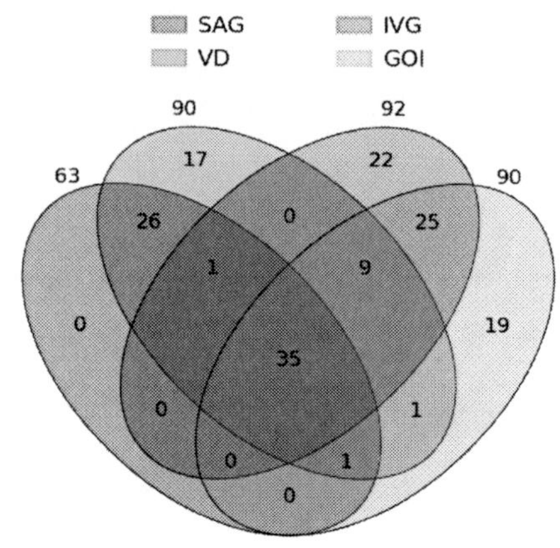

Figure 3: Phone set overlaps for SAG, VD, IVG, and GOI

4 Experiments

Building upon the methods described above, the experiments aim to evaluate the performance of the proposed approach in classifying phonetic and articulatory features, along with variety and speaker groups, across diverse Austrian varieties.

4.1 Data overview

Dataset. The dataset consists of 16 kHz WAV recordings with corresponding labels in the format of HTS (Zen et al., 2007) label files containing detailed temporal-aligned phone annotations in addition to linguistic and prosodic information. The dataset comprises four distinct varieties, each contributing unique linguistic characteristics.

- The SAG variety utilizes data extracted from the Wiener Corpus of Austrian Varieties for Speech Synthesis (WASS) (Pucher et al., 2015; Toman and Pucher, 2015).
- The Viennese (VD) variety draws from the Viennese Sociolect and Dialect Synthesis (VSDS) corpus (Pucher et al., 2010).
- Additionally, the dataset includes Innervillgraten (IVG) and Bad Goisern (GOI) varieties, both sourced from the Goisern and Innervillgraten Dialect Speech (GIDS) corpus (Schabus et al., 2014).

The dataset is reduced to achieve balance among varieties, ensuring that each variety has an equal number of data points and approximately the same number of speakers (SAG: 5, VD: 3, IVG: 4, GOI: 4). Upon segmenting the utterances into labeled units utilizing the provided time-codes from the annotations, the training set comprises 185,496 quinphones (90%), while the test set contains 20,610 quinphones (10%). To ensure a balanced evaluation, the test set was further refined for each feature to include an equal representation of 1-targets and 0-targets. The mean duration of a quinphone is 500 ms.

Variety description. All four varieties have shared phones and (except for SAG) between 17 and 22 unique phones. The numbers of overlapping phone sets are illustrated in Figure 3.

- SAG is the standard variety of German spoken in Austria. In SGG, for example, the high vowels [i] - [ɪ], [y] - [ʏ], and [u] - [ʊ] are clearly differentiated by quality (Davis and Mermelstein, 1990). This difference in quality is rather small to non-existent in SAG, though these phones still exist in SAG. A difference in vowel quality between SAG and SGG is the low vowel [ɑ] in SAG, which is [a] in SGG. In general, the transition between standard and dialect can be described by different processes that do not necessarily result in unique phones. For our analysis on the phonetic level, we are focusing on the different phones.
- The VD is an East Bavarian sociolect, nowadays mainly spoken by older, male, working class German speakers in Vienna, and has characteristic processes like monophthongization, which result in unique phonetic differences. The Viennese monophthongization is a form of assimilation, whereby one part of the diphthong is assimilated to the other (Moos-

müller, 2011).

1. <Haus> (Engl. “house"): [hɑɔ̯s] → [hɒːs]
2. <weit> (Engl. “wide"): [vɑɛ̯t] → [væːd̥]

- The GOI dialect is a Central Bavarian dialect spoken in the region of Bad Goisern and has a significant number of diphthongs that arise through diphthongization of vowels, as shown in Example 1 below for the word <Schwester> (Engl. “sister"). Another source of new diphthongs is the vocalization of the lateral (/l/-Vocalization), as shown in Example 2 for the word <bald> (Engl. “soon"). This is a prominent feature in the Central Bavarian varieties and accours in word-medial and word-final positions. The vocalization of the lateral is perceived as a dialect feature and thus widely suppressed by standard variety speakers, including those who strive for a standard variety. Another characteristic phone of GOI is the uvular trill [ʀ].

1. <Schwester> (Engl. “sister"): [ʃvesda] → [ʃvɛesda]
2. <bald> (Engl. “soon"): [bɑld] → [bɔed]
3. <recht> (Engl. “right"): [reçd] → [ʀɛeçd]

- The IVG dialect is a South Bavarian dialect spoken in East Tyrol and uses a fricativized trill [ʀ] or the uvular fricative [χ] as a characteristic phone, transcribed as [ʀχ] in our data. Another distinctive phone of IVG is the palatal approximant [ʎ].

1. <warten> (Engl. “to wait"): [vɑːdn] → [vɔːʀχdn]
2. <Zahl> (Engl. “number"): tsɑl] → [tsɔːʎ]

4.2 Phone classification

In the phone evaluation, positive classification targets in the dataset indicate the presence of at least one phone within a quinphone instance. Following the exclusion of exceedingly rare instances, the evaluation yields a total count of 132 phones from the initial pool (24 phones are excluded). The computed average F1-score stands at 0.42 with a standard deviation of ± 0.1. The phones with the highest F1-scores, after subtraction of associated dummy scores (denoted in brackets), are delineated in Table 1. The characteristic [æː] monophtongs described in Section 4.1 achieve an F1-score of 0.63 (0.0), while [ɒː] achieves 0.1 (0.0). For a full list of all phone classification results see Figure 6 in the appendix.

The phone category exhibits the second-best results, demonstrating significant variations among different phones. Notably, the distinct [ʀ] and several diphthongs from the GOI phone set attain a commendable score. Within the IVG phone set, the phones [ʀχ] and [ʎ] exemplify that phones incorporating language-specific features contribute to an elevation in the classification score and are especially well classified. This phenomenon is similarly observed for the VD monophthong [æː]. The specific vowel quality [ɑ] of SAG on the other hand, is not well classified. Given that the dummy classifier yields a score close to 0, these results demonstrate a classification performance significantly surpassing random chance for the dialect/sociolect varieties.

4.3 Classification of articulatory and phone categories

Within the 54 articulatory and phone classes, the average score is 0.23 with a standard deviation of ± 0.2. Only the categories retroflex (0.69), affricates (0.66), aspirated (0.64), voiced fricative (0.6), syllabic (0.55), and ʊ-vowel (0.52) achieve F1-scores over 0.5, indicating moderate classification (see Figure 4). Other categories, such as vowel types (low, high, closed, etc.), consonant types (front, fortis, short, etc.), and fricative types (central, back, front, unvoiced), consistently exhibit values below 0.5.

The group of articulatory and phone classes has the lowest score, indicating that this category is not well represented within the embedding in the case of quinphones. Only six out of 54 categories achieve F1-scores over 0.5. The other 48 categories lack sufficient information for a reliable classification in this quinphone setup. Compared to the variety, phone, and speaker categories, the articulatory and phone categories achieve the lowest average score over all features. It is proposed that the task of Language Identification (LID) does not effectively train models to represent these features in a compound manner in quinphones. Moreover, the setup of using quinphones is likely to contain

Table 1: Phones with highest F1-scores

Phone	F1-score (dummy)	Phone	F1-score (dummy)
[ʀ]	0.70 (0.0)	[ɛɑ]	0.66 (0.0)
[ʎ]	0.69 (0.0)	[ɕ]	0.66 (0.0)
[f]	0.67 (0.02)	[ʀχ]	0.66 (0.0)
[ɔɛ]	0.66 (0.0)	[ɛ]	0.66 (0.01)
[ɑɛ]	0.66 (0.0)	[ɔe]	0.65 (0.0)

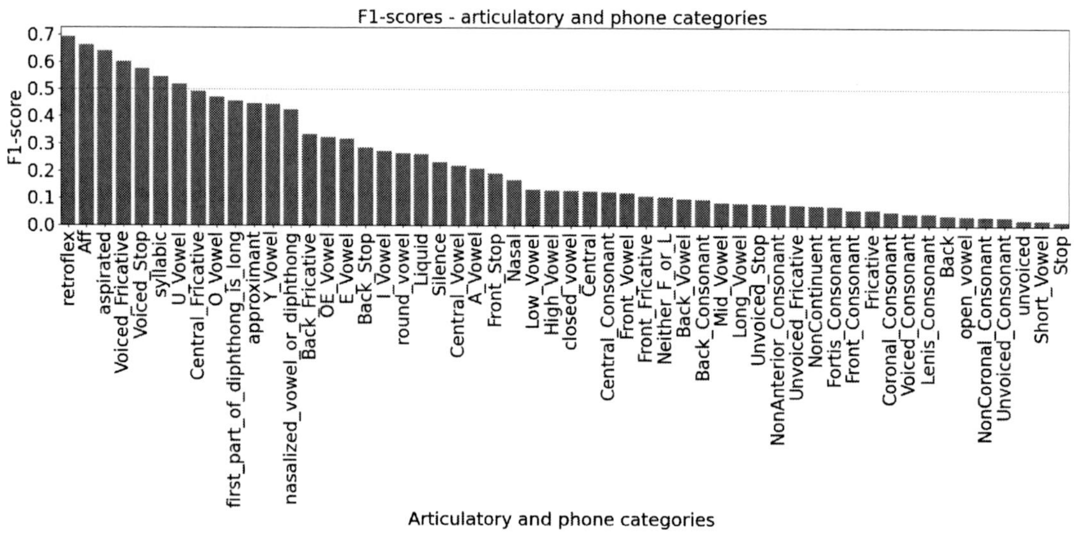

Figure 4: F1-scores for classification of articulatory and phone categories

Table 2: F1-scores for Austrian varieties

Variety	F1-score (dummy)
IVG	0.9 (0.04)
GOI	0.89 (0.03)
SAG	0.84 (0.05
VD	0.68 (0.04)

more features within one quinphone (for example, consonants and vowels), making the training set very unbalanced.

4.4 Variety classification

The variety category comprises four distinct varieties, achieving an average score of 0.83 $\pm$ 0.1. As illustrated in Table 2, IVG attains the highest F1-score of 0.9 (0.03), followed by GOI with 0.89 (0.03), SAG with 0.84 (0.05), and VD with 0.68 (0.04).

The classification outcomes for quinphones demonstrate significant language-related cues within the variety category. While this phenomenon was demonstrated at the utterance level in Figure 2, it is noted that the representations of utterance embeddings from IVG and GOI show fewer outliers and less overlap compared to VD and SAG. This distinctiveness potentially contributes to improved classification results for IVG and GOI at the quinphone level. The authors suggest that the decreased performance of VD stems from the proximity of small speech units to SAG, leading to misclassifications in certain instances.

4.5 Speaker classification

The final group reflects speaker-related information embedded in the quinphone audio data. The average score is 0.36 with a standard deviation of $\pm$ 0.22. Notably, SPO (SAG) and HPO (VD) stand out with the highest scores of 0.9 and 0.73, respectively, while the remaining 14 speakers exhibit scores ranging from 0.51 to 0.07 (see Figure 5). The dummy classifier consistently yields a score of 0 in all cases.

The speaker classification achieves the second-lowest accuracy, suggesting that the embedding does not effectively capture information about the

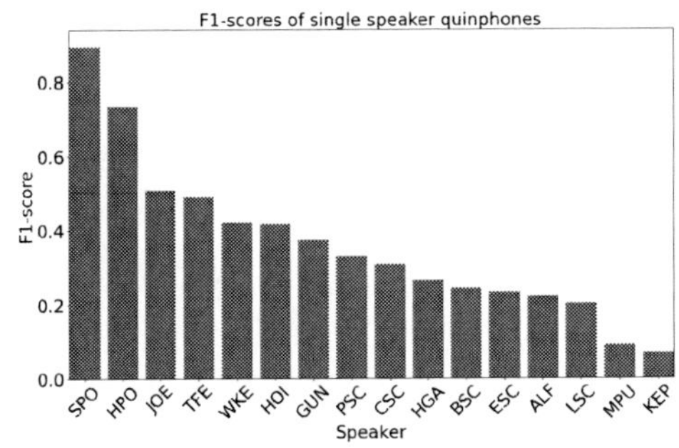

Figure 5: F1-scores for single speaker classification

speaker's voice, which is expected for a model trained on the task of LID. Speaker classification only exceeds F1 values of 0.5 for the SPO (SAG), HPO (VD), and JOE (VD) speakers. SPO and HPO, both professional radio and TV speakers, could potentially exhibit distinct speaking styles due to their professional backgrounds. This divergence in speaking style is likely manifested in the embeddings, leading to a more pronounced separation between these two speakers compared to others. JOE, as the singular youth voice in the corpus, could impart a unique linguistic imprint to the embeddings, potentially resulting in distinguishable language characteristics.

5 Conclusion

Understanding the intricacies of multilingual language embeddings in capturing phonetic features for unseen language varieties holds significant importance in advancing the capabilities of automated language processing systems. This study explores the efficiency of multilingual language embeddings derived from short audio segments (quinphones) in capturing phonetic features for Austrian German varieties. It shows that the multilingual wav2vec 2.0 model (fine-tuned on the task of LID) disentangles speaker and language information for unseen varieties of Austrian German. Furthermore, it indicates that individual phones within a quinphone are sufficient for the model to group or model specific varieties. This supports the utilization of comprehensive multilingual language identification embeddings in diverse applications, including automatic speech recognition, accent recognition, and language identification. It is particularly relevant for low-resource languages, where fine-tuning poses challenges.

6 Limitations

In this study, we opted to split utterances into non-overlapping segments to mitigate the potential issue of similar embeddings arising from overlapping segments. However, it is important to note that despite this precaution, instances of repeated single words between training and testing splits may still arise, albeit infrequently. Furthermore, a noteworthy limitation of our methodology pertains to its applicability to languages that lack closely related counterparts in the pre-trained model, unlike German and Austrian German. This discrepancy may hinder the extension of our findings to languages not adequately represented in the model's training data.

7 Ethical Considerations

No new data was recorded in this study. The datasets utilized are anonymized, employing pseudonyms and removing identifying information to ensure the privacy and confidentiality of the speakers. Explicit consent was obtained from each individual speaker for the use of recordings for research purposes. The findings do not marginalize any dialects or reinforce any power dynamics. Furthermore, the explainability of models that can be achieved through an analysis on the phonetic level contributes to making deep learning models more transparent to the potential user.

References

A. Babu, C. Wang, A. Tjandra, K. Lakhotia, Q. Xu, N. Goyal, K. Singh, P. von Platen, Y. Saraf, J. Pino, A. Baevski, A. Conneau, and M. Auli. 2022. XLS-R: Self-supervised cross-lingual speech representation learning at scale. In *Proc. Interspeech 2022*, pages 2278–2282.

Yonatan Belinkov and James Glass. 2017. Analyzing hidden representations in end-to-end automatic speech recognition systems. In *Neural Information Processing Systems (NIPS 2017)*, volume 2017-December, pages 2442–2452.

Johannes Bjerva and Isabelle Augenstein. 2018. From phonology to syntax: Unsupervised linguistic typology at different levels with language embeddings. In *Proc. NAACL HLT 2018 - 2018 Conference of the North American Chapter of the Association for Computational Linguistics: Human Language Technologies*, volume 1, pages 907–916.

Alexis Conneau, Alexei Baevski, Ronan Collobert, Abdelrahman Mohamed, and Michael Auli. 2021. Unsupervised cross-lingual representation learning for speech recognition. In *Proc. Interspeech 2021*, pages 2426–2430.

Alexis Conneau, Kartikay Khandelwal, Naman Goyal, Vishrav Chaudhary, Guillaume Wenzek, Francisco Guzmán, Edouard Grave, Myle Ott, Luke Zettlemoyer, and Veselin Stoyanov. 2020. Unsupervised cross-lingual representation learning at scale. In *Proceedings of the 58th Annual Meeting of the Association for Computational Linguistics*, pages 8440–8451. Association for Computational Linguistics.

Steven B. Davis and Paul Mermelstein. 1990. German. *Journal of the International Phonetic Association*, 20:48–50.

Brecht Desplanques, Jenthe Thienpondt, and Kris Demuynck. 2020. ECAPA-TDNN: emphasized channel attention, propagation and aggregation in TDNN based speaker verification. In *Proc. Interspeech 2020*, pages 3830–3834.

Matthijs Douze, Alexandr Guzhva, Chengqi Deng, Jeff Johnson, Gergely Szilvasy, Pierre-Emmanuel Mazaré, Maria Lomeli, Lucas Hosseini, and Hervé Jégou. 2024. The faiss library. *arXiv preprint 2401.08281*.

Stephan Elspaß and Stefan Kleiner. 2019. Forschungsergebnisse zur arealen Variation im Standarddeutschen. In Joachim Herrgen and Jürgen Erich Schmidt, editors, *Deutsch: Sprache und Raum. Ein internationales Handbuch der Sprachvariation*, pages 159–184. De Gruyter.

Patrick Cormac English, John D. Kelleher, and Julie Carson-Berndsen. 2023. Discovering phonetic feature event patterns in transformer embeddings. In *Proc. Interspeech 2023*, pages 4733–4737.

Lorenz Gutscher, Michael Pucher, and Víctor Garcia. 2023. Neural speech synthesis for austrian dialects with standard german grapheme-to-phoneme conversion and dialect embeddings. In *Proc. 2nd Annual Meeting of the ELRA/ISCA SIG on Under-resourced Languages (SIGUL 2023)*, pages 68–72.

John Hewitt and Christopher D. Manning. 2019. A structural probe for finding syntax in word representations. In *Proc. of the 2019 Conference of the North American Chapter of the Association for Computational Linguistics: Human Language Technologies, Volume 1 (Long and Short Papers)*, pages 4129–4138. Association for Computational Linguistics.

Wenxin Hou, Yue Dong, Bairong Zhuang, Longfei Yang, Jiatong Shi, and Takahiro Shinozaki. 2020. Large-scale end-to-end multilingual speech recognition and language identification with multi-task learning. In *Proc. Interspeech 2020*, pages 1037–1041.

Herman Kamper, Yevgen Matusevych, and Sharon Goldwater. 2021. Improved acoustic word embeddings for zero-resource languages using multilingual transfer. In *IEEE/ACM Transactions on Audio, Speech, and Language Processing*, volume 29, pages 1107–1118.

Andrea Kleene, Alexandra N. Lenz, Hans Bickel, Ulrich Ammon, Juliane Fink, Andrea Gellan, Lorenz Hofer, Karina Schneider-Wiejowski, Sandra Suter, Jakob Ebner, and Manfred Michael Glauninger. 2016. Variantenwörterbuch des Deutschen – die Standardsprache in Österreich, der Schweiz, Deutschland, Liechtenstein, Luxemburg, Ostbelgien und Südtirol sowie Rumänien, Namibia und Mennonitensiedlungen. In *Variantenwörterbuch des Deutschen*. De Gruyter.

J. Linke, M.S. Kádár, G. Dobsinszki, P. Mihajlik, G. Kubin, and B. Schuppler. 2023. What do self-supervised speech representations encode? An analysis of languages, varieties, speaking styles and speakers. In *Proc. Interspeech 2023*, pages 5371–5375.

S. Moosmüller. 2011. Sound changes and variation in the Viennese dialect. In *On Words and Sounds: A selection of papers fromt the 40th PLM, 2009*, pages 134–147. Cambridge Scholars Publishing.

Michael Pucher, Friedrich Neubarth, Volker Strom, Sylvia Moosmüller, Gregor Hofer, Christian Kranzler, Gudrun Schuchmann, and Dietmar Schabus. 2010. Resources for speech synthesis of viennese varieties. In *Proc. of the Seventh International Conference on Language Resources and Evaluation (LREC'10)*. European Language Resources Association (ELRA).

Michael Pucher, Markus Toman, Dietmar Schabus, Cassia Valentini-Botinhao, Junichi Yamagishi, Bettina Zillinger, and Erich Schmid. 2015. Influence of speaker familiarity on blind and visually impaired children's perception of synthetic voices in audio games. In *Proc. Interspeech 2015*, pages 1625–1629.

Dietmar Schabus, Michael Pucher, and Gregor Hofer. 2014. Joint audiovisual hidden semi-markov model-based speech synthesis. *IEEE Journal of Selected Topics in Signal Processing*, 8(2):336–347.

Yaman Kumar Singla, Jui Shah, Changyou Chen, and Rajiv Ratn Shah. 2022. What do audio transformers hear? Probing their representations for language delivery & structure. In *2022 IEEE International Conference on Data Mining Workshops (ICDMW)*, pages 910–925.

Markus Toman and Michael Pucher. 2015. An Open Source Speech Synthesis Frontend for HTS. In *Proc. of the 18th International Conference on Text, Speech, and Dialogue - Volume 9302*, pages 291–298.

Jörgen Valk and Tanel Alumäe. 2021. VoxLingua107: a dataset for spoken language recognition. In *Proc. IEEE SLT Workshop*.

Ashish Vaswani, Noam Shazeer, Niki Parmar, Jakob Uszkoreit, Llion Jones, Aidan N. Gomez, Łukasz Kaiser, and Illia Polosukhin. 2017. Attention is all you need. In *Advances in Neural Information Processing Systems*, pages 6000–6010.

Heiga Zen, Takashi Nose, Junichi Yamagishi, Shinji Sako, Takashi Masuko, Alan W. Black, and Keiichi Tokuda. 2007. The HMM-based speech synthesis system (HTS) version 2.0. In *6th ISCA Workshop on Speech Synthesis, SSW 2007*, pages 294–299. The International Society for Computers and Their Applications (ISCA).

Juan Zuluaga-Gomez, Sara Ahmed, Danielius Visockas, and Cem Subakan. 2023. CommonAccent: Exploring Large Acoustic Pretrained Models for Accent Classification Based on Common Voice. In *Proc. Interspeech 2023*, pages 5291–5295.

Robert Östling and Murathan Kurfalı. 2023. Language embeddings sometimes contain typological generalizations. *Computational Linguistics*, 49(4):1003–1051.

A Appendix

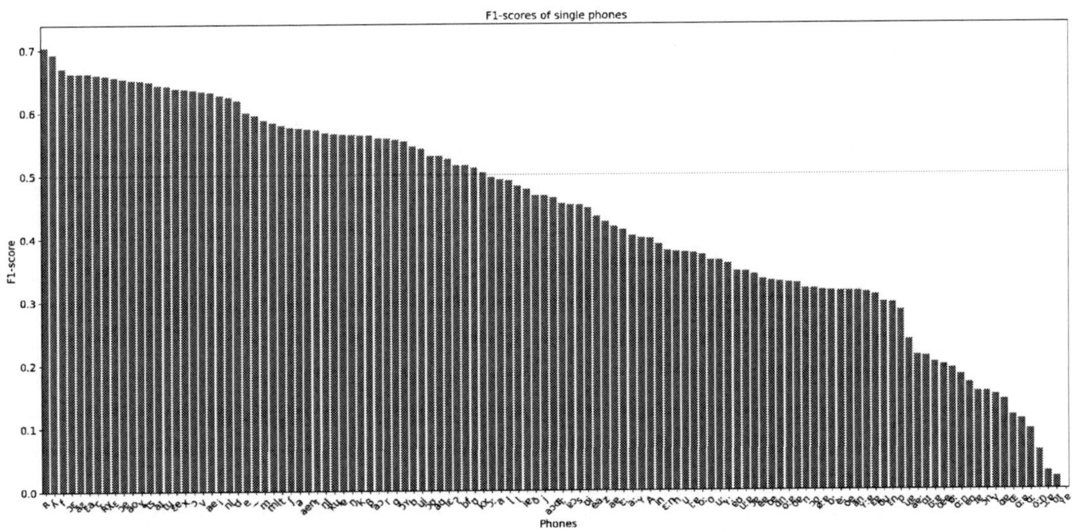

Figure 6: F1-scores for classification of all phones

A Multilingual Dataset of Adversarial Attacks to Automatic Content Scoring Systems

Ronja Laarmann-Quante, Christopher Chandler, Noemi Incirkus, Vitaliia Ruban, Alona Solopov and Luca Steen
Ruhr University Bochum, Faculty of Philology, Department of Linguistics, Germany
noemi.incirkus@edu.rub.de
{ronja.laarmann-quante, christopher.chandler, vitaliia.ruban, alona.solopov, luca.steen}@rub.de

Abstract

Automatic content scoring systems have been shown to be vulnerable to adversarial attacks, i.e. to answers that human raters would clearly recognize as incorrect or even nonsense but that are nevertheless rated as correct by an automatic system. The existing literature on this topic has so far focused on English datasets. In this paper, we present a multilingual dataset of adversarial answers for English, German, French and Spanish based on the multilingual ASAP content scoring dataset introduced by Horbach et al. (2023). We apply different methods of generating adversarial answers proposed in the literature, e.g. sampling n-grams from existing answers or generic corpora or inserting adjectives and adverbs into incorrect answers. In a baseline experiment, we show that the rate at which adversarials are rejected by a model depends on the adversarial method used, interacting with the language and the prompt-specific dataset a model was trained on.

1 Introduction

One of the prerequisites for automatic scoring tools to be usable in educational settings, besides an overall good performance, is the robustness against cheating behavior. In this paper, we deal with automatic content scoring, also known as automatic short answer grading (ASAG), which refers to the task of scoring students' answers to prompts like the following: `[An experiment about the stretchability of different polymer plastics is outlined]` *Task: Describe two ways the experimenter could have improved the experimental design and/or validity of the results.*[1] The answers to such prompts are typically short, ranging from a few words to a few sentences and the focus of the scoring is on content rather than form or style.

Previous work has shown that automatic scoring models for such tasks can be tricked by different kinds of adversarial answers, meaning answers that are clearly wrong or even nonsense for human raters but that are nevertheless graded as (partly) correct by automatic scoring models. For example, Ding et al. (2020) showed that shallow and deep learning models can be fooled by randomly sampled n-grams taken from real answers, the prompt or even from generic corpora. Willms and Pado (2022) found that increasing the answer length by repeating the answer once or twice can deceive a transformer model into scoring incorrect answers as correct. Filighera et al. (2023) inserted random adjectives and adverbs into wrong answers, which did not turn the answer into a correct answer but it nevertheless increased the likelihood that it would be scored as correct by a transformer model.

The experiments in the literature have so far focused on English datasets. However, different languages pose different challenges to automatic content scoring (see e.g. Padó et al., 2023 for German) that may also influence the vulnerability towards adversarial attacks. Furthermore, automatic content scoring has been tackled from a cross-lingual perspective (Horbach et al., 2023) but so far, there is no multilingual dataset of adversarial answers available that could be used to test the robustness of a model for different language settings.

The aim of this paper is twofold: Firstly, we present a comprehensive multilingual dataset of adversarial answers that comprises English, German, French and Spanish. The adversarial answers are based on the multilingual ASAP dataset introduced in Horbach et al. (2023) using the adversarial methods proposed by Ding et al. (2020) and Filighera et al. (2023) with some extensions (Sec. 3). Secondly, we provide a baseline experiment with a shallow baseline model as used by Ding et al. (2020), showing that not only the language but also the prompt-specific

[1] See prompt 2 of the ASAP-SAS dataset: https://www.kaggle.com/c/asap-sas/.

Dataset	Lang.	Prompt		
		1	2	10
$ASAP_{orig}$	English	2,229	1,704	2,186
$ASAP_{orig300}$	English	300	300	300
$ASAP_{en}$	English	330	328	330
$ASAP_{de}$	German	301	301	301
$ASAP_{fr}$	French	274	187	211
$ASAP_{es}$	Spanish	325	297	393

Table 1: Number of answers per dataset and prompt in the multilingual ASAP corpus of Horbach et al. (2023).

dataset that a model was trained on and the specific adversarial method has a large influence on a model's capability of rejecting adversarial answers (Sec. 4). The code and data from this study is available under the following link:
`https://gitlab.ruhr-uni-bochum.de/vamos-cl/multilingual-adversarial-dataset-konvens-2024`

2 Data

First, we present the content scoring dataset and second the generic corpora used as background corpora for each language, e.g. for constructing prompt-independent adversarial answers.

2.1 Content Scoring Data

We use the English, German, French and Spanish part of the multilingual content scoring dataset introduced by Horbach et al. (2023). The English part consists of three datasets: $ASAP_{orig}$, which comprises answers to prompts 1, 2 and 10 of the original ASAP-SAS dataset (see footnote 1) collected from high school students; $ASAP_{orig300}$, which contains a random sample of $ASAP_{orig}$ with 300 answers per prompt so that it roughly matches the datasets in the other languages in size; $ASAP_{en}$, comprising answers to the same prompts collected from crowd workers, matching the data collection process for the other languages, i.e. German ($ASAP_{de}$), French ($ASAP_{fr}$) and Spanish ($ASAP_{es}$). Table 1 shows the number of answers per dataset and prompt. All answers come with an adjudicated gold score produced by human raters. Prompts 1 and 2 were scored on a scale from 0 (incorrect answer) to 3 (perfect answer), prompt 10 on a scale from 0 to 2. More information about the dataset can be found in Horbach et al. (2023).

2.2 Generic Corpora

For each language, we use a generic corpus as background corpus. Following Ding et al. (2020) and Filighera et al. (2023), we use the Brown Corpus (Kučera and Francis, 1967) for English available via the NLTK library (Bird et al., 2009). For German and French, we use the newest available corpora from the Leipzig Corpora Collection[2] (Goldhahn et al., 2012) that were compiled from randomly chosen websites, which are "deu-com web" from 2021 for German and "fra-ch web" from 2020 for French. For Spanish, we use the CESS-ESP corpus (Martí et al., 2007) available via the NLTK. Basic statistics for the generic corpora are summarized in Table 4 in Appendix A.

3 Adversarial Methods

We use three different types of methods for generating adversarial answers: (1) word-based and character-based n-grams from either real answers or generic corpora following Ding et al. (2020). These methods assume knowledge of n-gram probabilities in either real answers or in generic texts of a language. This is not what a student who wants to cheat is assumed to know but nevertheless a trustworthy system has to be robust against such (nonsense) answers (Ding et al., 2020). (2) Sampling either n-grams or only nouns from the prompt material. These methods also create nonsense answers but they could mimic real cheating of a student who just copies material from a prompt. (3) Inserting either adjectives or adverbs into wrong answers as proposed by Filighera et al. (2023). They found that such answers looked more unnatural to human raters but not like suspicious cheating attacks. Nevertheless, some of the answers fooled a neural model into scoring incorrect answers as correct.

For each method in each set, we generate 1,000 adversarial answers for each prompt. Table 7 in Appendix A shows an example adversarial for each method. Where part-of-speech (POS) tags are needed, texts are first tagged with spaCy (Honnibal et al., 2020), using the small core model for each language. For the Brown Corpus, the POS tags that come with the corpus are used.

3.1 Random N-Grams

In this method, we create adversarial answers by a weighted random sampling of 1-5 grams based on either words or characters from either the real answers to a prompt (correct as well as incorrect answers, henceforth called ASAP-based adversarials)

[2]`https://wortschatz.uni-leipzig.de/en/download/`

or the generic corpus. To make the generic corpora comparable in size, we use a randomly sampled subset of 5,000 sentences for each corpus.

For word-based n-grams, we follow the procedure described in Ding et al. (2020) with a few changes to make the adversarials more similar to the real answers: Firstly, we keep punctuation marks and secondly, we determine the lengths of the answers differently: In Ding et al. (2020), an answer ends when the last n-gram contains the special end-of-sentence token or when a pre-defined maximum length is reached. We also use the end-of-sentence marker to stop the generation process for an answer but besides that, we use a random length for each answer that lies in the range of plus/minus one standard deviation around the mean number of tokens in the real answers to the prompt. We do the same for character-based n-grams, where additionally, we take the mean token length (plus/minus one standard deviation) into account to generate word boundaries. In addition, we add spaces before capital letters and after punctuation marks.

3.2 Random Prompt Material

The following two adversarial methods could resemble real cheating behavior of students, namely randomly picking and rearranging either n-grams or only nouns from the given prompt. Table 5 in Appendix A shows the number of words and nouns, respectively, in the prompt material as used in the data collection for each language.

Prompt N-Grams Firstly, we generate adversarials by randomly sampling 1-5 grams from the prompt material. We sample with replacement and generate separate adversarials for each *n*. Of course, in real cheating, it would be odd to assume that a student would always pick exactly *n* adjacent words but this allows us to systematically study the role of greater context. We keep words occurring in graphics or tables in the prompt material but we remove punctuation marks and also do not mark the beginning or end of a sentence. Each adversarial answer has a random length between minus/plus one standard deviation around the mean number of words in the real answers to a prompt, with a minimum length of 5 words. Our rationale is that students would roughly know from experience how long answers are expected to be.

Prompt Nouns In this method, we create answers only consisting of nouns from the prompt, which is equivalent to the 'Content Burst' method in Ding et al. (2020) applied only to the prompt and not the student answers. The idea is that nouns carry most of the semantic value of an answer. We first extract all the common nouns (including nouns occurring in tables and graphics) and then randomly sample nouns (with replacement) based on their token frequency up to an average maximum length of 44 characters (following Ding et al., 2020), resulting in answer lengths of 6-7 words.

Dataset	Prompt		
	1	2	10
ASAP_{orig}	380 (23%)	168 (13%)	290 (18%)
$\text{ASAP}_{orig300}$	68 (23%)	43 (14%)	51 (17%)
ASAP_{en}	178 (59%)	176 (59%)	115 (38%)
ASAP_{de}	151 (50%)	97 (32%)	121 (40%)
ASAP_{fr}	125 (46%)	76 (41%)	70 (33%)
ASAP_{es}	82 (25%)	84 (28%)	74 (19%)

Table 2: Number of answers scored 0 by human raters.

3.3 Inserting Adjectives and Adverbs

For this set of adversarials, we use the method of inserting adjectives or adverbs into incorrect answers as proposed by Filighera et al. (2023). To this end, we first extracted all answers scored with zero points by the human raters, see Table 2.

Inserting Adjectives Following Filighera et al. (2023), we filtered the 100 most frequent adjectives occurring with nouns and pronouns in the generic corpus of a language. To do so, for the Germanic languages German and English, where adjectives precede nouns, we extracted all bigrams consisting of a word form tagged as adjective as first element and a noun, pronoun or proper noun as second element, e.g. `(('general', 'ADJ'), ('purposes', 'NOUN'))`, `(('occasional', 'ADJ'), ('meetings', 'NOUN'))`. For the Romance languages French and Spanish, where adjectives follow nouns, we looked for the respective bigrams with adjectives as the second element. We then identified the 100 adjectives occurring most frequently in this set of bigrams. To create an adversarial answer, we insert a random adjective from this list before every noun (for English and German) and after every noun (for French and Spanish), respectively, in each incorrect answer. In order to get 1,000 adversarials for every prompt in every language, we create different versions of each incorrect answer by randomly choosing different adjectives.

It is important to note that we do not adjust the inflection of the adjectives to the grammatical context. Adjectives have to agree in grammatical gender and number with nouns in German, Spanish and French (and additionally in case in German), which is not relevant for English. Therefore, the generated answers in these languages may be perceived as more unnatural to human raters. However, since non-native speakers are likely to produce the same kinds of grammatical errors, it should not affect their ratings. Likewise, we do not check semantic appropriateness which leads to expressions like *the experimental* ***christian*** *design* or *the* ***dark*** *experiment* that could in fact look suspicious to human raters.

Inserting Adverbs For inserting adverbs into wrong answers, we again largely follow Filighera et al. (2023). Working only with English, they first identified bigrams in which adverbs preceded verbs based on the Brown Corpus, and extracted the 100 most frequent adverbs from this set. The adversarials were then created by choosing a random adverb from this list and inserting it before the verb in every sentence of a wrong answer.

For English, we adopt this procedure but for the other languages, we first empirically determined common positions for adverbs as they could differ from English. From the German, French and Spanish generic corpora, we extracted the five most frequent trigrams containing adverbs in the middle position, e.g. (`NOUN, ADV, VERB`).[3] The result is shown in Table 6 in Appendix A. For each language, we determined the 100 most frequent adverbs occurring in these positions. Next, we transformed the extracted POS-trigrams into bigrams by removing the ADV tag. To create the adversarial sentences, we iterate over the POS tags of the answers and, for the first POS-bigram from this list of bigrams that we encounter, add a random adverb from the pool between the two words. After a manual review of the thusly created adversarials, we added an additional rule for German wherein we place adverbs after auxiliary verbs to create more natural-sounding sentences. Note, however, that as with adjectives, we did not check the adversarials for grammatical or semantic correctness, yielding also answers that human raters might find unnatural. In all languages, answers that do not contain verbs or any of the aforementioned POS-bigrams are modified by inserting an adverb at the beginning of the sentence. To get 1,000 adversarial answers per language and prompt, we create different versions of each incorrect answer by inserting a different random adverb.

[3]Tags are taken from the simple UPOS tagset (`https://universaldependencies.org/u/pos/`).

Dataset	Lang.	Prompt		
		1	2	10
ASAP_{orig}	English	.73	.49	.65
$\text{ASAP}_{orig300}$	English	.56	.35	.56
ASAP_{en}	English	.52	.15	.56
ASAP_{de}	German	.54	.49	.55
ASAP_{fr}	French	.68	.67	.59
ASAP_{es}	Spanish	.72	.46	.63

Table 3: Performance of the models based on ten-fold cross-validation on real answers measured in QWK.

4 Scoring Adversarial Answers

We provide a baseline experiment concerning the ability of a baseline scoring model to reject the different kinds of adversarial answers. Ding et al. (2020) used an SVM-based shallow model that was shown to be more robust against adversarials than a neural model, therefore we decided to use a shallow scoring model with a similar setup. Note that the goal of this paper is not to find the best model but rather to gain some insights into the behavior of different kinds of adversarials for different prompts and languages. We train a separate model for each prompt in each dataset. Following Ding et al. (2020), we use an SVM classifier with default kernel and the following features: the top 10,000 character 2-5 grams, the top 10,000 word 1-5 grams, and answer length. Our model is implemented with *scikit-learn* (Pedregosa et al., 2011).

To measure the performance of each model when scoring real answers, we calculate quadratically-weighted kappa (QWK) based on 10-fold cross-validation. QWK is typically used for content scoring as it takes the distance between the gold score and the predicted score into account. The results are given in Table 3, showing some variance between the languages but also between the prompts.

Like Ding et al. (2020), we measure the robustness of a model against adversarial answers with the adversarial rejection rate (ARR): A perfect model should reject every adversarial answer, i.e. assigning a score of 0. This would yield an ARR of 1.0. Every adversarial scored 1 or higher is regarded as not-rejected, i.e. accepted. A model that accepts all adversarials would have an ARR of 0.0, i.e. the higher the score, the better.

Note that for English, we always train three dif-

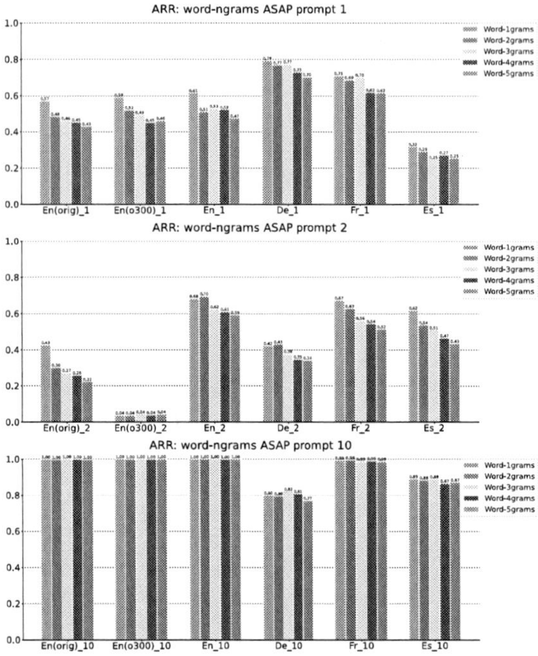

Figure 1: ARRs for the adversarials based on word n-grams from the ASAP corpora.

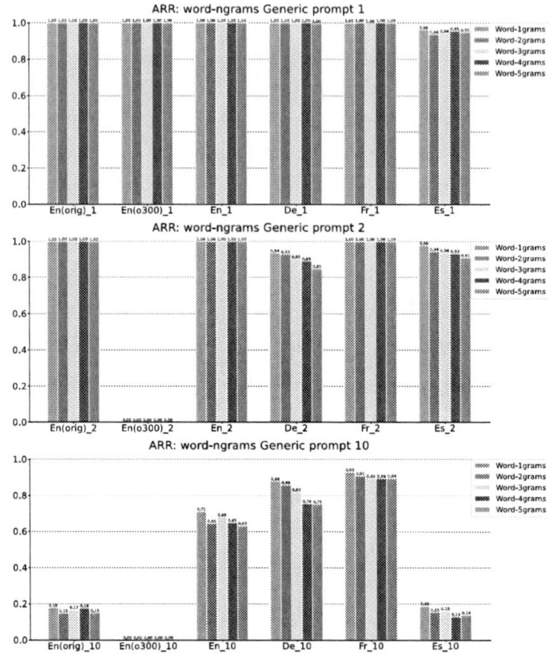

Figure 2: ARRs for the adversarials based on word n-grams from the generic corpora.

ferent models, based on ASAP$_{orig}$, ASAP$_{orig300}$ and ASAP$_{en}$, respectively. This means that for English adversarials that are based on a generic corpus or the prompt material rather than a specific dataset, each model is given the same adversarials and the difference in ARR can be attributed to a difference training material rather than the adversarials. An overview of all results is given in Table 8 in Appendix A.

4.1 Results for Random N-Grams

4.1.1 Word-Based N-Grams

First, we summarize the results for the word-based n-grams shown in Figure 1 (ASAP-based) and Figure 2 (generic). Regarding the **size of *n***, across all prompts and languages, the ARR tends to be highest for the adversarials generated with unigrams and lowest for those generated with 5-grams, which is in line with the results of Ding et al. (2020). The ARR of adversarials generated from the **generic** corpora tends to be higher than that of the **ASAP-based** ones, which is also in line with Ding et al. (2020). Only for prompt 10, we see a different pattern with ASAP-based adversarials being more consistently rejected than generic ones across all languages. Regarding **language**, it is notable that the ARRs of the French adversarials are mostly in the upper range compared to the other languages, especially for the generic adversarials. In contrast, the Spanish adversarials tend to have the lowest ARRs compared to the other languages.

The greatest variance can be seen among the different **prompts**, partly interacting with the language: While for prompt 1, the ARR for the generic adversarials is close to 1.0 for each language and each n, the other prompts behave differently. In prompt 10, ASAP$_{orig}$, ASAP$_{orig300}$, ASAP$_{en}$ and ASAP$_{es}$, have strikingly low ARRs. Especially ASAP$_{orig300}$ sticks out, with all generic adversarial answers being accepted in prompt 10 and all generic as well as most ASAP-based adversarials in prompt 2 (also for character-based n-grams).

To investigate this further, we performed different checks: We first used the adversarials created from ASAP$_{orig300}$ prompt 2 with a scoring model trained on one of the other English datasets, i.e. ASAP$_{orig}$ and ASAP$_{en}$. The system trained on ASAP$_{en}$ yielded an ARR of almost 1.0 for each n. The ARRs for the ASAP$_{orig}$ model were similar to the ones generated from ASAP$_{orig}$, which is expected since ASAP$_{orig300}$ is a subset of ASAP$_{orig}$. From this, we conclude that there is nothing odd with the ASAP$_{orig300}$ adversarials but rather that the scoring model trained on ASAP$_{orig300}$ is in-

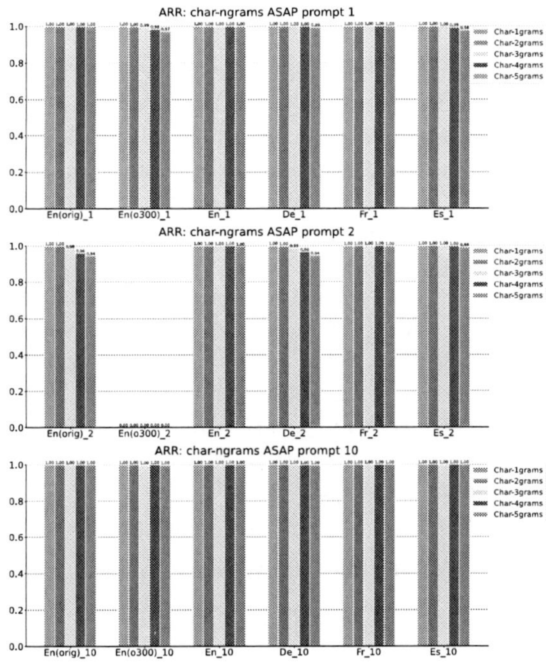

Figure 3: ARRs for the adversarials based on character n-grams from the generic corpora.

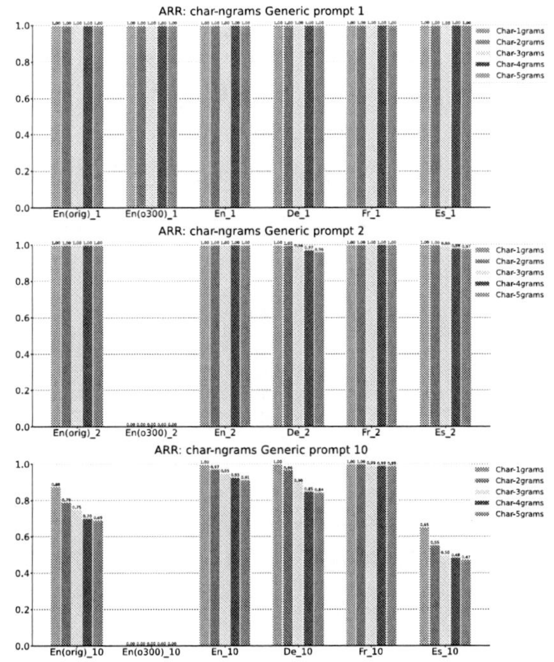

Figure 4: ARRs for the adversarials based on character n-grams from the ASAP corpora.

sufficient. This was confirmed by the following check: We used the German, French and Spanish generic adversarials to calculate the ARR of the model trained on ASAP$_{orig300}$. As the (shallow) model has not seen any of these languages during training, all the answers should clearly be scored 0. While for prompt 1, the ARRs were indeed close to 1.0 as expected, the ARRs for prompt 2 and prompt 10 were all close to 0.0. Hence, the scoring model built from ASAP$_{orig300}$ for these prompts must be insufficient. One possible explanation for this is that the dataset is too skewed, with only 14% and 17% of the answers in ASAP$_{orig300}$ prompt 2 and 10, respectively, having a (gold) score of 0, which may mean that the model built from these prompts failed to learn to detect incorrect answers at all. This is not so much apparent from the aggregated cross-validation performance on real answers (see Table 3) than for the ability to reject adversarial answers and it emphasizes the need to evaluate model performance from different perspectives.

4.1.2 Character-Based N-Grams

For the character-based n-grams the picture is much more homogeneous than for the word-based n-grams with most ARRs being (close to) 1.0 across languages and prompts, see Figure 3 (ASAP-based) and Figure 4 (generic). One notable exception is the ASAP$_{orig300}$ model with an ARR of 0.0 for prompts 2 and 10 already discussed in Section 4.1.1. The other exception are the generic adversarials scored with the models built on prompt 10: Except for French, the ARRs are notably lower than 1.0. The degree differs by language, but the patterns are similar. This suggests that there is something about this prompt that makes the resulting models less robust against (generic) adversarial answers. However, neither the score distribution nor the answer length nor type-token ratio analyzed in Horbach et al. (2023) are strikingly different for this prompt so this would need further investigation in future work.

4.2 Results for Random Prompt Material

4.2.1 Prompt N-Grams

Figure 5 shows the results for the adversarials generated from random n-grams from the prompt material. Regarding the size of *n*, we do not see the same clear pattern as for the generic or ASAP-based n-grams from Section 4.1.1, where the ARRs decreased with increasing *n*: For the prompt-based n-grams, this pattern only occurs for prompt 10. For prompt 2, especially for ASAP$_{fr}$, we even observe the opposite, namely that answers based on

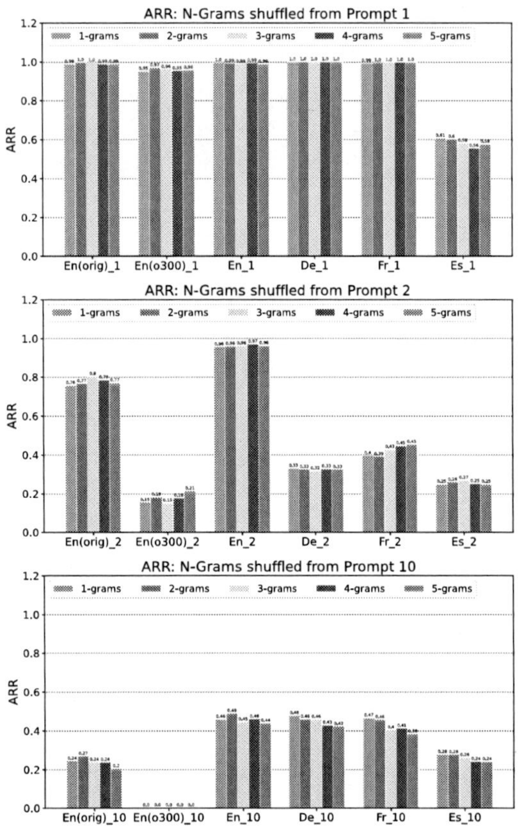

Figure 5: ARRs of adversarials generated from random n-grams taken from the prompt material.

4- or 5-grams are more often rejected than those based on uni- or bigrams. We see that only the ASAP$_{de}$ model for prompt 1 has a perfect ARR of 1.0, i.e. no German adversarial was accepted for any n. In general, we see a clear influence of the prompt, with prompt 1 being the one with the highest ARRs across languages (all $> 90\%$ except ASAP$_{es}$) and prompt 10 the one with the lowest ARRs (no $> 50\%$). For prompt 2, the results differ largely by language. Regarding language, the Spanish models are consistently among the weakest ones. Even in prompt 1, the ARRs are only close to 60%. Here, it is noteworthy that almost all of the accepted Spanish adversarials were even assigned a score of 3, i.e. the highest score. In contrast, the ASAP$_{en}$ models are among the most robust ones across all prompts. We also find again a very weak performance of ASAP$_{orig300}$ for prompts 2 and 10 that was already discussed in Section 4.1.1.

4.2.2 Prompt Nouns

With only random nouns sampled from the prompt rather than n-grams, it was hardly possible to deceive the scoring models. Except for ASAP$_{orig300}$ prompts 2 and 10, where the ARR was again close to 0.0 (see the discussion in Section 4.1.1), the lowest ARRs were 0.985 for ASAP$_{es}$ prompt 10 and 0.988 for ASAP$_{fr}$ prompt 1. But only for German, none of the adversarials was accepted. A total of 13 answers even received a score of 3, i.e. they would have been judged as perfect answers. Recall that the answers generated with this method were considerably shorter than those from the other methods, which might influence the result and would need further investigation.

4.3 Results for Adjectives and Adverbs

4.3.1 Inserting Adjectives

Figure 6 shows the results for adversarials created by the insertion of adjectives into wrong answers. Although our shallow model only uses surface n-grams as features and may not have seen the adjectives during training, these adversarials do indeed fool the model in many cases.

We see that prompt 1 is more robust against these adversarials compared to the other prompts across all datasets. In terms of language, overall, the ASAP$_{fr}$ and ASAP$_{en}$ models are most robust while ASAP$_{orig}$ and ASAP$_{orig300}$ have the lowest ARRs. For ASAP$_{orig}$ this is rather surprising given the large amount of training data and the comparably high QWK values when scoring real answers. The main difference between ASAP$_{en}$ and ASAP$_{orig}$, besides the size, is that ASAP$_{orig}$ was collected from students whereas ASAP$_{en}$ was collected from crowd workers. Potentially, this means that the kind of writing differs. Again, answer length could be an influencing factor, since answers in ASAP$_{orig}$ tend to be longer than answers in ASAP$_{en}$ (Horbach et al., 2023). The fact that the ARRs are lower for ASAP$_{orig}$, where the adjectives fit the grammatical context, than for German, French or Spanish, where adjectives are sometimes wrongly inflected, shows that grammatical correctness is not important for the model. Note also that most of the answers that received a score > 0 were scored with 1 point, but there are also answers that went from originally 0 points to the maximum score.

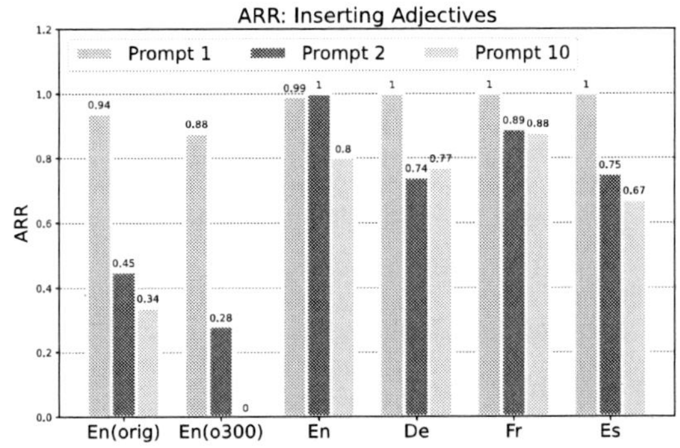

Figure 6: ARRs of adversarials produced by inserting adjectives into wrong answers.

4.3.2 Inserting Adverbs

For the insertion of adverbs, the results show similar patterns as for the insertion of adjectives, see Figure 7: Again, prompt 1 mostly has higher ARRs (all $> 90\%$) than the other prompts for all languages. Furthermore, ASAP$_{orig}$ and ASAP$_{orig300}$ again have the lowest ARRs: While the ARR for all other models stays consistently above 80%, the rejection rate for prompts 2 and 10 in the original student answer corpora ranges only between 0% and 54%. In terms of language differences, the ASAP$_{fr}$ model is again among the most robust models, with ARRs $> 97\%$ for all prompts. However, it is worth noting that for prompts 1 and 2, although the overall rejection rate is close to 1.0, those adversarial answers that were accepted received a score of 3, i.e. the highest score possible. (For prompt 1, all of these adversarials were based on the same student answer but received different adverbs during their creation.) As with adjectives, some adversarial answers would be both syntactically and semantically incorrect but nevertheless be accepted by the system.

Comparing the two insertion methods, adjectives seem to generate answers that more often fool the scoring system than adverbs do. One of the reasons may be that more adjectives are inserted into an answer than adverbs, yielding higher answer lengths. It is possible that the scoring models simply pick up on this (compare the results of Padó et al., 2023). However, while on average, wrong answers are shorter than correct answers in each dataset, there is a high variation within each score (see Horbach et al., 2023). Hence, the interplay of the insertion methods and answer length should be more thoroughly investigated in future work.

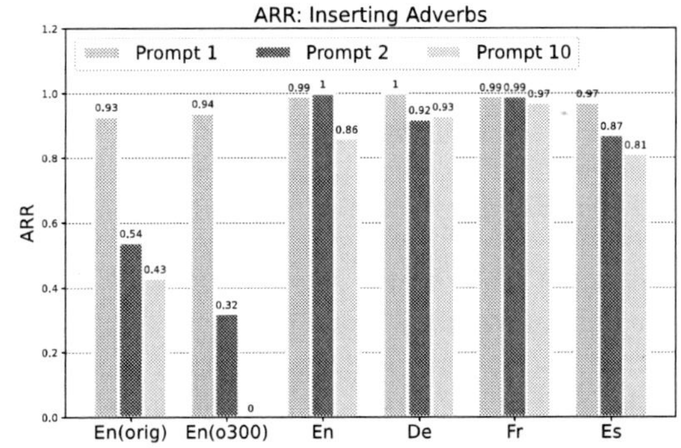

Figure 7: ARRs of adversarials produced by inserting adverbs into wrong answers.

5 Conclusion and Future Work

We presented a multilingual dataset of adversarial answers for English, German, French and Spanish based on the multilingual ASAP content scoring dataset introduced by Horbach et al. (2023). In total, 468,000 adversarial answers were generated following different methods proposed in the literature (Ding et al., 2020; Filighera et al., 2023). In a pilot experiment, we tested the rate at which a baseline classifier rejects the adversarial answers.

While the exact results only reflect the specific classifier that we used, some important general conclusions can be drawn: We saw that a classifier may behave differently depending on the adversarial method used, strongly interacting with language and prompt: For example, for adversarials generated from n-grams sampled from the prompt, the performance of the Spanish ASAP$_{es}$ model is much worse than those of the other languages but only for prompt 1. For the word-based n-grams sampled from the real answers, ASAP$_{es}$ performs much worse on prompt 1 than on prompt 10 but for generic n-grams it is vice versa. Another example is that the English ASAP$_{en}$ model has rather high ARRs across all adversarial methods but for the generic word-based n-grams it is very low but only for prompt 10. We can conclude that in the future, when testing content scoring models for robustness, these complex interplays have to be taken into account and classifiers should be tested against various kinds of adversarial answers and also on various prompts. The dataset we presented here could be used as a benchmark dataset for such endeavors.

In future work, we want to test the behavior of state-of-the art classifiers on the adversarial dataset and more thoroughly analyze the influence of the prompt and features like answer length.

Ethical Considerations

Discussing the ethical implications of developing automatic content scoring systems for real-world scenarios is beyond the scope of this paper. While the aim of the present study is to help detect vulnerabilities of such systems and make them more robust, the insights could also be used maliciously for developing more elaborate methods for cheating purposes. Our adversarial dataset does not include any newly collected data but derives data from already existing corpora and datasets, hence it could inherit biases that may be present in these sources.

Limitations

One clear limitation of this paper is that we draw conclusions from only one content scoring model, which does not produce state-of-the art results when scoring real answers. Other models, especially neural models that do not rely on surface n-grams as features, may behave differently and should be tested in future work. Furthermore, all experiments are based on prompts from the original ASAP-SAS dataset. Other datasets focusing on different kinds of topics and questions are not considered. Finally, our adversarial dataset is not exhaustive in that it (a) only comprises a small set of European languages and (b) only includes a limited number of adversarial methods, whereas more methods are conceivable, e.g. systematically varying the answer length.

References

Steven Bird, Ewan Klein, and Edward Loper. 2009. *Natural Language Processing with Python: Analyzing Text with the Natural Language Toolkit*. O'Reilly Media, Inc.

Yuning Ding, Brian Riordan, Andrea Horbach, Aoife Cahill, and Torsten Zesch. 2020. Don't take "nswvtnvakgxpm" for an answer –The surprising vulnerability of automatic content scoring systems to adversarial input. In *Proceedings of the 28th International Conference on Computational Linguistics*, pages 882–892, Barcelona, Spain (Online). International Committee on Computational Linguistics.

Anna Filighera, Sebastian Ochs, Tim Steuer, and Thomas Tregel. 2023. Cheating Automatic Short Answer Grading with the Adversarial Usage of Adjectives and Adverbs. *International Journal of Artificial Intelligence in Education*.

Dirk Goldhahn, Thomas Eckart, and Uwe Quasthoff. 2012. Building large monolingual dictionaries at the leipzig corpora collection: From 100 to 200 languages. In *Proceedings of the 8th International Language Resources and Evaluation (LREC'12)*, pages 759–765. International Committee on Computational Linguistics.

Matthew Honnibal, Ines Montani, Sofie Van Landeghem, and Adriane Boyd. 2020. spaCy: Industrial-strength Natural Language Processing in Python.

Andrea Horbach, Joey Pehlke, Ronja Laarmann-Quante, and Yuning Ding. 2023. Crosslingual Content Scoring in Five Languages Using Machine-Translation and Multilingual Transformer Models. *International Journal of Artificial Intelligence in Education*.

Henry Kučera and Winthrop Nelson Francis. 1967. *Computational Analysis of Present-day American English*. Brown University Press.

M. Antonia Martí, Mariona Taulé, Lluís Márquez, and Manuel Bertran. 2007. *CESS-Cat Project: CESS-ECE: A Multilingual and Multilevel Annotated Corpus*. Originally available from http://www.lsi.upc.edu/~mbertran/cess-ece/publications.

Ulrike Padó, Yunus Eryilmaz, and Larissa Kirschner. 2023. Short-Answer Grading for German: Addressing the Challenges. *International Journal of Artificial Intelligence in Education*.

F. Pedregosa, G. Varoquaux, A. Gramfort, V. Michel, B. Thirion, O. Grisel, M. Blondel, P. Prettenhofer, R. Weiss, V. Dubourg, J. Vanderplas, A. Passos, D. Cournapeau, M. Brucher, M. Perrot, and E. Duchesnay. 2011. Scikit-learn: Machine learning in Python. *Journal of Machine Learning Research*, 12:2825–2830.

Nico Willms and Ulrike Pado. 2022. A Transformer for SAG: What Does it Grade? In *Proceedings of the 11th Workshop on NLP for Computer Assisted Language Learning*, pages 114–122, Louvain-la-Neuve, Belgium. LiU Electronic Press.

A Appendix

Corpus	Lang.	#Sents.	#Tokens	#Types
Brown	English	57,340	1,161,192	56,057
deu-com web	German	10,000	179,093	32,206
fra-ch web	French	10,000	216,787	29,975
CESS-ESP	Spanish	6,030	192,686	25,464

Table 4: Basic statistics of the generic corpora for each language.

Lang.	Prompt		
	1	2	10
English	87 (22)	95 (25)	168 (32)
German	135 (34)	123 (35)	201 (58)
French	121 (34)	127 (38)	195 (57)
Spanish	82 (19)	95 (25)	163 (30)

Table 5: Number of words in the prompt material for the different languages. The number in brackets refers to the number of nouns.

Lang.	Trigram			Count
German	NOUN	ADV	PUNCT	271
	NOUN	ADV	VERB	270
	ADV	ADV	PUNCT	235
	PRON	ADV	ADV	230
	NOUN	ADV	ADP	227
French	VERB	ADV	ADP	324
	VERB	ADV	DET	274
	AUX	ADV	VERB	230
	NOUN	ADV	VERB	212
	NOUN	ADV	NOUN	202
Spanish	VERB	ADV	ADP	404
	NOUN	ADV	ADJ	333
	NOUN	ADV	VERB	331
	VERB	ADV	DET	267
	NOUN	ADV	AUX	250

Table 6: Top 5 POS-trigrams including adverbs per language based on the generic corpora.

Method		Example
Correct student answer		Based on the student's data, plastic B stretched more. b The students could have improved the experiment by resting the plastics at the same length also by doing more than just two trials using sam. Putting same amount of weight in the type of plastic bag. (score 3)
ASAP Word N-Grams	1	most ways how the the what plastic of highest the been trail consistent stretch the have but could trial time. design that most to much the plastic expirement, this
	2	The stretch the was very average not stretched the plastic type tell us D stretched the strengths to add plastic type Based on a few 50% 3.a. allowed the
	3	This to stretch because the same length in both trials The conclusion I conclude that plastic flexible as it In conclusion plastic two ways: The it to the the weights were,
	4	a. Plastic experiment D have the before it stratched. the two tries. this data and the mm it stretched in used three kinds of should improve the experiment type B is the
	5	3 trials are always in the starting length of ability to stretch was plastic the most weight, without stretching. they were the same length can conclude that plastic type
Generic Word N-Grams	1	separators what have one School have Zeising, posts District Democrats wilderness in Vikings Mantle are committee more the from non-profit the Faced you teeth. Grapefruit well is The The a Karen,
	2	plane to hopes to Central Catholic The go-go-go without after information how this crowding horses what to volunteered an has brought and Mrs. high-sounding titles When bouncy show received a to work. (*)
	3	Suddenly also have to in 1885 concluded terminate special sessions The United average. years a slave to Mantle is the Atlanta area Cotten construed might allow the to go up about who said
	4	said. Bursts him, was retracted before On the last March, a mighty primary and the fall bit lost at least four-year terms will expire law could not suspend among Democratic district leaders (*)
	5	the state. The from Texas A& I College a peak this year, came an expanding share of the proposal modest $8,250 to provide Christmas gifts vehicle traffic on Eddy Street " to have these laws
ASAP Char N-Grams	1	h2hrth ttis os tma lsb he hste a Tu. ha tbft sud hoeds ao otnuf Btiic is. te t. v xorel gt oce atp Ihe Hhse d Pwwe aob hlyo fn pi , atl edd anc spsv og vnltm trrtle 2o)e chwi wa elu afite itss mo as trut ot nebtsa llf ols tne eayer tr eac h Apcyr asda ha
	2	TananM t. tiro tsefi ckehe hehty pal of st igf ingri asntl eud deea er Ac he hedtpM be rir eesm eh2 co ic as T2veh e Anve hecst ild rofpos sho te desl dlat sss os thas exs tcts tono uvamm plls tcld hei s Awr sypt utcI tpl clca we et inbyns igm aueti
	3	Ils testt heei guttem eestch te su ro vpe rnto Alhe oa yst resti rim, plla sistnd iexp tco chafon tdu cs Ati cra le ise igan dsti st td atheu ng sat cali ches could tthdh aft h Fro rese ta cs showb . Otc hnd2ul dterto nyreed ob es Twl dbis tnc l
	4	Tmost sedb ndpedb eture oic tywe igret cprovg usth ertu ldbh etyde nt lasts edt ype Agt h, nc lu heycve imicp ou ldbw eigste dcw eiex pe sticex peorei tud ewhat edthla sto uplthe emproh efohe rea tatth ei chths, bestic plas ia lsig nin oftt af o
	5	Ifhave aperim used. sthatt retcme to fu nto fo, in sargr ay mo rei mental de sofpla efore ictyp untof there rialsa 3rdts tthet ingte Dplald havges toepl asm to13 nthovf th efretc het heps ts tro wing Ty peB d23mm lastis wast dt heswhi ch opemu
Generic Char N-Grams	1	: ewto . t aneape lnhrcs apeaoae geef wnnttdu eyes cg roniooe nanms trraer ynn aaren Mnhah eey8ryn rni. sns (*)
	2	Tonn tedolli ioe Ia yme Ola eeinxp th nd, ssc thttone bh1re unrcti il as leisw he s: 5nuhe ate d Amalhe ms y. l. at ats eof asa se Hseso edi tse Mailnd otiers veftg rm istna in tr' 'tsU dmalP ltte Du tolsr pe'. ma itrig hlmua -ht al tu tuprefi 3, tse aym ngreto hai nldc aB . o rami t Tholno
	3	PofarL anyl e Coin1a vear k Mindov er ott hurihem tinspe wil"d ea anad edalol evckti npneecl ahel Whi guy pi cdo ze Cawo -a tir daendP riB lupuras swhohe f Ad mher pla ibltwa orb kslint vicuca nee tob thef irbroic aewa dere codedon gray atn Pen ted (*)
	4	Bipinv erc iceo tw itse, Piveta reeke thd sligr ouispl t, bosi tya tor, i fa ve rsfl amt he Ssf in Aru nr th ahamp nghergu eo rac tywi tfalemo reby hiontti onin th Misi onf lcondam epin g', he lkert o8pelv eo ratpita e Na titthe la trgemel dtmal dte19dS ouytoms ary er ste. (*)
	5	ff erege tp etor ea er cones ev easemie sneapla ceerth eri ve w Secr estartl ttobo vert and Bead esi atio nons lir Ti bea consht fou hers mh erdaon ledsco nt ajor -s pro cntendn cingi ngalkwa sde Un ivM artir, altsuna nhata less , sesda yere cotly pu Th eye cni ca tsay sver y1t hemi 20intei gnf (*)

Table 7: Examples of a correct student answer and generated adversarials for each method for prompt 2 of the original ASAP-SAS corpus. All adversarial answers, except for the ones marked with (*), were given at least a score of 1 based on the $ASAP_{orig}$ or $ASAP_{orig300}$ model. (Table continued on next page)

Method		Example
Prompt N-Grams	1	student's the the side a remove the five of and plastic the like freely on of allow and experimental one the and/or have and down table on following ways and/or
	2	the procedure student's data remaining three following investigation clamp to of the its length the following is hanging hanging freely type of from the edge of length tape ways the types repeat one type bottom edge the clamp student recorded the student validity of of plastic the experimental length tape student recorded
	3	for five minutes different polymer plastics a second trial student recorded the table so that of one type the student recorded exactly like the measure the length take a sample stretchability procedure take have improved the different polymer plastics could have improved
	4	student recorded the following to test four different have improved the experimental the length of the side of the table and/or validity of the the plastic types repeat recorded the following data them to hang for performed the following investigation improved the experimental design to the bottom edge to the bottom edge
	5	for stretchability procedure take a and/or validity of the results of the table attach a clamp to the bottom edge exactly for the remaining three remaining three plastic samples perform the length of the plastic of the plastic types repeat the top edge of the
Prompt Nouns		minutes procedure student plastics ways validity
Inserting Adjectives		Based on the **physical** student 's **right** data , **similar** plastic **southern** D stretched the same **common** length for both **christian** trials . Two **red** ways the **last** student could have improved the experimental **fine** design would be to on the **central** data **little** table , say how long each **last** type of **complete** plastic is before the **american** student started the **normal** experiment . Another **central** way the **high** student could of improved the experimental **open** design would be to have done only one **nuclear** trial instead of two.
Inserting Adverbs		**certainly** To improve this experiment the student should have mentioned the 4 different types of plastic if mentioned , it would give a more accurate reason as why one type of plastic is more / less stretchable than the other . [...]

Table 7: (continued) Examples of a correct student answer and generated adversarials for each method for prompt 2 of the original ASAP-SAS corpus. All adversarial answers, except for the ones marked with (*), were given at least a score of 1 based on the $ASAP_{orig}$ or $ASAP_{orig300}$ model.

Method	English (orig) Prompt			English (orig300) Prompt			English (en) Prompt			German (de) Prompt			French (fr) Prompt			Spanish (es) Prompt		
	1	2	10	1	2	10	1	2	10	1	2	10	1	2	10	1	2	10
ASAP Word 1-grams	0.57	0.427	0.998	0.591	0.037	1.0	0.614	0.683	0.999	0.793	0.423	0.8	0.71	0.673	0.993	0.317	0.618	0.891
ASAP Word 2-grams	0.484	0.303	0.997	0.519	0.037	0.999	0.51	0.696	1.0	0.768	0.431	0.796	0.688	0.628	0.995	0.291	0.537	0.884
ASAP Word 3-grams	0.46	0.274	1.0	0.492	0.042	1.0	0.528	0.625	1.0	0.774	0.379	0.821	0.701	0.562	0.987	0.246	0.509	0.89
ASAP Word 4-grams	0.452	0.26	0.999	0.45	0.039	0.999	0.522	0.611	0.999	0.73	0.349	0.809	0.618	0.544	0.99	0.272	0.465	0.866
ASAP Word 5-grams	0.429	0.224	0.997	0.461	0.043	1.0	0.473	0.593	1.0	0.704	0.343	0.771	0.617	0.515	0.987	0.254	0.435	0.871
Generic Word 1-grams	1.0	0.998	0.178	1.0	0.0	0.0	1.0	1.0	0.711	1.0	0.935	0.878	0.999	1.0	0.93	0.962	0.978	0.189
Generic Word 2-grams	1.0	1.0	0.148	1.0	0.0	0.0	1.0	1.0	0.645	1.0	0.929	0.858	1.0	1.0	0.909	0.936	0.944	0.154
Generic Word 3-grams	1.0	0.999	0.167	1.0	0.0	0.0	1.0	1.0	0.68	1.0	0.9	0.819	0.997	0.999	0.894	0.942	0.938	0.162
Generic Word 4-grams	1.0	1.0	0.176	1.0	0.0	0.0	1.0	1.0	0.65	1.0	0.889	0.755	1.0	0.999	0.894	0.954	0.933	0.129
Generic Word 5-grams	1.0	0.998	0.149	1.0	0.0	0.0	1.0	1.0	0.633	0.996	0.848	0.752	1.0	0.999	0.895	0.948	0.91	0.139
ASAP Char 1-grams	1.0	0.999	1.0	1.0	0.0	1.0	1.0	1.0	1.0	1.0	1.0	1.0	1.0	1.0	1.0	1.0	1.0	1.0
ASAP Char 2-grams	1.0	0.999	1.0	0.997	0.0	1.0	1.0	1.0	1.0	1.0	0.997	1.0	1.0	1.0	1.0	1.0	1.0	1.0
ASAP Char 3-grams	1.0	0.982	1.0	0.994	0.0	0.998	1.0	0.999	1.0	0.999	0.983	1.0	1.0	1.0	1.0	0.997	1.0	1.0
ASAP Char 4-grams	1.0	0.954	1.0	0.984	0.0	0.999	1.0	1.0	1.0	0.999	0.964	0.998	1.0	0.999	1.0	0.994	0.998	1.0
ASAP Char 5-grams	0.999	0.938	1.0	0.972	0.0	0.998	1.0	0.996	1.0	0.994	0.942	0.999	0.999	0.998	1.0	0.977	0.99	1.0
Generic Char 1-grams	1.0	1.0	0.889	1.0	0.0	0.0	1.0	1.0	0.998	1.0	1.0	0.998	1.0	1.0	0.999	1.0	1.0	0.653
Generic Char 2-grams	1.0	0.999	0.795	1.0	0.0	0.0	1.0	1.0	0.97	1.0	0.996	0.956	1.0	1.0	0.999	0.999	0.997	0.553
Generic Char 3-grams	1.0	1.0	0.754	1.0	0.0	0.0	1.0	1.0	0.945	1.0	0.98	0.893	1.0	1.0	0.992	0.997	0.993	0.5
Generic Char 4-grams	1.0	1.0	0.711	1.0	0.0	0.0	1.0	1.0	0.92	1.0	0.969	0.847	1.0	1.0	0.99	1.0	0.979	0.489
Generic Char 5-grams	1.0	1.0	0.695	1.0	0.0	0.0	1.0	1.0	0.907	1.0	0.954	0.844	1.0	1.0	0.991	0.999	0.973	0.475
Prompt 1-grams	0.988	0.757	0.244	0.952	0.154	0.001	0.996	0.957	0.459	1.0	0.331	0.478	0.993	0.396	0.466	0.607	0.249	0.278
Prompt 2-grams	0.997	0.766	0.269	0.97	0.183	0.002	0.992	0.96	0.489	1.0	0.325	0.459	0.996	0.391	0.457	0.602	0.259	0.277
Prompt 3-grams	0.996	0.803	0.238	0.961	0.151	0.001	0.989	0.962	0.445	1.0	0.317	0.458	0.997	0.428	0.404	0.581	0.269	0.262
Prompt 4-grams	0.989	0.785	0.238	0.954	0.177	0.001	0.994	0.971	0.46	1.0	0.328	0.428	0.998	0.447	0.412	0.555	0.252	0.241
Prompt 5-grams	0.989	0.77	0.205	0.958	0.214	0.001	0.988	0.963	0.439	1.0	0.325	0.422	0.998	0.454	0.383	0.576	0.249	0.241
Prompt Nouns	0.995	1.0	0.998	1.0	0.01	0.0	0.999	1.0	0.998	1.0	1.0	1.0	0.99	1.0	1.0	1.0	1.0	0.989
Inserting Adjectives	0.941	0.448	0.336	0.884	0.276	0.0	0.99	1.0	0.797	1.0	0.736	0.767	1.0	0.89	0.876	0.999	0.751	0.669
Inserting Adverbs	0.929	0.535	0.43	0.939	0.319	0.0	0.994	1.0	0.859	1.0	0.912	0.93	0.992	0.986	0.974	0.975	0.874	0.808

Table 8: Adversarial Rejection Rate (ARR) for each model for each adversarial method.

Towards Improving ASR Outputs of Spontaneous Speech with LLMs

Manuel Karner[1], Julian Linke[2], Mark Kröll[1], Barbara Schuppler[2], Bernhard C. Geiger[1,2]

[1]Know-Center GmbH, Sandgasse 34, 8010 Graz, Austria,
[2]Signal Processing and Speech Communication Laboratory,
Graz University of Technology, Inffeldgasse 16c, 8010 Graz, Austria

Correspondence: geiger@ieee.org

Abstract

This paper presents ongoing work towards an initial understanding of how large language models (LLMs) can assist automatic speech recognition (ASR) tasks. More concretely, we investigate if LLMs can improve hypotheses obtained from ASR systems, and if so, which patterns in the hypothesis allow for a correction. Our results show that LLMs can mainly correct syntax errors or errors caused by ASR systems splitting long words. We further find that in the majority of cases the word error rates with respect to the human annotation increase when an LLM is applied, while the semantic similarity with the human annotation improves.

1 Introduction

As artificial intelligence continues permeating our lives, reliable performance of automatic speech recognition (ASR) of conversational and spontaneous speech becomes more and more important as an enabler for natural conversations with social robots and automatic meeting transcripts, among other things. While ASR systems now achieve human-level performance for read or prepared speech (Szymański et al., 2020a), for which multiple benchmark datasets are available (Librispeech (Panayotov et al., 2015), Common Voice (Ardila et al., 2020), Multilingual Librispeech (Pratap et al., 2020)), ASR performance is still unsatisfactory for spontaneous speech. This is particularly true for face-to-face conversations of less-resourced languages, where word error rates (WERs) of 21.0-16.3% for Hungarian (Mihajlik et al., 2023, 2024) and up to 35.71% to 16.09% for Austrian German (Linke et al., 2022) are common.

Modern ASR systems like wav2vec (Baevski et al., 2020) or Whisper (Radford et al., 2023) rely on transformer architectures and often achieve excellent performance on read speech without requiring an explicit, powerful language model (LM). Indeed, common implementations of wav2vec contain only a simple n-gram LM. At the same time, large LMs (LLMs) have shown impressive performance on a variety of natural language tasks. Llama2 was even shown to be capable of ASR, if it is provided with embeddings of the acoustic signal (Fathullah et al., 2024).

In this paper, we investigate if LLMs can be used to correct errors in ASR outputs (Section 3) and which error patterns are easiest to correct (Section 4). Since we find that WERs are insufficient to fully evaluate original and corrected ASR outputs, we also analyze how the semantic similarity to the ground truth changes if an LLM is applied. In the future, we will incorporate LLMs into ASR systems based on the results presented here, aiming at coupling the power of LLMs with the acoustic signal available to the ASR system (cf. discussion in Section 5).

2 GRASS corpus and ASR systems

The experiments of this paper are based on data from the Graz Corpus of Read and Spontaneous Speech (GRASS) (Schuppler et al., 2014, 2017). More concretely, we used the conversational speech component of GRASS, which contains one hour long conversations from 19 pairs of speakers, summing up a total of 220.000 word tokens. Since the speakers knew each other well prior to the recordings and since they chatted with each other without topic instruction and without any experimenter in the recording room throughout the whole conversation, the speaking style of GRASS is highly spontaneous and casual compared to other data sets used in speech technology (Linke et al., 2023). Its challenging characteristics for ASR are the high degree of pronunciation variation and dialectal pronunciation, the highly varying speech rate, and the highly frequent occurrence of broken words, fillers, incomplete and/or grammatically wrong

p1	I will give you a part of an Austrian German sentence. Please correct it for me.
p2	I will give you a part of a german sentence. Please correct it for me but preserve austrian dialect.
p3	I had to write down this text in austrian german I heard, but it could be that excactly one word is wrong.
p4	I had to write down this Austrian German text I heard, but there could be one or two errors in it. I need your help to correct it. I will provide you the text and you approach the problem step by step. First check if the sentence is grammatically correct. Secondly decide which word is probably wrong, in rare cases there could be two wrong words. Thirdly exchange the wrong word with what you think is the right word and would make the sentence grammatically correct.
p5	I have to write down a sequence of Austrian words I listened to, but there are some problems with it. Since my hearing is bad it could be that I split a long word like "holzbungalows" into two smaller words that sound similar together like "halt" and "pomelos". I make other errors too, often they are grammar related. Therefore, I need your help to correct my mistakes.
p6	I have a part of a sentence in austrian german but it is grammatically incorrect. I need your help to improve it but there are three problems with it. The principal part of every word could be wrong, a word could be missing and in rare cases you have to delete a certain word. Do the best you can to form a grammatically correct sequence of words while preserving anything that you think is true.

Table 1: Prompts that were investigated in our experiments. We only report results for base prompts p1, p4, p5.

utterance structures, laughter and non-lexical tokens. Moreover, the lively turn-taking dynamics result in disrupted turns, overlapping speech, one-word-utterances (e.g., *hmh, ja, sicher*) and overall shorter utterances than for instance in spontaneous interviews. We use GRASS as an example for a database that 1) contains speech from a language variety that is low-resourced, and 2) for a speaking style that is highly casual and spontaneous, both posing (different types of) challenges to ASR systems. Reason to use GRASS for this study is not only to improve WER, but also to gain insights with respect to how an LLM in general deals with disfluent and even grammatically wrong structures that are highly frequent in GRASS.

Here, we compare ASR results for GRASS from four ASR systems comprising Whisper (Radford et al., 2023), Kaldi (Povey et al., 2011), and wav2vec2 (Baevski et al., 2020) with and without a lexicon and LM (w2v/w2vLM). For all experiments, we excluded utterances containing laughter, singing, imitations/onomatopoeia, unintelligible word tokens, and artefacts leading to 33734 utterances (14.4h).

Training/fine-tuning these ASR systems as described in Appendix C, we achieved similar conversation-dependent WERs with high-resourced zero-shot Whisper (41.78% $\pm$ 8.23%) and low-resourced Kaldi (42.86% $\pm$ 4.78%), while best WERs were achieved with the fine-tuned w2v (29.81% $\pm$ 4.80%) and w2vLM (22.79% $\pm$ 4.02%). Interestingly, mean WERs with Whisper were worst for utterances including only two word tokens (approx. 55%) but decreased for utterances with more word tokens (mean WER was approx. 30% for utterances with 15 word tokens).

3 Approach

We are interested in whether and to what extent generative capabilities of LLMs can be utilized to correct hypotheses obtained from ASR systems. As we are analyzing German utterances, we opted for a recent version of SauerkrautLM specifically fine-tuned for the German-speaking region as well as aligned to human preferences by direct preference optimization (Rafailov et al., 2023). The SauerkrautLM-Mixtral-8x7B-Instruct model, optimized to follow instruction-based prompting, is a Mixture of Experts model with the foundational model being Mixtral-8x7B-Instruct[1]. Each of the 8 experts is using the Mistral-7B architecture; resource efficiency was achieved by using a quantized variant of the LLM, i.e., `gptq-4bit-32g-actorder_True`.

Effective prompt engineering remains an open research challenge (Gonen et al., 2022). LLM outputs can vary significantly and unpredictably, for instance, depending on choice (Zhang et al., 2022) as well as on ordering (Lu et al., 2022) of (in-context) examples.

Informed by best practices from the literature, we initially designed six instruction base prompts (BP) from which we selected three for our experiments (see Table 1). Prompt p1 only emphasizes that GRASS contains Austrian German. Prompt p4 was inspired by (Zhang et al., 2023), where the authors recommended to add the phrase "Let´s think step by step" to "facilitate the reasoning chains in LLMs". Prompt p5 emphasizes an error pattern we named "long word splitting error" (cf. Observation 1 in Section 4). A typical example of this would be that the ASR system splits the word "*erzähle*" into the words "*er*" and "*zählt*". The three omitted prompts were either redundant or suffered from performance issues. For example, the omitted prompt p2 used the wording "preserve Austrian dialect" instead of "Austrian German" (hence is redundant) and yielded worse corrections than p1.

[1]Model Card: `https://huggingface.co/VAGOsolutions/SauerkrautLM-Mixtral-8x7B-Instruct` last accessed: 19.7.2024

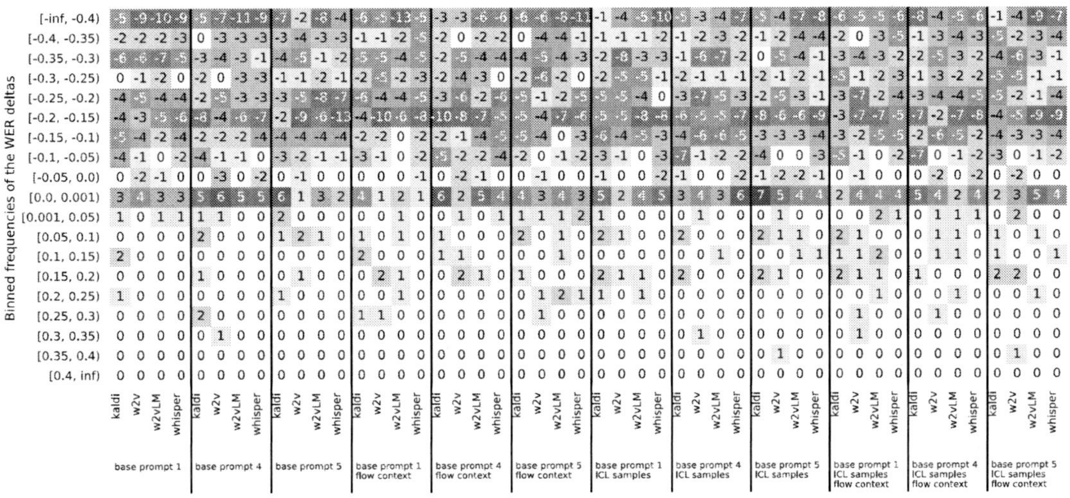

Figure 1: Effect of LLM corrections (instructed by 12 prompt combinations) on outputs of four ASR systems: Binned differences (deltas) are illustrated between the WERs of ASR hypotheses and the WERs of 1776 LLM corrections (4*12*37 = #ASR models * #experiments * baseline dataset size). Negative differences (counts in red) indicate a WER increase - positive differences (counts in blue) indicate a WER decrease.

We provided the LLM with two types of context. Flow Context (FC) represents short-term information dependencies from the conversation flow, i.e. the last 350 characters before the hypothesis to be corrected. In-Context Learning (ICL) leverages the ability of the LLM to learn from task demonstrations without fine-tuning the model. Thus, SauerkrautLM was provided with four hypothesis/reference pairs to better understand the correction task. Those were matched to the source of the input utterance, to incorporate the differences of the four ASR systems, i.e. in how they apply substitution, deletion, and insertion operations. While most of these differences are too subtle and diverse for a proper qualitative analysis, we noticed that Whisper sometimes keeps >70% of the letters in the correct order if it substitutes a word.

Combinations of three BPs with either FC, ICL, or both, led to a total of 12 experiments. Figure 2 in Appendix C shows an example for one full prompt used in the experiments including a system prompt, base prompt p1, FC, and one input utterance.

4 Results

After an initial data analysis and a preliminary experimental phase, one conversation from the GRASS corpus was selected to test how LLMs respond to different kinds of inputs. From this conversation, a baseline dataset (Table 4) was built, consisting of 37 utterances that 1.) contain at least three words, 2.) lead to (mostly) wrong ASR hypotheses, and 3.) appear to be improvable by a human. While the third criterion is quite subjective, we differentiated between utterances that probably contain enough information (within themselves and/or within the FC) to be improvable and those utterance for which a human correction would certainly not be possible with a high confidence. For a detailed explanation and examples on this matter we refer to the Appendix C.4.

Figure 1 shows differences between the WERs of the ASR hypotheses and the LLM corrections. These differences are binned into WER ranges and counted; each column represents resulting WER differences for the 37 utterances in the baseline dataset. Negative differences (counts in red) indicate a WER increase - positive differences (counts in blue) indicate a WER decrease. As a general result, WERs rather increased for the majority of considered utterances, independent of prompts, the amount of provided context, or the ASR system that generated the hypotheses. Notably, some hypotheses were amenable to correction by the LLM's inherent language understanding capabilities. In the remainder, we will analyze these utterances in detail to better understand under which circumstances LLMs can contribute to correcting ASR outputs. The results look qualitatively similar for independent execution of the chosen prompts and even when using a different LLM. To allow for

Index	Reference	ASR Hypothesis	LLM Correction	WER		Similarity	
				ASR	LLM	ASR	LLM
1.1	sich was einprägen und auswendig lernen	sich was einprägen und auswenn die lernen	sich etwas einprägen und auswendig l	0.29	0.33	0.90	0.93
1.2	sich was einprägen und auswendig lernen	sich was einprägen und aus wenn die lernen	sich etwas einprägen und es auswendig lern	0.38	0.43	0.89	0.98
2	und es verschickt natürlich automatisch	und es war schickt natürlich automatisch	und es wäre natürlich automatisch	0.33	0.2	0.79	0.70
3	und danach ist er scheinbar irgendwie	und dann nach ist er schon immer irgendwie	und dann ist er danach irgendwie gewesen	0.5	0.43	0.79	0.89
4	wenn_du jetzt einen fehler machst beim eingeben	wenn du jetzt einen fehler machst beim einsteigen	wenn du nun bei der eingabe einen fehler	0.38	1.0	0.76	0.90
5	die haben im hafen irgendein anderes boot	die haben im hafen irgendein anderes bus	die haben im hafen ein anderes schiff	0.14	0.29	0.68	0.89
6	sogar mitten in der nacht am hafen unten	sogar mitten in der nacht am haufen unten	sogar mitten in der nacht am hafen unten	0.12	0.0	0.90	1.0
7	zu ihrer verteidigung nur der kapitän hat eine schusswaffe falls piraten	zu ihrer verteidigung hat der kapitän eine schusswaffe falls es möglich ist	zu ihrer verteidigung hatte der kapitän eine schusswaffe falls nötig	0.38	0.27	0.90	0.89
8	ja ich frage mich auch immer	ja ich frag mich auch immer	ja ich frage mich auch immer	0.17	0.0	0.99	1.0
9	so wie die dort hausen	so wie die dort hause	so wie die dort hausen	0.2	0.0	0.94	1.0
10	das schiff zu entern	der schiff zu entscheiden	das schiff zu ents	0.5	0.25	0.77	0.82

Table 2: Experiments showing the effect of LLMs on ASR outputs. We refer to Observations 1 - 4 for more details on used prompts as well as respective ASR systems.

another perspective, we introduce the semantic similarity between reference and ASR hypothesis as well as reference and LLM correction as additional metric. The similarity values are calculated by first creating embedding vectors using `German_Semantic_STS_V2 model`[2], followed by calculating the cosine similarity. In Table 2, we illustrate selected utterances, the WERs as well as the semantic similarities before and after correction with LLMs. While the WERs in many cases increase, so does the semantic similarity (see Figure 3 in Appendix C for a heatmap similar to Figure 1, but with a focus on semantic similarity).

Observation 1: ASR Systems Split Long Words (Index 1-3). All ASR systems except Whisper tend to split long words. Since Kaldi and w2v (idx 1.1) often introduce syntactic errors into the split words, these errors are easier to correct, in comparison to w2vLM (idx 1.2) which only produces correct syntax. For w2vLM, this "long word splitting error" increases the number of words in the utterance, which makes correction even harder. This can lead to cases where the WER improves but the semantic overlap decreases (idx 2), or to different wordings with correct semantics (idx 3)

Observation 2: Relevance of FC (Index 4-7). Providing conversational context (FC) can lead to situations where the LLM output is semantically closer to the reference. While in some cases this also leads to fewer word errors (idx 6, idx 7), sometimes the WER increases for the sake of correcting the semantics of the hypotheses (idx 4, idx 5). Referring to Figure 1, FC had this positive effect in only approx. half of the used prompts.

Observation 3: Syntax Errors Are Easy to Correct (Index 8-10). As expected, syntax errors in the hypotheses produced by Kaldi and w2v are easily corrected by the LLM (idx 8, 9). The same holds for wrong articles (idx 10). These types of errors are corrected quite reliably (in our small set of experiments), which suggests a direction for future prompt engineering efforts.

Observation 4: Whisper is Rarely Corrected. SauerkrautLM almost never improved hypotheses resulting from Whisper. The main reason behind this is that our dataset consists mainly of (comparably) long utterances, and we can observe that for Whisper the WERs decrease with utterance length.

5 Discussion and Outlook

Our attempts at correcting ASR hypotheses with LLMs led us to rethink what it means to "correct ASR output". The main goal of an ASR system might depend on the application scenario: (i) it could be to transcribe a conversation as accurately as possible (e.g., in case of court protocols), or (ii) it could be to summarize the content of a conversation in a comprehensive, inclusive way (e.g., in case of meeting minutes). This appears to be highly relevant for setting up the ASR framework with respect to LLM selection as well as prompt engineering. To give an example, the German verb *"frag"* (idx 8 in Table 2) may be adequate for one, but inadequate for another scenario. This directly relates to the used metric to evaluate ASR outputs. WER as a metric may be inappropriate in certain scenarios

[2]Model card: `https://huggingface.co/aari1995/German_Semantic_STS_V2` last accessed: 19.7.2024

(and indeed, WER has often been criticized in the literature (Aksënova et al., 2021; Szymański et al., 2020b; Wang et al., 2003)). For these other scenarios, utilizing semantic similarity as metric might be better suited as it generally measures whether an output shares more (idx 4) or less (idx 2) meaning with the reference.

Our preliminary analyses indicate that LLMs may indeed be capable of improving certain error patterns in ASR outputs (such as syntax errors or errors due to long words being split). While the results of these analyses still must be reproduced using a larger variety of prompts and confirmed with statistical tests, we take the liberty to reflect on promising directions for future work. On the one hand, targeting only specific error patterns could lead to more stable corrections, by using Chain of Thought (Wei et al., 2022) or even Tree of Thought (Yao et al., 2023) based prompting. On the other hand, in our current implementation, LLMs attempt to correct ASR hypotheses without taking into account the speech signal, i.e. decoupling acoustics from text. Ignoring this important piece of information may be one of the reasons behind the sub-par performance exhibited in Figure 1. Having shown that LLMs can nevertheless improve ASR outputs in some cases suggests that including LLMs in ASR systems, thus coupling acoustic and language models, is a promising approach for automatic recognition of conversational speech. Conducting respective experiments, especially with longer hypotheses for which LLMs should be most useful, is within the scope of future work.

Acknowledgments

The work by M. Karner and B. C. Geiger was funded by grant P-32700 from the Austrian Science Fund.

References

Alëna Aksënova, Daan van Esch, James Flynn, and Pavel Golik. 2021. How might we create better benchmarks for speech recognition? In *Proceedings of the 1st Workshop on Benchmarking: Past, Present and Future*, pages 22–34. Association for Computational Linguistics.

Rosana Ardila, Megan Branson, Kelly Davis, Michael Kohler, Josh Meyer, Michael Henretty, Reuben Morais, Lindsay Saunders, Francis Tyers, and Gregor Weber. 2020. Common voice: A massively-multilingual speech corpus. In *Proc. of the 12th Language Resources and Evaluation Conference*, pages 4218–4222.

Alexei Baevski, Yuhao Zhou, Abdelrahman Mohamed, and Michael Auli. 2020. wav2vec 2.0: A framework for self-supervised learning of speech representations. In *Advances in Neural Information Processing Systems*, volume 33, pages 12449–12460.

Alexis Conneau, Alexei Baevski, Ronan Collobert, Abdelrahman Mohamed, and Michael Auli. 2021. Unsupervised Cross-Lingual Representation Learning for Speech Recognition. In *Proc. Interspeech 2021*, pages 2426–2430.

Facebook Research. 2022. Fairseq Model (XLSR). `https://github.com/facebookresearch/fairseq/tree/main/examples/wav2vec`. Last Accessed: 2024-03-05.

Yassir Fathullah, Chunyang Wu, Egor Lakomkin, Junteng Jia, Yuan Shangguan, Ke Li, Jinxi Guo, Wenhan Xiong, Jay Mahadeokar, Ozlem Kalinli, Christian Fuegen, and Mike Seltzer. 2024. Prompting large language models with speech recognition abilities. In *Proc. IEEE Int. Conf. on Acoustics, Speech and Signal Processing (ICASSP)*, pages 13351–13355.

Hila Gonen, Srini Iyer, Terra Blevins, Noah A Smith, and Luke Zettlemoyer. 2022. Demystifying prompts in language models via perplexity estimation. *arXiv preprint arXiv:2212.04037*.

Alex Graves, Santiago Fernández, Faustino Gomez, and Jürgen Schmidhuber. 2006. Connectionist temporal classification: labelling unsegmented sequence data with recurrent neural networks. In *Proceedings of the 23rd International Conference on Machine Learning*, ICML '06, page 369–376.

Kenneth Heafield. 2011. KenLM: Faster and smaller language model queries. In *Proceedings of the Sixth Workshop on Statistical Machine Translation*, pages 187–197.

Tom Ko, Vijayaditya Peddinti, Daniel Povey, and Sanjeev Khudanpur. 2015. Audio augmentation for speech recognition. In *Proc. Interspeech 2015*, pages 3586–3589.

Julian Linke, Philip N. Garner, Gernot Kubin, and Barbara Schuppler. 2022. Conversational speech recognition needs data? Experiments with Austrian German. In *Proc. of the 13th Language Resources and Evaluation Conference*, pages 4684–4691.

Julian Linke, Saskia Wepner, Gernot Kubin, and Barbara Schuppler. 2023. Using Kaldi for Automatic Speech Recognition of Conversational Austrian German. *arXiv preprint arXiv:2301.06475*.

Yao Lu, Max Bartolo, Alastair Moore, Sebastian Riedel, and Pontus Stenetorp. 2022. Fantastically ordered prompts and where to find them: Overcoming few-shot prompt order sensitivity. In *Proceedings of the 60th Annual Meeting of the Association for Computational Linguistics*, pages 8086–8098.

Péter Mihajlik, Máté Soma Kádár, Gergely Dobsinszki, Yan Meng, Meng Kedalai, Julian Linke, Tibor Fegyó, and Katalin Mády. 2023. What kind of multi- or cross-lingual pre-training is the most effective for a spontaneous, less-resourced asr task? *2nd Annual Meeting of the ELRA/ISCA SIG on Under-resourced Languages (SIGUL 2023).*

Péter Mihajlik, Yan Meng, Máté Soma Kádár, Julian Linke, Barbara Schuppler, and Katalin Mády. 2024. The Microsoft 2017 conversational speech recognition system. In *Accepted for presentation at Interspeech 2024.*

OpenAI. 2023. Whisper Model (large-v2). https://github.com/openai/whisper. Last Accessed: 2024-03-05.

Vassil Panayotov, Guoguo Chen, Daniel Povey, and Sanjeev Khudanpur. 2015. Librispeech: An asr corpus based on public domain audio books. In *2015 IEEE International Conference on Acoustics, Speech and Signal Processing (ICASSP)*, pages 5206–5210.

Daniel Povey, Arnab Ghoshal, Gilles Boulianne, Lukas Burget, Ondrej Glembek, Nagendra Goel, Mirko Hannemann, Petr Motlicek, Yanmin Qian, Petr Schwarz, et al. 2011. The Kaldi Speech Recognition Toolkit. *Workshop on Automatic Speech Recognition and Understanding.*

Daniel Povey, Vijayaditya Peddinti, Daniel Galvez, Pegah Ghahremani, Vimal Manohar, Xingyu Na, Yiming Wang, and Sanjeev Khudanpur. 2016. Purely Sequence-Trained Neural Networks for ASR Based on Lattice-Free MMI. In *Proc. Interspeech 2016*, pages 2751–2755.

Daniel Povey et al. 2022. Kaldi ASR TDNN Recipe Script. https://github.com/kaldi-asr/kaldi/blob/master/egs/wsj/s5/local/chain2/tuning/run_tdnn_1i.sh. Accessed: 2022-01-03.

Vineel Pratap, Qiantong Xu, Anuroop Sriram, Gabriel Synnaeve, and Ronan Collobert. 2020. Mls: A large-scale multilingual dataset for speech research. *ArXiv*, abs/2012.03411.

Alec Radford, Jong Wook Kim, Tao Xu, Greg Brockman, Christine Mcleavey, and Ilya Sutskever. 2023. Robust speech recognition via large-scale weak supervision. In *Proc. of the 40th International Conference on Machine Learning*, volume 202 of *Proc. of Machine Learning Research*, pages 28492–28518. PMLR.

Rafael Rafailov, Archit Sharma, Eric Mitchell, Christopher D Manning, Stefano Ermon, and Chelsea Finn. 2023. Direct preference optimization: Your language model is secretly a reward model. In *Proc. Advances in Neural Information Processing Systems (NeurIPS)*, volume 36, pages 53728–53741.

B. Schuppler, M. Hagmüller, J. A. Morales-Cordovilla, and H. Pessentheiner. 2014. GRASS: The Graz corpus of Read And Spontaneous Speech. In *Proc. of LREC*, pages 1465–1470.

Barbara Schuppler, Martin Hagmüller, and Alexander Zahrer. 2017. A corpus of read and conversational Austrian German. *Speech Communication*, 94C:62–74.

Andreas Stolcke. 2002. SRILM - an extensible language modeling toolkit. In *Proc. Interspeech 2002.*

Piotr Szymański, Piotr Żelasko, Mikolaj Morzy, Adrian Szymczak, Marzena Żyła-Hoppe, Joanna Banaszczak, Lukasz Augustyniak, Jan Mizgajski, and Yishay Carmiel. 2020a. WER we are and WER we think we are. In *Findings of the Association for Computational Linguistics: EMNLP 2020*, pages 3290–3295. Association for Computational Linguistics.

Piotr Szymański, Piotr Żelasko, Mikolaj Morzy, Adrian Szymczak, Marzena Żyła-Hoppe, Joanna Banaszczak, Lukasz Augustyniak, Jan Mizgajski, and Yishay Carmiel. 2020b. WER we are and WER we think we are. In *Findings of the Association for Computational Linguistics: EMNLP 2020*, pages 3290–3295, Online. Association for Computational Linguistics.

Ye-Yi Wang, A. Acero, and C. Chelba. 2003. Is word error rate a good indicator for spoken language understanding accuracy. In *2003 IEEE Workshop on Automatic Speech Recognition and Understanding (IEEE Cat. No.03EX721)*, pages 577–582.

Jason Wei, Xuezhi Wang, Dale Schuurmans, Maarten Bosma, brian ichter, Fei Xia, Ed Chi, Quoc V Le, and Denny Zhou. 2022. Chain-of-thought prompting elicits reasoning in large language models. In *Proc. Advances in Neural Information Processing Systems (NeurIPS)*, volume 35, pages 24824–24837.

Shunyu Yao, Dian Yu, Jeffrey Zhao, Izhak Shafran, Tom Griffiths, Yuan Cao, and Karthik Narasimhan. 2023. Tree of thoughts: Deliberate problem solving with large language models. In *Proc. Advances in Neural Information Processing Systems*, volume 36, pages 11809–11822.

Susan Zhang, Stephen Roller, Naman Goyal, Mikel Artetxe, Moya Chen, Shuohui Chen, Christopher Dewan, Mona Diab, Xian Li, Xi Victoria Lin, et al. 2022. Opt: Open pre-trained transformer language models. *arXiv preprint arXiv:2205.01068.*

Zhuosheng Zhang, Aston Zhang, Mu Li, and Alex Smola. 2023. Automatic chain of thought prompting in large language models. In *Proc. Int. Conf. on Learning Representations (ICLR)*, Kigali, Rwanda.

A Limitations

The manuscript presents work in progress and initial steps towards evaluating whether LLMs can be useful for correcting ASR utterances of conversational speech. While we performed experiments also with a different LLM (zephyr7B[3]) and ob-

[3]Model card : https://huggingface.co/HuggingFaceH4/zephyr-7b-beta last accessed: 19.7.2024

1 You are a linguist with expertise in the austrian german language. Your answer only contains the solution to the tasks you are given and nothing else. To be clear, this is very important, do not add anything else in your answer, it should only consist of the solution to the task and nothing else.

2 Task Instruction:
I will give you a part of an austrian german sentence. Please correct it for me.

3 In order to help you with your task here is some context of the text I want you to improve on. There should be helpful information in there:
unterschied ist ja der mir aufgefallen ist ist natürlich die kathi hat mhm zum reinigen wahrscheinlich ne doktor oetker die arbeitet seit {...}

4 Please only apply changes when you are confident about them and only answer with the improved german text. This is the text I want you to improve on:
5 sie weiß einprägen und auswendig lernen

Figure 2: Example of one prompt consisting of system prompt (1), base prompt p1 (2), flow-context (3), additional instructions (4), and the ASR hypothesis to be corrected (5).

tained qualitatively similar results, it is certainly not clear how our results generalize to other LLMs, different prompt techniques, or different corpora of conversational speech. Our manuscript should thus be interpreted as presenting anecdotal, instead of statistical, evidence.

B Ethical Considerations

In this work no human participants were involved in experiments. It uses the GRASS corpus, a datasets already published for academic research prior to this work, which collected following the international ethical requirements as suggested by the American Psychological Association. The speaker's privacy was protected in several ways: 1) Each speaker received an ID and their names are not mentioned anywhere. 2) When using audio examples for illustration, the snipplets need to be shorter than 8s duration to avoid an understanding of the pragmatic context. 3) Each user of the GRASS corpus has to sign a confidentiality agreement, including a statement to obey to the ethical requirements agreed upon when collecting the data.

C Appendix

C.1 Technical Details of the ASR Systems

Results with Whisper were achieved in a zero-shot manner with the model large-v2 (OpenAI, 2023) by setting the language parameter to `German`, the `suppress_tokens` parameter to -1 and the `temperature_increment_on_fallback` parameter to `None`. For Kaldi and wav2vec2 we trained or fine-tuned 19 ASR systems with GRASS in the sense of leave-p-out cross-validation by selecting one conversation as the test split and the remaining conversations as the training split (Linke et al., 2022, 2023). The Kaldi recipe (Povey et al., 2022) was based on an acoustic model trained with speed-perturbed 3-fold augmented data (Ko et al., 2015), 40-dimensional MFCCs+Δ+$\Delta\Delta$, 100-dimensional i-vectors, a network with 12 TDNN-F layers and the LF-MMI criterion (Povey et al., 2016). For the language model we trained 3-grams with the SRILM toolkit (Stolcke, 2002) and a Witten-Bell discounting. The pronunciation model included only most likely pronunciations for each word in GRASS given broad phonetic forced-alignments (Linke et al., 2023). For wav2vec2, we fine-tuned the pre-trained XLSR model (Conneau et al., 2021; Facebook Research, 2022) with a CTC loss (Graves et al., 2006) for character sequences. For w2vLM we used a character-based lexicon by mapping each word in GRASS to characters and a 3-gram language model based on the KenLM toolkit (Heafield, 2011) with Kneser-Ney smoothing and default pruning.

C.2 Baseline Dataset

Table 4 lists the whole baseline dataset, i.e. the 37 utterances (human annotations) selected to conduct our experiments.

C.3 Example Prompt

Figure 2 shows an example for one full prompt, including a system prompt, BP p1, FC, and one input utterance.

C.4 Human-Improvable Utterances

As already mentioned, whether an utterance is "human improvable" is quite subjective. We nevertheless suggest to categorize utterances into four cases, while admitting that the assignment of an utterance to each class is not always obvious. These cases can be described as follows (see Table 3 for an example):

C1 The ASR hypothesis is identically to the reference.

C2 The ASR hypothesis itself contains enough information to be human improvable with a

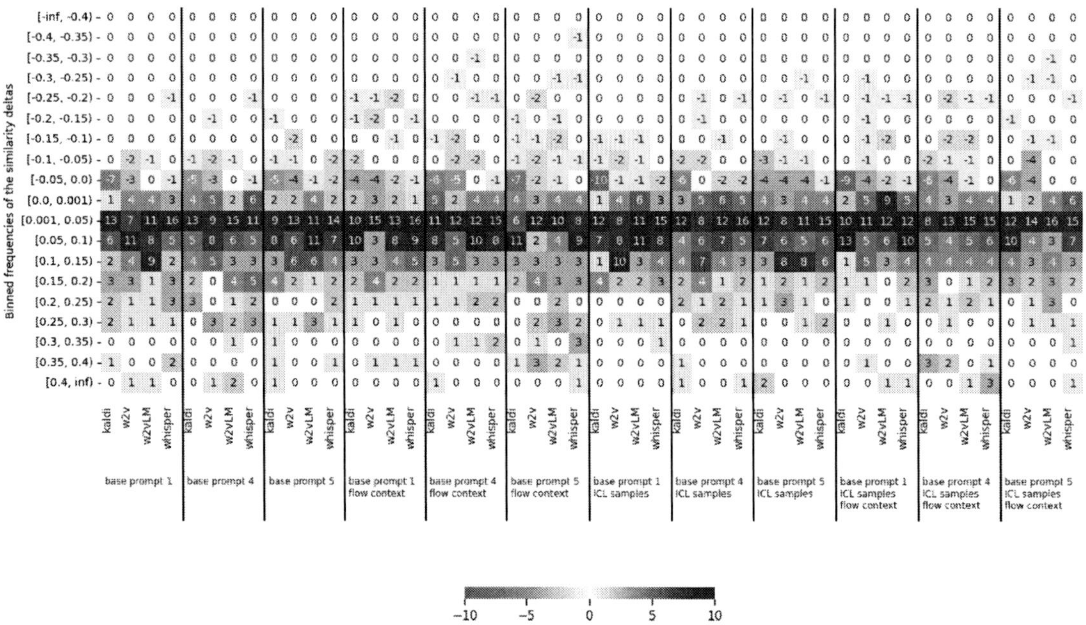

Figure 3: Effect of LLM corrections (instructed by 12 prompt combinations) on outputs of four ASR systems: Binned differences (deltas) are illustrated between the cosine similarities of the sentence embeddings of ASR hypotheses and the similarities of the 1776 LLM corrections (4*12*37 = #ASR models * #experiments * baseline dataset size). Negative differences (counts in red) indicate a similarity increase – positive differences (counts in blue) indicate a similarity decrease.

	Reference	ASR Hypothesis	LLM Correction
C1	die haben im hafen irgendein anderes boot	die haben im hafen irgendein anderes boot	die haben im hafen irgendein anderes boot
C2	die haben im hafen irgendein anderes boot	die haben im hafen irgendein anderes bus	die haben im hafen irgendein anderes schiff
C3	sogar mitten in der nacht am hafen unten	sogar mitten in der nacht am haufen unten	sogar mitten in der nacht am hafen unten
C4	ja das sind dann arme schweine	ja das sind dann anschaue	-

Table 3: Examples for different cases of human correctability. C1 is already correct; C2 can be corrected without FC; C3 needs FC to be correctable; C4 is not correctable, even when looking at the FC.

high likelihood and without any additional information such as FC.

(a) In C2 in Table 3, the word "hafen" together with the grammatical error "anderes bus" lead to a high probability of for the substitution of "bus" with "boot" (lowers WER) or with "schiff" (increases similarity).

C3 The ASR hypothesis itself does not contain enough information to be human improvable with a high likelihood, but within the FC there is enough information to do so.

(a) In the example in Table 3, "Boote" and a "hafen" are mentioned within the FC.

C4 Neither the ASR hypothesis nor the FC contain enough information for the hypothesis to be human improvable with a high likelihood.

(a) In C4 in Table 3, in the FC there is no mentioning of "schweine" or "armut". The term "schweine" is employed here as part of a German idiomatic expression. We do not believe that the FC indicates the usage of this phrase.

C.5 Semantic Similarity

Figure 3 shows a heatmap similar to Figure 1, but with a focus on semantic similarity. As it can be seen, applying an LLM often improves the semantic similarity to the reference compared to the ASR hypotheses.

1	sich was einprägen und auswendig lernen
2	ja ich frage mich auch immer
3	ich meine die machen das zwar aber
4	und es verschickt natürlich automatisch
5	haben eh alle versicherut
6	so wie die dort hausen
7	krankenhauskabine hat er ihn
8	und dann eine lehre gemacht
9	die müssen immer wache stehen oder wache gehen um das schiff und schauen ob da irgendwelche piratenboote von links oder rechts oder sonst wo kommen
10	das schiff zu entern
11	aha das heißt jetzt ist die neu die nächste bestellung ist hochdruckschläuche
12	so außen so aufschriften machen wo dann drauf steht wir führen nur
13	aber das ist halt eine andere art sich was einprägen und so weiter und auswendig zu lernen als wenn_du
14	naja das war einmal halt
15	musst du das eingeben
16	wenn_du jetzt einen fehler machst beim eingeben
17	die das programm geschrieben haben
18	gesperrter hafen war weil weil es ein
19	ohne dass irgendwas passiert ist
20	und normalerweise ist da unten ja jemand zuständig vierundzwanzig stunden am tag on call
21	sogar mitten in der nacht am hafen unten
22	die haben im hafen irgendein anderes boot
23	in diesen regionen
24	und alles andere müssen sie halt von außen hertransportieren deshalb ist auch alles so teuer
25	im pool hängst
26	im pool hängst
27	viel viel länger nicht mehr gemacht und ich glaube deshalb fällt?_es ihr schwerer als der kathi
28	als wenn_du seit zehn jahren nichts mehr gelernt hast
29	ja aber ich meine eine lehre lernst ja auch
30	ich meine ich weiß es nicht ich habe nie eine lehre gemacht aber
31	tragisch aber es ist natürlich umständlich dass du für korrekturen eh dich immer an wen andern wenden musst
32	da ersparst_dir sicher viel arbeit aber
33	und danach ist er scheinbar irgendwie
34	das ist ja nicht so
35	zu ihrer verteidigung nur der kapitän hat eine schusswaffe falls piraten
36	und das schlimmste sind die engen schleusen weißt eh diese engen kanäle weil da kannst halt relativ gut
37	mit insel also auf jedem von ein jeder insel ist ein hotel und die haben sogar noch swimmingpool und sie hat gesagt sie hat nie verstanden warum die leute wenn du draußen den schönsten ozean überhaupt hast

Table 4: All human annotations from the baseline dateset.

OneLove beyond the field - A few-shot pipeline for topic and sentiment analysis during the FIFA World Cup in Qatar

Christoph Rauchegger[1] and **Sonja Mei Wang**[2] and **Pieter Delobelle**[3]
[1] Technische Universität Berlin, Germany
[2] University of Wuppertal, Germany
[3] Department of Computer Science, KU Leuven; Leuven.AI, Belgium

Abstract

The FIFA World Cup in Qatar was discussed extensively in the news and on social media. Due to news reports with allegations of human rights violations, there were calls to boycott it. Wearing a OneLove armband was part of a planned protest activity. Controversy around the armband arose when FIFA threatened to sanction captains who wear it. To understand what topics Twitter users Tweeted about and what the opinion of German Twitter users was towards the OneLove armband, we performed an analysis of German Tweets published during the World Cup using in-context learning with LLMs. We validated the labels on human annotations. We found that Twitter users initially discussed the armband's impact, LGBT rights, and politics; after the ban, the conversation shifted towards politics in sports in general, accompanied by a subtle shift in sentiment towards neutrality. Our evaluation serves as a framework for future research to explore the impact of sports activism and evolving public sentiment. This is especially useful in settings where labeling datasets for specific opinions is unfeasible, such as when events are unfolding.

1 Introduction

In December 2010, it was announced that Qatar will host the FIFA World Cup in 2022 (BBC News, 2010). This announcement was met with concerns and criticism, including the effect of high temperatures during June and July (Matzarakis and Fröhlich, 2015), and accusations of bribery (Panja and Draper, 2020). Important political topics were allegations of human rights violations, such as withholding wages from migrant workers and their unexplained deaths (Heerdt and Roorda, 2023; Human Rights Watch, 2023), as well as abuse endured by LGBT people (Crane, 2022; Human Rights Watch, 2022).

As one of the biggest sport events of 2022, the FIFA World Cup in Qatar was followed by football fans and social media users who expressed their enthusiasm, but also critique towards this sporting event on the microblogging platform X, formerly known as Twitter (Pak and Paroubek, 2010; Fan et al., 2020). FIFA claims that there were over five billion "engagements" with the World Cup on social media (FIFA, 2023). The FIFA World Cup is one of the most followed sporting events worldwide – a mega-event (Müller et al., 2023).

While calls for boycotts became public before the World Cup and initiatives like "Boycott Qatar 2022" were established (Sportschau, 2022), there were planned protest activities during the World Cup, such as the OneLove captain's armband. Ten European teams announced their intention to wear the colored armband (KNVB Media, 2022). Announcements of sanctions made national teams cancel these plans, with threats of receiving a yellow card for wearing it becoming known on November 21st, 2022 (DW, 2022). Teams released statements expressing that it had been their intention to wear the armband to stand for inclusion, diversity and mutual respect, but chose not to in order to avoid negatively impacting the players (Ramsay and Nabbi, 2022). Instead of wearing the armband, the German national team held their hands in front of their faces to make a statement (ZDF heute, 2022). The sanctions against the German team's protest activity and the backing down of teams were discussed on social media, such as Twitter.

We conducted an analysis of 132k Tweets about the FIFA World Cup in Qatar to analyze topics dominating discussions on this event and opinions on one particular topic, namely the OneLove armband. By conducting this analysis, we also evaluate if our proposed method can replace supervised pipelines to analyze and measure public opinions. Supervised machine learning models play a crucial role in measuring sentiment online (Dang et al., 2020) by classifying user-generated texts (Lheureux, 2023; Rustam et al., 2021; Scott et al., 2021). However,

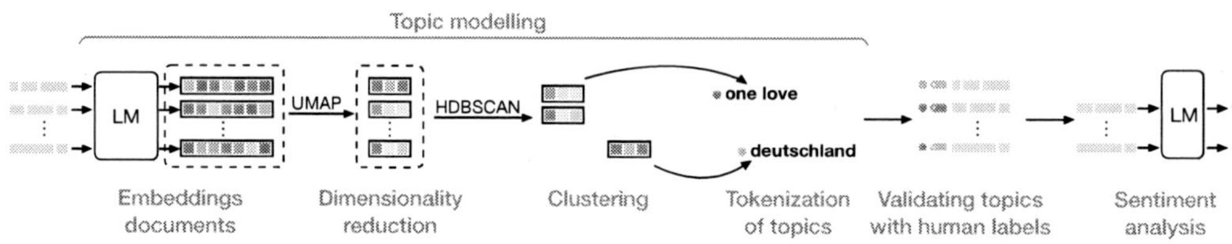

Figure 1: Topic modeling and sentiment analysis pipeline.

training these models requires labeled data, which involves significant time and resources. Thus, some projects are limited to using existing models, for instance when there is no annotation budget, or when monitoring events or crises, where there is no time to create a labeled dataset (Bruyne et al., 2024). Another limitation is that most studies of sentiment of specific events on social media happen after the event has passed, instead of while an event is unfolding, which is possible with our proposed method.

We specifically aim to answer the following research questions, both related to the World Cup in Qatar and for monitoring opinions on social media:

RQ1 Which topics related to the OneLove armband were discussed on Twitter? (§ 3.1)

RQ2 What is the sentiment on Twitter towards FIFA's ban of the OneLove armband? (§ 3.2)

RQ3 How suitable is a zero-shot or few-shot language model-based pipeline for measuring public sentiment from Twitter/X? (§ 4)

2 Background and Related Work

Numerous studies have conducted analyses on Twitter data for FIFA World Cups, including Meier et al. (2021), Patel and Passi (2020), Nuñez Franco (2023), Hassan and Wang (2023), and Fan et al. (2020). Controversies surrounding countries hosting these events were a focus of previous research. Meier et al. (2021) who analyzed Twitter data on the 2018 FIFA World Cup in Russia describe that it was controversial due to the annexation of Crimea in March 2014 and subsequent military conflicts in Ukraine. The authors argue that mega-events are used by host countries to portray a positive national image for domestic and global audiences. They also mention that in the past, countries have come under scrutiny when hosting such events, as civil society has increasingly focused on human rights and civil liberties of host countries, and demanded accountability and political reforms.

Brannagan and Giulianotti (2018) predicted that Qatar intended to use the global attention received from hosting the FIFA World Cup to show Qatar's pursuits of peace, security and integrity, and boister their attractiveness for international tourists. However, the criticism due to the news coverage of alleged human rights violations lead to calls for boycotts and planned protest activities. Hassan and Wang (2023) found that political discussions surrounding the FIFA World Cup in Qatar initially dominated but then gradually declined, shifting the focus to sporting achievements and cultural exchange. Findings from the sentiment analysis conducted by Nuñez Franco (2023) include that more than 66% of Tweets showed a positive sentiment and that the majority of data contained neutral hashtags, with only around 6% of Tweets containing a negative hashtags.

Similarly to (Meier et al., 2021), we argue that a sentiment analysis can be an indicator of whether the public is aware of contested issues around mega sports events such as FIFA World Cups and whether protest activities to raise awareness of human rights issues are supported. Further analysis, such as a qualitative content analysis of non-supportive Tweets, can inform future protest activities.

Differently from previous Twitter analyses on the FIFA World Cup in Qatar, we focus not only on finding out what topics were discussed, but also how users perceived the protest activity of wearing the OneLove armband, a much discussed protest activity. In addition, we analyze German Tweets, while previous research has focused on English Tweets.

3 Method

All analyzed Tweets were collected by the authors through the formerly freely available, official Twitter API. This API allowed access to all public Tweets of the last 30 days. To find Tweets with certain characteristics, we used the following filter:

```
-is:retweet -is:reply -is:quote lang:de
-liveticker -newsticker (#WM2022 OR
```

Table 1: Performance of different sentiment analysis models. All models were evaluated on our manually labeled test set, as discussed in § 3.2. We link to the publicly available models and indicate if they are multilingual (🌐) or only for German (🇩🇪).

	Model	Predicted labels	Acc [%]	F_1 [%]
🌐	`nlptown/bert-base-multilingual-uncased-sentiment`	1 to 5 stars	46.4	19.6
🇩🇪	`oliverguhr/german-sentiment-bert`	Positive, negative, neutral	62.6	43.9
🌐	`mistralai/Mistral-7B-Instruct-v0.2`	In favor, against or neutral	64.9	47.3
	+ 3-shot prompt (examples)		67.1	50.7
	+ translation to English		69.8	54.7
	+ Chain of Thought (CoT) reasoning (Kojima et al., 2022)		74.3	61.5
	+ all three techniques		76.1	64.2
🌐	`gpt-3.5-turbo`[1] (3-shot prompt, translation, CoT)	In favor, against or neutral	59.9	39.9
🌐	`gpt-4-turbo`[1] (3-shot prompt, translation, CoT)	In favor, against or neutral	**80.2**	**70.3**

```
#FIFAWorldCup OR FIFA OR WM OR (WM (Katar
OR Qatar)) OR ((Fußball OR Fussball)(Qatar
OR Katar OR Weltmeisterschaft)))
```

This string contains the German and English spelling variant of Qatar and Football. Weltmeisterschaft (abbr. WM) is the translation for "World Cup" in German. These hashtags and words were selected to ensure that Tweet topics are connected to the World Cup. Tweets that only contain content about football or only Qatar should be excluded through this search. Retweets, replies and quotes were excluded from the collection of data, as context needs to be taken into account when interpreting such Tweets (see Limitations). The language was set to German and liveticker and newsticker were excluded to avoid Tweets only about news regarding this event, as they are not relevant for sentiment analysis. The data set consists of 132,150 Tweets that were Tweeted in a time period from November 20 to December 18, 2022.

3.1 Topic modeling

To get an overview of important topics in our data set, we performed unsupervised topic modeling. We used BERTopic (Grootendorst, 2022) with a multilingual model and a CountTokenizer with n-grams of length 1 to 3, to also include bi-grams like 'one love' and tri-grams like 'One Love Binde'. The BERTopic library only includes stopwords in English, so we iteratively wrote our own short list to improve the clusters (see Appendix A).

We validated the discovered topics using a separate test set, where we manually annotated 600 Tweets belonging to seven topics: irrelevant, game Tweet, news, boycott, human rights, OneLove Binde and general politics. The highest amount of Tweets were news and reporting of the game progress, which are not interesting for our analysis.

The OneLove armband was relevant to Twitter users and our topic model found this topic and the issues related to this. As mentioned before, due to the media attention and controversy surrounding this protest activity, we decided to focus on Tweets about the OneLove armband. We manually annotated 200 Tweets that contain the word OneLove or a spelling variation (one-love and one love) as being for, against or neutral towards wearing the armband. Another of the authors annotated 100 Tweets to calculate Inter-Annotator Agreement (IAA). Of the 200 annotated Tweets on OneLove, 88 were annotated as for OneLove and 20 against OneLove. We did this by selecting the topics from our BERTopic pipeline that were associated with the Tweets that we manually labeled as 'OneLove Binde' (see Figure 2).

The topics found by our topic modelling pipeline align well with different aspects related to the OneLove armband, such as the penalty for wearing the armband despite the ban (a yellow card), discussions about politics in sports and various OneLove-related topics.

3.2 Few-shot sentiment analysis

We used sentiment analysis to analyze the Tweets on the OneLove topic, which is a commonly used method to extract subjective information, such as opinions and attitudes (Medhat et al., 2014; Mäntylä et al., 2018). However, our task is to gauge support for wearing the OneLove armband, which is distinct—and often the opposite—of support for the ban that FIFA implemented. This task, often referred to as stance detection (Alturayeif et al., 2023), is different than what publicly available sentiment analysis models are trained on, so we perform an evaluation of different language models.

[1]GPT-3.5 and GPT-4 are not fully supported with `select`-queries in Guidance, so unconstrained generation is used and this affects the accuracy.

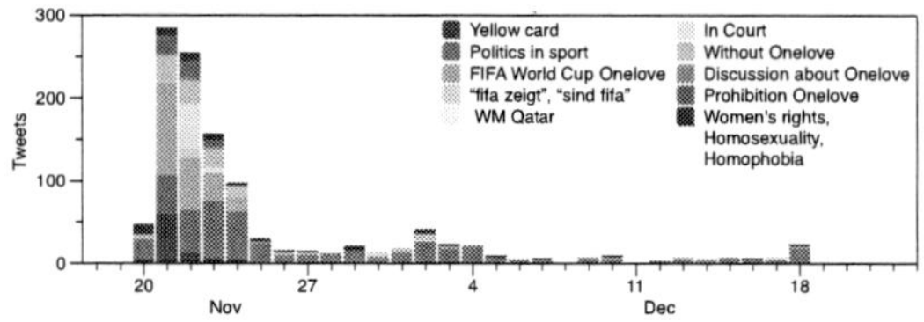

Figure 2: Timeline of discussed topics related to OneLove. The topics are found by topic modeling (§ 3.1) and linked to OneLove with manual annotation of a subset of Tweets.

In addition, we focus on evaluating zero-shot and few-shot methods to answer RQ3. Because of this focus, our approach could be directly applicable for new studies following other events, which in turn also allows for a faster reaction to develop a pipeline while an event is still unfolding.

We first create a set of gold labels by having two native German speakers annotate 148 randomly sampled Tweets using Doccano[1]. Our annotation labels are 'in favor of the OneLove Binde' ($n = 63$), 'against the OneLove Binde' ($n = 15$) and 'neutral' ($n = 70$). Some of the Tweets did not directly contain an opinion in the text, but used tags like #WMderSchande (World Cup of Shame) and #BoycottQatar. Other Tweets were commenting on how the OneLove armband is only a replacement for a real rainbow-colored armband and a compromise, these Tweets were also annotated as being for the armband. The inter-annotator agreement is $\kappa = 0.68$, which indicates significant agreement (Viera et al., 2005).

We evaluate two already finetuned BERT-based models and validate them by calculating macro-averaged accuracy and micro-averaged F_1 scores between the predicted labels and the gold labels. However, both models are finetuned for sentiment analysis on different domains, mostly reviews with a star-based rating system. As a consequence, the observed error rates are too high when applied to our dataset, as shown by the F_1 scores of 20% and 44% in Table 1.

To address this, we test a similar setting using generative LMs, where we tested Mistral, GPT-3.5 and GPT-4. For the publicly available model Mistral 7B (Jiang et al., 2023), we evaluated several variations of a prompt: (i) only the base prompt with the coding instructions, (ii) with 3 examples for 3-shot classification, (iii) with additional instructions to translate the Tweet to English, (iv) Chain of Thought (CoT, *"let's think step by step"*) reasoning (Kojima et al., 2022) and (v) a combination of all prompts. We also test the conversation-tuned GPT-3.5 and GPT-4 models by OpenAI using all aforementioned prompting techniques, as they proved to increase the performance on the Mistral model. We also note that the models struggle most with the 'against OneLove binde' class, for instance GPT-4 has an AUC score of 0.697 for this class, while the others are slightly higher with 0.769 (in favor) and 0.747 (neutral).

Based on this evaluation (see Table 1), we find that an optimized prompt with examples, Chain of Thought reasoning and a translation all improve the Mistral-based labeling. Interestingly enough, a BERT-based classifier performs almost as well (62.6% accuracy) as Mistral without prompting techniques (64.9%), at a lower inference cost. Nevertheless, by optimizing the prompt Mistral achieves 76.1% accuracy, which outperforms GPT-3.5 and is only slightly worse than the relatively expensive GPT-4 model, so we use Mistral with all prompting techniques to classify all Tweets on OneLove.

4 Discussion

Opinions on the OneLove armband. We first analyzed the topics found in the Tweets, where we found multiple topics related to OneLove (see Figure 2). There are more Tweets about the game itself, but 'one love' and 'boycott' are the first political topics we found with our topic modeling. The range of topics is broad, and include for instance discussions of the consequences of wearing the OneLove armband, women's rights and politics in sports. Initially, the discussion was about OneLove and related topics, such as women's rights, homosexuality and homophobia, as well as the mention of 'legal action'. Interestingly enough, most of the Tweets after the ban, on November 21, 2022, shifted to focus on politics in sports in general, as opposed to the armband itself or banning it.

The sentiment of the Tweets slightly shifted towards a more neutral stance, however there are more supportive Tweets for wearing the OneLove armband (see Figure 3). We also observe an initial spike of Tweets as a reaction on the ban of the OneLove armband, but this quickly ebbed away. The overall sentiment correlates with some surveys, e.g. Dörner (2022), although we observe more Tweets taking a neutral stance.

[1]https://doccano.github.io/doccano/

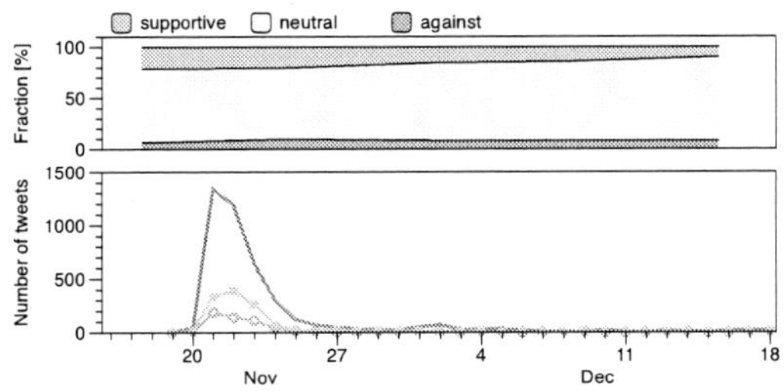

Figure 3: Sentiment of Tweets related to OneLove.

Few-shot analysis pipeline. In this paper, we also presented a few-shot pipeline to cluster Tweets using topic modeling and analyze them using zero-shot and few-shot language models. We found that both aspects of the pipeline work sufficiently well to use for events and crises: First, the topics discovered by BERTopic aligned with our manual labels (see § 3.1). Second, large language models, such as Mistral-7B, are surpassing finetuned BERT models (see § 3.2) and allow for in-context learning with few examples (Kojima et al., 2022), meaning classification pipelines are quicker to set up.

Comparison to Surveys Some social media users do not post their opinion publicly or post nothing, even if they have an opinion. The imagined audience, lurking behavior and deletion of Tweets impact the availability of social media data (Litt and Hargittai, 2016; Gong et al., 2016; Almuhimedi et al., 2013; Zhou et al., 2016). Our analysis can be used as an additional data point alongside other sources of information. Many surveys conducted by newspapers and other media outlets observed similar trends in the fraction of people supporting a boycott as our analysis does. A 2022 survey conducted by a local newspaper shows that 46% of German citizens who responded intended to boycott the 2022 FIFA World Cup, while 28% were against a boycott (Dörner, 2022). Another survey's results showed that 72% of respondents were in favor of a boycott (NDR, 2022). There was also a non-representative survey which German government officials responded to and approximately half favored a boycott (Merkur, 2022).

While surveys with fixed responses can give an overview of agreement and disagreement with an issue, an advantage of social media data compared to such surveys is that it is possible to analyze how individuals form or explain their stance on a topic. Topic modeling and sentiment analysis can also be combined with a qualitative analysis of Tweets if particular topics are of interest. Further analyses could focus on whether there are any group differences among those supporting or boycotting protest activities, as previous research has focused on inferring demographic data from information provided on Twitter (Sloan et al., 2013; Culotta et al., 2015; Sloan et al., 2015).

5 Conclusion

The FIFA World Cup 2022 in Qatar was accompanied by controversies, among them allegations of human rights violations of migrant workers and LGBT people. Football teams planned to wear the OneLove armband as a protest activity, however the FIFA threatened to sanction wearing the armband. We conducted topic modeling and found that Twitter users talked about the ban of the OneLove armband for a few days after the ban. We then focused on Tweets about OneLove and the subsequent ban of the OneLove armband, to gauge whether Tweets were for or against wearing the armband. Our analysis shows that there was more support for wearing the armband than not, although the support did fade over time, which could indicate that Twitter users perceived the protest as unsuccessful. We identified a shift from the armband-specific discourse to a broader discussion on politics in sports. A purpose of this protest activity was to raise awareness of human rights violations. If a sentiment analysis reveals negative public perception towards a particular protest activity, this suggests a potential need for reassessment and modification of the protest strategy which is possible while an event takes place through our proposed few-shot pipeline.

Limitations

The data set we analyzed consisted of German Tweets, which means that results only allow us a glimpse into German-speaking Twitter users' opinions on the FIFA World Cup in Qatar. X, formerly known as Twitter, has users from certain demographics and is not used by every German-speaking person, thus the results are not generalizable to all German-speakers. We did not try to infer demographics from our data. Nonetheless, our work contributes to research on social media data centered on languages other than English and goes beyond Germany's borders, as German is also spoken in other countries, such as Austria and Switzerland.

We elected to not include replies, which means there might be posts in threads that are for or against the OneLove armband that we did not cover with our analysis. Since the added context (the original Tweet) might make interpreting these Tweets more difficult[2], we decided to leave out these replies. Future work could focus to include these replies with the original Tweet.

Finally, we evaluated multiple models to classify Tweets. De Bruyne et al. (2021) showed that different BERT-based models performed differently with regard to emotion detection or sentiment analysis, which might be the case for the models we tested as well. Biases in the model might affect the classification as well (Talat et al., 2021). However, an analysis of these issues for the models we used is out of scope for this work.

Ethical considerations

We only used publicly available data and did not interact with human subjects, which means our work did not classify as human subjects research by our IRBs. Since this research did not seek informed consent, data were taken from a public online venue. On X, formerly known as Twitter, users have different privacy options, such as posting public and private Tweets. We collected only public Tweets which were easily accessible for all users through the search function. Following the conditions of the Twitter API, we cannot publish the full dataset that we used, instead we publish a "dehydrated" version which requires access to the API to receive full information on each Tweet. For our analysis and collection of data, we only used the Tweet, no further information on the person who posted it was collected.

Acknowledgments

Pieter Delobelle received funding from the Flemish Government under the "Onderzoeksprogramma Artificiële Intelligentie (AI) Vlaanderen" programme and was supported by the Research Foundation - Flanders (FWO) under EOS No. 30992574 (VeriLearn). He also received a grant from "Interne Fondsen KU Leuven/Internal Funds KU Leuven".

References

Hazim Almuhimedi, Shomir Wilson, Bin Liu, Norman Sadeh, and Alessandro Acquisti. 2013. Tweets are forever: a large-scale quantitative analysis of deleted tweets. In *Proceedings of the 2013 Conference on Computer Supported Cooperative Work*, CSCW '13, page 897–908, New York, NY, USA. Association for Computing Machinery.

Nora Alturayeif, Hamzah Luqman, and Moataz Ahmed. 2023. A systematic review of machine learning techniques for stance detection and its applications. *Neural Computing and Applications*, 35(7):5113–5144.

BBC News. 2010. England miss out to Russia in 2018 World Cup vote.

Paul Michael Brannagan and Richard Giulianotti. 2018. Soft power and soft disempowerment: Qatar, global sport and football's 2022 world cup finals. In *Leveraging Mega-Event Legacies*, pages 89–105. Routledge.

Luna De Bruyne, Toni G.L.A. van der Meer, Orphée De Clercq, and Véronique Hoste. 2024. Using state-of-the-art emotion detection models in a crisis communication context. *Computational Communication Research*, 6(1):1.

Jonathan Crane. 2022. HRW report alleges abuse of LGBTQ qataris.

Aron Culotta, Nirmal Kumar, and Jennifer Cutler. 2015. Predicting the demographics of Twitter Users from website traffic data. *Proceedings of the AAAI Conference on Artificial Intelligence*, 29(1).

Nhan Cach Dang, María N Moreno-García, and Fernando De la Prieta. 2020. Sentiment analysis based on deep learning: A comparative study. *Electronics*, 9(3):483.

Luna De Bruyne, Orphee De Clercq, and Veronique Hoste. 2021. Emotional robbert and insensitive bertje: Combining transformers and affect lexica for dutch emotion detection. In *Proceedings of the Eleventh Workshop on Computational Approaches to Subjectivity, Sentiment and Social Media Analysis*, pages 257–263.

Jan Dörner. 2022. Katar: So viele Deutsche wollen die WM boykottieren.

DW. 2022. OneLove campaign hit by threat of FIFA sanctions.

Minghui Fan, Andrew Billings, Xiangyu Zhu, and Panfeng Yu. 2020. Twitter-based BIRGing: Big data analysis of english national team fans during the 2018 FIFA World Cup. *Communication & Sport*, 8(3):317–345.

FIFA. 2023. One month on: 5 billion engaged with the FIFA World Cup Qatar 2022™.

Wei Gong, Ee-Peng Lim, Feida Zhu, and Pei Hua Cher. 2016. On unravelling opinions of issue specific-silent users in social media. In *Proceedings of the International AAAI Conference on Web and Social Media*, volume 10, pages 141–150.

[2]Is positive or negative sentiment towards the ban or the OneLove Binde or towards the original Tweet?

Maarten Grootendorst. 2022. BERTopic: Neural topic modeling with a class-based TF-IDF procedure. *arXiv preprint arXiv:2203.05794*.

Ahmed A. M. Hassan and Jia Wang. 2023. The qatar world cup and twitter sentiment: Unraveling the interplay of soft power, public opinion, and media scrutiny. *International Review for the Sociology of Sport*, 0(0).

Daniela Heerdt and Lucas Roorda. 2023. Lessons learned in Qatar: The role of the Netherlands and its businesses in addressing human rights abuses in mega-sporting events. *Netherlands International Law Review*, pages 1–46.

Human Rights Watch. 2022. Qatar: Security forces arrest, LGBT people.

Human Rights Watch. 2023. Qatar: Six months post-World Cup, migrant workers suffer.

Albert Q Jiang, Alexandre Sablayrolles, Arthur Mensch, Chris Bamford, Devendra Singh Chaplot, Diego de las Casas, Florian Bressand, Gianna Lengyel, Guillaume Lample, Lucile Saulnier, et al. 2023. Mistral 7b. *arXiv preprint arXiv:2310.06825*.

KNVB Media. 2022. Ten countries embrace the Dutch OneLove campaign.

Takeshi Kojima, Shixiang Shane Gu, Machel Reid, Yutaka Matsuo, and Yusuke Iwasawa. 2022. Large language models are zero-shot reasoners. *https://arxiv.org/abs/2205.11916*.

Yasemin Lheureux. 2023. Predictive insights: leveraging twitter sentiments and machine learning for environmental, social and governance controversy prediction. *Journal of Computational Social Science*, pages 1–22.

Eden Litt and Eszter Hargittai. 2016. The imagined audience on social network sites. *Social Media+ Society*, 2(1):2056305116633482.

Mika V Mäntylä, Daniel Graziotin, and Miikka Kuutila. 2018. The evolution of sentiment analysis—a review of research topics, venues, and top cited papers. *Computer Science Review*, 27:16–32.

Andreas Matzarakis and Dominik Fröhlich. 2015. Sport events and climate for visitors—the case of FIFA World Cup in Qatar, 2022. *International Journal of Biometeorology*, 59:481–486.

Walaa Medhat, Ahmed Hassan, and Hoda Korashy. 2014. Sentiment analysis algorithms and applications: A survey. *Ain Shams engineering journal*, 5(4):1093–1113.

Henk Erik Meier, Michael Mutz, Julia Glathe, Malte Jetzke, and Martin Hölzen. 2021. Politicization of a contested mega event: The 2018 FIFA World Cup on twitter. *Communication & Sport*, 9(5):785–810.

Merkur. 2022. Sollte die deutsche Politik die Katar-WM boykottieren? Exklusive Bundestags-Umfrage zeigt gespaltenes Bild.

Martin Müller, David Gogishvili, Sven Daniel Wolfe, Christopher Gaffney, Miriam Hug, and Annick Leick. 2023. Peak event: the rise, crisis and potential decline of the Olympic Games and the World Cup. *Tourism Management*, 95:104657.

NDR. 2022. Umfrage zur WM in Katar: Mehrheit im Norden für Boykott.

Luis Fernando Nuñez Franco. 2023. On sentiment analysis of Twitter content related to the FIFA World CUP 2022 in Qatar.

Alexander Pak and Patrick Paroubek. 2010. Twitter as a corpus for sentiment analysis and opinion mining. In *LREc*, volume 10, pages 1320–1326.

Tariq Panja and Kevin Draper. 2020. U.S. says FIFA officials were bribed to award World Cups to Russia and Qatar.

Ravikumar Patel and Kalpdrum Passi. 2020. Sentiment analysis on twitter data of world cup soccer tournament using machine learning. *IoT*, 1:218–239.

George Ramsay and Zayn Nabbi. 2022. England's Harry Kane and several other European captains told not to wear 'OneLove' armband at World Cup.

Furqan Rustam, Madiha Khalid, Waqar Aslam, Vaibhav Rupapara, Arif Mehmood, and Gyu Sang Choi. 2021. A performance comparison of supervised machine learning models for Covid-19 tweets sentiment analysis. *PloS one*, 16(2):e0245909.

Kristen Scott, Pieter Delobelle, and Bettina Berendt. 2021. Measuring shifts in attitudes towards covid-19 measures in belgium. *Computational Linguistics in the Netherlands Journal*, 11:161–171.

Luke Sloan, Jeffrey Morgan, Pete Burnap, and Matthew Williams. 2015. Who tweets? deriving the demographic characteristics of age, occupation and social class from twitter user meta-data. *PloS one*, 10(3):e0115545.

Luke Sloan, Jeffrey Morgan, William Housley, Matthew Williams, Adam Edwards, Pete Burnap, and Omer Rana. 2013. Knowing the tweeters: Deriving sociologically relevant demographics from twitter. *Sociological Research Online*, 18(3):74–84.

Sportschau. 2022. Erneut Fan-Proteste gegen WM in Katar,.

Zeerak Talat, Smarika Lulz, Joachim Bingel, and Isabelle Augenstein. 2021. Disembodied machine learning: On the illusion of objectivity in nlp. *arXiv preprint arXiv:2101.11974*.

Anthony J Viera, Joanne M Garrett, et al. 2005. Understanding interobserver agreement: the kappa statistic. *Fam med*, 37(5):360–363.

ZDF heute. 2022. DFB-Team hält sich den Mund zu.

Lu Zhou, Wenbo Wang, and Keke Chen. 2016. Tweet properly: Analyzing deleted tweets to understand and identify regrettable ones. In *Proceedings of the 25th International Conference on World Wide Web*, pages 603–612.

A Stopwords

- der
- dem
- das
- und
- er
- ein
- den
- ist
- es
- die
- ich
- man
- zu
- nicht
- so
- wie
- was
- auch
- aber
- wenn
- als
- noch
- mal
- sich
- dass
- nur
- oder
- dann

B Prompts

```
[INST] Rate German Tweets as 'supportive', 'against' or 'neutral' of wearing the One Love bracelet or one love binde in German. These Tweets were posted during the world cup in Qatar.

Coding instructions:
- Critique for the FIFA policy of banning the bracelet or wishing players could wear it should be interpreted as support for the one love binde.
- Similarly, if support for the one love binde is slightly implied, that is sufficient for it to be supported.
- If the tweet is factual without any sentiment, consider it neutral.
- If the tweet uses negative connotations with the one love binde and what it stands for (the LGBT community), the tweet is against.

Tweet: "lul und ich werde angefeindet weil ich den tv anmache hugo lloris weigert sich bei der anstehenden fußball weltmeisterschaft in katar die one love binde zu tragen er wolle die kultur des gastgebers respektieren so die begründung des frankreich kapitäns boykottqatar" [/INST]
Support for wearing the one love binde: supportive
[INST] Tweet: "dfb torwart neuer hält an one love binde bei wm in katar fest" [/INST]
Support for wearing the one love binde: neutral
[INST] Tweet: "soso die scheiß will wohl die onelove binde verbieten ihr habt echt nicht mehr alle latten am zaun infantino und seine geldsäcken sollte man in die wüste schicken fifaworldcup qatarworldcup qatar dopa" [/INST]
Support for wearing the one love binde: against
[INST] Tweet: "{tweet}" [/INST]
English translation: {translation}
[INST] Now look at the previous tweets and analyze the similarities with the latest tweet that we want to label and if that tweet expresses support for wearing the one love binde. Let's think step by step:[/INST] {reason}
[INST] Therefore the tweet expressed the following sentiment towards wearing the one love binde:[\INST] {decision}
```

Listing 1: **Prompt for Mistral-7B**

Linguistic and extralinguistic factors in automatic speech recognition of German atypical speech

Eugenia Rykova[1, 2, 3] **Mathias Walther**[2]
[1] University of Eastern Finland, Joensuu, Finland
[2] University of Applied Sciences TH Wildau, Wildau, Germany
[3] Catholic University Eichstätt-Ingolstadt, Eichstätt, Germany
eugenryk@uef.fi

Abstract

Automatic speech recognition (ASR) has been already used in speech and language therapy, including diagnostic tasks and practice exercises for people with aphasia (PWA). The lack of relevant data makes it difficult to evaluate the algorithms' suitability for German-speaking PWA. For the current project, four open-source ASR models were selected based on their performance on other types of atypical speech, and the details of their evaluation are presented in this paper. The four selected models are generally robust to speakers' gender and age. The one-word recognition yields better results for words of moderate length. Speech rate should be neither too slow nor too quick for lower error rates both in words and phrases, and the latter should be also of moderate length.

1 Introduction

Automatic speech recognition (ASR) has become part of many everyday services, including digital health. In particular, speech and language therapy (SLT) can benefit considerably from ASR usage – for example, when in-person therapy is supplemented with digital therapy solutions used independently (van de Sandt-Koenderman, 2011; Des Roches & Kiran, 2017; Braley et al., 2021).

Aphasia is a relatively common language disorder that occurs after completed language development because of brain damage, which in 80% of the cases is caused by a stroke (Wiehage & Heide, 2016). People with aphasia (PWA) benefit from high-intensity SLT (Bhogal, Teasell, & Speechley, 2003; Brady et al., 2016) and express the necessity of digitalized speech production exercises with appropriate feedback (Kitzing et al., 2009). However, commercial systems with excellent ASR results in applications for typical speakers demonstrate poor performance when processing impaired speech (Green et al., 2021).

In general, deteriorated condition of speech, high variability among speakers, and insufficiency of data make it difficult to use automatic speech recognition for aphasic speech. Errors in oral speech production, such as imprecise articulation and phonemic structure distortions, are mostly inconsistent and unpredictable, which hinders error modelling (Abad et al., 2013). Aphasia can be also comorbid with motor speech disorders, which bring further disfluencies and decrease speech intelligibility (Qualls, 2012). Besides, age is a risk factor for stroke and aphasia (see Schulz & Werner, 2019), and older individuals tend to recover from aphasia more slowly and to a lesser extent. Age per se can influence speech production on various linguistic levels, including acoustics and prosody (e.g., slower speech rate) (Johnson et al., 2022). Changes in acoustic features are reflected in poorer ASR performance for older speakers, which might be more drastic for female voices (Vipperla, Renals, & Frankel, 2008). On the other hand, aphasia generally affects more men than women (see Schulz & Werner, 2019), and some studies report higher ASR error rates on the speech of males (Adda-Decker & Lamel, 2005), while others note that ASR systems might perform poorer for female speakers because of the deviations from the data on which the systems have been historically trained (see Hirschberg, Litman, & Swerts, 2004).

Slower speech rate, increased duration of the utterances, and hyperarticulation in general – the features typical for aphasic speech – have been reported as factors decreasing the conventional ASR performance on typical speech in various languages, for example, English (Siegler & Stern, 1995; Hirschberg, Litman, & Swerts, 2004; Goldwater, Jurafsky, & Manning, 2008), Japanese (Shinozaki & Furui, 2001) and German (Soltau & Weibel, 1998), and contexts.

While different authors explore the possibility of making ASR systems more suitable for the recognition and assessment of aphasic speech (see for review Adikari et al., 2023; Azevedo et al., 2024; Pottinger & Kearns, 2024), to the best of authors' knowledge, there are currently three systems that use ASR for feedback on correctness/incorrectness in naming-oriented semantic exercises (Abad et al., 2013; Ballard et al., 2019; Barbera er al., 2021). In the apps for German-speaking PWA this option is under research (Lin et al., 2022; Heide et al., 2023). AphaDIGITAL (TDG, 2021) project focuses on developing a solution for German-speaking PWA that will provide detailed phonemic/phonetic and semantic feedback in naming and other exercises (see Rykova & Walther, 2024). For this purpose, four open-source ASR solutions have been selected as the most suitable for PWA's speech recognition based on their performance on other types of atypical speech. In the absence of necessary data from PWA, test material from other corpora with atypical speech was considered for evaluation. This paper presents the analysis of the models' robustness to extralinguistic factors and the effects of linguistic features on recognition rates.

2 Materials and methods

2.1 ASR models

The performance of four open-source ASR models, selected for the future pipeline of PWA's speech analysis, was subject to the current experiments. The models are presented in Table 1.

Name in the current paper: description	Reference
jonatas53: fine-tuned Facebook's Wav2Vec2-XLSR-53 model (Conneau et al., 2021) on German CV 6.1 dataset.	Grosman, 2023
mfleck: fine-tuned Facebook's Wav2Vec2-XLS-R-300M model (Conneau et al., 2021) on German CV dataset.	Fleck, 2023
nvidia2: a "large" version of Conformer-Transducer model, trained on several thousand hours of German speech data, NeMo toolkit.	NVIDIA, 2023
oliver9: fine-tuned Facebook's Wav2Vec2-XLSR-53 on German CV 9.0 dataset.	Guhr, 2023

Table 1: Evaluated open-source ASR models

2.2 Speech corpora

In the absence of necessary data from PWA, test material from other corpora with impaired speech was considered for the present evaluation, namely speech of adult cochlear implants (CI) users from CI Articulation Corpus (Neumeyer, 2009) and speech under intoxicated condition from Alcohol Language Corpus (ALC) (Schiel et al., 2008). The deteriorated features of CI users' and intoxicated speakers' speech resemble those of PWA's. In particular, decreased vowel exactness and precision of articulators' movements characterize the speech of adult CI users, which is also reflected in lower automatic recognition rates (Ruff et al., 2017; Arias-Vergara et al., 2022). Speakers in intoxicated condition demonstrate decreased speech rate and weakened speech motor control, noticeable both for human perception and digital applications (Pisoni & Martin, 1989; Tisljár-Szabó et al., 2014).

Naming-oriented exercises in the existing solutions are oriented on one-word recognition. AphaDIGITAL will include advanced exercises that entail phrase production (e.g., picture description), so the evaluation included both single words and phrases. The analysis included the following audio recordings from ALC and CI corpora:

NA_phrases – 641 phrases uttered by sober speakers from ALC corpus;

A_phrases – 702 phrases uttered by intoxicated speakers from ALC corpus;

NA_words – 1976 words, automatically segmented out of the tongue-twisting lists uttered by sober speakers from ALC corpus;

A_words – 2249 words, automatically segmented out of the tongue-twisting lists uttered by intoxicated speakers from ALC corpus;

NORM_words – 1032 words, automatically segmented out of the sentences uttered by normal-hearing speakers from CI corpus;

CI_words – 1021 words, automatically segmented out of the sentences uttered by CI users from CI corpus.

Due to the requirements of some ASR models, all audio recordings described below were (if necessary) converted to one channel and resampled to 16 kHz.

2.3 Measurements

Character Error Rate (CER) and HITS measurement (the number of precisely recognized words) were used to evaluate the models' performance. CER values were not normalized, meaning that if there were too many substitutions and/or insertions in the ASR transcription, the CER value could be higher than 1 (or 100%). CER and HITS values were computed with the help of the JiWER Python library (Python Software Foundation, 2023). In word sets, the percentage of empty outputs was also taken into consideration.

The results of recognition were not only compared among the models but also according to the following factors (when applicable):

atypicality: intoxicated/sober condition, usage of cochlear implants;

demographics: gender, age group (young vs old, with 50 years old taken as the division line);

linguistic and speech factors (hereinafter "linguistic"): duration of the analyzed segment in seconds, length of the segment in words or syllables, speech rate measured in words/minute (w/m) or syllables/second (syll/s) – for comparison, intended normal speech rate in German is on average 5.4 syll/s (Dellwo et al., 2006).

CER values according to atypicality were subject to the Student's t-test. Groups based on demographic factors were compared with the help of analysis of variance (ANOVA) with a post-hoc Tukey's Honest Significant Difference (Tukey's HSD) test.

The dependencies between linguistic factors were analyzed via Pearson and Spearman correlation tests. The differences between HITS with respect to linguistic factors were analyzed with a pairwise Wilcoxon signed-rank test. Decision (regression) trees with ANOVA as a fit method (Therneau and Atkinson, 2022) were used to assess the dependency of error rates on linguistic factors. They were created with *rpart* function. The leaf nodes were the mean error rate values for the group of observations selected according to the decision node(s). All the analyses were performed in R (R Core Team, 2023) at 95% confidence.

3 Results

3.1 Atypicality

In phrase recognition, the alcohol intoxication of the speakers affects the performance of all four models, increasing the CER values. In word recognition, alcohol intoxication of the speakers affects the performance of the jonatas53 and oliver9 models, while the CER values of mfleck (the lowest among the four models) and nvidia2 (the highest among the four models) do not change significantly. All four models have lower performance on the speech of CI users. The p-values for the Student's t-test in case of significant difference can be seen in Figure 1.

3.2 Robustness of the selected models to extralinguistic factors

For the four selected models, a graphical representation of the robustness to demographic factors can be seen in Figure 1. The absence of a statistically significant difference in ANOVA and post-hoc Tukey's HSD tests (p-value > 0.05) between CER values of demographic groups is understood under robustness. The significant differences and the corresponding p-values are marked in orange.

In the experiments with NA_phrases, all four models are robust to gender, age, and their interaction. In the experiments with A_phrases, mfleck is not robust to gender: CER values for female speakers are higher.

Mfleck and oliver9 are robust to gender, age, and their interaction in the experiments with NA_words. Jonatas53 is robust to gender, but not to age. Tukey's HSD shows that the underlying difference is CER values for the MO group, which are significantly higher than CER values for both FY and MY groups. In the experiments with A_words, jonatas53, mfleck, and oliver9 are robust to gender, but show significantly higher CER values for the older group. With both datasets, nvidia2 is robust to age, but shows significantly higher CER values for the female group, for A_words, in particular, the difference between FY and MY groups is significant.

Since there is only one normal-hearing young male speaker in the CI corpus and the recognition results for his data do not differ from the corresponding FY group, only age differences are discussed for this dataset. The oliver9 model is robust to age in the experiments with

NORM_words, and jonatas53 and mfleck are robust to age in the experiments with CI_words. In the rest of the comparisons, the CER values for younger speakers are significantly higher.

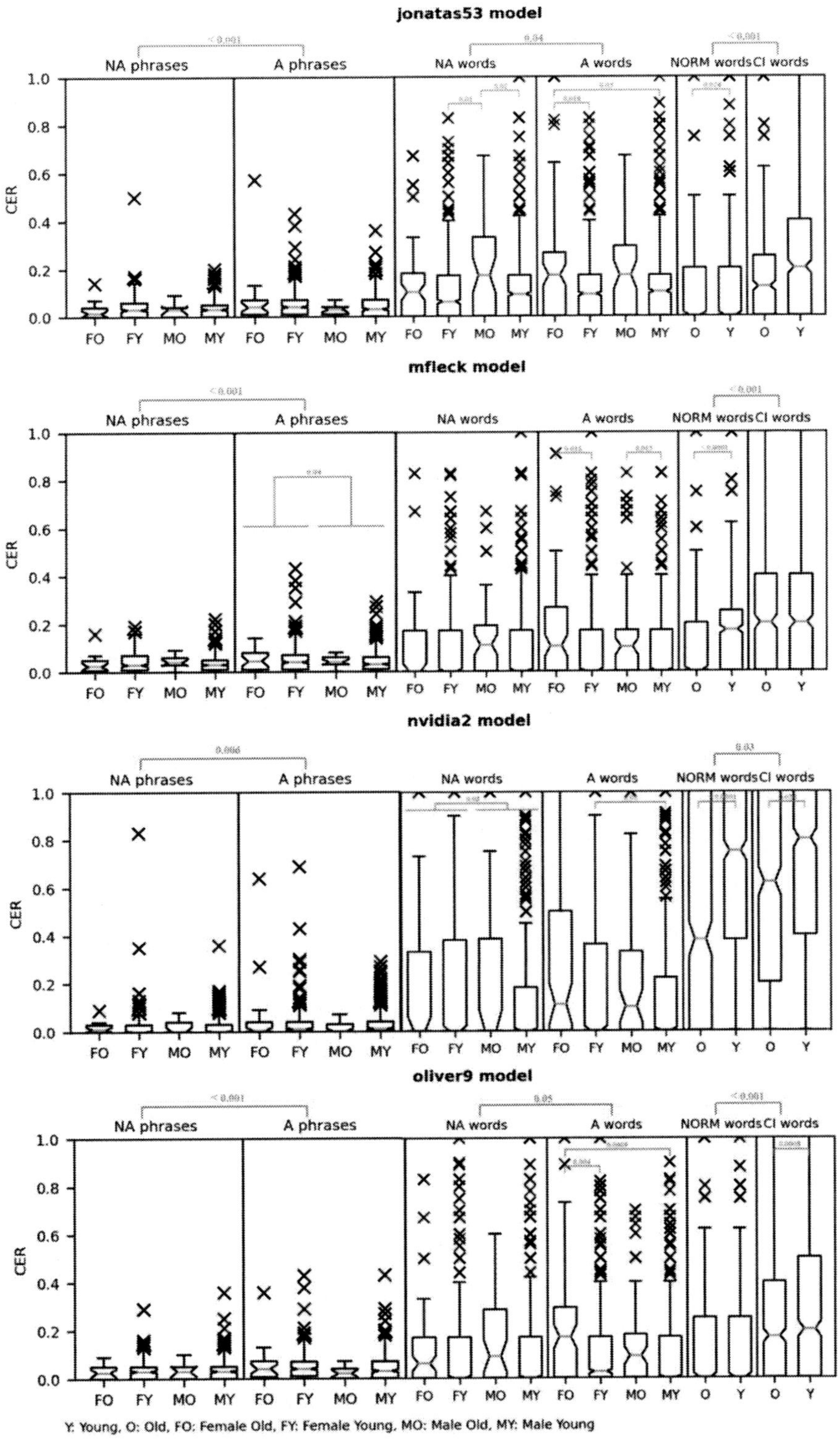

Figure 1: Robustness of the four selected models to gender and age.

3.3 Effect of linguistic factors on the performance of the selected models

3.3.1 Feature description

The numeric values of linguistic parameters are summarized in Table 2. In the ALC phrases datasets, the phrase length correlates strongly with audio duration (ρ = 84%) and speech rate (ρ = 86%). In the ALC words datasets, the word length strongly correlates with audio duration (ρ = 79% for NA_words, ρ = 73% for A_words). In the CI corpus, duration and speech rate have a moderate negative correlation (PCC = 68%). Both alcohol intoxication and CI usage have the following effect on linguistic characteristics: the duration of the same phrases or words becomes longer and the average speech rate becomes slower, but these differences are significant only among young speakers. In the ALC phrases and CI corpus, the speech rate of younger speakers is quicker than that of older speakers, and the duration of the same phrases/words is longer when uttered by the latter.

Dataset	Duration (s)				Speech rate (w/m)				Number of words		
	min	max	M	SD	min	max	M	SD	min	max	med
NA_phrases	1.5	17.5	6.3	2.7	24.2	184.2	89.8	32.8	2	23	10
A_phrases	1.7	17	7	3	22.5	170.4	84.4	31	2	27	10
	Duration (s)				**Speech rate (syll/s)**				**Number of syllables**		
	min	max	M	SD	min	max	M	SD	min	max	med
NA_words	0.3	2.5	0.7	0.3	1.7	7.4	3.9	0.9	1	6	2
A_words	0.3	3	0.8	0.3	1	10	3.8	0.96	1	10	2
NORM_words	0.14	1.1	0.4	0.13	1.8	8.3	4.6	1.2	1	2	
CI_words	0.1	1.6	0.5	0.16	1.2	9.1	4.2	1.3	1	2	

Table 2: Linguistic parameters of the testing datasets

3.3.2 Decision trees for CER

An example of a decision tree for mfleck performance on NA_words can be seen in Figure 2. Following the split according to the speech rate in the root node, and the split according to the duration in the following decision node, the leaf node contains 1705 words, for which the mean CER is the lowest. Combining the tree partitions for several models means choosing the maximum value for greater than and greater than or equal to splitting conditions (> and ≥), and choosing the minimum value for less than and less than or equal to splitting conditions (< and ≤).

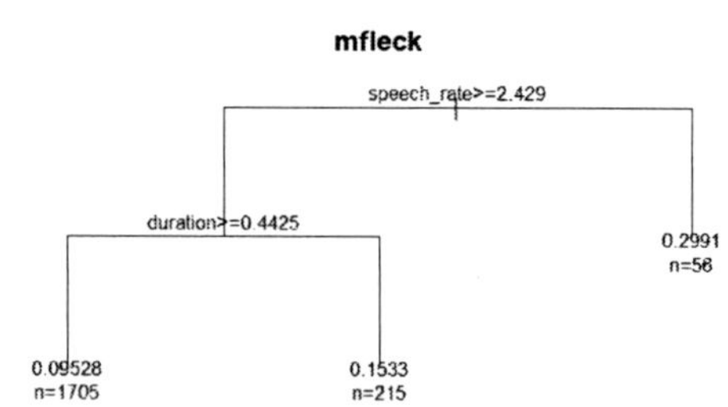

Figure 2: Decision (regression) tree for mfleck performance on NA_words.

Figure 3 presents an extract from the summary of the *rpart* function used for decision tree creation. The condition in the primary split is considered as an alternative one if the difference in the improve between it and the condition chosen for the tree is not greater than 0.01. Thus, in the presented example the number of syllables would be an alternative condition for decision node number 2.

In the experiments with NA_phrases, the most important condition for lower CER (root node) for nvidia2 is speech rate < 60.3 w/m or, alternatively, duration < 4.4 s. For the other three models, it is the phrase length < 6.5 words or, alternatively, sample duration < 4.2 s. In A_phrases, the most important condition is sample duration < 3.2 s (combined for all four models).

Combining the decision trees partition of jonatas53, mfleck, and oliver9 for NA_words and A_words brings out speech rate ≥ 2.9 syll/s and duration ≥ 0.44 s as the two most important conditions, followed by the length of the word ≥ 3.5 syllables for NA_words and word ≥ 4.5 syllables for A_words (this dataset includes longer words). For nvidia2, both speech rate and duration should be higher: > 5 syll/s and ≥ 0.9 s, respectively.

```
Node number 1: 1976 observations,     complexity param=0.03985966
  mean=0.1073684, MSE=0.02690127
  left son=2 (1920 obs) right son=3 (56 obs)
  Primary splits:
      speech_rate < 2.429   to the right, improve=0.03985966, (0 missing)
      n_syllables < 1.5     to the right, improve=0.01170752, (0 missing)
      duration    < 0.4275 to the right, improve=0.01091140, (0 missing)
  Surrogate splits:
      n_syllables < 1.5     to the right, agree=0.972, adj=0.018, (0 split)

Node number 2: 1920 observations,     complexity param=0.01209242
  mean=0.101776, MSE=0.02515304
  left son=4 (1705 obs) right son=5 (215 obs)
  Primary splits:
      duration    < 0.4425 to the right, improve=0.013310100, (0 missing)
      n_syllables < 2.5     to the right, improve=0.009555333, (0 missing)
      speech_rate < 4.528   to the left,  improve=0.005342128, (0 missing)
  Surrogate splits:
      n_syllables < 1.5     to the right, agree=0.895, adj=0.060, (0 split)
      speech_rate < 5.5305 to the left,  agree=0.892, adj=0.037, (0 split)
```

Figure 3: Extract of the rpart function summary for mfleck performance on NA_words.

In the CI corpus, CER values are lower for two-syllable words than for monosyllabic ones. Based on decision trees for NORM_words, the most important condition for jonatas53, mfleck, and oliver9 is duration $\geq$ 0.27 s in combination with speech rate > 2.1 syll/s. For nvidia2, the duration should be longer than 0.44 s.

For lower CER values in the recognition of CI_words by jonatas53, mfleck, and oliver9, the most important condition is speech rate $\geq$ 4.3 syll/s, followed by duration $\geq$ 0.24 s. For nvidia2, the duration should be longer than 0.62 s.

3.3.3 HITS and empty outputs

In the experiments with NA_words and A_words, HITS analysis for jonatas53, mfleck, and oliver9 shows that precisely recognized words are shorter than those with CER > 0. For nvidia2, the empty output is produced for the shortest words uttered at the fastest speech rate.

For the NORM_words, there is a general tendency for precisely recognized words to be longer and uttered at a slower speech rate. The shortest words uttered at the quickest rate are more likely to produce empty output.

The analysis of HITS for CI_words shows a general tendency for precisely recognized words to be longer and uttered at a faster speech rate. The shortest words uttered at the quickest rate are more likely to produce empty output.

4 Discussion

In the experiments with phrases from the ALC corpus, the four models are robust to the gender (as in Goldwater, Jurafsky, & Manning, 2010) and age of the speakers, except for one case: the CER values obtained with mfleck model are higher for female speakers (cf. Vipperla, Renals, & Frankel, 2008). Such results are in contrast with those obtained by Adda-Decker & Lamel (2005), which could be caused by non-natural speech and atypicality in case of intoxication, so that the differences in disfluency, durations, and alternate pronunciations were evened out. Most of the speech material consisted of tongue twisters that had to be pronounced as quickly as possible. The model that performed best for these datasets (nvidia2) yields better results for slower speech rate in NA_phrases. The speech rate is also higher in phrases with more words, and (predictably) the more words a phrase has, the longer its duration is. Thus, one can conclude that extremely high speech rates hinder automatic recognition, which is in line with the studies by Siegler & Stern (1995); Shinozaki & Furui (2001); and one corpus analysed by Hirschberg, Litman, & Swerts (2004). A lower number of words (no more than 6) or shorter duration (generally < 3.2 s) are other decisive factors for better performance in phrase recognition. As stated by Hirschberg, Litman, & Swerts (2004), it is possible that longer phrases just present more space for errors that shorter ones.

In CI_corpus, the speech rate of younger speakers is greater than that of the older speakers, and the duration of the same words is longer when uttered by the latter. That could explain, why in 62.5% of the cases, the models are not robust to age in an unexpected way: lower CER values for older speakers. Excluding nvidia2 (the weakest model for these datasets), ASR systems generally perform better on audio samples of greater duration (greater than 0.27 s) in combination with speech rates: the lower threshold for normal hearing speakers is 2.1 syll/s, and for the CI users it is 4.3 syll/s. Two-syllable words are recognized with lower CER values on average and are more likely to be recognized precisely, but they should not be uttered too quickly or too slowly, which is in line with the results described by Siegler & Stern (1995), Shinozaki & Furui (2001), and Goldwater, Jurafsky, & Manning (2008).

The experiments with the three models (excluding nvidia2) on words from the ALC corpus confirm that for better single-word recognition the audio samples should be not too short and not too slowly pronounced: duration ≥ 0.44 s and speech rate ≥ 2.9 syll/s (values comparable with NORM_words), correlating with the results on German hyperarticulated speech (Soltau & Waibel, 1998). These datasets contain much longer words than the CI corpus, and there are more relatively shorter words among those that are precisely recognized. The four models are mostly robust to gender, and partially – to age. The CER values for speech samples of older speakers are often higher as in the study by Vipperla, Renals, and Frankel (2008).

Summarizing the above, one can expect that words of moderate length will be recognized better than one-syllable or long words. Speech rate plays an important role in ASR. Thus, in one-word recognition, speech samples uttered at the rates below average of the corresponding datasets, which are lower than intended "very slow" (Dellwo et al., 2006), are more likely to produce higher CER values. Faster speech rates – the maximum values in ALC and CI corpora are higher than intended "very fast" (Dellwo et al., 2006) – also lower the recognition quality, both for words and phrases. For better results with the latter, it is also important to keep the number of words moderate or even low: in the analysed data, the threshold is six words. In the experiments with different datasets, recognition results show inconsistent, and sometimes contrasting, influence of the demographic factors, which might be a consequence of interaction with speech rate. In those datasets, where older speakers speak slower than the younger ones, the CER values of the former are either lower or do not differ from their counterparts. In those with no difference, the CER values for older speakers are higher.

5 Conclusion

The four selected ASR models are generally robust to speakers' gender and age. In fact, the differences might be caused by speech rate rather than by demographic factors per se. Since the models do not necessarily present disadvantages for the speakers of certain gender or age older users, they can be implemented in the error analysis pipeline of the aphaDIGITAL app without a concern that certain users would be treated unfair because of the demographics.

The recognition error rates suggest that words of moderate length are recognized better than one-syllable or long words, which should be taken into consideration when choosing target words for the exercises. Phrase recognition can be included in exercises without drawbacks for the ASR – in fact, phrase recognition might even be more accurate than one-word with the current models.

For better ASR rates, the speech rate of the speaker should be neither too slow (lower than conventional intended "very slow") nor too quick (intentionally speeded up). This knowledge could and should be incorporated into the app instructions ("Please speak at your usual pace") and feedback. For example, if a higher speech rate is detected, the user is asked to speak slower. The findings also suggest that the tasks to produce speech as quickly as possible might not be suitable for assessment with ASR (yet). On the other hand, compensating mechanisms for too slow speech should be elaborated: for example, treating ASR output segments as syllables of one word or adjusting the vowel length and quality.

Ethical Consideration

In the current paper, two speech corpora are explored. Both corpora were downloaded from BAS CLARIN repository (https://clarin.phonetik.uni-muenchen.de/BASRepository/) under free access for scientists.

The app that served as the motivation for current research is viewed as a supplement to in-person SLT and is not to replace SLT practitioners but to allow them to spend more time on complex tasks, which cannot be automatized, during the therapy sessions.

Limitations

The greatest limitation of the current work in general is the lack of relevant data. In the present paper, ASR solutions were tested with atypical speech, but not with the speech of speakers with aphasia.

Acknowledgments

AphaDIGITAL project is sponsored by German Federal Ministry of Education and Research via the TDG innovation ecosystem (Translationsregion für digitale Gesundheitsversorgung [Translational region for digital healthcare]) and „WIR! – Wandel durch Innovation in der Region" [Change through innovation in the region] program.

References

Alberto Abad, Anna Pompili, Ângela Costa, Isabel Trancoso, José G. Fonseca, Gabriela Leal, Luisa Farrajota, and Isabel P. Martins. 2013. Automatic word naming recognition for an on-line aphasia treatment system. *Computer Speech and Lang*uage, 27(6):1235-1248.

Martine Adda-Decker and Lori Lamel. 2005. Do speech recognizers prefer female speakers? *Proceedings of INTERSPEECH 2005*: 2205-2208.

Achini Adikari, Nelson Hernandez, Damminda Alahakoon, Miranda Rose, and John Pierce. 2023. From concept to practice: a scoping review of the application of AI to aphasia diagnosis and management. *Disability and Rehabilitation,* 46(7):1288-1297.

Tomás Arias-Vergara, Anton Batliner, Tobias Rader, Daniel Polterauer, Catalina Högerle, Joachim Müller, Juan-Rafael Orozco-Arroyave, Elmar Nöth, and Maria Schuster. 2022. Adult cochlear implant users versus typical hearing persons: An automatic analysis of acoustic–prosodic parameters. *Journal of Speech, Language, and Hearing Research,* 65(12):4623-4636.

Nancy Azevedo, Eva Kehayia, Gonia Jarema, Guylaine Le Dorze, Christel Beaujard, and Marc Yvon. 2024. How artificial intelligence (AI) is used in aphasia rehabilitation: A scoping review. *Aphasiology*, 38(2):305-336.

Kirrie J. Ballard, Nicole M. Etter, Songjia Shen, Penelope Monroe, and Chek Tien Tan. 2019. Feasibility of automatic speech recognition for providing feedback during tablet-based treatment for apraxia of speech plus aphasia. *American journal of speech-language pathology,* 28(25):818-834

David S. Barbera, Mark Huckvale, Victoria Fleming, Emily Upton, Henry Coley-Fisher, Catherine Doogan, Ian Shaw, William Latham, Alexander P. Leff, and Jenny Crinion. 2021. NUVA: A naming utterance verifier for aphasia treatment. *Computer Speech & Language,* 69(101221).

Sanjit K. Bhogal, Robert Teasell, and Mark Speechley. 2003. Intensity of aphasia therapy, impact on recovery. *Stroke*, 34(4):987-993.

Marian C. Brady, Helen Kelly, Jon Godwin, Pam Enderby, and Pauline Campbell. 2016. Speech and language therapy for aphasia following stroke. *Cochrane database of systematic reviews*, CD000425(6).

Michelle Braley, Jordyn Sims Pierce, Sadhvi Saxena, Emily De Oliveira, Laura Taraboanta, Veera Anantha, Shaheen E. Lakhan, and Swathi Kiran. 2021. A virtual, randomized, control trial of a digital therapeutic for speech, language, and cognitive intervention in post-stroke persons with aphasia. *Frontiers in Neurology*, 12:626780.

Alexis Conneau, Alexei Baevski, Ronan Collobert, Abdelrahman Mohamed, and Michael Auli. 2021. Unsupervised cross-lingual representation learning for speech recognition. In *Proceedings of INTERSPEECH 2021*, pages 2426-2430.

Volker Dellwo, Emmanuel Ferragne, and François Pellegrino. 2006. The perception of intended speech rate in English, French, and German by French speakers. In *Proceedings of the 3rd International Conference of Speech Prosody Speech Prosody 2006*, pages 101-104.

Carrie A. Des Roches and Swathi Kiran. 2017. Technology-based rehabilitation to improve communication after acquired brain injury. *Frontiers in Neuroscience*, 11:382.

Michael Fleck. 2023. Wav2vec2-large-xls-r-300m-german-with-lm. https://huggingface.co/mfleck/wav2vec2-large-xls-r-300m-german-with-lm (last accessed 12.09.2023).

Sharon Goldwater, Dan Jurafsky, and Christopher D. Manning. 2008. Which words are hard to recognize? Prosodic, lexical, and disfluency factors that increase ASR error rates. In *Proceedings of ACL-08: HLT*, pages 380-388.

Jordan R. Green, Robert L. MacDonald, Pan-Pan Jiang, Julie Cattiau, Rus Heywood, Richard Cave, Katie Seaver, Marilyn A. Ladewig, Jimmy Tobin, Michael P. Brenner, Philip C. Nelson, and Katrin Tomanek. 2021. Automatic speech recognition of disordered speech: Personalized models outperforming human listeners on short phrases. In *Proceedings of INTERSPEECH 2021*, pages 4778-4782.

Jonatas Grosman. 2023. Fine-tuned XLSR-53 large model for speech recognition in German. https://huggingface.co/jonatasgrosman/wav2vec2-large-xlsr-53-german (last accessed 12.09.2023).

Oliver Guhr. 2023. Wav2vec2-large-xlsr-53-german-cv9. https://huggingface.co/oliverguhr/wav2vec2-large-xlsr-53-german-cv9 (last accessed 12.09.2023).

Judith Heide, Jonka Netzebandt, Stine Ahrens, Julia Brüsch, Teresa Saalfrank, and Dorit Schmitz-Antonischki. 2023. Improving lexical retrieval with LingoTalk: an app-based, self-administered treatment for clients with aphasia. *Frontiers in Communication, 8:1210193*

Julia Hirschberg, Diane Litman, and Marc Swerts. 2004. Prosodic and other cues to speech recognition failures. *Speech communication,* 43(1-2):155-175.

Lisa Johnson, Samaneh Nemati, Leonardo Bonilha, Chris Rorden, Natalie Busby, Alexandra Basilakos, Roger Newman-Norlund, Argye E. Hillis, Gregory Hickok, and Julius Fridriksson. 2022. Predictors beyond the lesion: Health and demographic factors associated with aphasia severity. *Cortex*, 154:375-389.

Peter Kitzing, Andreas Maier, and Viveka Åhlander. 2009. Automatic speech recognition (ASR) and its use as a tool for assessment or therapy of voice, speech, and language disorders. *Logopedics Phoniatrics Vocology*, 34(2):91-96.

Yuchen Lin, Philipp Klumpp, Jakob Pfab, Abdelaziz Abdelioua, Daniel Gebray, and Mona Späth. 2022. Eine automatische Sprachbewertung für die neolexon Aphasie-App mithilfe Künstlicher Intelligenz [automatic language assessment with artificial intelligence. for the neolexon aphasia app.] Poster session presentation at Sprachtherapie aktuell: Forschung - Wissen – Transfer 9(1): XXXIV. *Workshop Klinische Linguistik e2022-11*, April 2022.

Veronika Neumeyer. 2009. Phonetische Untersuchungen der Artikulation von CI-Trägern [phonetic examination of the CI users' articulation]. Master's Thesis, Ludwig-Maximilians-Universität München, Germany.

NVIDIA. 2023. Conformer-Transducer Large (de). https://huggingface.co/nvidia/stt_de_conformer_transducer_large (last accessed 12.09.2023).

David Pisoni and Christopher Martin. 1989. Effects of alcohol on the acoustic-phonetic properties of speech: Perceptual and acoustic analyses. *Alcoholism: Clinical and Experimental Research*, 13(4):577-587.

Gordon Pottinger and Áine Kearns. 2024. Big data and artificial intelligence in post-stroke aphasia: A mapping review. *Advances in Communication and Swallowing*:1-15.

Python Software Foundation. 2023. JiWER: Similarity measures for automatic speech recognition evaluation. https://jitsi.github.io/jiwer (last accessed 15.12.2023).

Constance Qualls. 2011. Neurogenic disorders of speech, language, cognition-communication, and swallowing. In *Communication Disorders in Multicultural and International Populations*, pages 148–163, Mosby. Elsevier.

R Core Team. 2023. *R: A Language and Environment for Statistical Computing.* R Foundation for Statistical Computing, Vienna, Austria.

Suzan Ruff, Tobias Bocklet, Elmar Nöth, Joachim Müller, Eva Hoster, and Maria Schuster. 2017. Speech production quality of cochlear implant users with respect to duration and onset of hearing loss. *ORL, Journal of Oto-Rhino-Laryngology and its Related Specialties,* 79(5):282–294.

Eugenia Rykova and Mathias Walther. 2024. AphaDIGITAL – Digital Speech Therapy Solution for Aphasia Patients with Automatic Feedback Provided by a Virtual Assistant. In *Proceedings of the 57th Hawaii International Conference on System Sciences*, pages 3385-3394.

Florian Schiel, Christian Heinrich, and Sabine Barfüsser. 2008. Alcohol language corpus: the first public corpus of alcoholized German speech. In *Proceedings of the Sixth International Conference on Language Resources and Evaluation (LREC'08)*, pages 1641-1645.

Jörg B. Schulz and Cornelius J. Werner. 2019. *Statistischer Jahresbericht 2018 [Statistical Annual Report 2018].* Aphasia Station, Neurology Clinic, Aachen University Hospital.

Takahiro Shinozaki and Sadaoki Furui. 2001. Error analysis using decision trees in spontaneous presentation speech recognition. In *IEEE Workshop on Automatic Speech Recognition and Understanding, ASRU'01*:198-201.

Matthew A. Siegler and Richard M. Stern. 1995. On the effects of speech rate in large vocabulary speech recognition systems. In *Proceedings of the 1995 International Conference on Acoustics, Speech, and Signal Processing*, vol. 1:612-615.

Hagen Soltau and Alex Waibel. 1998. On the influence of hyperarticulated speech on recognition performance. In *Proceedings of the International Conference on Spoken Language Processing-98*, pages 225-228.

TDG - TRANSLATIONSREGION FÜR DIGITALE GESUNDHEITSVERSORGUNG. 2021. *AphaDIGITAL: Entwicklung einer digitalen, dezentralen sprachtherapeutischen Versorgung [Development of digital, decentralized speech therapy solutions]*. https://inno-tdg.de/projekte/aphadigital/ (last accessed 25.01.2022).

Terry Therneau and Elizabeth J. Atkinson. 2022. *Introduction to recursive partitioning using the rpart and routines.* Technical report, Mayo Foundation.

Eszter Tisljár-Szabó, Renáta Rossu, Veronika Varga, and Csaba Pléh. 2013. The effect of alcohol on speech production. *Journal of Psycholinguistic Research*, 43(6):737-748.

Wilhelmina Mieke E. van de Sandt-Koenderman 2011. Aphasia rehabilitation and the role of computer technology: Can we keep up with modern times? *International journal of speech-language pathology*, 13(1):21-27.

Ravichander Vipperla, Steve Renals, and Joe Frankel. 2008. Longitudinal study of ASR performance on ageing voices. In *Proceedings of INTERSPEECH 2008,* pages 737-748.

Anne Wiehage and Judith Heide. 2016. *Aphasie Informationen für Betroffene und Angehörige. [Information on aphasia for affected individuals and relatives]*. German federal association of academic speech therapists.

LLM-based Translation Across 500 Years. The Case for Early New High German

Martin Volk, Dominic P. Fischer, Patricia Scheurer, Raphael Schwitter, Phillip B. Ströbel
University of Zurich
Department of Computational Linguistics
volk@cl.uzh.ch

Abstract

The recently developed large language models (LLMs) show surprising translation capabilities for modern languages. In contrast, this paper investigates the ability of GPT-4 and Gemini to translate 500-year-old letters from Early New High German into modern German. We experiment with a corpus from the 16th century that is partly in Latin and partly in ENH-German. This corpus consists of more than 3000 letters that have been edited and annotated by experts from the Institute of Swiss Reformation Studies. We exploit their annotations for the evaluation of machine translation from ENH-German to German. Our experiments show that using the lexical footnotes by the editors in the prompts or directly injected into the text leads to high quality translations.

1 Introduction

Early New High (ENH) German marks the period in the history of the German language between the mid-14th and the mid-17th century. During this time the language experienced significant linguistic, cultural, and social changes that lay the foundation for modern German. Several characteristics distinguish ENH-German from both its predecessor, Middle High German, and its successor, New High German.

Native German speakers can grasp texts in ENH-German after some time of training or customization. Often, the overall gist is clear, although some words remain puzzling because they were spelled differently, have shifted meaning considerably or have fallen out of use. For example:

- ENHG: *unverschempter fravel* → unverschämter Frevel (outrageous offence)
- ENHG: *fast yfrig* (= literally: fest eifrig) → sehr entschieden (very determined)
- ENHG: *in die harr liden* → auf die Dauer ertragen (bear in the long run)

Translating Early New High German into modern German looks easy at first sight. But how good are machine translation systems on this task? It is a positive property of recent MT systems that they are robust against spelling variations (Bergmanis et al., 2020) which abound in ENH-German (Dipper and Schaffer, 2021). Subword segmentation and subsequent embeddings have resulted in MT systems that can handle learner language and dialectal spellings. Therefore, neural MT systems like Google Translate or DeepL can translate e.g. Swiss German dialect tweets or texts with word order variation and spelling errors into well-formulated English. If we then reverse the translation direction, we will obtain correctly spelled and well-worded German texts. And LLMs are even better at this text rewriting task than MT systems.

So this all indicates that MT for ENH-German into modern English or German should be possible. We compare DeepL and Google Translate with GPT-4 and Gemini in different configurations: adding lexical information to the prompts and inserting lexical information into the ENH-German sentences. We conclude with some translation experiments on sentences with ENH-German - Latin code-switching that abound in our corpus.

2 Related Work

2.1 Previous Work on NLP for ENH-German

For many years, the processing of historical languages depended on a normalization step. All spelling variants of a word were mapped to a normalized word form (e.g. ENH-German *wyn*, *win* were mapped to modern German *Wein* (wine)). Bollmann et al. (2017) applied an encoder-decoder architecture (a form of character-based rather than word-based neural MT) for text normalization of ENH-German. Their best models had an average word accuracy of 82.7%.

Schulz and Kuhn (2016) presented a Part-of-Speech tagger for historical German texts and evaluated it on a small testset. Ortmann (2021) developed a chunker for various stages of historical German including ENH-German. She evaluated the recognition of four phrase types (noun, prepositional, adjective, and adverb phrases). Sapp et al. (2023) built a parser for ENH-German by exploiting cross-dialect training from a middle low German treebank. Detecting code-switching between Latin and ENH-German was introduced by Volk et al. (2022).

2.2 Previous Work on MT for Ancient Languages

The first attempts to exploit MT for ancient languages aimed to normalize spelling variations. For an example, see Hämäläinen et al. (2019) for the normalization of Early English letters. But more recently, directly using neural MT for historical languages has been studied in various directions. Wang et al. (2023) organized a shared task for MT of Ancient Chinese. Park et al. (2022) worked on neural MT of ancient Korean.

Volk et al. (2024) investigate LLM-based MT for Latin and ENH-German. They focus on Latin but also touch upon MT and summarization for ENH-German. They compare GPT-4 based translations from ENH-German to German and English against human-written summaries. Despite low overlap scores with the summaries, they argue that GPT-4 is clearly better in translating ENH-German into English and German than Google Translate.

We found no other literature on MT from ENH-German to modern languages. We believe there exist no dedicated MT systems for ENH-German as source language. Our paper is the first systematic study of MT for ENH-German.

3 Our Corpus of Letters in ENH-German

We work on a large corpus of 16th-century letters (Volk et al., 2022; Ströbel et al., 2024). 3100 letters have been professionally edited by the Institute for Swiss Reformation Studies[1], and another 5400 have been manually transcribed. Three quarters of the letters are in Latin, the rest is in ENH-German, many letters contain code-switching between the two languages. This means we have a corpus of roughly 900,000 tokens in ENH-German (and 3 million tokens in Latin). In addition, our corpus comprises 2500 letters that have automatic transcriptions produced by Handwritten Text Recognition (HTR).

The letters include historical characters like ę, ů, å, ô, û. Abbreviations have been spelled out by the editors and transcribers, for instance *U a w b* is spelled out as *U[wer] a[ller] w[illige] b[rüeder]* (your all devoted brothers). In our translation experiments we use the spelled-out words without the brackets.

Paragraph boundaries are set by the transcribers, sentence boundaries have been automatically added. We automatically assigned a language tag to each sentence based on a self-trained language identifier that is able to distinguish between ENH-German and Latin with high accuracy (Volk et al., 2022).

The letters are part of the correspondence to and from the Zurich reformer Heinrich Bullinger. They deal with politics, theological debates, regional and European news as well as education and family matters. Bullinger's correspondence network extended from Zurich throughout Europe.

The 3100 edited letters have been published in 20 volumes of a "critical edition" (Gäbler et al., 1974–2020). They come with 81,573 footnotes in German that contain various types of comments by the editors. For instance, we were able to classify 3740 of these as biographical footnotes. They contain biographical information on some person mentioned in the letter (e.g. date and place of birth or profession). And – this is of relevance for the current work – we marked 8000 footnotes as lexical, most of them with the translation of a word or a short phrase from ENH-German to modern German. See Table 1 for examples.

For high precision, we marked only footnotes with one or two words as lexical. One-word footnotes account for 83% of the marked footnotes. 12% are two-word footnotes with a phrase (*in Richtung, gestern Abend, zu gehen* (in direction, last night, to go)), and 5% are two words separated by a comma which denote translation alternatives (*Gewehr, Waffen; abermals, erneut; verbergen, vorenthalten* (gun, weapon; again, anew; hide, withhold)).

Even though the footnote information is concise, the automatic application of this lexical information is challenging. Example footnote 19 in Table 1 shows the simple case of one modern German word that corresponds to one word in the ENH-German sentence. But footnote 38 has a German compound

[1] https://www.irg.uzh.ch/

Sentence in ENH-German	Footnote in modern German
... min hehen[19] heigind inn můßen dar zů zwingen *... my lords had to force him to do this*	19: Herren
Item den Fellix Müller, den důch scherer[38]. *Like Felix Müller, the cloth shearer*	38: Tuchscherer
... und den doff[70] [u]nnd daß nacht mall den heren, wie maß[71] hie zů Zürich brucht ... *... and the baptism and the last supper of the lord, as one uses it here in Zurich*	70: die Taufe; 71: man es
Alles dis ich üch verschiben[81] han, dem ist aso. *Everything that I recorded for you, is so.*	81: verschrieben, aufgezeichnet

Table 1: Sentences with examples of lexical footnotes, taken from letter 794 in (Gäbler et al., 1974–2020), Konrad Wirz to Heinrich Bullinger, April 1536. The letter was published in volume 6 of the edition in 1995.

that corresponds to two words in ENH-German. Footnote 70 is a two-to-two words correspondence, whereas 71 is a one-to-two mapping. Footnote 81 lists two alternative translations for the ENH-German word in the text.

4 LLM-based MT for ENH-German

4.1 Evaluating against Lexical Footnotes

As a first experiment, we translated 50 random ENH-German sentences into modern German with GPT-4 and checked whether the given German words from the lexical footnotes were in the translations. For instance, when we translate the second example sentence from Table 1 which has the lexical footnote *Tuchscherer*, we check whether this target word is in the modern German translation. The hypothesis is that the presence of these target words are evidence for good translations. This hypothesis is supported by the fact that the lexical footnotes comment on "non-intuitive" or difficult ENH-German words, as deemed by the editors.

We translated our ENH-German letters by prompting GPT-4 with: `Transfer this letter from old German into modern German, sentence by sentence: [letter here]. Output only the transferred sentences, one by one. Do not use any numbering.`

We found that 198 out of 743 target words (27%) are in the GPT-4 output of the 50 letters. This is considerably higher than the 10% of target words that we find when we translated via the pivot language English with Google Translate (ENH-German → English → German; cf. section 5).

4.2 Creating a Testset for MT Evaluation

In order to evaluate the MT quality for the ENH-German letters we need human reference translations. To create such a a testset efficiently we randomly selected 10 ENH-German letters from our corpus and pre-translated them with GPT-4 into modern German with the prompt: `Translate the following letter from Early New High German to modern German.`

We realized that GPT-4 preserves the historic style of the letters, and we therefore translated the German output again with the prompt: `Reformuliere folgende Sätze in flüssigem, modernem Deutsch.` (Reformulate the following sentences in fluent, modern German.) See Table 2 for an example of how the sentence changes in the two translation steps.

We then asked an expert in medieval linguistics (Latin and ENH-German) to correct the second output, which we then regarded as the gold standard human reference translation.

We realize that this method biases the human reference translation towards GPT-4. This approach, however, enabled us to produce reference translations for 10 letters (201 sentences) with a reasonable effort.

To counteract the bias, we asked another expert to correct the same sentences. The evaluation showed that comparing GPT-4's translations against the two different references yielded only minimal discrepancies.

4.3 Evaluating against our Testset

We translated the test set, letter by letter, from ENH-German to modern German by using GPT-4 (through the API) with the same prompt as in Sec-

Original ENH-German	Ich weiß nitt, kans och nitt erfaren, wo si sind, dann sy an keinem ort sich summend[28]. [28: verweilen]
Human Reference German	Ich weiss nicht und kann auch nicht herausfinden, wo sie sich aufhalten, da sie nirgendwo lange bleiben.
English	I don't know and can't find out where they are, as they don't stay anywhere for long.
MT System	**Automatic Translation**
GPT-4	Ich weiß nicht, kann auch nicht herausfinden, wo sie sind, denn sie zeigen sich an keinem Ort.
GPT-4 with lexical info in prompt	Ich weiß nicht, kann auch nicht erfahren, wo sie sind, denn sie verweilen an keinem Ort.
GPT-4 with lexical info inserted in text	Ich weiß nicht, kann auch nicht erfahren, wo sie sind, denn sie verweilen an keinem Ort.
GPT-4 two-step translation	Ich weiß nicht und kann auch nicht herausfinden, wo sie sich aufhalten, denn sie bleiben nirgendwo lange.
Google Gemini	Ich weiß nicht, und kann es auch nicht erfahren, wo sie sich befinden, da sie sich an keinem Ort aufhalten.
DeepL	Ich weiß es nicht, ich kann nicht herausfinden, wo sie sind, dann sind sie nirgendwo brummen.
GoogleTranslate	Ich weiß es nicht und kann es auch nicht herausfinden, wo sie sind, dann brummen sie nirgends.

Table 2: An ENH-German sentence taken from a letter of Berchtold Haller to Heinrich Bullinger, 28.10.1535, translated to modern German by different systems.

tion 4.1. For every letter, we computed the lowercase BLEU score and then averaged the scores. This results in a BLEU score of 28.2.

For comparison, we also translated the test set letters with Google Gemini (through the website). Just asking it to translate the letter resulted in boilerplate additions. Therefore, we sharpened the prompt to: `The following letter is in old German (Early New High German). Please translate it into modern German line by line. Please provide only the translation in German. No explanations.`

This worked for eight out of the ten files from our test set and resulted in an average BLEU score of 26.8. Gemini refused to translate the other two files, without any reasonable explanation. In repeated attempts Gemini did not produce any output for these letters.

4.4 Adding Lexical Information to the Prompt

Similar to the integration of terminology to a prompt (as in Bogoychev and Chen (2023)), we add the translation suggestions from the lexical footnotes to the prompt. Our general prompt is: `Translate the following letter from Early New High German into modern German.` For instance, when we translate the first sentence from Table 1, we add to the prompt `Translate 'hehen' as 'Herren'.` Since we do not know to how many ENH-German words a lexical footnote item refers, we use the heuristic that we specify the same number of words as in the lexical footnote. This means we add `Translate 'scherer' as 'Tuchscherer'.`, `Translate 'den doff' as 'die Taufe'.`, and `Translate 'wie maß' as 'man es'.` Unfortunately, this introduces some noise into the translation suggestions.

In a first evaluation we checked how often the desired target words (which were specified in the lexical footnotes) are in the automatic translation. We found that 533 out of 743 target words (72%) are contained in the translations. This count is based on exact matching the words from the lexical footnotes in the translations. Inflected forms would not match. The two human reference translations contained 52 resp. 53% of the lexical footnotes, while prompting GPT-4 without lexical information contained 27% (cf. Section 4.1).

In a second evaluation, we compared the GPT-4 output of our 10 letter test set with the human reference translation. This resulted in an average BLEU score of 33.2 (the scores range from 29.9 to

System Configuration	BLEU
GPT-4	28.2
GPT-4 with lexical info inserted in text	29.5
GPT-4 with lexical info in prompt	33.2
GPT-4 two-step translation*	51.9
GoogleTranslate (ENHG → EN → DE)	13.1
DeepL (ENHG → EN → DE)	16.7
Google Gemini	26.8

Table 3: Averaged BLEU scores (computed with the SacreBLEU tool) on the test set (10 ENH-German letters) when translating ENH-German to modern German. *The two-step translation served as the basis for the human reference translation.

38.9).

One may view adding lexical information to a prompt as an unrealistic setting since ENH-German texts do not usually come with specific translation suggestions. We argue that this setting resembles the use of a bilingual dictionary[2] (ENH-German to modern German) as an information source for steering the LLM translation.

4.5 Inserting Lexical Information into the Sentence

Rather than adding the lexical information as translation suggestions to the prompt, we now insert them directly into the source sentence by replacing the original word with the modern target word. This means we replace "hehen" with "Herren" in our ENH-German example sentence from Table 1 which then looks like "... min Herren heigind inn můßen dar zů zwingen" before we feed it to GPT-4 for translation.

We evaluated in the same way as above, both against the lexical footnotes and the test set. Interestingly, the evaluation with the target words from the lexical footnotes showed that fewer of them occurred in the translations: 467 out of 743 (63%). This means that adding the lexical translation information to the prompt preserves this information better than inserting it into the source sentence, which, in turn, suggests a better translation.

This result is confirmed by our evaluation against the test set (cf. Table 3).

The lexical footnotes in our corpus suggest target words for content words and function words. We would argue that the correct translation of content words is more important. Therefore, we automatically classified all our lexical footnotes into content vs. function words. Two-word footnotes were split and their parts classified.

When translating with the above simple prompt, the percentage of content words in the contained footnotes is 11% lower than in the missing footnotes (62.2% vs. 73.2%). With the footnotes directly inserted into the text when prompting, the difference is only marginal with the percentage of content words in the contained footnotes being 0.7% lower (69.4% vs. 70.1%). Finally, with the footnotes included in the prompt: the percentage of content words is 11.1% higher in the contained footnotes (71.4% vs. 60.3%). This shows that the quality of the contained footnotes increases when the lexical information is included in the prompt.

5 Comparison to Neural MT Systems

We cannot directly compare our LLM-based MT results to neural MT systems like DeepL or Google Translate since they do not offer ENH-German as source language. But we can pretend that the input is German and ask for a translation into some other language. We chose English as the pivot language. If we subsequently reverse the translation direction, we will get a modern German version.

When we applied this two-step translation with DeepL (and UK-English as pivot) for the 10 ENH-German letters in our test set, we obtained an average BLEU score of 16.7 (ranging from 11 to 21.9 for the 10 files). We see that DeepL interprets the words on the surface, e.g. translating ENH-German "rowen" into English as "rowing" instead of "robbing" or "stealing". DeepL allows the integration of a glossary which we did not use since we would need ENH-German to English correspondences, while our lexical footnotes provide ENH-German to modern German mappings.

[2]For examples see Frühneuhochdeutsches Wörterbuch at https://fwb-online.de/ or the Reference Corpus Early New High German at https://www.linguistics.ruhr-uni-bochum.de/ref/

Original ENH-German and Latin	**Philippum nostrum amicissime salutabis;** dices illi, das man ein latinische, schöne, wol yngebundne bibel gäbe umb try guldin.
Human Reference English	Give my warmest greetings to our Philipp; tell him that a beautifully bound Latin Bible can be purchased for three florins.
Translated by GPT-4	You will greet our dear Philip most kindly; tell him that one can get a Latin, beautiful, well-bound Bible for three guilders.
Translated by Gemini	Greet our Philip most kindly; tell him that a beautiful, well-bound Latin Bible is offered for three guilders.
Original ENH-German and Latin	Ich han ein pflägeri im huß; deren gib ich alle wuchen 1 fl. **(sic et alii)**, on spyß und tranck;
Human Reference English	I have a servant at home; I give her 1 fl. every week without food and drink (so do others as well).
Translated by GPT-4	I have a care facility in the house; to which I give 1 florin every week (and others do the same), without food and drink;
Translated by Gemini	I have a nurse in the house; I give her 1 florin every week (and so do others), not including food and drink.
Original ENH-German and Latin	Die **seniores illius ecclesiae** habend inn bschickt.
Human Reference English	The leaders of his church have sent him.
Translated by GPT-4	The elders of that church have been sent in.
Translated by Gemini	The elders of that church have put them in charge.

Table 4: Sentences with code-switching (i.e. mixing ENH-German and Latin) taken from our letter collection, translated by Open AI's GPT-4 and Google Gemini.

We also observe that occasional Latin sentences in our ENH-German letters are left untranslated by DeepL.

We are aware that DeepL offers a rewriting system ("DeepL Write") in addition to their MT system. In principle, this rewriting system can turn ENH-German texts into modern German. It allows one to select among four styles (simple, business, academic, easy) and four tones (enthusiastic, friendly, sovereign, diplomatic). It is unclear which style and tone combination would be most suitable for our letters. Rewriting also restructures the text, leading to additional challenges for evaluation, which is why we did not evaluate this system.

6 Evaluating Sentences with Code-Switching

So far, we have concentrated on sentences that are exclusively in ENH-German. But our corpus contains many sentences with code-switching. Therefore, we selected 61 sentences with a mix of Latin and ENH-German from our corpus and had them translated into English by an expert. We used English as the target language here because we know from previous experiments (Volk et al., 2024) that it results in high quality translations from Latin source texts.

We then asked the LLMs to translate these sentences (without context) into English with the prompt: `The following sentences are a mixture of Latin and old German (Early New High German). Translate them into modern English line by line.`

For GPT-4, this resulted in a BLEU score of 23.2 and a ChrF score of 46.3. Gemini scores slightly higher with a BLEU score of 25.4 and a ChrF score of 48.2 The online MT systems are unable to handle a mixture of the two languages in question here.

Table 4 shows two example sentences with impressive translations, slightly more fluent and idiomatic in the Gemini output than in in GPT-4. But we should keep in mind that sometimes the translation for presumably simple sentences has serious errors, as in our third example where GPT-4 translates an active sentence with a passive one, and thus gets the agent wrong, and Gemini produces a plural pronoun where the input pronoun is in singular.

7 Conclusion

This paper argues that LLMs like GPT-4 and Gemini are the first useful systems to translate ENH-German into modern German automatically. We showed how to exploit footnotes that specify lexical information in an edition of letters from the 16th century. These lexical footnotes map "non-intuitive" ENH-German words from the letters to modern German words (and thus provide translation suggestions). We used these lexical footnotes to evaluate the translations and then to steer the translations. We show that a two-step translation process with GPT-4 leads to high-quality translations in modern German.

We limited our work by automatically identifying only the most apparent lexical footnotes, i.e. footnotes with only one or two words. In future work we will identify and use lexical footnotes that are longer. A glance at our corpus reveals that there will be more than 1000 such footnotes which are more informative but also more complicated to exploit. It is often unclear to how many tokens from the ENH-German sentence they correspond.

Our study focused on commercial MT systems and multilingual LLMs. In future work we will also investigate open LLMs like LLaMA which we can then finetune to our specific needs.

Limitations

The most obvious limitation is our choice of building a test set based on LLM pre-translations. Independent human translations would be better (but are more time-consuming to produce). We counterbalance this approach by having three persons check and correct the pre-translations.

Secondly, we are aware that we regard ENH-German as a static block, although there are likely personal or regional variants that differ in distance to modern German and are thus harder to translate. In future work we will exploit the sender locations to cluster the ENH-German letters.

Thirdly, we argue that using lexical footnotes resembles the use of a bilingual dictionary. This is a simplification since these footnotes contain translation suggestions that were selected by the editors. A bilingual dictionary might contain multiple senses for a given word which must be disambiguated for use in translation.

Ethics Statement

Given the age of the ENH-German texts, its use does not pose an ethical challenge.

Acknowledgments

We gratefully acknowledge project funding provided by various sponsors through the UZH Foundation (see `www.bullinger-digital.ch/about`).

References

Toms Bergmanis, Artūrs Stafanovičs, and Mārcis Pinnis. 2020. Robust neural machine translation: Modeling orthographic and interpunctual variation. In *Human Language Technologies – The Baltic Perspective*.

Nikolay Bogoychev and Pinzhen Chen. 2023. Terminology-aware translation with constrained decoding and large language model prompting. In *Proceedings of the Eighth Conference on Machine Translation (WMT)*, pages 890–896, Singapore. Association for Computational Linguistics.

Marcel Bollmann, Joachim Bingel, and Anders Søgaard. 2017. Learning attention for historical text normalization by learning to pronounce. In *Proceedings of the 55th Annual Meeting of the Association for Computational Linguistics (Volume 1: Long Papers)*, pages 332–344, Vancouver, Canada.

Stefanie Dipper and Jan Christian Schaffer. 2021. Identifikation von Vorkommensformen der Lemmata in Quellenzitaten frühneuhochdeutscher Lexikoneinträge. In *Proceedings of the 17th Conference on Natural Language Processing (KONVENS 2021)*, pages 62–72, Online.

Ulrich Gäbler, Endre Zsindley, Kurt Maeder, Matthias Senn, Kurt Jakob Rüetschi, Hans Ulrich Bächtold, Rainer Heinrich, Alexandra Kess, Christian Moser, Reinhard Bodenmann, Judith Steiniger, and Yvonne Häfner, editors. 1974–2020. *Heinrich Bullinger Briefwechsel*. Heinrich Bullinger Werke. Theologischer Verlag Zürich.

Mika Hämäläinen, Tanja Säily, Jack Rueter, Jörg Tiedemann, and Eetu Mäkelä. 2019. Revisiting NMT for normalization of early English letters. In *Proceedings of the 3rd Joint SIGHUM Workshop on Computational Linguistics for Cultural Heritage, Social Sciences, Humanities and Literature*, pages 71–75, Minneapolis, USA. Association for Computational Linguistics.

Katrin Ortmann. 2021. Chunking historical German. In *Proceedings of the 23rd Nordic Conference on Computational Linguistics (NoDaLiDa)*, pages 190–199.

Chanjun Park, Seolhwa Lee, Jaehyung Seo, Hyeonseok Moon, Sugyeong Eo, and Heuiseok Lim. 2022. Priming Ancient Korean neural machine translation. In *Proceedings of the Thirteenth Language Resources and Evaluation Conference (LREC)*, pages 22–28, Marseille, France.

Christopher Sapp, Daniel Dakota, and Elliott Evans. 2023. Parsing Early New High German: Benefits and limitations of cross-dialectal training. In *Proceedings of the 21st International Workshop on Treebanks and Linguistic Theories (TLT, GURT/SyntaxFest 2023)*, pages 54–66, Washington, D.C. Association for Computational Linguistics.

Sarah Schulz and Jonas Kuhn. 2016. Learning from within? Comparing PoS tagging approaches for historical text. In *Proceedings of the Tenth International Conference on Language Resources and Evaluation (LREC'16)*, pages 4316–4322, Portorož, Slovenia.

Phillip Benjamin Ströbel, Lukas Fischer, Raphael Müller, Patricia Scheurer, Bernard Schroffenegger, and Martin Volk. 2024. Multilingual workflows in Bullinger Digital: Data curation for Latin and Early New High German. *Journal of Open Humanities Data*, 10.

Martin Volk, Dominic P. Fischer, Lukas Fischer, Patricia Scheurer, and Phillip B. Ströbel. 2024. LLM-based machine translation and summarization for Latin. In *Proceedings of the Third Workshop on Language Technologies for Historical and Ancient Languages – LT4HALA (at LREC/COLING)*, Torino.

Martin Volk, Lukas Fischer, Patricia Scheurer, Raphael Schwitter, Phillip Ströbel, and Benjamin Suter. 2022. Nunc profana tractemus. Detecting code-switching in a large corpus of 16th century letters. In *Proceedings of LREC-2022*, Marseille.

Dongbo Wang, Litao Lin, Zhixiao Zhao, Wenhao Ye, Kai Meng, Wenlong Sun, Lianzhen Zhao, Xue Zhao, Si Shen, Wei Zhang, and Bin Li. 2023. EvaHan2023: Overview of the first international Ancient Chinese translation bakeoff. In *Proceedings of ALT2023: Ancient Language Translation Workshop*, pages 1–14, Macau SAR, China. Asia-Pacific Association for Machine Translation.

Association for Computational Linguistics
209 N. Eighth Street
Stroudsburg, Pennsylvania 18360

ISBN 979-8-3313-0484-3

CURRAN ASSOCIATES INC.
proceedings.com